THE ENCYCLOPEDIA OF

SENIOR HEALTH AND WELL-BEING

THE ENCYCLOPEDIA OF

SENIOR HEALTH AND WELL–BEING

Joseph Kandel, M.D.

Christine Adamec

Facts On File, Inc.

The Encyclopedia of Senior Health and Well-being

Facts On File, Inc.
132 West 31st Street
New York NY 10001

Library of Congress Cataloging-in-Publication Data

Kandel, Joseph.
The encyclopedia of senior health and well being / Joseph Kandel, Christine Adamec.
p. cm.
Includes bibliographical references.
ISBN 0-8160-4691-3
1. Aged—Health and hygiene—Encyclopedias. 2. Geriatrics—Encyclopedias. I. Adamec, Christine A., 1949– II. Title.
RA777.6 .K357 2003
613′.0438′03—dc21   2002010485

Facts On File books are available at special discounts when purchased in bulk quantities for businesses, associations, institutions, or sales promotions. Please call our Special Sales Department in New York at (212) 967-8800 or (800) 322-8755.

You can find Facts On File on the World Wide Web at http://www.factsonfile.com

Text and cover design by Cathy Rincon

Printed in the United States of America

VB FOF 10 9 8 7 6 5 4 3 2 1

This book is printed on acid-free paper.

This book is dedicated to my wife, Merrylee,
for her continued support, love, caring, and patience.
Her insight, wit, and wisdom make this and
every other project so worthwhile.
Always,

—Joseph Kandel

I dedicate this book to my husband, John,
who is always supportive and immensely helpful
to me in all my endeavors.

—Christine Adamec

CONTENTS

FOREWORD

Our population is getting older. It's no secret. Senior adults are becoming the very old, and more people are becoming senior adults. Many problems and issues have arisen with this development, not the least of which is a concern over health care and health maintenance.

Thus, this book is more necessary now than ever before. As a board-certified clinical neurologist, I deal with senior patients every single day. The questions they ask, the concerns they have, are strikingly similar, although they may express them differently.

Some of these concerns include, "Will I become ill and frail?" "Will I have enough money?" "Will I become infirm and have to live in a nursing home?" "What's a nursing home like?" "Who is going to take care of me?" "Will I have enough money to live, or will I run out of money before I die?"

These are just a few of the questions that I hear repeatedly, and certainly they are cause for alarm. Although this book does not attempt to solve social problems or many of the ills that face our senior adults, it does attempt to be a comprehensive encyclopedia of elder care of the myriad issues from A to Z confronting senior adults. It also provides a wealth of information and knowledge that can be very helpful, particularly as a reference source, for agencies in answering these and other similar questions.

On a personal level, as a parent of young children and caregiver to two senior adults, I am a member of the "sandwich generation." The stresses that places on a family, on time commitments, and on the emotions are immense. Balancing the different aspects of care between my children and my parents is often difficult.

My mother-in-law is 86, and my father is 80. Certainly their medical conditions play a prominent role in my day-to-day life. My mother-in-law is vision and hearing impaired, and although she is certainly bright, these profound medical conditions clearly have had a dramatic impact on her independence. My father has a memory impairment that has led to a host of different issues. In this book, we address these very real-world concerns, as well as many, many other issues as they relate to senior adults.

With aging, one acquires a wealth of experience, of knowledge, and of understanding of our culture and our world. However, with advanced age also come multiple problems—financial, social, emotional, medical, and legal, to list just a few. All of these issues are dealt with in this encyclopedia. We hope that readers will find it of great benefit in providing the information they need to understand their concerns regarding senior adults and to make the best choices possible when faced with difficult decisions.

—Joseph Kandel, M.D.

ACKNOWLEDGMENTS

We would like to thank the following people for their assistance with researching this book: William A. Petit, M.D., FACP, FACE, medical director of the Joslin Diabetes Center affiliate of New Britain General Hospital (a University of Connecticut teaching hospital) in Connecticut and section chief for endocrinology, metabolism, and diabetes; and Peter Zabinski, M.D., FACS, a urologist with Melbourne Internal Medicine Associates (MIMA) in Melbourne, Florida.

Thanks also to the following state officials who provided information on state driving laws: Joyce A. Abbott, manager, Driver Services, West Virginia Division of Motor Vehicles; Lynn Armour, unit supervisor, Missouri Department of Revenue, Division of Motor Vehicle and Driver Licensing, Customer Assistance Bureau; James Barwick, supervisor, Driver Improvement, South Carolina Department of Public Safety; Terry A. Blevins, regions chief examiner, North Carolina Division of Motor Vehicles; Pat Carr, Medical/Driver License Records Technical Unit supervisor, Idaho Transportation Department, Division of Motor Vehicles; Scott R. Falb, driver safety specialist, Office of Driver Services, Motor Vehicle Division, Iowa Department of Transportation; Kerry Hennings, driver licensing and partnership development manager for the Division of Motor Vehicles, Department of Administration in Alaska; Deb LaBrie, program assistant II, Office of Driver Licensing, South Dakota Department of Commerce; Sean J. Martin, esq., assistant counsel, New York State Department of Motor Vehicles; Melody Sheffield, driver safety programs coordinator, Oregon Driver and Motor Vehicle Services and Regulation; and Fred Zwonechek, administrator, Nebraska Office of Highway Safety.

Special thanks to reference librarian Marie Mercer at the DeGroodt Public Library in Palm Bay, Florida, and to Mary Jordan, Interlibrary Loan librarian in Cocoa, Florida, for their dedicated assistance in obtaining hard-to-find journal articles and other important materials.

An additional thanks to James Chambers, our editor on this project, for his hard work in editing as well as his strong support of the book in the first place.

INTRODUCTION

U.S. and Global Issues of
Senior Health and Well-being:
Past, Present, and Future

All changes bring both new opportunities and challenges, and the global increase in the population of people age 65 and older, which is surprisingly rapid in some countries, is no different. Today, because of the increased longevity of many older people in the United States and Canada, as well as among older people in many other countries around the world, many adult children and even grandchildren and great-grandchildren have the chance to continue to interact with and love their relatives and to gain from their years of accumulated wisdom and experience.

At the same time, many (but not all) older individuals have a variety of serious problems with which they may need help; consequently, attention needs to be paid to their general medical and health needs, as well as to their housing and transportation needs, their nutritional requirements, medications that they need, and other problems that they may face. Yet, assistance should not be imposed on individuals merely because of their age: many older people continue to function as healthy and mentally competent individuals.

One of the conundrums of the modern age lies in providing enough help to those who need it while at the same time not forcing dependency on those who do not require such assistance. Respecting a senior adult's personal rights is therefore a difficult balancing act.

The globally aging population and its problems and issues affect nearly everyone, directly or indirectly, whether a person is a senior citizen, a caregiving relative, a medical or health professional, or a citizen whose taxes pay for the programs and services that are needed by older individuals. In fact, many people fit more than one of these categories; for example, some individuals who are older than age 65 are themselves family caregivers to their own parents in their 80s and 90s or to their ailing spouses. Some also continue to work, and many continue to pay taxes whether they work or not. Many people of all ages are involved in one of the many service industries that some senior citizens require.

The scope of the change in the life spans of older people during the past century has been startling. For example, according to the U.S. Census Bureau, in the year 1900, the average life expectancy for Americans born that year was 49 years (48 years for men and 51 for women). A person was born, and then he or she died by the age of 49; this was considered to be the normal way of things.

By 1940, the average life expectancy had increased to about 64 years for Americans born then (age 62 for men and 66 for women). By the year 2000, the average American born in that year can expect to live to the age of 77 years (74 years for men and 80 for women), 28 years longer than the person living in 1900 could hope for and 13 years longer than the person born in 1940.

How old is "old" continues to be redefined by experts and by average people in the population.

Many senior adults feel that old is someone at least 10 years older than they are. However, nearly all definitions set the age of 65 years as the entry level to the senior years in the United States and many other countries. The age of 65 is also used in this book as the beginning of the senior years.

A 65-year-old man or woman today is generally much healthier than a 65-year-old person from 1900 or 1940 and anticipates many more years of life. When the age of 65 was set as a retirement standard by the Social Security Act of 1935, most people died well before they ever attained that age. Today, many people live to their 65th birthday and well beyond that point.

Evolving Attitudes Toward Older People

Another emerging reality is that of societal attitudes toward older people, which not only affect how they are perceived but also how well (or ill) they are treated. Such attitudes affect everyone, even physicians. Some medical professionals say things such as "Why bother doing that test, especially at his age!" Why indeed! If nearly everyone in a culture devalues and demeans older people, this attitude inevitably "spills over" and affects doctors, lawyers, social workers, and others who interact with older people. Fortunately, there are indications that attitudes toward older people have improved in recent years.

One way to regard this changing attitude toward older people is to consider a possible parallel to the attitudes formerly evinced toward children. Until about the mid-20th century, many people basically regarded children as small adults; children were not perceived as individuals with specific needs. Attitudes changed, and children were perceived as having health and social needs that were very different from those of adults.

As with changing attitudes toward children, society began to realize in the latter part of the 20th century that older people are not merely older adults who are deteriorating rapidly but that many have their own unique needs that can and should be resolved. It was acknowledged that the health problems of older people are often more severe and of longer standing; however, at the same time, most older adults can enjoy dramatically improved health

with treatment. The field of geriatric medicine and gerontology (the study of older people) arose in the 20th century.

Another long-accepted belief was that the same types and dosages of medicine that were fine for a person who was 40 years old would work just as well for a person who was 80. Lately, experts have realized that the same drugs or dosages could be dangerous or fatal for an older person whether because of a slowed-down metabolism, because of aging kidneys that work more slowly, or for other medical and health reasons.

It is important to point out that the needs of older people are not roughly equivalent to the needs of children. To believe so is to infantilize older adults, an "ageist" error that can have many repercussions, such as needlessly causing older people to feel helpless when they may be competent at many or all tasks.

It was not necessarily that people in the past were cold and uncaring toward older people or that older people were essentially "written off" when they became ill, although it may appear that way from a contemporary perspective. Most people died before reaching the age of 70 until the latter part of the 20th century; consequently, most people considered disability and death among older people normal and acceptable.

Of course, it *is* normal for older people to become ill and eventually to die. However, most modern physicians today consider it important to identify existing illnesses among older people and to treat them whenever possible and desired. (Some treatments are considered too painful and debilitating by older individuals and their physicians.) Improving the quality as well as the length of life has become a major focus of modern medicine.

This change in attitude that developed in the United States, Canada, and most other countries around the globe is a radical departure from past years. This attitudinal shift is partly responsible for the increased longevity of many older people, as are new medical advances that are available to doctors.

Although certainly there are still ageist individuals and doctors who believe that older people should not be treated or that they should be treated only minimally, most medical experts seek to provide complete medical care and health advice to people of age 65 and older.

Changes in Killing Diseases of the Aged

It is also true that the types of illnesses that kill older people have changed significantly since 1900. (At that time, people of age 65 and older represented only 4 percent of the population in the United States, in contrast to about 13 percent today.)

About a hundred years ago, infectious diseases were the major killers of older people. For example, in 1900, both pneumonia and influenza (flu) were major killers of people of age 65 and older in the United States. In contrast, heart disease, which is today the number-one killer of older Americans, was the fourth-most-common cause of death in 1900. Another example: the number-two killer in 1900 was tuberculosis, which has since been combated successfully in the United States and most developed countries and is no longer a leading cause of death of older people. However, tuberculosis is still a major risk factor in many underdeveloped areas of the world.

The third-leading cause of death among older people in 1900 was diarrhea, which is no longer a major cause of death in the United States and other countries because of improved infection control and medications.

In further contrast, diabetes was not among the top 10 killers of older people in the United States in 1900, nor was Alzheimer's disease. There was no cure for diabetes in 1900, and people who had Type 1 (insulin-dependent) diabetes died in childhood or early adulthood. Few people had Type 2 diabetes because most people didn't live long enough to develop it, as also with Alzheimer's disease.

Housing Older People Through Time: Almshouses, Board-and-Care Homes, Hospitals, and Nursing Homes

Many older people in the United States and other countries today live in their own homes, or they live with their family members. Only a small percentage of older people reside in skilled nursing facilities (nursing homes). However, in the late 19th century, many older people lived in poorhouses (also known as almshouses), especially if they had no family members but sometimes even when they did still have living family members.

Often, older people were housed with orphaned children and mentally ill people. Sometimes, the juvenile delinquent population or the unemployed poor were mixed together with the other populations to form a group whose problems society could not resolve. Diseases such as cholera and pneumonia were rampant in these crowded quarters, and deaths were common events.

Social reformers decried the abuses and problems of almshouses, and by the 1930s, many almshouses had closed. Institutions were created for older people, orphans, and other groups who had formerly lived in the almshouses.

Many older poor individuals moved to "board-and-care" homes in the early 1900s and subsisted on state funds or private charitable donations. Other seniors who were very ill resided in hospitals, and by the early 1950s, long-term stays in hospitals were common.

The Social Security Act of 1935 banned old age assistance payments to people who lived in the few remaining almshouses in 1935, and this action encouraged people to relocate to board-and-care homes.

In 1954, federal laws were passed that offered grants for companies to build nursing homes that were based on the model of hospitals rather than on board-and-care homes. Consequently, the care of seniors who were unable to function on their own shifted from hospital-based care to nursing homes in the mid-1950s.

A new option became popular in the late 20th century, that of "assisted-living facilities." This term describes a place that offers a lower level of care than a nursing home but a higher level than the no-care offered in a private residence. The care in an assisted-living facility may be as minimal as a call button in the resident's apartment and a few other amenities, or it may include a physician in residence, a dining hall, numerous activities, and other options. Assisted-living facilities vary dramatically in the services that they offer their residents, but one thing is clear: most older people would rather live in an assisted-living facility than in a nursing home.

State regulations of assisted-living facilities vary drastically. In contrast, both state and federal guidelines bind nursing homes, largely because most patients in nursing homes are on Medicaid or Medicare.

Many people who would otherwise have entered nursing homes have chosen assisted-living facilities, although few assisted-living facilities accept Medicaid or Medicare. However, despite the explosive development of assisted-living facilities, nursing homes continue to exist, and in 1997 (latest data available), there were about 1.6 million nursing-home residents living in 17,000 facilities in the United States, most of them older white women (older than age 80). The National Center for Health Statistics projects that at current rates and with the growing elderly population, the nursing home population will *double* by 2030.

As of this writing, nursing homes in many states and as an institution in general are under close scrutiny by federal and state investigators, who are concerned about problems with the abuse and neglect of older residents. Many people have filed lawsuits against nursing homes, and some attorneys specialize in nursing-home litigation. Despite these issues, it is apparent that nursing homes will continue to be needed in the United States, and adaptations will be made by nursing-home owners, as well as by the agencies that regulate them.

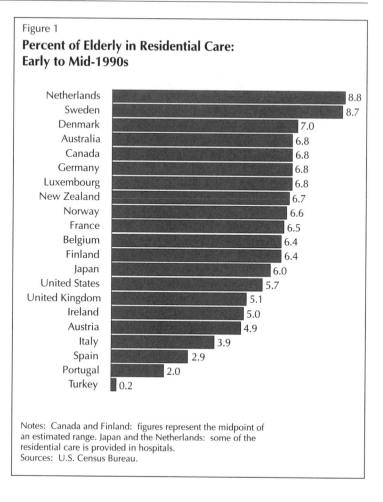

Figure 1

Percent of Elderly in Residential Care: Early to Mid-1990s

Country	Percent
Netherlands	8.8
Sweden	8.7
Denmark	7.0
Australia	6.8
Canada	6.8
Germany	6.8
Luxembourg	6.8
New Zealand	6.7
Norway	6.6
France	6.5
Belgium	6.4
Finland	6.4
Japan	6.0
United States	5.7
United Kingdom	5.1
Ireland	5.0
Austria	4.9
Italy	3.9
Spain	2.9
Portugal	2.0
Turkey	0.2

Notes: Canada and Finland: figures represent the midpoint of an estimated range. Japan and the Netherlands: some of the residential care is provided in hospitals.
Sources: U.S. Census Bureau.

Residential Care in Other Countries

How do other countries handle nursing homes (residential care) for their older citizens? This issue was addressed in the Centers for Disease Control and Prevention (CDC) report *An Aging World.* According to the CDC, some countries have a higher rate of using residential care than the United States. For example, in the Netherlands, an estimated 8.8 percent of the elderly were in residential care in the 1990s. The high rate in the Netherlands was followed by Sweden,

at 8.7 percent, Denmark at 7.0 percent, and Australia, Canada, Luxembourg, and Germany all at 6.8 percent. In contrast, the U.S. percentage of all older people living in nursing homes was 5.7 percent. Lower rates of institutionalization were also seen in some countries, such as Turkey at less than 1 percent (0.2 percent) and Portugal at 2 percent. (See the chart above for further information.)

In some countries, large numbers of very old people reside in institutions. The CDC reports that more than 50 percent of all Norwegians of age 85 and older live in institutions, as do one-third or more in Australia and New Zealand. In the United States, about 13 percent of the 4.2 million older people who were age 85 and older reside in nursing homes.

According to the CDC, rates of the institutionalization of older people are low among developing countries, in large part because it is considered culturally inappropriate to place out elderly family members. However, this does not mean there is no long-term care in developing countries. Some areas, particularly among those in Southeast Asia with a rapidly growing elderly population, are beginning to embrace the long-term-care institution or nursing-home concept.

Medical Advances

The importance of dramatic improvements in infection control and in the treatments of diseases, along with amazing technological advances in diagnostic equipment, magnetic resonance imaging (MRI), and other radiological devices, and the use of computers must be considered in any discussion of older people. These advances have significantly improved the health status of millions of older people in the United States, Canada, and other countries throughout the globe.

Staggering improvements have also occurred in the care of chronically ill people. Older people today receive knee or hip replacements when those areas have been ravaged by arthritis or other illnesses. They also receive lens implants to replace eyes damaged by glaucoma, cataracts, and other diseases of the eye, now forgoing the blindness that was the accepted standard 50 years ago. Cochlear implants for the ears are implanted to restore hearing to many individuals who have lost this ability, and others use sophisticated hearing aids that would amaze and dazzle people from the recent past.

Life-Saving Advances of the 20th Century

When Doctors Banting and Best of Canada discovered insulin as a treatment for Type 1 diabetes (an illness requiring insulin) in 1921, this finding largely benefited children and young adults because anyone with the disease died in childhood or early adulthood. There were no older people with Type 1 diabetes. Few people developed Type 2 diabetes, another form of diabetes, because few were obese (as most people with Type 2 diabetes are) and also because most people in earlier populations died before reaching their senior years or even attaining middle age.

Today, some older people have Type 1 diabetes, for which they receive insulin. In addition, many older people suffer from Type 2 diabetes, and after years of the disease, oral medications are no longer sufficient to sustain life. Many of them need insulin, too. As a result, the discovery of insulin, along with other discoveries long past, now enable many older people to enjoy extended life spans.

The development of tests and vaccines and medical treatments for many killing infections have also enabled people to live longer. The number of medical discoveries that have enabled long life in the past century is staggering in scope. Doctor Fleming's discovery of penicillin allowed doctors to fight against diseases such as pneumonia and other life-threatening bacterial infections. Medications for heart disease and drugs now battle cancer with some success. Vaccines were developed to immunize people against pneumonia and influenza (flu), the major killers of the past.

Astonishing medical breakthroughs occurred in the 20th century. After Dr. Christian Barnaard, a cardiac surgeon from South Africa, performed the first heart transplant in 1967, physicians learned to perform other life-saving transplants. Advances were made in antirejection technology, such that individuals who were previously doomed to certain death could sustain life for years after receiving a transplanted lung, heart, kidney, or other organ. In some cases, multiple organs are transplanted, such as both a pancreas and a kidney.

Improvements in Detection of Disease and Equipment

Detection methods of disease are far superior to those of past years. Laboratory and X-ray tests and other procedures that doctors have available to them now can identify previously undiagnosed and life-threatening diseases, such as heart disease or kidney disease. In comparison to the past, when only painful and invasive studies were available, now with modern diagnostic testing, doctors can quickly and painlessly diagnose a wide spectrum of illnesses. When such an illness is identified in its early stages, it can often be aggressively treated with a variety of medications as well as with lifestyle recommendations given to individuals for exercising, weight loss, and nutritional changes.

Preventable Illnesses Still Exist

Yet, at the same time that such remarkable medical progress has occurred that enable so many people to live longer and healthier lives, it is also true that many of the same old scourges of older age continue to impinge on the nerve of progress. These include heart disease and cancer, the number-one and -two life takers; despite powerful new medications and treatments, millions of people still succumb to these key threats. In addition, many individuals still die from pneumonia or influenza, although there are vaccines that are readily available to most people in the United States, Canada, and many other countries. Too many people still fail to get their shots, even though Medicare in the United States covers these injections.

Other correctable health problems are not corrected by older people. About 10 percent of older people continue to smoke, leading to deaths from lung cancer, throat and oral cancer, emphysema, and many other diseases. An enormous amount of suffering and billions of dollars in health-care costs would be saved if people ended their addiction to tobacco and stopped smoking.

Preventive actions become even more compellingly important when we look at racial differences. For example, African Americans smoke slightly less than Caucasian Americans do, and yet they have a higher rate of lung cancer and are much less likely to survive for five years after diagnosis. African Americans are less likely to receive medical care, although it's unclear why this is true and whether this problem is a function of low income, distrust of the medical profession, lack of access to medical care, or genetic issues that are linked to race.

Some Medical Problems Still Mystify Doctors

Some medical problems continue to elude medical science. For example, most people who develop pancreatic cancer have a very short life span (months) because by the time the disease is detected and the individual is showing apparent signs of illness, such as jaundice, it is too late to save the person. Yet, other forms of cancer are seeing major breakthroughs, and it is likely that the diagnostic riddle of pancreatic cancer will be broken as well in the near future. For example, researchers have developed a test to detect ovarian cancer, and it is being evaluated as of this writing. Medical breakthroughs with cancer treatments will continue as will cures.

Other medical problems and illnesses require individuals to take specific actions that may be difficult for them to take. For example, the majority of older people in the United States and Canada are clinically obese, a medical problem that often leads to many other illnesses, such as diabetes, cardiovascular disease, stroke, and chronic low back pain. Obesity is usually very difficult to treat, and many people who lose weight eventually gain it back again.

Researchers are searching for a means to identify and control the appetite "thermostat" of the body. When such a breakthrough does come, as it will, then the number of older people will rise still further because more individuals will be healthy and will live longer lives.

A Global Look at Seniors

The United States is not the only country whose population of older citizens is increasing; instead, the benefits and problems of a burgeoning elderly population are of global scope. Another factor affecting the increased percentage of older people in many countries is declining fertility. As fewer babies are born, younger people represent a smaller proportion of the total population. However, medical advances are the key factors in an increasingly aging global population.

Countries with Large Elderly Populations
Some countries have much larger percentages of older people than others do. For example, in Italy, 18.1 percent of the entire population was age 65 and older in 2000; Italy was followed by Greece and Sweden, both at 17.3 percent, and then Japan at 17.0 percent.

In contrast, in the United States, less than 13 percent of the population was age 65 or older in 2000 (about the same percentage as in Canada), and the United States is not among the world's oldest countries. Figure 2 illustrates the percent of population for the world's oldest countries in 25 countries worldwide.

The situation is changing in many developing countries as well, where the older population will increase dramatically from 2000 to 2030. According to the U.S. Census Bureau in its report *An Aging World: 2001,* more than half (59 percent) of all senior citizens on the globe live in developing countries. This percentage is projected to increase to 71 percent by 2030. This large increase of older citizens means that developing countries will face similar needs as developed countries in providing help for older people with health, medical, housing, and other needs.

The greatest increase in the number of older people is found in Asia. It is estimated that by 2025, more than two-thirds of the entire world population older than age 65 will reside in poor countries.

According to the U.S. Census Bureau, "Less developed countries as a group have embarked on a demographic transition from high fertility and [high] mortality to lower fertility and [low] mortality." At the same time, many countries struggle with the health problems of their aging population. For example, because of the very high number of smokers in China, where nearly two-thirds of all men smoke, this country faces very high numbers of aging individuals with cancer, emphysema, and other smoking-related illnesses. Millions of Chinese men will die from smoking-related illnesses.

In Singapore the population of individuals age 65 and older is projected to almost quadruple by 2030, increasing by 372 percent, the largest worldwide increase of any country in the world. Singapore's increase is projected to be followed by Malaysia (277 percent), Colombia (258 percent), and Costa Rica (250 percent). During this same

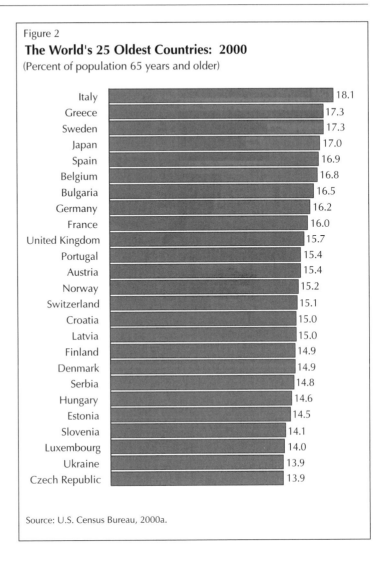

Figure 2

The World's 25 Oldest Countries: 2000

(Percent of population 65 years and older)

Country	Percent
Italy	18.1
Greece	17.3
Sweden	17.3
Japan	17.0
Spain	16.9
Belgium	16.8
Bulgaria	16.5
Germany	16.2
France	16.0
United Kingdom	15.7
Portugal	15.4
Austria	15.4
Norway	15.2
Switzerland	15.1
Croatia	15.0
Latvia	15.0
Finland	14.9
Denmark	14.9
Serbia	14.8
Hungary	14.6
Estonia	14.5
Slovenia	14.1
Luxembourg	14.0
Ukraine	13.9
Czech Republic	13.9

Source: U.S. Census Bureau, 2000a.

period, the increase in the elderly population is projected at 126 percent in Canada and 102 percent in the United States.

Some countries will have low increases in the percentages of older citizens; for example, Bulgaria is projected to have the lowest increase of 52 countries, or 14 percent. Other countries with low projected increases are Ukraine (21 percent), Hungary (37 percent), and Malawi (41 percent).

Figure 3 illustrates the percentage change of both developing and developed countries over a 30-year span in the 21st century.

Figure 3

Percent Increase in Elderly Population: 2000 to 2030

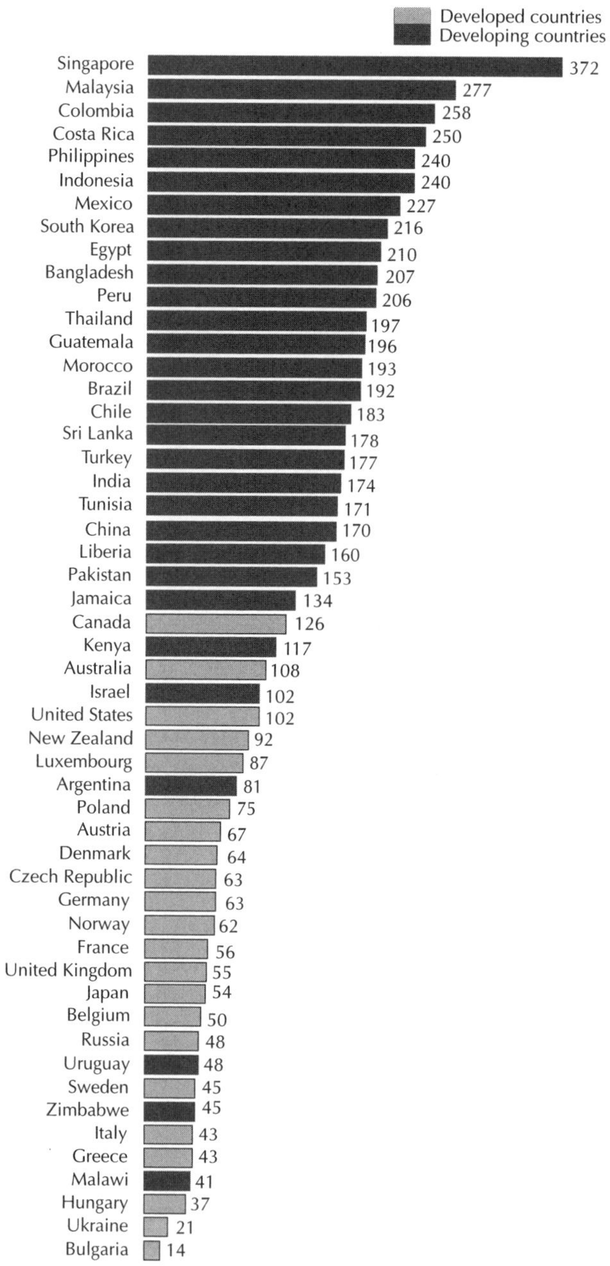

Developed countries
Developing countries

Country	Percent
Singapore	372
Malaysia	277
Colombia	258
Costa Rica	250
Philippines	240
Indonesia	240
Mexico	227
South Korea	216
Egypt	210
Bangladesh	207
Peru	206
Thailand	197
Guatemala	196
Morocco	193
Brazil	192
Chile	183
Sri Lanka	178
Turkey	177
India	174
Tunisia	171
China	170
Liberia	160
Pakistan	153
Jamaica	134
Canada	126
Kenya	117
Australia	108
Israel	102
United States	102
New Zealand	92
Luxembourg	87
Argentina	81
Poland	75
Austria	67
Denmark	64
Czech Republic	63
Germany	63
Norway	62
France	56
United Kingdom	55
Japan	54
Belgium	50
Russia	48
Uruguay	48
Sweden	45
Zimbabwe	45
Italy	43
Greece	43
Malawi	41
Hungary	37
Ukraine	21
Bulgaria	14

Source: U.S. Census Bureau, 2000a.

Increased Population of Older People Brings New Issues and Problems

As a result of the demographic changes that are seen in the world today, many adult children, grandchildren, and others are far less likely to lose their relatives to an early death, and they can instead continue to enjoy relationships with their aging relatives.

But at the same time that greater numbers of older people live on, the probability increases that they will experience a variety of serious chronic ailments, such as diabetes, hypertension, cardiac problems, stroke, and a host of other debilitating medical conditions. In addition, advancing age also leads to an increase risk of psychiatric and neurological problems, such as Alzheimer's disease, dementia, Parkinson's disease, and other mental and physical illnesses that make older people increasingly dependent on others for their care.

In addition to medical concerns, there are many issues of basic well-being that affect older people. Older individuals and their caregivers often have special needs when it comes to housing, transportation, legal issues, and an array of other aspects of daily life.

There are also unexpected and distressing consequences of even the most well-meaning actions toward older individuals. The fact that some older people need assistance does not mean that all or most require such assistance. As Carole Haber pointed out in her 1983 book, *Beyond Sixty-Five: The Dilemma of Old Age in America's Past*, and which is still true 20 years later;

It has become a widely shared expectation that the old will require specialized care and attention. The irony of these policies and ideas, though, is that in attempting to assist the poverty-stricken and ailing, they have ensured the dependence of a large proportion of the elderly. The measures mandate the separation of the old from the very factors that once guaranteed their continued prestige.

Housed in an "old folks" home or retired on a small pension, the elderly have little hope of controlling their work, family or possessions. As a result, the entire age group . . . has acquired the characteristics of the colonial era's ancient and broken. And not surprisingly, like that eighteenth-century group of aged persons, they too receive little respect. But this is not simply because we live in a youth-oriented society or one that at some point had suddenly come to detest the aged. Rather, over the course of a century, demographic and economic realities have combined with professional policies to enforce the powerlessness of old age. Once beyond sixty-five, most persons are bureaucratically characterized as diseased and dependent.

More Seniors and More "Old Old" Seniors

Several factors are pivotal to any discussion of senior health. First, there are many more older people in the United States, Canada, and the world today than in years past, and there are also greater numbers of people who are much older than seniors in the past. Additionally, many older people of today are far healthier than the fewer older people who lived in the past. The man or woman of age 65 in 1900 had a different health status and life expectancy than the 65-year-old person of 1950, who was also very different from the person who has attained 65 years in the early 21st century.

Radical population shifts in the latter part of the 20th century continue as many more older people live beyond age 65. The numbers of people who live to age 80 and beyond is expanding. According to the U.S. Census Bureau, the United States comprises 13.1 percent of all individuals age 80 and older in the world. However, one other country has greater numbers of very old (also called old-old) people: in 2000, China was the home for 16.3 percent of all people age 80 and older in the world.

People who are 100 years old or more (centenarians) are no longer a rarity in our society. For example, in the United States in 2000, there were 68,000 people who were centenarians, according to the U.S. Census Bureau, up from 37,000 centenarians in 1990, an increase of 84 percent in 10 years. In contrast, the population for individuals of all ages increased by about 11 percent during the same 10-year period.

This trend of very old people is likely to continue. In many cases, society is seeing people age 65 and older who are responsible for caring for their aged parents. They may feel daunted by their own increasing health problems, and this task can be a very difficult one to bear. Additionally, sometimes elderly parents care for their senior-age children. In one reported case, a 97-year-old mother helps to care for her 68-year-old daughter.

Social Security and Medicare in the U.S.

No historical overview or even a discussion of the health issues of older people would be complete without a description of the Old-Age, Survivors, and Disability Insurance (OASDI) Program administered by the Social Security Administration in the United States, a program that initially passed because of the nationwide devastation of the Great Depression of the early 1930s.

Since the passage of the Social Security Act of 1935, programs of social security for the aged and later for the disabled as well have played an increasingly important role in the national landscape of health care.

In the United States, the legislation signed by President Franklin D. Roosevelt on August 14, 1935, which created the Social Security Administration, provided a stopgap for older individuals who had no retirement income or any other income and who could no longer work. Since that time, the program has burgeoned into a multibillion-dollar program.

The addition of Medicare in 1965, which provided health coverage to Social Security recipients, added another layer of protection. Although it did not and still does not provide coverage for outpatient (outside the hospital) medications, Medicare pays for the large part of hospital and nursing care, as well as outpatient visits.

The first Social Security numbers were registered in 1936, and Grace Dorothy Owen of Concord, New Hampshire, received the lowest recorded Social Security number: 001-01-0001. By 1937, 35 million Social Security cards had been issued to people of all ages in the United States. Credits for "old age" insurance were first tabulated in January 1, 1937. From 1937 to 1942, retired individuals received one lump sum rather than a monthly payment for the rest of their lives. Motorman Ernest Ackerman retired one day after the program began, and he received a lump sum of 17 cents.

In 1939, Congress amended the Social Security Act, to provide for benefits to both the spouse and the minor children of the retired worker.

The first monthly benefits check was released in January 1940 to a retired secretary, Ida May Fuller from Ludlow, Vermont. Ms. Fuller's first check was for $22.54. She lived 100 years and collected more than $22,000 in Social Security retirement benefits.

In 1956, the Social Security Act was amended yet again, this time to provide for the coverage of disabled workers ages 50–65 and also to cover adult children who were disabled. Within the next two years, the age floor of 50 was dropped, and indigent disabled workers younger than age 50 could apply for benefits.

The next change was to create a program that has had massive repercussions to date: Medicare. The Amendments of 1965 created this health insurance program for retired workers, and an estimated 20 million beneficiaries enrolled in the program within the initial three years of its passage. Medicare was later expanded to cover disabled workers as well. The Social Security Administration administered the program until 1977 when the Health Care Financing Administration (HCFA) was created to run Medicare. HCFA was renamed the Centers for Medicare and Medicaid Services (CMS) in 2000.

The next major federal social-welfare program created was Supplemental Security Income (SSI), which was passed in 1972. This program was created for individuals who were disabled and had low income, but who had *not* worked sufficient time periods to qualify for Social Security retirement or disability benefits. More than 6 million individuals of all ages received SSI benefits in 2002.

Another change came in 2000. Before that date, monthly benefits were reduced for retired workers receiving Social Security benefits and who chose to work. The Senior Citizens' Freedom to Work Act of 2000 ended the "retirement earnings test" for most older people. The one exception was among older people who chose to retire at an early age and for whom the income limitations still applied.

The first organization to oversee the Social Security program was the Social Security Board. In 1946, the Social Security Board was given a new name: the Social Security Administration. In 1953, this organization was subsumed under the newly created Department of Health, Education, and Welfare (HEW), which was later renamed the Department of Health and Human Services in 1980. In 1995, the Social Security Administration became its own independent organization, under the administration of President Clinton.

In 2000, the Older Americans Act, which reauthorized legislation that extended coverage for older people, was signed into law.

The Role of Alternative Medicine

The increased popularity of alternative remedies and treatments has affected older people. In a sort of "back to the future" development, scientists are discovering that some herbs, supplements, and other alternative remedies are effective at extending and improving the lives of many seniors. For example, a deficiency in Vitamin B_{12} could cause an individual to exhibit symptoms of dementia. If vitamin levels are not checked, an individual could be misdiagnosed with Alzheimer's disease, a tragic error that could be easily rectified if identified. Giving the individual Vitamin B_{12} would alleviate the dementia.

Some individuals benefit from taking magnesium or other minerals or herbs. It is extremely important, however, that seniors inform their doctors of their plan to take supplements or that they are already taking them. Some herbs can cause negative effects, especially in interaction with other drugs. For example, people taking blood-thinner drugs should be careful if taking ginkgo biloba because this herb will thin the blood further and could be dangerous or fatal. Other herbs, such as ephedra, can increase blood pressure, which is counterproductive among people with hypertension and who may be taking drugs to lower their blood pressure.

Drug-to-drug interactions are common. This means that one or more drugs can increase, decrease, or otherwise change the effect of other medications the individual is taking. The change may be a small one, or it could be as major as a life-threatening event. As people live longer, they have more illnesses and require more medications, and the possibility for a negative interaction increases. It becomes even more important for people to inform their physicians about all drugs that are taken, whether prescription medicines, cold medicines, vitamins, nutrients, or supplements.

Family Caregivers and Their Importance

Family caregiving is another issue of paramount importance. Most family caregivers to the elderly are middle aged or even seniors themselves, and many are still employed while they attempt to provide assistance and care to fragile parents and relatives.

When the caregiver is older than 65 and is providing assistance to someone who is 85 or 90, the quality of health of both individuals may be compromised. Family caregivers need to realize that they cannot provide good care if their own health is compromised. Yet, studies indicate that family caregivers are likely to neglect their own health and to limit their exercise when they begin to care for aging relatives. Family caregivers are also prone to stress and depression.

To acknowledge the challenges of family caregivers, this issue was added to the Older Americans Act when it was amended in 2000. The reauthorized act included the National Family Caregiver Support Program and funded $125 million in grants to state agencies in 2001 so that states could provide information and assistance to family caregivers of older people.

The reauthorized bill also acknowledged the unique needs of grandparents who are raising their grandchildren. In addition, it also established the Native American Caregiver Support Program to help caregivers of Native American elders who are ill or disabled.

Elder Abuse and Neglect

Abuse or neglect of older citizens is a problem today, whether the abuse occurs at the hands of an angry and overworked nurse's aide in a nursing home or it results from the behavior of a distraught adult child. In the United States, reported cases of abuse and neglect of older people increased by 150 percent from 1986 to 1996, although the older population increased only 10 percent during that time. About 30 percent of the nursing homes in the United States were cited for abuse violations during the 1999 to 2001 period.

Elders are also severely neglected in some cases. In fact, neglect is more likely to lead to death than abuse is. If older people can no longer prepare their own food or even feed themselves, then they will starve. If an older person is denied needed medical care, then he or she will sicken and die. Elder abuse and neglect is a problem in countries worldwide and is likely to be an increased problem as senior populations continue to grow. In the United States, each state has its own policies for how elder abuse and neglect should be handled.

Psychiatric/Psychological Issues Among Older People

Many older people face problems with severe depression or anxiety as spouses see their partners sicken and die and as their own health frailties become more accentuated through the years. In 1998, an estimated 15 percent of the older population in the United States aged 65 to 79 were severely depressed. This percentage worsened with age, and 21 percent of those aged 80 to 84 were depressed, with the rate increasing to 23 percent of the elderly population age 85 and older.

Depression is also associated with health problems and physical illness. People who are depressed ignore proper nutrition, don't take their medications, and often fail to participate in social activities; theirs is a negative downward spiral.

Although the majority of older people do not have Alzheimer's disease or dementia, the physical, mental, and emotional toll is great among those who do, as well as upon those who care for them. As we write this essay, former President Ronald Reagan has reached his 91st birthday but probably doesn't know or appreciate its significance because he is entrapped in the net of Alzheimer's disease.

Many baby boomers (born between 1946 and 1964) are terrified of Alzheimer's disease because they wonder if this illness lies ahead in their own futures. Policy makers also worry, knowing that someone will have to provide the care and pay the bill if the boomers do develop Alzheimer's at the current rate and if they cannot be treated more effectively than as of this writing in 2002.

Fortunately, new developments and medications may hold the secret to resolving the much-feared scourge of dementia. Researchers are testing vaccines that may hold the key to dissolving the brain plaques associated with the mental lapses and deterioration of Alzheimer's disease. Others speculate that shortages of substances such as folate (iron) or other minerals or vitamins may be a cause or a contributor to the development of Alzheimer's disease. If research shows this to be true, many people will choose to take supplements as preventive medications.

Gender Issues Among the Aging

Another key aspect of any discussion of senior health is the impact of gender differences. For example, some illnesses are more dangerous or fatal for men or for women. Older men are more likely to contract cancer, and older women are more likely to suffer from arthritis, osteoporosis, and hypertension.

Also, women generally live longer than men do, and the majority of nursing home residents in the United States (75 percent) are female. Older women are also more likely to live alone than older men are. In 1998, only 17 percent of older men lived alone, compared to 41 percent of older women.

Yet, older men are less likely to live with their relatives than older women are. In 1998, 7 percent of senior men lived with a relative, versus 17 percent of older women who lived with relatives. However, older men are more likely to be married than are older women. Seventy-three percent of older men lived with a spouse in 1998, compared to only about 40 percent of older women who lived with a spouse.

Racial Issues

Race should not be ignored in any discussion of older people, for the primary reason that race affects longevity and health. For the most part, Caucasians (whites) fare the best when it comes to health matters, although older white women are more likely to suffer from osteoporosis and Alzheimer's disease than their African-American, Asian-American, or Hispanic counterparts. However, for most other illnesses, elderly nonwhites are sicker and die younger than whites.

Some people jump to the conclusion that nonwhites are poorly treated because of their race and their inaccessibility to medical care. This may be true, but it is not clear if it is. Often, nonwhites exhibit behavioral patterns that can lead to health problems, such as consuming alcohol or overeating, which can exacerbate medical problems such as diabetes or even cancer.

Nonwhite, older individuals may be suspicious of medical practitioners, or the problem could be that they lack the means (money, transportation, or other factors) to go to a doctor's office when they're sick. As a result, they may only use medical services when it is an emergency, and their medical care is provided in a fragmented fashion by a hospital emergency room.

Difficult Ethical Questions with which Society Struggles

As the population ages and the percentage of older people increases, many ethical issues become increasingly more pressing to consider and resolve. At the same time that technology leaps forward, physicians, families, and society at large struggle with ethical dilemmas. For example, who is responsible for the care of older people who need financial assistance or care? Is it primarily their family's "job," or is it instead a societal responsibility? Or should the care of needy older people be a shared responsibility between the family and society?

Paying for prescription drugs is a pivotal issue in society today and one that is hotly debated by politicians, physicians, and others who are actively interested in problem solving. Medicare does not pay for medications as of this writing; yet, some older people need their medicines to live. Some older people who take many drugs and are on limited finances may have to choose which drugs to purchase of all the medications that they take. Some seniors have difficulty affording any drugs and should ask their physician about prescription assistance programs.

On the other hand, there are some seniors who *choose* to purchase pleasure items or take a vacation rather than obtain their medically necessary medications.

Many pharmaceutical companies offer free or very low-cost drugs for low-income older people; eligibility and application requirements vary. But the larger problem of a rapidly aging population needing medications looms on.

Beyond medications, there are also costs for medical treatments. At what age is a person "too old" for a heart or kidney transplant? And who should make this decision: the government, the family, the doctor, or someone else? These are moral and ethical dilemmas that continue to rack the conscience of good citizens in the United States and in the world.

Another issue is a life-and-death one. Older people in the United States and many other countries may elect ahead of time to choose or not choose life-sustaining treatment should they become severely ill. In other societies, doctors and/or families can make this decision for the older person.

But what of the older person's rights? Should society be able to terminate a life when a person wishes to live, even though it would cost society a great deal to sustain that life? Turning the issue around, does society have the right to end a person's life merely because he or she can no longer produce in our society, despite all the work he or she may have achieved in years past?

The issue is even more complicated than it may appear on the surface; for example, can decision makers be sure that their laws and regulations are not colored by ageist perceptions of older people as universally sick and unproductive? In reality, many older people continue to live independently and to work until well beyond the arbitrary retirement age of 65 years. As a result, it is very difficult for legislators to know what, if any, action to take in many arenas.

Consider the issue of driving. Many individuals older than age 80 are physically or mentally impaired. Yet, there are still many such individuals who continue to hold a driver's license and who continue to drive their vehicles.

Although older people don't have the high accident rates of teenagers, when only the number of miles is considered, the car-crash rate is very high.

Some experts think that all older people should have an eye examination or a complete driving test; others say that such requirements would be a form of age discrimination.

Most states ignore the issue altogether, although some states have eliminated mail-in drivers license renewals or have required vision testing for all people older than a given age. As the population continues to age, this issue, too, will loom larger and will need to be addressed.

The Need to Acknowledge That Older People Are Diverse

Another myth that needs to be exploded is that all older people are alike. In fact, they are more unlike (heterogeneous) than they are alike. They are enormously diverse. Seniors may be white, African American, Hispanic, Asian, or Native American, or have mixed racial heritages.

Older people are also wealthy, middle class, and poor. Some are very ill while others are quite healthy. Some older people are well educated; others are high school graduates, and some attained only a few years of grade school. Their interests vary radically as well. Some seniors are very active and healthy, and they love to travel and socialize; others are far more introverted and, even though well, would rather stay home with a good book.

Yet, the general public often perceives older people through an ageist spectrum, seeing them as sick, unhappy, slow moving, and slow witted. This negative perception colors the views of how older people should be treated in terms of the care they need or deserve.

The 21st Century and What Lies Ahead

Medical breakthroughs continue to improve the life span as well as the life quality of older Americans. Within the next generation, it is likely that cures, not just treatments, will be found for diseases such as diabetes and obesity, as well as for Alzheimer's disease and other forms of dementia.

Chronic ailments that continue to rob many people of their life quality, such as the many different forms of arthritis, will become less painful for individuals as these disabling illnesses become more treatable. Cures for diseases such as diabetes and cancer lie ahead on the near horizon for many seniors. Genetic manipulation may make it possible to perform further and even more startling medical advances than have been already seen. The future looks bright indeed, as long as society acknowledges the future needs of older citizens and prepares a plan to provide them.

Gratton, Brian. *Urban Elders: Family, Work, and Welfare Among Boston's Aged, 1890–1950.* Philadelphia: Temple University Press, 1986.

Haber, Carole. *Beyond Sixty-Five: The Dilemma of Old Age in America's Past.* Cambridge, England: Cambridge University Press, 1983.

Kane, Robert L., M.D., Joseph G. Ouslander, M.D., and Itamar B. Abrass, M.D. *Essentials of Clinical Geriatrics.* New York: McGraw-Hill, 1999.

Kinsella, Kevin, and Victoria A. Velkoff. *An Aging World: 2001.* Washington, D.C.: U.S. Census Bureau, 2001.

Petit, William, Jr., and Christine Adamec. *The Encyclopedia of Diabetes.* New York: Facts On File, 2002.

Porter, Ray, ed. *Cambridge Illustrated History of Medicine.* Cambridge, United Kingdom: Cambridge University Press, 1996.

Sahyoun, Natalie R., Ph.D., RD, et al. "The Changing Profile of Nursing Home Residents: 1985–1997," *Aging Trends* 4 (March 2001), National Center for Health Statistics.

Social Security Administration. "A Brief History of Social Security." SSA Publication No. 21-059 (August 2000).

ENTRIES A–Z

AARP The largest private organization for retired individuals, and an active lobby for seniors. Formerly known as the American Association of Retired People, the AARP dropped the words but kept the letters of their name, apparently hoping to appeal to younger baby boomers and other individuals older than age 50 who do not regard themselves as elderly or retired.

AARP produces many publications and reports for members and nonmembers on a wide variety of issues of interest to older people, such as health topics, insurance, retirement living, and travel. They also produce two magazines: *Modern Maturity* (oriented to those older than age 65) and *My Generation* (oriented to those younger than age 65 years).

Contact the AARP at:

601 E Street, NW
Washington, DC 20049
(800) 424-3410 or (202) 434-2277
http://www.aarp.org

abuse/neglect Purposeful action or inaction that causes harm or death to an older person, whether the abuse is inflicted by a spouse or other family member, by a home-care worker, by an employee in a hospital, nursing home, or other location, or by any other person.

Abuse and neglect of seniors are very serious problems in the United States, and institutional abuse is only recently receiving attention. Some experts estimate that as many as 10 percent of individuals older than age 65 experience some form of abuse or neglect. Congressional experts and the General Accounting Office reported in their 2002 report on nursing-home abuse that there were known incidents of abuse in 30 percent of investigated nursing homes during the period 1999–2001.

Forms of Abuse

Abuse may be physical, such as a beating; sexual, as when an older person is raped or otherwise sexually assaulted; or financial, as in unreasonably withholding funds from an individual or misusing the financial assets or property of an older person.

Neglect can be the most severe form of abuse an older person faces because when needed food, clothing, shelter, or medication are withheld, eventually, the person will sicken and die.

Sometimes, abuse is even self-induced, such as when older people fail to eat enough (or any) food or to provide their own basic needs, usually because they are physically or cognitively unable to do so, although sometimes the underlying problem is DEPRESSION.

Emotional abuse also afflicts many older people, although generally in society, the most attention is paid to physical or sexual abuse or to neglect.

Physical Abuse Physical abuse refers to harm that is directly imposed upon a person, such as beating, striking, slapping, or other violent acts. Physical abuse may cause bruising, fractured bones, or even death.

Note: bruising is *not* always a sign that the older person has been abused. Some older individuals bruise very easily, and yet no one has caused them any harm. At the same time, however, just because a person is older than 65 does not automatically mean that he or she must bruise easily. Consequently, any severe or extensive bruising should be questioned because it may be an indicator of abuse.

Sexual Abuse Sexual abuse does not appear to occur frequently, but it does occur to some older people. Sexual abuse includes forcing the person to receive and/or to perform unwanted sexual acts. Sexual abuse may be as extreme as rape, but it also includes the unwanted touching by another of the victim's genitals, breasts, buttocks, and other body areas.

If an older person with ALZHEIMER'S DISEASE or DEMENTIA is sexually assaulted by another person, the abuse is as illegal as when the older person is mentally competent. It is necessary to state this because some people have the wrong idea that uninvited sexual contact with an older person who is not competent is not quite as bad as when the older person is in full possession of his or her mental faculties.

Both men and women are sexually victimized, although women are more likely to be victims of sexual abuse. In one extreme case, an extremely confused older man was raped so repeatedly that he asked investigators if he was a man or a woman.

The sexual abuse may occur in a nursing-home setting, at home, or elsewhere. Wherever it occurs, it is against the law.

Emotional Abuse   Sometimes abuse is emotional, in which case the older person is constantly berated or verbally attacked. An example of emotional abuse is frequently shouting at or deriding individuals in a consistent pattern, such as constantly telling the individual that he or she is stupid, crazy, useless, or should die, as well as other forms of verbal abuse. Emotional abuse may also accompany physical or sexual abuse.

Neglect   Neglect is the withholding of needed items, such as food, clothing, shelter, or medicine. Neglect can be passive or active; for example, *abandonment* is a form of passive neglect. If an older person who needs help is left alone and cannot seek help on his or her own, this constitutes abandonment. The neglectful person can predict that the older person will suffer and die but is not there to see it happen.

Active neglect, on the other hand, involves refusing to provide food, shelter, clothing, or medication to a person who lives with the abuser or who is cared for by the abuser in an institution. The evidence of the neglect is clearly apparent. Purposeful withholding of needed medical treatment may be also called medical neglect. An example of medical neglect is failing to take an obviously very sick person to see the doctor, to take the person to an emergency room, or to call for an ambulance.

It is also neglectful for a caregiver to provide food to the older person that cannot be consumed; for example, giving older people food that they cannot chew or leaving food with them when they are incapable of feeding themselves.

State Laws and Abuse/Neglect   In the United States, each state law provides for how alleged incidents of abuse and neglect of seniors should be handled and to whom it should be reported, whether to a division of the state aging department, the state health department, or to another organization. In general, abuse or neglect should be reported to the police department as well as to the adult protective services unit of the state social services office in the area where the elderly person lives. Police and/or social workers will subsequently investigate the allegation and presumably will take the appropriate action.

Nursing-Home Abuse   In recent years, there has been increasing concern about the abuse or neglect of older people living in nursing homes. Seniors have been physically and sexually assaulted in nursing homes, and they have also been neglected by the withholding of food and/or medical care. Lurid newspaper and magazine articles have documented shocking cases of very poor care, in which the residents are starving, covered with severe bed sores, and basically ignored.

Many lawsuits have been filed against nursing homes, and some states, such as Florida, have placed a cap on the upper limit that may be recovered from a nursing-home lawsuit. This action was probably taken to avoid the financial ruin of many nursing homes in the state.

There are many reasons why abuse and neglect may occur in nursing homes, and the subject is very complex. One possible reason is that many people who live in nursing homes are on MEDICAID, which returns a lower rate to the nursing-home owners than the fees received from private payers. MEDICARE pays only for short-term stays in nursing homes, often after patients are released from hospitals and it is assumed that they will be able to return to their homes after recovery.

It is also true that most nursing homes pay low salaries to the workers and have difficulty attracting skilled or experienced employees. Most nursing homes have a very high turnover of staff.

Many older people who live in nursing homes require extensive care and may suffer from Alzheimer's disease or dementia; thus, it is very difficult for the often underpaid and overworked staff to provide care. Of those older people who are still cognitively intact and who live in nursing homes, most are very ill and require a great deal of care.

The combination of low financial return to nursing-home owners, low pay to workers, and "high maintenance" patients are key issues contributing to the abuse of patients in nursing homes, although other issues may also be involved, such as the oversight or lack of oversight of state and federal government agencies, the difficulty in finding physicians to treat nursing-home patients, the insufficient number of visitors that many nursing-home residents receive, and other issues.

Of course, it is important to emphasize that abuse and neglect are not acceptable in any nursing home. Nursing homes are answerable to state inspectors for violations to the rights of their residents as well as for violations of building and health codes.

Some studies indicate that when abuse or neglect occurs in a nursing home, it is most likely to occur during the evening hours when there are fewer staff members available. In addition, single men in their early 20s who are on staff are more likely to be physically abusive to patients than older men or females. People who have been convicted of violent crimes in the past are more likely to be abusive again, and nursing homes should screen their staff before hiring any workers, including hourly workers.

Yet, studies performed by the GAO and released in 2002 revealed that many nursing homes do *not* perform FBI checks of workers. As a result, an abusive person can leave a nursing home from where he is fired in one state and move to another state and get a job at another nursing home.

The best route to prevent an older resident from suffering from abuse in a nursing home is for family members to visit the individual on a regular basis. Aware of regular visits from family members, the nursing-home staff will be more likely to provide at least a basically acceptable standard of care to the older person because they will know that poor care will be noticed and complained about. If family members are unable to visit the loved one, they may be able to contact religious organizations or clergy and to request assistance with providing visitors.

The National Elder Abuse Incidence Study

The National Elder Abuse Incidence Study is probably the most comprehensive study of elder abuse that has ever been performed in the United States or anywhere else. The study results were released in 1998, and the findings were based on data collected from state agencies nationwide in 1996. The researchers found that there were 236,479 reports of abuse, neglect, and self-neglect in 1996. Of this number, 115,110 reports were substantiated by an investigation as valid complaints, and analyses were then made on the substantiated cases.

Among these substantiated cases, the largest category of maltreatment was physical abuse (61.9 percent), followed by abandonment (56.0 percent), emotional/psychological abuse (54.1 percent), financial/material abuse (44.5 percent), and neglect (41.0 percent). (Some older people experienced more than one form of maltreatment.)

Traits of Abusers When considering the age of abusers, according to *The National Elder Abuse Incidence Study: Final Report,* the age category that included the highest percentage of abusers were 41 to 59 years (38.4 percent). Interestingly, however, more than one-third of the perpetrators (34.3 percent) were *themselves* age 60 or older. As the population continues to age, it is increasingly likely that greater numbers of people who are age 60 and older will themselves become FAMILY CAREGIVERS to their aging parents and spouses.

Most of the abusers (77.4 percent) in the study were white, and a minority (17.9 percent) were African American. ADULT CHILDREN were the most likely perpetrators (47.3 percent) of substantiated maltreatment, followed by spouses of the victims (19.3 percent).

Other research has been performed on characteristics of the abusers of older individuals. Some researchers have identified several basic characteristics and patterns among both abusers and the older individuals that they abuse. For example, most abusers, whether they are family members who are caregivers or are employees at a nursing home, feel "burned out" and may also feel that they have little or no time for themselves.

If the abusers work in an institution such as a nursing home, they may feel that the work is difficult and that they are underpaid, unappreciated, and have little or no career prospects for the future (which may be an accurate perception, unless they go back to school or change careers). They may have contempt for older persons in general, particularly for those who are very helpless. If they regard the residents as "like children," and if they tend to infantilize nursing home residents, studies indicate that they are also more likely to abuse them.

Characteristics of Abused Persons Abused individuals are most likely to be female and physically weak. People older than age 80 have a much higher risk of abuse than younger individuals. According to *The National Elder Abuse Incidence Study: Final Report,* people older than age 80 comprised about 19 percent of the elder population, but they represented more than half of all the substantiated cases of neglect in the study (51.8 percent), and nearly half of the cases of physical abuse (43.7 percent).

Older people who are unable to care for themselves are more likely to be abused than are those who are independent individuals. Sadly, abused people may be fearful of their abusers, but at the same time, they may also be fearful (or do not know how) to report the abusive behavior to others. Physicians and other individuals are more likely to report such abuse.

Medical Indicators of Abuse or Neglect

According to Dr. Krouse in her article on elder abuse on eMedicine on the Internet, the following clinical findings indicate a strong probability of elder abuse:

- More than one injury in various states of healing
- Injuries that are unexplained
- A delay in seeking treatment
- Explanations for the injury that differ between the caregiver and the injured person
- Bruises, burns, rope marks, or lacerations
- Presence of venereal disease or genital infections

- Malnutrition
- Dehydration
- Laboratory finding of under- or overdose of medications
- Decubitus (skin) ulcers

For further information on the abuse and neglect of older individuals, contact:

National Center on Elder Abuse (NCEA)
1225 I Street, NW
Suite 725
Washington, DC 20005
(202) 898-2586
http://www.elderabusecenter.org

Brogden, Mike, and Preeti Nijhar. *Crime, Abuse and the Elderly.* Portland, Oreg.: Willan Publishing, 2000.

Collins, Kim A., M.D. et al. "Elder Abuse and Neglect," *Archives of Internal Medicine* 160, no. 11 (June 12, 2000).

Decalmer, Peter, and Frank Glendenning, eds. *The Mistreatment of Elderly People.* London: Sage Publications, 1997.

General Accounting Office. "Nursing Homes: More Can Be Done to Protect Residents from Abuse," GAO-02-312 (March 2002).

Krouse, Laurel H., M.D., Ph.D. "Elder Abuse," eMedicine. Available online. URL:http://www.emedicine.com/emerg/topic160.htm, posted June 5, 2001.

Marshall, Charles E., M.D., Donna Benton, Ph.D., and Joselynn M. Brazier, M.D. "Elder Abuse: Using Clinical Tools to Identify Clues of Mistreatment." *Geriatrics* 55, no. 2 (2000): 42–53.

Tatara, Toshio, Ph.D., principal investigator, et al. *The National Elder Abuse Incidence Study: Final Report.* Washington, D.C.: The National Center on Elder Abuse, 1998.

accessibility to facilities Refers to the enabling of the use of facilities for people who are older than age 65 or those who are disabled. For example, people who use wheelchairs should have access to ramps in most public buildings and shopping centers. In addition to stairs, there should also be elevators. Some facilities provide escalators, but they may be difficult for disabled people to manage.

The AMERICANS WITH DISABILITIES ACT requires that private and public establishments provide accessibility to disabled individuals. Restaurants must have bathroom stalls that can accommodate a wheelchair and that have grab bars for people who may be unsteady on their feet.

Parking spots must be available close to the entrance for people who carry disabled stickers on their cars. These stickers are usually provided by the state department of motor vehicles after receipt of a letter from the disabled individual's doctor. They can also often be made available for temporary use, such as when someone is recovering from an injury or illness (such as from a hip FRACTURE or open heart surgery), or they can be made available on a longer basis for more chronic conditions, such as STROKE or PARKINSON'S DISEASE.

accidental injuries/deaths Physical harm or death that occurs as a result of FALLS, fires, motor vehicle crashes, or other accidents in or away from the residence. Accidental injuries are a leading cause of death among people older than age 65, and according to a report in *MMWR,* unintentional injuries are the seventh cause of death among adults age 65 and older.

Among older people, the greatest number of deaths from accidental injuries result from falls, and about 8,500 older adults in the United States died from falls in 1996. The majority (60 percent) were adults who were 75 years or older. See Table 1. (See also EYE PROBLEMS, another leading cause of falls and other injuries.)

As can be seen from Table 1, white males have the greatest rate of death from falls, followed by white females. Black males have about half the risk of death from a fall as white males, and the risk is even lower for black females (10.1 per 100,000).

For older males and females of all races, the rate of death from falls was the greatest in the Midwest and was lowest in the Northeast, although it is unclear why this is true.

House Fire Deaths Are Higher Among Older People

According to a study reported in 2001 in the *New England Journal of Medicine,* based on 7,190 fires and 223 injuries and deaths in the Dallas, Texas, area, injuries were highest among individuals older than age 65 and among blacks. The fatality rate was highest among people age 65 and older and also

TABLE 1   NUMBER AND RATE OF FALL-RELATED DEATHS AMONG ADULTS AGE 65 OLDER AND IN THE UNITED STATES, 1996

Characteristic	Men		Women	
	Number	Rate per 100,000	Number	Rate per 100,000
Age				
65–74 years	960	11.5	544	5.3
75–84	1,563	34.8	1,618	23.3
Older than age 85	1,372	128.3	2,417	89.8
Race				
White	3,649	29.3	4,349	24.4
Black	180	16.7	170	10.1
Region				
Northeast	684	23.4	784	17.8
Midwest	1,086	32.9	1,327	27.5
South	1,294	26.8	1,612	23.1
West	831	29.5	856	22.7

Derived from: Judy A. Stevens, M.S., M.PH., Ph.D., et al. "Surveillance for Injuries and Violence Among Older Adults," *Morbidity & Mortality Weekly Report* 48, no. SS-8 (December 17, 1999): 27–50.

children younger than age 10. A lack of a smoke detector in the home was another major factor in injuries and deaths from house fires.

Fracture Injuries, Especially Hip Fractures

Accidental injuries are the primary cause of FRACTURES and injuries involving the brain and spinal cord. Hip fractures are also a serious type of fracture, and adults age 65 and older in the United States sustain an estimated 212,000 fall-related hip fractures per year. Skull fractures leading to bruising of the brain, epidural or subdural hematomas, are very serious. Rib fractures can be dangerous if a lung is punctured.

Although more men die from falls than women, when it comes to fractures, women who fall are much more likely to suffer from fractures. In fact, older women suffer about 80 percent of hip fractures. The risk for hip fracture increases with age and women age 85 and older are about eight times more likely to require hospitalization after a fall than women who are ages 65–74 years. (See Table 2.)

As can be seen from the table, the rate of hip-fracture hospitalization steadily increases with age for both men and women. The rate of hospitalization is also much higher for white older women than for black older women. The data is not available for black older men, but it can be assumed that the rate is probably lower than for white men because the death rate from falls is much lower for black men.

Hip fractures are a very serious problem because an estimated half of older adults who experience hip fractures will never recover their previous level of functioning.

TABLE 2   RATE OF HOSPITALIZATION PER 100,000 POPULATION FOR HIP FRACTURE AMONG ADULTS AGE 65 AND OLDER IN THE UNITED STATES, 1996

Characteristic	Men	Women
Age (years)		
65–74 years	168.0	501.1
75–84	682.1	1,620.3
Older than 85 years	2,256.2	3,958.3
Race		
White	413.0	1,174.0
Black	Not available	230.0
Region		
Northeast	466.9	1,191.2
Midwest	519.5	1,514.7
South	540.7	1,354.4
West	419.7	1,347.3

Derived from: Judy A. Stevens, M.S., M.PH., Ph.D., et al. "Surveillance for Injuries and Violence Among Older Adults," *Morbidity & Mortality Weekly Report* 48, no. SS-8 (December 17–1999): 27–50.

Motor Vehicle Accidents

Older people are more likely to sustain serious injuries or deaths in car crashes than younger people. Although drivers age 65 and older represent about 13 percent of the population, they also represent 17 percent of all car crash fatalities. A small percentage of car crash fatalities among older people (16 percent) are pedestrians.

See also DRIVING.

Istre, Gregory R., M.D. et al. "Deaths and Injuries from House Fires," *New England Journal of Medicine* 344, no. 25 (June 25, 2001): 1,911–1,916.

Stevens, Judy A., M.S., M.PH., Ph.D. et al. "Surveillance for Injuries and Violence Among Older Adults," *Morbidity & Mortality Weekly Report* 48, no. SS-8 (December 17, 1999): 27–50.

activities of daily living   Refers to the basic activities that most individuals can accomplish for themselves, such as feeding themselves, bathing, and managing their own toileting. With disability and disease, these activities may become increasingly difficult or even impossible for an older person to achieve, and for this reason, they may be unable to meet their own basic nutritional or personal hygiene needs. As a result, they must rely on others to provide this care. Some older people neglect their health and nutrition and can die as a result.

Some disabled people also have difficulties with "instrumental activities of daily living," (IADLs) as well. This phrase refers to activities that are not necessary for daily living but that are still important tasks to most people. IADLs include such tasks as being able to use the telephone, drive a car, shop alone, prepare meals, handle money, and walk a half-mile unassisted.

Some individuals move to ASSISTED-LIVING FACILITIES so that they can still live independently but also have access to assistance if they need it. Others move in with their families and receive help from them. Some people move to NURSING HOMES if they need a higher level of care. Various support services exist to help minimize the impact of illness on these activities.

Administration on Aging (AoA)   Federal organization in the United States that is tasked with policy development, planning, and delivering assistance to older people and their caregivers. Under the OLDER AMERICANS ACT, the AoA provides funding to states and to area agencies and tribal organizations that assist elders with issues related to NUTRITION, TRANSPORTATION, elder-abuse prevention, and other services.

The AoA administers the National Eldercare Locator, a toll-free number that can direct people to assistance in their local areas, available at (800) 677-1116 from 9 A.M. to 8 P.M., Monday through Friday, Eastern time.

The organization also provides pension-counseling programs, long-term care OMBUDSMAN programs to investigate complaints of nursing home fraud and abuse, and a broad array of other programs designed to provide assistance to older people. In addition, the AoA funds many efforts to help older people. For example, in fiscal year 2000, grants were provided to 16 states to assist older people facing DISASTERS, such as hurricanes, floods, and other natural disasters.

The AoA offers the National Aging Information Center, a service with abstracts on aging research, summaries, policy reports, and other data related to other people. (*www.aoa.gov/naic*).

Contact this organization at:

AoA
330 Independence Avenue, SW
Washington, DC 20201
(202) 619-7501
http://www.aoa.gov

adult children   Generally refers to adults who provide partial or comprehensive assistance and care to their elderly parents. In most cases, women are the FAMILY CAREGIVERS to their aging parents, although males may also provide caregiving. The average person who provides care to a parent older than age 65 is an adult female in her 50s; however, some "adult children" are younger than in their 50s. Other adult children are themselves older than age 65, sometimes struggling to provide care for their parents in their 80s and 90s.

Adult children often still have children who are living at home, and consequently, they may feel that they must choose between their own children and the needs of their older parents. Should the parents come to live with the adult children, the change affects everyone who lives in the home. Some studies indicate that adolescents can become more positive toward their grandparents when they share a home with them. Most research, however, concentrates on the burden that adult children face when they provide caregiving.

See also BABY BOOMERS; LONG-DISTANCE CARE; SANDWICH GENERATION.

adult day centers   Facilities that provide care, usually during daylight hours, to individuals who are older than age 65. Generally the term *day center* is preferred to *day-care center* because centers for adults are very different from child-care facilities. Also, the phrase may seem demeaning, ageist, and infantilizing to some older people.

Adult day-center care is provided to people who cannot be left alone but who are not so sick that they require continuous nursing-home care. They may suffer from DEMENTIA or ALZHEIMER'S DISEASE, or they may be mentally sound but be medically fragile.

There are an estimated 4,000 day centers for adults in the United States, nearly double from the numbers available in 1989. Most day centers are nonprofit organizations, and are associated with medical centers, home-care agencies, nursing homes, or other organizations.

See also BABY BOOMERS; RESPITE SERVICES.

adverse drug event   Negative consequence of taking a medication, which may range from mild discomfort to death. Some doctors may be overly fearful of adverse drug events: some experts believe that some older people are undertreated because of physicians' fears that medication could lead to an adverse event, such as a STROKE or a HEART ATTACK. In this case, patients may fail to gain benefit from drugs because of excessive fear among doctors.

Because so many older people are likely to be taking more than one and sometimes many medications, their risk for an adverse drug event is heightened. In addition, many patients have multiple physicians and often receive prescriptions and take medications ordered by one or more doctors without the other physicians' knowledge. (This is not recommended. Patients should advise every doctor about all drugs, prescribed, over-the-counter, or herbs or SUPPLEMENTS that they take at each and every office visit.)

It has also been scientifically established that older peoples' bodies often react differently from younger individuals' bodies to the same dose of medication. Also, in most cases, medications have not been tested on individuals older than age 65 prior to the pharmaceutical company receiving approval for the medication to be sold. Rates of metabolism, degrees of body fat (which acts as a storage reservoir for many medications), and liver or kidney diminished function are just a few reasons for erratic responses to some medicines in the senior population.

For example, a dose of digoxin for the heart that is considered a normal dose for the average person younger than age 65 can sometimes induce a cardiac arrhythmia in an older person. The older person may also have symptoms such as nausea, vomiting, confusion, and other side effects not seen in younger people. One key reason for this particular difference is that older people have less-healthy hearts.

According to Dr. Rosanne M. Leipzig in her 2001 article for *Geriatrics*, sometimes adverse events caused by drugs are mistaken by doctors for aging-related problems, such as INCONTINENCE or even DEMENTIA or CONFUSION. Leipzig says that risk factors for an adverse drug reaction in an older person who is taking many drugs (polypharmacy) should be considered, as should the dosage of the drug.

Some Drugs Are Less Advisable for Older People

Leipzig advises against the prescribing of certain drugs to people age 65 and older; for example, she recommends against prescribing the antidepressant Elavil (amitriptyline), the sedative Valium (diazepam), the muscle relaxant Flexeril (cyclobenzaprine), and the nonsteroidal antiinflammatory (NSAID) Indocin (indomethacin), among other drugs that she feels are inappropriate or dangerous for many older people. Instead, she recommends choosing another drug in the same class; for example, rather than Elavil, prescribing Pamelor (nortriptyline) because it is more readily tolerated by older people and has fewer side effects.

Leipzig concludes, "Familiarity with the drug classes and particular agents that are generally contraindicated in older persons also will help reduce the potential risks and side effects."

Many doctors do not realize that they need to take the age of their older patients into account when determining both which drug to use and what dosage to prescribe. In a review of studies on medications prescribed for older people, reported in a 2000 issue of *The Annals of Pharmacotherapy*, the researchers found that about 14 to 24 percent of patients had been prescribed medications that were not recommended for older people.

Commonly prescribed inappropriate medications included Elavil (amitriptyline), an antidepressant, the painkiller Darvon (propoxyphene), and Valium (diazepam), a long acting antianxiety medication. Women older than age 80 and patients on MEDICAID were the most likely to be prescribed inappropriate drugs. Nursing-home patients were also more likely than others to receive inappropriate drugs for older people.

Chronic Pain and Adverse Drug Events

Many older people take medications for the chronic pain of ARTHRITIS or other painful medical problems. When some painkillers are taken on a regular basis, patients may experience side effects, such as severe stomach upset or even ULCERS. According to Dr. Steven D. Feinberg, in his 2000 article for *Geriatrics*, care should be taken in prescribing painkillers. He believes that muscle relaxants and drugs in the benzodiazepine (sedative) class are sometimes overprescribed to older patients.

Dr. Feinberg also points out that although acetaminophen is well tolerated, it can cause liver damage over the long term and says that doctors should test the liver function of patients who regularly take high doses of acetaminophen. Aspirin is another drug that people may take for granted, but it can cause gastrointestinal bleeding, rashes, and even shock, all of which are adverse drug events.

Nonsteroidal antiinflammatory medications are frequently prescribed for chronic pain, but they may cause ulcer disease. If the patient also consumes alcohol, the risk for gastrointestinal bleeding is increased further.

Medications in the opium class drugs relieve pain, but older people are more likely to be overly sensitive to drugs such as morphine. They may also be resistant to taking such drugs, fearing they will become addicted to these medications. They may become habituated or addicted to these medications, and careful physician supervision is important.

Corticosteroid drugs such as Prednisone, prescribed for inflammation, also can cause adverse drug events; for example, they can cause high blood sugar (hyperglycemia) in older people, loss of calcium from bones, and even CATARACTS.

Topical drugs (applied to the skin) may be effective for treating pain, and they generally have limited adverse effects and are safer than oral medications. Zostrix (capsaicin) is one such medication (used for pain control after an attack of shingles), and there are other prescribed and over-the-counter topical agents.

See also MEDICATION INTERACTIONS; PAIN MANAGEMENT.

Aparasu, Rajender R., and Jane R. Mort. "Inappropriate Prescribing for the Elderly: Beers Criteria-Based Review," *The Annals of Pharmacotherapy* 34 (2000): 338–346.

Feinberg, Steven D., M.D. "Prescribing Analgesics: How to Improve Function and Avoid Toxicity When Treating Chronic Pain," *Geriatrics* 55, no. 12 (2000): 44–62.

Hanlon, Joseph T., Leslie A. Shimp, and Todd P. Sernia. "Recent Advances in Geriatrics: Drug-Related Problems in the Elderly," *The Annals of Pharmacotherapy* 34 (2000): 360–365.

Leipzig, Rosanne M., M.D., Ph.D. "Prescribing Keys to Maximizing Benefit While Avoiding Adverse Drug Effects," *Geriatrics* 56, no. 2 (2001): 30–34.

African Americans   Blacks living in the United States. Aging African Americans have significantly higher rates of many diseases and serious conditions than are experienced by other races, such as higher rates of CORONARY HEART DISEASE, DIABETES, OBESITY, HYPERTENSION, and STROKE, although the reasons for these higher rates are unclear and are actively debated. There were about 2.8 million African Americans age 65 and older in the United States in 2000, according to the U.S. Census Bureau. The majority (1.7 million) were female.

Deaths

Black Americans have about the same rate of negative habits such as SMOKING as whites, but they are more likely to develop cancer, and they are also more likely to die from cancer. African Americans have higher rates of kidney disease than people of other races do, and they experience about four times as many new cases of kidney failure as experienced by CAUCASIANS. Many African Americans have problems with both hypertension and obesity, which are also linked to the development of kidney disease.

Among all races, African Americans have the greatest risk for developing PANCREATIC CANCER, although the reason for this is unknown. They are also more likely than Caucasians to develop STOMACH CANCER, and African American males have a very high rate of PROSTATE CANCER.

Illnesses

In looking at ASTHMA, African Americans with asthma have about three times the rate of death than white Americans. Another high-risk area is GLAUCOMA: African Americans have a risk of developing glaucoma that is three to four times greater than the risk experienced by whites.

Although MEDICARE provides coverage for immunizations against flu and pneumonia, only about 14 percent of all African Americans age 65 and older actually receive these vaccines. It is unclear whether there is a problem with accessibility to facilities, whether there is a lack of belief in the importance of such immunizations, or if some other factors (or possibly multiple factors) are at work. What is clear is that failure to receive immunizations against flu and pneumonia leads to poorer health, and this problem needs to be resolved.

Life Expectancy

African Americans, particularly African-American males, have a shorter LIFE EXPECTANCY than that of Caucasians or individuals of other races; for example, African-American men have a life expectancy of about 66 years, compared to about 74 years for all men.

Many of the medical problems faced by African Americans (as with white Americans who have similar medical problems) are interrelated; for example, an African-American person with high blood pressure (hypertension) has a greater risk of suffering from a heart attack or stroke than those without hypertension. A person who is obese has a greater risk of having both diabetes and hypertension.

Gender Issues

There are some differences in the health risks of African-American women and men, compared to other races, or compared to each other, that is, black women compared to black men.

African-American Women

Black women in the United States have a markedly higher risk of death from HEART ATTACK and stroke than white women. In fact, some age groups of black women have a higher risk of death than that faced by their African-American male counterparts. Black women are also at much greater risk for developing diabetes than white women.

African-American Men

Black men have a higher rate of diabetes, stroke, and other serious health problems than experienced by white men.

Poverty

According to the U.S. Administration on Aging, more than 68 percent of older African Americans are poor, marginally poor, or economically vulnerable. They are about one and one-half times more likely than whites to live in poverty. About 25 percent of older African Americans (age 65 and older) have an income below the poverty line.

Benefits of Blackness

There are not only negative health and well-being aspects to being an African American in the United States, but there are also some health *benefits;* for example, black males have about half the risk of death from a fall as white males, and the risk is even lower for black females. African-American men and women also have significantly lower rates of OSTEOPOROSIS than that experienced by whites and other races.

U.S. Administration on Aging. "The Many Faces of Aging: Serving Our African American Elders." 2001.

ageism   Stereotyping of individuals based solely on their age and usually centering on individuals older than age 65. Said psychiatrist Robert Butler, to whom the coining of the term *ageism* is attributed, "Ageism, the prejudice of one group against another, has been applied mostly to the prejudice of younger people toward older people. Underlying ageism is the awesome dread and fear of growing older, and therefore, the desire to distance ourselves from older persons who are a proxy portrait of our future selves. We see the young dreading aging and the old envying youth. Ageism not only reduces the status of older people but of all people."

If older people are viewed as helpless and hopeless or as useless individuals in society despite their individual circumstances and their personal past or present contributions, they may eventually assume these negative roles in a form of LEARNED HELPLESSNESS.

Neutral and Negative Stereotyping

Ageism need not be negative but may be superficially positive, as in assuming that all older women are "grandmotherly" and hence kindly and sweet, or that all older men are "grandfatherly." However, ageist stereotyping is far more likely to be negative.

A View of All Older People as Sick and Senile

Often, an overriding perception of the basic lifestyles of older people colors how people age 65 and older are viewed by younger individuals. For example, an "ageist" stereotypical perception is of the older woman who sits in a rocking chair, knits all day, and constantly complains about her ailments.

The key features of the ageist stereotype are often frailty, inactivity, and a cause of problems or annoyance to others. In fact, some older people actually *are* in poor health and are physically inactive; however, it is also true that many older people are active and vigorous.

Complaints of ARTHRITIS, HYPERTENSION, dizziness, and other medical problems generally increase with aging. However, most people who are even very elderly can receive medical care that will improve their medical conditions. Many people believe that all or most older people suffer from DEMENTIA, another ageist assumption. Although it is true that the risk for dementia increases with age, the majority of older people do *not* have dementia.

Language That Demeans Older People

Older people may be infantilized, and terms such as *second childhood, old boys* or *old girls, old coot, old codger, geezer,* and many other words and phrases are used to either pointedly or subtly deride older individuals.

Negative words were once used by many people to demean some racial and ethnic groups, but such words and phrases are now considered by most people to be unacceptable terms. It is hoped that most people will realize that ageist terms are also unacceptable.

Doctors and Ageism

Ageism is not necessarily malevolent or hate based but instead may stem from a lack of knowledge about older people, as well ingrained cultural perceptions; for example, even many physicians assume that it is "normal" for older people to feel ill, and they may treat their older patients less aggressively than they would a person who is 40 or 50 years old. One possible indicator of such a bias can be seen when a doctor frequently cites age as the cause of every medical problem that a patient has or if a doctor always dismisses all major or minor complaints as age based.

An older woman with pains in one of her legs was told by her doctor that because she was 85, she had to expect that such pains would occur. She told him that both her legs were 85 years old but that only one of them hurt, redirecting his attention to her physical complaint rather than her age.

Most older people can also make lifestyle changes that will help improve health, such as increasing their physical activity and eating a healthy diet. The difference between acknowledging such differences and ageism comes when doctors and others generalize from all older people to one older person.

Measuring Ageism

Geriatric researchers have developed a tool to measure ageist attitudes. Some ageist events are such items as "a doctor or a nurse assumed ailments caused by age," "called an insulting name," "assumed I could not hear well," and "ignored or not taken seriously." According to Erdman Palmore in his report on his ageism survey in a 2001 issue of *The Gerontologist,* the most commonly occurring form of ageism reported (by 58 percent of respondents) was "I was told a joke that pokes fun at old people."

Palmore found that less-educated individuals (a high school education or less) reported more incidents of ageism than college graduates.

Sometimes therapists exhibit ageist bias. In a study of therapists' attitudes toward older individuals, reported in a 2000 issue of *Family Process,* researchers analyzed the responses of practicing therapists, therapists in training, and nontherapists who were given case histories of older individuals who were ages 74 and 69 and to case histories of younger individuals ages 29 and 34. Except for age, the marital problems described in the case histories were the same. For example, both young and older females were fearful of a lack of sexual activity stemming from their unattractiveness. Both younger and older males in the case histories were behaving defensively and had increased their use of alcohol.

The researchers found a significant age bias across therapists, nontherapists, and therapists in training. The problems of the younger individuals in the case histories were seen as more important and pressing. Said the researchers,

Substance abuse, sexual problems, and conflict escalation tend to be construed as indicative of more serious relationship difficulty and greater personal dysfunction when client age is younger. Vulnerability to age-related stereotypes and perceptions does not appear to be substantially reduced by clinical training and experience. It is evident that non-therapists, therapists-in-training, and experienced clinicians are alike prone to differential age standards. Given the finding that views vary in relationship to client age, a corollary vulnerability may exist for age-related discriminatory treatment.

Butler, Robert, M.D. "Global Ageing: Challenges and Opportunities of the Next Century," *Aging International* 23, no. 1 (1996): 12–32.

Grant, Lynda D. "Effects of Ageism on Individual and Health Care Providers' Responses to Healthy Aging," *Health and Social Work* (February 1996).

Ivey, David C., Elizabeth Wieling, and Steven M. Harris. "Save the Young—the Elderly Have Lived Their Lives: Ageism in Marriage and Family Therapy," *Family Process* (July 22, 2000).

Palmore, Erdman, Ph.D. "The Ageism Survey: First Findings," *The Gerontologist* 41, no. 5 (2001): 572–575.

aging in place   Remaining at home, despite aging and disabilities. Many people prefer to live in their homes and not be placed in a nursing home if they become medically fragile. Some people can "age in place" in an ASSISTED-LIVING FACILITY where meals and emergency care is provided to older or disabled individuals. The overwhelming majority of seniors would prefer an assisted-living facility to a nursing home; however, MEDICARE does not cover the cost of assisted living. In some cases, MEDICAID covers assisted living for low-income seniors if the state has received a Medicaid waiver; however, this option is available in few cases.

AIDS   Refers to Acquired Immune Deficiency Syndrome, a disease that is caused by the Human

Immunodeficiency Virus (HIV). An estimated 10 percent of all AIDS patients in the United States are age 50 and older (about 75,000). The majority, or about 52 percent, of these older individuals with AIDS, are either AFRICAN AMERICAN or HISPANIC AMERICAN, according to the National Institute on Aging. Among women alone, the percentages are much higher: of all females older than age 50 who have AIDS, 70 percent are either African American or Hispanic.

People who engage in risky sexual behavior such as anal sex and/or males who do not use a condom (and their sexual partners) are at risk for contracting HIV. Many older people consider condoms solely in the context of contraceptives, and women beyond menopause may mistakenly believe that condoms are unnecessary when they have sexual intercourse. Although pregnancy is not a risk for a postmenopausal woman, AIDS and other sexually transmitted diseases continue to be risks throughout life.

Some individuals contracted HIV through blood transfusions that occurred between 1978 and 1985 when the blood supply did contain blood tainted with the HIV virus. Other people have contracted HIV through sharing needles, not only for using illegal drugs but sometimes to inject insulin for DIABETES. Anyone who has shared needles with another person should be tested for HIV/AIDS.

Older people are sometimes embarrassed or afraid to be tested for HIV/AIDS, and consequently, they take no action. This is a mistake because in the early stages of the disease, medication can be taken to delay its progression. Also, the disease could be more virulent in older people than it is in younger individuals.

For further information, contact the following organizations:

AARP
601 E Street, NW
Washington, DC 20049
(202) 434-2260
http://www.aarp.org/griefandloss

Center for AIDS Prevention Studies at the University of California, San Francisco
74 New Montgomery Street
Suite 600
San Francisco, CA 94105
(415) 597-9100
http://www.ashastd.org/nah/nah.html

CDC National Prevention Information Network
P.O. Box 6003
Rockville, MD 20849
(800) 458-5231 (toll-free)

National Association on HIV Over Fifty
c/o Midwest AIDS Training and Education Center
808 S. Wood Street
MSC 779
Chicago, IL 60612
(312) 996-1373
http://www.uic.edu/depts/matec/nahof.html

Senior Action in a Gay Environment (SAGE)
305 7th Avenue
16th Floor
New York, NY 10001
(212) 741-2247
http://www.sageusa.org

National Institute on Aging. "HIV, AIDS, and Older People" (1999).

alcoholism An addiction to alcohol, including both physical and psychological components. Older people who drink to excess may have been drinking for years, or they may start drinking late in life due to DEPRESSION, BEREAVEMENT, PAIN and loneliness, or for other reasons. Often, their drinking is hidden and friends, and family members may not realize the source of physical and behavioral problems, attributing them instead to "old age."

Sometimes the symptoms of chronic alcoholism may be confused with the symptoms of ALZHEIMER'S DISEASE or DEMENTIA. These diseases should not be diagnosed in a person who is a heavy drinker until alcohol has been completely out of the system for at least four weeks.

Because many older alcoholics deny drinking at all, the doctor should not rely on self-report only but also needs to look for other characteristic signs of alcoholism, such as sudden and unexplained INCONTINENCE, sudden poor grooming, and worsening GOUT or DIABETES. Certain physical changes, including a protuberant abdomen ("beer belly"), enlarged breast size in men, and prominent blood vessel markings, are just a few of the outward signs of alcohol excess. Certain blood tests can be helpful with diagnosis. An unexpected reaction to a medication may also indicate that alcohol has interacted with the person's medicine.

Symptoms of Alcoholism

The National Institute on Alcohol Abuse and Alcoholism says there are four basic symptoms of alcoholism:

1. The first symptom is a compulsion to drink and a craving for alcohol. Alcoholics don't merely want to drink; they *need* to drink.
2. People afflicted with alcoholism cannot control their drinking. They cannot limit themselves to one or two drinks but instead, once started, must drink until intoxication and/or unconsciousness occurs.
3. Alcoholics are physically dependent on alcohol. If they do not drink, they suffer physical consequences, such as nausea, sweating, or shakiness. If they take a drink, these physical symptoms will disappear.
4. The final symptom of alcoholism is "tolerance," which means that the alcoholic needs to drink more than in past years to obtain the same effects from the alcohol.

Because many people can deny these symptoms to themselves and to others, experts have developed "CAGE," an acronym to help people know if they have a drinking problem. Experts say that CAGE is also an effective test for older people. The elements of CAGE are as follows:

C: "Have you ever felt that you should *cut* down on your drinking?
A: "Have people *annoyed* you by criticizing your drinking?
G: "Have you ever felt bad or *guilty* about your drinking?
E: "Have you ever had a drink the first thing in the morning (an *eye* opener) to steady your nerves or to get rid of a hangover?"

If a person answers "yes" to two or more of the CAGE questions, then he or she should be screened further for alcoholism.

Demographics of Alcoholics

Experts say that it is really not known how many older alcoholics there are because few people older than age 65 (and only about 15 percent of those who are alcoholics) actually seek treatment. However, it is estimated that from 2 to 4 percent of the elderly population does suffer from alcoholism. Most older alcoholics are men, although some researchers say that because problem drinking is so hidden by older people, there may be many more female alcoholics than is known. It is possible that society may be seeing only the "tip of the iceberg" when it comes to this illness.

Alcohol Can Affect Older People Differently

For a variety of reasons, alcohol can affect older people differently than it affects younger individuals. For example, older people usually have a decreased ratio of body water to body fat, which means that there is less fluid in which to dilute the alcohol. As a result, it is more concentrated in the body. This means that a small amount of alcohol can result in a higher blood alcohol level than the same amount would cause in younger people who weighed about the same. Basically, older people become intoxicated more quickly.

The liver is also often less efficient in most older people, and the older alcoholic risks more liver damage than the younger person.

Alcohol can also affect the brain of the older person more quickly. If an older person says that he or she feels "tipsy" after just a few drinks, he or she is probably telling the truth.

Health Problems Caused by Alcoholism

Virtually every body system is affected negatively by alcoholism, and years of heavy drinking take its toll on the body. Many serious illnesses are caused by or associated with alcoholism, such as cirrhosis of the liver, alcoholic hepatitis, brain damage, OSTEOPOROSIS, and cardiac and kidney diseases. Such diseases can be very dangerous; for example, about half of older alcoholics who have cirrhosis die a year from diagnosis.

Older alcoholics are also more likely to suffer from accidental injuries than nonalcoholics, and they also have an increased risk of hip FRACTURES. Not only does intoxication increase the risk of accidents, but the injuries can be more pronounced because of osteoporosis. They are also more likely to suffer from anemia stemming from iron and VITAMIN DEFICIENCIES, particularly a deficiency of Vitamin B_{12}. Unfortunately, this type of deficiency can cause memory loss and balance dysfunction; because these are also common symptoms of alcohol abuse, the effects can be additive. Deficiencies of Vitamin K may be present (which could lead to bleeding problems), as well as deficiencies of magnesium and phosphorus.

Alcohol interferes with the body's ability to produce white blood cells, particularly those that attack bacteria. It can damage the blood platelets and impair blood clotting. Alcoholics are more likely than nonalcoholics to suffer from a bleeding problem as simple as nosebleeds or as dire as STROKE from bleeding in the brain.

Excessive drinking can also damage the cardiovascular system. Alcoholism can cause HYPERTENSION, irregular heart rhythms, and heart muscle disorders (cardiomyopathies).

The immune system may be damaged by alcoholism, causing the alcoholic to become more vulnerable to bacterial infections such as pneumonia, tuberculosis, and other infections.

Alcoholism can lead to pancreatitis, an inflammation of the pancreas that is caused by a blockage of the ducts of the pancreas and causes damage to pancreatic tissue. If the case of pancreatitis is acute, the condition can be fatal. Symptoms of pancreatitis are vomiting and severe abdominal pain, which improves when the person leans forward. In some cases, there are no apparent symptoms.

Alcoholics are more prone to developing cancers, particularly of the head, the neck, and the esophagus. Liver-cancer risk is increased for the alcoholic. If the alcoholic also smokes, as the majority does, the risk for cancer is further accelerated.

Alcoholics are more likely to suffer from sleep disorders, such as insomnia or sleep apnea. This is a dangerous condition in which the person stops breathing for brief periods, which can be fatal. Many alcoholics attempt to treat insomnia with alcohol, which interferes with sleep patterns and is very unhealthy.

The brain is also affected by alcohol abuse. Magnetic resonance imaging (MRI) scans have shown both tissue damage and brain shrinkage in some people who are alcoholics. The emotions and the cognitive abilities of the alcoholic are affected by excessive drinking. Long-term alcoholics may also suffer from Wernicke-Korsakoff's syndrome, which is a short-term memory disorder in which the alcoholic forgets what has just happened and can only remember events that occurred years ago. These patients often confabulate or "make up" information to fill in the gaps of their missing memories. They are unable to store any new memories.

Alcoholics who have a deficiency of thiamin suffer from damage to the cerebral cortex of the brain, and they experience a variety of cognitive impairments and memory losses.

The gastrointestinal system is also often harmed by alcoholism, and the alcoholic person is more likely than nonalcoholics to suffer from heartburn and from GASTROESOPHAGEAL REFLUX DISEASE. Alcoholics are also more at risk for esophageal cancer due to damage caused by alcohol consumption to the mucous lining of the esophagus. Alcohol abuse can even harm the salivary glands and cause inflammations of the tongue and mouth.

The kidneys are also affected by alcoholism, which can actually change the structure of the kidneys and impair their function. Alcoholism also increases the amount of calcium and magnesium that are lost in the urine.

Late-Onset Drinkers

Many researchers categorize individuals into either lifelong problem drinkers or those who become alcoholics when they are in their late middle age (after age 50) or their senior years. Experts estimate that late-onset drinkers represent about 30–50 percent of all older problem drinkers. They also have a better prognosis and respond better to treatment than people who have been lifelong problem drinkers. However, they must actually seek treatment to recover from alcoholism.

Older Problem Drinkers versus Nonproblem Drinkers

In a study of 1,884 older individuals (ages 55 to 65 at the time of the study's onset), reported in a 1996 issue of *Alcohol Health & Research World*, researchers found that problem drinkers and nonproblem drinkers (social drinkers) showed certain patterns.

The following characteristics were found more frequently among older problem drinkers versus non-problem drinkers. Problem drinkers were:

- More likely to be unmarried/widowed
- Consumed twice as much alcohol
- More likely to use avoidance to deal with problems
- Less likely to have support from family or friends
- Much more likely to have suffered negative consequences related to drinking

Alcohol Interactions

Another risk of alcohol abuse is that alcohol interacts with many different categories of medications that older people may be taking, such as sedatives, painkillers, and muscle relaxants. Because older people are generally much more likely to be taking medications than younger people, they are also more likely to experience medication interactions if they consume alcohol. (See chart.)

Some medications, when taken along with alcohol, can result in a disulfiramlike reaction.

TABLE 1 INTERACTIONS BETWEEN ALCOHOL AND VARIOUS CLASSES OF MEDICATIONS

Drug Class	Generic Name	Brand Name	OTC or Rx	Interaction
Analgesics (pain relievers)	Aspirin Acetaminophen	various (e.g. Tylenol)	OTC and Rx	* Aspirin increases gastric emptying, leading to faster alcohol absorption in the small intestine. *Alcohol enhances acetaminophen metabolism into a toxic product, potentially causing liver damage
Antibiotics (for microbial infections)	Erythromycin	various	Rx	Erythromycin may increase gastric emptying, leading to faster alcohol absorption in the small intestine.
	Isoniazid	Nydrazid, Rifamate, Rifater	Rx	Alcohol increases the risk of isoniazid-related liver disease.
Anticonvulsants	Phenytoin	Dilantin	Rx	Chronic alcohol consumption induces phenytoin breakdown.
Antihistamines (allergies, colds)	Diphenhydramine Chlorpheniramine Clemastine Hydroxyzine Promethazine Cyproheptadine	e.g. Benadryl, various Atarax, Vistaril Phenergan Periactin	OTC and Rx	Alcohol enhances the effects of these drugs on the central nervous system, such as drowsiness, sedation, and decreased motor skills. These interactions are more pronounced in seniors.
Anticoagulants (prevention of blood clots)	Warfarin	Coumadin	Rx	Acute alcohol intake may increase anticoagulation by decreasing warfarin metabolism. Chronic alcohol ingestion *decreases* anticoagulation by increasing warfarin metabolism.

TABLE 1   INTERACTIONS BETWEEN ALCOHOL AND VARIOUS CLASSES OF MEDICATIONS *(continued)*

Drug Class	Generic Name	Brand Name	OTC or Rx	Interaction
Antidiabetic agents (blood sugar regulation)	Chlorpropamide Glipizide Glyburide Tolbutamide Metformin	Diabenese Glucotrol DiaBeta, Glynase, Micronase Orinase Glucophage	Rx	Alcohol consumption by diabetic patients taking these medications increases the risk of lower than normal blood sugars (hypoglycemia). Chlorpropamide, Glyburide and Tolbutamide can cause disulfiramlike interactions after alcohol ingestion. Metformin may cause increased levels of lactic acid in the blood after alcohol consumption.
Barbiturates	Phenobarbital	various	Rx	Alcohol enhances the sedative and hypnotic effects on the central nervous system.
Benzodiazepines (sedatives)	Alprazolam Chlordiazepoxide Clonazepam Diazepam Lorazepam Midazolam Oxazepam Temazepam Triazolam	Xanax Librium Klonopin Valium Ativan Versed Serax Restoril Halcion	Rx	Alcohol enhances the effects of these drugs on the central nervous system, such as decreased motor skills.
Histamine H2 blockers (ulcers, heartburn)	Cimetide Nizatidine Ranitidine	Tagamet Axid Zantac	OTC and Rx	These agents inhibit ADH in the stomach, increasing gastric emptying. Blood alcohol levels are higher than expected for a given alcohol dose and this effect increases over time.
Immune modulators (rheumatoid arthritis)	Methotrexate	Rheumtrex	Rx	Immune modulators (medications that affect immune cell function) are associated with a risk of liver damage, which is increased in combination with alcohol.
Muscle relaxants	Cyclobenzaprine Carisoprodol	Flexeril Soma	Rx	Alcohol consumption enhances impairment of physical abilities (such as driving) and increases sedation. Carisoprodol produces an opiatelike high when taken with alcohol. It is metabolized to meprobamate and sometimes abused as a street drug.

Drug Class	Generic Name	Brand Name	OTC or Rx	Interaction
NSAIDs (pain relief and inflammation)	Ibuprofen Flurbiprofen Fenoprofen Ketoprofen Naproxen Diclofenac	(Motrin, etc.) Nalfon Orudis Naprosyn Voltaren	OTC and Rx	Alcohol consumption increases the associated risk of gastrointestinal bleeding.
Opioids (pain relief)	Codeine Hydromorphone Fentanyl Morphine Meperidine Propoxyphene	various Dilaudid generic various Demerol Darvon, Wygesic	Rx	Alcohol enhances the effects of these agents on the central nervous system, such as drowsiness, sedation, and decreased motor skills.
Sedatives and Hypnotics	Chloral hydrate Meprobamate	Noctec Equanil, Miltown	Rx	Alcohol inhibits the metabolism of these agents and produces a depressant effect on the central nervous system that includes sleepiness, disorientation, incoherence, and confusion.
Tricyclic Antidepressants (depression)	Amitriptyline Clomipramine Despiramine Doxepin Imipramine Nortriptyline Trimipramine	Elavil, Endep Anafranil Norpramin Adapin, Sinequan Tofranil Aventyl, Pamelor Surmontil	Rx	Alcohol consumption increases the risk of sedation and a sudden drop in blood pressure when a person stands up (orthostatic hypotension).
Herbal Medications (Sleep aids)	Chamomile Echinacea Valerian	various preparations	OTC	Alcohol may accentuate the drowsiness that is associated with these herbal preparations.

Source: This material was excerpted from "Interactions Between Alcohol and Various Classes of Medications," *Alcohol Research & Health*, 23, no. 1 (1999): 46–47.

Disulfiram (Antabuse) is a drug that is given to treat some alcoholics. If the alcoholic consumes even a tiny amount of alcohol while taking disulfiram, he or she becomes violently ill with severe flushing, nausea, vomiting, and sweating.

See Table 2 for medications that can induce such a reaction when taken with alcohol.

Treatment of Alcoholism

An older person who has been a long-term alcoholic and who suddenly stops drinking may suffer such consequences as delirium tremens, a severe form of withdrawal that can result in seizures and even death. As a result, the older person who is going through "detoxification" (removal from alcohol) should receive treatment in a hospital or inpatient facility that is experienced with treating older alcoholics.

The aging alcoholic may be suffering from malnutrition, which should also be treated.

In general, the person who becomes alcoholic late in life has a much better prognosis for recovery than the person who has been a heavy consumer of alcohol since young adulthood.

TABLE 2   COMMONLY USED MEDICATIONS THAT CAN CAUSE DISULFIRAMLIKE REACTIONS (FLUSHING, NAUSEA, VOMITING, SWEATING)

Type of Medication	Generic Name	Brand Name
Analgesics	Phenacetin	various
(Nonsteroidal antiinflammatory drugs, also known as NSAIDs)	Phenylbutazone	
Antibiotics	Cefamandole	Mandol
	Cefoperazone	Cefobid
	Cefotetan	Defotan
	Chloramphenicol	various
	Griseofulvin	Fulvicin, Grifulvin, Grisactin
	Isoniazid	Nydrazidid, Rifamate, Rifater
	Metronidazole	Flagyl
	Nitrofurantoin	Furandantin, Macrodantin
	Sulfamethoxazole	Bactrim, Septra
Cardiovascular medications (Nitrates)	Isosorbide dinitrate	Dilatrate, Isordil, Sorbitrate
	Nitroglycerin	Nitro-Bid, Nitrostat
Diabetes medications (sulfonylureas)	Chlorpropamide	Diabenese
	Glyburide	DiaBeta, Glynase, Micronase
	Tolazamide	generic
	Tolbutamide	generic

Source: This material was excerpted from "Interactions Between Alcohol and Various Classes of Medications," *Alcohol Research & Health,* 23, no. 1 (1999): 46–47.

Many people of all ages have found success through volunteer programs offered by Alcoholics Anonymous. The major premise of Alcoholics Anonymous is that the person must give up all alcohol. Alcoholics work through "12 steps" in their efforts to achieve sobriety. They meet regularly and work to help each other stay off alcohol.

Because so many older people have problems with depression and loneliness, the social support provided by such organizations can be very helpful. However, if older individuals have problems with transportation and mobility, they may find it difficult to attend regular meetings. Another problem is that many older people refuse to acknowledge that they have a problem with alcohol.

Medications for Alcoholism

Antabuse (disulfiram) was the drug that was most used in the past to treat alcoholism. It is still used by some physicians, often in combination with other medications; however, it is generally not recommended for elderly patients because of the severity of the effects it can cause. This drug is used as an aversive treatment. When people taking Antabuse also consume alcohol, they become violently ill with nausea and vomiting, even when the amount of alcohol that was consumed was very small.

Trexan (naltrexone) is a newer medication to treat alcoholism and has been used for this purpose since the early 1990s. This drug inhibits the action of alcohol on the brain. As a result, if a person taking Trexan consumes alcohol and then drinks, he or she will not gain a pleasurable feeling that they had in the past. Trexan is also given to people who are addicted to opiates because it blocks the action of the opiate on the brain.

A key problem is that in order for Antabuse or Trexan to work, the patient must actually take them and compliance with the medication regimen can be spotty. If the person can be treated in a hospital or clinic, then staff can administer the medication, but many people cannot afford inpatient treatment and health insurance may not provide coverage.

Benzodiazepines are a class of drugs used to treat patients undergoing alcohol withdrawal, although no studies have been performed on their efficacy among older patients. In general, however, doctors use shorter-acting benzodiazepine drugs to avoid the prolonged sedative effect. As can be seen from the drug interaction chart, benzodiazepines interact with alcohol if the person continues to drink. This class of medicine can also have significant side effects, including the risk of habituation or addiction.

Apte, Minoti V., M.D., M. Med. Sci. et al. "Alcohol-Related Pancreatic Damage: Mechanisms and Treatment," *Alcohol Health & Research World* 21, no. 1 (1997): 13–20.

Ballard, Harold S., M.D. "The Hematological Complications of Alcoholism," *Alcohol Health & Research World* 21, no. 1 (1997): 42–52.

Bode, Christiane, Ph.D. and J. Christian Bode, M.D. "Alcohol's Role in Gastrointestinal Tract Disorders," *Alcohol Health & Research World* 21, no. 1 (1997): 76–93.

Brennan, Penny L., and Rudolf H. Moos. "Late-Life Drinking Behavior: The Influence of Personal Characteristics, Life Context, and Treatment," *Alcohol Health & Research World* 20, no. 3 (1996): 197–205.

Epstein, Murray, M.D. "Alcohol's Effect on Kidney Function," *Alcohol Health & Research World* 20, no. 3 (1996): 84–92.

Oscar-Berman, Marlene, Ph.D. et al. "Impairments of Brain and Behavior: The Neurological Effects of Alcohol," *Alcohol Health & Research World* 21, no. 1 (1997): 65–75.

Rigler, Sally K., M.D. "Alcoholism in the Elderly," *American Family Physician* 61 (2000): 1,710–1,716.

Standridge, John, MD, FAAFP, assistant professor, Department of Family Medicine, University of Tennessee, College of Medicine, Chattanooga, Tenn. "Alcohol Abuse in the Elderly." Continuing Medical Education activity, published by the Southern Medical Association (November 1998).

Weathermon, Ron, Pharm.D. and David W. Crabb, M.D. "Alcohol and Medication Interactions," *Alcohol Health & Research World* 20, no. 3 (1996): 40–54.

Zakhari, Sam, Ph.D. "Alcohol and the Cardiovascular System," *Alcohol Health & Research World* 21, no. 1 (1997): 21–29.

alternative medicine/complementary alternative medicine (CAM)   Medications and treatments that are considered nontraditional, such as the use of herbs and supplements, acupuncture, hypnosis, and other remedies that are rarely the first choice of most Western physicians who are treating patients.

Some experts believe that alternative medicine has become extremely popular in the West because many people are dissatisfied with remedies and treatments used for common and chronic problems, such as ARTHRITIS, OBESITY, HEADACHE, and other problems that provide incomplete, temporary, or inadequate relief.

A key misconception about alternative medicine that is shared by many people from all walks of life is the belief that alternative medicines are inherently safe because they are "natural." The reality is that some herbs and supplements can be dangerous or even fatal for some people. In addition, a common error that many patients make is not telling their physicians about the natural substances that they are taking. The prescribed medications that the patient already takes may interact with the alternative remedy, boosting or reducing its effect or changing it in some other way.

Examples of Drug Interactions

Ginkgo biloba is a blood thinner, and people who are taking ginkgo biloba as well as a blood thinner, such as Coumadin (warfarin), could suffer from internal bleeding and even death. The valerian root, sometimes taken as a sleep remedy, can interact with antiseizure drugs. Some herbs also interact with alcohol; for example, the drowsiness associated with alcohol is accentuated when the person also takes chamomile, echinacea, or valerian. These are just a few of the many possible interactions that may occur.

For these reasons, in all cases, seniors or their caregivers should be sure to inform the older person's physicians about any vitamins, herbal, or other alternative remedies the patient is taking.

Alternative medications are offered in "health-food" stores throughout the United States as well as in supermarkets and pharmacies and from many mail-order distributors. A proliferation of alternative medicines and remedies are also offered to consumers worldwide over the Internet.

In general, alternative medication encompasses such categories as:

- Herbal remedies
- Supplemental vitamin or mineral therapy
- Homeopathic remedies

Herbal Remedies

A wide variety of roots, teas, berries, and other items are sold as herbal remedies. The market for herbal remedies is estimated at about $5 billion in the United States alone.

The key impetus to the growth in sales of herbal remedies in the United States was the passage of the Dietary Supplement Health and Education Act of 1994. Based on this legislation, herbal remedies and vitamin supplements were thereafter regulated differently from both over-the-counter and prescribed medications.

In contrast to how herbs and supplements are approved and marketed in the United States, pharmaceutical companies who wish to sell new prescribed drugs must offer considerable proof in the form of clinical studies to the Food and Drug Administration (FDA) before their products may be offered to the public. These studies must indicate not only that a new drug is safe but also that it is efficacious and that it improves the condition that it treats—in other words, that the new drug actually does what it is said to do and in a safe and effective manner.

In contrast, the Dietary Supplement Health and Education Act of 1994 in the United States made the situation quite different for the sale of herbs and supplemental vitamins and minerals. In that case, the federal government, rather than the drug company, must provide proof of a problem. Also, to remove an herb or supplement from the market, the government must prove that it is dangerous. The herb or supplement may be ineffective, but if it is not actually dangerous, then it will remain on the market. To prove that a drug is dangerous can be difficult to achieve. Of course, the FDA can and does issue press releases when it believes that an alternative remedy may be harmful.

It is true that manufacturers are supposed to limit their medical claims under the law, but as of this writing, there seems to be little investigation or enforcement of this requirement, possibly because of the sheer volume of the thousands of products on the market.

Another issue of concern to consumers is that the purity of herbal remedies and supplements has been questioned in some cases, as have their actual contents. Some random studies have indicated that some herbal remedies have been adulterated with substances not described on the packaging; others have revealed that there is little or none of the substance that is purported to be included.

Sometimes, herbal remedies contain high doses of substances that may be harmful, such as ephedra (ma huang). In a person who already has hypertension, cardiac ailments, DIABETES, or other medical complications, taking ephedra and similar drugs can be very dangerous and even fatal.

Supplemental Vitamins   Individuals should always check with their physicians first before instituting any new medication regimen, including vitamin or mineral therapy. Some seniors may benefit greatly from vitamin supplementation; for example,

seniors have an increased risk for a serious Vitamin B_{12} deficiency. (Seniors should not take Vitamin B_{12} without consulting with their physician because taking this vitamin may be unnecessary.) It is also important to inform the doctor because as patient needs vary, doses of medicines may need to be adjusted.

Homeopathic Remedies   Homeopathy is a system that was developed by German physician Samuel Hahnemann in the early 19th century. This physician had stopped practicing medicine, but he continued experimenting on herbs. Hahnemann noted that large quantities of the drug quinine made healthy individuals feverish and shaky with malarialike symptoms. Much smaller doses, however, helped people who actually had malaria.

Most physicians in the United States discount the value of homeopathic remedies although doctors in Germany and other European countries accept them.

Hahnemann devised his concept of the "law of similars," which was based on his particular belief that large quantities of some substances may cause illness, but very tiny quantities of the very same substance may provide relief. For example, belladonna, a deadly drug for most people, is used by homeopaths in tiny quantities to cure migraine headaches. Some individuals have stated that they have gained migraine relief from homeopathic doses of belladonna. It is unclear whether they feel better because they *think* that they will feel better (the placebo effect) or if belladonna actually has some curative powers.

Other Alternative Treatments   Some practitioners recommend relaxation therapy, acupuncture, hypnosis, massage, chiropractic, Ayurveda, yoga, aromatherapy, TAI CHI, and a very broad array of other options to improve health and overall wellness. In the case of seniors, these remedies may be very helpful with muscle pain, BACK PAIN, arthritis, and generalized stress. Seniors who wish to use alternative treatments should consult with their physicians, and if there is no medical reason to avoid such alternative treatments, the treatments may be helpful. For example, tai chi has been shown to be extremely effective in improving balance among patients who have PARKINSON'S DISEASE.

To obtain more information on alternative remedies and complementary medicine, contact the National Institute's of Health Office of Alternative

Medicines Clearinghouse. The telephone number is toll-free: (888) 644-6226.

See also SUPPLEMENTS.

Physicians' Desk Reference. *The PDR Family Guide to Nutritional Supplements: An Authoritative A-to-Z Guide to the 100 Most Popular Nutritional Therapies and Nutraceuticals.* New York: Ballantine Books, 2001.

Alzheimer's disease   Also called "senile dementia of the Alzheimer's type" or SDAT. Alzheimer's disease is the most frequently occurring form of DEMENTIA. *Dementia* is a broad term that refers to a brain dysfunction that directly affects the intellect and that is much more common among older individuals, although the majority of senior citizens *do not* suffer from dementia. The cognitive abilities of afflicted individuals will continue to decline, eventually causing death. The rate of deterioration may be rapid or slow, depending on many different factors, but it generally occurs during a period of two to 20 years.

Discovery of Alzheimer's Disease

The disease was first diagnosed by German physician Alois Alzheimer in 1906 after an autopsy on a woman, Auguste D., who had reportedly said poignantly at some point before her death, "I have lost myself." Auguste D. had experienced increasingly difficult and severe problems with her memory and behavior, and she died at age 51. If August D. lived today, she would be diagnosed with early onset Alzheimer's disease.

The autopsy on Auguste D. startled Dr. Alzheimer, who discovered that the brain cells of Auguste D. were very differently shaped from the normal cells that are found in the cerebral cortex. This is the area of the brain that is responsible for memory and reasoning. Dr. Alzheimer also found extensive tangles of a plaque substance, which are not seen in a normal brain.

Today these plaques are a clear indicator that a deceased person had Alzheimer's disease. Currently, they cannot be identified in brain tests on living individuals without a brain biopsy, although researchers are working on ways to diagnose the disease definitively and as early as possible so that patients can be treated. As of this writing, researchers are closing in on a classic pattern of patients with Alzheimer's disease in a brain-imaging study using a positronic emission tomograph (PET) scan.

In the United States, about 4 million people have Alzheimer's disease; in Canada, about 317,000 Canadians have been diagnosed with the disease. Experts say that there will be 14 million people with Alzheimer's disease in the United States by the mid-21st century unless a way to halt or cure the disease is found. Scientists and pharmaceutical companies are currently actively testing various forms of treatment to prevent or treat dementia.

Risk Factors

A 1996 study of thousands of families that include a relative with Alzheimer's disease found that the risks of developing Alzheimer's are as follows:

11 percent if neither parent has Alzheimer's
36 percent if one parent has the disease
54 percent if both parents have the disease
40–50 percent if an identical twin has Alzheimer's disease

Another factor, which may be causal, is an individual's neurochemical (brain chemical) composition and interaction with other neurochemicals. There are neurochemical changes to the brains of people with Alzheimer's disease. For example, the level of acetylcholine is greatly reduced in the brains of people who have Alzheimer's disease.

Although many people think that older people inevitably lose their cognitive abilities and will unfailingly develop dementia as they age, this is a myth. The risk for developing Alzheimer's disease (or other forms of dementia) does increase with age, but many senior citizens do not have this impairment. Looking at all the people who are older than age 65 in the United States, about 10 percent have Alzheimer's disease. The percentage of those afflicted with the disease increases to 30–50 percent of people who are older than age 85. This also means that 50–70 percent of those 85 years are older do *not* have Alzheimer's disease.

Possible Causes of Alzheimer's Disease

Medical researchers actively dispute among themselves what causes Alzheimer's disease; however, there appear to be several major camps of theorists. One group believes that the disease is caused by an amyloid protein, which causes the sticky plaque formations that are characteristic of the brains of those with Alzheimer's disease. Other groups say these plaque formations are only a byproduct of the "true" cause. Some of these individuals believe the real culprit is another brain substance called tau, a substance they believe is responsible for killing brain cells. Actively ongoing research should bring new medical breakthroughs.

There are also genetic susceptibilities to Alzheimer's disease, although much of the disease cannot as yet be attributed to heredity; consequently, having a parent or even parents with dementia does not condemn their children to developing the illness when they are older. The key susceptibility gene for Alzheimer's disease is APOE4, as of this writing.

Centenarians and Dementia

Because of a general belief that all or most older people develop dementia, Danish researchers studied CENTENARIANS (people age 100 or older) and reported on their findings in 2001 in the *Journal of Gerontology: Psychological Sciences.* The researchers found that only about half of the centenarians (51 percent) had mild to severe dementia. The researchers' conclusion was that dementia was common among older people but is by no means inevitable.

Of 105 centenarians who had previously been diagnosed with dementia, the researchers found that 13 of them actually had other diseases that could have contributed to a dementia diagnosis, such as Vitamin B_{12} and folic-acid deficiencies, hypothyroidism, and PARKINSON'S DISEASE.

Of further interest, in looking at the 92 centenarians who really had dementia, the researchers found that half of these subjects had two or more CARDIOVASCULAR or CEREBROVASCULAR DISEASES. These type of diseases are known to be linked with dementia, and they may cause or contribute to the development of dementia.

One unusual finding: The researchers found that HYPERTENSION was more common in the *non*-demented centenarians than among those with dementia. The researchers were not sure if hypertension was in some way a protective factor against dementia for very old people or if centenarians with dementia had developed

lower blood pressure for some unknown reason. Because other studies have come to the opposite conclusion that hypertension is linked to the development of dementia, further study is indicated.

Gender and Racial Differences

Gender plays a role in Alzheimer's disease: the majority (68 percent) of those who are afflicted with Alzheimer's disease in the United States are women. Most people diagnosed with Alzheimer's disease (85 percent) in the United States are white.

Many Are in Poor Health but Still Live at Home

Many people with Alzheimer's disease have other serious medical problems, and an estimated 66 percent of elderly individuals with Alzheimer's disease are in fair to poor health. They may have other serious illnesses, such as DIABETES, ARTHRITIS, and HEART DISEASE. In addition, according to the federal government, about 20 percent of Medicare beneficiaries who have Alzheimer's also have CANCER.

Despite their ill health and, contrary to popular belief, instead of residing in nursing homes, most people with Alzheimer's disease in the United States (70 percent) live at home and are cared for by their spouses or other family members. Yet, people with Alzheimer's still represent a large portion of all nursing-home residents: 50 percent or more of nursing-home residents have Alzheimer's disease.

Symptoms of Alzheimer's Disease

There are mild, moderate, and severe stages of Alzheimer's disease. It can be difficult for even trained physicians to diagnose Alzheimer's disease in the very early stages, although doctors may be suspicious of the onset of the disease. It is also important for family members to realize that the symptoms listed here could indicate another medical problem altogether, and thus a careful evaluation by an experienced medical doctor is essential.

Some examples of symptoms of a mild dementia are:

• Personality changes, such as depression, agitation, and anxiety

• Frequent and unexplained mood swings

- Difficulty or inability to perform daily tasks that the person was capable of performing in the past
- Temporary confusion while still in the normal environment (such as in one's own neighborhood)
- Problems finding words or changes in the ability to carry on a casual conversation

Alzheimer's disease at the moderate stage is less difficult to diagnose for the physician and may also be more readily noted by family members. Some key symptoms of SDAT at the moderate level are:

- Difficulty or an inability to recognize friends and family friends or to know their names
- Aggressive or combative behavior
- Difficulty with speech, often with a reluctance to participate in conversations that require more than a one- or two-word answer
- Inability or confusion with tasks that were easy in the past, such as bathing or toileting (Some people with Alzheimer's disease are also afraid of water.)
- Loss of good personal hygiene, for example, wearing the same clothes day after day (often stained)
- Severe resistance to changes in routine or changes of any type

When Alzheimer's has reached a severe level, it is not difficult for the medical doctor or even for family members to identify the medical problem as dementia. That said, it is still important to obtain a careful diagnosis in the event that the cause of the problem is something else altogether or that it may be complicated by another ailment that could be treated.

Some examples of symptoms that are seen in people in the severe stage of Alzheimer's disease are:

- Speech that is very slow or cannot be understood at all, often with the production of made-up or nonsense words (neologisms)
- Complete incontinence of bowels and bladder
- Extreme suspiciousness or paranoia

- RAGES for no apparent reason
- Getting lost in a formerly familiar place, such as one's own street
- Trouble with simple tasks that could have been performed easily in the past, such as tying shoes, or dressing and that are unrelated to any physical disabilities
- Wandering aimlessly around the house (or outside) at night and being sleepy or lethargic during the day (often called the reversal of the day–night cycle)
- Aphasia (Difficulty in speaking or understanding the meaning of words used by others

This does not mean that people who have one or two of these symptoms of severe Alzheimer's disease (or symptoms in the other stages) must invariably have Alzheimer's disease or another form of dementia; for example, people who have difficulty speaking may have had mild strokes. People who are incontinent could have other medical problems that are related to the bladder or the colon. What is important is that physicians look at the totality of the person's experience and that they compare the current lifestyle of patients with their recent past performance. To do this, they may need to consult with family members and spouses.

A Degenerative Disease

People with Alzheimer's become increasingly worse, although medications can delay the deterioration in some cases. However, extensive ongoing medical research is expected to result in dramatic improvements in treatment and possibly even a cure within the next decade. The onset of Alzheimer's is not always noticeable, and experts report that the disease may begin years before any symptoms occur. For this reason, scientists are seeking ways to identify Alzheimer's disease as early as possible because the earlier that treatment can begin, the better the prognosis for the patient.

Other Diseases with Symptoms Similar to Alzheimer's Disease

The symptoms of dementia or observable symptoms that resemble dementia may have many different causes other than Alzheimer's disease. Some diseases that can mimic dementia are STROKE, end-stage Parkinson's disease, head trauma, chronic ALCOHOLISM, certain nutritional deficiencies, and other illnesses.

Dementialike symptoms may even result from the taking of some medications, such as opium-based painkillers or from medication interactions. In addition, those with symptoms of an apparent Alzheimer's disease or dementia may instead be suffering from a vitamin deficiency, such as a deficit of Vitamin B_{12} or a folic-acid deficiency. They may also have another correctable medical problem, such as a THYROID DISEASE, particularly hypothyroidism.

Diagnosing Alzheimer's Disease

It is very important for the treating physician to perform a thorough evaluation, including a careful medical history, thorough physical examinations, and appropriate laboratory tests, before diagnosing patients with any form of dementia. Doctors need to realize that despite their age and an increased probability that they may have dementia because of an advanced age, older patients may have another medical problem that is altogether different from dementia.

As of this writing, Alzheimer's disease can only be diagnosed with certainty after death through an autopsy. To diagnose a living patient, physicians perform a physical examination and also ask the individual a series of predetermined questions to determine the likelihood of the illness. They also observe the behavior of the person.

Doctors use such screening tests as the Mini-Mental State Examination (MMSE) to determine both short- and long-term memory capabilities as well as the patient's functioning in writing and speaking. They may also ask the patient to perform simple tasks such as drawing a circle for a clock face and then asking the patient to draw a time, such as 3 P.M. This would be an easy task for most adults but it is an impossible chore for a person with moderate or severe Alzheimer's disease. More elaborate paper-and-pencil testing may also reveal even subtle dementia changes.

Diagnostic Breakthroughs

In 2000, researchers developed a blood test that appeared to be sensitive to the early stages of Alzheimer's disease, and it is hoped that ultimately the test will be able to detect the illness. The test looks for a special protein that is present in high concentrations in the brains of people with Alzheimer's but is found in unusually low concentrations in their blood. The advantage of early identification is that physicians can treat individuals in the early stages of the disease so that brain function can be preserved for a longer period.

A new breakthrough in the area of brain imaging can now predict dementia changes 12–24 months before a patient may be clinically symptomatic. MRI high-field-strength scanning with "spectroscopy" and positronic emission tomography (PET) scanning can measure how the brain uses certain brain chemicals. Based on the pattern of chemical metabolism that is viewed, doctors can make certain predictions of brain function. However, these tests are not widely available as of early 2003.

Delaying the Degeneration with Treatment

Although Alzheimer's disease is not curable as of this writing, physicians are working to delay the severity of the deterioration with medications. Many pharmaceutical companies are testing drugs for dementia; they are in the trial stage as of this writing.

Medications to Slow the Progression of Alzheimer's

As of 2002, three primary medications are used to slow down the memory loss experienced by patients diagnosed with Alzheimer's disease, including Aricept (donepazil HCl), Exelon (rivastigmine tartrate), and Reminyl (galantamine HBr).

These medications cannot "cure" Alzheimer's disease, but they may be effective at slowing down the deterioration.

There is some indication that some medications may delay or even prevent the development of Alzheimer's disease, although the research is very preliminary as of this writing. A study on the use of antiinflammatory drugs (NSAIDs), and their impact on Alzheimer's disease, reported in a 2001 issue of the *New England Journal of Medicine*, indicated that long-term use of NSAIDs may protect against Alzheimer's disease, although not against dementia.

Mental Exercises May Help

Some physicians recommend that patients "exercise" their minds, by using crossword puzzles and games. Some companies produce toys and games that are made specifically for people who suffer from Alzheimer's disease.

Another extremely effective approach is to "retrain" the mind formally and to recruit additional areas of the brain that are being underutilized. Working with a psychologist and technicians, patients can learn to use adaptive devices, such as a paper and pencil to write down appointments, an alarm wristwatch to remind them to take their medicines, and picture cards to outline the events of the day. These tools can be very helpful, depending on the stage of the illness.

Future Outlook

Some scientists are testing a vaccine that, if it works, may actually prevent the development of Alzheimer's disease. This vaccine contains amyloid, the substance that forms plaques in the brain. In mice that were specifically bred to develop Alzheimer's disease and that subsequently developed the disease, when they were injected with the vaccine, their behavior and maze performance dramatically improved.

In the mice that did not yet have the disease, after the vaccine was injected, dementia did not develop. Apparently, the vaccine destroyed amyloid plaques that had already formed in the brain and also prevented them from developing. Human trials in the United States and the UNITED KINGDOM are ongoing as of this writing.

Another possible solution developed from research in 2002. According to a release from the NATIONAL INSTITUTE ON AGING, some studies have indicated that in experiments, mice with low levels of folic acid have higher levels of homoscysteine. These higher levels may have caused damage to nerve cells in the brain. It is also true that people with Alzheimer's disease often have low levels of folic acid in their blood, although it is unclear whether this is a cause or effect of the disease or is unrelated to the disease. Researchers speculate that perhaps consumption of greater amounts of folic acid in the diet or in supplements could act as a preventive measure to Alzheimer's disease.

Folic acid is found in citrus fruits and juices, whole wheat bread, dry beans, and green leafy vegetables. Folic acid is also an additive in enriched breads, cereals, flours, cornmeals, pastas, rice, and other grain products. Supplemental folic acid is also an option, although patients with Alzheimer's and their caregivers should consult with their physicians before adding folic acid to a patient's diet.

Fear of Having or Developing Alzheimer's Disease

Many middle-aged and older individuals, particularly if their own parents have been diagnosed with dementia, may fear that they too are "showing" early signs of Alzheimer's disease merely because they misplace their car keys or forget someone's name at a party. It is important to understand that these are common memory errors and are not indicative of Alzheimer's disease. Forgetting an appointment time, is a memory lapse. No longer understanding the concept of time or the function of a watch is an indication of dementia.

Often, doctors are asked if being unable to think of certain words could indicate an early onset of Alzheimer's disease. This problem is common among senior adults and is often called tip-of-the-tongue aphasia. It is not an indicator of Alzheimer's. However, a family member's report of a patient's inability to form sentences is a matter of major concern.

Caregiving Issues

Most people with Alzheimer's disease continue to live at home with FAMILY CAREGIVERS, although care may be supplemented by medical aides and some states offer RESPITE CARE, which gives the caregiver a break from the task of watching over the Alzheimer's patient. This is important because experts say that at least 10 percent of caregivers to people with Alzheimer's disease become injured or sick themselves as a direct consequence of caregiving. In addition, nearly half of them (43 to 46 percent) suffer from depression.

Some states provide ADULT DAY CENTERS for people with Alzheimer's, enabling family members to continue to work and to avoid having to place their family member in a nursing home. However, experts say that most adult day centers are not suitable for Alzheimer's or dementia patients because these patients require extra care.

Housing Issues

For those people with Alzheimer's who do not live with family members, the choices are ASSISTED-LIVING FACILITIES or NURSING HOMES. Some assisted-living facilities offer special units for people with Alzheimer's disease, as do some nursing homes. According to a report from the National Conference of State Legislatures in 2000, 26 states set requirements for assisted-living facilities that provide housing to people with Alzheimer's disease. They are: Arizona, California, Delaware, Florida, Georgia, Idaho, Kansas, Maine, Maryland, Massachusetts, Nebraska, Nevada, New Mexico, North Carolina, Ohio, Oklahoma, Oregon, Pennsylvania, Rhode Island, South Carolina, South Dakota, Texas, Vermont, Virginia, Washington, and Wyoming.

Caregivers and Home Modifications

Because most people with Alzheimer's disease continue living at home, their family caregivers (usually spouses or other family members) are well advised to plan for ways to modify the home so it will be safe and accessible. The 1993 booklet "Alzheimer's and Related Dementias: Homes that Help: Advice from Caregivers for Creating a Supportive Home," based on a study by Richard V. Olsen, Ph.D. et al. of the Architecture and Building Science Research Group at the New Jersey Institute of Technology, provided numerous practical suggestions for home modifications.

For example, the authors strongly recommend bathing the person with Alzheimer's disease using a hand-held shower. This will enable the caregiver to determine the water temperature and to avoid scalding the patient and will also allow for moving the device around the patient. The disabled person will also have fewer instructions to follow when a hand-held shower is used.

If a patient is afraid of water, a gentle mist can be used, starting with the feet and slowly moving up. The patient should be able to hold onto a grab bar or may need to sit in a special chair made for the bath/shower, depending on the level of physical disability. Grab bars in the shower often give the patient a sense of security. To avoid slipping in the bath or shower, nonskid safety strips or even a bath mat should be placed inside the tub/shower.

Locks should be removed from the bathroom door so that people with Alzheimer's cannot lock themselves in and then forget how to unlock the door. If Alzheimer's patients are able to bathe themselves, caregivers should check their water heaters to make sure the water temperature cannot exceed 120 degrees to avoid the danger of scalding.

Some Alzheimer's patients may be confused by the "gearshift" type of water tap that is turned one way for hot water and another way for cold water. They may need one tap for hot water and another for cold water. Others, however, do better with one tap to manipulate.

To avoid the problem of flooding the bathroom (because the individual forgot to turn the water off), it may be a good idea to install (or have a plumber install) automatic faucet timers or shutoffs.

The authors also had recommendations for other rooms within the home, such as the kitchen and bedrooms. For example, in the kitchen, it is best to remove sharp objects or items that are breakable. Cleaners and dangerous household items should be placed behind childproof latches. To avoid the person leaving the stove on, some caregivers place an aluminum cover over the entire stove so that the burners cannot be seen. If the person is still capable of boiling water for tea or coffee but may forget to shut off the burner, then caregivers can buy a kettle that shuts itself off automatically when the water is hot.

Left to their own devices, people with Alzheimer's may often eat unhealthy or inappropriate food, such as raw chicken or even pet food. Some caregivers place snacks in colorful containers and tell family members that they can eat anything from these containers. They also try to restrict use of the refrigerator, and they put pet food out of sight.

To prevent people with Alzheimer's from coming into the kitchen while meals are being prepared, some caregivers install half doors so that the patient can see and talk to caregivers and do not feel that they must also enter the room.

For the bedroom, some caregivers purchase hospital beds so that a person with Alzheimer's will not fall out of bed or climb out of bed at night and wander off. Others put comforters or blankets on the floor around the bed to cushion any falls.

To avoid confusion at night, some caregivers put night lights along the route to the bathroom, to help show the way. Others place a commode at the bedside by a night light.

To resolve problems with wandering, some caregivers employ very creative means. For example, one caregiver placed a scenic mural over the front door so that the door could not be seen at all. The door handle was behind a flap, and the patient didn't see it. Out of sight is often out of mind for patients with Alzheimer's disease. The patient liked the mural so much that when she needed to enter a nursing home, she wanted it to go with her. Some people fence in their yards so that their ill family members can walk around outside.

Important: people who live with others who have Alzheimer's should ensure that *no* medications are accessible to the person with Alzheimer's. Both over-the-counter and prescribed medications should be removed from the medicine cabinet and locked up. Old medicines should be discarded. People with Alzheimer's disease cannot be allowed to have any responsibility for taking their own medications. They are at serious risk of not taking their medications at all or of taking the wrong dosages. As a result, they risk underdosing or overdosing themselves.

It is also very important that any medications that are taken by caregivers or other family members should also be locked up because the person with Alzheimer's may mistakenly take prescribed or over-the-counter medications that are meant for others. This could result in a serious ADVERSE DRUG EVENT.

Programs for Lost Patients with Alzheimer's

Because people with Alzheimer's are noted for wandering off and getting lost, which can be very dangerous and even life-threatening for them, the ALZHEIMER'S DISEASE AND RELATED DISORDERS ASSOCIATION with the U.S. Justice Department created a "Safe Return" program. The patient is given a special ID bracelet and is also registered in a national database.

Thousands of people have been found and returned home because of this program. The program operates in all 50 states; however, some states have provided extra funding and training in support of the program. These states are: California, Connecticut, Delaware, Georgia, Kansas, Massachusetts, New Jersey, Pennsylvania, Tennessee, Texas, and Virginia.

For further information about Alzheimer's disease, contact the Alzheimer's Disease and Related Disorders Association, a nationwide organization that has local chapters at:

Alzheimer's Disease and Related Disorders
    Association, Inc.
919 North Michigan Avenue
Suite 1100
Chicago, IL 60611-1676
(800) 272-3900 (toll-free) or (312) 335-8700
http://www.alz.org/

Andersen-Ranberg, Karen, Lone Vasegaard, and Bernard Jeune. "Dementia Is Not Inevitable: A Population-Based Study of Danish Centenarians," *Journal of Gerontology: Psychological Sciences* 56B, no. 3 (2001): 152–159.

Fox-Grage, Wendy, Judith Riggs, and Suzanne Linnane. "Alzheimer's Disease and Related Dementias: A Legislative Guide," National Conference of State Legislatures (March 2000).

In't Veld, Bas A., M.D., Ph.D. et al. "Nonsteroidal Antiinflammatory Drugs and the Risk of Alzheimer's Disease," *New England Journal of Medicine* 345, no. 21 (November 22, 2001): 1,515–1,521.

National Institutes of Health News Release. "Folic Acid Possibly a Key Factor in Alzheimer's Disease Prevention" (March 1, 2002).

Olsen, Richard V., Ph.D. et al. "Alzheimer's and Related Dementias Homes That Help: Advice from Caregivers for Creating a Supportive Home," Newark, N.J.: Architecture and Building Science Research Group, School of Architecture, New Jersey Institute of Technology, 1993.

Shirey, Lee, et al. "Alzheimer's Disease and Dementia: A Growing Challenge," *Challenges for the 21st Century: Chronic and Disabling Conditions* 1, no. 11 (September 2000): 1–6.

Alzheimer's Disease and Related Disorders Association, Inc.   Founded in 1980, this organization provides leadership to eliminate ALZHEIMER'S DISEASE through the advancement of research, while also enhancing care and support services for individuals and their families. The Alzheimer's Disease and Related Disorders Association is the largest private funder of research on Alzheimer's disease. The organization has a network of chapters throughout the United States that provide access to local services. The organization offers a catalog of consumer publications and a free consumer newsletter.

For more information, contact the Alzheimer's Disease and Related Disorder Association, Inc. at:

919 North Michigan Avenue
Suite 1100
Chicago, IL 60611
(800) 272-3900 or (312) 335-8700
(312) 335-8882 (TTY)
http://www.alz.org

American Association for Geriatric Psychiatry (AAGP)   National association that promotes the mental health and well-being of older people and is dedicated to improving the care of those with late-life mental disorders. Founded in 1978, AAGP has about 1,800 members. Publishes *The American Journal of Geriatric Psychiatry.* Also publishes consumer pamphlets, such as "The Role of the Geriatric Psychiatrist," "Depression in Late Life: Not a Natural Part of Aging," and "Alzheimer's Disease: Understanding the Most Common Dementing Disorder."

For more information about this organization, contact:

American Association for Geriatric Psychiatry
7910 Woodmont Avenue
Suite 1050
Bethesda, MD 20814
(301) 654-7850
http://www.aagpgpa.org

American Association of Homes and Services for the Aging (AAHSA)   Organization of not-for-profit NURSING HOMES, continuing-care retirement communities, ASSISTED-LIVING and senior housing facilities, and community service organizations. Founded in 1961, the purpose of AAHSA is to advance the interests of its 5,600 members through leadership, advocacy, networking, education, and research. Publishes several consumer publications, including "Quality in Long-Term Care: The Not-for-Profit Difference" and "The Value of Accreditation."

For further information, contact AAHSA at:

2519 Connecticut Avenue, NW
Washington, DC 20008
(202) 783-2242
http://www.aahsa.org

American Bar Association Commission on Law and Aging   An organization that is part of the American Bar Association (ABA). Started in 1979, the commission examines and responds to law-related issues of aging, including Social Security and MEDICARE due process, long-term care, housing, guardianship and alternatives, court access, and the rights of older persons, in general. The commission's 15 members are appointed annually by the president of the ABA. The organization has a director and a staff of seven attorneys, as of August 2001.

For further information about this organization, contact:

ABA Commission on Law and Aging
740 15th Street, NW
Washington, DC 20005
(202) 662-1000
http://www.abanet.org/aging

American Cancer Society (ACS)   Key national organization in the United States on the issue of CANCER and its cure and treatments.

Founded in 1913 by 15 physicians and business-people in New York City, the organization now funds major research studies and also provides extensive information and advocacy for people with all types of cancer and their families and friends. Many publications are available through the American Cancer Society.

The ACS has more than 3,400 local offices, and according to their mission statement, the organization is "dedicated to eliminating cancer as a major health problem by preventing cancer, saving lives, and diminishing suffering from cancer, through research, education, advocacy, and service."

The ACS also works with cancer organizations in other countries worldwide.

For further information, contact the organization at:

American Cancer Society
1599 Clifton Road, NE
Atlanta, GA 30329
(800) 227-2345 or (404) 320-3333
http://www.cancer.org

American Diabetes Association   Formed in 1940 by physicians concerned about diabetes treatment and research, this organization supports clinical research on both Type 1 and Type 2 DIABETES and provides important information to physicians, nurses, patients with diabetes, and others. The ADA has offices in each state and the District of Columbia. According to information provided by the American Diabetes Association, their mission is to prevent and cure diabetes and improve the lives of everyone affected by diabetes.

The ADA is also an active advocacy organization, providing support and information on discrimination and violations of the AMERICANS WITH DISABILITIES ACT in the school and the workplace. It has also provided court briefs in several successful lawsuits on behalf of children and adults who have diabetes. In addition, the ADA lobbies in Congress and with other groups over the issues of importance to those who have diabetes.

The ADA has been a cosponsor with major federal agencies on very large clinical trials of patients with diabetes, such as the Diabetes Control and Complications Trial (DCCT), as well as many other vitally important studies.

The American Diabetes Association provides information to diabetes professionals and consumers with diabetes. The ADA also produces four professional peer-reviewed journals, including *Diabetes, Clinical Diabetes, Diabetes Care,* and *Diabetes Spectrum.*

For further information, contact the organization at:

American Diabetes Association (ADA)
1701 North Beauregard Street
Alexandria, VA 22311
(800) 342-2383 (DIABETES) or (703) 549-1500
http://www.diabetes.org/

American Geriatrics Society   Nationwide, not-for-profit association of geriatric-health-care professionals, research scientists, and others who concentrate on health improvements, independence, and quality of life of older people. Founded in 1942, the organization has about 6,000 members.

The AGS produces several publications, including the *Journal of the American Geriatrics Society, Annals of Long Term Care,* and *AGS Newsletter.*

For further information, contact the organization at:

American Geriatrics Society
350 Fifth Avenue
Suite 801
New York, NY 10118
(212) 308-1414
http://www.americangeriatrics.org

American Heart Association (AHA)   The leading U.S. authority on diseases of the heart and blood vessels (cardiovascular disease). Founded in 1924 by six cardiologists as a scientific organization, the national organization, a health agency, currently has affiliates in states nationwide. The AHA provides information and statistical data on all forms of HEART DISEASE and STROKE to enable prevention of these diseases and effective treatment when they occur. According to the AHA, their mission is to "reduce disability and death from cardiovascular diseases and stroke."

The American Heart Association produces a broad array of informational pamphlets, as well as an annual statistical update on heart and stroke statistics.

For more information, contact the organization at:

American Heart Association
7272 Greenville Avenue
Dallas, TX 75231-4596
(800) AHA-USA1 (242-8721, toll-free)
http://www.americanheart.org

See also AMERICAN STROKE ASSOCIATION.

American Parkinson Disease Association   Advocacy, informational, and research organization in the United States that concentrates on promoting a better quality of life for individuals with PARKINSON'S DISEASE, using numerous "information and referral centers" nationwide. The organization also seeks to find a cure for Parkinson's disease through research.

For further information, contact the organization at:

American Parkinson Disease Association (APDA)
1250 Hylan Boulevard
Suite 4B
Staten Island, NY 10305
(800) 223-2732 or (718) 981-8001
http://www.apdaparkinson.org

American Society on Aging   Organization that provides education and training to professionals in the field of aging. Founded in 1946, the primary purpose of the organization is to enhance the lives of older adults and their families. The organization has 6,000 members. It publishes *Aging Today* and *Generations.*

For further information, contact:

American Society on Aging
833 Market Street
Suite 511
San Francisco, CA 94103
(415) 974-9600
http://www.asaging.org

American Stroke Association   A division of the American Heart Association created in 1998 to help emphasize the importance of STROKE prevention and to strengthen the American Heart Associations' effort to reduce disability and death from stroke through research, education, fund raising, and advocacy. The American Stroke Association is the leading source of stroke information. During 1999–2000, the American Stroke Association spent $61 million on stroke-related research and programs. The organization also publishes *Stroke: Journal of the American Heart Association.*

For further information, contact the organization at:

American Stroke Association
7272 Greenville Avenue
Dallas TX 75231
(888) 4-STROKE
http://www.strokeassociation.org

Americans with Disabilities Act (ADA)   Signed into law in 1990 in the United States, the Americans with Disabilities Act prohibits discrimination against disabled individuals in the workplace, public facilities, and other areas that are used by disabled individuals of all ages.

Prior to the passage of the ADA, the rights of disabled individuals fell under a broad range of state statutes that varied greatly from state to state. The ADA, a federal law, provided one prevailing standard for all children and adults with DISABILITIES, although many lawsuits have tested the law since its passage.

The ADA is helpful for many older and disabled people because it requires ACCESSIBILITY TO FACILITIES through the use of ramps or other options.

For further information on the ADA, go to the Department of Justice website at: http://www. usdoj.gov/crt/ada/adahom1.htm

See also FAMILY AND MEDICAL LEAVE ACT.

anemia   Disease characterized by insufficient red blood cells. Many older people suffer from anemia resulting from chronic diseases, deficiencies of Vitamin B_{12} and iron, and gastrointestinal bleeding; however, anemia is not always present in older individuals and should never be considered a "normal" aspect of aging. Some medical treatments, such as chemotherapy or radiation therapy for CANCER, can also result in anemia. Individuals with anemia may require medication or blood transfusions.

There are three primary types of anemia, including the anemia found with chronic diseases, iron-deficiency anemia, and a deficiency of Vitamin B_{12}. The anemia found with chronic disease is usually mild to moderate but should be treated before the condition worsens.

Iron-deficiency anemia may stem from gastrointestinal blood loss caused by nonsteroidal antiinflammatory medications, which are often prescribed for ARTHRITIS. Blood loss may also stem from cancer or other disorders. In some cases, older people become deficient in iron because of poor diets or the inability of their bodies to absorb iron in the food that they eat.

A Vitamin B_{12} deficiency, which represents about 9 percent of the various forms of anemia diagnosed among older people, is treated with either injections of Vitamin B_{12} or with oral tablets of B_{12}. There are tests to determine if patients have lost the ability to absorb B_{12} from their normal dietary intake, but most physicians simply choose to treat the problem with weekly injections for four weeks and monthly injections thereafter.

Risk Factors

The risk for developing anemia increases with age, and men age 85 and older have the highest risk for developing any form of anemia.

Symptoms of Anemia

Older individuals with anemia have symptoms that may be mistakenly attributed to the aging process. Some primary symptoms and signs of anemia among older individuals are as follows:

- Fatigue
- Weakness
- Worsening of other illnesses, such as heart diseases or cognitive impairment
- Worsening dizziness
- Frequent infections
- CONFUSION
- Chest pain

Diagnosis and Treatment

If anemia is suspected, it can be detected through a complete blood count (CBC). Doctors should also consider anemia as a possibility if the older person has cancer, OSTEOARTHRITIS, RHEUMATOID ARTHRITIS, TUBERCULOSIS, or hepatitis.

In anemia caused by chronic disease, iron is not prescribed because it will not improve the condition. Instead, the anemia is monitored by physicians. Some patients take erythropoietin.

With iron-deficiency anemia, the iron must be replaced. Patients may be given iron or iron sulfate. If the patient is deficient in Vitamin B_{12}, then Vitamin B_{12} is administered.

Smith, Douglas L., M.D. "Anemia in the Elderly," *American Family Physician* (October 1, 2000).

antioxidants   Cancer-fighting substances that are often added to food or taken as SUPPLEMENTS. Some examples of antioxidants are Vitamin C and Vitamin E. Individuals who have previously had HEART ATTACK or STROKE sometimes take antioxidants as a form of prevention of future occurrences.

Butler, Robert N., et al. "Anti-Aging Medicine: Efficacy and Safety of Hormones and Antioxidants," *Geriatrics* 55, no. 7 (2000): 48.

anxiety disorders   Feelings of panic or restlessness, often combined with a vague need to act, but a lack of confidence about one's actions. Anxiety disorders are chronic feelings and may include panic disorder, social phobia, obsessive-compulsive disorder (such as the need to constantly wash the hands or to perform repetitively other acts that the person knows are meaningless), agoraphobia (fear of being helpless in a situation, a condition that is often manifested by people staying in their homes and shunning others), generalized anxiety disorder (GAD), and other forms of anxiety disorders.

The individual with an anxiety disorder often has suffered from the disorder before reaching the senior years, and the problem is often a recurrence, a continuation, or a worsening of previous symptoms (that were often undiagnosed in the past).

Experts say that anxiety disorders are very common among older people and often coexist with DEPRESSION, although they are often untreated. Said psychologist Ariel J. Lang, Ph.D., and psychiatrist Murray B. Stein, M.D., in their 2001 article on anxiety for *Geriatrics*, "Anxiety is one of the most common psychiatric symptoms in older adults; yet it has been studied less than depression or dementia. As a result, the diagnosis and treatment of late-life anxiety are evolving and may be based more on a physician's clinical experience than on scientific evidence."

According to psychiatrist Gary Kennedy in his book, *Geriatric Mental Health Care: A Treatment Guide for Health Professionals*, agoraphobia may be more common than depression among physically healthy older women, affecting about 6 percent of women and about 4 percent of healthy older men.

Kennedy says that the symptoms of anxiety disorders evinced by older individuals are similar to those seen in younger people with the same diagnosis, with the exception that older people with obsessive-compulsive disorder are more likely to fear that they have sinned.

Says Kennedy of geriatric patients with anxiety disorders:

> Anxious persons are apprehensive and tense and have a sense of dread. They may be irritable, startle easily, feel restless or on edge, and find it difficult to fall asleep. As with depression, they have physical symptoms. They have difficulties with gastrointestinal function, including trouble swallowing, indigestion, excessive flatulence, and either too frequent or too few bowel movements. They may worry excessively about their health, their memory, their money, the safety of the neighborhood, and falling or being mugged while out of the house.

Medical Problems and Medications That Can Cause Anxiety

Some medical problems can cause symptoms of anxiety disorders, including THYROID DISEASE, congestive heart failure, DEMENTIA, PARKINSON'S DISEASE, Cushing's disease, CHRONIC OBSTRUCTIVE LUNG DISEASE (COPD), ASTHMA, and hypoglycemia (low blood sugar).

Some medications can also induce anxiety, such as thyroid hormones, caffeine, and ephedra.

Symptoms of Various Forms of Anxiety Disorder

Individuals who suffer from generalized anxiety disorder (GAD) are often irritable, tense, or restless or keyed up. They may have difficulty sleeping or concentrating. Older individuals with GAD are more likely to worry excessively about their health; younger people with GAD usually worry about money.

Panic disorder is another form of an anxiety disorder. Physical symptoms of a panic attack include sweating, shortness of breath, heart palpitations, DIZZINESS, nausea, a feeling of unreality or of losing control, and an imminent fear of dying. These are also symptoms seen with many medical problems that older individuals may have, such as with CORONARY HEART DISEASE or STROKE. Older individuals may accelerate their panic by imagining that they are suffering from a HEART ATTACK. (Heart attack should be ruled out first in anyone with symptoms of heart failure.)

Coexistence of Anxiety and Depression

As mentioned earlier, many people who suffer from anxiety disorders also have depression, and both conditions should be diagnosed and treated. According to authors Forrest Scogin, Mark Floyd, and Jennifer Forde in their chapter on anxiety in older adults in *Psychopathology in Later Adulthood,* when patients have both an anxiety disorder and depression, they are often very negative, have feelings of inferiority and rejection, are hypersensitive to criticism, are self-conscious, and are distressed in social situations.

Diagnosis and Treatment

Chronic anxiety should be diagnosed by a psychiatrist, who will take a complete medical history and question the patient closely. If medications are indicated, antianxiety drugs are usually prescribed.

Some medications in the benzodiazepine class that are often prescribed to treat anxiety include Ativan (lorazepam), Serax (oxazepam), Klonopin (clonazepam), and Xanax (alprazolam). Doctors may also prescribe antidepressants, such as Serzone (nefazodone), Zoloft (sertraline), Luvox (fluvoxamine), Paxil (paroxetine), or Effexor (venlafaxine).

According to Dr. Kennedy, adults age 65 and older represent 21 percent of all the users of benzodiazepine (antianxiety) prescriptions, and about 11 percent of men and 25 percent of women ages 60 to 74 are taking antianxiety drugs.

Risks of Antianxiety Drugs Kennedy states that older adults on antianxiety drugs are at risk for car crashes while driving. Obviously, the dangers of driving while taking sedating drugs should be emphasized to patients and to their family members or family caregivers. It is also true that such drugs may contribute to the risk of FALLS. Other drugs, particularly Xanax, can be habit forming.

Physicians also need to keep in mind that some drugs may affect older people very differently than younger individuals. In addition, many older people are already taking two or three (or more) medications, and it is important to consider the impact of these drugs on each other to avoid an ADVERSE DRUG ADVENT.

Scogin, Floyd, and Forde said, "Drug treatment with older adults can be increasingly difficult due to age-related change in drug absorption, distribution, metabolism, and sensitivity to side effects. Older adults typically are taking several prescription and over-the-counter medications that may have interaction effects with psychotropic medications. All of these factors make dosing difficult for seniors. Some suggest starting at half the recommended dose to begin treatment."

Psychotherapy may also be effective in treating older individuals with anxiety disorders. Cognitive behavioral therapy (CBT), in which the individual is trained to challenge irrational or damaging thoughts, has been shown to be helpful to some older individuals. Lang and Stein said,

> A number of studies have found that relaxation training reduced overall anxiety in older persons who report anxiety symptoms. In case studies, CBT has been used successfully to treat anxiety disorders (including GAD [generalized anxiety disorder], panic disorder, specific phobia and OCD) in older patients. Results of controlled trials of cognitive-behavior therapy for GAD are promising.

Kennedy, Gary. *Geriatric Mental Health Care: A Treatment Guide for Health Professionals.* New York: Guilford Press, 2000.

Lang, Ariel J., Ph.D., and Murray B. Stein, M.D. "Anxiety Disorders: How to Recognize and Treat the Medical Symptoms of Emotional Illness," *Geriatrics* 56, no. 5 (2001): 24–34.

Scogin, Forrest, Mark Floyd, and Jennifer Forde. "Anxiety in Older Adults," in *Psychopathology in Later Adulthood,* Susan Krauss Whitbourne, ed. New York: John Wiley & Sons, 2000.

arteriosclerosis/atherosclerosis Arteriosclerosis is a general term used to describe several conditions in which substances accumulate on the walls of the arteries. The term *atherosclerosis* is also used interchangeably with *arteriosclerosis.* Depending on where the blockage is located and how extensive it is, arteriosclerosis can be either disabling or deadly.

Atherosclerosis affects one in four Americans and claimed 14,413 lives in 2000. Older people are at high risk for developing atherosclerosis, particularly if they have risk factors such as SMOKING, OBESITY, DIABETES, and other risk factors.

Some substances that may clog the arterial walls include:

- CHOLESTEROL
- Calcium
- Cellular waste products

These deposits (plaque) cause the arteries to thicken, harden, and lose their basic natural elasticity. The deposits can partially or completely obstruct (occlude) blood flow to the heart, the brain, and other vital organs. Arteries in the arms, legs, hands, and feet can also be affected.

Arteriosclerosis is a factor in many diseases that affect the heart and circulatory system and that may cause CARDIOVASCULAR DISEASE. Coronary artery disease (CAD) is one type of arteriosclerosis that affects only the inner linings of arteries; it is responsible for most HEART DISEASE.

Risk Factors

SMOKING or exposure to tobacco smoke can stimulate the development of atherosclerosis. Other risk factors include:

- Normal aging
- HYPERTENSION
- Elevated cholesterol levels (or triglycerides)
- Diabetes
- Obesity
- Physical inactivity

Age and Gender Risks Two of every five men older than age 40 have significant coronary artery obstruction. Among white men, CAD causes nearly 10 deaths in 10,000 between the ages of 55 and 64.

At younger ages, atherosclerosis is more common among men; however, after the onset of MENOPAUSE, the condition occurs as often among women as men.

Other Risks Genetic risk factors for atherosclerosis involve an individual's inability to process cholesterol-containing low-density lipids.

Survival Rates

A patient with a 70 percent blockage of one coronary artery has a 2 percent risk of death from atherosclerosis within five years. Obstruction of three arteries increases the risk for death from 2 percent to 11 percent. A patient with a 70 percent blockage of the carotid artery has an annual 2 percent risk of death and a 15 percent risk of STROKE.

Screening for Arteriosclerosis

Screening for C-reactive protein (CRP) blood levels can identify at-risk patients who have a family history of premature heart disease despite currently healthy cholesterol levels. Screening may also be appropriate for patients who have chronic disorders or who take medications that raise their homocysteine levels, as well as for patients who have an unexplained deep vein thrombosis (DVT).

The AMERICAN HEART ASSOCIATION (AHA) considers fasting plasma homocysteine screening appropriate for people who smoke or who have:

- High blood pressure
- Atherosclerotic vascular disease despite not having any typical risk factors
- Atherosclerotic disease before the age of 60
- A family history of premature vascular disease in one or more first-degree relatives

The AHA is not expected to recommend more widespread screening for elevated homocysteine levels until clinical trials demonstrate that reducing these levels significantly reduces the risk of developing atherosclerosis.

Symptoms of Atherosclerosis

Symptoms of atherosclerosis develop gradually and do not usually appear until:

- Arteries narrow enough to restrict blood flow
- A blood clot (thrombus) develops in an artery or travels to another part of the body (embolus)
- An aneurysm develops in an artery wall

Symptoms are determined by the arteries affected and the parts of the body damaged by insufficient blood flow. Blockage of the arteries that nourish the heart can cause:

- Chest pain
- Shortness of breath
- Sweating
- Nausea
- Dizziness
- Light-headedness
- Rapid heartbeat (palpitations)
- Heart attack

If an artery leading to the brain is obstructed, the patient may experience:

- Headache
- Confusion
- Dizziness
- Weakness or paralysis on one side of the body
- Sudden, severe numbness of any part of the body
- Vision problems
- Difficulty walking
- Lack of coordination in the arms and hands
- Inability to speak or to speak clearly
- Memory loss
- Stroke

Narrowing of arteries leading to the intestines can cause:

- Abdominal aching or cramps, usually beginning 15–30 minutes after eating
- Severe abdominal pain
- Vomiting
- Diarrhea
- Constipation

People whose legs and feet are not getting enough blood may experience muscle cramps, especially when exercising. They may also experience a loss of leg hair, toenail thickening, and skin that feels cool to the touch and is pale or bluish in color (cyanotic).

A limited blood flow in the arteries leading to the kidneys can result in high blood pressure and KIDNEY DISEASE.

Diagnosing Atherosclerosis

In addition to a complete medical history and physical examination, doctors may use any or all of several techniques to diagnose atherosclerosis.

The coronary arteriogram (angiogram) involves injecting a dye (contrast agent), and then taking X rays to locate any narrowing in the arteries as well as any blockage or other irregularities in the arteries through which the blood travels on its way to the heart.

Doppler sonography uses a transducer to channel sound waves into a blood vessel to assess blood flow. If it is difficult or impossible to hear the sound of blood moving, then the artery may be obstructed.

The doctor may perform a blood pressure comparison by taking the blood pressure in both the arms and ankles to determine whether circulation is impaired.

Radionucleotide angiography (MUGA scan) uses radioactive tracers to determine if the heart wall moves and to measure the amount of blood each heartbeat expels while the patient is resting.

Myocardial perfusion imaging (thallium scanning), performed after exercise or when the patient is resting, may reveal areas of the heart where the blood supply is inadequate.

Doctors should consider the possibility of premature atherosclerosis in any patient who has had a heart attack or has experienced the following symptoms or signs:

- Transient ischemic attack
- Angina pectoris (chest pains)
- Leg pain caused by walking and relieved by rest (intermittent claudication)
- Fatty yellowish thicknesses, small knots of tissue or tumors (xanthomas) in creases of the hands or elbows or along the sleevelike membrane that encases connective tissue (tendon sheath)
- Yellowish fatty deposits (xanthelasmas) around the eyes
- Recurring pancreatitis
- A family history of high cholesterol levels (hyperlipidemia) or family members who had coronary vascular disease before the age of 60.

Stages of Atherosclerosis

Beginning in childhood, atherosclerosis progresses with age. Some scientists believe atherosclerosis starts when elevated cholesterol and triglyceride levels, high blood pressure, and tobacco smoke damage the innermost layer (endothelium) of an artery and when plaque subsequently stimulates the cells to produce other substances that add to the overall accumulation.

When this process occurs, blood pressure increases. Plaques thicken, and the walls of the affected artery harden. The artery narrows. Blood clots develop near the plaque, slowing down or stopping blood flow altogether.

It may take decades for an artery to become partially blocked, but a partially blocked artery can become completely occluded within minutes.

Treatment for Atherosclerosis

Atherosclerosis cannot be cured. Treatment, which is designed to prevent the arteries from becoming narrow enough to damage the vital organs, includes lifestyle modifications, medication, and surgery.

Dietary Changes   Patients who have atherosclerosis should exercise regularly, stop smoking, and control their diets, particularly by limiting their consumption of meats, dairy products, chocolate, and fried foods. A low-fat diet is usually best, with emphasis on consuming fruits, vegetables, whole grain cereals, and legumes. Such a diet can help to prevent plaque from accumulating, and it may also work to eliminate any existing deposits.

Low-dose ASPIRIN THERAPY may be used to lower CRP levels. One of the statin drugs may be prescribed to treat high cholesterol aggressively.

Surgical Treatment   Coronary angioplasty improves blood flow by using a flexible tube (catheter) to widen the opening of an artery. Balloon angioplasty involves inflating a balloon that has been inserted into a blood vessel to flatten plaque that is obstructing blood flow.

Another procedure, percutaneous transluminal coronary angioplasty (PTCA), is performed on coronary arteries so that blood can flow into the heart.

Atherectomy is a procedure in which a tiny implement is used on the tip of a catheter to shave material that is narrowing the inside of an artery.

Laser angioplasty uses a thin beam of light to vaporize blockage within an artery.

Coronary artery stenting involves expanding a tiny coil implanted inside a blocked artery to clear the artery and to keep it open.

Current and Future Advances

Researchers are studying the possibility that inflammation in the bloodstream may play an important role in heart attack and stroke, and they are investigating the relationship between atherosclerosis and the following factors:

- Fibrinogen and other elements that allow blood to clot (coagulation factors)

- Homocysteine, a product generated during amino acid metabolism and believed to damage artery walls and contribute to premature vascular disease

- Lipoprotein a (Lp a), a modified version of "bad" cholesterol (LDL) that makes blood clot more quickly

- C-reactive protein (CRP), which indicates the likelihood of heart attack or stroke

- Viral or bacterial infection

The possibility of growing new blood cells to replace those damaged by disease is also being investigated by researchers.

For further information, contact the following organizations:

National Heart, Lung, and Blood Institute (NHLBI)
Building 31
Room 4A21
Bethesda, MD 20892
(800) 575-WELL
http://www.nhlbi.nih.gov

National Stroke Association
9707 East Easter Lane
Englewood, CO 80112-3747
(800) STROKES
http://www.stroke.org

Starr, Cynthia. "Emerging Cardiac Risk Factors," *Patient Care* 35, no. 10 (May 30, 2001): 38–50.

arthritis   Refers to an estimated 100 different types of conditions that affect the joints and, therefore, the associated muscles, ligaments, and connective tis-

sues of the body. Arthritis causes pain, inflammation, and swelling of the joints, as well as pain in the muscles, bones, tendons, and ligaments that support the joints. Some patients experience periods with severe acute pain. Others have low-grade pain and inflammation on a chronic and continuing basis, which usually worsens as they age. The most commonly experienced forms of arthritis are as follows: OSTEOARTHRITIS, RHEUMATOID ARTHRITIS, and GOUT.

Arthritis is the primary cause of DISABILITY among Americans of all ages and is the most common chronic condition among people in the United States older than age 65, afflicting about 49 of every 100 older adults. About half of all men in the United States older than age 70 and two-thirds of all women older than age 70 have some form of arthritis, usually osteoarthritis. Arthritis is a minor annoyance for some older individuals; for others, it devastates their lives. Patients with severe cases of arthritis may need joint replacements, usually of the knee or the hip.

Risk and Age

The risk for developing some form of arthritis increases with age; for example, according to the CENTERS FOR DISEASE CONTROL AND PREVENTION (CDC), the rate among men ages 45 to 64 years developing arthritis was 193.0 per 1,000 persons in 1996. That rate of arthritis nearly doubled (to 394.6) for those ages 65 to 74, and it increased still further to 437.9 per 1,000 for men who were age 75 years and older. (See Table 1.)

The rate of arthritis among women is higher than that found among men, and it also increases with age. Women ages 45 to 64 have a rate of arthritis of 284.0 per 1,000. As can be seen from the chart, the rate for women age 65 to 74 is higher than that for men in that age group, as well as among men age 75 and older, or 500.3 versus 437.9. This rate increases further still to 576.4 for those women who are 75 years old and older.

TABLE 1 RATE OF ARTHRITIS PER 1,000 PEOPLE IN THE UNITED STATES BY GENDER AND AGE			
	45 to 64	**65 to 74**	**75 and Older**
Men	193	394.6	437.9
Women	284	500.3	576.4

Source: Centers for Disease Control and Prevention (CDC)

Arthritis and Death

Although arthritis is not usually a direct cause of death, the condition is associated with other serious conditions. For example, people with rheumatoid arthritis have an increased risk of death from developing an INFECTION or from respiratory ailments that they have developed. People with osteoarthritis are more prone than those without arthritis to slipping and falling and to breaking a hip or suffering from another life-threatening fracture. Such fractures frequently lead to DISABILITY and even death. Also, with decreased activity due to pain, many patients gain weight and develop problems with HYPERTENSION and other medical conditions, such as OBESITY.

Symptoms

The symptoms of arthritis vary considerably, depending on the form of arthritis that is diagnosed, but there is usually some form of pain and inflammation. There may be difficulty and slowness with movement, apparent to the layperson. The individual may have swollen and red joints, which may also be enlarged and malformed from chronic arthritis.

Diagnosis

Most doctors can diagnose and treat the more common forms of arthritis, although it is the RHEUMATOLOGIST who specializes in arthritic diseases. Neurologists, orthopedic surgeons, and physical medicine (physiatrists) physicians also treat arthritis.

Some forms of arthritis, such as rheumatoid arthritis, lupus, and others, can be diagnosed through laboratory tests that detect a specific factor in the blood. If the factor is present in the blood, then the individual usually has arthritis.

Other forms of arthritis, such as the far more common osteoarthritis, can be diagnosed through X rays. In fact, the initial X rays may be used as a baseline later on so that the doctor can compare them to later X rays that are taken as the patients age. Doctors may also order a CT scan (computerized tomography) or a magnetic resonance imaging (MRI) scan to determine the degree of damage that has occurred to the joints and to the supporting soft tissue structures.

Treatment of Arthritis

Physicians cannot cure arthritis, but they can treat the pain and some of the other symptoms that it causes, such as swelling or inflammation.

Medications for Arthritis Many doctors prescribe PAINKILLING MEDICATIONS to treat arthritis, such as nonsteroidal antiinflammatory drugs (NSAIDs). Stronger painkilling medications, such as narcotics, may also be needed. Sometimes, doctors will perform "trigger point" injections of cortisone into the inflamed area when the patient is in severe pain. In other cases, particularly if the discs between the vertebrae are severely inflamed and painful, the doctor may perform an epidural injection of cortisone or lidocaine into the affected area.

Heat and Cold Therapies Doctors also often recommend that patients with arthritis employ the use of heat or cold over the inflamed area. For example, an ice pack may be placed on the affected area, with a towel between the ice pack and the patient's skin provided for protection.

Massage Therapy and Physical Therapy Massage therapy may help patients with arthritis. Physical therapy may also enable some improvement, particularly to help strengthen muscles that have become deconditioned because of a lack of EXERCISE stemming from severe pain. The weaker the muscles become, the less able they are to support the joints. Patients can get locked into a negative downward spiral of pain. Typically, the patient does not exercise or even move around very much because of pain. This causes the muscles to become weak, which exacerbates the pain. The patient is then even less likely to exercise at that point.

This spiral can be broken. Medications can help patients feel well enough to exercise, which will improve their muscles and make it less likely that they will cause further pain. Starting with water exercises may be an easy way to begin an exercise program. Of course, there is no magic formula of exercise and medication that will completely eradicate arthritis. It is a chronic disease, much as HYPERTENSION, DIABETES, and other illnesses that cannot be cured (to date) but can be treated.

Weight Loss Weight loss is also helpful if patients are overweight or obese because less weight means less physical pressure on joints.

Sufficient Sleep   Many patients with arthritis suffer from insufficient sleep. This problem may occur because of their pain and stiffness or because of other medical or psychological problems that they suffer from. Inadequate sleep can worsen the symptoms of arthritis, and patients who are not sleeping at least six or seven hours per night should inform their doctors. They may need a mildly sedating drug. Sometimes, the avoidance of caffeine (coffee, cola, chocolate) for at least several hours before going to bed can help the person fall asleep more easily.

Alternative Medicine   The use of ALTERNATIVE MEDICINE, such as recommending supplemental doses of glucosamine and chondroitin, may benefit some patients with arthritis. Acupuncture may be helpful for some patients; clinical studies run by the U.S. government are currently being held to test the efficacy of acupuncture.

For further information, contact the following organizations:

American Academy of Orthopaedic Surgeons
P.O. Box 2058
Des Plaines, IL 60017
(800) 824-BONE (toll-free)
http://www.aaos.org

American Chronic Pain Association
P.O. Box 850
Rocklin, CA 95677
(916) 632-0922
http://www.theacpa.org

American College of Rheumatology
1800 Century Place, Suite 250
Atlanta, GA 30345
(404) 633-3777
http://www.rheumatology.org

American Pain Society
4700 West Lake Avenue
Glenview, IL 60025
(847) 375-4715
http://www.ampainsoc.org

American Physical Therapy Association
1111 North Fairfax Street
Alexandria, VA 22314
(800) 999-2782 (toll-free) or (703) 684-2782
http://www.apta.org

Arthritis Foundation
1330 West Peachtree Street
Atlanta, GA 30309
(800) 283-7800 or (404) 965-7537
http://www.arthritis.org

National Institute on Arthritis and Musculoskeletal and Skin Diseases Information Clearinghouse
1 AMS Circle
Bethesda, MD 20892
(301) 495-4484 or (877) 226-4267 (toll-free)
http://www.nih.gov/niams

Kandel, Joseph, M.D., and David B. Sudderth, M.D. *The Arthritis Solution.* Rocklin, Calif.: Prima Publishing, 1997.

McAlindon, Timothy E., DM et al. "Glucosamine and Chondroitin for Treatment of Osteoarthritis: A Systematic Quality Assessment and Meta-analysis," *Journal of the American Medical Association (JAMA)* 283, no. 11 (March 15, 2000): 1,469–1,475.

National Institute of Arthritis and Musculoskeletal and Skin Diseases (NIAMS). "Questions & Answers about Arthritis Pain," National Institutes of Health, NIH Publication No. 01-4856 (February 2001).

Arthritis Foundation   Key national nonprofit organization in the United States that funds major research on arthritis and provides advocacy and information on more than 100 different forms of arthritis to arthritis sufferers and their families. The organization has statewide support chapters throughout the United States. The Arthritis Foundation also publishes *Arthritis Today.*

For further information, contact the organization at:

Arthritis Foundation
1330 West Peachtree Street
Atlanta, GA 30309
(800) 283-7800 or (404) 965-7537
http://www.arthritis.org

art therapy   The use of drawing, painting, sculpting, or other forms of art expression to enable older people to draw on their own creativity and to feel better about themselves and their lives.

Asian Americans/Pacific Islanders (AAPI)   Individuals of Asian or Pacific Islands ancestry who were born in or move to the United States. Asian Americans include Chinese, Japanese, Asian Indians, Koreans, and people of Filipino genetic ancestry. Pacific Islanders include people from Micronesia, Polynesia, and Melanesia. In 2000, there were about 801,000 Asians age 65 and older living in the United States, according to the U.S. Census Bureau. Of these, about 460,000 were female.

Many older Asian Americans and Pacific Islanders do not obtain immunizations against flu or PNEUMONIA. Although Medicare provides coverage for these vaccines, only about 27 percent of older Asian Americans and Pacific Islanders actually receive these injections.

About 12 percent of AAPI seniors live beneath the poverty line, compared to 5 percent of the Caucasian non-Hispanic elderly population. Many AAPI seniors live with their adult children or with their grandchildren.

According to the ADMINISTRATION ON AGING (AOA), the average family CAREGIVER of older Asian American or Pacific Islander seniors is a woman who is age 39 and is working either part-time or full-time. The AOA says these particular caregivers are the least likely of family caregivers in any group to seek professional assistance with caregiving.

Administration on Aging. "Serving Our Asian American and Pacific Islander Elders," 2001.

aspirin therapy   Taking low doses of aspirin daily to avert a HEART ATTACK or a STROKE. Numerous studies have shown that taking low doses of aspirin each day is very beneficial to both older individuals who are either at risk for a heart attack or a stroke as well as for those who have already experienced a heart attack or a stroke. Before starting any medication regimen, however, including taking over-the-counter medications or any SUPPLEMENTS, it is very important to first consult with a physician to confirm that the therapy is indicated and will not cause any MEDICATION INTERACTIONS.

assets   Generally refers to items of marketable value owned by an individual, such as a house, automobile, stocks, bonds, and cash. Programs such as MEDICAID and SSI have income and asset limitations on those who are eligible for them. One effect is that if people needing nursing-home care have accumulated assets beyond a specific predetermined amount (which is set by federal and state governments), then they will usually need to spend their own money or liquidate some of their assets to pay for that care. In many cases, a person's owned residence is excluded as a "countable" asset.

In past years, older individuals who needed nursing care but who did have assets chose to turn over their money or resources to adult children or others to make themselves appear financially insolvent. This practice has been condemned by the federal government, which has set rules that income or asset transfers must occur well before the time when the person seeks to apply for Medicaid, SSI, or any other state programs for low-income individuals.

Some older adults who would otherwise choose MARRIAGE or REMARRIAGE stay single because of the effect on their finances that would occur; for example, if a couple chose to marry, then the assets of both would be considered if one of them needed to move to a NURSING HOME and sought eligibility for Medicaid to pay for the nursing-home cost. However, if they remained single, only the individual's own assets would be considered with regard to eligibility.

assistance programs   Programs that provide cash benefits, food, or other assistance to individuals. MEDICAID is an example of an assistance program. This program provides for medical coverage for poor individuals who meet both state and federal criteria. Some assistance programs provide for free or low-cost prescription drugs. SSI (Supplemental Security Insurance) is another such program. SSI provides for a low monthly payment to eligible individuals. Individuals who receive SSI are automatically eligible to receive Medicaid in addition. Individuals receiving Medicaid will also receive medication benefits. (Medicare does not cover outpatient medications.)

Some older individuals who are at the poverty level and who are receiving MEDICARE will also qualify for SSI and Medicaid. Some retired individuals are unable to meet their basic needs with their Social Security retirement check alone, and they are unable to pay for their medications and other expenses. As a result, such assistance programs offer what some have called a "safety net." Eligible individuals will usually also qualify for low-income housing programs, food stamps, and other governmental programs for poor individuals.

assisted-living facility (ALF)   An organization that provides housing and some level of care to older and disabled individuals. It does not provide the much higher-skilled level of medical care that is found in a NURSING HOME or a rehabilitation center. If such care is needed, the individual is usually discharged. However, some assisted-living facilities have units set aside for patients who require a great deal of care.

An assisted-living facility may provide rooms or apartments, and they may range from very simple to very lavish and costly arrangements. Generally, an assisted-living facility provides a dining facility with meals, emergency call buttons in the residents' rooms or apartments, transportation to doctor's offices and shopping, and other options. As of 2000, there were about 600,000 people in the United States living in about 30,000 assisted-living facilities.

Some states use other terms to denote assisted-living facilities, such as *personal-care facility* or *residential-care home.*

State Laws on Assisted Living Vary Widely

State laws on assisted-living facilities vary greatly from state to state; some states provide a great deal of oversight, while others have minimal regulation. Often, it is either the state department of health or social services that provides oversight, although the state department of aging or consumer affairs may be the organization that oversees assisted-living facilities.

Some states require licensing and certification of assisted-living facilities while others do not. Some states have set criteria on admissions as well as on involuntary discharges from an assisted-living facility. According to the National Conference of State Legislatures, the following states set requirements for assisted-living facilities that provide housing for residents who have ALZHEIMER'S DISEASE: Arizona, California, Delaware, Florida, Georgia, Idaho, Kansas, Maine, Maryland, Massachusetts, Nebraska, Nevada, New Mexico, North Carolina, Ohio, Oklahoma, Oregon, Pennsylvania, Rhode Island, South Carolina, South Dakota, Texas, Vermont, Virginia, Washington, and Wyoming.

Most Assisted-Living Residents Are Women

According to a summary of a report in a 2000 issue of *Contemporary Longterm Care,* most residents (75 percent) of assisted-living facilities are female. The average age of residents is 84 years for women and 83 years for men. An estimated 41 percent of residents are wheelchair users. About 10 percent of ALF residents receive special assistance with managing their DIABETES, and about 29 percent of residents receive help with managing their medications.

Advantages of Assisted-Living Facilities

Older individuals may find it difficult or impossible to live completely independently, and yet they may also be fairly self-sustaining and not need the level of care provided by a nursing home. The midlevel care offered in an assisted-living facility may be sufficient for their needs unless or until they require more assistance than the facility can provide. The social activities and sense of community that these facilities can provide are also tremendous benefits in this era of the loss of the nuclear family.

Disadvantages of Assisted Living

As of this writing, most assisted-living facilities are "private pay," and thus MEDICARE or MEDICAID will not cover the cost of residence fees. Consequently, residents must use their own income and savings or must liquidate assets or find some other means to afford fees.

In 2000, the average daily rate for a private studio apartment in an ALF was estimated at about $2,000 per month, although fees vary greatly from area to area. The cost also depends heavily on the type of facility that is chosen and the services provided; for example, some ALFs provide gourmet meals to residents; in others, the meal fare is much more simple.

Medicaid Waivers and ALF Fees

In many states and in assisted-living facilities that wish to participate and are approved, a limited number of units are set aside in a special program for Medicaid recipients. In this "Medicaid waiver" program, requested by the state to the federal government, individuals who receiving Medicaid benefits may have all or part of their rent paid for out of Medicaid funds. This program may be expanded in the future; however, as of this writing, it represents only a tiny portion of all assisted living units.

See also AMERICAN ASSOCIATION OF HOMES AND SERVICES FOR THE AGING (AAHSA).

"ALF Overview Preview," *Contemporary Longterm Care* 23, no. 6 (June 2000).

Edelstein, Stephanie, and Karen Gaddy of the American Bar Association, Commission on Legal Problems of the Elderly. *Assisted Living: Summary of State Statutes. Volume I: Guide and Table to State Summaries.* Washington, D.C.: AARP, 2000.

assisted suicide   Causing or enabling the death of a person who wishes to commit suicide but who is unable to do so or does not wish to do so without assistance. Usually, the person who is "assisted" is very ill and in pain and may have a TERMINAL ILLNESS, although that is not always the case.

Assisted suicide is illegal in many states. It is also very controversial. There are powerful arguments used by both sides on the assisted suicide issue. Proponents argue that a terminally ill person in severe pain who wishes to die should be released from suffering. They also say that even if an illness is not terminal or not extremely painful, the person should still have the right to end his or her life, with or without assistance. This was the position taken by former Michigan doctor Jack Kevorkian, who is serving a jail sentence as of this writing for performing assisted suicides in violation of state law.

Dissenters say that the terminally ill person who is in severe pain should be given strong narcotics or other medications to combat the pain and that the decision of life and death should not be solely left up to family members or doctors. In addition, sometimes, the person who wishes to die has a treatable illness, such as DEPRESSION, which may be complicated by their feelings of loss if a spouse or other family members or friends have died. If treated, say dissenters, then the person can often lead a normal life.

As of this writing, the state of Oregon has an assisted-suicide law; however, the law has been challenged by federal authorities who assert that physicians may not administer medication for the purpose of causing death.

See also SUICIDE.

assistive devices   Items that enable people with DISABILITIES to better function in society. Assistive devices include such items as HEARING AIDS, WHEELCHAIRS, back braces, artificial limbs, and other devices. Such simple items as prescription eyeglasses could also fall into this category.

Assisted-living devices may be anatomical devices, as with an artificial hand or foot. They may also be mobility devices, such as walkers, wheelchairs, crutches, and other devices that help patients move about. Hearing devices include hearing aids, amplified telephones, and the use of an interpreter. Vision devices include a white cane, readers, and other vision technology.

TABLE 1 NUMBER OF PERSONS USING ASSISTIVE TECHNOLOGY DEVICES BY AGE OF PERSON AND TYPE OF DEVICE: UNITED STATES, 1994

Assistive device	All ages	44 years and younger	45–64 years	65 years and older
Anatomical devices		Number in thousands		
Any anatomical device [1]	4,565	2,491	1,325	748
Back brace	1,688	795	614	279
Neck brace	168	76	78	*13
Hand brace	332	171	119	42
Arm brace	320	209	86	*25
Leg brace	596	266	138	192
Foot brace	282	191	59	31
Knee brace	989	694	199	96

**TABLE 1 NUMBER OF PERSONS USING ASSISTIVE TECHNOLOGY DEVICES
BY AGE OF PERSON AND TYPE OF DEVICE: UNITED STATES, 1994** *(continued)*

Assistive device	All ages	44 years and younger	45–64 years	65 years and over
Anatomical devices		Number in thousands		
Other brace	399	239	104	56
Any artificial limb	199	69	59	70
Artificial leg or foot	173	58	50	65
Artificial arm or hand	*21	*9	*6	*6
Mobility devices				
Any mobility device [1]	7,394	1,151	1,699	4,544
Crutch	575	227	188	160
Cane	4,762	434	1,116	3,212
Walker	1,799	109	295	1,395
Medical shoes	677	248	226	203
Wheelchair	1,564	335	365	863
Scooter	140	12	53	75
Hearing devices				
Any hearing device [1]	4,484	439	969	3,076
Hearing aid	4,156	370	849	2,938
Amplified telephone	675	73	175	427
TDD/TTY	104	58	*25	*21
Closed caption television	141	66	*32	43
Listening device	106	*26	*22	58
Signaling device	95	*37	*23	35
Interpreter	57	*27	*21	*9
Other hearing technology	93	*28	*24	41
Vision devices				
Any vision device [1]	527	123	135	268
Telescopic lenses	158	40	49	70
Braille	59	*28	*23	*8
Readers	68	*15	*14	39
White cane	130	*35	48	47
Computer equipment	*34	*19	*8	*7
Other vision technology	277	51	76	151

* Figure does not meet standard of reliability or precision.
[1] Numbers do not add to these totals because categories are not mutually exclusive; a person could have used more than one device within a category.

The probability of needing an assistive device usually increases with age, particularly with mobility devices, hearing devices, and vision devices. (See Table 1.)

Assistive devices may also include modifications or accommodations provided in public facilities or in the workplace, as required by the AMERICANS WITH DISABILITIES ACT. For example, providing telephone devices for the deaf on hotel telephones is one form of an assistive device/accommodation.

Russell, J. Neil, Ph.D. et al. "Trends and Differential Use of Assistive Technology Devices: United States, 1994," Centers for Disease Control and Prevention, National Center for Health Statistics, Advance Data Number 292 (November 13, 1997).

asthma Chronic narrowing of the bronchial passages of the nose and throat, making breathing difficult. People of all ages may develop asthma,

TABLE 1   ASTHMA DEATHS IN THE UNITED STATES, 1998 (RATE PER MILLION)

Age Groups, 1998	Children Younger Than Age 5	Children 5–14	People ages 15–34	Adults 35–64	Adults 65+
TOTAL	2.1	3.3	5.0	17.8	86.3
Black/African American	8.1	9.7	16.6	52.3	130.4
White	Unknown	2.0	3.0	13.3	81.1
Hispanic/Latino	Unknown	Unknown	3.7	16.4	84.5
Female	1.4	2.7	4.3	22.3	99.1
Male	2.8	4.0	5.7	13.0	68.1

Source: Centers for Disease Control and Prevention. "Respiratory Diseases," in *Healthy People 2010,* National Institutes of Health, 2000.

although it is the most dangerous and potentially fatal for older people with this medical problem. The condition may be aggravated by some climates. Infections, such as bronchitis or pneumonia, can also cause a worsening of asthma.

People who are diagnosed with asthma need to make an advance plan of what to do in the event of an asthma attack, and they should also be sure that family members and friends are also aware of this plan in the event that the person with asthma needs assistance. Asthma is a condition that requires prompt action in the case of an emergency. Wearing an identifying bracelet or necklace could save the life of an individual with asthma.

Causes

Asthma may be caused by allergies or infections, and may be triggered by sudden weather changes or air pollution. SMOKING may also trigger asthma in some people. Environmental toxins may also play a role, such as "Red Tide." Often, the cause is difficult to determine.

Risk Factors for Death

Asthma may be mild, but it can also be a life-threatening disease. According to the American Lung Association, females have a 25 percent higher mortality (death) rate from asthma than males. African Americans with asthma have about three times the rate of death found among white Americans. The risk for death increases with age and is highest for people older than age 85.

According to the CENTERS FOR DISEASE CONTROL AND PREVENTION (CDC), the asthma death rate is 86.3 per million for adults older than age 65. This contrasts with the next highest death rate of only 17.8 per million for people ages 35 to 64 years. The death rate is also much higher for older Americans, who are African Americans (130.4 per million). (See Table 1.)

Diagnosis and Treatment

Asthma is diagnosed by a physician, based on the patient's symptoms and the results of the physical examination. It needs to be distinguished from CHRONIC OBSTRUCTIVE PULMONARY DISEASE (COPD), which is a combination of both chronic bronchitis and EMPHYSEMA.

People who have asthma should see their doctors on a regular basis, as frequently as the physician says it is necessary. Chronic asthma is treated with prescribed bronchial inhalers that are used on a regular (usually daily) basis. These drugs will help to reduce the inflammation that comes with asthma and consequently reduce the risk of a serious asthma attack; however, if a severe attack occurs anyway, the individual may need to be hospitalized.

attitudes toward elderly   See AGEISM.

attorneys   Individuals who are educationally qualified and licensed by their states to provide legal assistance. Older individuals may need attorneys to provide assistance to them with drawing up WILLS, with LEGAL GUARDIANSHIPS, and with preparing other legal documents. If individuals are considered to suffer from mental incompetency (an inability to manage their own legal or financial affairs or all their affairs) by family members or others, then attorneys may represent the family in court. Con-versely, attorneys may also represent older individuals who are disputing with others whether they are mentally incompetent.

Competent attorneys may enable individuals to save a great deal of time, money, and emotional distress; incompetent attorneys can create financial ruin and emotional hardship.

baby boomers   Refers to the large group of people in the United States born between 1946 and 1964 and considered by some people as similar to a sort of population bulge in a python because of the large numbers of births that occurred during those years. As the baby boomers continue to age into the 21st century, its members and many other people are concerned about the health care, retirement, housing, and other needs that this group will present to themselves as well as to society.

As of this writing, baby boomers are increasingly responsible as FAMILY CAREGIVERS to their parents and other aging relatives.

See also ADULT CHILDREN; SANDWICH GENERATION.

back pain   Usually refers to moderate to severe discomfort in the spinal column or in the general back area. Back pain may be caused by trauma to the back or to the supporting discs, ligaments, or muscles. Back pain may also be caused by many illnesses, such as KIDNEY DISEASE, CANCER, INFECTIONS, OSTEOARTHRITIS. Often, the pain is concentrated in the low back because it is this area that receives the most weight and stress of the body. Fortunately, in many cases of back pain, the problem goes away on its own, and as many as 90 percent of back-pain patients will recover in a few weeks or months. However, low back pain can also become a chronic illness requiring attention.

Many people older than age 65 have back problems, and back pain is actually common among people of all ages. According to the CENTERS FOR DISEASE CONTROL AND PREVENTION (CDC), 70 to 85 percent of *all* people suffer from back pain at some point in their lives. According to Doctors Cohen and Chopra in their 2001 article in *Geriatrics* on the primary care work-up of back symptoms, in a survey of 3,000

Americans older than age 65, 20 percent of the respondents reported problems with low back pain.

Looking at the Back
The spinal cord comprises the vertebrae of the cervical spine (neck area), the thoracic spine (middle back), and the lumbar-sacral spine (the lower back). There are discs between each vertebrae, and sometimes these discs become inflamed because of ARTHRITIS, normal aging, or from other causes.

Most back pain is "mechanical," which means that it stems from a structural problem (some part of the elements that make up the back), rather than from infections or diseases. However, when low back pain occurs in individuals age 65 and older, it is important to rule out other possible causes as well, such as cancer. This is particularly important if patients have previously had cancer, have had pain for a month or longer, and have experienced an unplanned weight loss.

Symptoms
Back pain varies from person to person, and pain may be mild or moderate to very severe. Some individuals also experience weakness or numbness in their legs, as well as pain.

Diagnosis
The physician attempts to determine where the patient is feeling pain. The area where the pain is felt may also be the origin of the problem, or the pain could be a "referred pain," which is pain that stems from another part of the body but which is felt elsewhere.

Most physicians will perform a basic neurological examination, including testing the patient's reflexes, to determine if there is any basic weakness or a lack of feeling, as well as asking the patient to perform simple maneuvers, such as standing on the toes or walking on the heels. The patient is often asked to lie flat, and the physician will perform the "straight leg test." In this test, the patient raises one leg as high as possible and then steadily lowers it. Then the same test is performed on the other leg. The doctor is looking for any pain with this movement, which may indicate inflammation or lower back damage.

Most patients are also asked to rate their pain on a scale of 1 to 10, with 1 being very mild to 10 being the worst pain they ever experienced. This self-rating can help the doctor gauge the seriousness of the problem. Patients may also be asked what activities they have had to restrict because of their pain and what activities they cannot perform at all because of it. It is also important to determine what, if any, activities occurred around the time of the onset of the back pain; for example, if the patient had just moved heavy furniture or had recently been involved in a car crash.

The medical history of the patient is also very important, including whether or not there were previous surgeries, medications that the patient is taking, previous illnesses, and whether close relatives have had similar problems.

In cases of moderate to severe back pain, the physician usually orders further testing, such as a complete blood count (to check for ANEMIA or infection), an erythrocyte sedimentation test (to check for RHEUMATOID ARTHRITIS, lupus, or other autoimmune diseases), and a urinalysis (to check for bladder infection).

The physician may also decide that plain X rays of the back are indicated or may opt for magnetic resonance imaging (MRI) of the area of the spine that is causing pain. Patients with pacemakers, however, cannot have an MRI, although a CT scan is a diagnostic possibility, as is an ultrasound test.

A physical examination of the patient with back pain is essential. The doctor needs to know how much it hurts and where it hurts, as well as whether or not the pain extends into the legs. Various movements by the patient will be evaluated, such as having the patient bend sideways, forward, and backward. The doctor may also observe the patient's gait to see if he or she can walk relatively normally or not.

Treatment for Back Pain

How the condition is treated depends on the diagnosis. Bed rest is recommended far less than in the past; however, older patients may require at least a few days of bed rest if they are suffering from acute to moderate pain.

Medications   Drugs may be prescribed to treat the condition, such as nonsteroidal antiinflammatory drugs (NSAIDs) or painkilling medications. Physicians must be careful in their choice of medications because many medications pass through the liver, the kidneys, or the stomach. If the older person is having problems with any of these organs, then the physician will need to consider which drug to prescribe as well as to tailor the dose to the needs of the individual.

Even if there are no diseases other than the back pain, older persons' bodies may process drugs at a much slower rate than when they were young, which is another factor the doctor needs to consider in determining drugs and dosages. Many patients with back pain are given NSAID medications, and the physician usually asks the patient to report any gastrointestinal problems that may develop.

If the patient is known to have had previous problems with taking NSAIDs, the doctor may try a COX-2 inhibitor, such as Celebrex (celecoxib) or Vioxx (rofecoxib). A prostaglandin analog, Cytotec (misoprostol) may be prescribed with an NSAID drug, to help protect the stomach lining.

Some patients have such severe pain that they may require an opium-based narcotic, such as morphine sulfate, methadone, OxyContin, or Duragesic (fentanyl). As of this writing, many physicians are extremely hesitant to prescribe OxyContin because it has become a drug of abuse for some individuals. However, patients with pain generally do not abuse OxyContin or other narcotics.

Doctors may also prescribe low doses of antidepressants for pain control, such as Elavil (amitriptyline) or Sinequan (doxepin Hcl). The antiseizure drug Neurontin (gabapentin) may be prescribed to relieve pain. Other antiseizure drugs that have been used to treat back pain include Dilantin (phenytoin sodium), Tegretol (carbamazepine) Topamax (topiramate), and Lamictal (lamotrigine).

Other drugs that may be helpful are the muscle relaxant Flexeril (cyclobenzaprine) or dextromethorphan (commonly used for cough but also helpful in pain control).

Some patients may receive epidural injections of corticosteroid drugs, which can provide short-term (weeks or months) relief from pain. During the less painful period after receiving the injection, most patients are strongly encouraged to make lifestyle changes to strengthen their backs and reduce the probability of having another severe flare-up of their pain.

Lifestyle Changes Many patients with back pain are advised to make lifestyle changes, such as instituting an exercise program as soon as the pain becomes tolerable. Physicians may recommend physical therapy to enable patients to learn exercises that will help their specific problem. Doctors may also use transcutaneous electrical nerve stimulation (TENS), formal electrical stimulation, ultrasound, and related therapies. Aquatic exercise is often very helpful because water reduces the pressure on the body and enables many patients to move around more easily.

Most patients are advised to treat their own pain with ice or heat. They are also advised to wear comfortable shoes. Women are told to carry light pocketbooks rather than heavy shoulder bags.

Many patients with back pain may find that their sexual activities are curtailed. However, some sexual positions are less painful than others, according to Doctors Kandel and Sudderth in their book, *Back Pain: What Works! A Comprehensive Guide to Preventing and Overcoming Back Problems.* Positions which do not place physical stress on backs are generally the best, such as sideway positions.

If Surgery Is Needed Some patients will require back surgery. The surgery may be relatively limited or may be very complex, depending on the patient's needs. Back surgery should only be performed by a very experienced back surgeon.

For further information, contact the following organizations:

American Academy of Orthopaedic Surgeons
6300 North River Road
Rosemont, IL 60018
(800) 346-2267 (toll-free)
http://www.aaos.org

American Association of Neurological Surgeons
5550 Meadowbrook Drive
Rolling Meadows, IL 60088
(847) 378-0500 or (888) 566-2267 (toll-free)
http://www.aans.org

American Back Society
St. Joseph's Professional Center
2647 International Boulevard
Suite 401
Oakland, CA 94601
(510) 536-9929
http://www.americanbacksoc.org

Arthritis Foundation
1330 West Peachtree Street
Atlanta, GA 30309
(404) 872-7100 or (800) 283-7800 (toll-free)
http://www.arthritis.org

Cohen, Robert I., M.D., Pradeep Chopra, M.D., and Carole Upshur, Ed.D. "Low Back Pain, Part 2: Guide to Conservative, Medical, and Procedural Therapies," *Geriatrics* 56, no. 11 (November 2001): 38–47.
———. "Low Back Pain, Part I: Primary Care Work-up of Acute and Chronic Symptoms," *Geriatrics* 56, no. 11 (November 2001): 26–44.
Deyo, Richard A., M.D., M.P.H., and James N. Weinstein, D.O. "Low Back Pain," *New England Journal of Medicine* 344, no. 5 (February 1, 2001): 363–370.
Kandel, Joseph, M.D., and David B. Sudderth, M.D. *Back Pain: What Works! A Comprehensive Guide to Preventing and Overcoming Back Problems.* Rocklin, Calif.: Prima Publishing, 1996.

baldness Generally refers to the permanent loss of hair on the head. Male pattern baldness is a hereditary condition. Some men choose various hair restoration techniques such as hair transplant, while others wear hairpieces. Others use elaborate methods of using still-growing strands of hair to comb over bald spots. There are also over-the-counter medications that may help hair to grow again, such as Rogaine (minoxidil). Some men take no action to hide their baldness.

Some women experience hair loss and baldness. They may wear wigs or may also use Rogaine to increase hair growth.

There is no health risk to baldness other than the increased exposure of the skin to the sun and the risk of developing SKIN CANCER. People who are bald or who have very thin hair should wear hats if they are out in the sun to protect the skin on their scalps.

People who are taking anticancer drugs during treatment for cancer may temporarily lose their hair.

In most cases, the hair growth returns to normal when chemotherapy ends.

Barrett's esophagus   A precancerous condition that can occur in the lower part of the esophagus and that usually follows many years of untreated GASTROE-SOPHAGEAL REFLUX DISEASE (chronic heartburn).

bereavement   Deep sorrow experienced at the time of the death of a loved one. Because of their age, older individuals are more likely to have to face the deaths of those they care about, including family members and friends. Some people experience bereavement over the death of beloved pets upon whom they have depended. Bereavement may develop into DEPRESSION. Some bereaved people develop a problem with late onset ALCOHOLISM.

See also DEATH; FUNERALS; WIDOWS/WIDOWERS.

bladder cancer   A malignant tumor of the bladder, the organ that stores urine. Bladder cancer is diagnosed in about 38,000 men and 15,000 women in the United States each year. In the United States, it is the fourth-most-common form of cancer that men experience and the eighth-most-common among women. The five-year survival rate for bladder cancer is high: 71 percent for patients who are age 75 and older, compared to 86 percent for patients who are younger than age 65.

According to the National Cancer Institute in the United States, bladder cancer is found more frequently in some industrialized nations, such as the United States, Canada, France, Denmark, Italy, and Spain. The rates of bladder cancer incidence are lower in the United Kingdom and Eastern Europe, and they are lower still in Asia and South America, where their citizens have about one-third the incidence of bladder cancer cases found in the United States.

Location of the Cancer

The bladder wall includes both transitional cells and squamous cells. According to the National Cancer Institute, when bladder cancer occurs, the majority of the time (90 percent) it develops in the transitional cells. This is also called transitional cell carcinoma.

In other cases of bladder cancer, the cancer develops in the squamous cells, and it is called squamous cell carcinoma. In a minority of cases, cancer forms in the lining of the bladder. This type of bladder cancer is referred to as superficial bladder cancer, or carcinoma in situ.

Known Risks for Bladder Cancer

Researchers have found patterns among patients diagnosed with bladder cancer. They are more likely to fit the following categories:

- People who are older than age 40
- Male (men have a two to three times greater risk of developing bladder cancer)
- White (CAUCASIANS develop bladder cancer at about twice the rate of AFRICAN AMERICANS and HISPANIC AMERICANS. Asians have an even lower rate of bladder cancer)
- Tobacco user (Cigarette smokers have double to triple the risk of contracting bladder cancer. Pipe and cigar smokers also have a higher risk. Some researchers believe that tobacco smoke damages the DNA. An estimated half of all bladder cancers in men and one-third in women are attributed to smoking)
- Occupational exposure caused by employment in rubber, textile, dye, and leather industries
- Having other family members who have had bladder cancer
- Previous history of bladder cancer (If a person has had bladder cancer before, it may recur)

Symptoms of Bladder Cancer

People with bladder cancer may have blood in their urine, experience pain during urination, and feel a need to urinate frequently. The bladder may also feel very irritated. However, these are also symptoms of a common and easily treatable bladder infection.

Anyone with these symptoms should ask a doctor, preferably a urologist, to diagnose and treat the problem. Also, because bladder infections are relatively uncommon in men, any of these signs merit immediate attention among those males who experience them.

Diagnosis

If the doctor suspects bladder cancer, he or she will check the abdomen and pelvis for tumors and may also perform a rectal exam. A woman may also receive a vaginal examination. Other tests that can detect a possible tumor are the intravenous pyleogram (IVP) in which dye is injected into a blood vessel to make the bladder show up clearly on special X rays.

A UROLOGIST may also perform a cystoscopy, which is a procedure in which a special tube is inserted into the bladder so that the doctor can inspect it from the inside. It is also possible for the doctor to remove tissue during this procedure, which can be biopsied to check for cancer.

In 2001, physician researchers at Yale University reported on a urine test that they had developed to detect cancer cells. The test detects a protein called survivin, which researchers found in patients with new and recurring bladder cancer. It was not present in normal patients or in patients with other forms of cancer. This test may simplify detection, once approved for general use.

Staging of Bladder Cancer

In Stage 0 (zero) of bladder cancer, the cancer cells are only on the surface of the interior lining of the bladder. This type of cancer may also be called superficial cancer, or carcinoma in situ. About 70 percent of all bladder cancers are diagnosed at this stage.

In Stage I, the cancer cells are located more deeply in the bladder lining but have not spread further.

In Stage II, cancer cells have invaded the muscle of the bladder.

In Stage III, the cancer cells have further spread throughout the bladder and may have gone beyond the bladder to the prostate gland in men or the uterus or vagina in women.

In Stage IV, the most advanced stage of bladder cancer, the cancer cells have extended to other sites of the body as far away as the lungs or other organs.

Treatment of Bladder Cancer

If bladder cancer is diagnosed from a biopsy, further tests may be needed to help determine the course of treatment. Computerized tomography (CT) scans or magnetic resonance imaging (MRI) scans may help determine the stage of the bladder cancer. Bone scans may also help with staging, as may other tests that the doctor orders.

Bladder cancer may be treated with surgery, chemotherapy, radiation therapy, or biological therapy.

Surgery In most cases of bladder cancer, the doctor chooses some form of surgery. Superficial bladder cancer may be treated with transurethral resection, in which the doctor uses a cystoscope and special tools to remove the cancer. Radiation therapy or chemotherapy may be recommended after this procedure.

In some cases, such as when the cancer is confined to only one section of the bladder, then only the cancerous part of the bladder is removed. This is called a segmental cystectomy.

If the cancer is more advanced, the patient may need the entire bladder removed (radical cystectomy). The doctor will take out the whole bladder, the lymph nodes in the area, part of the urethra, and any organs nearby that may contain cancer, such as the prostate gland in men or the uterus, ovaries, fallopian tubes, and part of the vagina in women.

If the entire bladder is removed, the surgeon must form another way for urine to be collected. The doctor may be able to create a new pouch for urine inside the body, using some of the patient's own intestine, or patients may need to wear a bag on the outside of their bodies.

A cystectomy may make men impotent after the surgery, but in some cases, this complication can be avoided. For women, sexual intercourse may become difficult if the surgeon has had to remove part of the vagina. Patients who have had segmental cystectomies may need to urinate more frequently, at least at first, although the effect may be permanent.

Chemotherapy The use of cancer-killing drugs may be the recommended therapy for bladder cancer. In some cases, the chemotherapy medication is inserted into the bladder and left there for several hours (intravesical chemotherapy). This treatment may occur once a week or once a month for several weeks or up to a year, depending on the doctor's recommendation.

For cases in which the cancer is deeply embedded in the bladder, patients who receive chemotherapy may need intravenous therapy, in which the drugs are administered through the vein. How frequently intravenous chemotherapy is needed depends on the individual case.

Radiation Therapy   If the cancer cells are to be irradiated, the radiation can be introduced by a special machine located in a hospital or clinic. Another option is for the doctor to insert radioactive substances surgically. Patients must be hospitalized for a few days during this procedure and treatment. Radiation therapy may cause nausea and vomiting. It may also cause ERECTILE DYSFUNCTION in men and vaginal dryness in women. Usually these effects are not permanent.

Biological Therapy   Doctors who choose biological therapy use a Bacille Calmette-Guerin (BCG) solution (or another form of weakened bacteria), introducing it into the bladder with a catheter. The patient is instructed to retain the solution in the bladder for several hours. The goal is for these bacteria to stimulate the person's immune system and thus kill not only the bacteria but also the cancer cells. A minority of patients (about 5 percent) have developed a severe reaction to this form of therapy such as a high fever. It is not generally used in patients with low-stage tumors.

Future Outlook

Doctors are seeking genetic markers for bladder cancer to facilitate an early diagnosis. They are also investigating genetic therapies and other forms of treatments.

Little, D'Arcy, M.D., CCFP, and Munir A. Jamal, M.D., FRCSC. "Damaged DNA and Cellular Apotosis: The Story on Bladder Cancer in the Elderly," *Geriatrics and Aging* 4, no. 2 (2001): 14–15, 19.

National Cancer Institute. "Bladder Cancer," NIH Publication No. 01-1559 (September 7, 2001).

Smith, S. D., et al. "Urine Detection of Survivin and Diagnosis of Bladder Cancer," *Journal of the American Medical Association (JAMA)* 285 (2001): 324–328.

blindness/severe vision impairment   Complete or nearly complete loss of sight. The risk for blindness increases with age, especially after the age of 75 years. Some states have a definition of *legal blindness,* in which the individual's sight is too impaired to drive a vehicle. These states set their own standards for the level of vision impairment that constitutes legal blindness.

In the United States, experts estimate that there are more than a million people age 40 and older who are blind, including 712,000 women and 335,000 men. Of these individuals, most (884,000) are white, followed by 112,000 individuals who are AFRICAN AMERICAN. (Blacks have a disproportionately high rate of blindness compared to their numbers in the population.)

Blindness or severe vision impairment may be the result of long-term DIABETES or may be caused by CATARACTS, GLAUCOMA, MACULAR DEGENERATION, or other EYE DISEASES.

According to "Vision Problems in the U.S.," a 2002 report on blindness published by the organization Prevent Blindness America under contract to the National Eye Institute of the NATIONAL INSTITUTES OF HEALTH, the overall national average of poor vision and blindness for adults age 40 and older is 2.85 percent. Alaska has the lowest rates of poor vision and blindness, at 1.3 percent.

Those states with the largest proportion of individuals age 40 and older with both vision impairment (poor eyesight) and blindness are as follows:

- North Dakota (3.74 percent)
- Iowa (3.73 percent)
- South Dakota (3.70 percent)
- Nebraska (3.42 percent)
- Kansas (3.43 percent)
- Florida (3.42 percent)

Prevention of Blindness

In many cases, prevention of blindness is possible if older adults have annual checkups to detect glaucoma, cataracts, and other eye diseases. There are also certain programs in place for people with diabetes, who are, by the nature of their disease, at very high risk for developing eye diseases that lead to blindness.

The National Diabetes Eye Examination Program, launched in 2001 by the CENTERS FOR MEDICARE AND MEDICAID SERVICES (CMS), formerly the Health Care Financing Administration (HCFA), is a program to encourage people with diabetes to obtain eye examinations.

In this program, patients older than age 65 who have not had a dilated eye examination for three or more years may be matched with an ophthalmologist or optometrist in their area to receive a comprehensive eye examination as well as a year of follow-up care for the conditions diagnosed during that examination. The only cost is the MEDICARE copayment, which may be waived if a financial need exists. (For further information or to locate a participating ophthalmologist, call the 24-hour toll-free number (800) 222-3937.)

Emotional Impact of Blindness

It is usually extremely difficult for a formerly sighted person to lose his or her vision. The person may feel that he or she has lost independence, the enjoyment of seeing family and friends, and the ability to perform tasks that were easily performed in the past. The person may suffer from DEPRESSION or ANXIETY, and psychological counseling is often indicated. However, older people are often resistant to receiving therapy, seeing it as a weakness or as only for someone who is severely mentally ill.

Prevent Blindness America. "Vision Problems in the U.S.: Prevalence of Adult Vision Impairment and Age-Related Eye Disease in America" (2002).

brain tumor A cancerous growth in the brain. Also known as an intracranial tumor. Brain tumors may be life threatening and may cause many health problems. About 16,800 brain tumors are diagnosed in the United States per year, and brain tumor is the cause of death in about 13,000 people per year.

Symptoms

About half of the people who have brain tumors experience severe headaches, and these are generally headaches that are worse in the morning and that dissipate during the day. Some people have migraine headaches. Some patients also experience seizures that involve a loss of consciousness. Changes in balance, in movements, or in motor strength and changes in concentration and attention can all be signs of a brain tumor.

Diagnosis

The physician may suspect a brain tumor, but it cannot be definitively diagnosed until a magnetic resonance imaging (MRI) scan is performed.

Treatment

If a brain tumor is diagnosed, generally it is the NEUROLOGIST, or expert in the brain and spinal cord, who treats the disease. If surgery is needed, a neurosurgeon performs the procedure. Sometimes, the tumor is treated with radiation therapy. Some patients are also followed with chemotherapy, depending on the type of tumor.

Technology has advanced to the point that some of the newer and higher functioning MRI scanners can be used to follow patients with brain tumors after they have had surgery or radiation treatment. Using a technique called MRI Spectroscopy, the physician can now distinguish between brain tissue that has a residual tumor versus brain tissue that is scarred or irritated from a STROKE or radiation. Ultimately, following up with a specialist is still mandatory.

For further information, contact the following organizations:

American Brain Tumor Association (ABTA)
2720 River Road
Suite 146
Des Plaines, IL 60018
(847) 827-9910 or (800) 886-2282
http://www.abta.org

The Brain Tumor Society
124 Watertown Street
Suite 3-H
Watertown, MA 02472
(617) 924-9997 or (800) 770-8287
http://www.tbts.org

DeAngelis, Lisa M., M.D. "Brain Tumors," *New England Journal of Medicine* 344, no. 2 (January 11, 2001): 114–123.

breast cancer The most commonly diagnosed malignant tumor found among women and the second leading cause of death from cancer among women in the United States and Canada. (Contrary to popular belief, it is lung cancer that is the leading cause of cancer death among women in the United States and Canada.) About 183,000 women are diagnosed with breast cancer each year in the United States, and nearly 41,000 die from the disease each year. In Canada, an estimated 5,500 women died of breast cancer in 2001, according to the National Cancer Institute of Canada.

Risk Factors

Middle-aged and older women are at the greatest risk of facing breast cancer, although younger women may also be diagnosed with the disease. Complicating the treatment for breast cancer among older women is the fact that many of them also have other diseases, such as DIABETES, ARTHRITIS, and HEART DISEASE. For this reason, some physicians may be hesitant to treat breast cancer aggressively in older patients.

Age Risks   The risk for breast cancer increases with age. According to the National Cancer Institute, the risks for being diagnosed with breast cancer are as follows:

From age 30 to age 40: 1 out of 257
From age 40 to age 50: 1 out of 67
From age 50 to age 60: 1 out of 36
From age 60 to age 70: 1 out of 28
From age 70 to age 80: 1 out of 24

Men with Breast Cancer   The overwhelming majority of breast cancer patients are female, although a tiny percentage (less than 1 percent) of breast cancer victims are males; about 400 men die of breast cancer each year. Some risks for men developing breast cancer are the use of estrogen, dysfunction of the testicles, gynecomastia (breast enlargement), a family history of breast cancer, and diseases such as cirrhosis or Klinefelter's syndrome.

Racial Risks   White women have a greater risk (13.2 percent) of being diagnosed with breast cancer, compared to the lower risk of 9.7 percent faced by black women, according to 1996 data. Yet, despite their lower risk of being stricken with breast cancer, black women have a slightly higher rate of death, or 3.62 percent compared to 3.47 percent for white women.

This higher death rate from breast cancer may occur because black women are more likely to be diagnosed with breast cancer at a later stage than white women. They may also receive poorer quality health care than white women or they may lack access to medical care.

They may also have adequate access but do not seek regular checkups and MAMMOGRAMS, tests which may detect tumors in the breast. It is also possible that black women may suffer from more aggressive cancers; researchers are studying this possibility as well.

Other Risks   Other risks for breast cancer are as follows:

- Having had breast cancer in the past (If a woman has had breast cancer in one breast, her risk is increased for the other breast becoming cancerous.)
- Family history of breast cancer (If a mother, sister, or daughter has had breast cancer, a woman has a greater risk.)
- Late childbearing (Women who had their first baby after age 30 have a greater risk for developing breast cancer.)
- Radiation therapy (Women who were exposed to radiation to their breasts have an increased risk, for example, women who had radiation therapy for Hodgkin's disease.)
- Alcohol consumption (Some studies indicate that drinking alcohol increases the risk for breast cancer.)

Survival Rates

The five-year survival rate for breast cancer has improved significantly in the United States since 1979 when the survival rate was 75 percent for white women and 63 percent for black women. According to the National Cancer Institute, the five-year survival rate for 1989–95 (the latest figures as of this writing) are 86 percent for white women and 71 percent for black women. (Black women have a poorer survival rate than white women in most forms of cancer.)

Screening for Breast Cancer

Gynecologists and family doctors check women's breasts for lumps during annual physical examinations, and women should also perform regular self-examinations to check themselves for breast lumps.

In addition, women older than age 50 should also obtain an annual mammogram, which is a special X ray for breast cancer.

Mammography can detect cancer about 1.7 years before the woman feels any lump in her breast. According to the CENTERS FOR DISEASE CONTROL AND PREVENTION (CDC), timely mammography screening among women older than age 40 could prevent as many as 30 percent of all deaths from breast cancer.

In the U.S., MEDICARE provides annual coverage for mammograms for Medicare recipients. In addition, most health insurance companies also pay for mammograms. However, based on a concern that poor women might not be receiving breast cancer screenings, Congress passed the Breast and Cervical Cancer Mortality Prevention Act in 1990. This law established the National Breast and Cervical Cancer Early Detection Program in the CDC. This program provides for screening services, breast examinations, Pap tests, and pelvic examinations to low-income women. From its inception in 1990 to 2001, the program has provided more than 2.7 million screening examinations for low-income women. The CDC says that as a result of this program, 8,600 breast cancers have been diagnosed.

Breast Cancer Screening in Women Age 70 and Older

There is some continued controversy about whether breast cancer screening should continue for women age 70 and older. Most organizations continue to recommend an annual screening, but some doctors believe that it is not necessary to order annual mammograms for women after age 69. They believe that if an older women does have breast cancer, it is unlikely to be an aggressively growing cancer. Opponents argue that the failure to continue to screen women for breast cancer could lead to an undertreatment of older women and to their early deaths.

According to the American Society for Therapeutic Radiology and Oncology, in study results presented in 2000 in Boston, researchers who studied breast cancer patients found that the disease was just as aggressive in older women as in women ages 40 to 70 years. Consequently, the researchers recommended that breast cancer be treated actively in all women, regardless of their age.

Based on these findings, it would thus seem logical that women age 70 and older should continue to receive annual mammograms as well, particularly in light of the increased rate of breast cancer in this age group.

Symptoms/Breast Changes to Watch For

In the very early stages of breast cancer, there are no symptoms. As the cancer continues to grow, however, there are often detectable signs. Some signs are:

- Thickening or a lump in or by the breast or in the underarms
- Change in the shape or size of breast
- Nipple discharge or tenderness
- Changes in the skin of the breast or nipple, such as redness or scaliness

Diagnosing Breast Cancer

If a physical examination and/or a mammogram indicates the presence of cancer, doctors will perform a needle or surgical biopsy. With a needle biopsy, the doctor removes tissue with a needle. With a surgical biopsy, the surgeon makes an incision and removes tissue while the woman is under anesthesia.

A biopsy will confirm if cancer is present and will help determine how advanced the cancer is, as well as how fast it is growing. The doctor may also use an ultrasound to assist with diagnosis. Based on this information, the doctor can recommend what actions the woman should take next.

Stages of Breast Cancer

Doctors divide breast cancer into basic stages, depending on the severity of the cancer and how fast it is growing. In Stage 0 (zero), the very earliest stage, the cancer is very confined and has not spread within or without the breast. This stage is sometimes called noninvasive cancer.

In Stage I, the cancer is 1 inch or less in size and has not spread beyond the breast.

In Stage II, the cancer is either an inch or smaller, but it has spread to lymph nodes under the arm, OR it is 1 to 2 inches in size but it has not spread to underarm lymph nodes, OR it is larger than 2 inches but has not spread to the lymph nodes under the arm.

Stage III is divided into two stages, IIIA and IIIB. In Stage IIIA, the cancer has spread to the lymph nodes. It may be smaller or larger than 2 inches.

In Stage IIIB, the cancer has spread to the tissues located near the breast, such as the chest wall, the ribs, and the chest muscles, OR the cancer has spread to lymph nodes inside the chest wall.

In Stage IV, the cancer has reached other organs, such as the lungs, the liver, and the brain, or it has spread to the skin and the lymph nodes inside the neck. This is the most advanced form of breast cancer.

Treatment for Breast Cancer

As with most other forms of cancer, surgery, chemotherapy, or radiation therapy are all possible options that may be chosen to combat the cancer. Women who are treated by radiation will see radiation and medical ONCOLOGISTS (cancer doctors) and will also continue to see their primary physicians.

Surgical Treatment Some form of surgery is usually the chosen course of action for breast cancer. Either a lumpectomy (removal of the breast lump containing cancer) or a complete removal of all or most of the breast (mastectomy) are the surgical options. If a lumpectomy is performed, the surgeon will also usually remove lymph nodes from the underarm area near the affected breast. Radiation therapy, in which special high-intensity X rays irradiate the affected area, is also often performed to try to ensure that the cancer is completely eradicated.

If a mastectomy is performed (either a partial or total mastectomy), the surgeon removes the cancerous area and at least some breast tissue, as well as lymph nodes under the arm. Radiation therapy usually follows surgery.

According to the National Cancer Institute, doctors may recommend a mastectomy when the following conditions are present:

- There is cancer in more than one section of the breast.
- The breast is small and a lumpectomy would leave little tissue.

- The woman refuses radiation therapy.
- The woman chooses mastectomy.

If the woman has a mastectomy, after recovering from the surgery, she may decide to use breast forms that fit into the bra or may opt to use a padded bra. She may also opt for a plastic surgeon to reconstruct the breasts. Some women choose against special bras or reconstruction.

Radiation Therapy Radiation is another way to try to kill or contain the cancer cells. Radiation is either provided by a machine, or it is implanted. If the radiation is provided by a machine, the woman goes to the clinic or the hospital for about five days a week for several weeks. If the material is implanted into the breast, the woman remains in the hospital for several days, and the radiated implants are removed before her discharge from the hospital.

Chemotherapy Another option to treat cancer is to use strong anticancer drugs that are pills or injections. These drugs may cause nausea and vomiting, although new medications help control some of the side effects.

Biological Therapy A newer way to treat breast cancer is called biological therapy. This treatment is an attempt to stimulate the body's natural defenses. Patients are treated with a drug called Herceptin (trastuzumab), which may stop or slow the growth of cancer cells. Biological therapy may accompany chemotherapy.

Joining a Clinical Trial Another option for the breast cancer patient may be to join an ongoing clinical trial that is testing a medication or a procedure. This may enable her to use experimental therapies or treatments that would otherwise be unavailable to her.

Questions to Ask
Before Surgery

The National Cancer Institute says that women considering surgery for breast cancer should ask the surgeon the following questions before surgery:

- What kind of surgery is recommended?
- How much of my breast needs to be removed?
- If I have a mastectomy, can I later have breast reconstruction?

- Do you recommend breast reconstruction at the time of surgery or later?
- Will you remove any lymph nodes?
- Where will the surgery be performed?
- Will I have general or local anesthesia?
- How will I feel after the operation?
- If I have pain after surgery, how can I obtain relief?
- What side effects should I report?
- Where will the scars be, and what will they look like?
- How long will I be in the hospital, and will I need care after I am discharged?
- When will I be able to return to my normal activities?

Emotional Aspects

The diagnosis of breast cancer and the removal of part or all of a breast is an emotionally devastating experience for women of any age, whether they are sexually active or not. Participating in a support group of other women who have faced the same problem may also help women deal with the problem.

Physicians should not automatically assume that women who are in their senior years will not "mind" having to undergo breast surgery, any more than they should assume that men with prostate cancer would not become upset if they were to lose their sexual potency from a prostatectomy (removal of the prostate gland, usually because of prostate cancer).

Support from a psychologist or therapist may be warranted, and support groups may help as well.

Current and Future Advances

Scientists seek to diagnose breast cancer as early as possible to facilitate the best chance of a cure. For example, in 2001, among women already diagnosed with breast cancer, British researchers tested a tiny camera that can be inserted through a woman's nipple to check for cancer in the milk ducts of the breast. This can be very helpful because when breast cancer occurs, it usually starts in the milk duct area and then spreads outward. The camera can detect whether the already diagnosed cancer is contained or if it is spreading.

For further information, contact the following organizations:

National Alliance of Breast Cancer Organizations
9 East 37th Street
10th Floor
New York, NY 10016
(212) 889-0606 or (888) 806-2226 (toll-free)
http://www.nabco.org

National Breast Cancer Coalition
1707 L Street, NW
Suite 1060
Washington, DC 20036
(202) 296-7477 or (800) 622-2838 (toll-free)
http://www.stopbreastcancer.org

Y-ME National Breast Cancer Organization
212 W. Van Buren
Chicago, IL 60607
(312) 986-8338 or (800) 221-2141 (toll-free)
http://www.y-me.org

Centers for Disease Control and Prevention. "At a Glance. The National Breast and Cervical Cancer Early Detection Program, 2001" (2001).

Fox, Sarah A., Ed.D., M.S.P.H., et al. "Targeted Mailed Materials and the Medicare Beneficiary: Increasing Mammogram Screening Among the Elderly," *American Journal of Public Health* 91, no. 1 (2001): 55–61.

National Cancer Institute. "Breast Cancer," NIH Publication No. 00-1556 (December 12, 2000).

bruising   Older people are more likely to have broken capillaries and to bruise more easily than younger individuals. Bruising may also be a sign of ABUSE.

calcium deficiency   Overly low levels of calcium in the blood, also known as hypocalcemia. Older individuals may be at risk for a calcium deficiency because of medications they take, as well as some diseases for which they may be at risk, such as KIDNEY DISEASE, liver disease, or ALCOHOLISM. Mild hypocalcemia may mimic the symptoms of early ALZHEIMER'S DISEASE or DEMENTIA. Patients may also experience muscle pains and cramping. Severely ill patients who are in the intensive care unit of a hospital are also at risk for developing hypocalcemia, as are individuals who have had thyroid surgery due to damage that may have occurred to the parathyroid glands embedded in the thyroid.

Should the physician suspect hypocalcemia, blood tests can verify whether the calcium levels are within the normal range or not. If they are not, the cause is treated. The patient may also need to take supplemental calcium and prescribed Vitamin D. Periodic retesting is indicated to make sure the patient's calcium levels do not become excessively high, or hypercalcemic.

Canada   As with the rest of the world, the population of Canada is aging, and Canadians are facing and will continue to face a wide range of problems associated with older individuals, as well as opportunities to draw upon the experience and knowledge of their senior citizens.

Most older Canadians receive a pension from the Old Age Security (OAS) program, available to those age 65 and older and adjusted to provide increased payments to low-income seniors. The Canada and Quebec Pension Plans (C/QPP) is another source of retirement income to eligible individuals. Canada has a public health-care system that provides medical care for patients. It is known as Medicare and is administered by Health Canada.

According to a 2002 report from the Division of Aging and Seniors of Health Canada, which is entitled "Canada's Aging Population," one in eight Canadians was 65 years old or older in 2001. This number is projected to increase to one in five by the year 2026. Most older Canadians (about 83 percent) live in Ontario, Quebec, British Columbia, and Alberta.

In addition, the most rapid growth is among Canadians age 85 and older (the OLDEST OLD). In 2001, there were 430,000 Canadians in this age group, which is more than twice the number of very old Canadians in 1981. By 2041, it is estimated that the oldest old Canadians will increase to 1.6 million people.

Canadians enjoy a higher LIFE EXPECTANCY than some other countries. For example, according to a 2001 report from *Aging Trends,* published by the CENTERS FOR DISEASE CONTROL AND PREVENTION (CDC) in the United States, the life expectancy of Canadians is 75.2 years, compared to 74.1 years for people in the United States. (There are also some countries with higher life expectancies than Canada: see LIFE EXPECTANCY for a table of countries and life expectancies.)

Health Issues

Medical problems of older individuals are an increasing concern in Canada, and Canadian sources report that there are about 317,000 Canadians diagnosed with ALZHEIMER'S DISEASE. But a worse threat comes from CARDIOVASCULAR DISEASE, which is the biggest killer.

Cardiovascular disease, which primarily comprises CORONARY HEART DISEASE, STROKE, and HYPERTENSION, affects the health of many older Canadians. According to Health Canada, in their 1999 report, *The Changing Face of Heart Disease and Stroke in Canada,* a third or more of all deaths were due to cardiovascular disease in 1997.

Many older Canadians also experience chronic health problems, primarily arthritis, hypertension, allergies, back pain problems, chronic heart problems, CATARACTS, and DIABETES.

There are also gender differences, when considering medical problems. As can be seen from Table 1, Canadian women ages 65–74 have a lower rate of death from cardiovascular disease than men, or 31.7 percent of all deaths compared to 36.3 percent for men.

In considering women age 75 and older, they surpass men in the rate of deaths from cardiovascular disease; for example, 42.3 percent of the deaths to women ages 75–84 die were from cardiovascular disease, compared to 40.8 percent for men. The gap widens further for women age 85 and older. Nearly half (49.2 percent) of all Canadian women in this age group die from cardiovascular disease, compared to 44.1 percent for men.

TABLE 1   PERCENTAGE OF DEATHS FROM CARDIOVASCULAR DISEASE IN CANADA, BY AGE AND SEX, 1997

Age	Men	Women
65–74 years	36.3	31.7
75–84 years	40.8	42.3
85 and older	44.1	49.2

Source: *The Changing Face of Heart Disease and Stroke in Canada*

About 11 percent of Canadian women ages 65–74 have heart problems, and 17 percent of men in the same age group experience heart problems. This percentage of heart disease increases dramatically for women age 75 and older: 22 percent of the women in this age group have heart problems. The percentage of heart problems for men age 75 and older is the same as for women: 22 percent.

Cancer

Another major threat for older Canadians is illness and death from various forms of CANCER, the second leading cause of death in Canada after cardiovascular disease. About 134,000 new cases of cancer were diagnosed among Canadians in 2001, according to the National Cancer Institute of Canada. Many older people are stricken with cancer, and people older than age 60 represent the largest proportion (82 percent) of all cancer deaths in Canada.

The most prominent form of cancer among Canadians with cancer is LUNG CANCER. Many women also contract BREAST CANCER, and for some, it is fatal. The National Cancer Institute of Canada estimated that 5,500 Canadian women died of breast cancer in 2001.

Living Situations

According to Health Canada, most older Canadians live in private residences, and only about 7 percent of them reside in an institution. Of all people who do live in institutions, about 85 percent live in care homes for elderly and disabled people, and the remaining 15 percent live in hospitals, religious institutions, or other institutions.

Older women are more likely than men to live in an institution, as with older women in the United States. According to Health Canada, the public health agency in Canada, in 1996, of all Canadian women who were age 85 and older, 38 percent lived in an institution, compared to 24 percent of males the same age. Among women ages 75 to 84, 10 percent resided in an institution, compared to 7 percent of men the same ages. However, the percentage of men and women ages 65 to 74 who lived in an institution in 1996 was the same: 2 percent.

For further information, contact:

Division of Aging and Seniors
Health Canada
Address locator: 1908A1
Ottawa, Ontario
K1A 1B4
(613) 952-7606

Websites of interest to Canadians:

Canadian Health Network: http://www.canadian-health-network.ca

Health Canada: http://www.hc-sc.gc.ca

Health Canada's Division of Aging and Seniors: www.hc-sc.gc.ca/seniors-aines/

Seniors Canada Online: http://www.seniors.gc.ca

Statistics Canada: http://www.statcan.ca

Veterans Affairs Canada: http://www.vac-acc.gc.ca

See also Appendix VIII for a listing of health agencies in Canada.

Division of Aging and Seniors, Health Canada. "Canada's Aging Population" (2002).

Heart and Stroke Foundation of Canada. *The Changing Face of Heart Disease and Stroke in Canada.* Ottawa, Canada: Heart and Stroke Foundation, 1999.

cancer   A malignant overgrowth of cells that can lead to death if untreated. According to the AMERICAN CANCER SOCIETY, about 1.3 million new cases of cancer were diagnosed in the United States in 2001, and about 553,400 people died of some form of cancer (about 1,500 per day). Cancer is the second most prominent cause of death for all causes in the United States after HEART DISEASE, and more than half of all new cancer cases are diagnosed among patients who are age 65 or older.

In Canada, about 134,100 new cases of cancer were diagnosed in 2001, and cancer claimed the lives of an estimated 65,300 people, including 34,600 males and 30,700 females in 2001, according to the National Cancer Institute of Canada. Many older people are stricken with cancer, and people older than age 60 represent the largest proportion (82 percent) of all cancer deaths in Canada.

Cancer may occur in many different parts of the body; however, most cancer patients (both male and female) in the United States and Canada who die have LUNG CANCER. The second-most-dominant form of cancer death varies by gender and is BREAST CANCER for women and PROSTATE CANCER for men. (Contrary to popular belief, more women die of lung cancer than of breast cancer in the United States.)

Some cancers are more common than others are, and some cancers are more virulent than others are; for example, SKIN CANCER is very common, but it is usually only the rare malignant melanomas that are fatal. Conversely, PANCREATIC CANCER and OVARIAN CANCER are far less commonly diagnosed, but many victims die.

However, there are hopes for medical advances. For example, in 2002, researchers tested a blood test that can identify ovarian cancer in the early and treatable stages. In most cases of ovarian cancer, the survival rate is very low (about 20 percent of women diagnosed with ovarian are alive after five years) because the disease is often diagnosed too late. However, if the illness is diagnosed in the early stages, the prognosis radically improves to a survival rate of 95 percent after five years. Once the test is developed and approved, it can be used on women who are considered at high risk because of their family history. Presumably, tests with similar results will be developed for diseases such as pancreatic cancer.

Causes of Cancer

The cause of the cancer varies with the type, and in many cases, the cause is unknown. In the case of lung cancer and many cases of ORAL CANCER, the cause of the disease is usually SMOKING. Sometimes, the cause may be external to the person, such as an exposure to dangerous chemicals or materials in the workplace. In the past, exposure to asbestos in the home and the workplace (used as an insulation) led to a unique type of lung cancer, mesothelioma. This problem, combined with inflammatory airway changes, led to patients having severe respiratory problems.

Some forms of cancer carry a genetic risk, such as breast cancer, while others do not appear to carry such a risk. Some experts believe that a genetic predisposition to cancer may be triggered by environmental factors. For example, a person who has many family members with cancer may further increase his or her risks by smoking. However, often the cause of cancer in an individual is unknown.

Diagnosis of Cancer

The diagnosis depends on the site of the cancer. Some forms of cancer have few, seemingly minor, or advance symptoms, such as pancreatic cancer, prostate cancer, or ovarian cancer. Other forms of cancer usually do have some warning signs, such as with lung cancer or breast cancer. At least annual physical examinations that are performed by a medical doctor can help allay the risks of cancer because the doctor will not only inspect the body but will also order diagnostic tests for cancer, such as a colonoscopy to detect COLORECTAL CANCER or a mammogram to detect breast cancer. The doctor will usually perform a digital rectal examination on a man to detect prostate cancer.

Treatment of Cancer

Treatment varies according to the area of the body that is affected by cancer as well as how advanced the cancer is and how fast it is growing. In many cases, surgical removal of the cancerous tumor and the organs it affects is the chosen option. Surgery may be relatively minor, such as with the excision of a small skin cancer, or it may be major surgery, as with the removal of a lung in lung cancer, the removal of the prostate gland in prostate cancer, or the excision of the ovaries in ovarian cancer.

In many cases, radiation therapy may also be used. In most cases when radiation treatment is given, the individual receives radiation from a machine in a hospital or clinic. The individual may go to the facility for five days a week for several weeks, or another regimen may be recommended by the physician. If the cancer is localized, radioactive material sometimes can be inserted directly into the cancerous area. This is commonly done in some patients with prostate cancer, who receive radiation through "seed" implants. The side effects of radiation therapy vary, but some effects may include nausea, redness to the affected area, and fatigue.

Chemotherapy is another option for some patients with cancer. Cancer-killing drugs are given to the patient, often intravenously, although in some cases pills may be taken. Often, the drugs make patients feel ill, and patients may also lose their hair. When the drug therapy is ended, the patient may feel better. The chemotherapy regimens in place today are much better tolerated than those of just a few years ago. Antinausea medications, medications to raise the blood count, and numerous additional adjunct treatments are available to give patients the best chance possible at a successful chemotherapy regimen.

There are also a variety of biological or hormonal treatments for cancer. For example, men with prostate cancer may be treated with hormones to suppress their own male hormones. The rationale behind this treatment is that their male hormones will cause the tumor to grow faster; thus if male hormones are suppressed, then the cancer growth may be delayed.

Usually No Longer a Death Sentence

Although the reaction of most people who are diagnosed with cancer is to assume that they will die soon, many people live for years after the diagnosis, and most die of other ailments. Sophisticated medical and technological advances have greatly improved the prognosis for cancer patients. However, it is important to diagnose the cancer as soon as possible so that effective treatments can be started. To achieve this end, patients need to inform their doctors of symptoms they are experiencing, and they also need to comply with requests for diagnostic tests.

Most people dislike or even refuse to undergo medical tests, and their lifesaving importance should be emphasized to patients. For example, many people dislike the colonoscopy, which is an internal examination of the colon with special instruments. The patient must have a clean bowel before the examination is performed and thus must experience diarrhea that is induced with medication. The patient may be mildly sedated during the procedure. Colonoscopies, as with other screening tests, save lives because they can detect cancers at an early stage. The doctor can often remove the early cancer before it spreads to neighboring organs. Precancerous polyps can also be identified and removed.

Older People May Be Treated Less Aggressively

Some studies indicate that although older people respond well to chemotherapy and other forms of cancer treatment, they may be receiving less-aggressive treatment than younger people. One reason for this may be that older people are more likely to have other diseases as well, and doctors consider them harder to treat.

Limiting Risk for Cancer

Although some key health factors are beyond the control of individuals, such as their genetic makeup, there are actions older people can take to limit their risk for developing cancer. The single most major step is to give up smoking and alcohol. Maintaining a nutritious diet, exercising, and losing weight if weight loss is indicated can all help decrease the odds of developing cancer.

Risk and Survival Factors

Some individuals who fit specific patterns have a greater risk of death from cancer than others do.

For example, AFRICAN AMERICANS who develop cancer have a lower survival rate than whites, although researchers are not sure why this is true. Males and females also vary in their risks for various types of cancer. Males are more likely to contract lung cancer, although many women also suffer from this disease. In general, women have a higher survival rate from cancer than men. Education may also play a factor in survival from cancer. In general, more highly educated people have a greater chance of surviving cancer. This may be because they are more likely to visit their physicians and to have their disease detected at an earlier stage.

Racial Differences   The five-year survival rate for all cancers has improved in the United States since the period 1974–79; however, survival rates are still low for some forms of cancer, such as pancreatic cancer and cancer of the esophagus. Survival rates are the best for patients with prostate cancer, melanoma of the skin (skin cancer), and breast cancer. In most cases, the five-year survival rate is lower for blacks than for whites. (See Table 1.)

For example, the five-year survival rate for all types of cancer is 61.5 percent for whites but only 48.9 percent for blacks. In looking at some types of cancers, there are wide disparities. The survival rate for cancers of the oral cavity and pharynx (throat) is 56.2 percent for whites but only 34.6 percent for African Americans in the United States. In only one type of cancer is the survival rate for African Americans slightly higher than it is for CAUCASIANS. In the case of stomach cancer, the five-year survival rate for blacks is 21.6 percent versus a survival rate of 19.5 percent for whites.

It is not known why the survival rates for blacks are so much lower. It may be that African Americans do not have access to good medical care, or they may not seek out care in the early stages of the disease. It may also be true that more aggressive forms of cancer attack African Americans than those of other races. Further research is needed to establish the reasons for the racial differences in cancer survival rates.

Male and Female Survival Rates   There are differences between the survival rates of men and women with the same types of cancers. As can be seen from the chart, the 1989–96 survival rate for all

forms of cancer was 63 percent for white females and 60.1 percent for white males. Among African Americans, the survival rate for women was 49.3 percent and it was 48.5 percent for males.

Education Levels   Researchers have also found a difference in the survival rates of cancer patients, based on their educational status. For example, among high school graduates, the cancer death rate is 139.7 per 100,000 people. (This is about the same rate for those who have not graduated from high school, or 137.8 cancer deaths per 100,000 people.) However, the death rate drops dramatically to 79.6 for those with at least some college education.

It is likely that more-educated people are more aware than others of cancer risks, and they are also more likely to see their doctors. People with some college education are also less likely to smoke, and they have a greatly reduced risk of dying from lung cancer. The lung cancer death rate for the high school graduate is 41.8 per 100,000 compared to the much lower rate of 17.6 per 100,000 among people with at least some college education.

For further information, contact:

American Cancer Society
1599 Clifton Road, NE
Atlanta, GA 30329
(800) 227-2345 or (404) 320-3333
http://www.cancer.org

National Cancer Institute
6116 Executive Boulevard, MS 8322
Bethesda, MD 20892
(900) 4-CANCER (toll-free) or (800) 332-8615 (TTY)
http://cis.nci.nih.gov

Altman, Roberta, and Michael J. Sarg, M.D. *The Cancer Dictionary.* New York: Facts On File, 1999.

Muss, Hyman B., M.D. "Older Age—Not a Barrier to Cancer Treatment," *The New England Journal of Medicine* 345, no. 15 (October 11, 2001): 1,128–1,129.

National Cancer Institute of Canada. *Canadian Cancer Statistics 2001.* Toronto, Canada, 2001.

U.S. Department of Health and Human Services. *Healthy People 2010.* 2nd ed. "With Understanding and Improving Health and Objectives for Improving Health." 2 vols. Washington, D.C.: U.S. Government Printing Office, November 2000.

TABLE 1 FIVE-YEAR RELATIVE CANCER SURVIVAL RATES FOR SELECTED CANCER SITES, ACCORDING TO RACE AND SEX: SELECTED GEOGRAPHIC AREAS, 1974–79, 1980–82, 1983–85, 1986–88, and 1989–96

[Data are based on the Surveillance, Epidemiology, and End Results Program's population-based registries in Atlanta, Detroit, Seattle-Puget Sound, San Francisco-Oakland, Connecticut, Iowa, New Mexico, Utah, and Hawaii]

Sex and Site	White					Black				
	1974–79	1980–82	1983–85	1986–88	1989–96	1974–79	1980–82	1983–85	1986–88	1989–96
Both sexes	Percent of patients									
All sites	50.9	52.1	53.9	56.7	61.5	39.2	39.7	39.8	42.6	48.9
Oral cavity and pharynx	54.9	55.5	55.3	55.3	56.2	36.5	30.8	35.0	34.8	34.6
Esophagus	5.4	7.5	9.4	10.9	13.2	3.3	5.4	6.3	7.3	9.1
Stomach	15.4	16.4	16.2	19.1	19.5	15.9	19.4	18.8	19.0	21.6
Colon	51.8	55.7	58.4	61.5	62.6	47.3	49.1	49.3	52.6	52.2
Rectum	49.8	52.9	55.9	59.2	60.7	40.2	38.0	43.5	51.1	52.3
Pancreas	2.5	2.8	2.9	3.2	4.2	3.2	4.7	5.4	6.0	3.8
Lung and bronchus	13.1	13.5	13.9	13.5	14.4	11.3	12.2	11.4	11.9	11.3
Urinary bladder	75.1	79.0	78.3	80.6	81.9	51.9	58.9	59.3	62.0	63.7
Non-Hodgkin's lymphoma	48.2	51.9	54.4	52.9	52.6	50.5	50.0	44.9	49.9	41.9
Leukemia	36.7	39.6	41.7	43.9	45.4	31.0	33.2	33.4	37.2	34.0
Male										
All sites	43.5	46.7	48.5	51.8	60.1	32.1	34.4	34.6	37.7	48.5
Oral cavity and pharynx	54.3	54.4	54.5	52.2	53.7	31.2	26.3	30.0	29.3	29.0
Esophagus	5.0	6.6	7.8	11.4	13.1	2.3	4.6	5.2	7.1	8.6
Stomach	13.9	15.4	14.5	16.1	17.1	15.4	18.5	18.5	14.8	20.5
Colon	50.9	56.0	59.0	62.4	63.2	45.4	46.7	48.4	52.1	52.8
Rectum	49.0	51.4	55.3	58.8	60.2	36.9	35.9	42.3	46.7	52.4
Pancreas	2.7	2.6	2.6	2.9	3.8	2.4	3.6	4.8	6.5	4.0
Lung and bronchus	11.6	12.2	12.1	12.1	12.9	10.0	11.0	10.2	12.0	10.1
Prostate gland	70.4	74.5	76.3	82.7	94.1	60.8	64.7	63.9	69.3	86.7
Urinary bladder	76.0	80.0	79.6	82.2	84.0	59.1	63.5	64.8	67.5	67.3
Non-Hodgkin's lymphoma	47.1	50.9	53.5	50.2	48.7	45.0	47.0	43.6	46.7	37.4
Leukemia	35.8	39.6	41.3	45.2	46.5	31.0	30.4	32.3	35.9	31.9
Female										
All sites	57.5	57.1	58.8	61.5	63.0	46.8	45.9	45.4	47.8	49.3
Colon	52.6	55.4	57.9	60.7	62.1	48.7	50.9	50.0	53.1	51.8
Rectum	50.9	54.6	56.6	59.6	61.5	43.3	40.7	44.5	55.5	52.2
Pancreas	2.2	3.0	3.2	3.4	4.5	4.1	5.8	5.9	5.6	3.6
Lung and bronchus	16.7	16.3	17.1	15.9	16.6	15.5	15.5	14.2	11.8	13.5
Melanoma of skin	86.0	88.3	89.3	91.2	91.7	69.9	- - -	70.1	- - -	78.5
Breast	75.4	77.1	79.3	83.9	86.3	63.1	65.8	63.5	69.4	71.4
Cervix uteri	69.7	68.0	70.3	71.7	71.6	62.9	61.2	60.2	55.3	58.6
Corpus uteri	87.8	82.8	84.6	84.4	85.6	59.3	54.5	53.9	56.7	56.9
Ovary	37.2	38.8	40.2	42.0	50.1	40.1	38.3	41.7	38.5	47.5
Non-Hodgkin's lymphoma	49.3	52.9	55.4	56.1	57.5	57.6	53.6	46.5	54.1	49.4

- - - Data not available.

NOTES: Rates are based on followup of patients through 1997. The rate is the ratio of the observed survival rate for the patient group to the expected survival rate for persons in the general population similar to the patient group with respect to age, sex, race, and calendar year of observation. It estimates the chance of surviving the effects of cancer. Numbers have been revised and differ from previous editions of *Health, United States*.

SOURCE: National Institutes of Health, National Cancer Institute, Cancer Statistics Branch, Bethesda, Maryland 20892.

cardiac arrest Extremely dangerous situation in which the heart stops beating. Older individuals have an increased risk for this problem. If the heart is not restarted by CPR or by defibrillation, the patient will suffer from brain damage and death. Cardiac arrest is usually caused by CORONARY HEART DISEASE, including HEART ATTACK and other cardiac illnesses.

According to the AMERICAN HEART ASSOCIATION, if the cardiac-arrest victim receives treatment with electric shock (defibrillation) within several minutes, the chances of survival greatly increase. However, the chances of survival drop by 7 to 10 percent for every minute without treatment, and most resuscitation attempts fail 10 minutes or more after cardiac arrest occurs.

As many as 95 percent of all cardiac-arrest victims die before reaching the hospital, and it is essential to seek medical treatment within the home or on the way to the hospital. According to the American Heart Association in its 2002 statistical publication, "Early CPR and rapid defibrillation combined with early advanced care can produce high long-term survival rates for witnessed cardiac arrest. In some cities with public access defibrillation programs, when bystanders provide **immediate** CPR and the first shock is delivered **within 3 to 5 minutes,** the reported survival rates from VF [ventricular fibrillation] cardiac arrest are as high as 48 to 74 percent." (Bolding was provided by American Heart Association.)

Early Warning Signals of Cardiac Arrest

According to the American Heart Association, in the early warning signs of a cardiac arrest, the victim:

• Is unresponsive

• Stops normal breathing

• Loses pulse or other signs of circulation

American Heart Association. *2002 Heart and Stroke Statistical Update* (2001).

cardiologists Physicians who specialize in and treat heart disease. Cardiac surgeons perform heart surgery. HEART DISEASE is the number-one killer of older individuals of all races and ethnic groups. These physicians first complete an entire training program in internal medicine and then go on to do specialty training in the field of cardiology. Some cardiologists specialize even further, studying various invasive cardiac procedures or different types of cardiac testing.

cardiovascular disease (CVD) Diseases of the heart itself or of the blood vessels of the heart, including CORONARY HEART DISEASE, HYPERTENSION, and STROKE.

An estimated 61.8 Americans have one or more forms of cardiovascular disease. An estimated 24.8 million of this number are age 65 and older. According to the AMERICAN HEART ASSOCIATION, cardiovascular diseases together represent the number-one killer of Americans and were responsible for 958,775 deaths in 1999, compared to 549,838 deaths from CANCER. Coronary heart disease is the biggest killer in the United States among the diseases that represent CVD, claiming 55 percent of the lives of those who die from cardiovascular disease. The next-largest killer is stroke, at 17 percent of all deaths from CVD.

Cardiovascular disease is a major problem worldwide: according to the American Heart Association, CVD caused or contributed to one-third of all deaths, globally. In Latin America, for example, about 800,000 people die each year from cardiovascular disease, or 25 percent of all deaths. The numbers of men and women who die are about equal, according to the American Heart Association.

The World Health Organization has reported that 7.1 million people in the world died from coronary heart disease in 1999. About 5 million people in the world died from strokes, and 15 million additional people worldwide survived strokes. Many Europeans smoke, are obese, and have DIABETES, and these factors combine to increase the risk for cardiovascular disease.

CVD is also a problem in Canada, and according to the *Changing Face of Heart Disease and Stroke in Canada,* published by Health Canada, it is the leading cause of death for more than a third of Canadians.

The British Heart Foundation also reports that cardiovascular diseases are a major problem in Europe in their 2002 statistical compendium.

(Available at www.dphpc.ox.ac.uk/bhfhprg/stats/2000/index.html) According to this source, cardiovascular diseases are the leading cause of death for Europeans, causing 4 million deaths per year and almost half of all deaths. The highest death rates from coronary heart disease are found in northern, central, and eastern Europe.

The highest rates for a "coronary event" (certain or probable HEART ATTACK)—835 per 100,000—were found in men in Finland-North Karelia. The lowest rates for men, 81 per 100,000, were found in China. The highest event rate for women—265 per 100,000—was in the United Kingdom, and the lowest, 35 per 100,000 for each country, was in Spain and China.

Risks for Developing CVD

Some people are at particular risk for developing CVD, either because of their race or ethnicity, other illnesses that they have, or other factors. The key risk factors for developing CVD are:

- Diabetes
- AFRICAN-AMERICAN race (about 41 percent of African-American men and 40 percent of African-American women have CVD in the United States, and they face about a 40 percent higher risk of death than faced by CAUCASIANS)
- Mexican-American ethnicity (about 29 percent of Mexican-American men and 27 percent of Mexican-American women in the United States have CVD)
- Older individuals (the risk increases with age, with the greatest risk among people older than age 65)
- NATIVE AMERICAN race (many Native Americans are at high risk of death from CVD, particularly some tribes such as the Pima Indians in Arizona)
- People who smoke
- People who have a problem with OBESITY

Age Data

According to the American Heart Association in their *2002 Heart and Stroke Statistical Update,* for men, the prevalence of cardiovascular disease increases from 51 percent of men in the United States ages

55–64 years to an upward jump of 65.2 for men who are between the ages of 65–74. The percentage increases further still for those age 75 and older to 70.7 percent.

For women, the prevalence of CVD among women ages 55–64 is 48.1 percent. This percentage increases dramatically among women ages 65–74 years, to be the same as found among males, or 65.2 percent. Women who are age 75 and older have a *higher* rate of cardiovascular disease than experienced by men in the same age group, a rate of 79 percent.

PERCENTAGE OF PEOPLE WITH CARDIOVASCULAR DISEASE IN THE UNITED STATES, BY AGE AND GENDER

	Men	Women
Ages 55–64	51%	48.1%
Ages 65–74	65.2%	65.2%
Ages 75+	70.7%	79%

Source: American Heart Association, *2002 Heart and Stroke Statistical Update.*

Diagnosis and Treatment of CVD

Doctors diagnose cardiovascular disease based on blood pressure readings, electrocardiograms, magnetic resonance imaging (MRI) scans, stress tests, and various other means.

The treatment depends on the nature and the severity of the problem. EMERGENCY-CARE treatment is required in the case of a heart attack or stroke, usually followed by maintenance doses of medications, as well as recommended lifestyle changes, such as weight loss, better control of diabetes among diabetic individuals, and regular exercise. Smokers must stop smoking immediately. Individuals who have high cholesterol levels need to change their diets and often need to take cholesterol-lowering medications as well.

In the case of hypertension, the goal is to lower the blood pressure. Medication is often used. Patients are also advised to watch cholesterol levels and to lose weight if they have a problem with obesity.

Studies have shown that ASPIRIN THERAPY is effective at controlling the risk for both stroke and heart attack. Prescribed medications such as Mevacor (lovastatin), Pravachal (pravastatin), Lipitor (atorvastatin), and Zocor (simvastatin) are often ordered because these drugs can lower cholesterol levels and reduce the risk for heart attack. Some studies have shown that these drugs have reduced the risk of CVD by about a third. In patients with diabetes, the risk is decreased even more dramatically with these medications by 55 percent.

Other medications such as drugs in the beta-blocker class or in the angiotensin-converting-enzyme (ACE) inhibitor class may be indicated for patients with cardiovascular disease. In one study, the Hope Study, it was found that ramipril, an ACE inhibitor, decreased the risk of heart attack, stroke, and death so significantly for patients with diabetes that researchers ended the study early for diabetic patients so that the subjects taking a placebo (sugar pill) could take the real drug instead and obtain its benefits.

American Heart Association. *2002 Heart and Stroke Statistical Update.* Dallas, Tex.: American Heart Association, 2001.
Heart and Stroke Foundation of Canada. *The Changing Face of Heart Disease and Stroke in Canada.* Ottawa, Canada: Heart and Stroke Foundation, 1999.

caregivers Term usually used to denote family individuals who care for an ill member, although it is sometimes used to refer to private individuals who are paid to provide care in a nursing home or other environment. Many family caregivers are married middle-aged women who still have children in the home.

See also FAMILY CAREGIVERS.

Parks, Susan Mockus, M.D., and Karen D. Novielli, M.D. "A Practical Guide to Caring for Caregivers," *American Family Physician* 62 (2000): 2613–2620, 2621–2622.

cataract An eye illness that causes an opaqueness of the lens of the eye and can cause BLINDNESS if not treated. According to the 2002 report, "Vision Problems in the U.S.," produced by Prevent Blindness America, about 20.5 million Americans older than age 40 have cataracts, including 12.7 million women and 7.8 million men. More than half of all Americans age 80 and older have cataracts. The World Health Organization says that cataracts are the leading cause of blindness worldwide.

Risk for Developing Cataracts Increases with Age

Cataracts are increasingly common as people age; for example, among men in 1996, the rate of cataracts was 17.3 per 1,000 persons in the United States for those ages 45–64 years of age. The rate radically increased to 109.3 per 1,000 persons for people ages 65–74 years and increased yet again to 189.6 per 1,000 people for those who age 75 and older.

Among women, the rate of cataracts was 29 per 1,000 for those ages 45–64 in 1996. It increased to 186.4 for those ages 65–74 and still further to 203.9 per 1,000 women age 75 and older. Clearly, women in the United States have a higher risk of developing cataracts than men.

Other Risk Factors

People with DIABETES are also particularly at risk for developing cataracts. Some possible causes of cataracts are eye injuries or exposures to radiation or toxic substances. Other risk factors for developing cataracts are smoking or an excessive exposure to sunlight. However, the cause of cataracts is often unknown. The National Eye Institute, a part of the National Institutes of Health, is researching whether some minerals or vitamins may be effective in delaying the growth of cataracts or in preventing them from forming altogether. Results should be available in several years.

Symptoms of Cataracts

When cataracts first develop, there may be no symptoms, or the person may experience only a slight clouding in the field of vision. As the disease progresses, it becomes more and more difficult for the individual to see through the cloudy film of the cataract. Most people who have ignored the problem up to that point will seek help when their vision becomes severely impaired.

Some people do experience a few early warning symptoms. For example, the person with cataracts may find that sunlight seems more glaring than it did in the past. Oncoming headlights of a car at night may seem far too bright or have a distorted appearance. Colors may also seem duller than in the past.

Individuals who experience such symptoms may ignore them or may dismiss them as not important or as a normal part of aging. As a result, patients and even their doctors may not realize that these symptoms are indicators of cataracts. This is problematic because it is far preferable to be diagnosed and treated at an early stage of the disease when the prognosis is more favorable.

Diagnosis and Treatment

An OPHTHALMOLOGIST or optometrist can diagnose the existence of cataracts in an eye examination, and if surgery is required, the ophthalmologist can perform this procedure. The cataract and the natural lens will be removed, and an artificial clear plastic lens will be implanted in the eye in its place. The federal government spends about $3.4 billion per year for patients on MEDICARE who have cataract-removal surgery.

Cataracts can recur, and patients who have previously had cataracts are advised to have regular eye examinations and medical checkups. People who smoke should immediately stop smoking to reduce their risk of recurring cataracts. Individuals with diabetes need to work on maintaining their glucose levels to as close to normal as possible. People who have had cataracts should avoid excessive sun exposure and should wear sunglasses and hats when they must be out in the sun for a prolonged period. (It is also advisable to limit sun exposure to limit the risk for developing SKIN CANCER.)

See also EYE DISEASES.

Caucasians Racial grouping which usually refers to white non-Hispanics. In 2000, there were about 30 million Caucasians age 65 and older living in the United States, according to the U.S. Census Bureau. Of these, most were female, or about 17.8 million.

In the United States, Caucasians generally fare better than AFRICAN AMERICANS and other races in terms of longevity, housing, and rates of CANCER. They are also much less likely to live below the POVERTY line. However, there are some negative life/health aspects to being a member of this racial group. For example, bladder cancer is twice as common among Caucasians. Also, whites, especially white females, are more likely to die from ALZHEIMER'S DISEASE than women of other races. Whites have a greater risk for suffering from FRACTURES. Caucasian women have a higher risk of developing OSTEOPOROSIS.

centenarians Individuals who have lived to the age of 100 years or beyond. In the United States as of November 1, 2000, there were 68,000 people who were centenarians, according to the U.S. Census Bureau. There were 37,000 centenarians in 1990; thus, the number increased by about 84 percent in 10 years. In contrast, the population for individuals of all ages increased by about 11 percent during the same 10-year period. The global population of centenarians is also anticipated to be on the rise, with the global aging of citizens in many countries throughout the world.

In a Danish study of centenarians, reported in 2001, researchers found that only about half of the study subjects had Alzheimer's or another form of DEMENTIA. This largely disproves the generally accepted belief that nearly all very old people will develop some form of dementia.

See also ALZHEIMER'S DISEASE.

Centers for Disease Control and Prevention (CDC) A large and influential organization that is part of the NATIONAL INSTITUTES OF HEALTH and the primary federal government agency that oversees the other agencies that provide both research and information on a variety of serious diseases that affect older Americans as well as all Americans. For example, the National Center for Health Statistics compiles data and statistics on chronic diseases, death rates, and other statistical data, and it also publishes reports on findings.

For further information, contact the organization at:

CDC
1600 Clifton Road
Atlanta, GA 30333
(800) 311-3435 or (404) 639-3311
http://www.cdc.gov

Centers for Medicare and Medicaid Services (CMS) The federal government agency in the United States that is tasked with the rather daunting task of overseeing both MEDICARE and MEDICAID services, multibillion-dollar programs.

Formerly known as the Healthcare and Financing Administration (HCFA). In 2001, CMS spent an estimated $476 billion for medical services provided to 70 million individuals who were disabled, elderly, or poor. (Some individuals fit all three categories.)

Most Medicare payment claims are handled by private contractors, such as Blue Cross-Blue Shield. States manage Medicaid claims and receive partial federal reimbursement.

Inglehart, John K. "The Centers for Medicare and Medicaid Services," *New England Journal of Medicine* 345, no. 26 (December 27, 2001): 1,920–1,924.

cerebrovascular diseases Diseases that cause damage to the blood vessels in the brain and neck and that can lead to STROKE. Cerebrovascular diseases are high-risk illnesses that cause death and disability worldwide. People with DIABETES have a higher risk of developing cerebrovascular diseases than do nondiabetics.

Other key risk factors include an increased serum cholesterol level, certain inflammatory conditions of the blood vessels (vasculitis), and a family history of stroke.

Children of Aging Parents (CAPS) Nationwide organization for FAMILY CAREGIVERS that was launched in 1977. The organization provides information, education, and outreach to help people. According to CAPS literature, they receive about 10,000 requests for information each year.

For more information, contact the organization at:

Children of Aging Parents
1609 Woodbourne Road
Suite 302-A
Levittown, PA 19057
(800) 227-7294 (toll-free) or (215) 945-6900
http://www.caps4caregivers.org

cholesterol Refers to fats (lipoproteins) that circulate in the bloodstream, including low-density lipoproteins (LDL) and high-density lipoproteins (HDL). LDL is considered a "bad" form of cholesterol, while HDL is a "good" one. The reason for this is that LDL clogs the blood vessels, while HDL helps to clear them up. If excessive levels of LDL cause

fatty deposits to amass and remain in the arteries, this buildup can lead to STROKES or HEART ATTACKS. Conversely, high levels of HDL are good and it is best to have HDL levels greater than 40 mg/dl.

To test for lipoproteins, physicians order a lipoprotein profile, while provides data on the blood levels of LDL, total cholesterol, HDL, and triglycerides (another fatty substance found in the blood).

CLASSIFICATION OF LDL, TOTAL CHOLESTEROL AND HDL CHOLESTEROL (mg/dl)

LDL Cholesterol

<100	Optimal
100–129	Near optimal/above optimal
130–159	Borderline High
160–189	High
190–199	Very high

Total Cholesterol

<200	Desirable
200–239	Borderline high
240 or higher	High

HDL Cholesterol

<40	Low
60 or higher	High

Source: National Cholesterol Education Program, 2001

Treating High LDL Levels

EXERCISE, diet changes, and weight loss may all be effective tactics in helping patients bring down "bad cholesterol" levels that are high. Physicians may also treat patients with low doses of aspirin. In addition, they may use prescribed medications to bring a patient's cholesterol levels down. Often used are HMG CoA Reductase Inhibitor drugs, (or "statins"), such as pravastatin (Pravachol), simvastatin (Zocor), Mevacar (lovastatin), and Lipitor (atorvastatin). These medications can lower LDL cholesterol levels by about 15–40 percent.

In 2001, the Food and Drug Administration (FDA) removed Bayol (Cerivastatin), one of the cholesterol-lowering drugs, from the market after it was linked to deaths in 40 people worldwide. The drug had apparently caused a rare disease called rhabdomyolysis in a small number of people. This disease resulted in muscle damage that led to pain and that could also cause KIDNEY FAILURE. Apparently, this problem has not been as severe among other HMG medications that are on the market.

Intermediate-release niacin is another form of treatment that has also been used to treat individuals with high cholesterol levels; however, this medication must be used with caution. Intermediate niacin can affect the glucose levels of people with DIABETES. The drug can also cause an increase in the patient's uric acid levels, causing or exacerbating GOUT in some people. (Gout is a very painful acute inflammation of a joint, often in the foot or toe.)

See also CORONARY HEART DISEASE.

Aronow, Wilbert S., M.D. "Cholesterol 2001: Rationale for Lipid-Lowering in Older Patients with or without CAD," *Geriatrics* 56, no. 9 (2001): 22–30.
National Cholesterol Education Program, National Heart, Lung, and Blood Institute. "Detection, Evaluation, and Treatment of High Blood Cholesterol in Adults (Adult Treatment Panel III): Executive Summary," NIH Publication No. 01-3670 (May 2001).

chronic diseases   Refers to illnesses that are common and that are not usually curable, although they are generally treatable with medication and also with lifestyle changes, such as exercise and weight loss. The majority of people older than age 65 have one or more chronic diseases.

Examples of the key chronic diseases affecting many older people are:

- ARTHRITIS
- CORONARY HEART DISEASE
- HYPERTENSION
- DIABETES
- BACK PAIN

Chronic diseases, or the flare-up of medical problems that are associated with chronic diseases (such as pain or other symptoms), represent the reason for about half of all physician visits among people older than age 65. (See chart.) This is a greater percentage than experienced by younger groups. As can be seen from the chart, the percentage of visits for acute visits (visits for severe and sudden medical problems) actually declines with age, while the percentage of

visits for chronic medical problems rises, peaking at age 75 years and older. People older than age 65 have almost twice the percentage of routine chronic diseases as faced by people age 24 and younger.

Emergency room visits may be aggravated by underlying medical conditions, such as poorly controlled hypertension, SYNCOPE (fainting) with diabetes, and pain in the joints from OSTEOARTHRITIS. For this reason, it is best for older individuals to receive regular medical care and at least annual physical examinations.

PERCENTAGE OF PATIENTS SEEING DOCTORS FOR CHRONIC AND ACUTE DISEASES IN THE UNITED STATES, 1999

	Chronic problem, routine	Chronic problem, flare-up	Acute problem	Other
Age				
15–24	20.7	6.2	39.7	33.3
25–44	24.4	8.3	36.7	30.6
45–64	35.7	8.7	31.7	23.9
65–74 years	38.4	10.2	26.9	24.5
75 and older	43.5	7.9	27.2	21.4

Derived from: "National Ambulatory Medicare Care Survey: 1999 Summary," Advance Data from Vital and Health Statistics, no. 322, July 17, 2001.

chronic obstructive pulmonary disease (COPD)

A serious and incurable (although treatable) lung disease that causes a severe obstruction of a person's air flow and also is the cause of death for many older people in the United States and other countries. The disease occurs as a result of a combination of chronic bronchitis and EMPHYSEMA, although it can also result from emphysema alone. As with ASTHMA, the airways are hyperresponsive to stimuli and the illness can cause extreme and even life-threatening coughing and choking as the person attempts to catch a breath.

Risks for COPD

About 14 million people in the United States suffer from COPD. SMOKING is the cause in an estimated 90 percent of the cases of people who are diagnosed with COPD. Environmental exposure to chemicals can also cause or worsen COPD, and people who are in certain professions, such as miners, firefighters, and metal workers, have a higher risk to develop COPD.

The death rate from COPD is highest among white males who are age 65 and older.

Bacteria and Allergies
Can Worsen the Condition

Infections such as streptococcus pneumoniae and haemophilus influenzae can worsen the already existing medical condition, and some bacteria, such as pseudomonas, can severely exacerbate the condition. Allergies may also worsen the condition. COPD is different from asthma in that permanent damage to the lungs occurs with COPD.

Symptoms and Diagnosis
of COPD

Chronic coughing and frequent occurrences of shortness of breath are possible symptoms of COPD. The person with COPD is also more prone to developing colds and other infections.

Doctors may order a chest X ray to diagnose COPD. There are also breathing machines that can measure how effectively the lungs are working.

Treatment of COPD

When experiencing an attack of breathing difficulties, patients may use bronchodilators, which are inhaled medications. Antibiotics are administered to fight INFECTIONS. Steroid drugs may also be used for short periods of several weeks. For severe cases, steroids may be given intravenously. Some patients may need oxygen therapy, administered by special tubes (cannula) inserted through the nose. Oxygen therapy can occur at home, with HOME HEALTH-CARE workers providing assistance.

In some cases, surgery may be required, such as lung transplants. A lung reduction procedure may also be possible.

Lifestyle Changes

Anyone diagnosed with COPD who smokes needs to stop smoking immediately to increase odds of survival. Patients may also need antidepressants or smoking cessation products to stop smoking. Ending their smoking habit is the one most important action that COPD patients can take and it should be emphasized. People who smoke but who do not have COPD should also stop smoking immediately to avoid the future development of COPD.

Barnes, Peter J., D. Sc. "Chronic Obstructive Pulmonary Disease," *New England Journal of Medicine* 343, no. 4 (July 27, 2000): 269–280.

Hunter, Melissa H., M.D., and Dana E. King, M.D. "COPD: Management of Acute Exacerbations and Chronic Stable Disease," *American Family Physician* 64 (2001): 603–612, 621–622.

cognitive impairment   Difficulty in thinking that was not present in an individual in the past. The person may have ALZHEIMER'S DISEASE or DEMENTIA or may be cognitively impaired due to chronic ALCOHOLISM.

In some cases, a vitamin deficiency, such as a deficiency of Vitamin B_{12}, may cause a cognitive impairment. In other cases, a medication or a MEDICATION INTERACTION may be impairing a person's thought processes. If the impairment results from a vitamin deficiency, it will often be resolved when the underlying deficiency is corrected. If a medication is causing the problem, changing the medication or its dose may improve the person's ability to think clearly.

It is very difficult for older people in the early stages of Alzheimer's disease or dementia to accept that their cognitive abilities will continue to decline as they age. It is also extremely hard for the family members of the individual to cope with this fact. Many individuals have said that seeing a parent or loved one's mind deteriorate was much harder than observing an increase in physical disabilities. Relatives of people with problems of cognitive impairment also worry that they too may develop such problems when they are older.

Frisoni, Giovanni B., et al. "Mild Cognitive Impairment in the Population and Physical Health: Data on 1,435 Individuals Aged 75 to 95," *Journal of Gerontology: Medical Sciences* 55A, no. 6 (2000): M322–M328.

colorectal cancer   Malignant tumor of the colon and/or rectum. The colon is the large intestine, also known as the large bowel. The rectum is a passage connecting the colon to the anus. Colorectal cancer is the third leading cause of all cancer deaths in the United States. An estimated 75 percent of the people who are diagnosed with colorectal cancer have no family history of the disease (although family and personal history should be considered as a possible risk factor).

About 56,700 Americans die of colorectal cancer per year, and about 135,400 new cases are diagnosed annually. In Canada, an estimated 6,400 people died of colorectal cancer in 2001, and 17,200 new cases of colorectal cancer were diagnosed.

According to the National Center for Chronic Disease Prevention and Health Promotion, a division of the CENTERS FOR DISEASE CONTROL AND PREVENTION (CDC), one-third or more of all the colorectal deaths in the United States could be avoided if everyone who was age 50 and older had regular screening tests for the disease.

Gender and Race Factors

Although colorectal cancer has a high fatality rate, when considered in terms of the frequency of diagnosis, colorectal cancer follows skin, prostate, and lung cancer for men. For women, colorectal cancer diagnosis follows skin, breast, and lung cancer in frequency of diagnosis. Men have a higher risk of colorectal cancer than women do.

African Americans have a significantly higher risk for colorectal cancer than Caucasians in the United States. According to the National Cancer Institute, white men have a rate of 20.1 per 100,000, and black men have a greater rate of 27.2 per 100,000. White women have a rate of colorectal cancer of 13.7 per 100,000, compared to African-American women who face a higher rate of 19.5 per 100,000.

Risks for Contracting Colorectal Cancer

The risk for developing colorectal cancer increases with age. Other risks for colorectal cancer include:

- Family or personal history of polyps
- Inflammatory bowel disease (ulcerative colitis and Crohn's disease)
- Obesity
- Alcohol abuse
- Physical inactivity

Symptoms

A person may have no symptoms in the early stages of colorectal cancer. When symptoms occur, the key symptoms are:

- Blood in the stool
- A change in bowel habits
- Diarrhea or constipation
- Frequent unexplained stomach cramping
- Unexplained weight loss
- Stools that are more narrow than is usual for the person
- Sustained and unexplained fatigue

Other illnesses can also cause these nonspecific symptoms, and patients who experience them should see their doctors for an evaluation.

Diagnostic Tools

There are several ways that doctors may diagnose colorectal cancer. The most simple technique is the digital rectal examination, in which the doctor inserts a lubricated finger in the rectum to feel for any abnormalities. This test may also detect PROSTATE CANCER in men. If any abnormalities are detected, further studies will be ordered.

Fecal Occult Blood Test There are also laboratory tests for colorectal cancer, and the most commonly used test is the fecal occult blood test (FOBT). This test detects blood in the stool that cannot be seen by the individual and may indicate colorectal cancer. Individuals are given special cards on which to collect their own small stool specimens. The laboratory will then check the specimens on the cards for hidden (occult) blood.

Experts recommend that people older than age 50 should have the FOBT every year. Unfortunately, according to the CDC, only about 21 percent of whites and African Americans have annual FOBTs, and the percentages of those having annual FOBTs are even lower for HISPANIC AMERICANS (11 percent) and Asians/Pacific Islanders (10 percent). According to the CDC, if the fecal occult blood test were done every one to two years on people ages 50–80, it would reduce the death rate from colorectal cancer. However, it should be noted that a lack of occult blood does not definitively rule out colorectal cancer.

According to gastroenterology medical professor and author Anil Minocha, M.D., in his book for medical residents, *The Gastroenterology Resident Pocket Survival Guide,* only 20–40 percent of patients who have colorectal cancer also have occult blood in their stools. As a result, most people older than age 65 need further testing, despite the results of the FOBT.

Invasive Screening Procedures There are also several invasive procedures to detect colorectal cancer, including the flexible sigmoidoscopy, the colonoscopy, and the barium enema.

These procedures differ in how each one is performed and how much of the bowel can be inspected. They also differ in the actions that the surgeon may take, if any, should cancerous or precancerous growths be identified during the procedure.

The patient's level of consciousness also varies. For example, with the flexible sigmoidoscopy (using a flexible scope, which can go around turns in the lower one-fourth of the bowel), the patient is usually conscious during the procedure.

With a colonoscopy, a more extensive screening procedure in which the doctor visually inspects the entire colon, patients may be given "conscious sedation," or sedating drugs that may cause them to fall asleep. As of 2001, MEDICARE covers the colonoscopy as a screening tool.

During the double-contrast barium enema, patients are fully conscious. Patients are administered a barium dye that bathes and highlights the colon, making it opaque on X rays, and then air is introduced to give a double contrast and make the X ray view even clearer. (With a single contrast barium enema, only the barium is used.)

The preparation for both the colonoscopy and the barium enema is similar: patients will take special oral medicine that causes diarrhea and clears out their stools ahead of time so the bowel can be more easily examined during the procedure. The colon can also be "cleaned out" (emptied) prior to a sigmoidoscopy, but most doctors rely instead on a few enemas rather than on oral medication.

The actions that the doctor can take as a result of the findings during the procedure are also dependent on the type of procedure. For example, polyps (precancerous growths) can be detected during a sigmoidoscopy, but they cannot be removed unless the colon was completely cleaned out ahead of time. Also, if polyps are found during a sigmoidoscopy, the doctor will order a colonoscopy so that the entire colon can be checked for polyps and they can be removed. The assumption is that if one part of the colon has polyps, then the rest of the colon may also have polyps and should be checked.

A colonoscopy is considered the best procedure for finding polyps because the colonoscopy exam-

COMPARISON OF INVASIVE SCREENING PROCEDURES FOR COLORECTAL CANCER			
	Double-contrast barium enema	Flexible sigmoidoscopy	Colonoscopy
Medicine to clean out bowel given day before?	Yes	Not usually	Yes
Colon visualized?	Yes	Only part of colon	Yes
Polyps can be seen?	Yes, but cannot be removed with this procedure. Smaller polyps may be missed	Yes, in the area examined (about 1/4 of bowel)	Yes
Polyps can be removed?	No	Usually not	Yes
Sedation given?	No	No	Yes
Biopsy can be performed?	No	Yes	Yes

TABLE 1   PERCENTAGE OF ADULTS AGE 50 YEARS OR OLDER WHO HAD COLORECTAL CANCER SCREENING TESTS WITHIN THE RECOMMENDED TIME INTERVAL, BY RACE AND ETHNICITY, UNITED STATES, 1999

Race/Ethnicity	Fecal Occult Blood Test	Sigmoidoscopy or Colonoscopy
	(Received within the past year)	(Received within the past five years)
White	21%	34%
African American	21%	33%
Asian/Pacific Islander	10%	35%
American Indian/Alaska Native	18%	36%
Spanish/Hispanic Origin	11%	29%

Centers for Disease Control and Prevention (CDC). "At a Glance. Colorectal Cancer: The Importance of Prevention and Early Detection, 2001," 2001.

ines the entire large bowel and because the doctor can remove any polyps that are found. Polyps can also be detected with a barium procedure, but they cannot be removed. A colonoscopy would need to be ordered to achieve that goal, putting the patient through an additional procedure. Also, smaller polyps may be missed during a barium enema.

If the doctor wants to remove tissue to check for cancer (a biopsy), this procedure cannot be performed during a barium enema. The doctor may, however, perform a biopsy during either a colonoscopy or sigmoidoscopy.

Note: People who have precancerous polyps should be followed up even more closely than others should because polyps may recur.

Recommendations for Testing

With older adults, some experts recommend either an annual fecal occult blood test, combined with a flexible sigmoidoscopy every five years *or* a colonoscopy every 10 years. If the double-contrast barium enema is used, it should be performed every five to 10 years.

These procedures may be needed more frequently if there are risk factors for disease of the colon or if the doctor recommends so. However, only about a third of adults older than age 50 in the United States have had either a sigmoidoscopy or a colonoscopy within the recommended time frame. In fact, the CDC estimated that as of 1999, only about 44 percent of adults older than age 50 had *ever* had either procedure. (See Table 1.)

Colonoscopy Is Preferred by Some Experts

Some experts believe that a colonoscopy is the preferable diagnostic screening tool in asymptomatic older adults. In fact, Anil Minocha, M.D., chief of gastroenterology at the Southern Illinois University School of Medicine in Springfield, Illinois, says that having a sigmoidoscopy to screen for cancer is comparable to having only one breast examined in a mammogram because the sigmoidoscopy only can look at part of the bowel and thus can miss cancers beyond the scope of the exam.

One study, which offers strong support to this view, was reported in a 2000 issue of the *New England Journal of Medicine*. Researchers reported on more than 3,000 older male patients at Veterans Administration hospitals who had had colonoscopies. They found precancerous conditions in nearly half (47 percent) of the patients and cancer in about 1 percent. The researchers said, "Many of these neoplasms would not be detected with sigmoidoscopy." They also stated, "Most of the patients with cancer (73.3 percent) were identified before there was nodal involvement or distal spread and were therefore candidates for curative treatment."

Because most doctors want to treat patients when they are in the precancerous or early cancerous stages when they have a better prognosis, the colonoscopy appears to be the best diagnostic tool to achieve that goal.

Staging of Cancer

When colorectal cancer is detected, doctors "stage" it with a biopsy, or a tissue sample. *Staging* means that doctors determine how advanced the cancer is and how fast it is growing. Then they do a stage grouping.

With colorectal cancer and other forms of cancer, doctors use a system called the "TNM" system, developed by the American Joint Committee on Cancer. This system enables a classification of the tumor based on determinations for how advanced the tumor is, (the "T"), whether or not the tumor has spread to nearby lymph tissues (the "N"), and whether or not the cancer has metastasized to distant tissues (the "M"). For example, T1 means that the cancer is in its earliest stage. At the T1 point, the cancer is also known as carcinoma in situ or intramucosal carcinoma. There are also T2, T3, and T4 levels. When the cancer is considered at the T4 level, it has spread through the colon and to nearby organs or tissues.

There are three basic stages of "N" information. N0 means there is no lymph involvement, N1 means there are cancer cells that are in one to three lymph nodes, and N2 means that cancer is found in four or more lymph nodes.

As for "M" categories, there is either no spread to distant tissues or organs (M0), or there is spread (M1).

Once the TNM categories of the tumor are determined, the stage grouping can be made. With colorectal cancer, there are five stage groupings, starting with Stage 0 (zero), which is a stage of early cancer found only within the inner lining of the rectum or colon.

If the cancer is Stage I, this means more of the inner wall of the rectum or colon is affected by the cancer. This can be either T1, N0, M0 or T2, N0, M0.

With Stage II, the cancer has further advanced in the colon or rectum but has not spread to lymph nodes. This can be either T3, N0, M0 or T4, N0, M0.

In Stage III, the cancer has spread to lymph nodes but not to the rest of the body. This can be any stage of T, N1, M0 or any T, N2, and M0.

In Stage IV, the most advanced stage, the cancer has spread to distant tissues, such as the lungs or the liver. This is also characterized as any T, any N, and M1.

Treatment of Colorectal Cancer

Surgery Surgery is the only viable treatment for colorectal cancer and is the mainstay. Other options, such as chemotherapy and radiation therapy, are considered adjunctive. Surgery is often recommended even when the cancer has spread to the surrounding tissues and is advanced, primarily to stop bleeding and prevent obstruction.

When surgery is performed, doctors will remove all or part of the cancerous colon/rectum. Lymph nodes in the area are also removed. Usually, the colon's functioning can be maintained through reconnections; however, if this is not possible, the patient may need a temporary or permanent colostomy. This means that the waste material will go directly into a bag that is external to the body and that will be periodically emptied by the patient. This may be a temporary procedure if it is needed to allow time for the colon to heal. In about 15 percent of cases, a permanent colostomy is required.

Chemotherapy Some patients receive chemotherapy for colorectal cancer. It is generally only used in colon cancer if the cancer is advanced but is often used in rectal cancer at all stages.

Anticancer drugs are usually introduced intravenously or sometimes with a catheter. Some forms of drugs are available in pill form. During the course of chemotherapy, the patient may feel nauseous, tired, and dizzy, and the anticancer drugs may also cause hair loss.

Radiation Therapy Another adjunctive option in addition to chemotherapy is to irradiate the cancerous tissue. Radiation may be given through a medicine available at a hospital or an outpatient center. In some cases, radiation pellets may be internally inserted. Radiation therapy may cause loss of appetite, nausea, fatigue, and irritation at the site of the radiation.

Clinical Trials Another option for patients with colorectal cancer is to join a clinical trial in which new medications or other therapies are being tested. These medications and treatments are only available in clinical trials, and offer patients another choice.

Questions to Ask the Doctor

According to the National Cancer Institute and other experts, patients diagnosed with colorectal cancer should ask their doctor the following questions:

• What is my stage of cancer?

• What treatments do you recommend?

- What types of other doctors do I need to see? (Surgeon, medical oncologist, radiation oncologist, or other type of doctor)
- Will I need a colostomy? If so, will it be temporary or permanent?
- Will I have to go into the hospital for my treatment? If so, for how long?
- How will my normal activities be affected by my treatment?
- What will happen if I don't have the recommended treatment?
- What side effects should I expect from the treatments?
- What are the possible treatments for the side effects of therapy?

Pain Control

If the cancer becomes advanced, many patients will need pain control medication such as narcotics. There is little point in worrying about whether patients will become addicted when their lives are ending, and there is ample point in alleviating as much PAIN as possible. A thorough discussion regarding the risks and benefits of narcotic pain management with a physician may reduce any concern over addiction.

For further information, contact the following organization:

Colorectal Cancer Network
P.O. Box 182
Kensington, MD 20895
(301) 879-1500
http://www.colorectal-cancer.net
See also CANCER.

Bond, John H., M.D. "Polyp Guideline: Diagnosis, Treatment, and Surveillance for Patients with Colorectal Polyps," *American Journal of Gastroenterology* 95, no. 11 (November 2000): 3053–3063.

Centers for Disease Control and Prevention. "At a Glance: Colorectal Cancer: The Importance of Prevention and Early Detection, 2001" (2001).

Lieberman, David A., M.D. et al. "Use of Colonoscopy to Screen Asymptomatic Adults for Colorectal Cancer," *New England Journal of Medicine* 343, no. 3 (July 20, 2000): 162–168.

Minocha, Anil, M.D., FACP. *The Gastroenterology Resident Pocket Survival Guide.* McLean, Va.: International Medical Publishing, 1999.

———. Personal communication on November 12, 2001, with Christine Adamec.

National Cancer Institute. "Cancer of the Colon and Rectum," NIH Publication No. 99–1552 (1999).

companions   Paid or unpaid individuals who are not family members but who provide care and assistance to those older individuals who need it.

compassion fatigue   Refers to the "burnout" experienced by both professionals or FAMILY CAREGIVERS who have attended to the needs of others for many hours, months, and sometimes even years. At the point of compassion fatigue, the person loses all ability to provide empathy, understanding, and assistance to the ill person. This point may be reached because caregivers have ignored their own emotional or physical needs until they have become emotionally or physically ill themselves. The caregiver may be suffering from depression and may also be experiencing physical and emotional exhaustion.

Some family-member caregivers have delayed obtaining needed medical treatment because they did not wish to leave the older person with someone else or because they could not find anyone else to provide care. In some cases, the family caregiver cannot afford respite care but does not wish to place the ill person in a nursing home. If caregivers can receive respite (some time off or time away from providing caring), they may be able to return to an active caregiving role.

Increasing numbers of communities are providing day-centers for older individuals so that family members can work during the day and know that their elderly relative is safe and cared for. Then the older person is picked up after work and returns home with the caregiver.

In addition to adult day centers, families are once again looking to their religious centers, such as churches and temples, for respite. Often, religious organizations offer supervised functions for two to three hours at a time. This may be all the time that a caregiver needs to feel refreshed from caregiving responsibilities.

See also ADULT CHILDREN.

confusion Cognitive difficulty or inability to interpret or analyze information that could be perceived by the average person or by the individual him/herself at other points in time. Some level of emotional distress also accompanies this cognitive difficulty.

In the case of an older person who is suffering from DEMENTIA or ALZHEIMER'S DISEASE, the confusion becomes increasingly frequent. Confused people may not know who they are, who others are, where they are, and other basic facts. They may also know these facts briefly or when they are told them, but then the information is rapidly forgotten. Often, patients will repeat the same conversations, having forgotten that these discussions had already taken place.

The confusion of an older person with a cognitive impairment is one of the most difficult aspects for family members to accept and with which to deal. Fear, ANXIETY, DEPRESSION, and RAGE may also accompany the older person's confusion. Alternatively, depression may appear as confusion, making things even more complicated.

In some cases, confusion may be caused by an ADVERSE DRUG EVENT, which means that the medication is causing the problem rather than a form of dementia or other ailment. Often, when the problematic medication is removed, the person will recover. In other cases, confusion may be caused by a MEDICATION INTERACTION, which means that the confusion stems from a particular combination of drugs. The individual may need a different medication or a different dosage of medication.

Still another issue is the sudden withdrawal of medication (such as from forgetting to take medicines while on vacation). This inaction can trigger an attack of confusion.

See also COGNITIVE IMPAIRMENT; PARANOIA.

Congress, U.S. The U.S. House of Representatives and the U.S. Senate form the U.S. Congress. These legislative bodies enact laws directly affecting the health and welfare of older (and younger) people in the United States.

Congress also approves the annual budget of federal expenditures, which includes the massive outlays for MEDICARE, MEDICAID, and other federal programs that affect people older than age 65. Each year, individuals and organizations actively lobby members of Congress to change existing laws so that their constituencies will receive more favorable treatment.

constipation Difficulty or inability to have a bowel movement for at least 25 percent of the time or more. An occasional difficulty with bowel movements does not constitute constipation. Constipation also usually involves passing hard stools. In addition, patients often feel that they are not "empty" after they do have a bowel movement. Quantitatively, doctors view constipation as the inability to have more than two bowel movements per week. Constipation may also cause back pain and gastric pain, as well as a generalized feeling of discomfort. Often a trivial problem in younger individuals, constipation can become a serious health problem for older individuals, and they should seek treatment for it.

Constipation is a common problem among many seniors, and it may also become a chronic complaint. According to Dr. Schaefer and Dr. Cheskin, in their 1998 article on constipation for *American Family Physician,* about 26 percent of older men and 34 percent of older women suffer from constipation to the point that it affects their quality of life. This may seem like a high percentage, but the percentage of constipation is even higher in nursing homes, where about 75 percent or more of the elderly residents take laxatives on a daily basis to cope with their constipation.

Risk Factors

People with some diseases are more at risk for developing constipation, such as patients with PARKINSON'S DISEASE or who have spinal tumors. The risk for constipation also increases with age. Constipation may also be caused by THYROID DISEASE, particularly hypothyroidism, which is below normal low levels of thyroid hormone. Low levels of potassium may also cause constipation. Diet or insufficient fluids may cause constipation. A sluggish colon could be the cause of the constipation. This condition is often seen among patients with DIABETES.

Patients who are limited to WHEELCHAIRS or their beds are more likely to suffer from chronic constipation because of the lack of physical movement.

Medications, particularly PAINKILLING MEDICATIONS, may lead to chronic constipation. Some antidepressants can be constipating, as are some anti-hypertensive drugs.

Diagnosis and Treatment

Physicians take a history of the patient and do a physical examination, including a rectal examination. A rectal examination can reveal any obvious masses or recent bleeding. The physician will usually have the patient's stool analyzed for occult (hidden) bleeding, which may indicate CANCER. In some cases, and particularly if the older person has never had the procedure, a colonoscopy will be recommended so that the colon can be examined for polyps or other signs of disease. A sigmoidoscopy, or an examination of part of the colon, may be ordered in lieu of a colonoscopy.

In general, constipation can be resolved by increasing the amount of fiber in the diet or adding a very mild LAXATIVE. Stool softeners may also help patients to resolve their constipation. Often, EXERCISE, even as simple as walking, can help the system adjust and alleviate constipation.

Doctors may recommend bowel retraining, in which patients are urged to set aside specific times to use the toilet, particularly after meals, when they are more likely to be able to have a bowel movement.

At its most extreme, however, the feces may become impacted and will have to be manually removed by the individual, a caregiver, or a medical person.

Shaefer, David C., M.D., Ph.D., and Lawrence J. Cheskin, M.D. "Constipation in the Elderly," *American Family Physician* (September 15, 1998).

coronary heart disease (CHD) Diseases of the heart, primarily myocardial infarction (HEART ATTACK) and angina pectoris (chest pains from heart disease) that are due to blockages in the coronary arteries of the heart. Also known as coronary artery disease.

Heart disease is the number-one killer of older people, and according to the AMERICAN HEART ASSOCIATION (AHA), 84.5 percent of patients who die from coronary heart disease are age 65 and older. The AHA also says that of about 2.3 million Americans discharged from hospitals in 1999 with a first diagnosis of coronary heart disease, 57.6 percent were age 65 or older. Clearly coronary heart disease is a high-risk medical problem for older individuals.

An estimated 12.4 million people in the United States have coronary heart disease according to the American Heart Association. About 6.3 million people suffer from angina pectoris, including about 4 million women and 2.3 million men, and the risk for heart disease increases with aging. For example, in the United States, the rate of hospitalization due to heart failure is 13.2 per 1,000 people for adults aged 65–74 years.

That rate more than *doubles* to 26.7 per 1,000 for people ages 75–84. It nearly doubles yet again to 52.7 per 1,000 for adults age 85 and older. The rate is higher for many AFRICAN AMERICANS than for whites as can be seen from Table 1. (Racial data is not available for all races.)

TABLE 1	HEART FAILURE HOSPITALIZATIONS IN 1997, RATE PER 1,000		
	65 to 74 years	75 to 84 years	85+
All	13.2	26.7	52.7
African American	20.0	21.4	47.0
White	9.9	21.4	41.8

Source: "Heart Disease and Stroke," Healthy People 2010, Centers for Disease Control and Prevention, National Institutes of Health, 2000.

Risk Factors for Coronary Heart Disease

There are several major risk factors for heart disease. They include

- High CHOLESTEROL levels of low-density lipids (LDL or "bad" cholesterol)
- HYPERTENSION
- Race (African Americans are at greater risk than Caucasians.)
- SMOKING
- OBESITY
- Gender (Males have a higher risk of developing heart disease, but women have a greater risk of death.)

Cholesterol Levels and Their Impact on the Heart

There are two primary types of cholesterol levels, including "bad" cholesterol levels, which are low-density lipids (LDL), and "good" cholesterol, a phrase that refers to high-density lipids (HDL). The bad cholesterol chokes up the arteries. Conversely, the good cholesterol clears them up. As a result, older individuals (and most other adults) need to have low levels of LDL and high levels of HDL. In general, this means achieving an LDL of less than 130 and an HDL of more than 40.

High Blood Pressure and Heart Disease   People with hypertension have a greater risk of coronary heart disease than nonhypertensive individuals. Because the risk for hypertension increases with age, older people need to have their blood pressure checked at each visit to a physician. If their blood pressure levels are high, patients may need to take medications to lower their blood pressure, which will also in turn work to lower the risk for coronary heart disease.

Because African Americans as a racial group experience a much higher rate of hypertension than Caucasians (40 percent of blacks older than age 20 are hypertensive, versus 27 percent for whites older than age 20), their risk for developing heart disease is also greatly increased.

Smoking and the Heart   Tobacco use increases the risk of developing heart disease and of death. People who do not die of CANCER from smoking may instead suffer from congestive heart failure, while people who *stop* smoking reduce their death risk. For example, individuals who stopped smoking before the age of 50 cut their risk of dying in the next 15 years by 50 percent. But even people older than age 65 who smoke can gain benefit by ending their tobacco dependence.

Obesity and Coronary Disease   Excessive weight is another risk factor for developing coronary heart disease, and older people as well as people of all ages in the United States have a major problem with obesity. Older people in other countries also have an obesity problem. In many cases, the problem is not just overeating and high bad cholesterol levels but also a problem with a serious lack of physical exercise. Even simple exercises such as walking several times a week can help reduce excess weight and improve overall health.

Many people mistakenly believe that they must lose massive amounts of weight to benefit from weight loss; however, research has revealed that if a person who weighs 50 pounds more than the norm loses even 10 pounds, his or her risk for heart attack, stroke, and other diseases is significantly decreased.

Gender Differences   Although women have an overall lower rate of coronary heart disease, they have a greater risk of death when they do suffer from myocardial infarction (heart attack). Nearly half (44 percent) of the women in the United States who have a heart attack die within a year, versus 27 percent of men who die within a year of a heart attack. This is particularly problematic for older women, who have twice the risk of dying within weeks of a heart attack than faced by men.

Symptoms of Coronary Heart Disease

The most common symptom of cardiac disease is chest pain. Although all chest pain is not inevitably diagnosed as heart disease, this medical problem should be evaluated, and heart diseases should be ruled out first before other possible medical problems are investigated.

Some individuals have pain in one or both arms or in their stomach, back, neck, or jaw. Another common symptom is chronic shortness of breath. A sudden pallor from the normal skin tones may be another symptom of heart disease.

Diagnosis of Coronary Heart Disease

Doctors who suspect heart disease will usually order an electrocardiogram and a variety of laboratory tests. They may also order a treadmill test to determine the stamina of the individual and the stress that exercise puts on the heart (if the treadmill test is deemed safe enough for the patient to perform).

Treatment of Heart Disease

A variety of different medications may be ordered by the physician if heart disease is diagnosed. Many doctors also recommend the use of daily aspirin to fight heart disease in patients who have been diagnosed with heart disease or who are at high risk. ASPIRIN THERAPY has been found to be very effective in averting both heart attack and stroke for many people.

Doctors also frequently recommend lifestyle changes, such as simple exercises, weight loss, and dietary changes to improve cholesterol levels and to combat problems with obesity.

For further information, contact:

American Heart Association
7272 Greenville Avenue
Dallas, TX 75231-4596
(800) AHA-USA1 (242-8721) (toll-free)
http://www.americanheart.org

American Heart Association. *2002 Heart and Stroke Statistical Update,* American Heart Association (2001).

Centers for Disease Control and Prevention. "American Heart Month—February 2001," *Morbidity and Mortality Weekly Report* 50, no. 6 (February 16, 2001): 89–93.

Makalinao, Jose Mari R., M.D., and Suzanne D. Fields, M.D. "Chronic Heart Failure: Examining Consensus Recommendations for Patient Management," *Geriatrics* 55, no. 12 (2000): 53–58.

McLaughlin, Mary Ann, M.D., M.P.H. "The Aging Heart: State-of-the-Art Prevention and Management of Cardiac Disease," *Geriatrics* 56, no. 6 (2001): 45–49.

CPR   Cardiopulmonary resuscitation, a method of reviving a person whose breathing has stopped. CPR is a lifesaving treatment. Breathing may have stopped because of blocked air passages, a shock, high fever, or a variety of other reasons. CPR training is available through various charitable organizations.

There are two primary types of CPR. Basic CPR is important for everyone to know. This includes the basics about breathing and instruction on chest compressions to restart the heart once stopped. The second type is advanced cardiac life support (ACLS), which is a technique offered to health-care professionals and which requires additional training.

cremation   Disposal of human remains by burning them at extremely high temperatures in a special furnace. Cremated human remains weigh from 3 to 9 pounds and are composed primarily of bone fragments. They may be placed in a special urn or other container, depending on the wishes of the family. Some religions disapprove of or altogether ban cremation, such as Islam.

The remains may be buried in a cemetery plot, or, if in accordance with state laws, they may be strewn in a place that is meaningful to the deceased or to the family members. There are also some cemeteries that offer areas with special shelves or "niches" for funeral urns to be kept. Some people choose to retain the remains in an urn or other receptacle that they keep in their home.

The family may choose to hold a memorial ceremony to honor the deceased, ranging from a simple to a more elaborate ceremony. Before his death, Timothy Leary, the 1960s proponent of using drugs such as LSD, arranged to have his cremated remains shot into outer space with the remains of others.

Increasing numbers of deceased people are cremated in the United States, Canada, and other countries. The key reasons for this choice are that cremation is far less costly than in-ground burial in a cemetery and also saves land. In addition, it is considered simpler, more convenient, and less emotionally draining on the survivors of the deceased person.

According to the Cremation Association of North America (CANA), there were about 604,000 Americans cremated in 2000. Cremation was the choice in about 25 percent of deaths, up from 21 percent in 1990. Cremation was also chosen by a greater percentage of people in Canada. There were 90,200 cremations in Canada in 1998 (the latest data available) according to CANA, which was about 42 percent of all Canadian deaths. This percentage was up from about 31 percent in 1988.

It is expected that cremation will continue to grow as a choice for the disposal of human remains. A 1999 survey of 1,000 Americans older than age 30 found that 46 percent said they would choose cremation instead of burial for both themselves and their loved ones. This percentage is up from the response in 1990 when 37 percent said they would choose cremation.

The percentages of cremations in other countries vary considerably, according to statistics reported by CANA. For example, about 98 percent of deceased people were cremated in Japan in 1998, the highest rate among statistics collected. Other countries with high rates of cremations were the Czech Republic (76 percent), Hong Kong (79 percent), and Peru (75 percent). Countries with low rates of cremation, based on CANA data in 1998, were Ghana (2 percent), Italy (4 percent), and Ireland (5 percent).

For further information about cremation, contact:

Cremation Association of North America
401 North Michigan Avenue
Chicago, IL 60611
(312) 644-6610
http://www.cremationassociation.org

Wirthlin Worldwide. "Executive Summary of the Funeral and Memorial Information Counsel Study of American Attitudes Toward Ritualization and Memorialization: 1999 Update" (January 2000).

crimes against the elderly   Some groups target individuals age 65 and older to defraud them or harm them in other illegal ways. Many crimes are financial; others are physical, such as ABUSE.

According to a 1999 publication by Kelly Anders of the National Conference of State Legislatures, "Elder Fraud: Crimes Against the Elderly," there are high incidences of financial fraud against older individuals in California, Florida, and New Jersey, where there are also large populations of seniors. Seniors in New Jersey lose an estimated $180 million a year in frauds, and authorities are only able to reclaim about 10 percent of the seniors' money.

Most victims of financial frauds are females older than age 70, and as many as half are older than age 80. Common frauds include the following:

- Bills for items the customer never ordered
- Offers of discounts or free trips that are never provided
- Work-at-home plans offering large profits for people who buy special kits
- Magazine sales by people who do not really represent magazine publishers
- Prize offers for fake sweepstakes
- Home-repair scams

If older individuals (or anyone else) are confused about the terms and conditions of an offer, they should insist on more time to consider it. (Often seniors are pressured to decide immediately.) They should also demand to receive the offer in writing. If the service provider pressures the individual to decide "today," it is often a suspicious offer.

For further information, contact:

National Fraud Information Center (NFIC)
P.O. Box 65868
Washington, DC 20035
(800) 876-7060 (toll-free)
http://www.fraud.org

Anders, Kelly. "Elder Fraud: Financial Crimes Against the Elderly," National Conference of State Legislatures (July 1999).

D

dating   Attending social and romantic events with another person. Because many older individuals are likely to have experienced the death of their spouses or loved ones, they may be in the position to socialize again and to meet a new partner, if they should wish to do so.

Adult children and others are not always approving about the dating activities of older people. Sometimes, adult children resent the entry of a new person into their parents' lives, seeing it as an intrusion rather than a social opportunity for their parents. They may also fear that their parents will remarry, that they will be shut out of their parents' lives, and that they may lose their inheritances. In addition, they may fear that the new person will "take over" the parent's life and that the adult children will no longer be considered important by the parent.

Intimacy and sexual relations *do* occur with regular frequency in older couples, contrary to popular belief. Physical restrictions, medical conditions, and social norms may all play a role, but sexual relations between two consenting adults is often another point of great concern for ADULT CHILDREN. This issue can become quite problematic in nursing homes, as administrators may be just as concerned with this behavior. Open communication seems to be the best policy here. Of course, adults who are mentally incompetent cannot legally consent to sexual acts. It is also important to keep in mind that seniors are vulnerable to contracting sexually transmitted diseases when they engage in sexual activities. Physicians and others may fail to warn sexually active seniors about how to protect themselves against STDs.

See also AIDS; MARRIAGE/REMARRIAGE.

deafness   Partial or total inability to hear. Older people may have been born deaf, or they may have become deaf in one or both ears due to illnesses or to the deterioration of part of the ear.

See also HEARING DISORDERS; HEARING AIDS; HEARING LOSS.

death   Cessation of life. Heart disease is the most common cause of deaths among people older than age 65, followed by deaths from CANCER and then STROKE (CEREBROVASCULAR DISEASE). (See Table 1 for data on the deaths of older people in 2000).

The other primary causes of death among older individuals are chronic obstructive pulmonary disease (COPD), pneumonia or influenza (FLU), DIABETES, accidents, ALZHEIMER'S DISEASE, KIDNEY DISEASES, SEPTICEMIA, ATHEROSCLEROSIS, and HYPERTENSION. Most deaths resulting from COPD, a condition that includes chronic bronchitis and emphysema, are caused by SMOKING. Smoking causes or contributes to many other deaths.

Racial Differences

Some leading causes of death vary among some racial groups. For example, deaths from Alzheimer's disease are more frequent among Caucasians (especially white females) than among other races. Among AFRICAN AMERICANS, deaths from diabetes, kidney disease, septicemia, and hypertension are more frequent than among other races. Among all age groups, the death rate from cancer is higher among blacks, particularly male African Americans.

According to the Centers for Disease Control and Prevention in a 2001 report, heart disease is the number-one cause of death for older people of all races, and cancer is the second cause of death. There are some differences thereafter, which are summarized in the table below.

TABLE 1 CAUSES OF DEATH IN THE UNITED STATES, AGE 65 AND OLDER, ALL RACES, 2000

All causes	1,805,187
Heart disease	595,440
Cancer	392,082
Stroke	146,725
COPD	107,888
Flu/pneumonia	60,261
Diabetes	52,102
Alzheimer's	48,492
Kidney disease	31,588
Accidental Injuries	31,332
Septicemia	25,143
Other causes	314,134

Source: Arialdi M. Minino, M.P.H. and Betty L. Smith, B.S., Ed, Division of Vital Statistics. "Deaths: Preliminary Data for 2000," *National Vital Statistics Reports* 49, no. 12 (October 9, 2001).

Diabetes is a cause of death for both HISPANIC AMERICANS and whites, but it is the fourth leading cause among Hispanics, compared to the sixth leading cause of death among blacks and whites.

Gender Differences

Both women and men die of heart disease, but women have a slightly higher rate (47.6 percent of all deaths, in 1998) than men (44.6 percent). Men, however, have a higher rate of cancer, at 33 percent of all deaths among males, versus 26.2 percent of all deaths for females. Women are more likely to die from stroke (12.6 percent of deaths) than men (8.3 percent).

Other Causes of Death

Although not a leading cause of death, older people who fall are in danger of death, and FALLS represented about 2 percent of all deaths among people in the United States ages 65 and older in 1997.

Health Improvements

Some death rates have dropped, such as death rates from heart disease and stroke in the United States, as well as deaths from atherosclerosis, also known as "hardening of the arteries." Once a leading cause of death, atherosclerosis is no longer in the top 10 causes of death in the United States.

Minino, Arialdi M., M.P.H. and Betty L. Smith, B.S., Ed, Division of Vital Statistics. "Deaths: Preliminary Data for 2000," *National Vital Statistics Reports* 49, no. 12 (October 9, 2001).

Sahyoun, Nadine R., Ph.D., RD et al. "Trends in Causes of Death Among the Elderly," *Aging Trends* 1 (March 2001).

"death tax" Refers to the estate tax charged by federal and state governments in the United States upon the death of an individual whose estate exceeded a limit that was decreed by the state or federal government.

Some individuals believe that estate taxes are unfair because they are high and because they diminish the amount that the person can leave to family members. Others believe that the tax burden falls primarily on wealthy people, whose families can afford such a tax, and they also argue that these tax revenues are needed by society. It is clear that

TABLE 2 LEADING CAUSES OF DEATH FOR PEOPLE AGES 65 AND OLDER IN THE UNITED STATES, BY RACE

	White	Black	Native American	Asian/Pacific Islander	Hispanic
1.	heart disease	heart	heart	heart	heart
2.	cancer	cancer	cancer	cancer	cancer
3.	stroke	stroke	diabetes	stroke	stroke
4.	COPD	diabetes	stroke	pneumonia/flu	COPD
5.	pneumonia/flu	pneumonia/flu	COPD	COPD	pneumonia/flu

Source: Arialdi M. Minino, M.P.H. and Betty L. Smith, B.S., Ed, Division of Vital Statistics "Deaths: Preliminary Data for 2000," *National Vital Statistics Reports*, v. 49, no. 12, October 9, 2001.

the vast majority of money from death tax comes from the wealthiest 2 percent of individuals.

Whether there is a lack of equity in this matter is and will continue to be a hotly discussed topic among those with the most to lose: owners of small and large family businesses, small-farm owners, entrepreneurs, and big-business owners. This is a political issue that will continue to be debated as the population ages.

See also ESTATE PLANNING.

dehydration A severe and harmful lack of fluid intake, with the primary symptoms of thirst, dry skin and dry mucous membranes, and light-headedness and nausea. Dehydration can be a very dangerous and even fatal condition. In addition, individuals with DIABETES who are dehydrated are in serious risk of going into a hypoglycemic coma and need treatment immediately.

The primary causes of dehydration are as follows:

• Inadequate fluid intake
• Vomiting
• Diarrhea
• High fever
• Diuretic medications or other drugs
• High glucose levels (hyperglycemia)
• Bleeding

Symptoms

Weakness and pallor (in a white or Asian person) are symptoms of dehydration. Poor skin turgor is another (when skin on the arm is pulled gently, it does not rapidly go back to normal).

Diagnosis and Treatment

The diagnosis of dehydration is based on the physician's observations of the signs of dehydration in the patient. A blood test can be taken to check the Blood Urea Nitrogen (BUN) levels. High BUN levels indicate dehydration.

Doctors treat dehydration by determining the cause of the problem and, at the same time, by replacing lost fluids to an adequate level, usually intravenously. The patient is also urged to consume liquids orally, when possible. The dehydrated senior may need to be hospitalized for at least a day, depending on the severity of the dehydration. After discharge, the patient should continue to drink copious quantities of fluid for at least several days.

dementia Cognitive disorder that is characterized by CONFUSION, ANXIETY, and the inability to continue a normal life. One form of dementia is "senile dementia of the Alzheimer's type" (SDAT), which is also commonly known as ALZHEIMER'S DISEASE. However, there are other forms of dementia, including Multi-Infarct Dementia (MID), Dementia with Lewy Bodies, and Pick's disease. Some diseases also can cause symptoms of dementia, such as cerebral atrophy or advanced PARKINSON'S DISEASE. Chronic and untreated syphilis can cause dementia, and long-term AIDS may lead to dementia as well.

It is also true that some deficiencies, such as a deficiency of Vitamin B_{12}, can cause symptoms of dementia.

Multi-Infarct Dementia

In this form of dementia, the small blood vessels of the brain became blocked or occluded and brain tissue is destroyed, causing the dementia. The key risk factors for Multi-Infarct Dementia are HYPERTENSION and advanced age. Vasculitis, an inflammation of the blood vessels of the brain, may also play a role. The disease can also cause STROKE, severe headaches, and abnormal psychiatric behavior. The onset of the disease usually occurs between the ages of 60 and 75 and is more prominently found among older men. There is no known treatment for this disease, as of this writing.

Symptoms of Multi-Infarct Dementia, which are similar to those of Alzheimer's disease, include:

• confusion
• memory disturbance
• wandering
• bladder or bowel incontinence

Dementia with Lewy Bodies

Another form of dementia, this medical problem is associated with abnormal brain structures (Lewy bodies). Some researchers believe that this dementia is actually a subset of the dementia of Alzheimer's disease or that it can also be found in patients with Parkinson's disease, while others believe it is a distinctive form of dementia.

Experts say that with the onset of this form of dementia comes hallucinations, which may also be accompanied by delusions (false beliefs) and DEPRESSION. Patients also develop memory loss, confusion, muscle rigidity, a shuffling gait, and impaired thinking.

There is no treatment for this form of dementia, as of this writing, although research actively continues.

Pick's Disease

With this form of dementia, patients suffer from changes in social functioning, memory, language, and intelligence, as well as in personality. The key symptoms include memory loss, concentration problems, and speech difficulties. The disease is characterized by an atrophy of the brain in the frontal and temporal lobes. Imaging studies such as computerized tomography (CT) scans or magnetic resonance imaging (MRI) of the brain are often quite dramatic in appearance among patients with this illness.

The cause of this form of dementia, which can occur among younger or older individuals, is unknown, and there is no treatment for it, as of this writing.

Cerebral Atrophy

With the atrophy of the cerebrum comes dementia, muscle weakness, and speech and vision problems. The cause is unknown. Some medications may relieve some of the atrophy. If the cerebral atrophy is progressive, death will ensue. If it is limited to only part of the brain, it is not usually fatal.

Effects of Dementia on Family Caregivers and Others

The increasing loss of the ability to think and the loss of physical functioning can be profoundly distressing for family members who were used to the individual's former abilities. Some FAMILY CAREGIVERS may struggle to continue to care for a relative with dementia, neglecting their own health and personal needs. They may believe that placing the relative in a nursing home would be neglectful or cruel. Sometimes, only when the family caregiver becomes physically incapacitated will action be taken to place the person with dementia in a facility where he or she can be treated.

dental services   Professional care of the teeth and gums. Although they often need dental services, many older people fail to see a dentist once a year or even over many years. The reasons for not seeing a dentist may be that the person does not wish to see the dentist or may also be that it is difficult to obtain TRANSPORTATION to the dental office. The individual may also suffer from mental or physical disabilities that make it hard to arrange and keep appointments.

In addition, if the person lives in a SKILLED NURSING FACILITY, it is up to the staff of the facility to ensure that dental services are provided. Yet, the staff may concentrate instead on the more severe health problems that their residents are experiencing and may perceive dental services as a low priority.

Experts say that in addition to providing dental care, a dentist can note signs of serious illness that should be treated, such as oral cancers or infections that can lead to tooth loss, such as GINGIVITIS.

At least in part because of a lack of dental care, 39 percent of Americans who are older than age 65 and have less than a high school education have lost all of their natural teeth, compared to 13 percent of older adults who have had some college education and who have lost all their teeth. Blacks have a higher risk (30 percent) than whites (25 percent) of losing all their natural teeth between the ages of 65–74 years. In most cases, tooth loss is due to dental cavities and to periodontal (gum) disease, both treatable by regular dental care.

An even greater lack of dental care is evident in nursing-home facilities. According to the CENTERS FOR DISEASE CONTROL AND PREVENTION (CDC), only about 19 percent of all nursing home residents in the United States received dental services in 1997. Yet, nursing-home residents are highly likely to need such services. They may have difficulty brushing and flossing their teeth and may have diseases that increase the risk of dental disease, such as DIABETES.

Many nursing-home residents may need to take medications that cause dry mouth and thus increase the risk of dental cavities, gum disease, and oral yeast infections. When these treatable problems are not diagnosed and treated, the condition worsens and tooth loss is virtually inevitable.

The negative spiral continues as residents have difficulty or pain chewing their food, exacerbating other health problems that they may have. Tooth loss also contributes to low-self esteem and feelings of hopelessness.

Centers for Disease Control and Prevention, Health Resources and Services Administration, Indian Health Service, National Institutes of Health. "Oral Health," in *Healthy People 2010: Understanding and Improving Health.* Vol. 2, 2d ed. Washington, D.C.: National Institutes of Health, 2000.

dentures Replacements for natural teeth, also known as false teeth. Tooth loss is not inevitable with aging, and some surveys have shown that the majority (53 percent) of individuals 65 years old or older in the United States retain their own teeth. However, many seniors lose their teeth because of poor oral hygiene and their failure to obtain regular (or any) DENTAL SERVICES. As a result, they develop cavities and/or gum diseases, which lead to tooth loss.

It's very important that dentures fit properly. Ill-fitting dentures may make it difficult or even impossible for the individual to eat, and this problem could lead to malnutrition. Dentures should also be kept clean and should be brushed daily. During sleep, dentures should be soaked in an appropriate cleansing liquid. Individuals who have partial dentures should care for their "partials" in the same way as people with full dental replacements.

Sometimes, dentures need to be readjusted or repaired. Such actions should not be attempted by the denture wearer but instead should be undertaken by the dentist or other individuals that he or she recommends.

Some people who wear dentures believe they no longer need to see their dentists, but this is completely wrong. People who wear dentures should have regular checkups with their dentists to ensure that their gums are in good health and that no GINGIVITIS or other dental diseases are present. Dentists also check for cases of ORAL CANCER. The dentist will also check that the dentures are not defective.

depression A prolonged feeling of severe and profound sadness and hopelessness. Depression is also known as depressive disorder or major depressive disorder. People older than age 75 seem to be at greater risk for depression than those who are younger; however, an adult of any age may suffer from depression. According to the American Psychiatric Association, about 20–25 percent of people with serious diseases also suffer from depression, including patients with DIABETES, HEART ATTACKS, STROKES, and CANCER.

Physicians and therapists need to distinguish depression from temporary states such as BEREAVEMENT that occur when an older person loses a loved one to death. Depression must also be distinguished from the normal ups and downs of moods that everyone has.

For a diagnosis of depression, the depressed mode must have lasted at least two weeks and it must also be accompanied by three or more of the following signs: a weight change (up or down) of at least 5 percent within a month; a sleep disorder (not sleeping or sleeping constantly); low energy; poor concentration; feelings of worthlessness and repeated thoughts of suicide or death. The older person who is depressed may also suffer from delusions (false beliefs) and hallucinations (seeing things that are not there and hearing things that are not said). A loss of interest in once-pleasurable activities may also be an important indicator of depression.

In its most extreme state, depression can lead an individual to contemplate or even to carry out a plan for SUICIDE: older men in particular have a high suicide rate. Depression may also lead to ALCOHOLISM or DRUG ABUSE. (It is also true that alcoholism or drug abuse may lead to a depression.)

It may seem "natural" to some physicians and others when older people seem depressed. They may assume that failing health, loss of loved ones, and lack of stimulating activities would "depress anyone." However, depression is not a normal state for older people, and it should be treated. Depression can impair the person's health status and also affects others around the depressed person.

About 2–4 percent of people older than age 65 who live in the community experience depression, and this percentage increases to as high as 20 percent or more for people who are hospitalized, who have been recently hospitalized, or who live in nursing homes.

A Difficult Diagnosis

It can be difficult for doctors to diagnose depression in older individuals for several reasons. First, many older individuals are less likely than younger people to talk with a doctor about their feelings of sadness and distress. They may fear that the doctor will think that they are "crazy." Instead, they may "somaticize," or concentrate on their vague body aches and pains that do not appear to be serious medical problems to the doctor.

Another reason why diagnosis may be difficult is that depressive symptoms may resemble symptoms of other diseases, such as THYROID DISEASE or vitamin deficiencies. For example, the person who has an underactive thyroid gland (hypothyroidism) may be lethargic, have difficulty concentrating, and exhibit little emotion. In this case the patient needs thyroid hormone, not an antidepressant. Certain medications may also make patients lethargic or sluggish.

There are also many other diseases with symptoms that can mimic depression, such as PARKINSON'S DISEASE, HUNTINGTON'S DISEASE, stroke, CHRONIC OBSTRUCTIVE PULMONARY DISEASE (COPD), multiple sclerosis, Cushing's disease, and Addison's disease. Almost any major medical process can either have depression as a component or can mimic some of the signs of depression.

Even some infectious diseases can bring symptoms that resemble those of depression, such as hepatitis and the human immunodeficiency virus (HIV). It is very important for doctors to perform a complete workup of patients to first rule out other diseases and disorders.

Possible Triggers of Depression

Some older individuals have suffered from depression for years; others may experience depression late in life. Some problems that may trigger a depression in older people are:

- Serious chronic health problems or a new health problem, such as a fall or heart attack
- Biochemical changes
- Hormonal imbalances (hypothyroidism, hypoglycemia)
- Loss of a loved one
- Enforced life changes, such as having to move to a new home or to a nursing home
- Relationship strains with ADULT CHILDREN or others

Chronic or New Health Problems Many older people have chronic medical problems, and this increases the likelihood that they will also experience depression. Sometimes, it is difficult for the physician to sort out which symptoms are representative of depression and which relate to other medical problems.

New health problems can also trigger a depression, such as FALLS that cause injuries or a recent heart attack.

Biochemical and Brain Changes As individuals age, their biochemistry also changes and sometimes goes "out of balance." Some experts believe an increased level of cortisol is present in some older individuals, accelerating the risk of depression as well as that of anxiety. There may also be imbalances of neurotransmitters, such as serotonin and dopamine. Many medications can have an interaction with brain chemicals and can produce symptoms of depression.

There are also brain changes that may lead to depression. According to the American Psychiatric Association in the 2000 edition of the *Diagnostic and Statistical Manual of Mental Disorders, DSM-IV-TR,* "Among those with depression in later life, there is evidence of subcortical white matter hyperintensities associated with CEREBROVASCULAR DISEASE. These 'vascular' depressions are associated with greater neuropsychological impairments and poorer responses to standard therapies."

Some Medications Some medicines may induce a depressive state or may make a person appear to be depressed. Medications in the following classes can cause depressive symptoms:

- Antihypertensive drugs (Reserpine, Inderal [propranolol], clonidine)

- Cardiovascular medications (digitalis, diuretics)
- Sedatives (barbiturates, benzodiazepines)
- Steroids (corticosteroids, estrogens)

Bereavement It is understandable for people whose loved ones have died to feel profound sadness, and such behavior does not necessarily mean a person needs to be treated for depression (unless they exhibit suicidal signs). But if the high level of sorrow extends beyond two months and shows no signs of abatement, this could indicate a depression that should be treated.

Enforced Life Changes A depression may be triggered by a necessity to move to a new neighborhood, move in with an adult child, or move to a nursing home. Changes can be very difficult for older people.

Relationship Strains with Others Older people who are dependent on adult children may find it hard to achieve a new relationship and to accept that they are no longer "in charge" as they were in the past. Having adult children who control many of the routine life activities (handling the mail, checking account, transportation, and so forth) can also be a strain and may lead to a depression.

A Treatable Illness

Depression is highly treatable in many cases, according to psychiatrists. Older patients often respond well to drugs for depression as well as to psychotherapy and support groups.

Medications for Older People There are several primary classes of drugs used to treat depression in older people. However, it is important to keep in mind that older people may metabolize drugs at a different rate and also that they are more likely to be taking other medications that could interact with the antidepressant and cause further problems.

Some medications can affect the liver and other organs, and as a result, any drug should be chosen with extra caution. Also, patients should make absolutely certain that their physician has knowledge of all of their medications, including SUPPLEMENTS, and nutrients prior to starting any new medications.

Tricyclic antidepressants such as Elavil (amitriptyline) may be prescribed to help the individual over-

come the insomnia that may accompany depression. Medications in this class may be sedating and almost always produces a very dry mouth. Some experts consider Elavil an inappropriate medication for older people. (See ADVERSE DRUG EVENT.) Elavil can cause urinary retention in men. It may also cause dizziness and confusion and at higher doses may affect the heart's rhythm.

Another class of antidepressant medications is the serotonin selective reuptake inhibitors (SSRIs), which can be highly effective in treating depression. This class includes medications such as Prozac (fluoxetine) and Zoloft (sertraline).

Some doctors treat patients with depression with monoamine oxidase inhibitor (MAO) drugs; however, these medications are usually not prescribed for older individuals because they require a very strict dietary regimen that is difficult for most people to follow.

One key problem in treating depression (as well as a problem with treating many other illnesses) is that many older people fail to take their medicine. Charles F. Reynolds III, M.D., wrote in his article on elderly patients with depression for *Psychiatric Quarterly* in 1997, "The most important obstacle to adequate treatment of late-life depression is patient compliance. As many as 70% of elderly patients take only 50–75% of their prescribed dose."

Depression Can Affect Physical Health

The existence of depression can worsen a patient's condition by delaying recovery from an injury or an illness. In a study of 542 depressed and nondepressed elderly patients who had been hospitalized, reported in a 1999 issue of the *American Journal of Geriatric Psychiatry,* the researchers found that depressed patients saw their doctors more frequently after the hospitalization (although not for depression) and were more likely to need rehospitalization. The patients who were diagnosed with depression often failed to obtain mental health services.

The authors said, "The low usage of mental health services by depressed elderly patients in this study was particularly disturbing. The 160 depressed patients averaged less than one mental health visit for every 3 months of follow-up, even though most patients experienced persistent depression during the first 6 months after discharge. . . . This level of psychiatric services is consistent with the overall low rate of diagnosis and treatment of depression in elderly medical patients."

Who Treats Depression

Psychiatrists are medical doctors who treat emotional disorders such as depression. Although any physician may treat depression, psychiatrists are generally the most knowledgeable about psychiatric medications and treatments. In addition, because of their knowledge of the brain, neurologists are also skilled at diagnosing and treating depression. Psychologists are not medical doctors and cannot prescribe medicine, but they can provide assistance with improving coping skills and with other therapeutic options. They are a wonderful resource for nonmedication treatment options for depression.

Of course, it is very important for the treating doctor to coordinate any prescribed medication with the person's primary care physician and to ensure that any problem with medication interactions are prevented or minimized.

Depression and Anxiety May Go Together

Psychiatrists report that many older people who have depression also exhibit symptoms of clinical anxiety, such as obsessive worrying and fear of leaving the house. Anxiety is also a treatable disorder.

Caregivers Are Affected by a Relative's Depression

The depression of the older individual also affects others. The depression of a relative who is age 80 and older can also increase the stress of FAMILY CAREGIVERS who are female, according to a study reported in a 2001 issue of the *Journal of Gerontology*. (Male caregivers were not studied but presumably also experience stress.) Alleviating the depression of the senior would theoretically work to improve the stress of the caregiver.

For further information about depression or other emotional disorders, contact the following organizations:

American Association for Geriatric Psychiatry
7910 Woodmont Avenue
Suite 1050
Bethesda, MD 20814
(301) 654-7850
http://www.aagpgpa.org

American Psychological Association
750 Frost Street, NE
Washington, DC 20002
(202) 336-5500
http://www.apa.org

American Psychiatric Association
1400 K Street, NW
Washington, DC 20005
(202) 682-6000
http://www.psych.org

National Alliance for the Mentally Ill
Colonial Place Three
2107 Wilson Boulevard
Suite 300
Arlington, VA 22201
(703) 524-7600 or (800) 950-6264 (toll-free)
http://www.nami.org

National Institute of Mental Health
6001 Executive Boulevard
Room 8184
MSC 9663
Bethesda, MD 20892
(301) 443-4513 or (800) 421-4211 (toll-free)

See also ANXIETY DISORDERS; CONFUSION.

Administration on Aging. "Older Adults and Mental Health: Issues and Opportunities" (January 2001).

American Psychiatric Association. *Diagnostic and Statistical Manual of Mental Disorders, DSM-IV-TR.* Washington, D.C.: American Psychiatric Association, 2000.

Davis, Katherine M., MSN, CS, NP-C, and Elizabeth Mathew, MSN, NP-C, CS. "Pharmacologic Management of Depression in the Elderly," *Nurse Practitioner* 23, no. 6 (1998): 16018, 16026, and 16028.

King, Deborah A., and Howard E. Markus. "Mood Disorders in Older Adults," in *Psychopathology in Later Adulthood.* (Ed. Susan Krauss Whitbourne). New York: John Wiley & Sons, 2000.

Koenig, Harold G., M.D. and Maragatha Kutchibhatla, Ph.D. "Use of Health Services by Medically Ill Depressed Elderly Patients After Hospital Discharge," *American Journal of Geriatric Psychiatry* 7, no. 1 (1999): 48–56.

Reynolds, Charles F., III, M.D. "Treatment of Major Depression In Later Life: A Life Cycle Perspective," *Psychiatric Quarterly* 68, no. 3 (1997): 221–246.

diabetes   Serious medical problem that is primarily characterized by an absolute or relative lack of insulin activity or by resistance of the body to respond to insulin, leading to high glucose levels (hyperglycemia) and multiple metabolic abnormalities.

Most medical experts believe that individuals with diabetes should be treated by a team of medical experts, including an ENDOCRINOLOGIST, a registered dietitian, a certified diabetes educator, and other diabetes practitioners. However, the daily care must be maintained by individuals with diabetes themselves or by their caregivers, who need to manage home blood-glucose monitoring and take necessary action based on these results, for example, eating appropriate snacks if the person is hypoglycemic (the blood glucose is too low) or taking extra insulin or fluid if glucose levels are too high. In addition, individuals with diabetes or their caregivers must work to maintain a healthy diet in the person with diabetes and also to ensure that they EXERCISE as much as they are able to do so.

Diabetes is a serious disease and it is one of the six leading causes of death among people older than age 65 in the United States. In fact, the death rate from diabetes is probably considerably underestimated. Doctors say that death certificates are often incomplete and inaccurate and that the multiple metabolic abnormalities associated with diabetes lead to HEART ATTACK, STROKE, KIDNEY DISEASE and KIDNEY FAILURE, and other vascular problems, which may be listed as the cause of death on death certificates.

Risks for Diabetes

Some ethnic groups have a greater risk of death from diabetes; for example, it is the third-leading cause of death among NATIVE AMERICANS, and it is the fourth-leading cause of death among AFRICAN AMERICANS.

An estimated 11 percent of all Americans ages 65–74 years have diabetes, and this percentage continues to rise. Among those who are age 75 and older, an estimated 20 percent have diabetes, although only about half of them are aware that they have the disease. The rates are significantly higher for African Americans, HISPANIC AMERICANS, and Native Americans in the same age groups. Diabetes is also a risk for older individuals in countries around the world and will become an increasing burden as the global population ages and becomes more sedentary and overweight.

Key Symptoms

The primary symptoms of diabetes include:

• extreme thirst

• frequent urination

• slow healing cuts/wounds

• blurred vision

• unexplained weight loss

Types of Diabetes

Contrary to popular opinion, older people can develop both of the two types of diabetes: Type 1 diabetes and Type 2 diabetes; however, most seniors with diabetes have Type 2 diabetes. (Gestational diabetes is a third form of diabetes; however, it occurs only to some women who are pregnant, thus precluding individuals who are age 65 and older from this form of the disease.)

Type 1 diabetes, formerly called insulin-dependent diabetes or juvenile diabetes, can have an onset in childhood or early adulthood but can also be diagnosed later in life. People with Type 1 diabetes have pancreases that no longer produce insulin. Because insulin is necessary to life, they must receive insulin in another way. They nearly always inject the insulin, although in the near future, inhaled insulin and implantable insulin pumps may be commonly available options. Insulin pumps are available now, but most people continue to inject their insulin.

People with long-term Type 1 diabetes are at risk for many medical complications, including BLINDNESS, kidney disease, HYPERTENSION, HEART DISEASE, and DEPRESSION.

Type 2 diabetes is the other major form of diabetes and represents 90–95 percent of all cases of diabetes in the general population. Both an insufficient amount of insulin and the inability of the body to use efficiently the insulin that is produced are the causes of Type 2 diabetes. Type 2 diabetes was formerly called noninsulin-dependent diabetes or adult-onset diabetes. The name was changed because some people who have had Type 2 diabetes for many years may require insulin, particularly among people age 65 and older. Another reason for the name change was that it is possible for children and adolescents to develop Type 2 diabetes.

Lack of Diagnosis

A serious problem is that many seniors with diabetes have not been diagnosed, and thus they are not receiving treatment. For example of the estimated 18 percent of women ages 60–74 who have diabetes, about 4.5 percent remain undiagnosed. Of the estimated 20 percent of men ages 60–74 with diabetes, the problem of a lack of diagnosis is even greater: about 8 percent are undiagnosed.

This lack of diagnosis continues among people older than age 74: about 5 percent of women age 75 and older have undiagnosed diabetes, and about 8 percent of men age 75 and older are undiagnosed. Without diagnosis, these individuals are not treated and their health is compromised.

Race and Ethnicity

As mentioned, the rate of diabetes is much higher among African-American and Hispanic seniors. The Pima Indians of Arizona have a very high rate of diabetes. About one of every three African-American women between the ages of 65–74 have diabetes, an extremely high rate. This higher rate means that more African Americans are at risk of suffering from complications stemming from diabetes.

According to a study released in 2000 and published in the *Journal of Clinical Epidemiology,* African-American women with diabetes have a higher rate of coronary heart disease, cardiovascular disease, and death when compared to other racial groups.

African Americans with diabetes are twice as likely to suffer from blindness and three to five times as likely to experience kidney failure as are whites. Their risk of suffering from amputation is also twice as high as that for whites.

About 33 percent of Mexican-American women in the 60–74 age group and 32 percent of African Americans have diabetes, compared to only 16 per-

cent of white women in the same age group. This means that Mexican-American and African-American female seniors have more than twice the risk of having diabetes than white women of the same age have.

African Americans who know that they have diabetes generally receive suboptimal treatment, although it is unclear why this is true. Researchers have analyzed the care received by elderly African Americans on MEDICARE and who have diabetes and reported on their findings in a 1998 issue of *Diabetes Care.*

The researchers found that African Americans visited their physicians fewer times per year than did other individuals with diabetes. In addition, blacks were also much less likely to have had appropriate measurements of their blood glucose levels recorded by medical staff. They were also were more likely to use the emergency department of the hospital when they were ill rather than to see a physician in either an office or clinic. The authors stated, "These discrepancies may reflect a preference by African Americans to avoid medical testing and procedures, but they could also result from a less aggressive treatment style by physicians for African Americans or difficulties by African Americans in gaining access to the health care system."

Obesity and Hypertension

Most people with Type 2 diabetes have problems with OBESITY and hypertension, and along with their higher rate of diabetes, African Americans frequently have these problems. If their glucose levels are not brought into control, many obese and hypertensive people with diabetes risk developing coronary heart disease and kidney disease. Most doctors also screen for high levels of "bad" CHOLESTEROL or body fats that tend to clog the arteries.

Different Symptoms from
Younger People with Diabetes

According to authors Meneilly and Tessier, in their article in a 2001 issue of the *Journal of Gerontology,* often the common symptoms of hyperglycemia (frequent urination, thirst and blurred vision) are *not* the key indicators of diabetes among older individuals. Instead, elderly people are more likely to be diagnosed with diabetes after they have been hospitalized for a complication of diabetes such as a stroke or a heart attack.

Complications from Diabetes

People age 65 and older with diabetes are more likely than younger people with diabetes to suffer from the many complications that are related to diabetes, such as BLINDNESS, cardiovascular disease, and kidney failure.

According to the CENTERS FOR DISEASE CONTROL AND PREVENTION (CDC), lower extremity amputations are more common among people with diabetes who are older than age 65. In fact, individuals in this group experience 64 percent of all amputations.

Because individuals with diabetes frequently have a loss of sensation in their feet due to neuropathy (nerve damage), they are very susceptible to developing skin ulcers and infections of the feet. Regular foot examinations could prevent many of the undiagnosed infections that proceed to gangrene and then require amputations of toes, feet and limbs.

According to John R. White Jr. and R.K. Campbell, authors of the chapter on managing Type 2 diabetes in the book *Diabetes Mellitus in the Elderly,* "The [older] patient with diabetes is 25 times more likely to become blind, 17 times more likely to develop kidney disease, 20 times more likely to develop gangrene, and 2 times more likely to suffer a stroke or a heart attack than aged matched cohorts without diabetes. However, recent studies have demonstrated a tight correlation between development and progression of most of the chronic complications of diabetes and strict glycemic control."

Because of the risk for blindness, U.S. government officials and OPTHALMOLOGISTS offer Medicare recipients with diabetes a program of free eye examinations and treatment for individuals who are older than age 65 and who cannot afford eye examinations. It is called the National Diabetes Eye Examination Program. Interested people should contact their ophthalmologist for further information.

According to the Foundation of the American Academy of Ophthalmologists, 7,400 doctors have signed up for the program, and more than 16,000 seniors were referred to receive free eye examinations by March 2001. To locate an opthalmologist participating in this program, call the 24-hour toll-free number (800) 222-3937.

Diagnosis

In addition to a patient having symptoms of diabetes, the illness is confirmed with blood glucose levels. The diagnosis is made with a fasting glucose level of greater than 126 mg/dl on two different occasions or with a 2-hour glucose test that is greater than 200 mg/dl. For example, after fasting for 8–14 hours, plasma glucose levels are measured, and levels are taken again about one or two hours later after the individual ingests 75 g of glucose provided by the person administering the test.

The level for diabetes must be equal to or greater than 200 mg/dl two hours after taking the oral glucose. There is also a test that measures how well the body handles glucose after a three-month period of time; it is called the glycosylated hemoglobin level. This information can be quite helpful in measuring long-term diabetes control.

Treatment

Diabetes is treated with a combination of exercise, medications, and lifestyle recommendations. In addition, the patient's blood must be tested at least several times each day, at a minimum. Glucose levels must be monitored with home glucose tests.

Medication Treatment All patients with Type 1 diabetes need insulin; some patients with Type 2 diabetes will also require insulin. Many older people with Type 2 diabetes take oral medications recommended by their physicians.

Older individuals with diabetes have shown considerable improvements with some medications. For example, such studies as the Systolic Hypertension in the Elderly Program (SHEP) study have demonstrated that among older individuals who have both hypertension and diabetes, those individuals who used diuretics (drugs that reduce body water salt and that dilute blood vessels) dramatically reduced their risk for stroke.

Another study, the Heart Outcomes Prevention Evaluation (HOPE) study demonstrated that medications in the angiotensin-converting enzyme inhibitor (ACE) class could reduce the risk of complications and death among elderly individuals with diabetes.

There are currently four general classes of oral medications used to treat diabetes: 1) insulin secretagogues, which induce a greater secretion of insulin (sulfonylureas, meglitinides and phenylalanine derivatives), 2) biguanides (metformin), 3) alpha glucosidase inhibitors (miglitolol, acarbose), and 4) thiazolidinediones (TZDs), such as rosiglitazone and piogliazone.

Meglitinides represent a class of medication prescribed for people with Type 2 diabetes to maintain glycemic control. Prandin (repaglinide) and Starlix (nateglinidol) are available "secretagogue" medications, which means that these drugs induce a greater secretion of insulin. Sulfonylurea drugs also are secretatogues, but they are not recommended for this use, and they act differently on the body. Older patients must be careful with long-acting sulfonylurea drugs such as glyburide, which may cause hypoglycemia.

One category of drug used to treat people with Type 2 diabetes is the biguanides. As of this writing, the only drug in the class is Glucophage (metformin). Drugs in this class work to decrease the amount of glucose made by the liver and improve sensitivity to insulin. Caution must be used with older patients because diminished kidney function is a risk. Maintaining a well-hydrated state of sufficient fluids is essential.

Thiazolidinediones (TZDs) are another class of drug used to treat people with Type 2 diabetes. TZDs make the body more sensitive to existing insulin, allowing it to move glucose from the bloodstream into the cells more effectively. The drug takes 12–16 weeks to reach its maximal effects.

Some commonly prescribed medications for patients with Type 1 diabetes are the various forms of insulin, including regular, lyspro, NPH, Aspart, lente, ultralente, semilente, and glargine.

Dietary Recommendations   Contrary to popular belief, there is no one "diabetes diet" that is recommended for everyone who has diabetes. Another misconception is that people with diabetes should never eat sweets. Although a heavy diet of sweets or other carbohydrates is not recommended, a limited amount of "treats" may fit into the balanced diet of people who have diabetes.

Lifestyle Recommendations   Most experts recommend that people with diabetes who are overweight should lose weight by eating fewer calories and by exercising. In addition, exercise is good for people who are not overweight. Eating smaller portions but more frequently is also advisable.

Another critically important recommendation for people with diabetes is to perform daily foot examinations. An injury that is not felt can escalate into a severe wound that may cause the loss of a limb. People with diabetes should ensure that their shoes fit properly, and they should never go barefooted. If older people with diabetes in the United States need special shoes, they may be able to obtain them through Medicare from a special program that stems from the Medicare Therapeutic Shoe Act.

A Potential Medical Breakthrough

Islets Neogenesis Associated Protein (INGAP) refers to a naturally occurring protein that has been synthesized in the laboratory and that can theoretically stimulate the growth of the insulin-producing beta cells in the pancreas. In initial animal studies, INGAP increased insulin levels and appeared to cure the diabetes in the animals. INGAP is currently being tested in human patients because it has the potential to cure Type 1 diabetes by stimulating the patient's pancreas to produce new beta cells that make insulin. This treatment may or may not be suitable for people older than age 65 who have Type 1 diabetes.

For more information on diabetes, contact:

American Diabetes Association (ADA)
1701 North Beauregard Street
Alexandria, VA 22311
(800) 232-3472 or (703) 549-1500
http://www.diabetes.org/

Chin, Marshall H., MD, MPH. "Diabetes in the African-American Medicare Population: Morbidity, Quality of Care, and Resource Utilization," *Diabetes Care* 21, no. 7 (July 1998): 1090–1095.

Cooper, James W., Ed. *Diabetes Mellitus in the Elderly.* New York: The Haworth Press, 1999.

Hennessy, C. H., Ph.D., M.A. et. al. "The Older Years," in *Diabetes and Women's Health Across the Life Stages: A Public Health Perspective.* G.L.A. Beckles, P.E. Thompson-Reid, eds. Atlanta, Ga.: U.S. Department of Health and Human Services, Centers for Disease Control and Prevention, National Center for Chronic Disease Prevention and Health Promotion, Division of Diabetes Translation, 2001.

La, Shih-Wei, Chee-Keong Tan, and Kim-Choy Ng. "Epidemiology of Hyperglycemia in Elderly Persons," *Journal of Gerontology: Medical Sciences* 55A, no. 5 (2001): M257–M259.

Meneilly, Graydon S., and Daniel Tessier. "Diabetes in Elderly Adults," *Journal of Gerontology* 56A no. 1 (2001): M5–M13.

Morley, John W. "Editorial: Diabetes Mellitus: A Major Disease of Older Persons," *Journal of Gerontology: Medical Sciences* 55A, no. 5 (2000): M255–256.

Petit, Jr., William, M.D. and Christine Adamec. *The Encyclopedia of Diabetes*. New York: Facts On File, 2002.

diagnostic tests Tests that are administered to determine whether a person has a specific disease or may have the disease. Diagnostic tests are also used to rule out such diseases as autoimmune disorders, endocrine diseases, and blood diseases.

There are a broad variety of diagnostic tests. Laboratory tests may test the blood or urine for diseases or abnormalities. X rays may detect broken bones or soft-tissue injuries. Bone scans may detect inflammation in the bones or hidden FRACTURES that X rays cannot detect. Magnetic resonance imaging (MRI) or computerized tomography (CT) scans may detect tumors or other disorders and are a noninvasive way to look at various organs or structures.

Technology is changing in the health-care field at a very rapid rate. Tests now determine the chemical metabolism of various organs in safe, reliable, and noninvasive ways: certain kinds of heart testing and even brain imaging can measure how active certain parts of the brain are, even if a pattern consistent with DEMENTIA is present, predating any clinical symptoms that the doctor observes.

dialysis Filtering of the blood by machine. When people experience KIDNEY FAILURE, the only recourse to continued life is either kidney dialysis or a kidney transplant. Dialysis may be managed at a dialysis center or, in some cases, may be provided at home. When patients have a procedure called hemodialysis, they go to a dialysis center three times a week for three to four hours each time, and a machine filters their blood. Patients can have peritoneal dialysis accomplished in their homes; in this case, fluid is placed into the abdominal cavity to wash out the toxins and then is drained. This procedure can be done continuously or overnight.

See also KIDNEY DISEASE.

diarrhea Loose watery stools for more than a day. If it continues and is untreated, diarrhea can be life threatening. Diarrhea may be a temporary condition resulting from a minor or serious illness, indigestion, or contaminated food. It may also result from medication or from an acute or chronic disease. Infection with bacteria or parasites in the gastrointestinal tract may also cause diarrhea.

In the early 1900s, diarrhea was a common cause of death among people age 65 and older. Today, diarrhea can usually be treated with medications and is rarely a cause of death among senior citizens if they receive appropriate care. Replacement of fluids and electrolytes is also important. Some individuals may need to be hospitalized so that they can receive an intravenous replacement of fluids.

disability Lack of ability to perform important daily tasks that others can perform, including work or basic activities. According to the CENTERS FOR DISEASE CONTROL AND PREVENTION (CDC) in their report on "Disability and Secondary Conditions" in *Healthy People 2010,* there are 34.1 million adults in the United States age 65 and older who have disabilities, and they represent about 63 percent of all disabled people in the United States.

Gender Differences

In general, women are more likely to be disabled than men are, in part because women live longer than men. Another reason for the increased likelihood of disabilities among women is that they are more prone to developing chronic disabling diseases such as ARTHRITIS, THYROID DISEASE, and other medical problems than men are.

Federal data on the percentage of women who have two or more chronic medical problems have revealed that 61 percent of women ages 70–79 fit this category, compared to 35 percent of men in the same age group. Seventy percent of women age 80 and older have two or more chronic medical problems, compared to 53 percent of males.

Activities of Daily Living and Instrumental Activities of Daily Living

A disability may cause people to be unable to perform ACTIVITIES OF DAILY LIVING, such as feeding themselves, bathing themselves, or handling toileting on their own. Disabled people often also have difficulties with instrumental activities of daily living, (IADL) as well. These are activities that are not necessary for daily living but are important to most people. IADLs include such tasks as being able to use the telephone, drive a car, shop alone, prepare meals, handle money, and walk half a mile unassisted.

Higher Rate of Institutionalization

Because of their physical limitations, disabled older people are more likely to reside in a NURSING HOME or an ASSISTED-LIVING FACILITY. Some studies have found that a majority of older people with five or more ADL impairments (about 60 percent of them) have entered nursing homes. However, this also means that large numbers of older disabled people do *not* reside in institutions. Instead, many older disabled people receive assistance from FAMILY CAREGIVERS or from HOME HEALTH CARE.

Programs for Disabled People

Most older people in the United States who are disabled are eligible for Social Security benefits under the OLD-AGE, SURVIVORS, AND DISABILITY INSURANCE PROGRAM that is administered by the SOCIAL SECURITY ADMINISTRATION. Some are also eligible for SSI, a program for disabled people of all ages with low income. People on SSI are eligible for MEDICAID, a program that provides medical services and medications.

Although people receiving Social Security retirement benefits are usually eligible for MEDICARE, which is a government-funded health-insurance program, Medicare covers only about 80 percent of medical costs, and it does not pay for any medications as of this writing.

Conversely, the Medicaid program, which is administered by the states, usually has no or very low copayments for recipients and this program does include medication coverage for most medicines.

Housing and Disabled People

Housing is also impacted by an individual's disability. In the United States, the Fair Housing Act makes it illegal for anyone to discriminate against a disabled person who wishes to rent or buy a home or other dwelling. In addition, the Fair Housing Act requires owners to make reasonable accommodations. For example, a landlord with a "no pets" policy could be required to allow a blind person to have a guide dog living with him or her.

Complaints of Fair Housing violations should be filed with the U.S. Department of Housing and Urban Development. To contact this office, call toll-free: (800) 669-9777 (voice) or (800) 927-9275 (TTY). Write to this office at:

Office of Program Compliance and Disability Rights
Office of Fair Housing and Equal Opportunity
U.S. Department of Housing and Urban
   Development
451 Seventh Street, SW
Room 5242
Washington, DC 20140

Work and Disability

Disabled people clearly have a lower employment rate. According to information provided by the U.S. Census Bureau, 24.7 percent of all Americans ages 65–74 were employed in 2000. The rate for disabled individuals of the same ages was 10.8 percent.

A person with a disability may be unable to work altogether, although some disabled people may be able to work if accommodations are made to the disability. A simple example of a type of a public accommodation is a wheelchair ramp that enables a person using a wheelchair to enter a building that formerly had stairs only. Employers can also make accommodations for individual employees as well, and there are many types of accommodations that can be made under the AMERICANS WITH DISABILITIES ACT (ADA).

According to the U.S. Department of Justice in their 2001 booklet, "A Guide to Disability Rights Laws," the ADA requires employers of 15 or more people to "make reasonable accommodation to the known physical or mental limitations of otherwise qualified individuals with disabilities, unless it results in undue hardship."

For further information on disability and aging on the Internet, go to www.aoa.gov/NAIC/Notes/ disabilityaging.html.

Centers for Disease Control and Prevention (CDC), National Institute on Disability and Rehabilitation Research, U.S. Department of Education. "Disability and Secondary Conditions," in *Healthy People 2010,* National Institutes of Health (2000).

Ostir, Glen V. "Disability in Older Adults 1: Prevalence, Causes, and Consequences," *Behavioral Medicine* (winter 1999): 147–156.

U.S. Department of Justice, Civil Rights Division, Disability Rights Section. "A Guide to Disability Rights Laws" (August 2001).

disaster, natural   Severe act of nature such as a hurricane, flood, tornado, blizzard, or earthquake that displaces people from their workplace and homes. It can be very difficult for some older people to act quickly enough to cope with a natural disaster. They may be fearful, slow to act, and have insufficient resources, such as food or water.

State aging organizations coordinate programs to assist older individuals in the event of a disaster. Some states receive grants from the ADMINISTRATION ON AGING to create programs to help older people during a disaster. For example, in 2000, 16 states received grants to assist older people facing natural disasters, such as hurricanes and floods.

According to the Administration on Aging, older individuals who reside in a federal disaster area should contact the Federal Emergency Management Agency (FEMA) to register for the assistance that is available for a limited time following a disaster. The FEMA toll-free number is (800) 462-9029. Older persons and their family members can also seek help by calling the national Eldercare Locator toll-free at (800) 677-1116 to learn about services in the area.

Senior citizen centers in the local area may be able to provide assistance, as may local religious organizations and nonsectarian charitable organizations.

divorce   Legal dissolution of a marriage. Although divorce rates are not high among older people, they have increased over time. For example, in 1990, only 1.5 million older individuals were divorced or separated. By 2000, that number had increased to 2.6 million, and it represented 8 percent of all older persons.

It is unclear why rates of divorce and separation have increased. It is possible that people are less likely to stay in unhappy marriages. It is also possible that the value of marriage as an institution is devalued. Each position could be argued.

See also MARRIAGE/REMARRIAGE.

driving   Operating a motor vehicle, usually a private car. About 75 percent of Americans older than age 65 have driver's licenses, and as the population ages, the number of older drivers will increase. During the period 1985 to 1995, the number of licensed drivers who were 70 and older increased by 50 percent. It is expected that by 2025, the number of drivers age 65 and older will increase by 2.5 times over the number of older drivers in 1995.

A key reason for the continued rise in older drivers will be the sheer number of aging baby boomers (people who were born during the period 1946–1964). Also, most female baby boomers drive and expect to continue to drive when they are older than age 65.

Older drivers are not only more likely to have a driver's license, but they are also more likely to drive a car than in past years. For example, according to a study reported in 1990 by the National Highway Traffic Safety Administration, 77 percent of urban residents age 85 and older drove a car. This percentage increased to 86 percent by 1995. The percentage also rose for people ages 75–84 years. In 1990, the percentage of urban residents ages 75–84 years who drove a car was 85 percent; it rose to 90 percent by 1995.

Interestingly, the percentages of older people who transported themselves by walking have dramatically declined over the same time period. In 1990, 16 percent of those who were 85 and older used walking as their major mode of transportation. This percentage plunged to 9 percent by 1995. Among the younger seniors (ages 75–84 years), the percentage of those who walked instead of relying on cars also declined from 10 percent who walked in 1990 to 7 percent by 1995. The reasons for less walking and more driving may be fear of crime or difficulty with walking the distances to the areas they need to reach. The loss of the "neighborhood village" may also play a role.

Accident Rates

Many older people point to younger individuals as those who have the most accidents and fatalities, and looking at the numbers alone, they are right. However, older individuals generally drive far less frequently and also drive shorter distances than younger people do. As a result, some researchers have compared the accident and fatality rate by age in terms of the number of miles driven. When that yardstick is used, people older than age 65 have an accident and fatality rate that is equivalent to or worse than the rate for drivers younger than age 25.

Experts say that crash rates are especially high among seniors who are older than age 75: they have the highest risk of fatalities of any age group. This high death rate from car crashes is partly because of an increased number of crashes, but it is also due to the greater physical frailty of seniors.

In Thomas Bryer's report on a study of Pennsylvania drivers, he found that there were about four car crash deaths per 1,000 drivers among the population ages 20–69. However, the fatality rate steadily climbed after that age. The rate increased to nearly seven per 1,000 for those ages 70–74 years, surged up to 12 for those 75–79, and reached a high of about 19 per 1,000 deaths for those older than age 85 years. Thus, drivers older than age 75 had about a three to five times greater risk of death in an auto accident than younger drivers.

Bryer also found that with aging, the number of crashes that happened during 9 A.M. to 4 P.M. increased: two-thirds of the crashes to older drivers occurred within this time frame. He also noted that people of all ages lose their lives because of failure to use their seat belts.

Experts report that older people have their greatest risk of car crashes at intersections primarily because of greater difficulty in seeing, slowed responses, and judgment errors. The most troublesome maneuver for older drivers by far is making left turns at intersections.

Delayed Responses and Declining Vision

For most people, especially in North America, the ability to drive a car is very important. However, as most individuals age, their vision and response times also decline. They may also suffer from diseases such as CATARACTS or GLAUCOMA, impairing their vision. Often, visual acuity and depth perception diminish as well. Night vision may become much worse. They may suffer from a movement disorder, such as PARKINSON'S DISEASE, that may affect their response time.

As a consequence of their diminished visual acuity and slower physical responses, many older people voluntarily limit their driving to daytime hours only or to non-rush-hour traffic.

Some seniors will voluntarily stop driving altogether, although this is usually a difficult decision that will directly affect their mobility. Yet, some seniors who have DEMENTIA or ALZHEIMER'S DISEASE will continue to drive, despite their cognitive impairments. In most cases, seniors who continue to drive despite their mental and/or physical disabilities do not think that they are impaired and will not believe others who tell them that they should stop driving. Several studies in the early to mid-1990s indicate that as many as 23–30 percent of such cognitively impaired individuals continue to drive, and this estimate may be conservative.

It is important to keep in mind, however, that seniors are not one homogeneous group of very similar people; instead, they are very diverse people of very diverse abilities. As a result, it should *not* be concluded that all or most people are not capable of driving past a certain given age because this is not true. Another consideration is that the needs of the individual must be balanced against the safety of others in the general public who are also driving or are passengers on the roads, and it is this difficult balancing act that stymies many states as well as many countries.

Difficulty Driving at Night

Driving at night is more difficult for all age groups, due to reduced visibility; however, seniors may have even greater difficulty, depending on their individual situations. Studies have also shown that the steering ability of seniors declines with diminished levels of light. Fatality rates from car crashes are about three to four times higher at night than during the day.

When Others Intervene to Limit or Stop Seniors from Driving

Sometimes, family members, friends, or others seek to limit or altogether stop an older person from driving because they believe that he or she is too impaired to drive. Studies indicate that interveners are more likely to be a spouse or an adult child who believes that the relative's driving is so poor that it is dangerous.

In 2000, the state of Oregon's Driver and Motor Vehicles Services branch of the Department of Transportation performed a comprehensive study of older drivers, including an analysis of all drivers who were contacted for retesting on vision, driving and driving laws. According to the state, in the reexamination process, about 50 percent of older drivers pass the test. Twenty percent fail the examination and turn in their driver's licenses, and another 30 percent do not take the test and voluntarily give up their licenses. Apparently, the testing requirement brings an awareness and acceptance of driving difficulties among many older people who are having difficulties.

Based on data for 1998 provided by the Oregon Driver and Motor Vehicles Services, about 57 percent of drivers who were told they required retesting were age 66 and older, and the largest numbers in a single age group were ages 76–86. With regard to the particular organization asking for retests, the largest number of retests were requested by the state health department (31 percent). Doctors made up about 14 percent of the requests, and most of the doctor requests were for people older than age 65.

The state also analyzed medical conditions reported on all older drivers who needed to be retested. About 14 percent had stroke, 8 percent had heart problems, 7 percent had "mental conditions," and about 3 percent had Alzheimer's disease.

Because Oregon is roughly in the middle of all states with regard to its numbers of people who are age 65 and older, it seems likely that other states with greater populations of older drivers will have at least comparable numbers of older drivers who should be retested for the public safety. However, most states and most state laws continue to ignore this issue.

In his chapter for *Mobility and Transportation in the Elderly*, Jon E. Burkhardt said that there is hesitancy among family members and government agencies to take away a person's driver's license because of the importance of driving to so many members of society. They may not wish to take away the older person's independence, and they (particularly family members) may also fear that they will be expected to provide transportation to the older person who can no longer drive.

Burkhardt says,

When persons with diminished capabilities continue to drive, an increased safety risk is created for all members of society. But the older driver facing the prospect of reducing or terminating his or her driving (because of declining skills or for other reasons) often expects substantially reduced mobility. Such expectation leads in turn to reluctance among these older drivers, family members, and government agencies to terminate an older person's driving privileges. Thus, the point at which older persons voluntarily give up or are forced to relinquish their driving privileges is often seen by elders and those around them as a watershed event with large implications regarding independence, self-sufficiency, and social responsibilities.

Self-Limiting Driving

Many seniors limit their driving to daylight hours and drive during non-rush-hour periods. They may also drive slower than the speed limit, in part because they are trying to drive safely and also in part to compensate for their own difficulties with vision or their slowed responses.

According to a study on driving cessation among older people, reported in a 1993 issue of the *Journal of Gerontology*, driving cessation is associated with the following factors:

- Increasing age (Drivers older than age 75 drive less than younger drivers.)
- Education (Those with an elementary education or less are more likely to stop driving.)
- Residence in public or private housing complexes
- Low income
- Available alternate transportation
- Marital status (Married people were more likely to stop driving.)
- Inability to perform basic tasks, such as climbing stairs or performing housework
- No longer working

- Lack of participation in physical activities (exercising, gardening, walking)
- Lack of participation in social activities (going to restaurants, on trips, doing volunteer work, playing games)

In addition, some medical problems that were associated with driving cessation, were:

- Parkinson's disease
- STROKE
- ARTHRITIS
- Hip FRACTURE
- Cataracts
- Glaucoma
- Poor vision

Age-Related Rules for Senior Drivers

State laws are very different with regard to limitations on older drivers. Changing state laws is also difficult for states because seniors can accuse legislators of taking an "ageist" approach. Some states avoid this problem by having all people abide by certain laws; for example, in Missouri, all persons must pass a vision test and road-sign recognition test to renew their license. In Nebraska, every driver must pass a vision test to renew his or her driver's license. Also, the emphasis is on "medically unfit" drivers, regardless of age, according to Nebraska authorities.

Some states have age-related laws affecting seniors who wish to renew their licenses. For example, in Iowa, people older than age 70 may renew their licenses for only two years versus four years for those younger than age 70. In Hawaii, residents younger than age 72 renew their licenses for six years. However, for those who are 72 or older, their licenses expire in two years. In Oregon, all drivers older than age 50 must pass a vision test.

In some states, the family can ask the department of motor vehicles to evaluate the driving of an older person. Sometimes, the older person will be told who asked for the evaluation, which is the case in Iowa and other states. (This may discourage family members from reporting a relative who is a poor driver.) In other cases, although the person making the report must provide his or her name, the information will not be provided to the driver. This is the case in Missouri.

Mail-in renewals of driver licenses can also be a problem, enabling drivers who are no longer capable of safe driving to continue to drive. Some states that allow drivers to renew their driver's license by mail restrict mail-in renewals to those who are under a certain age; for example, Alaska and Idaho will not allow mail renewals by people who are older than age 69. Other states allow older drivers to renew by mail, but they must also mail in the results of a vision test performed by an optometrist. Many states, however, continue to allow people of any age to renew their driver's licenses by mail, with no vision test requirement or any other requirement.

Taking Away the Driving Privilege from Impaired Seniors

One issue that is very controversial and difficult for many states—and an issue that will only become more pressing as the number of seniors rises—is in deciding when an involuntary termination of an older person's driving privileges should occur, whether because drivers have dementia or because they are otherwise severely impaired.

Some states allow a traffic officer to make that decision based on driving behavior; others require that drivers be given notice that they must come in and take a driving test. If they fail to come in, their license is rescinded. In Alaska, if someone believes that an older person should no longer drive, he or she can request that the Division of Motor Vehicles evaluate the person's driving skills. They can also ask the older person's doctor to contact the Division of Motor Vehicles to request an evaluation.

California mandates that doctors report to the state health department, which in turn reports to the department of motor vehicles if a patient with dementia is still driving; the doctor is liable if he fails to take this action. If the dementia is moderate or severe, the individual's driver's license is suspended. In contrast, in other states, the physician could be regarded as violating patient confidentiality were he or she to take such an action.

More frequently, however, the issue of the driver with dementia who is still driving is not addressed by the motor vehicles department at all, except in vague terms; for example, some motor vehicle regulations state that a person with a mental disability should not drive. However, because most patients with dementia do not know or believe that they are ill, they do not believe that this provision applies to them and will not surrender their license or stop driving. If family members try to talk them out of driving, they may become very angry.

Studies of elderly drivers have, not surprisingly, found that drivers with dementia score lower on road tests and are more likely to have collisions and moving violations. One study reported in *Lancet* in 1997 studied the brains of 98 older drivers who were killed in car crashes. Of these drivers, one-third had brain plaques that revealed they had Alzheimer's disease, and in another 20 percent of the cases, it appeared likely the deceased driver had early Alzheimer's disease.

In some cases, and usually as a last resort, when family members believe that a relative's driving is dangerous to him or herself as well as to others, they may steal the patient's car keys, file the keys down, or disable the car in some way. Whether this is legal or not is unknown but does depend on state laws.

According to a pamphlet published by the Hartford Insurance Company in 2000 on people with Alzheimer's disease and driving, some people believe that they can serve as a "co-pilot" to the person with Alzheimer's and thus allow the older person to drive as long as they are there to provide helpful warnings and instructions. The insurance company says that this is not a good idea because "there is rarely enough time for the passenger to foresee the danger and give instructions, and for the driver to respond quickly enough to avoid the accident. Finding opportunities for the caregiver to drive and the person with dementia to co-pilot is a safer strategy."

The Hartford experts recommend discussing the problem with a person in the early stages of Alzheimer's, and they also offer a sample "Agreement with My Family about Driving," which indicates that the person will agree to stop driving when a specified person says that he or she should stop. It is not a legally binding document but may open the door to a touchy subject.

According to the American Academy of Neurology in its 2000 guidelines, people with even mild Alzheimer's disease should not continue to drive because of their increased risk of car crashes. One approach that many neurologists take is to test the patient with a simple in-office reaction time screening; if the patient performs marginally or poorly, the patient is sent on for a formal driver's evaluation or simulation. Based on these results, recommendations regarding future driving can be made.

A Driving Assessment

In his article for *American Family Physician,* Dr. Carr recommends that doctors perform a driving assessment if they think that a patient is impaired or if a family member tells the doctor that they think the patient is impaired. Carr says that part of that assessment should include a driving history and a medication review and should also include a consideration of medical conditions that may make it difficult for a patient to drive.

A driving history should take into account such aspects as the number of trips the driver makes and the reasons for them, where the trips are (urban versus rural), the types of roads used, and whether or not the driver is transporting other passengers. It is also important to consider whether the driver has already had car crashes, been issued tickets, had near misses of crashes, and has gotten lost while driving.

The medication review should include a review of all drugs, especially any medications that may impair driving, such as benzodiazepines, opioids, sedating antidepressants, antipsychotics, muscle relaxants, and glaucoma drugs. In some cases, the doctor may be able to switch a patient to a less sedating drug. In all cases, the doctor should warn the patient about medications that can impede their driving ability. One common cause of concern is painkilling medications, which frequently are associated with sleepiness.

Some illnesses that may impair an older person's ability to drive include Parkinson's disease, arthritis, cardiac disease, pulmonary disorders, alcoholism, dementia, visual and hearing impairments, CEREBROVASCULAR disease, and neuromuscular disorders.

Changing the Design of Roads and Highways

Because so many older people will be driving in the near future, some experts have decided that it is important to redesign the roads themselves,

STATE BY STATE ACTIONS FAMILY MEMBERS CAN TAKE IF THEY BELIEVE AN OLDER PERSON IS A DANGEROUS DRIVER

	Ask the Person's Doctor to Contact Department of Motor Vehicles to Request a Driving Evaluation	Call the Department of Motor Vehicles	Contact Local Police to Request Evaluation/Observe Driving of Person
AK	X	X	
HI	X	X	
IA	X	X	
ID	X		
MO	X*	X	
NC		X	X
NY	X**	X	X
OR	X	X	
NE	X	X	X
SC	X		
SD	X	X	
WV	X	X	

* In Missouri, physicians, police, and family members may fill out a form that states an individual is unsafe to drive. The Missouri Department of Motor Vehicles will evaluate the case and determine whether written or skills tests or a doctor's statement is needed.

** According to New York officials, few physicians contract the New York State Department of Motor Vehicles, apparently fearing lawsuits.

whenever possible. Many recommendations for road redesign were included in the "Older Driver Highway Design Handbook," published by the Federal Highway Administration in 1998.

The report recommends larger and clearer signs. Many recommendations provided in this report would appear to help older drivers but would also help drivers of all ages.

See also MOBILITY; TRANSPORTATION.

Bryer, Thomas. "Characteristics of Motor Vehicle Crashes Related to Aging," in *Mobility and Transportation in the Elderly* New York: Springer Publishing, 2000.

Burkhardt, Jon E., et al. "Mobility and Independence: Changes and Challenges for Older Drivers: Executive Summary," Administration on Aging (July 1998).

Carr, David B., M.D. "The Older Adult Driver," *American Family Physician* 61 (2000): 141, 146, 148.

Driver and Motor Vehicle Services Branch, Oregon Department of Transportation. "HB 2446: Older Driver Study. Preliminary Literature Review" (January 2000).

Glasgow, Nina. "Older Americans' Patterns of Driving and Using Other Transportation," *Rural America* 15, no. 3 (2000): 26–31.

The Hartford. "At the Crossroads: A Guide to Alzheimer's Disease, Dementia & Driving," Hartford, Conn. (2000).

Johansson, K., et al. "Alzheimer's disease and apolipoprotein E e 4 Allele in Older Drivers Who Died in Automobile Accidents," *Lancet* 349 (1997): 1,143–1,144.

Marottoli, Richard A., et al. "Driving Cessation and Changes in Mileage Driven Among Elderly Individuals," *Journal of Gerontology* 48, no. 5 (1993): S255–S260.

Office of Safety and Traffic Operations R & D, Federal Highway Administration. "Older Driver Highway Design Handbook" (January 1998).

Perrino, Carrol S., Ph.D. and Anthony Saka, Ph.D., P.E. "The Risky Driver: An Annotated Bibliography of Recent Research," Morgan State University National Transportation Center (April 1998).

Schaie, K. Warner, Ph.D. and Martin Pietrucha, Ph.D., eds. *Mobility and Transportation in the Elderly* New York: Springer Publishing, 2000.

drug abuse Taking illegal drugs or taking an excessive and medically unnecessary amount of legally prescribed drugs, such as painkillers. In addition, taking any medication that is not specifically recommended for a particular patient would also fall under this category. Patients should never share prescribed drugs.

Although most people associate drug abuse with adolescents or young adults, older people sometimes abuse drugs as well. They are more likely to abuse prescription drugs than to use heroin, cocaine, or other illegal drugs.

Prescription drug abuse may result from an overuse of painkillers, which has led to an addiction, or it may be due to a lack of management of the many drugs the person has been given by many different doctors. Many older people see more than one doctor, and often each doctor that they see will prescribe at least one medication. If the older person fails to tell each doctor about all medications that he or she takes (often because they forget to tell the doctor), an accidental overdose of drugs or an abuse situation can result.

Any use of any medication outside of the recommended regimen (either from an over-the-counter) bottle label or by prescription guidelines) can also be considered drug abuse. Senior adults often like to feel in control, and they may feel that if one pill helps them a little, then two might help them more. This is a common misconception and when acted upon often leads to additional medical problems.

Sharing medication with others is also a form of drug abuse. A medication that may help one person who has been diagnosed with HYPERTENSION, DEPRESSION, or other minor or serious health problems may just as easily worsen the same symptoms in another individual.

durable power of attorney/power of attorney Legal document which an adult has created in advance, usually with the assistance of an attorney, and which will transfer certain rights and responsibilities to another person. For example, an older person may wish to have a durable power of attorney drawn up in the event that he or she becomes physically or mentally incapacitated and unable to continue to handle personal and financial affairs.

A "regular" power of attorney presupposes the continued mental capacity of the individual, who is assumed to oversee or provide input to the person who is acting on his or her behalf. With a durable power of attorney, this power continues on even if the individual becomes mentally incompetent (see MENTAL COMPETENCY).

All states in the United States and in the District of Columbia have statutes regarding the durable power of attorney. Each state has its own laws regarding how durable powers of attorney may be set up and what restrictions apply. Some states allow different types of durable powers of attorney, such as one for financial affairs only or for health-care decisions only. An attorney in the individual's state should be contacted to learn about the laws in that state.

Some states have a "springing power of attorney." This is a power of attorney that can only be used at a specific future time or when a specific event occurs, such as the individual becoming mentally incompetent. According to *The Elder Law Handbook* by attorneys Peter J. Strauss and Nancy M. Lederman, the springing power of attorney is an option in the following states: Alabama, California, Delaware, Idaho, Illinois, Kansas, Massachusetts, Michigan, Montana, Nebraska, Nevada, New Jersey, New York, Washington, and Wisconsin.

Strauss, Peter J., and Nancy M. Lederman. *The Elder Law Handbook: A Legal and Financial Survival Guide for Caregivers and Seniors.* New York: Facts On File, 1996.

dysphagia Difficulty with swallowing. Dysphagia may accompany long-term and untreated GASTROESOPHAGEAL REFLUX DISEASE, also known as chronic heartburn. Dysphagia is sometimes associated with THYROID DISEASE and other illnesses. People with dysphagia should be evaluated by a physician to rule out the presence of CANCER or other serious ailments. Because swallowing is one type of muscle activity and movement, specific movement disorders need to be excluded as well.

eating disorders   Failing to eat normally and either eating insufficient amounts or consuming too much during a period of time. Refusing to eat (anorexia) is one form of eating disorder that is seen among older individuals; OBESITY is the primary eating disorder of overconsumption among seniors. Experts have not seen bulimia, or excessive eating and then purposeful vomiting, among older patients. However, some experts believe that some older individuals may use LAXATIVES as a way to purge themselves to lose weight, rather than taking them to control CONSTIPATION.

Although little research has been done on eating disorders among older individuals, researchers in Canada have found that seniors who are otherwise healthy may develop anorexia nervosa. Eating disorders should be treated because they can be fatal or contribute to fatality.

Causes of Eating Disorders

There is no one cause of eating disorders, and often it is difficult or impossible to determine the particular cause in an individual case. The aging process itself may be a contributing factor. Dana K. Cassell and David H. Gleaves, Ph.D., state in their book *The Encyclopedia of Obesity and Eating Disorders,*

> After the age of 50, physical changes such as a decrease in the basal metabolic rate, a decrease in lean body mass and an increase in percentage of body fat combine with common changes in psychosocial conditions to affect nutrition. For instance, decreasing financial resources and increasing social isolation may promote the development of poor eating patterns. Favorite foods may be financially out of reach; boredom may lead to decreased interest in meals; aging people may simply lack understanding of what their bodies require. Life stresses and trauma may also have an effect on the development of eating disorders in

the elderly. For example, research indicate that women who are newly grieving over the deaths of their husbands are likely to skip meals and resort to junk food.

Anorexia Among Older Individuals

Researchers and professors Paul Hewitt and Stanley Coren of the University of British Columbia in Canada researched anorexia among people of all ages, based on death records in the United States for the period 1986–90 that cited anorexia nervosa as a contributing factor in the death among people of all ages. Their initial and unexpected findings about older people were released in 1996.

Hewitt and Coren found a low death rate from anorexia, but their research revealed that when older people develop anorexia, they are more likely to die than are younger individuals. They also found that although anorexia in older individuals is more common among women, as with younger people, the rate for men with anorexia doubled among older men. Among younger individuals who died from anorexia, the anorexia victims were 90 percent female and 10 percent male. Among those older than age 45 years, women represented 78 percent of deaths from anorexia and males represented 22 percent.

A refusal to eat sufficient calories is usually accompanied by a state of DEPRESSION. The individuals may have experienced the loss of a loved one or a friend. It may also be an irrational attempt to seek control by individuals who feel powerless. If they feel that the only thing they have any choice over is whether or not to eat, they may decide to not eat.

Older individuals with anorexia may also be ill with an acute or CHRONIC DISEASE or with CANCER. They may be experiencing severe stress and may refuse to eat as a conscious or unconscious response to this STRESS. Older people who refuse to eat may also wish an end to their pain and suffering and use not eating as a form of SUICIDE. Hewitt and Coren's research on anorexia, however, carefully excluded the records of individuals who failed to eat because of a chronic or severe illness.

Some older people have little or no ability to taste their food, and this could also contribute to their inability or lack of desire to take in sufficient nutrition.

Another possible cause of a refusal to eat sufficient food is a ZINC deficiency, which makes eating less enjoyable.

Overeating

Excessive eating may also result from unhappiness or boredom. It also often stems from physical inactivity. In most cases, obese people both eat too much and exercise too little. For further information, see the entry on obesity.

Diagnosis and Treatment

Physicians can diagnose excessive undereating or overeating by weighing the patient and noting whether there has been a significant change of 20 pounds or more or a radical decrease or increase in the body mass index.

Individuals who are anorexic nearly always need psychological counseling and intervention, as well as a medical consultation with a physician experienced in (or willing to learn about) eating disorders. It is important for family members to stress to the physician that older people can and do starve themselves to death and that refusing to take action merely because the person is older is tantamount to AGEISM.

In addition, when anorexic individuals are age 65 and older, if such action is not taken, then death is likely to ensue. Relatives may be reluctant to intervene; however, failure to act could be a form of NEGLECT.

Obesity can be very hard to treat. In fact, a large proportion of Americans, Canadians, and Western Europeans of all ages are obese. Attention to the individual's diet is crucial, and a dietitian may need to be consulted. The obese senior may be subsisting on sweets and foods with many calories. Because obesity can cause or contribute to the development of DIABETES, HEART DISEASE, and many other ailments

and will worsen existing medical conditions, it is important to take the illness seriously and find ways to help the older person.

See also NUTRITION.

Blinder, J., Barry F. Chaitin, and Renee S. Goldstein, eds. *The Eating Disorders: Medical and Psychological Bases of Diagnosis and Treatment.* New York: Aperture, 1988.

Cassell, Dana K., and David H. Gleaves, Ph.D. *The Encyclopedia of Obesity and Eating Disorders.* New York: Facts On File, 2000.

University of British Columbia. "Anorexia Nervosa Also Claims Lives of Elderly," media release, November 28, 1996.

Elder-care Locator   Nationwide hotline staffed by the federal government in the United States and that can provide information and assistance on state and local agencies with regard to aging-related issues. Call the Eldercare Locator at (800) 677-1116, available Monday through Friday from 9 A.M. to 8 P.M. Eastern Time.

emergency department care   Care provided in the emergency department of a hospital and that is often required in a life-threatening or severely painful situation. Many older individuals may require emergency care because of a HEART ATTACK, STROKE, KIDNEY DISEASE, or accidental injury from FALLS, among some of the key reasons for visits to the emergency room of the hospital. Emergency care can save the life of a person who has had a heart attack or stroke.

Individuals who are age 75 and older had the highest hospital emergency-department rate in 1999 in the United States, according to the CENTERS FOR DISEASE CONTROL AND PREVENTION (CDC). About 42 percent of patients at this age arrive at the hospital in an ambulance. In considering patients age 65 and older, they represent the majority (about 56 percent) of all emergent (serious emergency) care. These visits are often for an acute flareup of a chronic condition.

McCaig, Linda F., M.P.H., and Catherine W. Burt, Ed.D., Division of Health Care Statistics. "National Hospital Ambulatory Medical Care Survey: 1999 Emergency Department Summary," National Center for Health Statistics, no. 320 (June 25, 2001).

emphysema   Severe degenerative lung disease that is nearly always caused by chronic SMOKING and that affects about 2 million Americans. The risk for developing emphysema increases with age. The CENTERS FOR DISEASE CONTROL AND PREVENTION (CDC) attributes more than 17,555 deaths to the disease each year. Emphysema also claims the lives of more than 1,100 Canadians every year.

Emphysema is an incurable disease. Although treatment can delay the deterioration that is caused by the disease, the symptoms from emphysema gradually worsen until the individual's lungs can no longer function. The American Lung Association ranks emphysema 15th among chronic activity-limiting conditions. Nearly half (44 percent) of those who have emphysema say that their lives are restricted because of it.

Causes of Emphysema

Most people who develop emphysema either are or were heavy smokers. Cigarette smoking is responsible for an estimated 80–90 percent of all cases of emphysema. Years of exposure to smoke, pollution, and other airborne irritants result in a disease-generating chemical imbalance in the lungs.

In a small number (1–3 percent) of all cases of emphysema, the disease results from an inherited condition that is caused by a deficiency of alpha1-antritrypsin (AAT), which is a protein that protects the lungs from infection and damage.

Researchers also believe that there are other as yet unknown additional factors that may cause emphysema in at least 15 percent of all cases because many heavy smokers never develop the disease, and few people have the hereditary deficiency that leads to emphysema.

Risk Factors

Some people have a greater risk of developing emphysema than others do. As mentioned, smoking is the greatest risk factor, but there are also lesser factors that can also lead to or contribute to the development of emphysema.

Age Risks   Almost all (92 percent) of Americans ever diagnosed with emphysema were at least 45 years old at the time of diagnosis, and the risk for developing the disease increases with age.

Gender Risks   Historically, emphysema has been found most commonly in older men; however, the disease is becoming increasingly prevalent among women. In 1994, males with emphysema outnumbered females by 54 percent. Within two years, that gender gap had narrowed to just 10 percent. Some experts believe that this increase in females with emphysema can be attributed to increases in the number of women smoking.

Racial Risks   Emphysema is more than three times more common in whites than in AFRICAN AMERICANS. It is also about 20 percent more common among African Americans than among HISPANIC AMERICANS.

Symptoms of Emphysema

Emphysema may destroy 50–70 percent of a person's lung tissue before any symptoms appear. When symptoms do occur, shortness of breath (dyspnea) following physical exertion is often the earliest sign of emphysema. Breathing becomes increasingly labored until even mild activity results in a sensation of not getting enough air.

In the later stages of the disease, patients may take longer than normal to exhale and may purse their lips while breathing. They may have overdeveloped neck and shoulder muscles and a barrel-chested appearance. Other symptoms of advanced emphysema include:

- Anorexia
- Anxiety
- Chronic and severe cough
- Depression
- Fatigue
- Heart problems
- Sleep disturbances
- Wheezing

Diagnosing Emphysema

An early diagnosis can eliminate or minimize exposure to risk factors and slow the disease progression. Beginning with a personal and family medical history and special attention to the patient's smoking habits, diagnosis includes examinations of the heart, lungs, hands, and feet to determine how difficult it is for the patient to breathe and whether or not the body is receiving sufficient oxygen. As mentioned, physical symptoms may not be evident during early stages of emphysema, and blood tests and chest X rays may also be normal.

A number of techniques are used to diagnose emphysema. The results are compared with values considered healthy for individuals who share the patient's age, gender, race, and other defining characteristics.

Spirometry can detect emphysema in its earliest stages. With this diagnostic tool, the patient takes a deep breath and exhales as quickly as possible into a tube that is connected to a machine. This machine registers how much air the patient's lungs can hold and how much air the patient expels in one second. This technique is the most effective way to determine whether a patient's airway is obstructed.

Another technique measures arterial blood gas (ABG) or the levels of oxygen and carbon dioxide in the blood that is leaving the lungs. Calculated by analyzing blood drawn from an artery, ABG is often used to evaluate advanced disease and determine whether a patient needs oxygen.

Pulse oximetry is a technique that uses a special light that is clipped onto the finger, the earlobe, or the forehead of the patient. This procedure measures blood oxygen levels. The clip may be left in place while the patient is asleep, awake, or walking.

Chest X rays may also be taken to diagnose emphysema. Because moderate-to-severe emphysema may make the heart appear smaller than normal, chest X rays often also reveal blood-vessel abnormalities and flattening of the diaphragm.

Stages of Emphysema

Prolonged exposure to cigarette smoke or other airborne pollutants gradually and irreversibly damages the walls of the lung's air sacs (alveoli) and destroys the elasticity that enable these structures to expand as they deliver oxygen to the bloodstream and then to shrink as they remove carbon dioxide from the blood. The patient's airways narrow, and bronchial tubes leading to the air sacs may collapse, trapping air in the lungs.

Destruction of the air sacs causes the following effects:

- Permanent holes in the lower lungs
- Reduced oxygen delivery to the bloodstream and limited removal of carbon dioxide
- Shortness of breath and difficult exhaling

The key complications of emphysema can include recurrent respiratory infections, an enlargement of the right ventricle of the heart (cor pulmonale), and also respiratory failure.

Treatment for Emphysema

The goal of treatment is to eliminate exposure to the conditions that aggravate symptoms, to delay disease progression, and to keep patients as active as they can be.

Everyone who has been diagnosed with emphysema must stop smoking immediately. Patients with emphysema should also see a doctor at the first sign of any respiratory infection. In addition, they should stay indoors when pollution levels are at an unhealthy high level.

Pulmonary Rehabilitation Combining EXERCISE, education, and counseling, pulmonary rehabilitation is a plan that is designed to improve the patient's quality of life and ability to participate in daily activities. The doctor may prescribe a walking program or other exercise routine to keep the heart and other muscles healthy, increase the patient's ability to function independently, and make a patient's hospital stays shorter and less frequent.

Medications for Emphysema Bronchodilators that relax the airway muscles are often the first medications prescribed for a patient whose airway tends to tighten. When inhaled as aerosol sprays, these medications travel directly to the lungs and begin to work almost immediately.

Antiinflammatory medications (corticosteroids) are another category of drugs that may be prescribed. Corticosteroids may soothe and repair the linings of air passages, making them better able to resist obstruction. These drugs also have side effects, such as depleting calcium from the bones, decreasing the function of the adrenal and pituitary glands, and raising the body's blood sugar level.

Antibiotics are usually used to clear up respiratory infections that have been diagnosed. Influenza and pneumococcal immunizations are encouraged to prevent flu and pneumococcal pneumonia among all seniors, particularly those who have been diagnosed with emphysema.

Supplemental Oxygen Therapy Supplemental oxygen can benefit patients whose severely damaged lungs cannot absorb enough oxygen from the atmosphere. Eventually, nearly all patients with emphysema will need supplemental oxygen to breathe.

Long-term oxygen therapy provides the following benefits:

- Reduces the excess red cells in the patient's blood
- Improves functioning of the heart and brain
- May eliminate exercise-related shortness of breath
- Extends the life span of patients with low blood oxygen levels (hypoxemia)

Surgical Treatment Lung-volume reduction surgery often improves a patient's breathing, eliminates the need for supplemental oxygen, and may relieve the other symptoms of emphysema. However, surgery is not often performed on individuals age 70 and older because it is considered highly risky for most patients.

After making two or three small incisions in the patient's chest, the surgeon inserts a tiny camera that provides a clear view of the lungs. A special stapling device that is inserted through another incision cuts away the most diseased portions of the lungs. This allows the remaining lung tissue and breathing muscles to function more effectively.

This minimally invasive experimental procedure may improve the patient's ability to exercise and enjoy life and relieve the debilitating symptoms of the disease.

Lung transplantation is another option which may extend and improve the quality of life in selected cases of very severe emphysema; however, it also exposes patients to the risk of organ rejection and infection.

Current and Future Advances

Researchers have learned that smokers who rarely eat fish are three times more likely to develop emphysema than smokers who eat fish regularly.

Scientists at the National Heart, Lung, and Blood Institute have demonstrated that retinoic acid, a derivative of Vitamin A, reverses emphysema in the lungs of laboratory rats. This finding may lead to the development of medication that would affect humans in the same way.

In another study that is scheduled for completion in 2002, the National Emphysema Treatment Trial is weighing the risks and benefits associated with lung-volume reduction surgery for patients with advanced emphysema.

For further information, contact the following organizations:

The American Lung Association (ALA)
1740 Broadway
New York, NY 10019
(212) 315-8700
http://www.lungusa.org

The National Emphysema Foundation (NEF)
15 Stevens Street
Norwalk, CT 06850
http://www.emphysemafoundation.org

Emphysema Foundation for the Right to Survive (EFFORTS)
Claycomo Plaza
41 NE U.S. Highway 69
Claycomo, MO 64119
http://www.emphysema.net
See also COPD.

endocrinologist Medical doctor who is an expert in the treatment of endocrine diseases, such as DIABETES, THYROID DISEASE, and other major medical problems. This specialist can often prevent borderline elevated blood sugar levels from turning into diabetes, with the combination of counseling, medications, and exercise. Endocrinologists are often the group of physicians that diagnose and treat calcium disorders, most notably OSTEOPOROSIS.

erectile dysfunction (ED) Inability to create or to maintain an erection of the penis. It may be caused by a medical problem or by general aging. It may also be caused by SURGERY, such as the removal of the prostate gland because of PROSTATE CANCER. Such removal inhibits the man's ability to have an erection. Some surgeons perform special surgery to attempt to maintain potency.

Erectile dysfunction is a common problem among men older than age 65, although it is less common in this population than is generally believed. About 45 percent of men ages 65–69 in the United States have some level of ED. Studies have proven that medication can significantly help some men, particularly the drug sildenafil citrate (Viagra). One study found that the efficacy of Viagra in older men was comparable to that found in all men older than age 18.

Before prescribing Viagra to a senior male, to avoid dangerous medication interactions, physicians should consider his general health as well as any other medications the man is taking. In particular, any individual using nitroglycerin or similar medications for chest pain should avoid this drug.

Medications That Can Cause Erectile Dysfunction

Many medications can cause a temporary problem with erectile dysfunction and experts estimate that up to 25 percent of all cases of ED are related to medications. Some examples of particular categories of drugs which have such a side effect are: HYPERTENSION medications (especially beta blockers and diuretics), antihistamines, tranquilizers, and most antidepressants. Even a common over-the-counter drug such as Tagamet, taken for stomach upset or heartburn, can impair a man's ability to have an erection.

Diseases or Conditions That Can Cause ED

Men with DIABETES have a higher risk of experiencing erectile dysfunction. Sometimes, the penile artery itself is blocked, a common problem among older men, especially men with diabetes. Additional common medical illnesses that may lead to ED are hypertension, increased serum lipids and thyroid disease.

When men are heavy consumers of alcohol, (two to three drinks per day or more), they increase their risk of ED. Chronic ALCOHOLISM can also subvert sexual relationships through decreasing arousal and lowering testosterone levels.

Diagnosing Erectile Dysfunction

Most cases of ED in the United States are first evaluated by the patient's primary care provider, internist, or endocrinologist. The patient may also be referred to a urologist for further evaluation and treatment.

The physician bases the diagnosis of erectile dysfunction on a combination of factors, such as the man's medical history, a physical examination, and a limited number of laboratory tests. For example, in some cases, the man may be low on testosterone, a male hormone that can be supplemented. The doctor will also examine the penis and the surrounding areas to check for any abnormalities and disease. Often, the doctor will also order a urinalysis to rule out a kidney or bladder infection as the cause for the impotence.

Treating Erectile Dysfunction

There are a variety of different treatments for ED. The most commonly known remedy is the drug sildenafil (Viagra). The FDA approved Viagra in 1998.

Older Men and Viagra A study of two groups of older men, including one group of men with ED but not diabetes and another group in which the subjects had both erectile dysfunction and diabetes, was reported in the *Journal of Gerontology* in 2001. There were altogether 293 subjects who took Viagra and 189 men who were on a placebo (no-Viagra pill).

The subjects were studied for three to six months and were asked questions about whether Viagra had helped them or not. Secondary assessments were done on the men's sexual desire, intercourse satisfaction, and other related items. In some cases, sexual partners also responded to a questionnaire provided by researchers about the efficacy of Viagra.

The researchers also tracked adverse events, such as the most serious one of death as well as the need for hospitalization or a prolonged stay in the hospital. The researchers took the blood pressure and pulse rates of subjects at each visit, and each person received several physical examinations over the course of the study.

Many of the patients were taking other medications in addition to the Viagra; for example, 68 percent of the patients with diabetes were taking medications for hypertension, compared to 35 percent of the nondiabetics who took hypertensive medicines.

The researchers found that 69 percent of the non-diabetic men receiving Viagra reported improvement versus 18 percent of nondiabetic men receiving a placebo who also said they had improved. Among the diabetic men, 50 percent reported improvement, versus 10 percent of the diabetic men who received a placebo. The drug was also well tolerated by most men, and the side effects were mild to moderate. Headaches were experienced by 17 percent, flushing (reddening of the body) was reported by 13 percent, and 8 percent said they had dyspepsia (stomach upset). A small number (4 percent) had temporary changes in their eyes, such as alterations to color vision, blurred vision, or light sensitivity.

Of these elderly patients, 22 had serious adverse events, including 11 patients taking Viagra and 11 taking a placebo. One subject died of a probable HEART ATTACK that the investigator believed was unrelated to the taking of Viagra. This subject had both hypertension and a history of alcoholism. Two other deaths were reported. The researchers concluded, "Oral sildenafil, which is efficacious and well tolerated by elderly men with ED and can be taken discreetly approximately 1 hour before sexual activity, is a welcome alternative to other treatment modalities currently available for ED."

Thinking About Sex Is a Necessary Component with Taking Viagra Although it may sound self-evident, some patients need to be told that sexual stimulation/sexual thoughts are still necessary to attain an erection when taking Viagra. In one case cited in *Clinical Diabetes,* a diabetes publication, a man's physicians could not figure out why the drug was not working until he told them that he took the drug and then proceeded to read a book about growing tomatoes afterward. The doctors told him he should concentrate on sex after taking Viagra.

Precautions About Viagra Viagra should only be prescribed for men who have problems with ED because it has no enhanced effect on actual sexual desire or on the ability to ejaculate/come to orgasm.

Viagra must never be used by a man who is taking any form of nitroglycerin because the combination of Viagra and nitrates could cause a fatal drop in blood pressure. For men who have underlying cardiac disorders who are not on nitrates, Viagra appears to be safe.

Other Treatment Drugs Viagra is not the only medication for erectile dysfunction. Other drugs can be injected directly into the penis to widen blood vessels. Caverject (alprostadil) and Genabid (papaverine) have been used, with a success rate of more than 70 percent. The patient learns to self-inject the drug about 10–15 minutes prior to planned intercourse. Patients have reported that the injection is not more painful than a brief pinching sensation.

An insertable pellet is another drug that may succeed. Muse (alprostadil) is a pellet that is inserted into the urethra, and is used 5–10 minutes before intercourse. It should not be used to have intercourse with a pregnant woman because it could be dangerous to the woman and/or the fetus. (Although few older men have sex with pregnant women, there are some who have pregnant wives and lovers.)

Nondrug Treatments Other nondrug treatments for erectile dysfunction are also available. For example, a mechanical vacuum device can be used to force blood into the penis and is reported to succeed for about 67 percent of men with erectile dysfunction.

Surgery for ED Surgery may be the answer for some men. The doctor may implant a device called a prosthesis, which can restore erection. The prosthesis may be an implant that is a rod that is inserted into the penis and that the man can manually adjust. There are also inflatable implants. According to experts, the primary problem with surgery is postoperative infection, which may be difficult to treat because of the location of the infection. Also, if the patient does have surgery, the other options, such as oral medications or vacuum devices, will no longer work.

For more information on erectile dysfunction, contact the following organizations:

Impotence Institute of America (IA)
Impotence World Association
119 South Ruth Street
Maryville, TN 337803
(865) 379-2154 or (800) 669-1603 (toll-free)
http://www.impotenceworld.org

Sexual Function Health Council
American Foundation for Urologic Disease
300 West Pratt Street
Suite 401
Baltimore, MD 21201
(800) 242-2383

Chu, Neelima V., M.D. and Steven V. Edelman, M.D. "Diabetes and Erectile Function," *Clinical Diabetes* 19, no. 1 (winter 2001): 45–47.

Wagner, Gorm, et al. "Sildenafil Citrate (VIAGRA ®) Improves Erectile Function in Elderly Patients with Erectile Dysfunction: A Subgroup Analysis," *Journal of Gerontology: Medical Sciences* 56A, no. 2 (2001): M113–M119.

estate planning Deciding upon and making a legal plan for how one's assets will be distributed after death. Making a will is part of estate planning, but there are other aspects involved as well, such as determining who will execute the will and what ATTORNEYS or law firms will draw up the proper documents.

Many older people mistakenly believe that only wealthy individuals need to perform estate planning; however, anyone who owns a house and has money in the bank, and who wishes these assets to pass on to relatives or others should perform at least basic estate planning. Such planning will enable the survivors to avoid sometimes huge tax liabilities to federal and state entities. It will also give family members and legal authorities specific directives of the patient's wishes, which can be very helpful at a particularly emotional time.

See also "DEATH TAX"; WILLS.

exercise Active or moderate movement, whether through sports, calisthenics, walking, or other actions. Most older Americans should be able to perform at least some exercise, even when they have DISABILITIES; however, many people older than age 65 are very physically inactive. Exercise is a health enhancer; however, the exercise should be tailored to the physical abilities of the individual. Studies indicate that even a simple exercise such as regular walking can improve the health of most people.

Adaptations to Older People's Abilities Can Be Made

According to an article by Robert Petrella, M.D., Ph.D. in a 1999 issue of *Physician & Sportsmedicine*, many medical problems can be improved or even prevented by exercise, including HYPERTENSION, DIABETES, OSTEOARTHRITIS, and OSTEOPOROSIS. Yet, he says that exercise is often not encouraged, and this may be in part due to AGEISM or erroneous perceptions.

According to Dr. Petrella, "Poor exercise adaptation and compliance in the chronically ill elderly may stem from the perception that chronic disorders are a part of normal aging. It is commonly believed the elderly cannot respond to lifestyle interventions and that aging and chronic disease are inevitable, even though both perceptions have been disproved."

Dr. Petrella says the form of the exercise can and should be tailored to the individual, and adaptations can also be made, such as smaller weights than lifted by younger people, fewer repetitions of exercises, and special shoes.

Disabled Patients Can Exercise

Even patients who have suffered from HEART ATTACK can benefit from controlled exercises. In a study of 27 heart-failure patients reported in a 2000 issue of the *European Journal of Heart Failure*, researchers placed 12 patients on a bicycle-training exercise program, followed by a home exercise program; the other 15 patients maintained their normal routines. The researchers found significant improvement in the health of the patients who exercised.

Family Caregivers and Exercise

It's also important for FAMILY CAREGIVERS to continue to exercise, although many previously active individuals become much more sedentary when they assume a caregiving role.

According to a 2001 news release from the NATIONAL INSTITUTES OF HEALTH (NIH), studies have shown that older women caregivers (ages 49–82 years) lowered their blood pressure and resolved serious sleep problems after they participated in a moderate exercise program of home-based exercising about five hours weekly. The study included 100 women, who were either in the home-based exercise group program (51 women) or they were in a group of older caregivers (49 women) who were provided with nutritional advice.

These women averaged 72 hours a week of caring for relatives with DEMENTIA, and most (92 percent) lived with their relatives. The average woman had cared for the impaired person for four years. According to the NIH,

At the end of the study, the exercise group showed significant improvements in stress-induced blood pressure levels and sleep quality compared to the women who received nutrition counseling. Exercisers spent 5 hours a week in physical activity by the study's end compared to the nutrition group who spent less than 3 hours per week in all forms of physical activity. The exercising caregivers showed significantly lower 12-month systolic and diastolic blood pressure levels in response to an emotional stress test compared to the nutrition group. Reduced blood pressure reactivity in response to stress is associated with fewer heart and blood pressure problems. Conversely, the nutrition participants' diet improved but the group showed no change in either resting or reactive blood pressure.

According to Dr. Sidney M. Stahl, chief of behavioral medicine within the National Institute on Aging's Behavioral and Social Research program, "Studies show that family caregiving accompanied by emotional strain is an independent risk factor for mortality [death] among older adults. The study gives us some evidence that a self-directed exercise program can reduce stress reactions and perhaps improve the health of caregivers."

It is important for individuals to consult with their physicians prior to initiating any type of exercise program. However, the studies are clear; exercise can be the elixir of health.

See also TAI CHI.

Kiilavuori, K., et al. "The Effect of Physical Training on Skeletal Muscle in Patients with Chronic Heart Failure," *The European Journal of Heart Failure* 2 (2000): 53–63.

National Institute on Aging, NIH News Release. "Moderate Exercise Program Benefits Health of Older Women Caregivers," National Institutes of Health (November 1, 2001).

Petrella, Robert J., M.D., Ph.D. "Exercise for Older Patients with Chronic Disease," *Physicians & Sportsmedicine* 27, no. 11 (October 15, 1999): 79–101.

eye diseases Disorders of the eye may be minor and temporary, such as an easily treatable eye infection, or may be major and threaten BLINDNESS, such as MACULAR DEGENERATION. All individuals age 65 and older should have at least an annual eye examination to screen for common eye diseases so that treatment can occur before it is too late.

According to Bruce P. Rosenthal, O.D. in his article on eye diseases for a 2001 issue of *Geriatrics,* macular degeneration is the most prominent cause of vision impairment among people older than age 75, and it is also the dominant cause of legal blindness for individuals older than age 65. In 2002, the National Eye Institute said that more than 1.65 million Americans age 50 and older had age-related macular degeneration. Of these individuals, most (about 1.1 million) are females. In addition, most are CAUCASIAN (about 1.5 million).

CATARACTS are another common problem among older individuals, and the National Eye Institute estimated that this eye disease affected about 20.5 million Americans age 65 and older in 2002. Medicare costs were about $3.4 billion per year for treated cataracts in 2002.

GLAUCOMA is another eye disease, and the National Eye Institute estimated that 2.2 million Americans age 40 and older had been diagnosed with the disease in 2002. Another 2 million people had glaucoma but were not yet diagnosed.

Risk Factors

The risk for developing an eye disease, such as cataracts or glaucoma, increases with age. AFRICAN AMERICANS have a risk of developing glaucoma that is three to four times greater than the risk experienced by whites.

As many as half of all Americans ages 65–74 have a risk of developing cataracts.

People who have DIABETES have a greater risk of developing all forms of serious eye diseases than others do. They also have a risk of suffering from diabetic neuropathy, a nerve-destroying eye disease that is unique to people with diabetes.

Annual eye examinations should be considered an essential part of health care for senior adults.

Prevent Blindness America. "Vision Problems in the U.S.: Prevalence of Adult Vision Impairment and Age-Related Eye Disease in America" (2002).

Quillen, David A., M.D. "Common Causes of Vision Loss in Elderly Patients," *American Family Physician* (July 1999).

Rosenthal, Bruce P., O.D. "Screening and Treatment of Age-Related and Pathologic Vision Changes," *Geriatrics* 56, no. 12 (December 2001): 27–31.

falls Accidents in which individuals lose their balance and usually land on a floor or a hard surface and may become injured. The person may break a bone or may damage muscles or organs. Falls are extremely common among people older than age 65 and can be very dangerous, even fatal, although many falls do not cause any permanent damage.

About one-third of all adults older than age 65 in the United States sustain falls each year. About 3 percent of these falls result in FRACTURES (broken bones); in fact, falls represent the cause of the majority (87 percent) of all fractures that occur among adults who are 65 years and older. Older adults who fall down are two to three times more likely to fall again within the next year.

Most falls (60 percent) occur in the home, 30 percent occur in a public place, and 10 percent occur in an institution such as a nursing home or a hospital. Falls are the second leading cause of spinal cord and brain injuries among adults older than 65 years.

Falls Can Be Fatal

According to the National Center for Injury Prevention & Control, a division of the CENTERS FOR DISEASE CONTROL AND PREVENTION (CDC) in their *Factbook Year 2000: Working to Prevent and Control Injury in the United States,* falls are the leading cause of injury-related deaths among people in the United States ages 65 and older. In 1998, about 9,600 people age 65 and older died from a fall. The risk for sustaining a fatal fall increases with age: about 60 percent of all deaths from falls occur to those 75 years old or older.

Older men are at greater risk for dying from a fall, and whites have a higher death risk from falls than blacks. According to the CDC, in terms of risk of death from fall, the order is: white men have the greatest risk, followed by white women, black men, and black women.

Hip Fractures

Of all the various types of fracture injuries resulting from falls that may occur to senior citizens, hip fractures are among the most likely fractures to cause severe injuries and deaths, although skull fractures are also extremely dangerous for older individuals. Patients who are hospitalized for hip fractures must usually remain in the hospital for about two weeks. At least 95 percent of all hip fractures result from a fall. There is also a distinct gender difference: women suffer about 80 percent of all hip fractures.

The problem of hip fractures is increasing in a worrisome way as the population ages; statistics show that fracture hospitalizations are on the increase. There were 230,000 hospital admissions for hip fractures in 1988, and that number increased to 340,000 admissions for hip fractures by 1996. Experts say the number of hospital admissions for hip fractures will exceed 500,000 per year by 2040.

Hip fractures often lead to a permanent loss of independence for the injured person. About half of all older individuals who are hospitalized for a hip fracture do not return home after the injury occurs because they are unable to care for themselves. Instead, they must rely on nursing-home care, assisted living, or the care of a relative or other person.

Other fractures that are commonly incurred from falls are fractures of the pelvis, vertebrae, arm, hand, leg, and ankle. These type of injuries can also lead to less independence for the injured person, although head, spine, or hip fractures are generally the most harmful.

Who Is Most at Risk for Falls

Both older women and older men are at risk for falls; however, men have a greater risk of death from a fall. Women, particularly white women, have a higher risk of incurring a nonfatal injury from falling. Some experts believe that this is due in part to the fact that white women have the greatest risk of having OSTEOPOROSIS. However, in the case of hip fractures resulting from falls, CDC research has established that it is the energy from the fall, rather than any inherent weakness of the bones themselves, that causes the fracture.

The risk of falling also increases with age, and those who are age 85 years and older have a 10–15 times greater risk of having a hip fracture from a fall than the risk experienced by those who are ages 60–65 years. This greater risk is probably due to worsening health that comes with aging.

Primary Reasons for Falls

There are many causes of falls in the senior population. One major cause is the inability to react quickly enough to stop a fall. The "righting reflex" may be significantly reduced due to joint changes, decreased appreciation of sensation, such as with nerve damage called "neuropathy" in patients with spinal-cord narrowing (spinal stenosis), and even in cases of nutritional deficiencies such as decreased levels of Vitamin B_{12} in the body.

Researchers have also found patterns of factors that appear to increase the risk for falls. Falls may be caused by external factors and by factors within the individual. A combination of both types of factors also cause or contribute to falls.

Environmental Factors   The key environmental factors that lead to falls include the following:

- Poor lighting
- Loose carpets or scatter rugs
- Slippery surfaces
- Objects on floors

Poor Lighting   Older individuals generally have poorer vision and need more illumination than is required by younger people. Insufficient lighting is another reason why some older people have trouble with DRIVING in the evening and why they may sustain injuries from car crashes.

Loose Carpets or Scatter Rugs   Carpets that are loose and on which a heel can easily be caught are dangerous for all people, but especially for older people. Flat carpet is preferable to area rugs. Scatter rugs can

easily bunch up and be tripped over and should be avoided or made skid free.

Slippery Surfaces   Bathtubs and bathroom floors may be slick; it is easy for an older person to slip on them. Most experts recommend skid-free mats and grab bars in the bathroom. Outside steps can be a problem because they may become slippery in rain or snow. Inside stairs may be slippery from cleaning or from loose carpeting and may also be steep. Experts recommend railings on both sides of the stairs, both inside and outside the home.

Objects on Floors   Items that are not put away, such as shoes and books, or many other items that may be in areas where people walk can cause or contribute to falls. If combined with poor illumination and the individual's poor vision or other problems, the risk of falling further increases.

Personal Medical Problems/Issues That Can Lead to Falls   There are many general factors that can cause falls. Some examples of problems faced by many older adults are:

- Problems with gait and balance
- Medications that cause or increase unsteadiness or dizziness
- Cataracts or other eye or vision problems
- Hypotension
- Neurological or musculoskeletal disabilities
- Dementia
- More than one chronic disease

Problems with Gait and Balance   If individuals are unsteady on their feet, then they may easily lose their balance, even in an otherwise safe environment. Experts recommend that people with gait and balance problems should take it slow and not allow others to rush them. Gait and balance training can often make a very positive impact on patients.

Medications That Cause or Increase Unsteadiness or Dizziness   There are many drugs that should be taken with caution, such as psychiatric drugs and painkillers. There are far too many drugs to list here, but a few examples of medications that older individual may take which are sedating are Inderal (propranolol) for blood-pressure patients, Lanoxin (digoxin) for heart disease, and Darvocet N100 (propoxyphene) for pain. These and other medications may lower blood pressure or may decrease a person's overall awareness and reactions.

Most of these medications come with a warning that the individual should not drive or operate any dangerous equipment while taking the drug. Such warnings should be heeded.

Cataracts or Other Eye or Vision Problems If individuals cannot see well, they are more likely to slip and fall. They simply do not see objects that are in the way.

Hypotension Some studies have shown that a sudden drop in blood pressure (hypotension) can lead to falls. In one study of older individuals in France, reported in 2000 in the *Journal of Gerontology*, the researchers found that a drop in blood pressure after eating (postprandial hypotension) greatly increased the risk for falls and for fainting (syncope).

The subjects who had postprandial hypotension had a 23 percent risk of falling or fainting, compared to an 8 percent risk among the control group subjects. In most cases, the subjects with postprandial hypotension had diabetes or took three or more medications. The risk for postprandial hypotension and falling was greatest after eating breakfast. Increasing overall hydration (consumption of fluid) and wearing support hose or stockings may be helpful in reducing this symptom.

Neurological or Musculoskeletal Disabilities Illnesses such as PARKINSON'S DISEASE increase the risk of falls among older people.

Dementia People who suffer from dementia have a greater risk of falling than seniors who do not have dementia, probably due to their impaired cognitive abilities.

Preventive Actions to Take for Seniors Who Live at Home

Most experts recommend that homes be checked for safety factors by the older individuals themselves and/or by other family members. Some common recommendations to improve safety in the home and reduce the risk of falls are:

- Add grab bars to bath tubs.
- Place handrails on both sides of stairs.
- Have the senior exercise regularly to build up strength, balance, and coordination.

- Install a night light by the bed, and install outside lights.
- Remove hazards that can be tripped over, such as scatter rugs.
- Schedule an annual vision check for the older person to exclude the possibility of a changed prescription or the presence of diseases such as cataracts.
- Ask the doctor to review all medications to check for interactions and side effects.
- Limit alcohol intake because even a small amount can impair reflexes.
- Have the senior arise slowly after eating or lying down, particularly if there is a problem with low blood pressure.

Strength Training to Reduce Falls

Studies have indicated that even very elderly people can learn to perform simple strength-increasing exercises and that these exercises can actually reduce the risk of falls. In a study reported in a 1997 issue of the *British Medical Journal*, researchers trained 116 women age 80 and older in exercises that improved strength and balance. Women in the control group made no changes in their lifestyles, but they were observed by the researchers. After one year, the exercise group had significantly reduced their risk of falling compared to the control group.

Other studies have bolstered the finding that exercise can reduce the risks for falls. Some studies have shown that TAI CHI, a simple form of Chinese martial art, can reduce the risk of sustaining falls.

Fears About Falling

Sometimes, the fear of falling can be as bad or worse than the results of an actual fall. The fear of falling can cause people to limit their activities greatly, either because they make this choice themselves or because their caregivers urge them to "take it easy." As a result, individuals who are fearful of falling may fail to move about and gain sufficient exercise. Ironically, this action may increase the probability of falling because restricting activity can weaken the muscles and the overall body strength so that when a person must move, the body is weaker and the risk of falling down is increased.

In a study reported in a 2000 issue of the *Journal of Gerontology: Medical Sciences,* researchers studied subjects in Australia who did not live in a nursing home and who had an average age of 77 years. They found that "nonfallers" (people who did not have a problem with falls but who feared that they would fall) had a significantly increased risk of being admitted to a nursing home when compared to subjects who actually did have a problem with falling.

The researchers said, "Fear of falling is a health problem among nonfallers as well as fallers. In fact, we found that being afraid of falling was predictive of admission to an aged care institution only among nonfallers."

They added, "Some nonfallers (and their caregivers) may have an image of falls as catastrophic events involving fractures, hospitalization, and nursing home admission. In contrast, many persons who have fallen (and their caregivers) are aware that most falls are fairly benign and do not cause any physical injury."

See also ALZHEIMER'S DISEASE.

Campbell, A. John, et al. "Randomised Controlled Trial of a General Practice Programme of Home Based Exercise to Prevent Falls in Elderly Women," *British Medical Journal* 315 (1997): 1065–1070.

Cumming, Robert G., et al. "Prospective Study of the Impact of Fear of Falling on Activities of Daily Living, SF-36 Scores, and Nursing Home Admission," *Journal of Gerontology: Medical Sciences* 55A, no. 5 (2000): M299–M305.

National Center for Injury Prevention & Control, a division of the Centers for Disease Control and Prevention (CDC). *Factbook Year 2000: Working to Prevent and Control Injury in the United States.* Washington, D.C.: Government Printing Office, 2000.

Puisieux, Francois, et al. "Ambulatory Blood Pressure Monitoring and Postprandial Hypotension in Elderly Persons with Falls or Syncopes," *Journal of Gerontology: Medical Sciences* 55A, no. 9 (2000): M535–M540.

Tideiksaar, Rein, "Preventing Falls: How to Identify Risk Factors, Reduce Complications," *Geriatrics* 51, no. 2 (1996): 43–51.

Family and Medical Leave Act (FMLA) A law in the United States that provides for the circumstances under which employees at most companies must be allowed to take unpaid time off from work because of their own illness or the sickness of a family member. Some individuals use the provisions of the FMLA to take time off to care for their aging parents who are ill or who need to be taken to doctor's appointments or for medical treatments.

Enacted by the U.S. Congress in 1993, the Family and Medical Leave Act went into effect on August 5, 1993, and the final regulations took effect on April 6, 1995. The law requires most employers in the United States to allow employees who have worked for them for at least a year (and have met other provisions of the law) to take up to 12 weeks of *unpaid* leave per year. The employee may also combine their paid sick leave from work with FMLA leave.

There are two primary reasons for taking leave: a serious health condition in oneself or in a family member who needs an employee's care and assistance. A *serious health condition* is defined as "an illness, injury, impairment, or physical or mental condition that involves inpatient care or continuing treatment by a health-care provider." As a result, if a person was hospitalized and then needed to recuperate at home for some period, the FMLA would generally apply.

The FMLA specifically lists diabetes under the law in 29 C.F.R. § 825.114(a)(1), (2), where it is one of five situations under "continuing treatment by a health-care provider." That situation is defined as follows: "any period of incapacity or treatment due to a chronic serious health condition requiring periodic visits for treatment, including episodic conditions such as asthma, diabetes, and epilepsy."

Thus, if a person or a family member becomes seriously ill, then the provisions of the FMLA could be used. The person may also take time off under the FMLA to take care of a spouse or a parent with a serious health condition.

Leave may be taken for 12 consecutive weeks, or it may be split up into smaller increments, according to the U.S. Department of Labor. It is the Department of Labor that enforces violations of the FMLA.

Many people do not use the entire 12 weeks because the leave is unpaid and they can afford to take only a few unpaid weeks off, at most.

The employee has certain responsibilities under the law. For example, the employer must be notified what the serious health condition is, although this can be done under confidential conditions. When the leave ends, the employer must allow the worker to come back to the same job or to a comparable job.

To learn more about the FMLA, the employer's human-resources office should be able to provide needed information. For background information on the FMLA and the Americans with Disabilities Act, the following website is useful: www.eeoc.gov/docs/fmlaada.html.

See also AMERICANS WITH DISABILITIES ACT; EMPLOYMENT.

family caregivers   Spouses, adult children, or other family members who provide care and assistance to individuals age 65 and older. The older person may live with the family caregiver or may reside elsewhere. Studies have revealed that most family caregivers in the United States are middle-aged females who are married and have children who still live at home.

In a study on family caregiving which was published in 2001, based on 236 members of the NATIONAL FAMILY CAREGIVERS ASSOCIATION (NFCA), researchers found that 44 percent of the respondents were providing care to a spouse, and 35 percent were caring for either a parent or a spouse's parent. (Others cared for children, siblings, other relatives, or friends.)

The large majority (74 percent) were between the ages of 36 and 64; however less than half (47 percent) were employed outside the home. Most (69 percent) were married. The researchers also found that "self-identification," or regarding themselves in the role of family caregivers, was an empowering identity. Those who perceived themselves as family caregivers felt more confident when talking with health professionals about their relative, with 47 percent saying that this self-identification contributed "a lot" and 36 percent "a little" to this self-confidence.

The large majority of respondents (91 percent) said that the message of "preserving your health" is important for all family caregivers. Twenty-two percent of the respondents said that it was "a lot" easier to pay attention to their own health when they

self-identified as a family caregiver. However, family caregiving can also affect healthy behavior.

In the survey, only 30 percent said they received regular exercise, although 61 percent did exercise regularly before taking on family caregiving responsibilities. They were also less likely to seek prompt medical attention for health problems after becoming a caregiver: 47 percent said they sought prompt attention after becoming a family caregiver, although before becoming a caregiver, 70 percent saw their doctors promptly when they were ill.

See also ADULT CHILDREN: BABY BOOMERS; COMPASSION FATIGUE.

National Family Caregivers Association. "Family Caregivers and Caregiving Families—2001," (2001).

fibromyalgia syndrome (FMS)   A medical condition, formerly known as fibrositis, that is characterized by widespread body pain, severe fatigue, and chronic difficulty with sleep. It may also be accompanied by other medical problems, such as irritable bowel syndrome. Although the syndrome appears to be more prominent among those younger than age 65, researchers are finding increasing incidences among older people.

It may also be true that the syndrome has not yet been identified very much among older people, in part because it is a relatively new phenomenon and also because physicians may have assumed that fibromyalgia did not occur in older people; thus doctors are not looking for it. In addition, the syndrome may have been present but was misdiagnosed as OSTEOARTHRITIS, THYROID DISEASE, or another medical problem.

Studies indicate that people with fibromyalgia experience pain at an earlier stage than others. In addition, the pain is felt more intensely, and it lasts longer than among people who do not have fibromyalgia. It is often poorly localized, affecting multiple muscle groups, thereby making a diagnosis even more difficult.

Causes

It is not known what causes fibromyalgia. It may be caused by a trauma to the body, a hormonal disturbance, an infection, or another cause. Some people may have a genetic predisposition to develop fibromyalgia, although no specific genetic location has been identified.

Symptoms

The symptoms of fibromyalgia are widespread pain, typically in the back and neck, although pain may be felt in the arms, the legs, and the trunk. Fatigue is another common symptom, as is chronic sleep disturbance. The individual with fibromyalgia may also suffer from depression, irritable bowel syndrome, and a host of other serious medical problems. Because of the chronic pain, the attention and memory of the individual with fibromyalgia are often affected.

Diagnosis

Laboratory tests and X rays to date cannot detect fibromyalgia but can only rule out other conditions, such as rheumatoid arthritis, osteoarthritis, thyroid disease, or systemic lupus. People with fibromyalgia have two to three times the level of Substance P, a pain neurochemical in their spinal fluid; however, it is not cost effective to use the amount of Substance P as a diagnostic tool.

Fibromyalgia is diagnosed by the presence of painful "tender points" on the body that are determined by the American College of Rheumatology. People who have been identified with at least 11 of the 18 tender points, in addition to widespread pain and fatigue that last at least three months, may have fibromyalgia.

Treatment of Fibromyalgia

Because pain is usually the key presenting medical problem, patients are treated with over-the-counter and prescribed painkilling medications, muscle relaxants, and nonsteroidal antiinflammatory drugs. Lifestyle changes, such as daily walks, exercise, and weight loss, can improve the condition. Exercise should not be overly vigorous because excessive exercising can cause a flare-up of symptoms. Exercise in water, including water walking and water aerobics, is often extremely helpful. Yoga and TAI CHI exercises that emphasize stretching and slow movements can also be beneficial.

Many people with fibromyalgia have other chronic medical problems as well, such as arthritis.

Physicians strive to treat them with medications and treatments that can help both conditions. Psychological support for the multitude of complaints can help and can also enable patients with fibromyalgia to learn appropriate coping mechanisms.

In general, rheumatologists and neurologists are the best qualified physicians to treat fibromyalgia, although physicians of other specialties may treat the condition.

For further information on fibromyalgia, contact the following organizations:

Arthritis Foundation
1330 West Peachtree Street
Atlanta, GA 30309
(404) 872-7100 or (800) 283-7800 (toll-free)

Fibromyalgia Alliance of America
P.O. Box 21990
Columbus, OH 43221
(614) 457-4222

Fibromyalgia Network
P.O. Box 31750
Tucson, AZ 85751
(800) 853-2929 (toll-free)

Kranzler, Jay D., M.D., Ph.D., Judith F. Gendreau, M.D., and Srinivas G. Rao, M.D., Ph.D. "The Psychopharmacology of Fibromyalgia: A Drug Development Perspective," *Psychopharmacology Bulletin* 36, no. 1 (2002): 165–213.

Mense, Siegfried, David G. Simons, and I. Jon Russell. *Muscle Pain: Understanding Its Nature, Diagnosis, and Treatment.* Baltimore, Md.: Lippincott Williams & Wilkins, 2001.

Staud, Roland, M.D. and Christine Adamec. *Fibromyalgia for Dummies.* New York: Hungry Minds/John Wiley & Sons, 2002.

flu/influenza and pneumonia   Infectious diseases that are very dangerous and even fatal for many older people. Deaths from flu and pneumonia remain a leading cause of many DEATHS among older individuals. This is tragic because although immunizations are available to most people in the United States, Canada, and other countries for individuals older than age 65, many older people, particularly nonwhite individuals, fail to obtain them, although it is unclear why this is true.

Medicare also covers immunizations for both flu and pneumonia. As a result, older people should be sure to receive immunizations for flu, as well as for pneumonia, a very serious disorder for anyone who has a chronic illness or a compromised immune system.

Flu shots are given annually; the pneumonia vaccine is generally administered once every five to seven years. The pneumonia vaccine is a very important immunization because pneumonia causes many deaths among older individuals. Pneumonia is the fifth-leading cause of death among whites, blacks, and Hispanics and is the fourth-leading cause of death among Asians.

Although a flu shot is generally a good idea for most older people, individuals should be sure to check with their physicians first before receiving the immunization. Someone who is acutely ill or feverish should not take the vaccine, nor should it be taken by anyone who is allergic to eggs or who has had a prior severe systemic reaction to the flu shot.

Frequency of Immunizations

Influenza is generally a problem between November through the following April, and pneumonia generally follows the same pattern. Most people who receive these immunizations obtain them sometime between October to mid-November. New flu shots are required each year, although pneumococcal immunizations may only need to be repeated every five to seven years, depending on the patient's physician's advice.

It may take three to four weeks for the body to develop antibodies against the flu or pneumonia. As a result, the timing of the injection is important. For example, people who received an injection on November 5 and were then exposed to the flu on November 11 could still develop the flu despite having received the injection. The body would not have had enough time to build up antibodies (the body's immune-system warriors) within that brief time frame.

Providers and Costs of Immunizations

Flu shots and pneumococcal vaccines are covered by Part B Medicare. If the immunization must be paid for, it is generally at a low cost. The state health department or local clinic may provide the shot for free or at low cost, or individuals may pay to obtain the immunization from their doctors.

Primary Symptoms of Flu and Pneumonia

Most people with the flu experience at least several of these symptoms:

- Fever that is greater than 101.5 degrees Fahrenheit
- Sore throat (pharyngitis)
- Chills
- Muscle aches (myalgia)
- Headache
- Cough, generally dry and nonproductive

Symptoms of Pneumonia Are:

- Fever
- Coughing up sputum (Generally greenish, brown, or blood-tinged, not white or clear)
- Chest pain, generally sharp
- Shortness of breath
- Fatigue

Categories of People Who Should Be Immunized

According to the CENTERS FOR DISEASE CONTROL AND PREVENTION (CDC), an annual flu shot is particularly recommended for people who fall in one or more of the following categories.

- Everyone older than age 50
- Nursing-home residents
- Those with long-term health problems, such as diabetes, heart disease, lung disease, asthma, kidney disease, or anemia
- Those with a weak immune system because of HIV or medications that weaken the system, such as cancer treatments or steroids

Minor and Major Reactions to Flu/Pneumococcal Injections

Many people have mild reactions to the injection, such as soreness at the injection site or redness. There may be some temporary achiness or slight fever for one or two days as well.

On rare occasions, individuals experience a bad reaction to the immunization. Anyone who experiences a fever of greater than 101.5 degrees Fahrenheit or who exhibits signs of an allergic reaction should obtain immediate medical attention. Some examples of an allergic reaction are:

- hives
- difficulty breathing/shortness of breath
- paleness/pallor
- wheezing
- rapid heartbeat
- light-headedness

A person who experiences such a severe reaction should also ask the doctor to file a Vaccine Adverse Event Reporting System (VAERS) form with the Centers for Disease Control or, upon treatment and recovery, patients may call the VAERS later themselves at (800) 822-7967.

Baine, William B., M.D., William Yu, M.A., and James P. Summe, M.S. "Epidemiologic Trends in the Hospitalization of Elderly Medicare Patients for Pneumonia, 1991–1998," *American Journal of Public Health* 91, no. 7 (2001): 1,121–1,123.

Sandhu, Satinderpal K., M.D. and Sherif B. Mossad, M.D. "Influenza in the Older Adult: Indications for the Use of Vaccine and Antiviral Therapy," *Geriatrics* 56, no. 1 (2001): 43–51.

Wallach, Frances R., M.D. "Infectious Disease: Update on Treatment of Pneumonia, Influenza, and Urinary Tract Infections," *Geriatrics* 56, no. 9 (2001): 43–47.

foot diseases Major and minor ailments that affect the feet. In some cases, diseases of the feet can cause severe harm; for example, if people who have DIABETES develop sores or lesions that they do not notice because of a lack of feeling in the feet, the wound could develop into gangrene, and the person could lose a foot or even lose a leg to amputation.

Another disease that often causes problems with the feet is GOUT. This is an excess of uric acid that settles into joints, often the toe or the ankle. Individuals who have gout should follow diets recommended by their physicians and may need to take allopurinol or other medications on a regular basis.

ARTHRITIS can cause deformities of the foot and the ankle, whether the illness is RHEUMATOID ARTHRITIS or OSTEOARTHRITIS.

Because older individuals are more likely to experience slips and FALLS, it is important that they wear comfortable shoes. Older women should avoid wearing high heels and should wear only low-heeled or flat shoes that fit comfortably.

fractures Broken bones. Fractures are common among older people who experience FALLS. An estimated 95 percent of all hip fractures are caused by falls. Fractures can be dangerous and even fatal: many older people who experience fractures never regain their former level of functioning, particularly in the case of individuals who have experienced a hip fracture.

Older people are also more likely to sustain severe fractures, such as breaking a hip bone. The enforced bed rest of such an injury can lead to increased problems with OBESITY and DEPRESSION.

According to the CENTERS FOR DISEASE CONTROL AND PREVENTION (CDC), about 3 percent of the falls experienced by seniors will result in fractures. Falls cause most (87 percent) of all the fractures experienced by adults who are older than age 65 years.

Types of Fractures and Danger Levels

Hip fractures are the most dangerous breaks that may occur to an older person; this type of fracture is most likely to lead to severe injuries and deaths. About half of older individuals who are hospitalized for a hip fracture cannot return home after the injury occurs. Other fractures that are commonly incurred from falls are fractures of the pelvis, vertebrae, arm, hand, leg, and ankle.

Women older than age 65 are more likely to experience fractures then men. Caucasian women are most at risk. Women are also more likely to be hospitalized for fractures than men.

funerals Ceremonies and rituals that are held to commemorate the death of a family member or loved one. These rituals are held to provide comfort to the bereaved family members and friends as well as to dispose of the remains of the deceased person. Funerals may be very elaborate rituals or they may be simple ceremonies attended by only a few people. Funerals may be held at the gravesite, or they may be primarily conducted at a funeral home, religious site, or other location.

Funerals often cause extreme emotional hardship for individuals, although they may also provide release and acceptance of the death of their loved ones. Sometimes, individuals try to protect older family members by trying to prevent them or actually preventing them from attending the funerals of their friends and others they love. Experts say that it is usually better to allow older individuals to attend the funerals and to grieve their losses actively.

Some people plan their own funerals prior to their deaths so that their loved ones will not have to make difficult decisions at a time when they are extremely bereaved and upset. People may also plan their funerals before their deaths because they do not want to place the financial burden of paying for the funeral on their grief-stricken relatives who may have difficulty affording the expenses. If such an advance plan is made, the individual should share the details of the funeral plan with family members.

See also BEREAVEMENT; CREMATION.

gait disorders Difficulty in walking normally, due to illness. Gait disorders may stem from many different diseases, most prominently diseases such as ARTHRITIS, OSTEOPOROSIS, or PARKINSON'S DISEASE. They may also result from medications the person is taking that impair balance and stability. Gait disorders are important to diagnose and treat because victims are at risk of further deterioration without treatment and also because they have a greater risk of injuries from FALLS than those without gait disorders. The majority of falls among older individuals are related to gait disorders.

Many gait disorders are not detected, usually because the physician does not observe the patient walking and because patients either do not realize that they are walking abnormally or they may think that this is a normal part of aging. In addition, patients often show their best effort and concentration at the physician's visit rather than the impaired gait that occurs in a more natural setting.

Risk Factors

Patients with Parkinson's disease, degenerative joint disease, and orthostatic hypotension are most at risk for developing gait disorders. Patients who have had a STROKE, peripheral neuropathy, or a Vitamin B_{12} deficiency are also at risk for developing gait disorders. The use of alcohol and some medications, such as diuretics, antiarrhythmics, antihypertensive drugs, or sedating medications, can further amplify the risk.

Symptoms

Gait disturbances are manifested in difficulty in walking and pacing and in unusually slow walking. Balance may also be impaired.

Diagnosis

The physician has a variety of tests that can be applied to evaluate a patient's gait. For example, the doctor may have the patient sit on a chair and then observe the patient standing and walking away from the chair. Neurological tests may be performed, such as having the patient walk (or attempt to walk) on the toes or on the heels.

The doctor should also look at possible problems with balance, which may be an indicator of an inner ear problem or a problem in the balance center of the brain.

Treatment

Physical therapy may be helpful to improving an individual's gait. Exercises also have value and have been shown in clinical trials to reduce the risk of falls. In one study of adults older than age 70, researchers found that aerobic exercises improved balance by about 20 percent. Strength training may also reduce the risk of falls. Walking programs have also been shown to improve mobility and reduce the risk of falls among those with gait disorders.

Some individuals may require assistive devices, such as canes or walkers. Some physicians use botulinum toxin (Botox) to treat muscle spasticity, although this treatment can be expensive.

Experts also strongly recommend that environmental areas where the patient lives should be assessed. For example, loose "scatter" rugs should be eliminated. Poor lighting should be upgraded. Stairways should be evaluated to make sure railings are available and that they are secure. Bathrooms and kitchen floors should not be overly slick.

Physicians should reevaluate medications that can contribute to gait disorders. A lower dose may still achieve the goal, or a different medication may be preferable. In some cases, however, the patient will need to continue to take the medication.

Duxbury, Andrew S. "Gait Disorders in the Elderly: Commonly Overlooked Diagnostic Clues," *Consultant* (September 1997): 2,337–2,351.

Gitter, Andrew, M.D. and Robert McAnelly, M.D. "The Value of Information Resulting from Instrumented Gait Analysis: The Physiatrist." Department of Veterans Affairs. Available online. URL:http://www.vard.org/mono/gait/gitter.htm. Updated May 10, 1999.

Rubenstein, Laurence Z., M.D., M.P.H., Christopher M. Powers, Ph.D., P.T., and Catherine H. MacLean, M.D., Ph.D. "Quality Indicators for the Management and Prevention of Falls and Mobility Problems in Vulnerable Elders," *Annals of Internal Medicine* 135 (2001): 686–693.

gall-bladder disease (cholecystitis) Inflammation of the gall bladder and/or the presence of gallstones within the gall bladder. This can be a very painful and even life-threatening illness. Surgery (a cholecystectomy) is usually required for an acute attack. About 500,000 cholecystectomies are performed each year in the United States. In most cases, gallstones, or tiny stones composed of crystallized cholesterol or other substances in the gall bladder, caused severe pain, requiring surgery. Gallstones are not always painful, however.

Risk Factors

Cholesterol gallstones are more common among older individuals, females, and those who are obese. Sometimes a rapid weight loss can cause the development of gallstones. Individuals taking some medications are at an increased risk for developing gallstones, including such drugs as estrogens or progestogens, which many women take subsequent to the onset of MENOPAUSE.

Some groups seem to be at greater risk than others for developing gallstones. For example, the Pima Indians of Arizona have the highest-known incidence of gallstones, and up to 75 percent of females in the Pima Indian tribe suffer from gallstones. (Many Pima Indians also have DIABETES, HYPERTENSION, KIDNEY DISEASE, and other medical problems.) Individuals of Scandinavian descent have a higher risk of developing gallstones than do African Americans or Asians.

Symptoms

Individuals who are suffering from a gall-bladder attack usually have severe abdominal pain, also known as biliary colic. Nausea and vomiting are other common symptoms of an attack. In the case of acute cholecystitis, a gallstone is stuck in the cystic duct, causing pain and inflammation and also causing infection in about half the cases.

Diagnosis

Physicians diagnose gall-bladder disease based on symptoms, as well as laboratory tests for bilirubin and amylase. Sometimes, ultrasound tests are also ordered to determine if the gall bladder wall is thickened.

Treatment

If patients are having an acute attack, they need to be admitted to the hospital. Surgery is usually performed. With chronic cholecystitis, surgery is usually eventually ordered as well. In some cases when the biliary system is obstructed, patients may develop a bacterial infection that is life threatening. Hypertension, mental confusion, pain, and JAUNDICE (yellowing of the skin), combined with laboratory studies that indicate biliary obstruction, are indicators of a bacterial infection that is an emergency. The patient needs to hospitalized and treated with antibiotics; the biliary system needs to be drained as well.

Agrawal, Sangeeta, et al. "Gallstones, from Gall Bladder to Gut," *Postgraduate Medicine* 108, no. 3 (September 1, 2000): 143–153.

Walling, Anne D. "Diagnosing Biliary Colic and Acute Cholecystitis, " *American Family Physician* 62, no. 6 (September 15, 2000): 1,386.

gambling Engaging in games of chance, ranging from playing bingo in a church hall to purchasing a lottery ticket to playing games in casinos. The rules surrounding gambling vary from state to state. Some states, such as Mississippi, Nevada, and New Jersey, allow organized gambling, and the state collects taxes. Many states run lottery games to generate tax revenues.

Older people may engage in gambling as an entertainment or a form of social interaction. A small number become "addicted" to gambling and spend all their money on lottery tickets, casino gambling, or other games of chance.

gardening Arranging and growing flowers, trees, and shrubs. A hobby enjoyed by many people of all ages, gardening may be beneficial for older individuals because it is a productive activity that requires attention and provides some EXERCISE, but it is also one that can be started and stopped depending on the desires and abilities of the individual. Window gardening takes up minimal space but can provide a great deal of enjoyment and continuous feedback. Herb gardening is also quite popular. Joining a gardening club can also be a very social event for seniors.

gastroesophageal reflux disease (GERD)   A disease characterized by a severe and chronic backflow ("reflux") of digestive acids into the esophagus and sometimes into the mouth as well. Many older people experience GERD, but large numbers of them rely heavily on over-the-counter antacids to resolve the problem and fail to see a physician about their condition. These over-the-counter drugs often cannot provide enough protection to the esophagus, nor can they resolve the problem, as could medications that a doctor would prescribe.

Chronic GERD that has lasted for many years can lead to inflammation and damage of the food tube known as the esophagus (esophagitis). It may also narrow the esophageal passage so that it is difficult for the individual to swallow (DYSPHAGIA). GERD that has been untreated for many years may also lead to Barrett's esophagus, a precancerous condition.

Risk Factors

Certain categories of people are more prone to developing GERD than others. They include such groups as people who:

- Have DIABETES
- Have hypothyroidism (low levels of thyroid hormone)
- Have a hiatal hernia
- Have chronic CONSTIPATION and straining to move the bowels
- Smoke
- Have asthma
- Are female (Older women are at greater risk than older men.)

- Have a decreased production of saliva (caused by medications and/or aging)
- Are overweight

Symptoms

The key symptoms of chronic GERD that are most likely to be found among older people are frequent heartburn, foul taste in the mouth, frequent belching, hoarseness, and cough. Some individuals have difficulty swallowing. Other common symptoms are frequent bouts with bronchitis and recurrent pneumonia. Some people who have GERD may have chest pain that is confused with a HEART ATTACK; however, heart attack should always be ruled out by a CARDIOLOGIST before GERD is considered as a possibility.

Diagnosis of GERD

GERD is often diagnosed based on the presence of chronic heartburn. The doctor should take a full medical history and should also perform a complete physical examination of the patient before prescribing any medications to treat GERD. Laboratory screening tests are also appropriate, and the patient should have a complete blood count (CBC) and any other appropriate tests that the doctor recommends.

The patient may also be diagnosed during an endoscopy, in which a special instrument is inserted down the throat and into the esophagus and then the stomach, to visualize the inner esophagus and stomach.

Treatment

People diagnosed with GERD may be treated with medications, lifestyle recommendations, and, if necessary, surgery, although surgery is not the usual treatment. The endoscopy can also detect other medical problems, such as HIATAL HERNIAS, ULCERS, or STOMACH CANCER.

Recommended Medications   Most patients are treated with a drug in the proton-pump inhibitor class, such as Prilosec (omeprazole) or Prevacid (lansoprazole). Some patients will also need to take a drug in the histamine-2 inhibitor class, such as Tagamet (cimetidine) or Zantac (ranitidine). If the patient also has KIDNEY DISEASE, the medication dosage may need to be adjusted.

Drugs to be Avoided Some medications should be avoided whenever possible by people with GERD because they may further aggravate the condition. Some examples of drugs that patients should try to avoid when possible are:

- Progesterone
- Calcium channel blockers
- Nonsteroidal antiinflammatory drugs
- Steroid medications
- Potassium
- Tetracycline

Some herbal remedies should also be avoided, particularly goldenseal and peppermint.

Lifestyle Changes Most doctors also strongly advise patients with GERD to make changes in their lifestyle, such as raising the head of their beds so that they are less likely to experience acid reflux at night. Patients who are overweight are urged to lose weight because obesity can worsen the symptoms of GERD. Patients are also urged to exercise but should avoid weightlifting and other strenuous exercises, instead, concentrating on walking, riding a stationary bicycle, or any other form of low-impact aerobic activity.

Dietary changes can also improve symptoms; for example, patients should forgo consuming chocolate, colas, and dairy products. Mint may also exacerbate the condition. Other foods may improve symptoms, such as ginger.

Carruthers-Czyzewski, Patricia, BscPhm, Msc. "Seniors' Health: GERD in Older Adults," *Canadian Pharmaceutical Journal* 132, no. 2 (1999): 28–32.
Minocha, Anil, and Christine Adamec. *How to Stop Heartburn: Simple Ways to Heal Heartburn and Acid Reflux.* New York: John Wiley & Sons, 2001.
Middlemiss, Carol. "Gastroesophageal Reflux Disease: A Common Condition in the Elderly," *Nurse Practitioner* 22, no. 11 (November 1998): 51–60.

geriatric specialists Individuals who are experts in dealing with the problems of people age 65 and older, such as gerontologists, geriatric psychiatrists, and physicians who specialize in providing care and treatment for older people. Many physicians have a keen interest in caring for senior adults, and this factor, in and of itself, often makes those doctors good choices.

Geriatric specialists who care for older patients usually understand the complexities that many patients face, such as multiple medical problems, multiple medications, separation from their children and friends, and emotional issues regarding their altered health and body image.

gingivitis Serious gum inflammation and infection. Gingivitis is an early stage of periodontal disease and is very common among seniors, especially those who do not see a dentist on a regular basis. If left untreated, gingivitis may lead to periodontitis, which can cause bone and tooth loss. Many older people must wear DENTURES because they failed to care for their teeth and gums and also failed to see a dentist on at least an annual basis.

Risk Factors

DIABETES is a risk factor for developing gingivitis. Another risk factor is SMOKING. This is yet another good reason for smokers to end their smoking.

Medications may be another cause of gingivitis; for example, many different medications have a side effect of creating chronic dry mouth (xerostomia), which can increase the risk for gingivitis.

Symptoms

The key symptoms of gingivitis are painful bleeding gums and separation of the gums from the teeth, although these symptoms are often minor and unnoticeable to the average person. This is another reason why it is important for older people to see a dentist at regular intervals.

Diagnosis of Gingivitis

Gingivitis is easily diagnosed by a dentist, who will then recommend treatment for the problem. In most cases, regular tooth brushing, flossing, and dental checkups will resolve the problem. If the disease has progressed further to periodontitis, then gum surgery may be needed.

Seniors should brush their teeth twice each day and floss once daily. A dentist should be called if any of the following problems is observed:

- Bleeding gums
- Puffy, swollen, tender gums
- Persistent bad breath
- Gums that appear to recess from teeth
- A change in the fit of dentures

National Institutes of Health. "21: Oral Health," in *Healthy People 2010.* National Institutes of Health (2000).

glaucoma Serious eye disease in which the fluid pressure inside the eye increases and may damage the optic nerve of the eye; the leading cause of blindness in the world. Glaucoma is highly treatable when it is diagnosed in an annual eye examination. For this reason, seniors should see an optometrist or OPHTHALMOLOGIST on an annual basis or more frequently if they notice any problems, such as more impaired version or eye pain. In 2002, MEDICARE announced a new benefit: individuals covered by Part B Medicare were eligible for annual glaucoma screenings.

About 3 million people in the United States have glaucoma, and an estimated 120,000 have become blind from the disease. Worldwide, an estimated 66.8 million people were affected by glaucoma in 2000, and of these people, about 6.7 million people became blind in both eyes. There are few or no symptoms of glaucoma in the early stages, although an eye professional such as an ophthalmologist or an optometrist could detect the disease with special equipment that is used in an annual eye examination. This is yet another reason for an annual eye examination.

Early Treatment Is Essential

Study results released in 2002 underlined the importance of early screening and treatment of glaucoma as very important for seniors. In a clinical study of 255 patients from Sweden and New York, all of whom were diagnosed with early glaucoma and were ages 50 to 80 years old (the Early Manifest Glaucoma Trial), researchers placed patients into two groups. In one group, patients were treated immediately with medications and laser treatments of their eyes. Patients in the second group were not treated. Both groups were followed carefully, and if a patient's glaucoma in the control/nontreatment group became worse, he or she was treated.

After six years, researchers found that disease progression was less common (45 percent) in the patients in the treated group than in those in the control group (62 percent). This finding indicates that early treatment can delay the progress of the disease for some patients. It also makes the need for annual eye screenings very clear, because most patients have no symptoms in the early stages of glaucoma, but an eye examination can detect early glaucoma.

Types of Glaucoma

There are two types of glaucoma: closed-angle and open-angle glaucoma. Open-angle glaucoma is more common and leads to painless progressive visual loss. Because it causes no pain, a patient easily ignores it. Closed-angle glaucoma refers to a narrowing of the angle of the eye such that the aqueous fluid does not flow properly. It is very painful to the patient, and it must be treated immediately.

Risk Factors

Glaucoma is the biggest cause of BLINDNESS among AFRICAN AMERICANS. The disease becomes increasingly likely to occur with aging and is most common among African Americans, people older than age 60, and those who have a history of glaucoma in their family. Among men older than age 75 in the United States, 85.3 per 1,000 men have glaucoma. The rate is lower among women who are older than age 75: 65.6 per 1,000 (still a very high rate).

The primary risk factors for developing the most common form of glaucoma, which is open-angle glaucoma, are advanced age, race (with African Americans at greatest risk), a family medical history of glaucoma, and raised intraocular pressure of the eye, a measurement that can be taken during an eye examination.

Unfortunately, many older people do not have these examinations. The consequences of not diagnosing and treating glaucoma can be very grim. The increased pressure in the eye caused by glaucoma can cause damage to the optic nerve and can result in vision impairment and even blindness.

Symptoms of Glaucoma

In the early stages of glaucoma, there may be no symptoms at all, although the disease is usually detectable by an eye professional during an eye examination. As the disease progresses, patients may notice a worsening of their peripheral (side) vision. Another symptom of open-angle glaucoma that may occur is worse night vision. Some symptoms of closed-angle glaucoma are pain, headache, and nausea/vomiting.

Diagnosis and Treatment

The diagnosis of glaucoma involves both the measurement of intraocular pressure as well as a determination of visual fields. An annual dilated-eye examination is recommended for all seniors to determine the presence of glaucoma, CATARACTS, MACULAR DEGENERATION, or other eye diseases. Patients with DIABETES should also be sure to tell their ophthalmologists or optometrists that they have this illness so that the eye professional can be even more aware of potential problems to look for.

If open-angle glaucoma is diagnosed, the treatment is usually prescribed eye drops. For closed-angle glaucoma, the patient is likely to require surgery or laser treatment of the afflicted eye.

According to Dr. Alward in his 1998 article in the *New England Journal of Medicine,* if topical medications don't work, other drugs are added. If these also fail to reduce the intraocular pressure, then lasers may be used. If lasers also fail, surgery may be required.

Many patients are first prescribed timolol maleate, a beta adrenergic antagonist drug. If necessary, a prostaglandin analogue may be added, such as latanoprost, or other drugs may be tried. Usually, one eye is treated at a time so that the untreated eye can be observed to compare against.

The oldest glaucoma drugs (used since the 1870s) are cholinergic agonist drugs. The most frequently used medication in this class is pilocarpine.

In the recent past, some doctors have noted that marijuana had the effect of reducing intraocular pressure. Some studies have shown a reduction in pressure; others have shown no such reduction. However, marijuana also causes other side effects, such as alternations in mental status, heart palpitations, low blood pressure (hypotension), and tachycardia. Dr. Wallace states, "There is concern that a deleterious effect on optic-nerve blood flow, resulting from systemic hypotension, might offset any benefit of reduced intraocular pressure."

For further information on glaucoma, contact the following organizations:

The Glaucoma Foundation
116 John Street
Suite 1605
New York, NY 10038
(800) GLAUCOMA (toll-free) or (212) 651-1900
http://www.glaucoma-foundation.org

Glaucoma Research Foundation
200 Pine Street
Suite 200
San Francisco, CA 94104
(800) 926-6693 (toll-free)
http://www.glaucoma.org

Alward, Wallace L.M., M.D. "Medical Management of Glaucoma," *New England Journal of Medicine* 339, no. 18 (October 29, 1998): 1,298–1,307.

global aging   The United States and Canada are not the only countries that are experiencing an aging population. As technology, medications, and better infection control enable treatment or prevention of the diseases that once killed so many people, populations all over the globe are aging.

As of 2000, ITALY was the country with the largest percentage of older people, with 18 percent of Italy's entire population age 65 and older. Greece and Sweden followed, both at 17.3 percent, and then Japan, at 17.0 percent. In contrast, less than 13 percent of the U.S. population was age 65 or older in 2000.

The global numbers of the OLDEST OLD (individuals age 80 and older) are also growing, with large percentages in China and the United States. In looking at all the people age 80 and older in the entire world in 2000, China had 16.3 percent of this population, and the United States had 13.1 percent.

Senior Population Not Projected to Be High in All Countries

Some countries are projected to experience low increases in the percentages of older citizens from 2000 to 2030; for example, Bulgaria is projected to have the lowest increase of 52 countries, or 14 percent. Other countries with low projected increases are Ukraine (21 percent), Hungary, (37 percent), and Malawi (41 percent). In contrast, during this same period, the increase in the elderly population is projected at 126 percent in CANADA and 102 percent in the United States.

Aging in Developing (Poor) Countries

Global aging is not limited to North America or Europe, contrary to popular opinion. The reality is that in many developing countries, the older population is large and is also growing. More than half (59 percent) of the entire world's population of people age 65 and older live in developing nations—an estimated 249 million people in 2000. This percentage is predicted to increase to 686 million people by 2030, based on information provided by the U.S. Census Bureau. This increased proportion of the older population in poor countries is based on several changes, such as decreased fertility (fewer babies are being born in many countries) and radically improved health measures that extend lives, such as better infection control and elimination of pestilence.

For example, the population of individuals age 65 and older is predicted to increase by 372 percent in Singapore, the largest increase of any country in the world. Singapore's increased and burgeoning senior population is projected to be followed by Malaysia (277 percent), Colombia (258 percent), and Costa Rica (250 percent).

Some poor countries will continue to have low life expectancies, primarily because of AIDS, particularly African countries such as Malawi, Swaziland, Zambia, and Zimbabwe.

An Increased Pace of Aging

According to the U.S. Census Bureau, the population of seniors in the world has been growing for centuries, but what has changed is the pace: it has speeded up.

According to authors Kevin Kinsella and Victoria A. Velkoff in their report for the U.S. Census Bureau, *An Aging World: 2001,*

> The global population ages 65 and over was estimated to be 420 million people as of midyear 2000, an increase of 9.5 million since midyear 1999. The net balance of the world's elderly population grew by more than 795,000 people each month during the year. Projections to the year 2010 suggest that the net monthly gain will then be on the order of 847,000 people. In 1990, 26 nations had elderly populations of at least 2 million, and by 2000, 31 countries had reached the 2-million mark. Projections to the year 2030 indicate that more than 60 countries will have 2 million or more people age 65 and over.

Adjustments to Large Numbers of Seniors

Countries with increasing numbers of seniors will also need to adapt to their needs in a variety of foreseeable as well as not yet foreseeable ways. Older individuals will require more medical care and medications. Interestingly, however, health costs may drop after a certain age and cannot be predicted to rise with every year of age. According to the Census Bureau, there are indications that health-care costs taper off after age 79. Perhaps people who live long lives are healthier than expected, or other factors may be at work.

Many Older People Live Alone

Although it is generally believed that most older people either live with their adult children or in a nursing home, the reality is that many seniors continue to live on their own in countries around the globe. The percentages of older people living alone vary greatly from country to country. For example, more than half (52 percent) of older women in Denmark live alone and not in an institution, followed by Germany at 50.8 percent.

In the United States, about 36.8 percent of older women live alone, and in Canada, that percentage is 33.7 percent. The percentages of older men living alone are much lower in nearly all countries, which may be because older men are much more likely to remarry than older women. (See HOUSING/LIVING ARRANGEMENTS.)

See also CARDIOVASCULAR DISEASE; DIABETES; HOME HEALTH CARE; HYPERTENSION; WORK.

Kinsella, Kevin, and Victoria A. Velkoff. *An Aging World: 2001.* Washington, D.C.: U.S. Census Bureau, 2001.

gout   A form of arthritis that usually affects one joint at a time, causing it to be extremely inflamed and painful. The joint may be anywhere in the body, although it often is located in the toe or ankle. Most gout sufferers are male, but women may also develop gout, especially when they have hypertension or kidney disease.

According to Joel R. Pittman, Pharm. D and Michael H. Bross, M.D., a key risk factor which is often (but not always) found in people with gout is a temporary buildup of uric acid (hyperuricemia) that concentrates in the joint. It is also true that some people with hyperuricemia do not have gout, and some people who do not have hyperuricemia develop gout.

Gout eventually dissipates, but a gout attack may recur in the same area of the body or in another joint. Repeated attacks in the same joint may ultimately destroy that joint. People with chronic attacks of gout are often placed on medication such as allopurinol, which dilutes the amount of uric acid circulating in the blood. Recurrent attacks can lead to the breakdown and destruction of the affected joint, and this situation is to be avoided if at all possible.

Gout was once thought to be a disease of rich people who ate and drank to excess; however, it can occur to people who are middle class or poor and who eat a normal diet. Individuals with chronic attacks of gout often also suffer from HYPERTENSION and may also have KIDNEY DISEASE as well.

Symptoms

Often, the onset of gout occurs at night and is extremely painful, waking the individual up. The affected area is inflamed and puffy, and the problem is clearly apparent to a layperson. If the gout is in the foot, toe, or ankle, the individual may have great difficulty walking or be unable to use that leg until the gout disappears, which may take a day or so.

Diagnosis

Gout is commonly seen by many physicians, particularly those who treat middle-aged and older people. The possibility of septic arthritis should also be considered. Doctors may aspirate crystals from the affected area; however, in practice, most physicians would not put patients through such a painful procedure, particularly if the diagnosis appears evident.

Treatment

Most physicians recommend dietary changes to patients with gout, such as the avoidance of shellfish and other foods with a high purine content. It is also important to gain better blood-pressure control and also to work on any problems with high CHOLESTEROL. However, most people with gout will also require medication. Doctors may prescribe a nonsteroidal antiinflammatory drug, such as Indocin (indomethacin), Anaprox (naproxen sodium), or Clinoril (sulindac). Alternatively, physicians may prescribe colchicine, or corticosteroid drugs.

For people with chronic recurrences of gout because of hyperuricemia, doctors often place patients on maintenance doses of drugs such as Zyloprim (allopurinol). This drug may have a side effect of causing gastrointestinal disturbance, skin rash, and leukopenia, which is a drop in the white blood-cell count. Patients who have kidney disease will need a careful adjustment of their dosage.

Other drugs that are used are Benemid (probenecid) and Anturane (sulfinpyrazone). These drugs are called uricosuric medications and are used in patients who are underexcretors of uric acid. They are contraindicated in patients with a low urinary output, which is often a problem among older individuals.

See also FOOT DISEASES.

Pittman, Joel R., Pharm. D. and Michael H. Bross, M.D. "Diagnosis and Management of Gout," *American Family Physician* (April 1, 1999).

government, federal   Refers to national government organizations in the United States. There are many federal organizations that directly affect the lives of older people, such as the SOCIAL SECURITY

ADMINISTRATION, which administers monthly payments of Social Security benefits, and the CENTERS FOR MEDICARE AND MEDICAID SERVICES (CMS), which oversees the MEDICARE system. THE NATIONAL INSTITUTES OF HEALTH (NIH) oversees a broad array of federal agencies that perform and analyze research, such as the CENTERS FOR DISEASE CONTROL AND PREVENTION (CDC).

The federal government also oversees programs that affect HOUSING, NUTRITION, and many other aspects of life for older individuals.

government, state   Refers to organizations within state government. Although federal government organizations are important to older individuals, state governments are also vitally important as well. States vary a great deal in the array of services that they provide to older individuals. Some states have many programs, while others have few. Some states provide benefits not mandated by federal law under their MEDICAID programs; others provide only what is required by federal law.

State laws vary considerably with regard to how ESTATE PLANNING may proceed, how MENTAL-COMPETENCY issues are managed, the extent of housing programs for older individuals, specific DRIVING rules for older individuals (if any), and numerous other areas that affect the lives of senior citizens.

grandparents/great-grandparents   Adults whose children (or grandchildren) have had children. In increasing numbers of cases, grandparents are rearing their grandchildren (or helping to rear them) and even their great-grandchildren. This may be because the parents are deceased, unemployed, ill, in jail, or for some other reason.

In 1970, there were 2.3 million children, which was 3.2 percent of all children, who lived in a household headed by a grandparent. By 1997, the number of children living with their grandparents had increased to 3.9 million, or about 5.5 percent of all children. (See Table 2.) In some cases, the children also lived with their parents (almost always their mother) in the grandparent's household; in other cases, their grandparents were raising them without the parent. (See Table 1.) In 1997, there were 1.3

million grandparent-only households, with no parents living with the family.

Differences Among Grandmothers and Grandfathers

Most grandparents maintaining households with children are grandmothers, and in 1997, there were 3.7 million grandmothers and grandfathers whose grandchildren lived with them. (Some of these families included the children's parents.) There are some gender and racial differences between grandmothers and grandfathers who maintain a household for their grandchildren; for example, grandfathers are more likely to be white and continuing to work. They are also less likely to be poor than grandmothers.

Children Living with Grandparents

Many of the children living with their grandparents are young, and about half (46 percent) are age six and younger.

Race also plays a factor among children living with their grandparents. Most children living in a grandparent-maintained home are white (42 percent) versus 36 percent who are African American and only 16.5 percent who are Hispanic. (See Table 2.)

Geographic area is also significant. The largest proportion of children living (co-resident) with their grandparents (with or without their parents present) are in the South (39.3 percent), followed by the West (24.5 percent), the Northeast (20.1 percent), and with the least in the Midwest (16.1 percent).

When children live with their grandparents, they are about three times *less* likely to have health insurance than when they live with one or both parents. Most children living with grandparents have either public insurance (welfare) at 31.3 percent, or they have no health insurance (29.2 percent). This factor is unaffected by race, and white, black, and Hispanic children are equally likely to be uninsured in this situation. However, black and Hispanic children who live with their grandparents are more likely to be living in poverty than are white children.

Casper, Lynn M., and Kenneth R. Bryson. "Co-resident Grandparents and Their Grandchildren: Grandparent Maintained Families." Washington, D.C.: Population Division, U.S. Bureau of the Census, Population Division Working Paper No. 26, March 1998.

TABLE 1 CHARACTERISTICS OF GRANDPARENTS WHO ARE CORESIDENTS WITH GRANDCHILDREN: 1997
(Numbers in thousands. Percent distribution of characteristics)

Characteristics	All coresident grandparent families	Grandparent-maintained families						Parent-maintained families				
		Total	Both grandparents, some parents	Both grandparents, no parent	Grandmother only, some parents	Grandmother only, no parent	Grandfather only	Total	Both grandparents	Grandmother only, two parents	Grandmother only, one parent	Grandfather only
Grandparents, total (number)	4,674	3,694	1,676	824	702	340	152	980	204	324	211	242
Grandmothers, total (number)	2,928	2,292	838	412	702	340	(X)	636	101	324	211	(X)
Percent distribution of grand-mothers	100.0	100.0	100.0	100.0	100.0	100.0	(X)	100.0	100.0	100.0	100.0	(X)
Race and Ethnicity												
White, non-Hispanic	46.9	48.0	56.7	62.8	38.6	27.9	(X)	42.8	40.7	51.0	31.2	(X)
Black, non-Hispanic	27.8	31.0	16.0	18.8	45.4	53.5	(X)	16.2	3.4	6.3	37.6	(X)
Hispanic	17.7	16.4	20.5	15.3	12.5	15.8	(X)	22.3	25.6	20.5	23.4	(X)
Other, non-Hispanic	7.6	4.5	6.8	3.2	3.5	2.8	(X)	18.7	30.2	22.2	7.8	(X)
Age												
Younger than 45	16.6	19.4	22.9	14.8	24.2	6.9	(X)	6.3	6.8	0.7	14.5	(X)
45 to 54	31.9	36.0	42.0	35.2	30.1	34.1	(X)	17.2	22.9	13.0	20.9	(X)
55 to 64	28.9	29.5	26.5	36.4	25.4	36.9	(X)	26.7	46.4	22.6	23.7	(X)
65 and older	22.7	15.1	8.6	13.6	20.3	22.2	(X)	49.8	23.9	63.7	40.9	(X)
Marital Status												
Married, spouse present	48.6	56.1	100.0	100.0	4.8	0.9	(X)	21.4	97.8	5.6	9.1	(X)
Divorced, separated	23.5	22.9	(X)	(X)	50.4	50.3	(X)	25.8	0.0	24.1	40.8	(X)
Widowed	22.0	15.4	(X)	(X)	32.9	36.1	(X)	45.5	0.0	66.1	35.8	(X)
Never married	5.9	5.5	(X)	(X)	11.9	12.7	(X)	7.3	2.2	4.3	14.3	(X)
Education												
Not high school graduate	38.0	35.5	27.7	41.0	36.6	45.9	(X)	46.8	41.9	49.6	44.8	(X)
High school graduate	39.8	40.2	45.9	39.3	38.5	30.4	(X)	38.6	46.1	35.0	40.4	(X)
At least some college	22.2	24.3	26.4	19.7	25.0	23.7	(X)	14.6	12.0	15.3	14.8	(X)
Work Experience in 1996												
Worked full-time, full-year	32.2	36.9	38.3	32.2	45.6	21.4	(X)	15.3	16.1	11.6	20.5	(X)
Less than full-time, full-year	17.2	19.6	22.5	21.5	16.3	16.8	(X)	8.6	18.6	3.9	11.1	(X)
Did not work	50.6	43.6	39.3	46.3	38.2	61.8	(X)	76.1	65.3	84.5	68.4	(X)
General State of Health												
Excellent	12.4	13.3	14.9	11.6	14.3	9.1	(X)	9.2	11.0	6.5	12.4	(X)
Very Good	21.2	21.9	22.6	27.2	22.9	12.0	(X)	18.5	15.6	22.4	14.0	(X)
Good	31.4	31.2	36.0	32.4	26.4	27.9	(X)	32.1	41.1	33.8	25.1	(X)
Fair or Poor	35.1	33.6	26.5	28.9	36.4	51.0	(X)	40.3	32.3	37.4	48.5	(X)
Poverty Status												
Poor	20.9	23.0	10.0	14.4	26.9	57.2	(X)	13.6	9.5	5.3	28.2	(X)
Not poor	79.1	77.0	90.0	85.6	73.1	42.8	(X)	86.4	90.5	94.7	71.8	(X)
Grandfathers, total (number)	1,746	1,402	838	412	(X)	(X)	152	344	103	(X)	(X)	242
Percent distribution of grand-fathers	100.0	100.0	100.0	100.0	(X)	(X)	100.0	100.0	100.0	(X)	(X)	100.0
Race and Ethnicity												
White, non-Hispanic	57.8	60.3	59.0	63.6	(X)	(X)	58.1	47.9	42.4	(X)	(X)	50.3
Black, non-Hispanic	15.6	18.3	16.2	19.5	(X)	(X)	26.0	4.8	3.4	(X)	(X)	5.4
Hispanic	19.7	17.3	19.2	14.6	(X)	(X)	14.1	29.7	24.2	(X)	(X)	32.1
Other, non-Hispanic	6.8	4.2	5.6	2.2	(X)	(X)	1.7	17.5	29.9	(X)	(X)	12.3
Age												
Younger than 45	13.3	14.9	16.9	11.0	(X)	(X)	13.8	7.2	11.7	(X)	(X)	5.2
45 to 54	28.3	32.0	38.4	23.7	(X)	(X)	19.3	13.2	12.4	(X)	(X)	13.6
55 to 64	30.8	32.6	29.9	38.8	(X)	(X)	31.0	23.6	34.3	(X)	(X)	19.0
65 and older	27.5	20.5	14.8	26.5	(X)	(X)	35.9	56.1	41.6	(X)	(X)	62.2
Marital Status												
Married, spouse present	79.8	90.1	100.0	100.0	(X)	(X)	8.6	38.1	96.7	(X)	(X)	13.2
Divorced, separated	9.9	6.1	(X)	(X)	(X)	(X)	56.0	25.5	0.0	(X)	(X)	36.3
Widowed	9.1	3.2	(X)	(X)	(X)	(X)	29.0	33.4	0.0	(X)	(X)	47.5
Never married	1.2	0.7	(X)	(X)	(X)	(X)	6.4	3.0	3.3	(X)	(X)	2.9
Education												
Not high school graduate	39.9	37.1	35.3	40.6	(X)	(X)	37.7	51.2	36.4	(X)	(X)	57.5
High school graduate	36.8	37.1	37.6	36.1	(X)	(X)	36.6	35.6	41.7	(X)	(X)	33.1
At least some college	23.3	25.8	27.1	23.3	(X)	(X)	25.6	13.1	21.9	(X)	(X)	9.4
Work Experience in 1996												
Worked full-time, full-year	48.1	54.5	59.9	49.5	(X)	(X)	38.7	22.0	33.7	(X)	(X)	17.0
Less than full-time, full-year	16.3	17.5	17.4	19.9	(X)	(X)	12.0	11.3	9.8	(X)	(X)	12.0
Did not work	35.6	27.9	22.7	30.6	(X)	(X)	49.3	66.7	56.5	(X)	(X)	71.0
General State of Health												
Excellent	14.1	15.4	15.3	14.7	(X)	(X)	18.0	8.4	8.3	(X)	(X)	8.5
Very Good	21.0	22.0	24.4	21.5	(X)	(X)	10.1	16.7	20.5	(X)	(X)	15.1
Good	33.5	33.9	35.6	31.1	(X)	(X)	31.9	31.9	35.3	(X)	(X)	30.5
Fair or Poor	31.5	28.7	24.6	32.7	(X)	(X)	40.0	43.0	35.9	(X)	(X)	46.0
Poverty Status												
Poor	12.0	12.4	10.0	14.4	(X)	(X)	19.9	10.5	9.4	(X)	(X)	11.0
Not poor	88.0	87.6	90.0	85.6	(X)	(X)	80.1	89.5	90.6	(X)	(X)	89.0

(X) Not applicable.   Source: U.S. Bureau of the Census, March 1997 Current Population Survey.

TABLE 2 CHARACTERISTICS OF GRANDCHILDREN WHO ARE CORESIDENTS WITH GRANDPARENTS: 1997
(Numbers in thousands. Percent distribution of characteristics)

Characteristics	All coresident grandparent families	Grandparent-maintained families						Parent-maintained families				
		Total	Both grandparents, some parents	Both grandparents, no parent	Grandmother only, some parents	Grandmother only, no parent	Grandfather only	Total	Both grandparents	Grandmother only, two parents	Grandmother only, one parent	Grandfather only
Grandchildren, total (number)	5,435	3,894	1,241	598	1,144	669	242	1,541	246	630	396	269
Percent distribution of grandchildren	100.0	100.0	100.0	100.0	100.0	100.0	100.0	100.0	100.0	100.0	100.0	100.0
Race and Ethnicity												
White, non-Hispanic	42.5	42.4	51.7	58.0	35.6	19.3	52.3	42.6	38.7	49.0	26.6	54.9
Black, non-Hispanic	30.1	35.9	18.8	22.3	48.6	62.7	23.8	15.2	3.2	7.9	40.7	5.9
Hispanic	18.2	16.5	21.0	15.2	12.5	14.7	20.6	22.6	20.0	21.4	23.7	26.5
Other, non-Hispanic	9.2	5.1	8.5	4.6	3.2	3.3	3.2	19.5	38.2	21.7	9.0	12.7
Age												
Younger than 6	46.0	50.8	66.3	36.1	56.7	27.1	45.6	33.7	49.0	25.8	39.4	29.7
6 to 11	30.9	28.8	24.5	28.9	26.6	40.0	29.8	36.4	33.8	38.5	33.7	38.2
12 to 17	23.1	20.4	9.2	35.0	16.7	32.8	24.7	29.9	17.2	35.7	26.9	32.1
Gender												
Male	48.8	48.3	51.1	43.3	48.6	45.8	50.8	50.1	39.9	55.5	43.1	57.2
Female	51.2	51.7	48.9	56.7	51.4	54.2	49.2	49.9	60.1	45.5	56.9	42.8
Nativity												
U.S. born, U.S. parents	77.7	86.7	80.1	87.8	90.2	92.7	84.2	55.0	43.7	48.1	68.1	62.1
U.S. born, 1 foreign parent	6.7	6.0	9.1	4.3	4.7	4.2	5.5	8.3	7.7	10.0	6.2	8.1
U.S. born, 2 foreign parents	12.8	5.8	9.6	6.1	3.5	2.1	6.1	30.5	45.7	32.4	22.4	23.9
Foreign born	2.9	1.5	1.1	1.7	1.6	0.9	4.2	6.2	3.0	9.5	3.3	5.8
General State of Health												
Excellent	40.7	39.6	42.2	40.4	42.3	34.6	24.9	43.4	53.4	42.1	35.7	48.8
Very good	29.0	27.8	28.1	30.3	25.7	26.5	33.0	32.2	26.9	35.1	27.0	38.2
Good	25.7	27.5	26.5	24.4	27.2	29.5	36.6	21.2	16.3	19.4	34.0	11.0
Fair or poor	4.6	5.2	3.3	4.9	4.8	9.4	5.5	3.1	3.5	3.4	3.2	2.1
Insurance Coverage												
Private insurance	39.5	30.3	38.2	18.6	38.1	14.0	27.5	62.5	66.4	75.3	42.6	58.2
Public insurance only	31.3	36.3	31.7	27.2	36.8	52.8	34.3	18.8	16.3	9.2	37.0	17.0
No health insurance	29.2	33.4	30.1	54.2	25.2	33.2	38.2	18.7	17.3	15.5	20.4	24.7
Region of U.S.												
Northeast	20.1	18.7	19.1	17.6	15.5	24.2	18.9	23.7	20.8	25.6	25.5	19.1
Midwest	16.1	16.9	15.0	19.1	18.7	17.7	9.4	14.3	7.2	12.6	21.2	14.3
South	39.3	43.3	38.2	44.8	49.6	44.0	34.8	29.0	23.8	22.8	41.2	30.4
West	24.5	21.1	27.7	18.4	16.2	14.0	37.0	33.0	48.2	38.9	12.1	36.2
Metropolitan Area Status												
Central city	37.8	38.9	31.1	23.9	44.2	60.4	31.2	35.1	33.3	29.7	50.4	26.6
Suburbs	44.5	41.3	51.4	43.4	35.6	26.6	51.8	52.5	50.7	62.6	35.1	56.1
Nonmetropolitan area	17.7	19.8	17.5	32.6	20.2	13.0	16.9	12.5	16.0	7.7	14.6	17.3
Household Members Under 18												
One	29.2	31.9	32.4	48.2	27.6	24.6	30.0	22.3	32.1	21.1	24.4	12.9
Two	31.8	29.2	34.8	15.2	31.4	24.7	37.9	38.2	26.9	37.8	39.1	48.3
Three or more	39.0	38.9	32.9	36.6	41.0	50.7	32.1	39.5	41.0	41.1	36.5	38.8
Earners in Household												
None	11.7	14.4	4.1	11.3	10.7	43.9	10.6	4.8	0.9	0.8	15.1	2.5
One	26.2	27.3	14.6	31.9	31.6	37.9	31.8	23.5	11.7	12.5	47.2	25.2
Two	32.4	28.0	22.7	35.1	37.7	11.3	37.1	43.5	38.9	57.3	27.3	39.4
Three or more	29.7	30.3	58.6	21.7	19.9	6.9	20.5	28.2	48.4	29.4	10.3	33.0
Family Income/Poverty Level												
Under 50 percent of poverty level	9.2	10.7	1.5	6.8	11.5	29.4	12.0	5.4	2.1	0.0	17.4	3.6
50 to 99 percent of poverty level	14.9	16.2	10.1	8.2	18.0	33.4	11.1	11.8	9.6	8.0	21.4	8.4
100 to 149 percent of poverty level	13.7	14.6	11.2	15.8	17.5	16.8	9.6	11.5	10.7	7.6	19.1	10.4
150 to 199 percent of poverty level	12.9	13.5	14.8	14.5	15.0	7.6	13.7	11.4	3.9	11.7	15.7	11.2
200 percent or more of poverty level	49.2	45.0	62.4	54.7	38.0	12.8	53.7	59.9	73.7	72.7	26.4	66.4
Household Public Assistance												
No public assistance	48.1	43.8	58.7	50.7	39.8	15.6	47.2	59.1	69.7	68.1	32.3	67.9
Any public assistance program	51.9	56.2	41.3	49.3	60.2	84.4	52.8	40.9	30.3	31.9	67.7	32.1
School lunch program	37.5	40.0	26.0	34.1	40.3	73.5	32.5	31.1	20.4	24.4	52.4	25.2
Food stamps	26.6	30.3	20.3	20.0	37.6	48.3	22.5	17.3	10.1	10.8	37.9	8.7
AFDC, ADC, TANF, GA	20.6	24.5	18.1	20.8	26.4	40.3	14.1	10.5	2.5	4.1	30.4	3.5
SSI	14.9	15.5	9.9	13.2	16.9	28.1	8.7	13.4	5.3	12.7	22.2	9.7
Housing assistance	7.4	8.5	2.0	3.6	7.5	26.3	9.4	4.5	0.0	3.6	11.2	0.9
Energy assistance	5.2	6.7	3.8	2.9	7.0	17.4	0.0	1.3	0.0	1.3	2.9	0.1

Source: U.S. Bureau of the Census, March 1997 Current Population Survey.

hair loss   See BALDNESS.

headache   Pain in any part of the head and that may be severe. A headache may be a temporary problem resulting from an illness or an infection, or it could result from a minor reaction to a medication.

A headache is sometimes a sign of a severe medical problem. A sudden searing pain should not be ignored. Instead, a physician should be consulted for an evaluation and a treatment plan. If the headache is extremely painful and it is the worst headache the individual has ever had, emergency medical treatment should be sought. Any change in the nature or frequency of a chronic headache condition warrants a medical evaluation.

Some people suffer from chronic tension or migraine headaches, but there are also other forms of headaches; for example, some headaches are associated with MENOPAUSE. Such chronic headaches may be alleviated with HORMONE REPLACEMENT THERAPY (HRT).

People of all ages, races, and ethnicities may suffer from headaches, as may both men and women.

Diagnosis

Physicians ask patients where their heads hurt most to help with the diagnosis. If the pain is in the locations where the sinus cavities are found and the patient is very stuffy and congested, then the doctor may diagnose a sinus infection. If the doctor is concerned about a potentially serious problem, a magnetic resonance imaging (MRI) may be ordered to rule out a BRAIN TUMOR.

The doctor will also ask other questions, such as how frequently the headaches occur, what are the location of the headaches on other occasions, how bad the current headache is, and if the patient has a headache when seeing the doctor. It is important to tell the physician about all medications that are taken, including PRESCRIBED MEDICATIONS, over-the-counter drugs, and any alternative remedies or SUPPLEMENTS. Sometimes, a particular medication or a combination of medications may be inducing the headaches.

The doctor will also ask the patient about events that occurred before the onset of the headache. Some patients with migraine headaches have an "aura" before the headache comes on. They may feel very tired, may see bright lights, or have other precursors to a headache. Stress may also bring on a migraine headache for people who are prone to migraines. Studies of people who suffer from migraines indicate that some people who are severely stressed have a delayed headache, and the migraine may develop as much as a day or so after the stressful event has occurred.

Treatment

Depending on the cause of the headache, the treatment may be medication or even surgery, should the condition be life threatening.

Medications for Headaches   People who have chronic headaches may need to take medication on a regular basis, or they may take medications on an as-needed basis, depending on the particular individual. A variety of different medications may be recommended, including over-the-counter or prescribed painkilling drugs. Nonsteroidal antiinflammatory medications may also be recommended.

Patients who suffer from chronic migraines may benefit from taking Imitrex (sumatriptan) at the first sign of an impending headache. Drugs in the "triptan" class have been proven very effective at stopping headaches.

Lifestyle Actions   Lifestyle changes are often indicated for people with chronic headaches. If STRESS is disrupting the life and health of patients, they need to reduce stress through RELAXATION THERAPY, TAI CHI, or other stress reduction methods.

Changes in Diet   Dietary changes may also be indicated. Caffeine and chocolate can induce headaches in some individuals. People who drink a lot of coffee and tea should generally not stop consuming these caffeinated beverages altogether in one day, but they should instead cut back the consumption slowly. Suddenly eliminating caffeine from the diet can cause a severe headache because the body is so used to receiving the caffeine.

Physical Therapy or Chiropractic Treatment   Physical therapy or chiropractic treatment may help some patients, particularly those who have neck pain along with their headaches. Exercises tailored to the individual by the physical therapist can often help alleviate or at least improve the headache symptoms.

Biondi, David M., D.O., and Josel R. Saper, M.D. "Geriatric Headache: How to Make the Diagnosis and Manage the Pain," *Geriatrics* 55, no. 12 (2000): 40–50.
Kandel, Joseph, M.D. and David Sudderth, M.D. *Migraine: What Works.* Rocklin, Calif.: Prima Publishing, 2000.

Health Care and Financing Administration (HCFA)
Former name of the CENTERS FOR MEDICARE AND MEDICAID SERVICES (CMS).

hearing aid   A form of ASSISTIVE DEVICE that is worn on or in the ear and that boosts sound and enables people with impaired hearing to hear significantly better. After hearing is tested, audiologists can determine whether or not a hearing device is needed, and if needed, they can advise the individual on the type that is recommended.

Many people are resistant to the idea of wearing a hearing aid or even considering that they may actually have a hearing impairment. They may see a hearing impairment as a sign that they are "old." Even when the individual is in his or her 70s or 80s, he or she may react this way, no matter how silly and self-defeating it may seem to others around them.

Assuming that such psychological barriers are not present or are overcome, before buying a hearing aid, a patient usually obtains a medical clearance, signed by a doctor, stating that the patient might benefit from wearing a hearing aid. It is important to buy a hear-

ing aid from a company that will provide advice and assistance during the adjustment process. Because it is often necessary for the patient to try several hearing aids before finding one that feels comfortable and works well, the sales contract should guarantee the patient a trial period of use so that the device can be turned back in if it is not effective for the patient.

Many patients wear their hearing aids incorrectly; for example, they wear the aids on occasion but frequently take the aids out during the course of the day. This is very confusing to the brain, much as would be the effect of taking eyeglasses off and on. Constantly taking off glasses would lead to dizziness and poor vision, just as the pattern of part-time hearing-aid use leads to suboptimal hearing.

See HEARING DISORDERS.

hearing disorders   A variety of acute and chronic hearing impairments that affect the ability to detect, recognize, or tolerate sound by distorting or amplifying sound. Hearing disorders may be minor, involving poor hearing that can be improved with assistance or diagnosis of the medical problem causing the poor hearing. It may also be as severe as a complete hearing loss.

Hearing disorders can affect concentration, impair sleep, and also affect an individual's ability to perform everyday tasks or even to maintain balance. The difficulty or inability to hear may occur in either one or both ears. The most common forms of hearing disorders are HEARING LOSS (the total lack of hearing ability), tinnitus (ringing in the ears), Ménière's disease, and hyperacusis.

HEARING AIDS may help many individuals to resolve their hearing difficulties; however, many older people are resistant to being tested for hearing disorders or to even considering the possibility of wearing a hearing aid. They may equate using a hearing aid with being older or more disabled than they perceive themselves to be.

Risks for Developing Hearing Impairment
The probability of developing a hearing impairment increases with age and also varies by gender. In general, men have a higher risk of developing a hearing impairment. For example, according to the

CENTERS FOR DISEASE CONTROL AND PREVENTION (CDC), among males ages 45–64 years old, the rate of hearing impairment was 183.4 per 1,000 men in 1996. (See Table 1.) This rate nearly doubled to 342.6 for men ages 65–74 and increased still further to 457.9 for males age 75 and older.

Among women, the rates of hearing impairment were lower than among men, but they also increased with aging. Women ages 45–64 had a hearing impairment rate of 82.9 per 1,000 women, which more than doubled to 184.5 for those ages 65–74. The rate increased dramatically to 315.5 for women older than age 75.

TABLE 1 NUMBERS OF HEARING IMPAIRED PER 1,000 FOR MEN AND WOMEN BY AGE IN THE UNITED STATES, 1996

Men		Women	
Ages		**Ages**	
45 to 64	183.4	**45 to 64**	82.9
65 to 74	342.6	**65 to 74**	184.5
Older than 75	457.9	**Older than 75**	315.5

Source: Centers for Disease Control and Prevention (CDC)

Tinnitus

Tinnitus is a constant or an intermittent ringing in the ears. The American Tinnitus Association estimates that approximately 50 million Americans hear ringing, hissing, or other sounds that other people usually cannot hear. Tinnitus occurs in 10–20 percent of the general population and is present in nearly one-third of adults older than 70.

Age-related nerve impairment is the chief cause of tinnitus among older individuals. Other risk factors for tinnitus include:

- Wax in the ear canal
- Stiffening of bones in the middle ear (otosclerosis)
- Allergy
- High or low blood pressure
- Tumor
- DIABETES
- Thyroid abnormalities
- Head or neck injury

Because the specific source of tinnitus can rarely be identified, the condition can rarely be cured. Strategies to relieve the symptoms include:

- Medications, such as antidepressants or antianxiety medications
- Avoidance of loud noises
- Electrical stimulation procedures
- Limiting of caffeine and tobacco
- Rest
- Biofeedback
- Hearing aids, sleep machines, and masking devices that offset symptoms

Ménière's Disease

A disorder of the inner ear, which controls balance. Ménière's disease is usually characterized by a sensation of spinning (vertigo); nausea and vomiting may also accompany the disorder. In about one patient in five, Ménière's disease involves both ears. The second ear often becomes affected two or three years after symptoms first appear.

In later stages of this disease, violent attacks of vertigo occur less often and then stop altogether. Sporadic bouts of tinnitus may become permanent. Doctors refer to these changes in the nature of the disease as "Ménière's burnout."

The following symptoms may also occur:

- tinnitus
- feelings of pressure inside one or both ears
- fluctuating hearing loss

Many scientists believe that Ménière's disease results from a tear in the membranous labyrinth, which is the site that regulates hearing and balance. Other suspected risk factors include:

- STRESS
- Excessive salt in the diet
- Endocrine or thyroid problems
- Abnormal sugar metabolism
- High CHOLESTEROL and/or triglyceride levels
- Excessive levels of alcohol, caffeine, and nicotine

Stages of Ménière's Disease   The early stages of Ménière's disease may last more than a year. During that time, symptoms may appear and subside unpredictably, with months or more between attacks. Symptoms of dizziness, nausea, or tinnitus that affect one ear may abate within 10 minutes, or they may last all day. In general, overall unsteadiness is more persistent than other symptoms, and it may last for days.

Diagnosing of Ménière's Disease   The diagnosis of Ménière's disease usually involves confirming the presence and cause of edema, measuring changes in sound recognition after drinking glycerine, and observing eye movements to evaluate balance (electronystagmography).

Electronystagmography is also used to evaluate patients who complain of dizziness. When posturography, another diagnostic tool, is used to diagnose balance disorders, the patient stands on a special platform. As the platform moves, the patient's body sway is recorded.

Treatment of Ménière's   Although Ménière's disease cannot be cured, medical management can control or eliminate the vertigo symptoms in about 70 percent of patients. Eliminating tobacco, alcohol, caffeine, and monosodium glutamate (MSG) a food additive, can also improve Ménière's symptoms. Other beneficial approaches include medication to reduce the retention of salt and water; control the symptoms of dizziness, nausea, and vomiting; and improve the circulation in the inner ear.

If Ménière's symptoms remain uncontrolled or debilitating after two months of medical treatment, surgery may be indicated if the physician believes that the older person can tolerate the procedure. The key surgical options include:

- Endolymphatic shunt or decompression procedure, which involves inserting a tiny silicone tube to drain excess fluid from the inner ear. This procedure usually preserves hearing and provides at least temporary vertigo control in 50–66 percent of patients.

- Selective vestibular neurectomy severs the balance nerve to prevent it from sending distorted signals to the brain. Vertigo is almost always permanently cured. Hearing is usually preserved.

- Labryinthectomy is an irreversible procedure that destroys the balance and hearing mechanism in the affected ear. More successful than other procedures in eliminating vertigo, labryinthectomy may cause other balance difficulties.

Hyperacusis

This disorder can transform sounds that do not annoy most people into sources of irritation and even pain. Some people who have hyperacusis are unable to tolerate ordinary noises such as a drawer opening or water running.

This heightened sensitivity to sound, which rarely affects people who do *not* have tinnitus, affects 20–45 percent of those who *do*. Occurring in people with normal hearing as well as in people whose hearing is impaired, hyperacusis can become painful enough to restrict ordinary activities.

Hyperacusis usually results from one-time or repeated exposure to excessive noise. Silence aggravates hyperacusis, which may also stem from:

- Head injury
- Bell's palsy
- Chronic fatigue syndrome
- Autoimmune disorder
- Epilepsy
- Medication
- Lyme disease
- Infection
- Temporomandibular joint syndrome (TMJ)

Hyperacusis management involves providing ear plugs, advising the patient to avoid loud noises, and recommending that patients replace or disable their doorbells, telephone ringers, and other annoying noisemakers. A low-frequency "pink noise" protocol may slowly improve noise tolerance by training patients to become accustomed to listening to sounds in a range slightly below their comfort level. Tinnitus retraining therapy, which combines individual counseling with enhanced background noise to make symptoms less noticeable, may also be effective.

For further information, contact the following organizations:

American Academy of Otolaryngology—Head and Neck Surgery
One Prince Street
Alexandria, VA 22314
(703) 519-1589 or (703) 519-1585 (TTY)
http://www.entnet.org

The American Hyperacusis Association, Inc.
545 NE 47th Street
Suite 212
Portland, OR 97213
http://www.americanhyperacusis.com

American Tinnitus Association
P.O. Box 5
Portland, OR 92702-0005
(800) 643-8783 (toll-free)
http://www.ata.org

Ménière's Disease Information Center
http://www.menieresinfo.com

Ruth, Roger A., and Hamill-Ruth, Robin. "A Multidisciplinary Approach to Management of Tinnitus and Hyperacusis," *The Hearing Journal* (November 2001).
Vernon, Jack A., ed. *Tinnitus Treatment and Relief*. Needham Heights, Mass.: Allyn & Bacon, 1998.

hearing loss   A limited ability or an inability to hear or understand speech. Hearing loss is the most common impairment in the United States and the third-most-prevalent chronic condition among older adults. More than 28 million Americans and 120 million people throughout the world are affected by some level of deafness.

Hearing loss may be temporary or permanent, partial or complete and may involve one ear (unilateral hearing loss) or both (bilateral) ears. Asymmetric hearing loss affects both ears but it is more pronounced in one than in the other.

Risk Factors

The primary environmental cause for hearing loss is exposure to noise loud enough to make the ears ring, to make it necessary to shout to be heard, and to make it hard to hear for several hours afterward. More than 30 million Americans are regularly exposed to dangerous noise levels, and about one-third of all hearing loss is at least partially caused by such exposure.

Ongoing noise that is close at hand damages the hearing most quickly, but even a single brief exposure to loud noise can be hazardous. Sources of excessive noise include power tools, yard equipment, snowmobiles, vacuum cleaners, and especially workplace exposure.

Age Risks   People older than age 50 may lose some hearing each year and may find it difficult to follow normal conversation. It is considered normal by many people for someone who has reached the age of 65 to need a hearing aid. Hearing loss affects one in three adults older than 60 and half of those older than 85. Hearing loss is generally more severe in women than in men. However, men are much more likely to suffer from some form of hearing loss than women. (See HEARING DISORDERS.)

Occupational Risks   People in some occupations have a greater risk of incurring a hearing loss. People who have served in the military, as well as construction and airport workers, machinists, and others who were routinely exposed to high noise levels, have a higher-than-average risk of developing early hearing loss and of becoming significantly impaired by the time they reach middle and older age.

Other Risks   An excessive accumulation of ear wax (cerumen), naturally produced in the outer ear, can cause temporary hearing loss, as can a cold or sinus infection or something that is stuck in the ear. People who dive or fly or travel in the mountains may have temporary trouble hearing when the middle-ear pressure is different from the outside air pressure.

Some types of hearing loss run in families. Other causes of hearing loss include:

- head injury or other trauma
- HEART DISEASE
- STROKE
- acoustic neuroma, a tumor that presses on the auditory nerve
- some chemotherapy drugs and other medications
- otosclerosis, a condition preventing sound from reaching the middle ear; the most common cause of hearing loss in older adults
- a cyst or flap of skin (cholesteatoma) growing into the middle ear

Screening for Hearing Loss

Screening for hearing loss begins when the patient responds to a doctor's questions or directions. Asking the doctor to repeat what has been said or speaking in a tone that either changes very often or doesn't change at all may indicate that a person has a hearing loss.

A mild hearing loss may block 25–40 percent of what is said. A person with a moderate hearing loss may miss 50–75 percent of what is said and may hear and understand speech only in face-to-face situations. Some people have a partial hearing loss and lose the ability to hear certain tones. Frequently, the higher tones are lost, but midrange sounds are preserved.

Someone with a severe hearing loss has trouble hearing under any circumstances, and a person whose hearing loss is profound is unable to hear speech and must read lips or rely on other visual clues.

Emotional Response

Hearing-impaired people may feel frustrated, frightened and, isolated by their inability to talk or interact with others. Frequently, those with moderate hearing loss will hear part of a conversation but will miss the main concept. They may "jump in" with comments that are not appropriate to the discussion, and others may think that the individual has a memory or a thinking disorder rather than the real problem, which is a hearing loss.

Many people with hearing problems are embarrassed to seek help, but studies show that wearing a hearing aid enables people with hearing loss to enjoy life more fully.

Symptoms of Hearing Loss

Although hearing loss usually develops gradually and painlessly, warning signs may include:

- ringing or buzzing (tinnitus) in the ears after an exposure to loud noise
- muffling of sounds after hearing an explosion
- difficulty understanding conversation after being in a noisy environment
- an inability to understand conversation except when reading lips in a quiet environment
- difficulty identifying the source of a sound

Diagnosis of Hearing Loss

After determining that ear wax, infection, or illness is not responsible for the hearing loss, a family doctor may evaluate the patient's ability to hear the ticking of a watch or to repeat or to respond to something said in a whisper. If hearing problems are apparent or likely, the doctor may then refer the patient to an audiologist trained to identify and measure hearing loss. The doctor may also send the patient to an otolaryngologist, a physician who treats diseases and conditions of the ear, nose, and throat.

Testing for Hearing Loss

Audiologists and otolaryngologists often use tuning forks to classify the type and degree of hearing loss that the patient has. Audiometry are tests that measure the person's ability to hear certain sounds. The patient is placed in a soundproof room and listens to sounds transmitted through padded earphones. Impedance testing uses a slim, flexible probe to check for middle-ear problems. A magnetic resonance imaging (MRI) scan may be ordered to detect tumors, scars, or injuries. CT scans may be ordered to detect abnormalities in auditory and vestibular pathways whose nerves send the brain sound vibrations and information about the body's position.

Types of Hearing Loss

About 90 percent of hearing loss is sensorineural hearing loss. Also called nerve deafness, this type of hearing loss occurs when nerves leading from the inner ear to the brain are irreversibly damaged. Present at birth or caused by illness, nerve deafness masks distant sounds and the high-pitched voices of women and children.

Sudden sensorineural hearing loss (SSHL) results from head injury, immune-system disease, medication or numerous other causes. SSHL usually involves only one ear, but this disorder requires immediate medical attention. Treatments include steroids, a low-salt diet, or inhaling a mixture of oxygen and carbon dioxide to improve the air and blood flow inside the ear.

About 4,400 cases of SSHL occur in the United States each year. Spontaneous recovery sometimes occurs within the first three days. Other cases improve within two weeks. Good-to-excellent recovery is common, but hearing continues to deteriorate in about 15 percent of patients.

Conductive hearing loss is caused by problems that involve the external or middle ear and can often be corrected with medication or surgery.

Another form of hearing loss is noise-induced hearing loss (NIHL), which results from repeated exposure to loud sounds and affects how completely and clearly a person hears. People with NIHL sometimes have tinnitus, which may diminish or disappear in time.

Mixed hearing loss is a combination of conductive and sensorineural hearing loss. It occurs when someone with a sensorineural hearing loss develops a conductive hearing loss, or the inner and outer ear are malformed. Doctors can treat conductive loss, but sensorineural damage is usually permanent.

Presbycusis, or age-related hearing loss, is the hearing problem that is most prevalent among older adults. To the person with presbycusis, speech sounds slurred, and sounds like *s* and *sh* sound the same. Most people who have presbycusis have trouble tolerating loud noise, and many have tinnitus in one or both ears.

Most doctors think presbycusis results from age-related changes in the middle and inner ear and along the nerve pathways to the brain. It is believed that presbycusis is caused by the cumulative effects of noise, health problems, and medications. People with presbycusis are generally advised to avoid loud noises and to wear ear plugs or special fluid-filled earmuffs to protect their remaining hearing. They are also advised to consider using hearing aids and telephone amplifiers.

Treatment for Hearing Loss

Depending on the cause of hearing loss, using warm water or a cerumen spoon to remove ear wax, medication to cure illness, or surgery to correct abnormalities can significantly improve hearing in many cases. When hearing cannot be restored, adaptive devices can help to amplify sounds and also to reduce background noise. For example, HEARING AIDS can be used to either amplify sounds or to distort aggravating sounds such as with people who have tinnitus, or ringing

in the ears, and who want the inner ear noise to be blocked by special hearing aids.

Another recently developed solution for hearing loss is the cochlear implant. A cochlear implant consists of a headpiece, worn behind the ear, that conveys sound to a speech processor that is kept in a pocket or worn on a belt. A small, round receiver, surgically implanted behind the ear, sends sound signals to the brain.

MEDICARE pays for the costs associated with cochlear implants. As of this writing, Congress is considering legislation in the United States to expand coverage to include the services of audiologists and to provide coverage of wearable, FDA-approved devices designed to compensate for hearing loss.

For further information, contact the following organizations:

American Speech-Language-Hearing Association (ASHA)
10801 Rockville Pike
Dept. AP
Rockville, MD 20852
(800) 638-8255
http://www.asha.org

Self Help for Hard of Hearing People, Inc. (SHHH)
7910 Woodmont Avenue
Suite 1200
Bethesda, MD 20814
(301) 657-2248 or (301) 657-2249 (TTY)
http://www.shhh.org

National Institute on Deafness and Other Communication Disorders (NIDCD)
National Institutes of Health
31 Center Drive
MSC 2320
Bethesda, MD 20892-2320
(800) 241-1044 or (800) 241-1055 (TTY)
http://www.nidcd.nih.gov

National Institute on Aging, U.S. Department of Health and Human Services, U.S. Public Health Service. "Age Page: Hearing and Older People" (1996).
National Institute on Deafness and Other Communication Disorders. "Health Information: Hearing and Balance." NIH Publication No. 01-4913 (January 2001).

heart attack/myocardial infarction Very dangerous and potentially fatal spasm of the heart muscles.
The risk for heart attack increases with age, and once
a person has had one heart attack, the risk for having another one is high. In the United States, about
a million people have heart attacks each year, about
half of which are fatal. In many cases, death occurs
as soon as an hour after the first symptom.

Rapid Treatment
Is Essential

A heart attack can lead to a CARDIAC ARREST, in
which the heart stops beating. Without treatment,
within four to six minutes of cardiac arrest, death
will occur. Even treatment cannot save all cardiac
arrest victims, but it greatly increases the odds of survival. Cardiac arrest patients are treated with electric shocks to the heart (defibrillation) to cause the
heart to resume beating. The symptoms of cardiac
arrest are a loss of consciousness and of normal
breathing and the loss of both pulse and blood pressure. Cardiopulmonary resuscitation (CPR) can
maintain life until emergency medical assistance is
administered.

Risk Factors for Heart Attacks
in Men and Women, by Race

Anyone of any age or race can have a heart attack,
but the risks are highest for older Americans and
they also vary by race and gender.

The AMERICAN HEART ASSOCIATION reports that
among nonblack men (males who were races other
than African American), the rate of new and recurrent heart attacks in 1999 was 39.7 per 1,000 for
nonblack men ages 75–84. This rate leaped upward
to 53.6 per 1,000 for those age 85 and older.

The heart attack rate for black men ages 75–84
was significantly higher than for nonblack men, or
54.9 per 1,000; however, the rate *dropped* for both
black men and black women age 85 and older, possibly because the most susceptible individuals died
before reaching the age of 85.

In contrast to the pattern seen among blacks
whose highest heart-attack rates were ages 75–84,
the heart attack rate was the highest for nonblack
men and women age 85 and older. (See Table 1 for
more data on black and nonblack men and women
and their heart-attack rates.)

Interestingly, NATIVE AMERICANS have a very low
rate of heart attacks, despite the other health problems from which many suffer, such as DIABETES,
HYPERTENSION, and OBESITY. According to the American Heart Association, the annual rates of heart
attacks for Native Americans ages 65–74 is 6.8 per
1,000 for men and 2.2 per 1,000 for women. The
reason for this low rate is unknown.

TABLE 1 HEART ATTACK RATES FOR NEW AND RECURRENT ATTACKS, PER 1,000 POPULATION FOR BLACK AND NONBLACKS, BY GENDER AND AGE, UNITED STATES, 1999				
	Black Men	Black Women	Nonblack Men	Nonblack Women
Ages 65–74	16.3	13.3	26.3	7.8
Ages 75–84	54.9	18.3	39.7	21.0
Age 85+	40.8	14.1	53.6	24.2

Because of the urgency of quick action, in 2001,
the National Heart, Lung, and Blood Institute
(NHLBI) in the United States began a new nationwide campaign "Act in Time to Heart Attack Signs"
to alert and educate Americans about the signs of a
heart attack and how they should react.

Heart Attack Symptoms

According to the NHLBI, common heart-attack
symptoms are:

- Sudden discomfort or pain in the arms, back,
  neck, jaw, or stomach
- Shortness of breath
- A cold sweat
- Chest pain
- Nausea and light-headedness

Treatment

The primary immediate treatments for heart attack
victims are providing thrombolytic drugs to destroy
clots that are blocking the heart. These drugs must
be administered within an hour of the onset of the
heart-attack symptoms. This can actually stop a
heart attack and prevent any permanent damage.
Patients may also need emergency surgery, such as
a coronary angioplasty (also known as balloon

angioplasty) or a coronary artery bypass graft (also known as bypass surgery).

With coronary angioplasty, the cardiac surgeon threads a tiny catheter though an artery and into the blocked heart vessel. The catheter has a special inflatable balloon on the end of it, and the doctor will inflate and deflate the balloon several times to dilate the artery. Often, a "stent" is also inserted, which is a wire mesh tube that helps to keep the artery open after the angioplasty procedure is completed. The stent is a permanent fixture.

With coronary artery bypass surgery, the surgeon takes a vein from some part of the patient, such as the leg or an artery in the chest. This tissue is then attached to the heart artery both above and below the narrowed area, making a bypass around the blockage. This is somewhat comparable to when highway bypasses are created around cities so that drivers can avoid the congestion of driving through the city. Sometimes, coronary bypass surgery needs to be repeated after about 10 years or so because the arteries become blocked again.

Long-Term Considerations

After the patient's survival from a heart attack has been established, there are other issues to consider. If the heart attack patient has HYPERTENSION, it needs to be treated. DEPRESSION is another risk for heart-attack patients, although treated depression is not a safeguard from future heart attacks. An estimated 20 to 40 percent of people who have had a heart attack will suffer from depression within six months after the attack.

EXERCISE and physical training can improve the conditions of people with chronic heart failure. A 2000 study reported in the *European Journal of Heart Failure* revealed that heart-attack patients may safely improve their overall health.

A comprehensive exercise and cardiac rehabilitation program can make a dramatic health improvement.

Kiilavuori, K., et al. "The Effect of Physical Training on Skeletal Muscle in Patients with Chronic Heart Failure," *The European Journal of Heart Failure* 2 (2000): 53–63.

Maheshwari, Alok, M.D. et al. "Acute MI: Age-Related Presentations and Treatment Options," *Geriatrics* 55, no. 2 (2000): 32–40.

heart disease   Chronic or acute malfunction of the heart. Heart disease is the number-one cause of death among all races of people older than age 65 in the United States.

See also CARDIAC ARREST; CARDIOVASCULAR DISEASE; CORONARY HEART DISEASE; HEART ATTACK.

heat exhaustion/heat stroke   Physical collapse due to excessively high body temperatures. In older people, severely hot weather can induce heat stroke and DEHYDRATION.

Risk Factors

People who are obese or who have cardiovascular diseases are more prone to heat stroke. Many people older than age 65 are physically inactive, which is another risk factor. Heat stroke can be fatal if untreated.

Symptoms of Heat Stroke

The following symptoms are indicators of possible heat stroke:

- Sudden onset of exhaustion
- High body temperature
- Accelerated heartbeat (tachycardia)
- Rapid breathing (hyperventilation)

In addition to physical signs, doctors may order blood tests and urinalysis. Blood tests may show abnormal liver results and hypoglycemia (low blood sugar), and the urine may show the presence of or an increase in protein (Proteinuria.) Special tests can also show if the muscles show any sign of damage from the heat stroke.

Treatment for Heat Stroke

Patients who are conscious are urged to drink fluids; if unconscious, fluids are administered intravenously. (Fluids may also be administered intravenously even if the person is conscious.) The person may be immersed in ice water in a hospital emergency-room setting or ice packs may be used to bring down the body temperature. Electrolyte imbalances will be corrected with intravenous fluids. Often, a cooling mist is used to slowly lower the body temperature.

Other Causes of High Body Temperature

Hyperthermia (unusually high body temperature) may also be caused by some medications, particularly amphetamine drugs. ALCOHOLISM may also increase heat intolerance and the risk of hyperthermia. Dehydration is another cause of hyperthermia.

Simon, Harvey B. "Hyperthermia," *New England Journal of Medicine* 329, no. 7 (August 12, 1993): 483–487.

hiatal hernia   A bulging of the stomach that extends into the diaphragm, which is the muscle that separates the abdomen from the chest. It is most commonly found among people who are older than age 50, and the hiatal hernia usually requires no treatment unless there are symptoms such as GASTROESOPHAGEAL REFLUX DISEASE (GERD) or the hernia is twisted and could cut off the blood supply to the stomach.

Risk Factors

Factors that may be related to the development of a hiatal hernia include:

- Physical exertion, particularly weightlifting
- An abdominal injury
- OBESITY
- Constant straining or coughing
- SMOKING

Symptoms

Most hiatal hernias do not cause any symptoms, although some people with gastroesophageal reflux disease (GERD), also known as heartburn, may develop a hiatal hernia. Some experts believe that GERD and hiatal hernia are linked together, although it is unclear which condition causes the other one.

Hiatal hernia may sometimes cause a slow chronic bleeding and may also cause ANEMIA.

Diagnosis

Hiatal hernia is usually diagnosed by a gastroenterologist, who orders a barium swallow or an endoscopy. A barium swallow is a test in which the patient swallows liquid barium and the physician observes its path down the esophagus. An endoscopy is a procedure in which the patient may be mildly sedated while a special scope is inserted down the throat and into the esophagus and the stomach.

Treatment

In most cases, lifestyle changes can improve a hiatal hernia. Doctors may recommend weight loss, especially if the patient has a problem with obesity. Patients are usually advised to eat smaller meals and to eat more frequently. They should avoid any foods or drinks that may cause GERD, such as caffeine and chocolate. Patients who smoke should immediately stop smoking, should avoid lying down until it has been at least three hours since they last ate, and should wear loose-fitting clothes.

If surgery is needed, it is usually performed laparoscopically, which means that the surgeon makes very small incisions in the abdomen.

For more information, contact the following organizations:

International Foundation for Functional Gastrointestinal Disorders (IFFGD)
P.O. Box 170864
Milwaukee, WI 53217
(888) 064-2001 (toll-free) or (414) 964-1799
http://www.iffgd.org

Intestinal Disease Foundation, Inc.
1323 Forbes Avenue
Suite 200
Pittsburgh, PA 15219
(877) 587-9606 or (412) 261-5888

Minocha, Anil, and Christine Adamec. *How to Stop Heartburn: Simple Ways to Heal Heartburn and Acid Reflux.* New York: John Wiley & Sons, 2001.

Minocha, Anil, M.D., FACP, FACG. *The Gastroenterology Resident Pocket Survival Guide.* McLean, Va.: International Medical Publishing, Inc., 1999.

Hispanic Americans   Americans of Spanish, Mexican, Cuban, Latin American, or South American origin. The largest percentage of Hispanic Americans (about 49 percent) are Mexican Americans. The Hispanic population in the United States is growing rapidly, as are the numbers of people older than age 65 who are Hispanic. According to the ADMINISTRATION ON AGING, Hispanic seniors will be the second-fastest-growing population among older people during the years 1990 and 2020.

The key health problems of older Hispanics in the United States are HEART DISEASE, CANCER, DIABETES, CEREBROVASCULAR DISEASE, HIV infection, FLU/INFLUENZA, and PNEUMONIA. Despite the fact that MEDICARE provides coverage for immunizations for pneumonia and flu, only about 15 percent of Hispanic seniors receive these vaccines. It is unknown why this is true.

Many Hispanic seniors have low income, and about 24 percent of older Hispanics live below the POVERTY level, more than twice the level of poverty for older individuals who are white.

According to the ADMINISTRATION ON AGING, the average FAMILY CAREGIVER of older Hispanics is a woman age 40 years.

Administration on Aging. "Serving Our Hispanic American Elders" (2001).

holidays, effect on elders   The effect of key national holiday celebrations on older people. Holidays such as Thanksgiving and Christmas or Hanukkah can be very difficult for older people whose spouses or partners have died and who may be living alone or in a nursing-home environment. Their own birthdays may be sad times for some older people who live alone. They may become extremely lonely and may also suffer from DEPRESSION. Being separated from family and loved ones during the holidays can be hard on anyone; it may be especially difficult on senior adults who may not have adequate support systems to cope with their feelings.

home health-care users   According to the 1996 data from the National Center for Health Statistics, most users of home health-care services in the United States age 65 and older were female (70 percent) and white (69 percent). Most lived in private residences (92 percent), and half of them lived with family members. Older women using home health care were much more likely to be widowed (59 percent) than

older men (19 percent). In addition, the percentage of older women living alone was higher (44 percent) than for older men (27 percent). One reason for the higher proportion of women living alone is that women live longer than men. Another reason may be that older men are much more likely to marry younger women than older women are to marry younger men, probably because of cultural reasons.

Interestingly, when considering the three age ranges studied, of 65–74, 75–84 and 85 years and older, the largest consumers of home health care were *not* the oldest individuals but instead were individuals ages 75–84. One reason for this may be that individuals age 85 and older may no longer be able to live at home and have moved to NURSING HOMES.

See Table 1 for a breakdown of age, race, marital status, living quarters, and living arrangements among older people using home health-care services.

Most home health-care users (50.9 percent) need help with ACTIVITIES OF DAILY LIVING, such as bathing and showering, followed by help with dressing (43 percent.) A large majority also need help with instrumental activities of daily living, such as shopping for groceries or clothes (79.5 percent). Many need assistance with performing light housework (34.1 percent).

Many home health-care users also have problems with INCONTINENCE, and 27.4 percent suffer from URINARY INCONTINENCE.

See table 2 for a breakdown of services that home health-care users need.

Private-Pay Home Care

Some older people or their families hire individuals to provide basic home care to the older person needing assistance. It is very important to check references of any person who is under consideration. Some people who have seemed very "nice" were actually cruel, and they have stolen money and property from the older person.

Medicare and Home Health Care

According to the Centers for Medicare and Medicaid Services, (formerly the Health Care Financing Administration, or HCFA), which is the organization that determines MEDICARE payments, there are several conditions that must *all* be met in order for Medicare to approve home health care. These conditions are:

TABLE 1   NUMBER AND PERCENT DISTRIBUTION OF ELDERLY HOME HEALTH-CARE CURRENT PATIENTS 65 YEARS AND OLDER BY SELECTED DEMOGRAPHIC CHARACTERISTICS, ACCORDING TO SEX: UNITED STATES, 1996

Demographic characteristic	Both sexes[1]		Male		Female	
	Number	Percent distribution	Number	Percent distribution	Number	Percent distribution
Total	1,753,400	100.0	528,300	100.0	1,224,800	100.0
Age						
65–74 years	527,900	30.1	180,400	34.2	347,500	28.4
75–84 years	820,500	46.8	253,500	48.0	566,800	46.3
85 years and older	404,900	23.1	94,400	17.9	310,600	25.4
Race						
White	1,215,300	69.3	353,900	67.0	861,400	70.3
Black and other	214,000	12.2	65,000	12.3	149,100	12.2
Black	190,900	10.9	56,200	10.7	134,700	11.0
Unknown	324,000	18.5	109,400	20.7	214,400	17.5
Hispanic origin						
Hispanic	47,300	2.7	*17,200	*3.27	*30,100	*2.5
Non-Hispanic	1,134,800	64.7	320,000	60.6	814,800	66.5
Unknown	571,200	32.6	191,000	36.2	379,900	31.0
Marital status						
Married	510,600	29.1	268,200	50.8	242,200	19.8
Widowed	820,200	46.8	102,600	19.4	717,700	58.6
Divorced or separated	49,700	2.8	*18,800	*3.6	*31,000	*2.5
Never married/single	144,100	8.2	*49,000	*9.3	95,100	7.8
Unknown	228,700	13.0	89,800	17.0	138,900	11.3
Living quarters						
Private residence	1,616,600	92.2	496,800	94.1	1,119,500	91.4
Rented room and board	*	*	*	*	*	*
Retirement home	37,700	2.2	*	*	*32,300	*2.6
Board and care or residential care facility	62,900	3.6	*	*	49,800	4.1
Health facility	*	*	*	*	*	*
Other or unknown	*15,900	*0.9	*	*	*	*
Living arrangement						
Family members	881,700	50.3	317,100	60.0	564,400	46.1
Nonfamily members	92,700	5.3	*24,100	*4.0	68,700	5.6
Alone	685,600	39.1	143,100	27.1	542,400	44.3
Other or unknown	*93,400	*5.3	*	4.0	*49,300	*4.0

TABLE 2 NUMBER AND PERCENT OF ELDERLY MEN AND WOMEN HOME HEALTH CARE CURRENT PATIENTS 65 YEARS AND OLDER RECEIVING SERVICES DURING THE LAST 30 DAYS: UNITED STATES, 1996

Service received	Both sexes[1]	Male	Female
		Number	
Total	1,753,400	528,300	1,224,800
		Percent	
Continuous home care	5.7	*4.5	6.3
Counseling	2.3	*2.5	*2.1
Homemaker-household services	28.1	23.0	30.3
Medications	9.8	7.5	10.8
Mental health services	*1.7	*	*2.0
Nursing services	84.2	84.8	83.9
Nutritional services	3.3	*	*3.4
Occupational therapy	4.9	*6.4	4.2
Physical therapy	19.8	22.0	18.9
Physician services	3.7	*4.5	*3.3
Social services	10.6	10.1	10.8
Speech therapy and/or audiology	*1.6	*	*
Transportation	*1.0	*	*
Volunteers	*	*	*
Other services	10.7	11.8	10.2

- The patient must be a Medicare recipient
- A physician must have determined that home health care is needed and have written a plan for care. This plan must be updated about every 30 days.
- The patient needs one or more of the following: skilled nursing care, intermittent nursing care, physical therapy, or speech therapy
- The patient cannot leave the house except with extreme difficulty and is essentially considered housebound
- The home health-care agency is approved by the Medicare program

If the above conditions have been met, Medicare will pay (as of this writing) for the following types of services:

- Skilled nursing care that is part time or intermittent and is provided by either a licensed practical nurse or a registered nurse (for example, help with taking medications or injections)
- Home health-aide services provided on a part-time or intermittent basis. Examples of services are help with dressing, bathing, toileting, and so forth.
- Physical therapy
- Speech language-pathology services
- Occupational therapy
- Medical social services, such as counseling or assistance in locating resources in the patient's area
- Assistance for people with DIABETES with blood glucose monitoring at home and reviews of medications
- Some medical supplies such as bandages but not to include prescribed medications
- Some medical equipment, toward which Medicare may pay 80 percent, such as a walker or a wheelchair.

Medicare will typically not pay for home-delivered meals, around-the-clock home care, or homemaker services, such as performing the laundry or doing light housekeeping.

*Medicaid and
Home Health Care*

For older patients who are poor and who are receiving MEDICAID services, home health care may be available to them as well. In some cases, Medicaid will cover services that are not paid for by Medicare, such as some home-care services, personal care, and other services. Each state decides if it wishes to provide more than basic services to its older citizens or not.

Gray, Shelly L., Jane E. Mahoney, and Dave K. Blough. "Medication Adherence in Elderly Patients Receiving Home Health Services Following Hospital Discharge," *The Annals of Pharmacotherapy* 35 (2001): 539–545.

Munson, Martha Little, M.S., Division of Health Care Statistics. "Characteristics of Elderly Home Health Care Users: Data from the 1996 National Home and Hospice Care Survey," National Center for Health Care Statistics, no. 309 (December 22, 1999).

home health/home care Health care and assistance that is provided to people within their own homes, rather than in NURSING HOMES, HOSPITALS, HOSPICES, clinics, or other settings. Home health

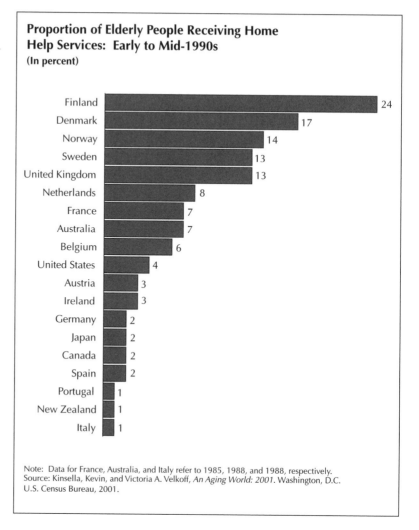

Proportion of Elderly People Receiving Home Help Services: Early to Mid-1990s
(In percent)

Note: Data for France, Australia, and Italy refer to 1985, 1988, and 1988, respectively.
Source: Kinsella, Kevin, and Victoria A. Velkoff, *An Aging World: 2001.* Washington, D.C. U.S. Census Bureau, 2001.

care may include injections, special treatments, or any other medical care that is indicated for a home-bound individual. Some people need home health-care aides to provide basic assistance, or they may need visits from nurses or other medically trained individuals. MEDICARE has strict rules on which particular home health-care services may be paid for by Medicare, and the rules continue to grow even stricter.

As of 1996 (the latest data available as of this writing), there were 1.75 million people age 65 and older who were using home health-care services, based on data provided in "Characteristics of Elderly

Home Health Care Users: Data from the 1996 National Home and Hospice Care Survey," published by the National Center for Health Statistics in late 1999.

Compared to older individuals in other countries, older Americans are relatively low users of home services; for example, in Finland, experts report that 24 percent of older individuals use home services, followed by seniors in Denmark at 17 percent, and Norwegian seniors at 14 percent. In the United States, only 4 percent of seniors use home services, and the percentage is 2 percent in Canada. The lowest users are in Italy, Portugal, and New

Zealand. Paradoxically, Italy has a rapidly growing elderly population. The chart on page 142 provides a comparison of older people using home care in different countries.

homelessness   Lack of a formal place to live. Older people may be homeless because they are mentally ill, have DEMENTIA or ALZHEIMER'S DISEASE, or have a problem with ALCOHOLISM. They may have no family members available to care for them, or they may refuse assistance from family members. It is unknown how many homeless people are age 65 and older.

hormone replacement therapy (HRT)   Hormones such as estrogen or progesterone that are prescribed for women after the onset of MENOPAUSE. These drugs may be synthetic compounds that are created in laboratories, or they may be derived from plants. HRT is available in pill form, transdermal patches applied to the skin, or creams that are inserted vaginally.

In the past, HRT has been presented as almost a "fountain of youth" to menopausal women. The reality is that HRT offers many benefits and also some risks to be considered as well. Every woman who is thinking about using HRT should consult with her physician and listen to the benefits and side effects before making the decision for or against using HRT.

In 2002, the Women's Health Initiative, a federally funded clinical study, released their results of a large-scale study of the effect of Prempro, a hormone replacement drug that included both estrogen and progestin and that was used as a common hormone replacement therapy. The Women's Health Initiative found a possible connection between Prempro and an increased risk for heart attacks, stroke, and breast cancer in women. Subsequent to that finding, sales of Prempro and many other hormone replacement drugs fell dramatically, according to the *Wall Street Journal* and other sources.

Another result of the Women's Health Initiative findings was that physicians began to consider each woman's need for HRT on a case-by-case basis,

rather than routinely recommending HRT for all or most menopausal women.

Any women who are taking Prempro are advised to contact their physicians to review whether they should continue taking the drug or they should take another HRT medication. (Or they should consider whether they stop taking HRT altogether, making sure to taper off on a gradual basis to avoid the severe symptoms that can result if the drug is abruptly stopped.)

Benefits of HRT

Some studies have indicated that HRT may provide protection against a variety of illnesses, including HEART DISEASE, STROKE, ALZHEIMER'S DISEASE, COLORECTAL CANCER, tooth loss, age-related MACULAR DEGENERATION, and OSTEOPOROSIS/FRACTURES. HRT may also provide relief from SLEEP DISORDERS, improving the quality and duration of a woman's sleep.

HRT is also used to alleviate the sudden severe flushing and sweating ("hot flashes") that can occur with menopause. In addition, women who take HRT may find relief from atrophy of the genitourinary tract. HRT may also bring relief from emotional problems such as DEPRESSION.

Risks of HRT

There are also some negative aspects to taking female hormones. Women who use HRT are more prone to developing GALL-BLADDER DISEASE, BREAST CANCER, migraine HEADACHE, and blood clots, as well as vaginal discharges. These problems are more likely if there is a family history for such problems, for example, if a woman's mother or sister has had them.

Another potential problem is that if the woman still has an intact uterus, HRT may present the risk of UTERINE CANCER. Added estrogen may also cause breast tenderness, fluid retention, and mild weight gain. These problems may abate after the woman takes the drug for a period of time.

For further information on hormone replacement therapy that is available on the Internet, go to the National Women's Health Information Center at www.4woman.gov/faq/hormone.htm. The NATIONAL INSTITUTE ON AGING also offers information on the pros and cons of HRT on the following website: www.aoa.dhhs.gov/aoa/pages/agepages/hormone.html.

Organizations with information on HRT are as follows:

American College of Obstetricians and Gynecologists (ACOG)
409 12th Street, SW
Box 96920
Washington, DC 20090
(202) 484-8748

National Institute on Aging
NIA Information Center
P.O. Box 8057
Gaithersburg, MD 20898

North American Menopause Society
Box 94527
Cleveland, OH 44101
(216) 844-8748
http://www.menopause.org

Planned Parenthood Federation of America, Inc.
810 Seventh Avenue
New York, NY 10019
(800) 230-PLAN (toll-free)
http://www.plannedparenthood.org

Fuhrmans, Vanessa. "HRT Worries Give Headaches to Drug Makers," *Wall Street Journal*, October 25, 2002, B1, B4.

hospice   Medical facility for individuals who are dying of a TERMINAL ILLNESS such as CANCER or AIDS. In the United States, the first hospice opened in 1974. According to the National Center for Health Statistics, there were 59,000 patients in hospices in 1996 (the latest information as of this writing).

Individuals who live in hospices are usually kept comfortable with PAINKILLING MEDICATIONS and are provided with food and/or fluids. However, other medications are not normally provided, nor are medical measures taken that would act to save the lives of residents. Sometimes, individuals remain in their own homes, and hospice care is given to them by hospice providers, such as nurses and social workers and other health-care professionals. Patients may also receive some care at a hospice facility and other care at home.

In Europe and especially in the United Kingdom, hospice care is often provided at facilities in rural areas, which are considered peaceful and pastoral. In England, the hospice movement began in the mid-1960s, when St. Christopher's Hospice opened.

Private insurance companies are increasingly likely to pay for hospice services, which are much less costly than active attempts to maintain the life of terminally ill patients. MEDICARE and MEDICAID also pay for some hospice services, although patients and their families should check for what is covered. Often, hospital social workers are knowledgeable about such programs.

For further information, contact:

Hospice Foundation of America
2001 S Street, NW #300
Washington, DC 20009
(800) 854-3402 (toll-free)
http://www.hospicefoundation.org

hospitalization   Admission to a hospital or medical center due to a serious illness. Many older individuals require hospitalization for illnesses such as FLU or PNEUMONIA or because of major illnesses such as STROKE or HEART ATTACK. Older individuals also are at greater risk than younger people of fractures sustained from FALLS, accidents, and from other causes. Aging brings an increased risk for hospitalization as well as for more-extended hospital stays than experienced by younger individuals. Even relatively mild problems, such as urinary-tract infections, can lead to hospitalization in the senior population. DEHYDRATION and CONFUSION can occur, requiring physician monitoring.

In an interesting study reported in 2001 in the *New England Journal of Medicine*, researchers reported on their findings of critically ill patients in Belgium who had agreed to participate in the study. Nondiabetic patients who became hyperglycemic (diabetic) while in the intensive-care unit were treated with either conventional therapy or intensive therapy.

The patients had a variety of illnesses such as cardiac diseases and CANCER. The subjects who were treated with intensive therapy had a significantly lower death rate: only 4.6 percent of this group died, compared to 8.0 percent who died among the conventional-treatment group. The significance of

TABLE 1   PERCENT OF ELDERLY POPULATION LIVING ALONE: DATA FROM 1990 TO 1999

Developed countries	Male	Female	Developing countries	Male	Female
Australia	13.7	29.3	Argentina	11.2	21.1
Canada	14.1	33.7	Aruba	12.5	15.4
Czech Republic	19.0	47.5	Bolivia	13.2	15.7
Denmark	23.3	52.0	Cyprus	10.6	24.8
Finland	19.5	46.5	Hong Kong	11.6	13.2
France	15.3	40.2	Mexico	7.5	14.0
Germany	16.9	50.8	Morocco (60+)	11.3	44.7
Greece	8.7	22.8	Philippines (60+) . . .	4.4	6.4
Ireland	18.9	27.7	South Korea (60+) . .	3.1	11.8
Japan	5.2	14.8	St. Lucia	20.9	18.9
New Zealand	17.8	38.0	Taiwan	13.0	7.4
Norway	21.3	44.7	Thailand (60+)	2.9	5.5
Portugal	9.4	23.9	Vietnam (60+)	2.5	8.1
Romania	12.4	31.7			
Sweden	25.1	49.9			
United States	15.1	36.8			

Note: Data for Mexico are for seven cities, and refer to 1989. Data are for household populations aged 65 and older, unless otherwise noted. Data for Morocco refer to urban areas only.

Source: U.S. Census Bureau.

this study was that people who suffer from severe hyperglycemia, whether they have previously been diagnosed with DIABETES or not, may experience an extended life if they receive intensive treatment during their hospital stay.

Van Den Berge, Greet, M.D., Ph.D. et al. "Intensive Insulin Therapy in Critically Ill Patients," *New England Journal of Medicine* 345, no. 19 (November 8, 2001): 1, 359–1,367.

housing/living arrangements   Older individuals may reside in their own homes or apartments, or they may live in ASSISTED-LIVING FACILITIES or SKILLED-NURSING FACILITIES (nursing homes).

Some older people live with their adult children or other relatives; others live in communities for individuals over a certain age, such as older than age 55 or age 60 or another age cutoff. These facilities may have a clubhouse and a variety of planned activities, but they do not offer the additional assistance that is offered in an assisted-living facility or a nursing home.

In many countries, the percentage of older women living alone is much higher than the percentage of older men living alone. Part of the reason for this is that women live longer than men. There may also be cultural reasons as well; for example, women in developed countries are more likely to live alone than are women in developing (poor) countries. However, even among developed countries, there are wide variations; for example, more than half (52 percent) of older women live alone in Denmark, versus 23.3 percent of older males who live alone. Germany and Sweden both have high rates of women living alone, including 50.8 percent for Germany and 49.9 percent in Sweden.

In contrast, a much lower percentage of 36.8 percent of older women live alone in the United States versus 15.1 percent of older men. In Canada, 33.7 percent of older women live alone, compared to 14.1 percent of older men. (See Table 1 to view the percentages of older men and women living alone in various countries around the globe.)

Huntington's disease (HD)   A degenerative neurological disorder, also called Huntington's chorea, that destroys patients' ability to walk, speak, reason, remember, and care for themselves. HD is the result of the genetically programmed degeneration of nerve cells in the areas of the brain that control movement, speech, thought, and memory. HD is almost always inherited. HD is more common among whites than African Americans. Symptoms of HD usually appear between the ages of 30 and 50, although they may occur in later years. About 10 percent of HD patients develop symptoms after the age of 65.

The NATIONAL INSTITUTES OF HEALTH (NIH) estimates that 30,000 Americans have HD, and at least 150,000 others have a 50 percent risk of developing it. Thousands more live with the realization that they could develop this devastating illness because of the genetic predisposition that they carry.

Risk Factors

A family history of HD is the only known risk factor for the disease; however, between one and three of every 100 people who have HD have no family history of the disease, nor do they have the defective gene that causes this disease. Everyone else who develops HD is born with the disease-causing gene. An adult who has the defective gene may pass it on to all, some, or no children. A child who does not inherit the gene will not develop HD and cannot pass it on to future generations.

Testing for Huntington's Disease

Predictive DNA analysis can determine, with 99 percent accuracy, whether an at-risk individual will develop HD. Presymptomatic testing indicates whether someone who has a family history of HD but who does not have symptoms of the disease will develop the disease. However, tests cannot predict the type or severity of symptoms that an individual will develop, when symptoms will appear, or how rapidly the disease will progress.

In general, at-risk individuals who choose to undergo presymptomatic testing for Huntington's disease should contact a neurology clinic whose multidisciplinary staff includes geneticists, neurologists, psychologists, and social workers.

Symptoms of Huntington's Disease

Members of the same family may develop different HD symptoms, and an individual's own symptoms may change during the course of the disease.

Some indicators of HD are:

- Changes in handwriting
- Tremor
- Seizures
- Sudden muscle spasms (myoclonus)
- Learning problems

Some HD patients exhibit muscular stiffness (rigidity) rather than the involuntary dancelike movements (chorea) that are characteristic of the adult-onset form of the disease. Uncontrollable movements of the fingers, face, feet or body may be the first signs of chorea. These types of movements tend to intensify when the patient is under emotional stress.

DEPRESSION is an initial symptom in many patients and may also occur during later stages of HD. Other emotional symptoms include mood swings, forgetfulness, irritability, apathy, and withdrawal from social activities, hallucinations, and paranoia.

Clumsiness and balance problems are also common symptoms of the disease. In addition, the ability to follow or focus visually on a moving target decreases as the illness progresses, and near-constant movement and swallowing difficulties can result in the patient suffering from a significant weight loss. Often, patients' judgment becomes impaired, and they may appear intoxicated.

Difficulties with communication are common. Because HD disrupts the thought processes, patients may have problems with starting conversations and with communicating spontaneously, expressing thoughts in words, and with grasping complex information.

Impaired comprehension and coordination make reading and writing difficult. There is a marked decline in the ability to absorb new information, learn new skills, recall the recent past, concentrate or pay attention, organize thoughts, and reason. These symptoms may be confused with ALZHEIMER'S DISEASE or DEMENTIA, although the long-term memory generally remains intact. Late-stage HD patients generally know where they are and recognize people they know well.

Individuals with HD may experience intensified involuntary movements and muscle spasms may seem to freeze the patient into abnormal postures and odd facial expressions. The patient's voluntary movements and reactions slow down. Patients with HD become unable to initiate movements or to control how fast or forcefully these movements occur.

Diagnosing Huntington's Disease

A thorough neurological examination and family history of HD are the basis of diagnosis. Laboratory tests may rule out other conditions, and MRI scans can show shrinkage and enlargement in parts of the brain that are most affected by HD.

The neurologist may use the Unified Huntington's Disease Rating Scale (UHDRS) to evaluate symptoms, stage, and severity of disease. This specialized research tool assesses:

- Chorea and rigidity
- Eye movements
- Pronunciation
- Mobility
- Irritability
- Behavior
- Coordination
- Ability to follow instructions and perform routine tasks

When symptoms of HD first appear after age 65, the diagnosis is especially challenging. Symptoms in older patients may be more moderate than with younger patients and may be masked by other health problems. In addition, the person may also exhibit some indications of senile chorea, which is a medical condition involving involuntary movements of the face, mouth, and tongue and sometimes also involving one or both arms or legs.

Sometimes a symptom of underlying disease, senile chorea can occur in people older than 60 who do not have the HD gene and who rarely have a family history of the disease. Some scientists believe senile chorea is a form of late-onset HD.

Stages of Huntington's Disease

The duration of Huntington's disease ranges from 10 to 30 years. As the disease progresses, chorea and dementia worsen. Unable to regulate emotional responses, the patient may become angry or belligerent. Patients' motor skills continue to decline, and the weakening of the muscles that regulate breathing and swallowing increase the risk of infection and choking.

In the final stages of HD, patients are severely debilitated and are confined to bed. Death usually results from:

- Prolonged immobility
- Malnutrition
- Pneumonia
- Heart failure
- Injuries sustained in falls or other accidents

Treatment for Huntington's Disease

There is no cure or effective treatment for HD. An interdisciplinary symptom-based approach is considered the best way to provide care and improve quality of life. Medications may be prescribed for the emotional problems, fatigue, restlessness, and excitability that are characteristic of the disease. Nonmedical management strategies may also be devised, implemented, and monitored by neurologists, physical/occupational therapists, speech/language pathologists, social workers, advocacy groups, adult day-centers, movement-disorder clinics, home-care agencies, long-term care facilities, and hospices.

Current and Future Advances

Studies involving a limited number of patients suggest that surgically implanting fetal tissue into damaged areas of the brain may prevent widespread nerve cell deterioration and maintain or improve motor skills and intellectual functions in HD patients.

Other current research focuses on the potential benefits of cystamine, a drug that seems to increase activity of the protons that prevent nerve-cell deterioration and minocycline, an antibiotic used to treat a variety of INFECTIONS, which seems to block the production of enzymes involved in disease progression.

For further information, contact the following organizations:

The Huntington's Disease Society of America (HDSA)
158 West 29th Street
7th Floor
New York, NY 10001-5300
(800) 345-HDSA
http://www.hdsa.org

National Institute of Neurological Disorders & Stroke (NINDS)
NIH Neurological Institute
P.O. Box 5801
Bethesda, MD 20824
(800) 352-9424
http://www.ninds.nih.gov/health_and_medical/disorders.huntington.htm

Ona, Victor O. et al. "Inhibition of caspase-1 slows disease progression in mouse model of Huntington's disease," *Nature* 399 (May 20, 1999): 263–267.
Prusiner, Stanley B., M.D. "Shattuck Lecture: Neurodegenerative Diseases and Prions," *New England Journal of Medicine* 344, no. 20 (May 17, 2001): 1,516–1,526.

hypertension Excessively high levels of blood pressure, usually defined as at least 140/90 mm Hg or a condition in a person taking antihypertensive medications. Also known as high blood pressure. Hypertension is a very common and very dangerous condition among people age 65 and older. It is also usually treatable, and many medical complications can be delayed or avoided with control of blood pressure. About 50 million people in the United States have hypertension, and about 75 percent of adults with hypertension are not controlling their blood pressure, thus unnecessarily increasing their risks for medical complications. Globally, an estimated 600 million people have hypertension, according to the World Health Organization (WHO). Some countries have a very severe problem; for example, more than 100 million people in China suffer from hypertension.

Most people with hypertension (95 percent) have "essential hypertension," which is high blood pressure with no clear-cut cause. Five percent of those with hypertension have "secondary hypertension," which is high blood pressure that is brought on by identifiable causes, such as medications they may take, from other causes, or from a combination of causes.

Hypertension is a very serious medical condition and is a chronic disease that is experienced by many people throughout the world. It can lead to severe complications such as HEART DISEASE, KIDNEY DISEASE, STROKE, BLINDNESS, and many other complications, up to and including death.

If the older person with hypertension also has DIABETES, as many do, then the risk for serious complications increases greatly. An estimated 42 percent of patients with hypertension who will ultimately need kidney dialysis or require kidney transplantation also have diabetes, according to the authors of a 2000 article in the *American Journal of Kidney Diseases*.

Causes of Hypertension

High blood pressure may be caused by a genetic risk, OBESITY, a stressful lifestyle, and a combination of these and other factors. Sometimes, medication is the cause of hypertension. The risk factor for hypertension is further exacerbated by SMOKING.

Risk Factors for Hypertension

Although people of any age, even children, can be hypertensive, most people with hypertension are middle-aged or older individuals, and the risk for developing hypertension increases with age.

Another key factor associated with hypertension is ethnicity: African Americans, New Zealand Maoris, and some Native American tribes in the United States, such as the Pima Indians, have higher rates of hypertension and greater risks for cardiovascular diseases than do individuals of other ethnicities.

According to a 2001 article on hypertensive risk factors, published in the *New England Journal of Medicine,* a study of more than 16,095 adults revealed that the key risk factors for hypertension were:

• Age (age 65 and older)

• Male (men were at greater risk than women)

• African American

• Not having seen a physician in the past 12 months

Age was the strongest risk factor for hypertension. In addition, people who were age 65 and older represented only 19 percent of the study population, but they were 45 percent of the individuals who did not know they had hypertension. Also, many people in this age group who knew they were hypertensive did not have their blood pressure under control.

According to the researchers, of those patients with hypertension who were being treated for their condition, the hypertension was under control in 65 percent of those who were ages 25–44 years. However, only 34 percent of those age 65 and older who were being treated for hypertension actually had their blood pressure under control. This is a distressingly low percentage, particularly because hypertension is linked to so many serious and potentially fatal illnesses.

Hypertension is a Chronic Condition

People with hypertension and their families need to realize that this is a chronic and lifelong condition. Although lifestyle changes and medication can vastly improve blood pressure measurements, it is still necessary to continue to monitor the condition for life. Many patients make a classic mistake of taking their medicine and noting their improved blood-pressure readings. They may conclude that they are "cured" and decide to stop taking their medication altogether. In such cases, the patient's blood pressure will typically go up yet again, and before individuals notice any difference in how they feel, serious medical complications can ensue.

Major Studies on Hypertension

Several major studies on individuals with hypertension are often cited by experts and researchers. These studies placed subjects in various groups with different medications that reduced blood pressure. The researchers worked to intensively reduce blood pressure in one group and to achieve a more moderate blood pressure goal in the other group. The blood pressure of the individuals in these groups were then compared to each other. Invariably, the group who brought their blood pressure down lower fared much better and had far lower rates of later serious complications in most categories.

TABLE 1 CLASSIFICATION OF BLOOD PRESSURE FOR ADULTS AGE 18 AND OLDER*

Category	Systolic (mm Hg)		Diastolic (mm Hg)
Optimal **	<120	and	<80
Normal	<130	and	<85
High–normal	130–139	or	85–89
Hypertension ***			
Stage 1	140–159	or	90–99
Stage 2	160–179	or	100–109
Stage 3	> or = 180	or	> or = 110

* Not taking antihypertensive drugs and not acutely ill. When systolic and diastolic blood pressure fall into different categories, the higher category should be selected to classify the individuals blood-pressure status. For example, 160/92 mm Hg should be classified as stage 2 hypertension, and 174/120 mm Hg should be classified as stage 3 hypertension. Isolated systolic hypertension is defined as SBP of 140 mm Hg or greater and DBP below 90 mm Hg and staged appropriately (for example, 170/82 mm Hg is defined as stage 2 isolated systolic hypertension). In addition to classifying stage of hypertension on the basis of average blood-pressure levels, clinicians should specify presence of absence of target organ disease and additional risk factors.

** Optimal blood pressure with respect to cardiovascular risk is below 120/80 mm Hg. However, unusually low readings should be evaluated for clinical significance.

*** Based on the average of two or more readings taken at each of two or more visits after an initial screening

Source: "The Sixth Report of the Joint National Committee on Prevention, Detection, Evaluation, and Treatment of High Blood Pressure, National Heart, Lung, and Blood Institute, National Institutes of Health, NIH Publication, No. 98-4080, November 1997.

Symptoms

Blood pressure is easily measured by the physician, nurse or even by the patient, using simple cuff devices. If the measurement is abnormal, it should be retaken to verify that no error was made and the individual truly is hypertensive. If individuals are diagnosed with hypertension, they may need to come in for weekly or more frequent visits to have the nurse recheck their blood pressure. If their blood pressure is excessively high, the doctor or nurse will inject medication or may have the patient admitted to the hospital.

Diagnosis

Physicians, nurses, staff members, and even a patient him- or herself can determine blood-pressure levels with a cuff device. Experts say that devices that take the blood pressure by insertion of a finger in a cuff are generally not as accurate as the devices that determine the blood pressure taken in the arm.

Before the blood pressure is taken, the person should avoid caffeine for several hours and also should not smoke. Just before the reading is taken, the person should rest for about five minutes, and his or her arm should be supported rather than hanging loose. It is also important to use the right cuff size. It may be difficult to obtain an accurate measure on either a very obese or an extremely thin person. Large or small devices may work better, depending on the size of the person.

Laboratory tests are also taken if hypertension is suspected, and doctors generally order a urinalysis and blood tests that measure hematocrit, serum electrolytes (especially sodium and potassium), BUN (blood urea nitrogen), creatinine and glucose levels, and plasma lipid levels. The patient's urine may also be checked for albumin excretion, and an electrocardiogram may also be ordered. A 24-hour urinary protein excretion level can provide important diagnostic information; for example, the normal range of urinary albumin excretion rate is less than 150 mg/day.

Spot urine levels can also be ordered. Levels of 0–30 mgs of albumin/grams creatinine are normal. If albumin levels are between 30–300, the person has microalbuminuria and needs to be treated. If the levels are greater than 300, then this is a sign of overt proteinuria (protein in the urine) and a problem that must be treated. This is an indicator of kidney disease.

Treatment of Hypertension

Lifestyle Changes   Hypertension can be treated by recommending to the patient improvements in diet, weight loss, and increased exercise. Individuals who smoke should *immediately* stop smoking. According to the World Health Organization and the International Society of Hypertension, in their WHO-ISH guidelines, "Smoking cessation is the single most powerful lifestyle measure for the prevention of both cardiovascular and non-cardiovascular disease in hypertensive patients."

People with hypertension who consume alcohol should either stop drinking altogether or should severely limit their alcohol intake. The Joint National Committee recommended that daily alcohol intake for the average person should not exceed 1 ounce (30 ml) of ethanol per day. People who are of smaller size and weight should not exceed 0.5 ounces (15 ml) of ethanol per day.

Dietary changes can also provide enhanced health benefits to the person with hypertension. Sodium can be decreased by avoiding highly salted foods and by not adding salt to foods. Some types of foods should be added to the diet of the hypertensive person. For example, it is important for the person with hypertension to ensure an adequate intake of potassium, and eating fresh vegetables or fruits such as bananas may provide sufficient potassium. However, sometimes people with hypertension become very low in potassium because of their medications (particularly diuretics) or for other reasons and may need to take a potassium supplement in addition. (Note: potassium should be taken only by prescription, because some drugs that are used to treat hypertension can raise potassium levels.)

Regular EXERCISE is another important lifestyle component of helping to keep hypertension within control. Even a brisk walk for 30–45 minutes for several days a week can be sufficient to improve an individual's health. According to the WHO-ISH 1999 report, 20 minutes per day of light to moderate exercise can enable those with hypertension to reduce their risk of death from cardiovascular disease by as much as 30 percent.

Some exercise, however, can be detrimental to the person who has hypertension; for example, heavy weightlifting or other isometric exercises can work to raise rather than lower blood pressure and consequently should be avoided.

Emotional stress can also raise blood pressure. People with hypertension may need to learn relaxation tactics to cope with their reactions to the problems of life. Stress cannot be altogether eliminated from life; however, it is the individual's reaction to stress that may be modified.

Medication   Many people who have hypertension will also need to take medication to lower their blood pressure. This is particularly true if they have other illnesses such as diabetes. Medication may also be needed to bring dyslipidemia (high cholesterol levels) under control.

Despite information that is provided to patients about the risk they face with hypertension as well as the emphasis upon the necessity to take their medication to decrease these risks, physicians still report many problems with nonadherence to their prescribed medication regimen. There are a variety of reasons why people with hypertension do not take their medicine.

The patient may not understand what is needed, and it is essential that doctors and patients attain clear communication. According to the WHO-ISH report, "Adequate information about BP and high BP, about risks and prognosis, about the expected benefits of treatment, and about the risks and side effects of treatment will be essential for satisfactory life-long control of hypertension, which is poor in many countries today."

Some patients do not take their medicine for hypertension regularly (or at all) for the same reason that they do not take their medicines for other illnesses. For example, they may forget to take the medicine or may minimize the extent of their problem.

Patients may fail to take their medication because they may not like the side effects of medication or they may not be able to afford the drugs. Other reasons for nonadherence may also be responsible.

Rechecking Blood Pressure

Doctors recommend follow-up measurements when patients have demonstrable hypertension. The Joint National Committee VI recommended the following guidelines for rechecks of blood pressure:

Systolic	Diastolic	Followup Recommended
130–139	85–89	Recheck in one year
140–159	90–99	Confirm in two months (based on past bp measurements, other cardiovascular risk factors, or target organ disease)
160–179	100–109	Evaluate or refer to source of care within one month
> or = 180	> or = 110	Evaluate or refer to source of care immediately or within one week, depending on clinical situation

"White Coat" Hypertension

Some individuals have a tendency to experience an elevated blood pressure when they are in a physician's office, presumably as a reflexive act of merely seeing a doctor and becoming anxious about what the physician may say or do. (The white laboratory coat of the doctor is the "white coat," the sight of which may induce a temporarily elevated blood pressure in some individuals.)

Because of this white-coat hypertension reaction, experts say that doctors should take at least several readings that are at least two minutes apart, and they should also take readings on different occasions before they diagnose hypertension—unless the blood pressure is so high that it would be dangerous to delay treatment. White-coat hypertension is also another reason why doctors advise people with hypertension to monitor their blood pressure at home.

See also ASPIRIN THERAPY; EYE PROBLEMS; GLAUCOMA; KIDNEY FAILURE.

Bakris, George L., M.D. et al. "Preserving Renal Function in Adults with Hypertension and Diabetes: A Consensus Approach," *American Journal of Kidney Diseases* 36, no. 3 (September 2000): 646–661.

Chalmers, John, et al., World Health Organization/International Society of Hypertension (WHO-ISH). "Practice Guidelines for Primary Care Physicians: 1999 WHO/ISH Hypertension Guidelines." Geneva, Switzerland, 1999.

Hyman, David J., M.D., M.P.H., and Valory N. Pavlik, Ph.D. "Characteristics of Patients with Uncontrolled Hypertension in the United States," *New England Journal of Medicine* 345, no. 7 (August 16, 2001): 479–486.

National Academy on an Aging Society. "Hypertension: A Common Condition for Older Americans," *Challenges for the 21st Century: Chronic and Disabling Conditions* 1, no. 12 (October 2000): 1–6.

Rigaud, Anne-Sophie, and Bernard Forette. "Hypertension in Older Adults," *Journal of Gerontology: Medical Sciences* 56A, no. 4 (2001): M217–M225.

World Health Organization and the International Society of Hypertension. "1999 World Health Organization-International Society of Hypertension Guidelines for the Management of Hypertension" (1999).

hypotension Refers to unusually low blood pressure. Hypotension may be caused by illness or by some medications. The person may feel dizzy when suddenly moving from a lying-down to a sitting-up position or from a sitting to a standing position. Hypotension can be dangerous because it can lead to an increased risk for FALLS. Studies have shown that hypotension that occurs after eating a meal (postprandial hypotension) is a high-risk indicator for falls, particularly among people who have DIABETES or those who take three or more medications.

Orthostatic hypotension refers to a sudden drop in blood pressure (about 20 mm Hg in the systolic blood pressure) that occurs when a person changes from a lying-down to a sitting-up position or from a sitting-up to a standing position.

Engstrom, John W., M.D., and Michael J. Aminoff, M.D. "Evaluation and Treatment of Orthostatic Hypotension," *American Family Physician* 56, no. 5 (October 1, 1997).

hypothermia An unhealthily low body temperature, often due to inclement or very cold weather conditions when the individual's home is not sufficiently heated. This can be a problem for those elderly individuals who live in very cold climates, particularly if they are not dressed warmly enough. Sometimes, older individuals try to save money on fuel bills by turning the thermostat down very low, but this can be risky for individuals prone to hypothermia. It is also true that even relatively mild temperatures of 60 degrees can trigger hypothermia in individuals who are prone to developing it.

In addition to hypothermia developed in the home, individuals who have ALZHEIMER'S DISEASE or DEMENTIA and who have a problem with WANDERING may develop hypothermia from the cold conditions in the outdoors.

Older people who are most at risk for developing hypothermia include those who suffer from the following medical problems:

- arthritis
- Alzheimer's disease and dementia
- THYROID DISEASE (low thyroid)
- STROKE
- PARKINSON'S DISEASE

In addition, individuals who take some medications, particularly sleeping pills, tranquilizers, or antidepressants, have a greater risk for suffering from hypothermia.

Symptoms of Hypothermia

Some common indicators of hypothermia, which unfortunately may sometimes be confused with the "normal" behaviors of older people, are as follows:

- Slowed speech
- Shallow breathing
- Confusion
- Behavioral changes
- Either excessive shivering or no shivering in a cold room
- Slowed reactions

Diagnosing Hypothermia

Experts say that the best way to diagnose hypothermia is to simply take the person's temperature. If the reading is at or below 96 degrees Fahrenheit, then emergency assistance should be called for immediately. (Most oral thermometers used in the home will not register below 96 degrees.)

In the meantime, the person should be wrapped up in warm blankets. If necessary, individuals can use their own body heat to warm up the hypothermic patient by hugging them closely but gently. The skin should *not* be rubbed roughly to get the older person's circulation going.

If Thermostats Are Set Low

Older people who feel that they must keep the thermostat at or below 60 degrees in cold weather (which is not advisable) should be sure to dress warmly and to wear warm clothes to bed, including socks. An electric blanket may also be helpful.

Alcohol should be avoided by anyone prone to hypothermia because it can worsen the condition.

Warm foods and fluids such as soups, tea, cocoa, or other items recommended by the physician may help to increase the individual's body temperature.

Low-Energy
Home-Assistance Programs

Many states have fuel-assistance programs for older people who cannot afford to pay their heating bills. The national Eldercare Locator (800) 677-1116 should be contacted to find out if such a program is available in a particular state so that the information that is gathered can ultimately help older people at risk to avoid hypothermia.

National Institutes of Health, National Institute on Aging. "Harsh Winter and High Energy Bills Raise Seniors' Risk of Hypothermia" (December 2000).

I

identification, wearable Necklaces, bracelets, watches, or other items that include identification that a person wears on some exposed part of the body. These forms of identification are very valuable for individuals with chronic severe diseases, such as DIABETES, HEART ATTACK, and STROKE. It is also valuable for older people suffering from ALZHEIMER'S DISEASE or DEMENTIA and who are prone to wandering and thus may become easily lost.

Wearable identification is better for medical purposes than identification information kept in a purse or wallet because individuals may become separated from their purse or wallet and also because it may take too long for others trying to provide help to locate such identification. Wearable identification can inform those who wish to help of medication and treatment needs, as well as the name and address of the wearer and a name and phone number of the person to call if the older person needs assistance. Medication allergies or needed medications are often found on these identification tags, and this information alone could prove to be life saving.

An older person may become very ill or unconscious and be unable to respond to questions from others. Wearable identification may provide life-saving information about the individual.

Some individuals may resist wearing medical ID bracelets or necklaces, but the life-saving importance of such items cannot be underestimated, and should be emphasized to the individual.

incontinence Loss of control of urinary or bowel functions. Incontinence may be a temporary and curable problem, or it may be a permanent condition caused by serious illness. URINARY INCONTINENCE is far more common than bowel incontinence. Urinary or fecal incontinence can be extremely embarrassing. Having to wear adult diapers to prevent "accidents" may make older people feel that they are incompetent or childlike. Often, there are treatments for such problems, but many feel that this is a natural part of aging and therefore do not seek medical attention that could help them.

infections Bacterial or viral invasions that cause minor to major illnesses. Some people are more susceptible to developing infections, such as individuals who have DIABETES, or those whose immune systems are weakened.

Pneumonia and influenza (FLU) are still dangerous infections in the United States and the rest of the world, and they may become very serious for older people, and can lead to death. Yet, these infections are largely preventable with immunizations. For this reason, doctors recommend that most people older than age 50 receive annual immunizations for flu and periodic immunizations for pneumonia. Often, however, many older people fail to receive these immunizations, although MEDICARE covers them.

Infections can cause back pain and other pain throughout the body. They can weaken individuals and make them more susceptible to more serious subsequent invasive infections, further weakening older people.

Sometimes, infections can be difficult to detect in older people, according to Dr. Mouton and his colleagues in their 2001 article for *American Family Physician*. Physicians and CAREGIVERS should be sure to be careful to look for subtle indicators. For example, a change in mental status that may be the only sign of an infection is often ignored.

The authors state,

Many signs and symptoms of infection that are common in younger adults, particularly fever and leukocytosis [high white-blood-cell count] present less frequently or not at all in older adults. While 60 percent of older adults with serious infections develop leukocytosis, its absence does not rule out an infectious process. Because frail older adults tend to have poorer body temperature response, elevations in body temperature of 1.1°C. (2°F.) from their normal baseline temperature should be considered a febrile [feverish] response. Fevers higher than 38.3°C (101°F.) often indicate severe, life-threatening infections in older adults, and hospitalization should be considered for these patients.

Mouton, Charles P., M.D., M.S. et al. "Common Infections in Older Adults," *American Family Physician* 63 (2001): 257–268.

intensive-care unit   Special section of the hospital that provides care for seriously or critically ill individuals who need constant attention and observation, such as HEART-ATTACK or STROKE victims. Special monitors take the temperature, pulse, and blood pressure of the patient, and alarms will go off if these readings fall below or above certain predetermined levels.

If patients' conditions improve, they are usually moved to another part of the hospital where the care is not so intensive.

Visits to patients in the intensive-care unit are usually restricted to family members only, and they must generally be brief visits.

The ratio of nurse to patient is very high in intensive-care units, often one to one or one to two, with aides available as well. This guarantees the opportunity for constant supervision.

Italy   This European country has the distinction of having the oldest population in the world, or 18.1 percent of the global population age 65 and older, in 2000, according to a report from the U.S. Census Bureau. In years past, Sweden had the oldest population.

See also GLOBAL AGING.

Kinsella, Kevin, and Victoria A. Velkoff. *An Aging World: 2001*. Washington, D.C.: U.S. Census Bureau, 2001.

J

Japan   An Asian country with a very large elderly population. Japan also had the world's highest life expectancy at birth in 2000, when 34 key countries were considered, or 84.1 years for women and 77.5 for men. (The life expectancy at birth in the United States is 79.9 years for women and 74.2 for men.)

See also GLOBAL AGING.

Kinsella, Kevin, and Victoria A. Velkoff. *An Aging World: 2001*. Washington, D.C.: U.S. Census Bureau, 2001.

jaundice   Yellow appearance of the skin, usually caused by a disease of the liver, such as hepatitis. PANCREATIC CANCER can also cause jaundice as can gallstones that are obstructing the gall bladder; such a condition is life threatening. All older individuals who are jaundiced should be sure to see their physicians immediately for an evaluation.

kidney disease Illnesses that stem from a malfunction of the kidneys, the organs that filter the impurities from the blood. Older individuals face an increased risk of developing kidney disease. The illness may be minor, such as a relatively minor kidney infection, or it can be a major problem that is also severely painful, such as kidney stones. In the face of an acute illness, the kidney function may slow down; this is called acute renal insufficiency (ARI).

In the most serious case, the kidneys fail to function altogether. This is called end-stage renal disease (ESRD), or KIDNEY FAILURE. The person whose kidneys fail must undergo kidney DIALYSIS, in which a special machine filters the blood, or they must have a kidney transplant. Dialysis may be performed in a clinic setting or sometimes in the home.

Risk Factors

People with DIABETES and/or HYPERTENSION are most at risk for developing serious kidney diseases, and it is extremely important for individuals diagnosed with one or both of these medical problems to work to attain as normal a level of functioning as possible. Other biological family members having kidney disease is another risk factor for the individual to develop kidney disease.

There are also racial risks to developing kidney disease; for example, AFRICAN AMERICANS, NATIVE AMERICANS AND ALASKA NATIVES, ASIAN AMERICANS, and HISPANIC AMERICANS have greater risks for developing kidney diseases than CAUCASIANS.

Age plays a factor in the development of kidney diseases, and with aging comes an increased risk for kidney disease.

Symptoms

Individuals with kidney disease may have no symptoms, mild symptoms, or extreme pain, depending on the nature of the illness. For example, kidney stones cause severe pain, causing most people to contact their physicians or to go to the nearest emergency room.

In the early stages of serious kidney disease, there are usually no symptoms; however, illness may be detected by a laboratory test that checks for creatinine levels. If creatinine levels are mildly abnormal, the patient can be treated, and kidney failure can usually be averted. At a later stage of kidney disease, there is still no pain, but laboratory tests detect the presence of albumin in the urine (albuminuria). At this point, the patient can still be treated for kidney disease.

Diagnosis

Physicians diagnose kidney disease based on the patient's symptoms as well as laboratory findings. A 24-hour urine collection test is usually ordered if the physician suspects kidney disease. A simple urinalysis can detect bacteria in the urine, and the urine can also be cultured to determine the presence of bacteria, as well as the type of bacteria.

Doctors can also order a blood urea nitrogen (BUN) test. BUN is a waste product produced by the kidneys. Increased levels of BUN may be an early warning sign of kidney disease and should be followed up. It can also indicate DEHYDRATION.

If kidney disease is detected, the patient is usually referred to a NEPHROLOGIST, a physician who is expert in the treatment of kidney disease as well as in treating hypertension.

Treatment

The treatment of kidney disease depends on the cause. If the illness is bacterial, then antibiotics will be administered. In other cases, medications can be administered to treat chronic kidney disease. In some cases, narrowing of the arteries leading to the kidneys may be playing a role. This condition is called renal-artery stenosis. Simple testing with an MRI can determine noninvasively if the condition is present. Angioplasty can then be performed, often producing a cure.

If the illness is very advanced and has led to KIDNEY FAILURE, the only therapy that will work is kidney dialysis, and eventually, a kidney transplant.

For further information, contact the following organizations:

National Institute of Diabetes and Digestive and
Kidney Diseases
National Institutes of Health
Building 31, Room 9A04
31 Center Drive, MSC 2560
Bethesda, MD 20892-2560
(301) 496-3583
http://www.niddk.nih.gov

National Kidney and Urologic Diseases Information
Clearinghouse (NKUDIC)
3 Information Way
Bethesda, MD 20892-3580
(800) 891-5390 or (301) 654-4415
http://www.niddk.nih.gov/health/kidney/kidney.htm

kidney failure/end-stage renal disease (ESRD)
The stage in chronic kidney disease in which either kidney DIALYSIS or the transplantation of a kidney from a recently deceased person or from a live donor is necessary for the person with kidney failure to continue to live. MEDICARE provides coverage to Medicare recipients for kidney-failure treatment. About 80,000 new cases of ESRD are diagnosed each year in the United States.

The kidneys can fail at any age, but the failure risk generally increases with age. In looking at new cases of kidney failure in 1997, the highest rates of kidney failure were found among people older than age 65.

The U.S. Renal Data System (USRDS), funded by the National Institute of Diabetes and Digestive Diseases (NIDDK) and the CENTERS FOR MEDICARE AND MEDICAID SERVICES (CMS), maintains a national database of information on treated chronic kidney-failure patients. This database includes information on an estimated 93 percent of all ESRD patients in the United States. ESRD costs about $50,000 per patient per year, and the costs exceed $2 billion for all patients in the United States.

When the kidneys work well, they filter out excessive fluid, minerals, and waste material from the blood. They also produce hormones that maintain strong bones and healthy blood. If kidneys fail, usually because of long-term disease, harmful materials are no longer filtered from the blood, blood pressure rises, and excessive fluid can build up (edema).

Risks for Kidney Failure
The most common cause of kidney failure is DIABETES, which is responsible for about 43 percent of all cases. Hypertension is the second leading cause of kidney failure. People with HYPERTENSION represent about 25 percent of those with ESRD. Because many people with diabetes also suffer from hypertension, people who have both diseases are at an even higher risk for kidney failure.

Racial and Ethnic Differences AFRICAN AMERICANS have about four times as many new cases of kidney failure as experienced by Caucasians. In 1996, African Americans represented about 13 percent of the population in the United States, but they were 30 percent of all kidney-failure patients.

Even more frightening, African Americans also develop the disease much earlier in their lives than Caucasians. For example, the average white person who develops kidney failure is about 62 years old. The average black person whose kidney has failed is about 56 years old.

NATIVE AMERICANS and ALASKA NATIVES are also at higher risk for suffering from kidney failure than Caucasians, developing kidney failure at about one-and-a-half times the rate for Caucasians.

Gender Risks In looking at people with diabetes who suffer from ESRD, men have a slightly higher rate of the disease than women.

Process of Kidney Failure
Most people have few or no symptoms in the early stages of kidney failure, although DIAGNOSTIC TESTING can often determine people who are at risk so that they can be treated early in the disease. Such early detection and treatment can be life saving.

Although there is usually no pain or other noticeable symptoms, in the first stage of kidney failure, blood flow through the kidneys increases and the kidneys enlarge. If a substance in the blood called creatinine is measured at this time, it is above normal and an early marker of kidney disease.

As the kidneys further deteriorate, the kidneys become more damaged. There are usually still no symptoms, but small amounts of a substance called albumin is detectable in the urine, if it is tested. When the disease progresses even further, the albumin and other substances can be found in a simple urinalysis.

The untreated kidneys will continue to deteriorate until the patient is in a stage of "advanced clinical nephropathy." At that point, patients will feel such symptoms as fatigue and weakness. Their urine will continue to have large quantities of protein (proteinuria). Patients often start to retain fluid, and they may have puffy faces and puffy ankles.

In the final stage of kidney disease, the kidneys fail altogether. Patients feel very ill at this point, and the fatigue and weakness is pronounced. Patients may also experience extreme itching and often have a loss of appetite. They may lose weight from not eating, but they may also gain weight from the large amount of retained fluid.

In the final stage of kidney disease and failure, all patients need dialysis, the use of a special machine to cleanse the kidneys, or a transplant of a kidney from a recently deceased donor or a live donor.

When patients have hemodialysis, they usually go to a dialysis center three times a week for three to four hours to have a machine filter their blood. The process takes three to five hours or longer, depending on the patient. Sometimes, dialysis for patients who live faraway from a hospital is performed in the home.

TABLE 1   AGE AND INCIDENCE OF ESRD

Total Population, 1997	New Cases of End-Stage Renal Disease Rate per Million
45 to 64 years	545
65 to 74 years	1,296
75 years and older	1,292

Source: "Chronic Kidney Disease," in *Healthy People 2010,* National Institutes of Health, 2000.

Cardiovascular Disease Kills Most People with ESRD

People who are ill with kidney failure are more likely to die from cardiovascular disease (CVD) than they are to die from actual kidney failure. CVD death among people with kidney failure is estimated at 30 times the rate for the general population. As mentioned earlier, patients with ESRD often have diabetes and/or hypertension to start with; in addition, many have a lipid disorder, and the toxins that are present due to their renal failure leads to a more aggressive form of ATHEROSCLEROSIS.

Preventing or Delaying Kidney Failure

People who have diabetes may be able to delay kidney failure by maintaining excellent glucose levels. Those who have hypertension need to keep their blood pressure as close to normal as possible and to be careful with their diet, especially avoiding a high intake of protein.

Kidney Transplantation

When a person's kidneys fail or are expected to fail imminently, the individual must be placed on kidney dialysis so that the impurities in the blood will be cleaned out mechanically. Another alternative is a kidney transplant. Physicians use kidneys from recently deceased people and sometimes from live donors. (A person needs only one kidney to live, and most people have two kidneys.) Transplants from live donors have a better success rate.

In 1997, there were 12,445 kidney transplants performed in the United States. Survival rates have steadily increased for kidney-transplant patients.

For further information, contact:

American Association of Kidney Patients
100 South Ashley Drive
Suite 280
Tampa, FL 33602
(800) 749-2257 (toll-free) or (813) 223-7099
http://www.aakp.org

American Kidney Fund
6110 Executive Boulevard
Suite 1010
Rockville, MD 20852
(800) 638-8299 (toll-free) or (301) 881-3052
http://www.akfinc.org

Life Options Rehabilitation Program
603 Science Drive
Madison, WI 53711
(800) 468-7777 (toll-free) or (608) 232-2333
http://www.lifeoptions.org

National Kidney Foundation (NKF)
30 East 33rd Street
New York, NY 10016
(800) 622-9010 (toll-free) or (212) 889-2210
http://www.kidney.org

National Institutes of Health. "Chronic Kidney Disease," in *Healthy People 2010,* National Institutes of Health. Washington, D.C.: Government Printing Office, 2000.

National Institutes of Health, National Institute of Diabetes and Digestive Diseases. *2000 Annual Data Report: Atlas of End-Stage Renal Disease in the United States.* Washington, D.C.: Government Printing Office, 2001.

National Kidney and Urologic Diseases Information Clearinghouse. "Kidney Failure: Choosing a Treatment That's Right for You," National Institute of Diabetes and Digestive and Kidney Diseases (NIDDK), NIH Publication No. 01-2412 (April 2001).

laxatives Over-the-counter or prescribed drugs that are taken by people who have a problem with CONSTIPATION. Some people who have difficulty maintaining regular bowel movements (daily or every other day) may also have a problem with passing hard stools, and they may use stool softeners to facilitate bowel movements. Others take laxatives that are combined with stool softeners.

It is possible to become physically dependent on laxatives; seniors should consult with their physicians if they feel that they must take a laxative to have a bowel movement. People who have chronic problems with constipation should be sure to increase their FIBER intake. Their doctors should also look at their medications to see if their dosages should be adjusted, in the event that the medications are constipating. Certain chronic medical conditions have a known effect on bowel function, such as DIABETES or PARKINSON'S DISEASE. Adjustments in activity, medications, dietary changes, and even the timing of medication can make a big difference in bowel habits for some seniors.

learned helplessness An induced feeling of powerlessness that leads to real powerlessness. The key premise of this concept is that when people are treated as if they are completely helpless, even though they actually are capable of performing at least some tasks, they often will eventually take on the attributes of helplessness. For example, if they are constantly urged to rest, even though they are capable of physical activity, they may give up on any EXERCISE. If they are fed, even though they can feed themselves, they may give up on attempting to self-feed. When people in a nursing home or other facility are capable of using the toilet if they receive some assistance in getting to the bathroom, but that assis-

tance is never or rarely received, then the affected people will become incontinent.

It is also true that learned helplessness in one task may generalize to an overall helplessness at many tasks. This means that if, for example, people feel that they cannot feed themselves, they may also feel that they cannot perform other activities, including tasks that they actually could have performed.

Sometimes well-meaning CAREGIVERS or attendants try to do many or most things for an older person, but study after study shows that the people who are the healthiest and the happiest are those who can perform at least some activities of daily living on their own.

Often, the helpers, or "enablers," have the best of intentions, but, nonetheless, they are doing a disservice to the senior adults whom they are trying to help. As a result, whenever possible, older people should be encouraged to maintain some level of control over their daily lives, even when they may take longer to perform these activities or it causes some inconvenience to a facility or caregiver.

legal guardianship Process whereby an individual is appointed to represent the interests of another person. In the case of older individuals, the guardian is usually one who acts for another who has been determined by a court to be mentally incompetent and thus is incapable of managing his or her own life and making major decisions. This is a different situation from when the DURABLE POWER OF ATTORNEY is used, in which an individual makes advance arrangements for another person to manage his or her affairs if and when the individual becomes mentally incompetent or physically incapacitated.

According to attorneys Peter J. Strauss and Nancy M. Lederman in their book, *The Elder Law Handbook,* "Guardianship is the judicial appointment of a person with the power and duty to make decisions concerning personal or financial affairs on behalf of another who is considered incapable of doing so for himself or herself. In this it is similar to a power of attorney, except that it is a judge—not you—who decides who is going to serve."

Sometimes, more than one legal guardian is appointed; for example, one legal guardian may be appointed to manage legal or financial affairs while another may be appointed to make medical or personal decisions for the individual. States vary greatly in their laws on legal guardianship, with some states maintaining considerable oversight and others requiring less governmental or judicial control once guardianship has been granted.

See also MENTAL COMPETENCY.

Strauss, Peter J., and Nancy M. Lederman. *The Elder Law Handbook: A Legal and Financial Survival Guide for Caregivers and Seniors.* New York: Facts On File, 1996.

life expectancy The number of years of life that an individual can expect to attain, on average. In the U.S., the projected life expectancy at birth, as of 2000, was 77.1, according to the U.S. Census Bureau, with a life expectancy of 81.0 years for women and 74.5 years for men. Statisticians will continue to hone these projections every year.

The United States does not have the highest life expectancy. Australia, Sweden, Italy, France, and other countries have higher life expectancies. (See Figure 1.) For example, of 34 countries, the highest life expectancy for women is in Japan, with a life expectancy at birth of 84.1 years. For men, Japan also offers the highest life expectancy from birth, or 77.5 years. Table 1 shows life expectancies for men and women in many countries worldwide.

Gender: Women Generally Live Longer

Another way to look at life expectancy is to project the number of years *more* that an adult or older person can expect to live. According to the Census Bureau, the average white woman (all races) in the United States who lived to the age of 65 in 2000 could

TABLE I LIFE EXPECTANCY AT BIRTH IN 34 COUNTRIES: 2000

Region/country	2000	
	Male	Female
DEVELOPED COUNTRIES		
Western Europe		
Austria	74.5	81.0
Belgium	74.5	81.3
Denmark	74.0	79.3
France	74.9	82.9
Germany [1]	74.3	80.8
Norway	75.7	81.8
Sweden	77.0	82.4
United Kingdom	75.0	80.5
Southern and Eastern Europe		
Czech Republic [1]	71.0	78.2
Greece	75.9	81.2
Hungary	67.0	76.1
Italy	75.9	82.4
Spain	75.3	82.5
Other		
Australia	76.9	82.7
Japan	77.5	84.1
United States	74.2	79.9

	2000	
DEVELOPING COUNTRIES	Male	Female
Africa		
Egypt	61.3	65.5
Ghana	56.1	58.8
Mali	45.5	47.9
South Africa	50.4	51.8
Uganda	42.2	43.7
Congo (Brazzaville)	44.5	50.5
Asia		
China	69.6	73.3
India	61.9	63.1
Kazakhstan	57.7	68.9
South Korea	70.8	78.5
Syria	67.4	69.6
Thailand	65.3	72.0
Latin America		
Argentina	71.7	78.6
Brazil	58.5	67.6
Costa Rica	73.3	78.5
Chile	72.4	79.2
Mexico	68.5	74.7
Venezuela	70.1	76.3

[1] Figures for Germany and Czech Republic prior to 1999 refer to the former West Germany and Czechoslovakia, respectively.

TABLE 2   EXPECTATION OF CONTINUED YEARS OF LIFE IN THE UNITED STATES, BY AGE, RACE AND SEX IN 2000

Age and Race	Male	Female
Age in 2000, in years	Expected Years More	Expected Years More
White		
65	16.3	19.2
70	13.0	15.5
75	10.1	12.1
80	7.6	9.1
85	5.5	6.6
90	4.0	4.7
95	3.0	3.3
100	2.2	2.4
Black		
65	14.6	17.5
70	11.8	14.1
75	9.4	11.2
80	7.4	8.7
85	5.8	6.5
90	4.5	4.9
95	3.6	3.6
100	.9	2.7

Source: Arialdi M. Minino, MPH and Betty L. Smith, B.S. Ed, Division of Vital Statistics. "Deaths: Preliminary Data for 2000," *National Vital Statistics Reports* 49, no. 12 (October 9, 2001): 1–39.

expect to live another 19.2 years, until she is 84 years old. The average man (all races) in the United States who lived to the age of 65 could expect to live another 16 years, until he is 81 years old. (See Table 2.)

Race: Most African Americans Don't Live As Long as Whites

As can be seen from Table 2, when considering older adults, AFRICAN AMERICANS in the United States have a shorter life expectancy than whites. For example, the average black male who is 65 years old can expect to live another 14.6 years, compared to 16.3 more years for the 65-year-old white man. The average black woman who is age 65 can expect to live another 17.5 years, compared to the 19.2 more years that a white woman of the same age can anticipate.

Improved Life Expectancies During Past Years

Life expectancies have increased considerably since 1900, and they continue to rise as science and tech-

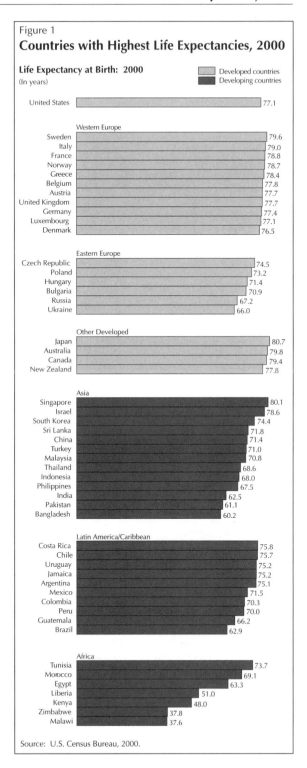

Figure 1

Countries with Highest Life Expectancies, 2000

Life Expectancy at Birth: 2000
(In years)

Developed countries
Developing countries

United States — 77.1

Western Europe
Sweden — 79.6
Italy — 79.0
France — 78.8
Norway — 78.7
Greece — 78.4
Belgium — 77.8
Austria — 77.7
United Kingdom — 77.7
Germany — 77.4
Luxembourg — 77.1
Denmark — 76.5

Eastern Europe
Czech Republic — 74.5
Poland — 73.2
Hungary — 71.4
Bulgaria — 70.9
Russia — 67.2
Ukraine — 66.0

Other Developed
Japan — 80.7
Australia — 79.8
Canada — 79.4
New Zealand — 77.8

Asia
Singapore — 80.1
Israel — 78.6
South Korea — 74.4
Sri Lanka — 71.8
China — 71.4
Turkey — 71.0
Malaysia — 70.8
Thailand — 68.6
Indonesia — 68.0
Philippines — 67.5
India — 62.5
Pakistan — 61.1
Bangladesh — 60.2

Latin America/Caribbean
Costa Rica — 75.8
Chile — 75.7
Uruguay — 75.2
Jamaica — 75.2
Argentina — 75.1
Mexico — 71.5
Colombia — 70.3
Peru — 70.0
Guatemala — 66.2
Brazil — 62.9

Africa
Tunisia — 73.7
Morocco — 69.1
Egypt — 63.3
Liberia — 51.0
Kenya — 48.0
Zimbabwe — 37.8
Malawi — 37.6

Source: U.S. Census Bureau, 2000.

nology overcome fatal diseases and prolong lives. For example, only about 39 percent of the boys and 43 percent of the girls who were born in the United Staes in 1900 could expect to live to the age of 65. By 1997, these percentages had increased greatly, and 86 percent of the girls and 77 percent of the boys born in that year could expect to live to the age of 65 years. The key reasons for these increased life expectancies were decreased death rates from acute infections.

Reasons for Improved Longevity

According to Dr. Christine Cassell in her article in a 2001 issue of *Geriatrics*, there are several key reasons for the improved life expectancy that many people enjoy today. Dr. Cassel says that in the United States, the number of people who are living beyond age 85 increased with the advent of the MEDICARE program in 1965 and with a greater access to health care.

She also points out that preventive medicine became an important issue and says that 100 years ago, for many people, the major causes of death were pneumonia, tuberculosis and intestinal disease. In modern times, science has made great strides in preventing or treating these infections. One commonality with the past, however, is that people still die of CANCER, HEART DISEASE, and STROKE, although they are usually dying from these illnesses at an older age than in the past.

Cassel concludes, "An increasing number of older persons enter old age in generally good health. Although they have circumnavigated chronic conditions such as heart disease and diabetes, they may be at increased risk for conditions that assault the brain. On various research fronts, we see provocative indications that diseases such as Alzheimer's and Parkinson's could be managed effectively or even prevented. Whether the best interventions come from natural compounds, genetically engineered biologics, or a combination of treatments remains to be seen."

Indeed, how modern science has allowed people to recover from many disease processes may also be critical in how long people live. Years ago, a major heart attack or a stroke would have killed a patient within the first 24 to 48 hours of onset. Now, with new protocols and medications, physicians can slow, stop, and in some cases even reverse the symptoms of a stroke or heart attack. This factor, combined with newer rehabilitation techniques, has played a role in increased longevity for many people.

Cassel, Christine K., M.D. "Successful Aging: How Increased Life Expectancy and Medical Advances Are Changing Geriatric Care," *Geriatrics* 56, no. 1 (2001): 35–39.

Minino, Arialdi M., M.P.H., and Betty L. Smith, B.S. Ed., Division of Vital Statistics. "Deaths: Preliminary Data for 2000," *National Vital Statistics Reports* 49, no. 12 (October 9, 2001): 1–39.

Sahyoun, Nadine R., Ph.D., R.D. et al. "Trends in Causes of Death Among the Elderly," Centers for Disease Control and Prevention, National Center for Health Statistics, *Aging Trends* 1 (2001): 1–9.

living will   A legal document that states the action a patient wants to have taken in the case of needed future medical care should the patient be unable to express his or her wishes at the time of severe illness. Some patients prefer that extreme measures be taken to save their lives, while others do not choose this option. Patients may have living wills drawn up by their attorney prior to their illness or incapacity to express their wishes. State laws vary on how the living will is to be handled.

The classic case of the reason for the living will is of the patient who is terminally ill or brain dead and who cannot express a desire to continue life. The living will may express that the person does not (or does) wish for medical care to continue in that event.

loneliness   Need and desire for absent companionship and friendship. Loneliness is likely to become an increasing problem as individuals age and lose spouses, friends, partners, and family members to death. Older people may also become lonely because they are ill or isolated, and it is difficult for them to see others socially. Severe loneliness can lead to DEPRESSION or ANXIETY (or both problems) and may even lead to SUICIDE.

long-distance care   Usually alludes to care planned by ADULT CHILDREN or other relatives for an older person who lives out of state or too far away for them to provide in-person care themselves to their relative. As a result, adult children or other relatives attempt to manage the care of an older person remotely. This generally involves hiring individuals in the state where the older person lives so that direct care can be provided. It can be very difficult and time consuming to oversee caregiving from a distance. Some people hire geriatric case managers, who are special social workers who can work to locate care for the older person and oversee the case for a fee.

Often, there are conflicts between various out-of-state adult children who are siblings, as well as between other family members. They may disagree on what type of care should be provided to the older person, who is best able to provide that care, and how aggressive to be with medical treatments. This is a very stressful situation for all involved, including the patient, the family members, and the treating physicians. Often, the doctor must speak to various family members who request opposite interventions, and the physician must work out a resolution as to treatment. As always, if patients are mentally competent, their wishes are the ones that need to be adhered to.

See also BABY BOOMERS; SANDWICH GENERATION.

longevity Refers to years of life.

See also CENTENARIANS; LIFE EXPECTANCY; OLDEST OLD.

long-term care Generally refers to skilled care provided in a NURSING-HOME setting. This term may, however, also refer to the requirement of a senior adult for an ongoing aide or assistance in his or her home or any other location.

long-term care insurance Insurance that is purchased ahead of time, usually to pay for nursing-home care in the future, should it be needed. There are many different companies that sell this form of insurance. It has many different pros and cons to take into consideration.

On the plus side, if the long-term-care insurance policy was created by a legitimate organization, it may provide needed benefits in the future so that a person can move to a nursing home without needing to liquidate his or her assets. On the negative side, most older Americans ultimately do not need to live in nursing homes, and thus, the payments may have been made with no eventual gain that results. The individual might have been better advised to invest his or her money in other ventures. There are also some companies that have behaved disreputably and that have bilked seniors of their SAVINGS.

lung cancer Malignant tumor on the lungs and the leading cause of cancer deaths in the United States. An estimated 160,000 men and women die from lung cancer, more than all the combined cancer deaths from PROSTATE CANCER, BREAST CANCER, and COLORECTAL CANCER. More women die from lung cancer each year in the United States than from breast cancer.

The survival rate after five years from the diagnosis of lung cancer is only about 14 percent. Many patients are not diagnosed until they are in the late stages of the disease. About 90 percent of lung cancer deaths are directly attributable to SMOKING.

There are two main types of lung cancer: nonsmall lung cancer (the more common form) and small-cell lung cancer. Small-cell lung cancer is more dangerous and aggressive than nonsmall lung cancer.

Risk Factors

Men have a higher rate of death from lung cancer than women, and African-American men have an even higher death rate from lung cancer than white men, according to the National Cancer Institute. White and African-American women have about the same rate of death, with white women having a slightly worse rate. (See Table 1.)

TABLE 1 DEATH RATES FROM LUNG CANCER, PER 100,000 PEOPLE, 1994–1998

Male		Female	
White	Black	White	Black
66.6	94.0	34.9	33.9

Source: National Cancer Institute. "Annual Report to the Nation on the Status of Cancer, 1973–1998, Featuring Cancers with Recent Increasing Trends," *Journal of the National Cancer Institute* 93, no. 11 (2001): 824–842.

**TABLE 2   SELECTED LUNG CANCER DEATH RATES IN TOP FOUR WORST STATES, 1994–1998
BY RACE AND SEX, RATE PER 100,000 DEATHS**

White Men		Black Men		White Women		Black Women	
Kentucky	98.8	Wisconsin	123.4	Nevada	48.8	Delaware	50.3
Arkansas	91.2	Kentucky	117.0	Kentucky	43.8	Rhode Island	48.8
Tennessee	90.5	Arkansas	115.4	Delaware	42.2	Pennsylvania	47.0
Mississippi	87.7	Tennessee	115.3	Maine	41.6	Indiana	45.3

Source: Derived from the National Cancer Institute. "Annual Report to the Nation on the Status of Cancer, 1973–1998, Featuring Cancers with
  Recent Increasing Trends," *Journal of the National Cancer Institute* 93, no. 11 (2001): 824–842.

Although adults of any age can contract lung cancer, those who are most at risk are as follows:

- Males older than age 60
- Black men
- People who have smoked a pack or more of cigarettes a day for 20 years or more
- People exposed to smoke from other smokers (second-hand smoke)
- People who were exposed to high-risk substances such as asbestos at work and who also smoke

Death Rates Vary By State

Lung cancer death rates vary radically in the United States, depending on the state in which a person lives, presumably because people in some states are much heavier smokers than in other states. For example, among white men, the lung-cancer death rates are highest for those living in Kentucky (98.9 per 100,000), Arkansas (91.2 per 100,000), and Tennessee (90.5 per 100,000).

Among African-American men, the lung-cancer death rates are highest in Wisconsin (123.4 per 100,000), Kentucky (117.0 per 100,000), and Arkansas (115.4 per 100,000). (See Table 2 for information on both men and women.)

Causes of Lung Cancer

Since 1964, when the Surgeon General's *First Report on Smoking and Health* was released, it has been known that smoking causes lung cancer. However, because nicotine is highly addictive, many people have tremendous difficulty in ending the habit that they usually started many years ago. Cigarettes lead to lung cancer, as do cigars and pipe tobacco.

It is also possible for a nonsmoker to develop cancer if often in the presence of others who smoke. According to the U.S. Surgeon General, nonsmokers develop 3,000 lung-cancer deaths per year from secondhand smoke.

Other causes of lung cancer include:

- Exposure to asbestos fibers
- Tuberculosis
- A previous lung cancer

Symptoms of Lung Cancer

Most people with lung cancer have symptoms of the disease, although they may not consider their symptoms serious or see the doctor until they are very ill. Some key symptoms are:

- A chronic cough
- Chronic chest pain
- Vomiting of blood
- Constant shortness of breath or hoarseness
- Frequent bouts with pneumonia or bronchitis
- Facial or neck swelling
- Appetite loss and weight loss
- Chronic fatigue

Other diseases may cause these symptoms, as well and only a physician can accurately determine whether a person has lung cancer or not.

Diagnosis

When doctors suspect lung cancer, they employ various tests to help with the diagnosis. For example, in one test, the doctor inserts a bronchoscope into the breathing passages to better inspect them. This procedure also enables the doctor to collect samples for a biopsy. It is also possible to remove biopsy tissue with a needle that is inserted directly into the chest.

The biopsy will determine whether cancer is present or not. If the patient does have lung cancer, the biopsy will also reveal how advanced the cancer is and how aggressively it is growing.

The doctor may also perform other tests, such as a bone scan to determine if cancer has advanced into the bones. A computed tomography (CT) scan or magnetic resonance imaging (MRI) scan may also help with diagnosis. A special procedure called a mediastinoscopy can also help to determine if cancer is also present in the lymph nodes of the neck. An incision is required for this procedure, which is performed under anesthesia.

There are other methods of early detection, such as analysis of saliva or samples of fluid from the bronchial area.

Treatment for Lung Cancer

Anyone who is diagnosed with lung cancer must stop smoking immediately and for good. (All others are well advised to quit smoking to avoid developing lung cancer and other smoking-related cancers and illnesses in the future.)

In many cases, surgery will be recommended. The surgeon will remove all or part of the lung. Sometimes, surgery cannot be done because it is too difficult to reach the tumor or because the patient is too ill for surgery. Surgery for lung cancer is a major procedure, and most patients will take at least weeks and probably months to recover from the procedure.

Chemotherapy is another treatment option. Cancer-killing drugs are introduced into the body intravenously or with a catheter. There are also some anticancer drugs available in the form of pills. Chemotherapy often causes nausea, fatigue, and hair loss, among some of the side effects.

Radiation therapy may also be recommended. In most cases, the patient receives radiation from a special machine that irradiates the cancerous area. The patient goes to a hospital or a clinic for these treatments. Radiation therapy for lung cancer may cause sore throat, trouble with swallowing, tiredness, and appetite loss.

Photodynamic therapy is another option to treat lung cancer. A special chemical is injected into the affected area, and then laser lights are used to activate the chemical and boost its cancer-killing ability. This therapy may be used to treat isolated tumors and also to treat some of the symptoms of lung cancer, such as difficult breathing or internal bleeding.

Photodynamic therapy causes patients to be very light-sensitive for at least six weeks, and they must avoid sunlight and even indoor bright lights. If they cannot stay indoors for six weeks, then they must wear protective clothing and sunglasses when going out very briefly during this restrictive period.

Cryosurgery is another option that is sometimes used to treat nonsmall-cell lung cancer. In this procedure, the area with the cancer cells is frozen so that they are destroyed.

National Cancer Institute. "Lung Cancer," NIH Publication No. 99-1553 (August 1999).

macular degeneration, age-related   Serious eye disease of the center part of the retina that can lead to BLINDNESS. Age-related macular degeneration is the primary cause of blindness in the United States and other developed countries. There is no cure for this form of macular degeneration, although there are treatments as of this writing. Ongoing clinical trials by the National Eye Institute and also by private organizations may bring new advances in therapy in the near future.

According to data produced by Prevent Blindness America for the federal government in its 2002 report "Vision Problems in the U.S.," there are an estimated 1.65 million Americans older than age 50 with age-related macular degeneration, including a 1.05 million females and 0.6 million males.

Age-related macular degeneration is categorized into early and late stages of the disease. In the early stage, visual impairment is not great, but abnormalities can be detected in the macula. The primary abnormality is the formation of "drusen" in the macula, which are accumulations of debris.

In the late stages of age-related macular degeneration, there are two forms, including the atrophic and the neovascular, exudative forms. Blindness can occur with either form.

Risk Factors

As might be expected, the risk for age-related macular degeneration increases with aging, and some studies have found that about 30 percent of those older than age 75 experience early-stage macular degeneration and that 7 percent older than age 75 experience late-stage macular degeneration. Other risk factors include:

- SMOKING
- A family history of this problem
- Being female
- Being white
- Having cardiovascular disease
- Having irises that are light in color
- Low intake of ZINC and antioxidant vitamins

Treatment of Macular Degeneration

The best treatment for age-related macular degeneration, as of this writing, is laser photocoagulation. However, there are some limitations to this treatment as well. For example, even when treatment is successful, about a 50 percent probability that leakage will happen again within two years exists. Also, central vision will be reduced with this treatment; however, it is less than would occur if the eye were not treated.

Other forms of surgery are also options. In addition, the drug thalidomide is being investigated as a possible treatment. Some studies are looking at whether the risks for developing age-related macular degeneration can be reduced by people taking antioxidants, either alone or in combination with zinc. Vitamin E is also often recommended as a treatment. Clinical results of these treatments are not available as of this writing.

Fine, Stuart L., M.D. et al. "Age-Related Macular Degeneration," *The New England Journal of Medicine* 342, no. 7 (2000): 483–492.

Fong, Donald S., M.D., M.P.H. "Age-Related Macular Degeneration: Update for Primary Care," *American Family Physician* 61 (2000): 3,035–3,042.

mammogram   Special screening X ray of breast tissue to determine if a woman may have BREAST CANCER. In general, women older than age 50 should have an annual mammogram to screen for breast cancer.

Some physicians do not test older women for breast cancer, and this issue is a controversial one. If the woman is up to age 75, she may have another 10 years of life. But if she were not tested for breast cancer, and if she has the disease and is not treated for it, she could be denied years of life. Studies indicate that breast cancer is as aggressive in older women as in younger women. If the woman is in very poor health, however, it might be difficult for her to cope with the treatments of breast cancer.

As the aging population continues to grow, this issue will become one that increasing numbers of women and their doctors will need to consider.

mania   Hyperexcited state. Some forms of DEMEN-TIA or ALZHEIMER'S DISEASE may cause an individual to behave in a manic, hyperactive, and out-of-control manner. The behavior is very disruptive and difficult to handle, even by experienced professionals. This is a key reason why it is very difficult for family members to provide care to elderly relatives suffering from dementia or Alzheimer's disease. With this disease, there can be dramatic and rapid mood swings, making some of even the most mild patients quite challenging and at times, even dangerous to deal with.

The individual may be delusional or paranoid, thinking that he or she is being threatened or that someone is trying to take away something that is theirs. In general, delusional people cannot be talked out of their delusion and at best they can be distracted by something else. Talking to the manic person in a calm voice can be helpful.

Some individuals will require sedating medication to control their mania, although whether and how much to drug older people is a controversial issue. This also brings up the issue of *chemical restraints,* another term to connote medications that are sedating and used for that purpose. These types of drugs, as with physical restraints, are meant to safeguard patients and prevent them from hurting themselves or others. However, caution should be taken to avoid the abuse of either chemical or physical restraints.

marriage/remarriage   Legal union of two people or the marriage of a person who has been previously married but is divorced or widowed. According to the Administration on Aging statistics amassed in 2001, older men are much more likely to be married than older women; 74 percent of older men were married, versus 43 percent of older women. Because so many older men are already married, and because women generally marry men who are the same age or older, it is generally more difficult for older women to remarry than it is for older men.

Older Individuals Living Together Without Marriage

Some older individuals choose to marry; however, increasing numbers are forgoing marriage because they wish to retain their own dental and medical benefits and other benefits that would be lost if they married. In addition, after marriage, if a spouse becomes ill, the joint assets and resources of both parties are at risk to cover costly nursing-home care or home health providers, as well as other medical expenses. But if the partners stay single and live together, only the assets of each person would be at financial risk if one became ill. In addition, there is a financial disincentive for senior adults to marry, as they almost always end up with higher taxes when they do.

Reactions of Adult Children to a Parent's Remarriage

Sometimes, adult children become upset when a parent remarries: they may feel that remarriage dishonors the memory of their deceased parent or that the parent will no longer need their assistance or heed their advice. Sometimes, adult children dislike the new spouse: they may believe that they should have been consulted before a parent remarried, or they may believe that the parent should only marry a person of whom the adult child approves.

Some psychiatrists say that adult children dislike the idea of a parent having sex, and a new marriage almost inevitably connotes the idea of sexual activities. The problem may be partly one of a feeling of disloyalty to the other parent, as well as a dislike of thinking about the sexuality of one's parent. The adult child may also think that older people should not have sexual relations, viewing this as an activity for younger individuals. As a result, adult children may be disgusted by seeing a parent display affection with a new spouse.

Adult children may also fear that they will lose an inheritance because they may think that it will go to the new spouse (or the spouse's children) if the parent dies. (This fear is not entirely unwarranted.) One way to avert such a concern is for the older person to do ESTATE PLANNING and to draw up a new will that stipulates how his or her assets should be handled upon death. Although this is a logical step, many older people ignore this choice. Yet even a small estate can cause considerable legal difficulties if the individual dies intestate (without a will).

In one case, bereaved adult children appeared at a garage sale at their stepparent's house, trying to buy a memento from their parent's belongings that were for sale. This case clearly illustrates that it is best for adult children and their parents to discuss issues with their parents and their stepparents candidly, such as what should happen to personal belongings that the adult child might want after the parent dies.

Some issues that adult children might consider in favor of remarriage are that the parent's health may improve, that he or she may be happier if he or she remarries, and that the parent's dependency on the adult child, which sometimes has been burdensome, may decrease. In addition, most studies show that married people are healthier and live longer than nonmarried individuals.

Adamec, Christine. "When Parents of Parents Remarry," *Single Parent* 27, no. 8 (October 1984): 20–21.

Meals on Wheels   Nationwide program in the United States of home-delivered meals that are provided to individuals who are homebound. Many recipients are elderly, and most are ill or disabled. In many cases, their relatives or friends cannot or do not provide assistance. Meals on Wheels is one of the largest and oldest programs providing nutritional assistance, although there are other meal delivery programs that are available as well. Meals on Wheels is partly funded by federal dollars.

In addition to providing nutrition, this program also provides social contact to meal recipients, which in many cases is just as important.

For further information, contact:

Meals on Wheels Association of America
1414 Prince Street
Suite 302
Alexandria, VA 22314
(703) 548-5558
http://www.projectmeal.org

media   Television, radio and print outlets, such as magazines and newspapers. The media often depict older individuals as either kindly grandparents or individuals suffering from dementia, and they often evince an ageist bias. In many cases, older people are not seen at all on television, nor are programs oriented to them, because television executives target most of their programming to adolescents and young adults, who they believe will buy the products advertised during commercials.

See also AGEISM.

Medicaid   The medical insurance program in the United States, under Title IX of the Social Security Act, and first enacted in 1965. This program is both federally and state funded in its mission to provide medical benefits to poor individuals who are disabled or elderly, (and for some dependent children and their parents) and who may be ineligible for other federal or private programs or who may receive insufficient funds or services from other programs. (For example, MEDICARE does not pay for outpatient medications as of this writing, while Medicaid does cover medications.)

In 1999, there were about 2.4 million people age 65 and older (about 7 percent of the older population) receiving Medicaid services; most of them were older women.

At the federal level, Medicaid (and also Medicare) is overseen by the CENTERS FOR MEDICARE AND MEDICAID SERVICES (CMS), formerly known as the Health Care and Financing Administration (HCFA). Medicaid affects many people who are elderly, disabled, and of low income.

To qualify for Medicaid, people must be "categorically eligible" for Medicaid, which means that low income is not sufficient by itself to guarantee eligibility. Instead, the person must also receive

Supplemental Security payment benefits (SSI) due to a disability or qualify in some other category of public assistance. Some Medicare beneficiaries who are indigent are also eligible for Medicaid benefits.

Types of Services

Medicaid provides coverage for the following forms of medical services:

- Inpatient hospital care
- Outpatient hospital care
- Medications
- Laboratory and X-ray services
- Skilled nursing-facility services

Some states also provide dental and optometric care in their Medicaid plans as well as other services. Another option chosen by many states is a form of managed care or HMO coverage for Medicaid enrollees, in which a particular physician or group will be the one(s) to provide care. This service has proven to be cost effective for both states and the federal government because it diverts individuals on Medicaid from seeking their routine medical care at hospital emergency rooms.

See also DISABILITY; GOVERNMENT, FEDERAL; GOVERNMENT, STATE.

medical records   Documents maintained by physicians that record health information on their patients. Medical records not only aid doctors in reviewing their patients' past history and treatments, but these records may also serve to provide information to any other doctors whom the patient sees.

Most medical records are held in paper form, but some records are computerized, particularly in larger clinics or hospitals.

If senior adults travel, they should carry a condensed copy of their medical records. Also, taking the time to write down their own chronological history of health events may be quite helpful, particularly if multiple physicians are involved in a patient's care.

Medicare   A large federal medical program in the United States for individuals who are eligible in rela-

tion to their retirement or disability benefits. Enacted in 1965 by Congress, Medicare provides medical coverage for an estimated 95 percent of the aged population in the United States, and it also provides medical coverage for many disabled adults of all ages.

In 1999, about 8.5 million people (about 26 percent of the population) age 65 and older received only Medicare coverage (with no MEDIGAP or extra health-insurance coverage), and Medicare payments totaled $213 billion for the year. The largest numbers of Medicare recipients are in the West (36.4 million in 1999). (See Table 1.)

Contrary to the SSI program, individuals who receive Medicare benefits need not be poor as a requirement of eligibility. Instead, they must meet age or disability requirements, among other conditions of eligibility.

The CENTERS FOR MEDICARE AND MEDICAID SERVICES (CMS), formerly known as the Health Care Financing Administration (HCFA), is the federal organization that oversees the Medicare program. CMS also administers the End-Stage Renal Disease Program to pay for DIALYSIS and kidney transplants in Medicare patients whose kidneys fail them.

At the outset of the program, Medicare was part of the Social Security Amendments of 1965, under Title XVIII of the Social Security Act. The program originally covered only eligible people who were age 65 and older. In 1973, the program was amended to include people younger than age 65 who were entitled to either Social Security disability benefits or Railroad Retirement disability benefits. At that time, most people with KIDNEY FAILURE were also added to the program, which is still a feature of the program today.

Parts of Medicare

There are two parts to Medicare, Part A and Part B. Medicare Part A covers inpatient hospital care and very limited periods of SKILLED-NURSING FACILITY care. Part B benefits primarily cover outpatient (office) physician visits. There is also a third part of Medicare known as the "Medicare+Choice" program, established by the Balanced Budget Act of 1997, which allows members to participate in private health-care plans. There are about 40 million people in the United States who are enrolled in Medicare and most have both Part A and B benefits. Of these, about 6 million participate in a Medicare+Choice plan.

TABLE 1 MEDICARE COVERAGE FOR PERSONS 65 YEARS OF AGE AND OLDER BY SELECTED CHARACTERISTICS, 1999

Characteristic	Medicare only[10]
	1999
	Number in millions
Total[4]	8.5
	Percent of population
Total, age adjusted[4,5]	26.3
Total, crude[4]	26.3
Age	
65–74 years	25.9
75 years and older	26.8
75–84 years	26.3
85 years and older	28.5
Sex[5]	
Male	26.2
Female	26.3
Race[5,6]	
White	25.1
Black	37.0
Hispanic origin and race	
All Hispanic[6]	42.5
White, non-Hispanic	24.0
Black, non-Hispanic	37.1
Percent of poverty level[5,7]	
Below 100 percent	32.7
100–149 percent	35.9
150–199 percent	31.5
200 percent or more	19.7
Geographic resgion[5]	
Northeast	25.5
Midwest	15.7
South	29.0
West	36.4
Location of residence[5]	
Within MSA[8]	28.0
Outside MSA[8]	20.6

Source: *Health, United States, 2001,* Centers for Disease Control and Prevention (CDC)

A third program, "TriCare," is offered to patients who are retired military people and have military medical benefits, in lieu of Medicare benefits.

Supplies and Equipment Covered and Not Covered by Medicare

Medicare pays for some HOME HEALTH CARE, as well as some approved medical equipment, such as wheelchairs, prosthetic devices, and oxygen equipment. As of this writing, prescription medications are not covered by Medicare, with the exception of immunizations for pneumonia, FLU, and hepatitis B, as well as some specific anticancer drugs.

Coverage for devices such as syringes, needles, supplies, and meters that are needed by some individuals with diabetes, particularly those with Type 1 diabetes who must self-inject insulin, are partly covered under Medicare. To receive coverage, the patient's doctor must fill out a form every six months. Medicare may cover special shoes as well, if needed. In general, the individual must pay for 20 percent of the Medicare-approved amount.

As of this writing, insulin and other medications taken outside the hospital are not covered under Medicare. Medicare also does *not* cover dental services, eyeglasses, or hearing aids.

Paying for Noncovered Items

Because Medicare does not cover all medical needs as of this writing, most seniors purchase what is called Medigap insurance, to pay for such items as chiropractic care. Some Medigap insurers provide prescription coverage. MEDIGAP INSURANCE also covers the "co-pay" fee for Medicare recipients.

If a retired person has health insurance from a private company, usually that insurance company pays for medical costs first, and then, if there are still costs remaining, Medicare will consider paying some of the balance.

For more information on Medicare, contact the local SOCIAL SECURITY ADMINISTRATION office, or contact the Centers for Medicare and Medicaid Services (CMS) at:

7500 Security Boulevard, C2-26-112
Baltimore, MD 21244
(800) 444-4606
http://www.medicare.gov

See also DISABILITY.

Social Security Administration, Office of Policy, Office of Research, Evaluation and Statistics. *Annual Statistical Supplement 2000 to the Social Security Bulletin*. Baltimore, Md.: Social Security Administration, 2000.

medication interactions The effect that medications may have on each other when taken by a person at about the same time or together. Some medications may boost ("potentiate") the impact of other drugs. They may also lower the efficacy of other medications. Some medications, when taken together, can result in medical problems that would not occur if they were not combined. These problem can be serious or even fatal adverse drug events.

Medication interactions are a potential problem for any person who takes any medicines, including over-the-counter drugs. Even alternative remedies can cause a problem; for example, ginkgo biloba can cause blood thinning, and it can also boost the impact of other blood thinners such as warfarin (Coumadin). If a physician was unaware that a particular patient was taking an herbal remedy, then he or she could not provide such a warning.

Many older people are likely to be on more than two or three medications for chronic conditions such as hypertension and cardiac problems. It is a good idea for patients to use just one pharmacy, if possible, so that the pharmacist can help track possible drug interactions. It is also a good idea for patients to keep a complete list of all medications and SUPPLEMENTS so that this information can be provided to new physicians or to pharmacists.

See also ADVERSE DRUG EVENT.

Hanlon, Joseph T., Leslie A. Shimp, and Todd P. Semla. "Recent Advances in Geriatrics: Drug-Related Problems in the Elderly," *The Annals of Pharmacotherapy* 34 (2000): 360–365.

Medigap insurance Supplemental insurance that individuals who are receiving MEDICARE in the United States purchase to cover the 20 percent of medical costs that are not covered by the Medicare system. Most Medigap policies do not include coverage for medications, although some do. Often, there are cer-

tain limits or exclusions, and patients are well advised to check into this prior to purchasing a plan.

meditation A method that is used to induce calmness and relaxation in an individual. Positive effects can include a lower heart rate and blood pressure, as well as an overall lowering of stress.

See also TAI CHI.

memory impairment Difficulty with recall of recent events or events past or with both. Memory impairment is a common problem for those who have DEMENTIA or ALZHEIMER'S DISEASE. However, some memory lapses are common for all people, and forgetting where one left the car keys or forgetting that it was someone's birthday does not indicate that a person is experiencing an onset of Alzheimer's disease. Instead, the person with memory impairment may forget how to get home from a formerly familiar place.

People suffering from DEPRESSION or ANXIETY are also more likely to have memory problems. In such cases, individuals are distracted or overwhelmed by their emotional problems. When the depression or anxiety is removed or at least improved, the memory will usually return to normal.

See also COGNITIVE DIFFICULTY.

menopause Refers to the process of the cessation of ovulation and the end of menstruation in the middle-aged or older woman. The average age for menopause is 51 years; thus, most women age 65 and older have gone through menopause a decade or more earlier. The number of incidents of urinary-tract infections, vaginitis, and yeast infections may increase during menopause as the lack of estrogen leads to vaginal-lining atrophy. Eating low-fat yogurt with active cultures (acidophilus) may help.

Many physicians prescribe HORMONE REPLACEMENT THERAPY to women who are menopausal and continue the therapy for many years. Some studies have indicated that combination medications (estrogen and progesterone) may cause medical problems in some women. There are many pros and cons to this choice, and each woman should discuss this decision with her gynecologist. Women who have DIABETES should remind their gynecologists about their diabetes in the event that a medication might affect their glucose levels.

For more information, contact:

American College of Obstetricians and Gynecologists
  (ACOG)
409 12th Street, SW
P.O. Box 96920
Washington, DC 20090
(202) 484-8748
http://www.acog.org

American Menopause Foundation
350 5th Avenue
Suite 2822
New York, NY, 10118
(212) 714-2398
http://www.americanmenopause.org

North American Menopause Society
P.O. Box 94527
Cleveland, OH 44101
(216) 844-8748
http://www.menopause.org

mental competency   A legal term that refers to an individual's ability to make rational daily and legal decisions about his or her life, such as where to live, what medical treatment to receive, and what to eat. State courts and state laws determine how the legal mental competency of individuals is to be determined, and laws vary considerably from state to state. This determination is usually made based on medical information provided by one or more physicians (often a NEUROLOGIST or a PSYCHIATRIST).

People with ALZHEIMER'S DISEASE, DEMENTIA, or other ailments that cause mental impairments may be regarded as mentally incompetent by their family or by other individuals. Concerned individuals may obtain a court order stipulating the mental incompetence of the patient, usually based on the finding of at least one medical doctor. The court may then appoint an individual to be the guardian of the mentally incompetent person. The guardian will make decisions on behalf of the mentally incompetent individual.

In general, mentally incompetent people do not retain their civil rights to vote or to marry. They may not drive a car, and they may not have complete access to their funds. The guardian may also receive access to monthly pension funds or other assets. To protect the mentally incompetent person, most courts require periodic reports from the guardian, and some states divide the guardianship responsibilities among several different people. For example, one person may oversee the financial assets of the mentally incompetent person, while another person may make medical decisions or day-to-day choices.

A person can have mild dementia but may continue to be mentally competent. It is important to remember that being declared mentally incompetent is a legal decision, whereas a diagnosis of dementia is a medical decision. The legal decision that a person is no longer mentally competent affects an individual's income, who controls his or her assets, and so forth. Courts generally rely on physicians for some direction with regard to mental competency, but they must also follow state law as well.

mobility   The capability of individuals to move about, with or without assistance. As many individual's age and develop chronic diseases such as ARTHRITIS or PARKINSON'S DISEASE, their physical mobility becomes increasingly impaired. People with BLINDNESS, DEMENTIA, and other ailments may also be physically impaired.

See also DRIVING.

MRI   Magnetic resonance imaging, originally called nuclear magnetic resonance (NMR) is considered by many health-care professionals to be the single greatest advance in diagnostic medicine in the last century. This unique tool is a noninvasive way to image healthy and damaged tissue without the risk of radiation. A magnetic field is set up, and then with a great deal of physics and computer savvy, special magnetic pictures are created.

Originally brought to the United States in 1985, MRI technology has been used extensively to diagnose all sorts of disease processes, such as brain tumors, joint or tissue damage (in the knees, shoulders, hips, and wrists), and jaw joint derangements, as well as neck and back disc herniations. New protocols are advancing this technology all the time, to the point that dementias and recurrent tumors can be teased out from STROKE and radiation changes.

Initially, the magnet strength of the MRI equipment was weaker, and the computer technology was also not as elaborate or sophisticated as it is as of this writing. But with recent breakthroughs in 2002, the magnetic scanners are much more open and "patient friendly," and the scanning times have also been drastically reduced from past years.

Some TV talk-show hosts have even promoted the idea of a whole body MRI scan as a diagnostic tool. Although this option is available, it is not particularly helpful at this time with the current level of technology.

muscle cramps   spasms of the muscles, not under voluntary control, that can be very painful. Cramps are more common in the legs and feet but may also occur in many other parts of the body. Older individuals have a greater risk for suffering from muscle cramps than younger people.

Causes of Muscle Cramps

Muscle cramps may be caused by a chemical imbalance, such as a vitamin or mineral deficiency; as a side effect of some medications; and also by a disease, such as ARTHRITIS or THYROID DISEASE. In addition, DIARRHEA or ALCOHOLISM may cause individuals to suffer from muscular cramps. Sometimes, strenuous exercise can induce muscle cramps.

People in some occupations are more likely to experience muscle cramps than others; for example, musicians and athletes are more prone to developing cramps because of the strenuous use of muscles.

In many cases, the cause of leg cramps cannot be determined.

Risk Factors

In general, leg cramps usually occur at night, although the reason for this is unknown. Nighttime leg cramps can be very painful.

In a study of patients age 65 and older, about half reported suffering from leg cramps; a higher percentage of women (56 percent) reported the problem than men (40 percent).

Diagnosis and Treatment

If a person has a chronic or continued problem with muscle cramps, the doctor will perform a physical examination to try to determine the root of the problem and also will usually order laboratory tests, such as thyroid tests and tests for fluid or electrolyte balances. If the physician can determine the cause of the cramps, then the treatment will be based on that cause. If the cause remains unknown, the patient with frequent leg cramps is often advised to use massage and stretching exercise. Physical therapy may be recommended as well. Often, cramping leg muscles may represent an underlying movement disorder, such as Restless Legs Syndrome.

Some studies indicate that Vitamin E is effective in people with chronic leg cramps. Muscle-relaxant therapy may be helpful.

In general, if cramps are chronically felt in the legs, doctors will recommend that patients sit or sleep with their legs raised on pillows or other devices.

It is important for patients with muscle cramps to seek medical attention, even possibly neurology specialty care, to determine ultimately the cause of the leg cramps.

Kanaan, Nbil, M.D., and Raja Sawaya, M.D. "Nocturnal Leg Cramps: Clinically Mysterious and Painful—But Manageable," *Geriatrics* 56, no. 6 (June 2001): 34–42.

National Family Caregivers Association (NFCA)
Organization that supports FAMILY CAREGIVERS and provides information and advocacy for their needs. Offers publications and assistance.

In 2001, a study of NFCA caregiving members was conducted by The Caregivers Advisory Panel, Inc./Mathew Greenwald & Associates and the Collaborative Partnership for Caregivers Research, and 239 respondents provided detailed information about family caregivers and their attitudes on a variety of issues.

Such issues as their own evaluation of their caregiving, if they regarded themselves primarily as family caregivers, if they felt they received enough training, and if they sought out financial assistance were explored in the survey by researchers. The survey results were provided in the *National Family Caregivers Association (NFCA) Survey of Self-Identified Family Caregivers,* and was released in September 2001.

For further information on NFCA or the survey, contact the organization at:

National Family Caregivers Association
10400 Connecticut Avenue
#500
Kensington, MD 20895-3944
(800) 896-3650 (toll-free)
http://www.nfcacares.org
See also CAREGIVERS.

Caregivers Advisory Panel. "National Family Caregivers (NFCA) Survey of Self-Identified Family Caregivers," P.O. Box 1206, Charlestown, RI 02813 (September 2001).

National Indian Council on Aging, Inc.
The foremost advocate for American Indian and Alaska Native elders. Founded in 1976, the National Indian Council on Aging, Inc., is an organization that was formed to bring about improved and comprehensive services for American Indian and Alaska Native elders. NICOA communicates and cooperates with service-provider agencies and advocacy organizations in the aging network. NICOA produces a quarterly newsletter entitled *Elder Voices,* which is mailed to organization members.

For further information, contact the National Indian Council on Aging, Inc., at:

10501 Montgomery Boulevard, NE
Suite 210
Albuquerque, NM 87111
(505) 292-2001
http://www.nicoa.org

National Institute on Aging (NIA)
One of 25 institutes and centers under the control of the NATIONAL INSTITUTES OF HEALTH (NIH). Formed in 1974, the NIA's mission is to support research on age-related diseases, the aging process, and the specific problems and needs of older individuals. The NIA also trains scientists on aging issues and provides information to the general public and other interested groups.

Contact the NIA at:

31 Center Drive, MSC 2292
Building 31, Room 5C27
Bethesda, MD 20892
(301) 496-1752
http://www.nia.nih.gov/

National Institutes of Health (NIH)
Federal health organization in the United States under which are umbrellaed many different institutes and organizations, such as the CENTERS FOR DISEASE

CONTROL AND PREVENTION (CDC), and the NATIONAL INSTITUTE ON AGING.

For further information, contact the NIH at:

National Institutes of Health
Bethesda, MD 20892
(301) 496-4000

National Osteoporosis Foundation Nationwide organization that provides information, research and assistance on OSTEOPOROSIS, a degenerative bone disease.

Contact the organization at:

National Osteoporosis Foundation
1150 17th Street, NW
Suite 500
Washington, DC 20036-4603
(202) 223-2226
http://www.nof.org/

National Stroke Association National organization that provides information and assistance for the victims of strokes and their families.

Contact the organization at:

National Stroke Association
9707 East Easter Lane
Englewood, CO 80112-3747
(303) 649-9299 or 800-STROKES (toll-free)
http://www.stroke.org

Native Americans/Alaska Natives/Native Hawaiians Racial group of individuals who are members of a Native American tribe in the continental United States, Alaska, and Hawaii. Also known as American Indians. In 2000, there were about 138,000 Native Americans age 65 and older living in the United States, according to the U.S. Census Bureau. Of these, about 79,000 were female.

Many older individuals in these racial groups have DIABETES, HYPERTENSION, KIDNEY DISEASE, KIDNEY FAILURE, STROKE, and OBESITY.

In 2000, under the OLDER AMERICANS ACT AMENDMENTS, the Native American Caregiver Support Program was created to aid Native Americans who need assistance. Regular grants are also made to tribes to provide congregate (group) and home-delivered meals, and the FY 2001 budget included $23.5 million for this purpose.

U.S. Administration on Aging. "The Many Faces of Aging: American Indian, Alaska Native, and Native Hawaiian Program" (2001).

neglect Failure of FAMILY CAREGIVERS or other caregivers to provide for the basic needs of a needful person, such as for food, shelter, or necessary medication. Neglect can be more dangerous than abuse because failure to provide food, shelter, and/or medication can lead to the death of an older person.

See also ABUSE.

nephrologist Medical doctor who is an expert at treating HYPERTENSION and KIDNEY DISEASE. Many older people suffer from a variety of kidney ailments that may be minor or may be as severe as KIDNEY FAILURE. If older persons have both hypertension and DIABETES, their risk for kidney disease increases, as does their need to consult with a nephrologist.

Many medical conditions require medications that are cleared through the kidneys. When there is kidney disease or decreased kidney function, these other illnesses can be affected, too. One of the most common problems in the senior adult population is the taking of multiple medications. With each medication, there is a certain risk of a side effect. With many medicines, there can be many side effects as well as a MEDICATION INTERACTION or a change in how the medication works and affects the body. Some medications can boost the actions of other drugs or reduce their action or change them in another way. The nephrologist will take all these problems in consideration when treating the patient.

neurologist Medical doctor who is an expert in diseases of the brain and spinal cord. Neurologists treat many older people, particularly those who have ALZHEIMER'S DISEASE, DEMENTIA, PARKINSON'S DISEASE, STROKE, and other illnesses that affect the brain and the spinal cord. A neurosurgeon is a specialist who is qualified to perform brain and spinal-cord surgery.

According to a review by the Academy of Neurology, most senior adults suffer from at least one ailment that could be diagnosed and treated by a neurologist. Some of these disorders include GAIT DISORDERS and balance problems, numbness and tingling in the extremities (often associated with pain), memory, speech or language problems, as well as many types of muscle and joint complaints.

Because of their training, neurologists are extremely well equipped to care for senior adults and their medical problems. Many primary-care physicians have learned to utilize neurologists as a valuable resource in consultation prior to ordering multiple expensive diagnostic tests.

night blindness   Difficulty seeing well in the evening hours, a common problem for many people who are older than age 65. People with such a problem should avoid DRIVING at dusk or later. The night blindness may stem from a treatable vitamin deficiency, such as a deficiency of Vitamin A, and it should be reported to the physician for evaluation. It may also be an early warning indicator of a serious eye disease, such as CATARACTS or GLAUCOMA.

Older people should receive annual eye examinations to maintain optimum vision. The adjustment of prescription lenses, treatment of increased eye pressure, and even simple surgery can help patients enjoy the evening hours as much as the daytime.

nursing homes   Term denoting facilities that provide care to elderly and/or disabled individuals. Also known as SKILLED-NURSING FACILITIES, or SNFs.

nutrition   Intake of food or another substance to maintain the body's basic caloric requirements. Often, older people receive insufficient nutrition (also known as undernutrition), either because they are incapable of preparing food or because they suffer from DEPRESSION and are not eating enough. The problem could be ill-fitting DENTURES or the lack of either dentures or natural teeth. Older individuals may have a lack of appetite because of medical prob-

lems that they are experiencing; for example, their senses of taste and smell, both important in eating, may be impaired. Other reasons may be the cause of poor nutrition.

Some diseases are directly affected by good or bad nutrition, most prominently, DIABETES. If the person with diabetes consumes excessive quantities of carbohydrates, he or she could suffer from severe hyperglycemia and even coma and death. Daily monitoring of the blood glucose is essential for all people who have diabetes, but many may be unwilling or unable to perform this monitoring. CAREGIVERS will often need to take over this task.

Some older individuals suffer from EATING DISORDERS, including some more typically associated with adolescent girls, such as anorexia nervosa; apparently, when it occurs among older people, it is primarily a desire for control rather than a wish to be thin that is at the root of the problem. Older people may feel that they have little or no control, other than to refuse food.

Undernutrition Among Seniors

According to *The Role of Nutrition in Maintaining Health in the Nation's Elderly,* a report on nutrition in the elderly by the Institute of Medicine, undernutrition is common among residents of SKILLED-NURSING FACILITIES as well as those who are hospitalized. The treatment for this undernutrition should depend on its cause or causes.

It is also true that some seniors do not receive sufficient vitamins or minerals. In a study reported in a 2000 issue of *Nutrition Insights,* a U.S. Department of Agriculture (USDA) publication, researchers reviewed data on 3,885 people age 66 and older. Their blood levels of vitamins and minerals were taken, as were their height, weight, and other data. The researchers found only a small number of "food-insufficient" (undernourished) older people in the sample and compared them to people receiving sufficient nutrition. Some key results are summarized below.

As can be seen from Table 1, the poorly nourished people were much more likely to have poor health, to be unmarried, and to have low levels of a variety of vitamins and minerals. (Marriage may bring a protective factor in that the partner encourages the person to eat better than a person alone would eat.)

TABLE 1   STATISTICALLY SIGNIFICANT MEAN DIFFERENCES BY FOOD SUFFICIENCY STATUS

Characteristics	Sufficient (3,768 people)	Insufficient (113 people)
Poor Health (percent)	30	65
Married (percent)	57	31
Dietary Assessment		
Calories	1,699	1,421
Protein (grams)	67.2	56.6
Carbohydrate (grams)	216	185
Thiamin (mg)	1.56	1.28
Niacin (mg)	20.8	16.0
Iron (mg)	14.9	10.6
Zinc	10.6	7.6
Meat (Servings)	1.7	1.4
Vegetables	3.2	2.3
Blood Serum levels		
Folate (nmol/L)	22.4	14.2
Vitamin C (mmol/L)	51.1	35.7

Source: U.S. Department of Agriculture. "Food Insufficiency and the Nutritional Status of the Elderly Population," *Nutrition Insights 18* (May 2000).

Overeating

Other seniors eat excessively, loading up on carbohydrates and skimping on vegetables and fruits. They may have a problem with OBESITY. It is also possible to be obese and yet at the same time to be deficient in many different vitamins and minerals.

Home meal-delivery services, such as provided by MEALS ON WHEELS, can provide a substantial portion of the nutrition needed by older people who live at home but who are isolated and cannot purchase and prepare their own meals for a variety of different reasons.

Feeding Through Food Tubes

Some very ill seniors may need to receive their nutrition through tubes inserted into the stomach because they are unable to consume food orally. This may be a temporary or permanent problem, depending on each individual case.

Long-term Impact of Poor Nutrition

Poor nutrition may weaken the immune systems of older people and make them more susceptible to developing infections, nutritional deficiencies, and a wide host of medical problems. A cascade effect may occur, and insufficient intake or a poor diet could ultimately cause sickness and death.

Committee on Nutrition Services for Medicare Beneficiaries, Food and Nutrition Board. *The Role of Nutrition in Maintaining Health in the Nation's Elderly.* Washington, D.C.: National Academy Press, 2000.

U.S. Department of Agriculture. "Food Insufficiency and the Nutritional Status of the Elderly Population," *Nutrition Insights 18* (May 2000).

obesity Excessive body fat for an individual's height and build, based on a body mass index measurement of 30.0 kg/m2 and higher. Body-mass index is a measurement used in the United States to determine if people are underweight, normal weight, overweight, or obese. (See Table 1 to view a chart of body mass indexes.) A body mass index of 30 or greater indicates a problem with obesity.

Many older individuals in the United States are overweight or obese. In considering Americans who are ages 60–69, from 62 percent to 80 percent are overweight, depending on race and gender. African-American women have the greatest risk of obesity (80 percent), and black men and white women have a lower rate of 62 percent each.

Usually a chronic disease, obesity can become very dangerous for many people because it may lead to or worsen Type 2 DIABETES, KIDNEY DISEASE, and GALL-BLADDER DISEASE and may even contribute to the development of CANCER.

Obesity is linked to many other serious illnesses, such as HYPERTENSION, CORONARY HEART DISEASE, and STROKE. Obesity can also exacerbate the symptoms of ARTHRITIS, BACK PAIN, and other medical problems. Fortunately, however, if an obese individual loses even a small amount of weight, often other medical problems will also improve, such as high blood pressure or high cholesterol levels. In some cases, a person with an early case of diabetes may even revert to normal levels of blood glucose if sufficient weight is lost.

BODY MASS INDEX (BMI) TABLE

BMI	19	20	21	22	23	24	25	26	27	28	29	30	31	32	33	34	35
Height							Weight (in pounds)										
4'10" (58")	91	96	100	105	110	115	119	124	129	134	138	143	148	153	158	162	167
4'11" (59")	94	99	104	109	114	119	124	128	133	138	143	148	153	158	163	168	173
5' (60")	97	102	107	112	118	123	128	133	138	143	148	153	158	163	168	174	179
5'1" (61")	100	106	111	116	122	127	132	137	143	148	153	158	164	169	174	180	185
5'2" (62")	104	109	115	120	126	131	136	142	147	153	158	164	169	175	180	186	191
5'3" (63")	107	113	118	124	130	135	141	146	152	158	163	169	175	180	186	191	197
5'4" (64")	110	116	122	128	134	140	145	151	157	163	169	174	180	186	192	197	204
5'5" (65")	114	120	126	132	138	144	150	156	162	168	174	180	186	192	198	204	210
5'6" (66")	118	124	130	136	142	148	155	161	167	173	179	186	192	198	204	210	216
5'7" (67")	121	127	134	140	146	153	159	166	172	178	185	191	198	204	211	217	223
5'8" (68")	125	131	138	144	151	158	164	171	177	184	190	197	203	210	216	223	230
5'9" (69")	128	135	142	149	155	162	169	176	182	189	196	203	209	216	223	230	236
5'10" (70")	132	139	146	153	160	167	174	181	188	195	202	209	216	222	229	236	243
5'11" (71")	136	143	150	157	165	172	179	186	193	200	208	215	222	229	236	243	250
6' (72")	140	147	154	162	169	177	184	191	199	206	213	221	228	235	242	250	258
6'1" (73")	144	151	159	166	174	182	189	197	204	212	219	227	235	242	250	257	265
6'2" (74")	148	155	163	171	179	186	194	202	210	218	225	233	241	249	256	264	272
6'3" (75")	152	160	168	176	184	192	200	208	216	224	232	240	248	256	264	272	279

Source: Evidence Report of Clinical Guidelines on the Identification, Evaluation, and Treatment of Overweight and Obesity in Adults, 1998. NIH/National Heart, Lung, and Blood Institute (NHLBI)

Obesity Is at Epidemic Levels Worldwide

Experts at the NATIONAL INSTITUTES OF HEALTH (NIH) and many other experts worldwide are concerned that obesity is at an epidemic level in the United States and in other developed countries such as CANADA, the UNITED KINGDOM, and Australia.

Rising Incidence of Obesity

Researchers have found that excessive fat, particularly fat that is concentrated around the waistline, is more predictive of diabetes, coronary artery disease, and other medical ailments than is fat that is concentrated in the hips or the lower body. Stated very simply, individuals who have an "apple" body shape face a greater risk for developing diabetes and other diseases than those with a "pear" body shape.

Causes of Obesity

It would seem obvious that the primary cause of obesity is that individuals take in more calories than they expend, thereby increasing their level of fat. However, it is not a simple problem for people who are obese, nor is it simple for those who treat them.

Some obese people insist that they eat no more than others, and in some cases, this is verifiably true. Older people who are ill and in physical pain may not get much exercise and thus may tend to gain weight if they continue to eat the same amounts that they consumed when they were able to exercise.

Sometimes, people may overeat as a result of DEPRESSION. This emotional disorder is easily treatable by medical doctors, particularly PSYCHIATRISTS, and it should not be ignored if present. However, many older individuals are reluctant to seek help for emotional disorders or even to acknowledge their existence.

In some cases, the obese individual may have an underlying medical problem such as a THYROID DISEASE, particularly hypothyroidism (low thyroid levels).

Some medications tend to cause individuals to gain weight, and if the individual is gaining a great deal of weight, this issue should be considered by the physician, who may wish to change the medication or the dosage.

Another possible cause of obesity may lie in hormones that are secreted by individuals. In 2001, scientists discovered a hormone called Resistin that may be linked to both obesity and the development of diabetes. Further study is ongoing, and it is hoped that along with knowledge of Resistin or other hormones that impact obesity will also come ideas for solutions to this problem.

Treating Obesity

Thousands of books and magazine articles have been written for people who need to lose weight; however, for most people, the basic answer still appears to lie in increased activity levels and decreased total amount of calories that are consumed.

When the older person who is overweight or obese is physically inactive because of medical problems, physical therapy may help; PAINKILLING MEDICATIONS may also be indicated. Some people who are 100 pounds or more overweight have bariatric surgery, which is surgery that limits the amount of food their stomachs can process. (It is popularly known as stomach stapling.) It is a procedure that is usually only considered for people who are severely obese. Older people with other medical problems may or may not be considered as viable candidates for this surgery.

Some individuals have had success with medications for weight loss, although some past weight-loss medications such as Redux were felt to be dangerous and were ordered by the Food and Drug Administration (FDA) to be removed from the market. Newer medications such as Xenical (orlistat) and Meridia (sibutramine) have been approved by the FDA. They appear largely ineffective at causing a significant sustained weight loss for most people and both drugs have side effects. For example, Xenical may cause fecal INCONTINENCE.

For further information on obesity and weight control, contact:

Weight-control Information Network (WIN)
1 WIN Way
Bethesda, MD 20892
(800) WIN-8098 or (301) 984-7378
http://www.niddk.nih.gov/health/nutrit/win.htm

Cassell, Dana K., and David H. Gleaves, Ph.D. *The Encyclopedia of Obesity and Eating Disorders.* New York: Facts On File, 2000.

Old-Age, Survivors, and Disability Insurance Program   A money payment program administered by the SOCIAL SECURITY ADMINISTRATION in the United States, which provides benefits to older individuals and also to disabled people of all ages who qualify. In addition, family members of the beneficiary, such as their spouses and minor children, may also be eligible to receive benefits.

The overwhelming majority of Americans age 65 and older are recipients of OASDI benefits. According to the Office of the Chief Actuary of the Social Security Administration, about 91 percent of the population age 65 and older received retirement benefits as of January 2002.

The numbers of beneficiaries receiving OASDI benefits are impressive. As of December 31, 2001, there were about 32 million people receiving retirement benefits, including 28.8 million retirees, 2.7 million spouses of the retired person, and about a half-million minor children. The average retired worker age 62 and older with a spouse received $1,455 per month. Retired workers with no spouse received an average monthly benefit of $860.

One problem that government officials are beginning to worry about is that the aging baby boomers (born 1946–64) will soon become eligible for Social Security benefits, and it may be difficult to fund this expense out of payments deducted from current workers. The oldest baby boomers were age 57 in 2003 and will become eligible for full retirement benefits at age 66, which will occur in 2012. Some of them may opt to retire at the younger age of 62, accepting lower monthly payments. The escalation of the number of beneficiaries will continue every year thereafter for 19 years.

See also OLDER AMERICANS ACT AMENDMENTS OF 2000 (PUBLIC LAW 106-501).

Office of the Chief Actuary, Social Security Administration. "Fact Sheet on the Old-Age, Survivors, and Disability Insurance Program" (December 31, 2001).

Older Americans Act Amendments of 2000 (Public Law 106-501)   Reauthorized and amended legislation affecting programs for seniors that was signed again into law by President Clinton in 2000 and extends the programs of the act until fiscal year 2005. The Older Americans Act in 2000 amended the Older Americans Act of 1965, which originally established the ADMINISTRATION ON AGING. Later amendments provided for programs for Native American elders, services for low-income minority elders, home-care services for very ill elders, the establishment of the long-term-care OMBUDSMAN program, and other services.

The reauthorized act included a new program, the National Family Caregiver Support Program. It provided funding of $125 million in grants to state agencies in 2001 so that states could provide information and assistance to family caregivers of older people. This program also acknowledged the needs of grandparents who are raising their grandchildren.

In addition, the new act also included an acknowledgment of the needs of older people who have developmental disabilities. It also established the Native American Caregiver Support Program to help caregivers of Native American elders who are ill or disabled.

See also OLD-AGE, SURVIVORS, AND DISABILITY INSURANCE PROGRAM.

older caregivers   As the population ages, there are more instances of seniors taking care of other seniors, for example, 65- or 70-year-old people who are FAMILY CAREGIVERS providing care for relatives, spouses and other people in their late 80s or 90s. Seniors sometimes also provide care to young children such as their grandchildren or even their great grandchildren when the children's parents are deceased or when they are unable to care for them for some reason.

See also GRANDPARENTS; OLDEST OLD.

oldest old   Individuals who are age 80 and older. The significance of the oldest-old population is primarily twofold. First, this population is growing rapidly in the United States and in the world. Second, individuals age 80 and older are most likely to require medical assistance, as well as help with HOUSING, TRANSPORTATION, and many other aspects of life. Most people age 80 and older cannot work and must rely on others for financial, medical, and other forms of assistance.

Although many older people who are ages 65–79 continue in relatively good health, the risk for severe health problems escalates with aging. The oldest old are much more likely to need mental-health services because of the development of such problems as ALZHEIMER'S DISEASE and various forms of DEMENTIA. Unless these diseases are conquered within the next decade (as may occur), the oldest old and their caregivers around the world will face considerable hardship.

A Global Look at the Oldest Old

In looking at the global population, the U.S. Census Bureau reported that 53 percent of the world's old-est-old population resided in six countries, including China, the United States, India, Japan, Germany, and Russia. In looking at individual countries and their percentage of all of the oldest old in the world in the year 2000, China led, with 16.3 percent of the global oldest-old population. China was followed by the United States (13.1 percent). (See Figure 1: Percent Distribution of World Population Age 80 and Older: 2000.)

Projected Worldwide Growth of the Oldest Old

Another way to regard the oldest old is to consider them as a percentage of all older people, age 65 and older. In 2000, the oldest old represented 17 percent of all people in the world older than age 65. Within individual countries, however, the percentages of the oldest old of all elderly varied. For example, in the United States, the oldest old were 26.5 percent of all elderly people in 2000. (This also means that 73.5 percent of the elderly were ages 65–79 in 2000.) In Argentina, in 2000, the oldest old were about 22 percent (21.7 percent) of the elderly population, and thus, about 78 percent of the elderly were ages 65–79.

However, by 2030, there will be dramatic changes in many countries, as predicted by the U.S. Census Bureau. The United States is projected to stay about the same, and in 2030, the oldest old will represent 26.4 percent of the entire elderly population in the United States. But other countries will see major increases in their oldest old populations. The most dramatic increases are projected to occur in Japan.

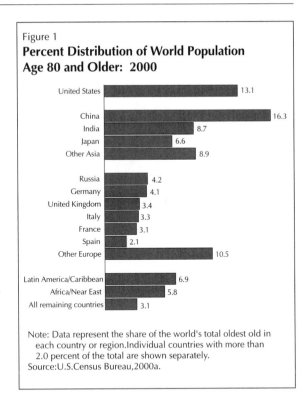

Figure 1

Percent Distribution of World Population Age 80 and Older: 2000

Note: Data represent the share of the world's total oldest old in each country or region. Individual countries with more than 2.0 percent of the total are shown separately.
Source: U.S. Census Bureau, 2000a.

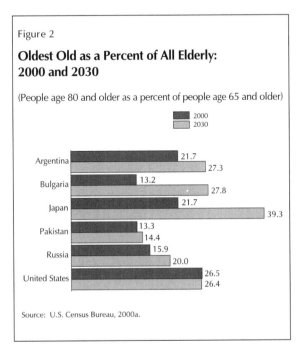

Figure 2

Oldest Old as a Percent of All Elderly: 2000 and 2030

(People age 80 and older as a percent of people age 65 and older)

Source: U.S. Census Bureau, 2000a.

In 2000, the oldest old represented 21.7 percent of Japan's elderly population. By 2030, the oldest old will almost double and will represent 39.3 percent of all elderly individuals in Japan.

Other countries will also have dramatic increases in their oldest old, if expert demographers are correct in their predictions. For example, in Bulgaria in 2000, the oldest old represented 13.2 percent of their entire elderly population, and thus about 87 percent of the elders were ages 65–79. By the year 2030, however, Bulgaria's oldest-old population percentage is projected to double, increasing to 27.8 percent of all elderly citizens in Bulgaria. Figure 2 illustrates population-growth changes in Argentina, Bulgaria, Japan, Pakistan, Russia, and the United States.

The challenge for countries around the globe is to appreciate and enjoy the benefits and wisdom of its oldest citizens, and at the same time, to provide the assistance and medical services as well as emotional care that will inevitably be needed by many of them.

See also GLOBAL AGING.

Kinsella, Kevin, and Victoria A. Velkoff. *An Aging World: 2001.* Washington, D.C.: U.S. Census Bureau, 2001.

ombudsman   Usually refers to an individual or an office that is designated to answer questions or perform investigations related to issues of aging, such as problems associated with HOUSING, SKILLED-NURSING FACILITIES, TRANSPORTATION, and other problems faced by older individuals.

The Long Term Care Ombudsman Program is administered by the ADMINISTRATION ON AGING, and its legislative authority is the OLDER AMERICANS ACT. Each state in the United States has an ombudsman office, usually located in the state capital. (See Appendix V for a state-by-state listing of ombudsmen nationwide.) According to the Administration on Aging, in 2000, 1,000 paid ombudsmen and 8,000 certified volunteer ombudsmen investigated 232,000 complaints made by or on the behalf of 137,000 people nationwide. The most frequently heard complaint was a lack of adequate staffing in nursing homes.

According to the Administration on Aging, skilled-nursing facility residents and other long-term care residents have the following rights:

- To be treated with respect and dignity
- To be free from chemical and physical restraints
- To manage their own finances
- To voice grievances without fear of retaliation
- To associate and communicate privately with any person of their choice
- To send and receive personal mail
- To have personal and medical records kept confidential
- To apply for state and federal assistance without discrimination
- To be informed fully prior to admission of their rights, available services, and all charges
- To be given advance notice of a transfer or discharge from the long-term care facility

Ombudsmen work to help protect the rights of older and disabled people and to investigate complaints. According to the Administration on Aging, ombudsman responsibilities include:

- Identifying, investigating, and resolving complaints made by or on behalf of residents
- Providing information to residents about long-term care services
- Representing the interests of residents before government agencies, and seeking administrative, legal, and other remedies to protect residents
- Analyzing, commenting on, and recommending changes in laws and regulations pertaining to the health, safety, welfare, and rights of residents
- Educating and informing consumers and the general public about issues and concerns related to long-term care, and facilitating public comment on laws, regulations, policies, and actions
- Promoting the development of citizen organizations to participate in the program
- Providing technical support for the development of resident and family councils to protect the well-being and rights of residents
- Advocating for changes to improve the quality of life and care for residents

For further information, contact:

National Long-Term Care Ombudsman Resource
  Center
1424 16th Street, NW
Suite 202
Washington, DC 20036

National Ombudsman Resource Center
National Citizens' Coalition for Nursing Home
  Reform
1424 16th Street, NW
Suite 202
Washington, DC 20036
(202) 332-2275
http://www.nursinghomeaction.org

oncologist   Medical doctor who is expert in
both CANCER diagnosis and treatment. Some doctors specialize in radiation treatments; other doctors deal with other aspects of cancer, such as
chemotherapy.

oral cancer   A malignant tumor of any part of the
mouth, lips, cheek, tongue, gums, salivary glands,
and the oropharynx (part of the throat at the back
of the mouth).

Risks

Most people who develop oral cancer are older than
age 45, and many are smokers.

Symptoms of Oral Cancer

The person with oral cancer may not notice any
symptoms; however, symptoms may include one or
more indicators. People who have any of these indicators should see their physicians for diagnosis and,
if necessary, treatment. Possible indicators of oral
cancer are:

- Sore on the mouth or lip that does not heal
- A lump on the lip or in the mouth or throat
- White or red patches on the tongue, gums, or
  inner lining of the mouth
- A constant sore throat
- Difficulty with swallowing (this is also a possible
  indicator of GASTROESOPHAGEAL REFLUX DISEASE)

- Swelling in the jaw, along with badly fitting
  dentures
- Change in the sound of the voice
- Ear pain

Diagnosis

Most patients with symptoms suspicious of oral cancer will see either an ear, nose, and throat surgeon
or an oral surgeon. The patient may need X rays or
a CT scan of the affected area to provide further
details. Sometimes, the doctor will also order an
ultrasound or a magnetic resonance imaging (MRI)
scan. The doctor will often biopsy the tissue so that
a pathologist can examine it and determine whether
cancer is present.

Treatment for Oral Cancer

The treatment for each patient depends on the location of the cancer and how advanced it is. Surgery
may be indicated, followed by radiation treatments.
Chemotherapy may also be given.

Surgery may affect the patient's appearance, and
it may be best to consult with a plastic surgeon as
well in concert with the surgeon treating the oral
cancer. Surgery may also affect the production of
saliva and the patient's ability to chew food,
although the immediate aftereffects of surgery
should improve within a few weeks. Patients may
need to use special toothbrushes and mouthwashes
until they regain better ability to chew their food.

Surgery of the face will also usually cause
swelling, which will go down with time. Unintended
weight loss may be another problem because patients
have considerable difficulty with eating after surgery
as well as during other treatments for oral cancer.

Patients who wear DENTURES will need their dentures refitted after recovering from surgery or may
need new dentures.

Speech therapy may also be needed postopera-
tively if the surgery was extensive. Patients who
smoke must stop smoking immediately.

osteoarthritis   A "wear-and-tear" degenerative
form of ARTHRITIS, and one that is experienced by the
majority of older Americans and people from other
countries, as well as by some younger individuals.

Osteoarthritis is the most prominent form of arthritis. The primary effect of osteoarthritis is on the joint capsule and the cartilage, the tissue that cushions the ends of bones at the point of a joint. Osteoarthritis causes the bony structures of the cartilage to wear down, and, in the most extreme cases, they may wear away completely.

About 20 million older people in the United States suffer from osteoarthritis, which is generally diagnosed when a person is older than age 60, although it can also be diagnosed in younger people. About 80 percent of people older than age 75 have osteoarthritis.

Osteoarthritis can cause disability and pain. In its more advanced stages, osteoarthritis can also cause the individual to require a joint replacement, most commonly of the hip or knee. An estimated 241,000 hip replacements and 245,000 knee replacements are performed each year in the United States, and most of these patients have osteoarthritis.

Causes of Osteoarthritis

Many people with osteoarthritis have family members who are also afflicted with this disease, and it is generally accepted that there is a genetic component to osteoarthritis. A prior history of joint injury may also play a significant role.

Symptoms of Osteoarthritis

Symptoms include pain in the joints and may also include referred pain to other parts of the body.

Diagnosis of the Condition

Physicians diagnose osteoarthritis based on symptoms as well as on X rays of the area that is causing pain. If physicians are looking for specific problems, they may order a magnetic resonance imaging (MRI) scan of the area of the body that is hurting. Doctors may also order blood tests to see if there is an underlying inflammation, such as an erthryocyte sedimentation rate blood test. They may also order other tests to see if the arthritis might be RHEUMATOID ARTHRITIS rather than osteoarthritis.

Treatments for Osteoarthritis

Treatments include a variety of medications and lifestyle recommendations. Osteoarthritis is a chronic disease that cannot be cured, but patients may be able to delay further deterioration by taking such actions as losing weight if they are overweight.

Medications Used to Treat Osteoarthritis   The most commonly known class of medication to treat arthritis are drugs in the nonsteroidal antiinflammatory (NSAID) category. These drugs can limit pain by reducing inflammation. Examples of such over-the-counter drugs are Motrin or Advil. Higher doses of NSAIDs may be prescribed. Because long-term use of NSAIDs can cause gastrointestinal distress and because they may even lead to the development of a gastric ulcer, physicians may prescribe other medications that are less likely to cause damage to the gastrointestinal system. Some examples are such drugs as Celebrex or Vioxx.

In cases of extreme pain, the doctor may inject corticosteroid drugs into the painful area. Corticosteroids are also available in oral form and in topical form that can be rubbed into the skin. Doctors disagree on how frequently patients may safely receive corticosteroid injections. Prednisone, cortisone, solumedrol, and hydrocortisone are all forms of corticosteroid drugs.

Long-term use of corticosteroids can be dangerous and may lead to OSTEOPOROSIS, HYPERTENSION, high blood sugar (hyperglycemia), infections, and CATARACTS.

Alternative Remedies   Some doctors recommend alternative remedies as well, such as the use of glucosamine and chondroitin, substances that have been shown to improve symptoms and delay further deterioration of the bones.

Some people have claimed benefit from receiving acupuncture, and studies are ongoing to determine if acupuncture is clinically valuable. As of this writing, it is unclear whether acupuncture helps patients with osteoarthritis, although preliminary results indicate that it may be helpful; however, at the same time, it does not appear harmful as long as the acupuncture practitioner is trained in the therapy and uses clean and disposable needles.

Lifestyle Recommendations   Cold or heat therapy may improve the condition, including gel packs that may be either heated or frozen as well as heating pads. Massage therapy may also help to mitigate muscle pain. Regular EXERCISE can help the patient to avoid further degeneration of the bones and soft muscle tissues.

Some patients find relief with transcutaneous electrical nerve stimulation (TENS), which provides low-dose and painless charges of electricity to the afflicted area. TENS treatment is usually administered by a physical therapist, although sometimes patients purchase TENS units so that the treatment can also be performed at home.

Patients who are obese are advised to lose weight so that there will be less stress on their weight-bearing joints. Some studies have shown that even a weight loss of 11 pounds has significantly diminished the effect of osteoarthritis in the knees.

Exercise is also commonly recommended. A physician may recommend an exercise program, or a physical therapist may help patients to develop a plan that is best suited for their lifestyles and medical problems.

Water therapy, such as exercising in a pool or even relaxing in a warm bathtub, may help to relax overly taut muscles and consequently to relieve pain. Relaxation therapy is another means to achieve pain relief. Patients can be taught to mentally relax one part of their body after another in a concerted manner.

Assistive Devices
May Be Needed

Some people with severe osteoarthritis may need ASSISTIVE DEVICES, such as splints or braces, to rest the damaged joint.

Surgery Is Sometimes Required

Sometimes, surgery is recommended to relieve the pain and symptoms of osteoarthritis. A torn joint may require surgery. Sometimes, bones are fused together. With arthroplasty, entire joints are replaced.

For further information, contact the following organizations:

Arthritis Foundation
1330 West Peachtree Street
Atlanta, GA 30309
(800) 283-7800 or (404) 965-7537
http://www.arthritis.org

National Institute of Arthritis and Musculoskeletal and Skin Disease Information Clearinghouse
National Institutes of Health

1 AMS Circle
Bethesda, MD 20892
(301) 495-4484 or (877) 22-NIAMS (toll-free)
http://www.nih.gov/niams

Kandel, Joseph, M.D. and David Sudderth, M.D. *The Arthritis Solution.* Rocklin, Calif.: Prima Publishing, 1996.

Lohmander, Stefan L., "What Can We Do About Osteoarthritis?" *Arthritis Research* 2 (2000): 95–100.

Manek, Nisha J., M.D., M.R.C.P. and Nancy E. Lane, M.D. "Osteoarthritis: Current Concepts in Diagnosis and Management," *American Family Physician* 61 (2000): 1,795–1,804.

McCarberg, Bill H., M.D., and Keela A. Herr, Ph.D., R.N. "Osteoarthritis: How to Manage Pain and Improve Patient Function," *Geriatrics* 56, no. 10 (2001): 14–24.

National Institute of Arthritis and Musculoskeletal and Skin Diseases (NIAMS). "Questions and Answers About Arthritis Pain," NIH Publication No. 01-4856 (February 2001).

osteoporosis A medical condition in which not only is total bone mass decreased but also tiny abnormalities in the bones lead to an increased risk for bone FRACTURES. There are about 4 to 6 million women and 1 to 2 million men in the United States with osteoporosis.

Osteoporosis increases the risk for bone fractures, as well as for a loss in height and for back pain. The hip and vertebral fractures that osteoporosis can cause are especially dangerous: about 24 percent of these patients die within a year, and 50 percent lose their independence. The rate of hospitalization for vertebral fractures caused by osteoporosis increases dramatically with age. For example, among people ages 65–74, there are 6.7 people per 1,000 who are hospitalized because of an osteoporotic vertebral fracture. This rate quadruples for people ages 75–84 to 26 people per 1,000. The rate of hospitalization for vertebral fractures rises still further for people age 85 and older, who have a rate of 39 people per 1,000.

Causes of Osteoporosis

Aging is clearly one factor in the development of osteoporosis, although middle-aged and younger people can develop osteoporosis. The disease may also be due to a genetic predisposition; for example, according to the NATIONAL INSTITUTES OF HEALTH, one study showed that women age 65 and older with the apolipoprotein E gene on chromosome 19 had twice the risk to experience fractures of the hip and wrist as did those without the gene.

In addition, the loss of naturally occurring sex steroid hormones among aging individuals, such as less estrogen in women and lower levels of testosterone in men, plays a pivotal role in the development of osteoporosis.

Lifestyle factors also clearly play a role in the development of osteoporosis, and less-active people are more likely to develop osteoporosis than are their more-active peers.

Individuals who have DIABETES have an increased risk for developing osteoporosis. Other secondary causes of osteoporosis include ALCOHOLISM, steroid use, and malnutrition.

Risk Factors

As mentioned, the risk for developing osteoporosis increases with age. In considering race and ethnicity, Caucasians and Hispanics have the highest risk of developing osteoporosis: 10 percent each, versus a risk of 7 percent for African Americans.

According to the National Resource Center for Osteoporosis and Related Bone Diseases, a subsection of the National Institutes of Health, other key risk factors for developing osteoporosis are:

- Gender (females are at greater risk)
- Thin or small-boned stature
- A family history of osteoporosis
- Postmenopausal status
- Eating disorders such as anorexia nervosa or bulimia
- Diets low in calcium
- Medications such as corticosteroids and anticonvulsants
- Smoking cigarettes

Diagnosis and Treatment

The doctor may strongly suspect a patient has osteoporosis because of a fracture that resulted from a minor fall or because the patient has risk factors for the disease. The only way to know for sure if the patient has osteoporosis is to run screening tests. Most

doctors order bone-mass density tests. In most cases, the dual-energy X-ray absorptiometry (DXA) is used to measure bone density, although other tests are available.

Medications are usually the treatment for osteoporosis. Many doctors prescribe estrogen for postmenopausal women, although studies indicate estrogen may serve better as a prevention from osteoporosis rather than a treatment for the disease after it is known to occur. All patients should be on adequate calcium and vitamin D, 1000–1500 mg/day and 400–800 IU respectively.

Men and women with osteoporosis may be treated with Fosamax (alendronate). In a two-year study reported in a 2000 issue of the *New England Journal of Medicine* on the effect of the drug on males, 241 men with osteoporosis were treated with Fosamax or a placebo. The researchers found that the drug significantly increased bone density and also helped the men to avoid fractures of vertebrae or losses in height.

Other drugs that are prescribed for osteoporosis are:

- Actonel (risedronate)
- Evista (raloxifene)
- Miacalcin (calcitonin)

Other treatments under investigation to treat osteoporosis are vitamin D metabolites, sodium fluoride, and injectable parathyroid hormone.

For more information on osteoporosis, contact:

National Institutes of Health
Osteoporosis and Related Bone Diseases—National
　Resource Center
1232 22nd Street, NW
Suite 500
Washington, DC 20037-1292
(202) 223-0344 or (800) 624-BONE (toll-free)
http://www.osteo.org

National Osteoporosis Foundation
1150 17th Street, NW
Suite 500
Washington, DC 20036-4603
(202) 223-2226
http://www.nof.org/
　　See also MENOPAUSE.

Baran, Daniel, M.D. "Osteoporosis: Efficacy and Safety of a Bisphosphonate Dosed Once Weekly," *Geriatrics* 56, no. 3 (2001): 28–32.

Orwoll, Eric, M.D. et al. "Alendronate for the Treatment of Osteoporosis in Men," *New England Journal of Medicine* 343 (2000): 604–610.

South-Paul, Jeannette E., Col., MC, USA. "Osteoporosis: Part I: Evaluation and Assessment," *American Family Physician* 63 (2001): 897–904, 908.

———. "Osteoporosis: Part II: Nonpharmacologic and Pharmacologic Treatments," *American Family Physician* 63 (2001): 1,121–1,128.

outreach Attempts to locate people with specific problems so that help can be provided. For example, many low-income women in the past have not received a diagnosis or treatment for BREAST CANCER. As a result, programs were created within the CENTERS FOR DISEASE CONTROL AND PREVENTION (CDC) to reach more women at risk for breast cancer and to provide help.

Older individuals may also need food or other types of assistance; there are various federal, state, and local outreach programs that work to seek out such individuals. In addition, charitable groups often also provide outreach services to needful people in their area.

ovarian cancer Malignant tumor of one or both ovaries, the organs that produce female hormones and eggs for reproduction. Ovarian cancer is a very dangerous form of cancer because the symptoms are not usually noticed until the disease is well advanced. Only about 25 percent of ovarian cancers are diagnosed in the early stages.

About 23,000 women are diagnosed with ovarian cancer each year in the United States, and it is the fifth-leading cause of cancer death for women. In Canada, about 2,600 women are newly diagnosed with ovarian cancer each year, and there are about 1,500 deaths from the disease per year. About half of all women diagnosed with ovarian cancer die within five years.

In 2002, researchers identified a blood test that could detect ovarian cancer in the early stages, when it is still treatable. This test must be further tested and developed but will hopefully be available to the public within several years.

Risk Factors

At an increased risk for developing ovarian cancer are women who:

- Have a mother, daughter, or sister with ovarian cancer or a family history of breast cancer or colorectal cancer
- Are older than age 50, with the greatest risk among women older than age 60
- Have never had children. (Also, the more children a woman has had, the lower the risk for ovarian cancer)
- Have had cancer before, especially breast cancer or colorectal cancer

Symptoms of Ovarian Cancer

Although symptoms may be vague (and there may be no symptoms at all in the early stages), women with ovarian cancer may experience the following symptoms. Note: these symptoms may also indicate a wide variety of other illnesses. For example, abdominal discomfort could indicate chronic heartburn (GASTROESOPHAGEAL REFLUX DISEASE), and diarrhea and constipation could indicate irritable bowel syndrome. Frequent urination could indicate an easily treatable bladder infection. To be sure, it is best to consult with a physician if these symptoms occur.

- Abdominal discomfort (chronic indigestion, bloating, and cramps)
- Diarrhea or constipation
- Frequent urination
- Weight loss or gain with no apparent reason
- Bleeding from the vagina (not menstrual bleeding)
- Bloated feeling even after eating a small meal
- Loss of appetite
- Unexplained low-grade fever

Diagnosis of Ovarian Cancer

The doctor will perform a pelvic examination to inspect the female reproductive system. The doctor may also order blood and urine tests, an ultrasound test, X rays of the rectum and colon (a barium enema), a computerized tomography (CT) scan, and other tests. If ovarian cancer is suspected, the doctor will perform a biopsy, which is a removal of tissue for the determination of whether cancer is present or not. If cancer is present, the biopsy will also determine how advanced the cancer is and how fast it is growing.

Treatment

In most cases, surgery is the choice of treatment for women with ovarian cancer. Both ovaries are usually removed, along with the fallopian tubes, uterus and cervix. The surgeon may also remove lymph nodes in the abdomen. Working with an oncologist (cancer specialist), the physician will determine to what degree, if any, that adjunct therapy is needed.

Chemotherapy may be recommended after surgery. Drugs used to kill remaining cancer cells are usually introduced into the body intravenously. In some cases, a catheter is used to place chemotherapy drugs directly into the abdomen (intraperitoneal chemotherapy).

Radiation therapy is another way to treat ovarian cancer. In most cases, women are treated by a special machine that irradiates the affected area. Another option is the use of radioactive liquid which is inserted directly into the abdomen through a catheter (intraperitoneal radiation therapy).

For further information contact:

Ovarian Cancer National Alliance
910 17th Street, NW
Suite 413
Washington, DC 20006
(202) 331-1332
http://www.ovariancancer.org

"Ovarian Cancer," National Cancer Institute, NIH Publication No. 00-1561 (June 16, 2000).

pain Severe or minor discomfort. In an older person, pain may stem from chronic diseases, such as ARTHRITIS or headache. The pain may also be acute, as in the case of a HEART ATTACK, or may be the severe pain that stems from diseases such as CANCER or ailments that cause pain over the short term, such as SHINGLES. Chronic illnesses may also cause extreme short-term pain, such as with GOUT.

It is unknown how many older people experience chronic pain, although studies indicate that from 20 percent to half of people older than age 60 suffer from pain on a regular basis. People in nursing homes are more likely to experience pain. Some studies have indicated that the most frequently occurring pain stems from the joint pain of arthritis. Leg pains are also common, as is BACK PAIN.

Diagnosis and Treatment

The first step for most physicians in treating pain is to examine the patient and take a medical history. Many physicians ask patients to describe the extent of their pain on a scale of 1 (almost no pain) to 10 (the worst pain they have ever felt). Some patients may respond better to simple pictures of people in pain, choosing the facial expression that best fits their pain. If the patient with pain has ALZHEIMER'S DISEASE or DEMENTIA, the doctor may need to deduce the severity of the pain by the patient's reactions during a physical examination. CAREGIVERS may be able to help the doctor interpret the patient's responses.

The cause for the pain may be immediately evident to the physician, or diagnosis may be delayed until needed laboratory tests and other tests can help the physician to ascertain the cause of the pain.

Once the cause is determined, the physician may choose to prescribe medications and/or therapies to help manage the pain. For some illnesses, the best remedy is rest; for others, exercising will improve the pain.

Medications may help resolve the pain, and there are a wide variety of medications from which doctors may choose. However, some older patients may be reluctant to take medications, particularly those that they consider possible drugs of abuse. They may fear becoming addicted to the drug or regard taking pain medications as a sign of personal weakness. Physicians should advise patients that the risk for addiction is generally very low when medications are used to treat pain.

Nonsteroidal antiinflammatory drugs (NSAIDs) may be the best choice for joint pain. However, NSAIDs have a risk of causing gastrointestinal pain and bleeding and may also lead to the development of an ULCER. Drugs in the newer Cyclooxygenase-2 (COX-2) inhibitor class are less likely to cause gastrointestinal distress, although they too present some risk for causing gastrointestinal problems.

A drug in the muscle relaxant class is another option. The patient may also need an analgesic (painkilling drug), ranging from a mild medication to a narcotic. Some older patients may have difficulty with drugs such as morphine, which may cause them to hallucinate and have other problems with cognitive impairment. Such drugs may also cause constipation. They are very sedating, and patients taking these drugs should be extremely cautious when driving.

Antidepressant drugs are also prescribed for PAIN MANAGEMENT, including such drugs as Elavil (amitriptyline). These drugs are generally given in doses lower than those prescribed for people who are clinically depressed. Some doctors consider Elavil inappropriate for seniors. See ADVERSE DRUG EVENT.

Anticonvulsant drugs may also reduce pain. There are many newer anticonvulsant drugs that are extremely effective in this regard.

Some patients with severe back pain respond well to trigger-point injections of steroids or lidocaine.

Injections of botox have also proven effective in reducing muscle spasm.

Undertreatment of Pain Is a Problem for Some Older People

Numerous studies have documented that older patients are often undertreated for their pain, even when the pain is severe. One possible reason for undertreatment is that many physicians are reluctant to prescribe controlled drugs such as narcotics; yet, these may be the only type of drugs that make the patient's pain tolerable.

Another reason may be AGEISM, or the belief that older people are supposed to feel pain because they are old. Pain is thus deemed a natural state for older people by ageist physicians. Although it is true that older people are more likely to suffer from painful conditions than younger people, it is not true that pain cannot be controlled with medications.

Patients in SKILLED-NURSING FACILITIES are at high risk for suffering from pain. Most people who live in nursing homes are medically fragile and require a great deal of care. Most also suffer from serious medical problems. If the treating physicians and nurses do not pay attention to the pain levels of nursing-home residents, then the patients can suffer greatly.

It is also true that sometimes it may be difficult to know if older residents are in pain because they may also be mentally or emotionally impaired and suffering from Alzheimer's disease or dementia. However, a competent physician is observant enough to detect when a patient is in severe pain, if only by the patient's response to touch.

Pain directly affects the quality of life of older people. If the pain is so debilitating that they cannot perform normal activities or the basic "activities of living" such as dressing themselves and bathing themselves, then they must rely on other people to perform these tasks for them. This can cause patients to spiral down into a greater level of dependency.

If the pain is made tolerable, however, many patients can maintain a higher level of functioning than when pain is the dominant force of their lives. They may be able to feed and bathe themselves and perform social and work activities that were impossible to achieve when they were overcome with pain.

Pain management is a concept that means that doctors seek to control the level of pain that stems from many chronic diseases. It is usually not possible to alleviate all the pain permanently, but it is frequently possible to decrease the pain levels significantly.

Physicians Expert in Pain Management

All doctors treat conditions of pain, but some doctors specialize in pain management. These doctors are usually NEUROLOGISTS or anesthesiologists, but they may also be physicians in other specialties as well.

Older Individuals and Pain Medications

Older people may need lower doses of narcotics and other painkillers than younger people because their digestive systems may be more sluggish and their body water is generally lower than that of younger people. Doctors also need to take into account the interaction of painkillers with other drugs the patients may take for various illnesses they may have.

Panda, Mukta, and Norman A. Desbiens. "Pain in Elderly Patients: How to Achieve Control," *Consultant* 41, no. 12 (October 1, 2001): 1,597–1,608.

painkilling medications   Drugs that stop or diminish minor, moderate, or major pain. Aspirin is a painkiller, as is morphine: the difference is in the degree of effect as well as the side effects that ensue. (Also, contrary to popular belief, even aspirin has side effects, such as stomach upset).

Some painkillers, such as acetaminophen (Tylenol), aspirin, and ibuprofen, can be purchased without a prescription. Other painkillers are not over-the-counter (OTC) drugs, and they require a doctor's prescription.

Which drug is used depends on where the pain is and what is causing it, as well as the physician's usual choice of medications. Some doctors primarily treat patients with pain with nonsteroidal anti-inflammatory drugs (NSAIDs), particularly for the pain of ARTHRITIS. Others rely on muscle relaxants. If pain is severe, doctors may prescribe a stronger painkiller, such as Ultram (tramadol) or Ultracet (tramadol with codeine). They may also choose to prescribe a narcotic drug. In the United States, these drugs are treated as "controlled drugs."

Controlled Drugs

Some painkillers are "controlled drugs" or "scheduled drugs," which means that there are strict controls on such medications. These drugs are considered potential drugs of abuse under the Controlled Substances Act (CSA), and as a result, they are restricted by the Drug Enforcement Administration. For example, a doctor may not call in to a pharmacy for some controlled medications but must instead provide a written prescription. Other restrictions may apply, such as how many pills may be prescribed over a certain period of time.

The CSA covers such painkilling drugs as Demerol, Percocet and Percodan (oxycodone), and OxyContin. It also covers some antianxiety drugs, such as Xanax, because they are considered habit forming. There are five schedules of controlled drugs. The drugs in Schedule I are drugs of abuse that are not legally used, such as heroin and marijuana. Some medications in Schedules II through IV are prescribed for pain; for example, methadone is a Schedule II drug, and it is used by some patients in pain. Often thought of as a drug given to drug abusers, to help them get off illegal drugs, methadone is now used by nonabusers for pain control.

It can become difficult for patients of all ages to receive a prescription for a controlled drug because of the considerable oversight that surrounds these drugs. Law-enforcement officials can scan the prescribing practices of physicians and challenge their decisions regarding controlled pain medications. In one case in Florida in 2002, a physician was charged with manslaughter because several patients died from overdoses of drugs the doctor had prescribed.

Undertreatment of Older People

People with extremely painful diseases such as severe arthritis or CANCER may need painkilling medications on a daily basis. However, studies have indicated that patients in the United States have been undertreated with pain medications because many physicians are fearful of prescribing these drugs. Some studies have also shown that older individuals, particularly those living in nursing homes, are likely to be extremely undertreated with pain medications.

Side Effects of Painkilling Drugs

Painkilling medications can have many side effects, such as CONSTIPATION and CONFUSION. They may also cause gastrointestinal diseases, such as ulcers. Painkillers should never be taken with alcohol because the combination could be fatal.

Even drugs that seem as harmless as Tylenol can be dangerous when the patient also consumes alcohol and can cause severe liver damage.

NSAID medications can cause gastrointestinal distress, ULCERS, DIARRHEA, and other stomach disorders. Muscle relaxants can also cause gastrointestinal diseases and sedation.

pain management   A phrase used by physicians to denote care that is provided to decrease an individual's pain to a tolerable level. Many chronic diseases cause moderate to severe pain, and, often, it is not possible or feasible to eliminate all pain completely. However, it is usually possible to lower the level of pain for most people, with the use of exercise, lifestyle changes, medications, and other therapies.

About 20 percent of Americans older than age 60 take over-the-counter or prescribed painkillers on a regular basis for the chronic pain of ARTHRITIS, low BACK PAIN, and other forms of pain. At least 20 percent also have tried a form of ALTERNATIVE MEDICINE to treat their pain, including herbal SUPPLEMENTS or RELAXATION THERAPY. Some patients take controlled PAINKILLING MEDICATIONS.

Older people, their caregivers, and their physicians need to be aware of all the medications that are taken by the person age 65 and older, including all over-the-counter drugs, alternative remedies, and prescribed medications. The reason for this is that the panoply of drugs can lead to a MEDICATION INTERACTION and even an ADVERSE DRUG EVENT (death or serious injury, as a result of medications that were taken).

Some pain medications, even when taken as directed, can cause harmful effects. This is particularly true of nonsteroidal antiinflammatory drugs or NSAIDs (whether they are over-the-counter or prescribed medications), which can lead to gastrointestinal bleeding, kidney dysfunction, and other side effects. Some experts have said that the side effects of NSAIDS have resulted in hospitalizations and even in deaths. However, when they are taken under the careful control of a competent physician to whom side effects or problems are reported, most individuals do not have permanent problems with NSAIDs.

Pain management guidelines in the United States require hospitals to monitor a patient's "pain level," and it is mandatory to address the pain of patients with medications, therapy, or some other form of treatment or intervention.

"Pain Drug Use Among American Elders," *Executive Health's Good Health Report* 34, no. 2 (November 1997): 1.

pancreatic cancer Malignancy of the pancreas, an abdominal pear-shaped organ about 6 inches long that is surrounded by the stomach and intestines and joined to the liver and gall bladder. The pancreas is a digestive organ that produces hormones such as insulin. It also generates pancreatic juices, which help digest food. According to the National Cancer Institute, pancreatic cancer is the fifth-leading cause of cancer, and most forms of this cancer start in the ducts carrying pancreatic juices.

Pancreatic cancer is a very dangerous and almost always fatal form of cancer. The disease usually has no symptoms until the patient is very ill.

About 29,000 people in the United States and 40,000 people in Europe die of pancreatic cancer each year. Black men and women have a rate of incidence and death that is about 50 percent higher than for white men and women. Asians have a lower rate of incidence.

According to the National Cancer Institute in the United States, pancreatic cancer represents only about 2 percent of all newly diagnosed cancers in the United States every year, but it causes 5 percent of all cancer deaths. The five-year survival rate is about 4 percent. If the cancer arises in the islet cells of the pancreas (as less than 2 percent do), the prognosis is better.

Risk Factors

Most people who develop pancreatic cancer are older than age 60. SMOKING is a known risk factor for the development of pancreatic cancer. People who smoke and then stop smoking will decrease their risk for pancreatic cancer within several years. DIABETES is another risk factor, and people who have diabetes develop pancreatic cancer at about twice the rate of nondiabetics.

Other risk factors for developing pancreatic cancer are:

- Gender (more men develop the disease than women)
- Race (African Americans have the greatest risk for developing pancreatic cancer)
- Family history (the disease is more likely if a parent or sibling has had pancreatic cancer)
- Presence of chronic pancreatitis, an inflammation of the pancreas

Symptoms

Most patients have no symptoms until the disease is very advanced. Some symptoms of pancreatic cancer are:

- Yellowish tinge to the skin and the whites of the eyes (JAUNDICE)
- Abdominal and upper back pain or discomfort
- Appetite loss
- Unintended weight loss
- Nausea and vomiting
- Weakness

The affected person may also notice that the urine is very dark in color. The skin may be very itchy because of a backing up of bile pigment. Islet cell cancer in the pancreas may cause the pancreas to overproduce insulin or other hormones. The patient's blood-sugar levels may be alarmingly low or high. People with any symptoms should see their physician immediately.

Diagnosis

During the physical examination, the doctor will check for jaundice and abdominal and back pain.

The physician will usually also check for an abnormal fluid buildup in the abdominal area.

Laboratory tests may be ordered to check for bilirubin. Normally bilirubin goes from the liver to the gall bladder to the intestine. But if a bile duct is blocked, the bilirubin can accumulate in the urine, blood, or stool.

The doctor will usually determine if pancreatic cancer is present with an upper gastrointestinal series (barium swallow) or endoscopy. The physician may also use computerized tomography (CT) testing or magnetic resonance imaging (MRI) as well as ultrasound or other tests. Ultimately, a biopsy will determine whether cancer is present. The biopsy can be performed with a needle through the abdomen or with the use of an endoscope, a tube that is inserted down the throat while the patient is under anesthesia.

Treatment

The most common treatment for pancreatic cancer is surgery to remove part of the pancreas and surrounding tissue. If all or part of the pancreas is removed, the patient may develop diabetes and require insulin injections. Some doctors attempt to create bypasses for the pancreas. This surgery has a very low success rate.

Doctors may also use radiation therapy to irradiate the cancerous area or chemotherapy to destroy the cancer cells. According to a 2001 issue in *Lancet,* a study of 541 patients with pancreatic cancer randomized patients into several groups, including one group in which patients received chemotherapy (cancer-killing drugs), one in which they received chemotherapy and radiation (chemoradiation), and another group in which no treatment was given. There was no apparent benefit to chemoradiation but some benefit was seen with chemotherapy, and further studies were recommended.

As of this writing, because the probability of successful treatment is so low, many doctors recommend that patients with pancreatic cancer participate in a clinical trial, in which they may receive medication or treatment that is otherwise not available to them because it has not yet been approved for general public use.

Doctors can control the pain with medications. Most patients with pancreatic cancer are treated by an ONCOLOGIST, or cancer specialist, as well as by their regular physicians.

National Cancer Institute. "What You Need to Know About Cancer of the Pancreas," NIH Publication No. 01-1560 (February 8, 2002).

Neoptolemos, J. P., et al. "Adjuvant Chemoradiotherapy and Chemotherapy in Resectable Pancreatic Cancer: A Randomised Controlled Trial," *Lancet* 358, no. 92993 (November 10, 2001): 1,576–1,585.

paranoia False belief (delusion) that others have a wish to cause harm to one. Many people with DEMENTIA or ALZHEIMER'S DISEASE exhibit symptoms of paranoia. They may behave aggressively or fearfully, based on this delusion. Individuals who suffer paranoia may need treatment with medications or, in some cases, PHYSICAL RESTRAINTS to prevent them from harming themselves or others.

Parkinson's disease A serious neurological disease that causes an increasing deterioration of the central nervous system. This deterioration stems from a decreasing supply of dopamine, a brain chemical that controls movement, as well as a breakdown in the nerve pathways that carry this chemical. Parkinson's disease was named after British physician James Parkinson, who identified the problem in 1817 in his work, "An Essay on the Shaking Palsy."

Risks for Developing Parkinson's Disease

Parkinson's disease affects about 1 million people in the United States among the millions throughout the world. About 50,000 new cases are diagnosed each year in the United States. An estimated 1 percent of individuals older than age 50 in the United States has the disease, which is found among all races. Both men and women are affected by Parkinson's disease, but the illness appears to be slightly more prevalent among men.

The large majority of people with Parkinson's disease are older than age 60, and the risk for developing the disease increases with age. But some individuals, such as television personality Michael J. Fox, become afflicted with the disease at a much younger age.

Symptoms of Parkinson's Disease

There are characteristic indicators of Parkinson's disease, and these symptoms generally worsen when the person is at rest and improve during activity. Some signs of Parkinson's disease include the following:

- Tremor of hands or feet
- A shuffling gait
- Akinesia (an inability to move)
- Bradykinesia (slowed movements)
- Rigidity and muscle stiffness
- Dyskinesia (uncontrollable and writhing movements)
- Dystonia (involuntary muscle contractions, causing repetitive motions)
- Stooped posture
- Retropulsion (tendency to fall backward)

Other Symptoms

SLEEP DISORDERS, particularly insomnia, are a major problem for many people with Parkinson's disease. In one study reported in a 2001 issue of the *Archives of Gerontology and Geriatrics,* 80 percent of 102 patients with Parkinson's disease reported that they experienced insomnia. There seems to be a common problem of fatigue in many of these patients, but the percentages of individuals who suffer from fatigue are unknown. About 40 percent of Parkinson's patients also suffer from DEPRESSION.

Another common problem is a "frozen" gait, in which the person starts to move, suddenly stops, and then resumes the action. This symptom is often associated with balance and speech problems but not with slowed movements. With facial muscle rigidity and a lack of spontaneous movements, these patients frequently suffer from drooling.

People with Parkinson's disease are at high risk from FALLS and are advised to wear crepe-soled shoes and to never carry items with both hands. At least one hand is needed for balance.

Digestion is also often slowed among people with Parkinson's disease, and it can be difficult for them to maintain a normal weight. They may need to con-sume liquid supplements to increase their calorie count. People with Parkinson's disease may also lose their sense of thirst and risk DEHYDRATION. As a result, they should be sure to consume sufficient fluids, whether they feel thirsty or not.

Individuals may also have speech impairments, particularly the classic hypotonia (soft whispery type of speech), and personality changes. Sexual difficulties are common.

Parkinson's disease can also be associated with a form of DEMENTIA (cortical dementia), which causes agitation and irritability. Some patients may become irrational and delusional. Another form of dementia experienced by some Parkinson's patients is subcortical dementia, which causes minor memory problems, distractibility, passivity, and delayed thought processes. It is also possible for a person to have both Parkinson's disease and ALZHEIMER'S DISEASE.

Speculation on Causes of Parkinson's Disease

Scientists are unclear on whether genetics or environmental causes are the primary driver of the development of Parkinson's disease. Studies of twins and families with Parkinson's disease indicate a strong genetic predisposition.

Icelandic researchers studied the medical records of 772 people with Parkinson's disease in Iceland (where it is much easier to obtain medical records of many people) and reported on their findings in a 2000 issue of the *New England Journal of Medicine.* They found that people who developed Parkinson's disease after age 50 had a significant number of relatives who also had the illness. The researchers added, however, that an environmental cause could not be ruled out, stating that "there is a noteworthy difference between the risk ratios for siblings and those for offspring. This may indicate a role for some shared environmental factor early in life, as has been suggested for Alzheimer's disease, or recessive inheritance of susceptibility."

Autopsies of deceased people with Parkinson's disease have revealed an excess of microscopic bodies in the brain that are known as Lewy bodies. Some researchers have speculated that the Lewy bodies are the cause of the disease, while others believe they are the result of it.

Diagnosis

A NEUROLOGIST is the best specialist to diagnose and treat Parkinson's disease because of training in nervous disorders and the brain. There are no diagnostic tests for Parkinson's disease. Physicians diagnose patients with Parkinson's primarily on their symptoms, from ruling out other disorders, and by their response to medications given to treat Parkinson's disease. Physicians also order computer tomography (CT) or magnetic resonance imaging (MRI) scans to rule out any disorders of the brain, such as brain tumors.

Treatment

The disease is not curable, but a variety of medications are given to patients with Parkinson's to control the symptoms of the disease. Levodopa is the most commonly prescribed drug. Levodopa is usually combined with carbidopa, a drug that boosts the effect of levodopa by allowing more of it to get into the brain tissues and not be broken down in the gut; the combination drug is called Sinemet. It is best taken on an empty stomach. A long-acting preparation is also available that actually may be better absorbed when taken with food.

Drugs for Parkinson's disease such as Sinemet cause many side effects. Some side effects are nausea and vomiting, low blood pressure, and hallucinations (usually only seen at the higher doses of medications). Longer-term effects are an increase in tremors and movement disorders. Keeping these serious side effects in mind, many physicians in the past would try to delay ordering medications for as long as possible. However, it is now fairly common practice to treat early at the lowest effective dose to alleviate symptoms.

Requip (ropinirole HCl) is an alternative medication to levodopa. It appears to have fewer side effects and less risk of movement disorders than do long-term levodopa or levodopa combinations. Other drugs that are related to Requip are Mirapex (pramipexole) and Permax (pergolide). These medications are known to produce sedation, with sudden "sleep attacks" reported in the literature.

Other medications that are also used to treat Parkinson's disease include Parlodel (bromocriptine), Eldepryl (selegiline), and Tasmar (tolcapone). Comtan (entacapone) is a more recent medicine that is touted to boost the effect of Sinemet and to smooth out any erratic fluctuations of dopamine chemicals in the brain. Patients need to consult with their physicians to learn which medications are best and what side effects may occur with these drugs. In severe cases of excessive movement and tremor, some doctors use the antipsychotic drug Clozaril (clozapine).

Brain Surgery

In some cases, neurosurgeons will perform brain surgery to ease the symptoms of Parkinson's disease as well as delay any further deterioration in the patient's condition. The pallidotomy was previously the usual surgical choice, although deep brain-stimulation surgery has gained in popularity for patients with severe problems with tremors. The pallidotomy is the surgical destruction of cells in the globus pallidus, a part of the brain that is involved with movements and that has gone awry in patients with Parkinson's disease.

With deep brain stimulation surgery, electrodes are implanted into the brain, and the patient is taught to manipulate the electrical stimulation through an implanted port in the body with the use of special magnets.

Experimental Procedures

Some surgeons have used experimental surgery to implant healthy dopamine-producing cells from aborted fetal tissue. In one study, surgeons performed a double-blind study, in which they performed partial brain surgery on the control group but did not implant fetal tissue. The treatment group had the brain surgery and was implanted with fetal tissue. (The control group was offered the tissue transplant after the study was completed, and most chose to have the procedure.)

The results of this study were mixed. Individuals younger than age 60 showed some improvement, while those older than age 60 did not improve. Some patients had adverse reactions about a year later when their involuntary movements increased rather than decreased, as was hoped for. The researchers believed that using less transplanted tissue in older patients might result in a better outcome. They also emphasized the differences in responses of younger and older patients.

The authors stated, "The fact that parkinsonism did not improve in the older patients during the first year after transplantation, despite the growth and development of dopamine neurons, may reflect a lower degree of plasticity of the brain or more diffuse brain disease in the older group. The fact that responses to drug therapy before surgery were worse in the older patients supports the contention that there are physiologic differences between younger and older patients."

The use of fetal tissues is replete with ethical dilemmas such as whether or not it is acceptable to use aborted fetal tissue and whether or not it is acceptable to provide what may be false hope to people who are very ill with Parkinson's disease. This debate continues.

Others have hoped that stem-cell transplantation, rather than neuronal tissue from healthy fetal tissue, would be effective, but as of this writing, it does not appear to provide any benefit to patients with Parkinson's disease. Some experts believe that transplantation of healthy adult stem-cell tissue may be an effective therapy in the future, and research is ongoing.

Daily Activities Can Be Impaired

Patients with Parkinson's disease may have increasing difficulties performing their basic ACTIVITIES OF DAILY LIVING, such as feeding themselves, dressing, and toileting, and lack of these abilities can be very distressing to most people. The Unified Parkinson's Disease Rating Scale is a measure designed specifically for Parkinson's patients to determine their daily functioning abilities.

Caregivers and Their Role

As with Alzheimer's disease and other degenerative diseases, although the illness is very hard on the person who has Parkinson's disease, it is also difficult for the spouse and other FAMILY CAREGIVERS to cope with it. They may need to hire extra help or make use of HOME HEALTH CARE.

For further information on Parkinson's disease, contact the following organizations:

American Parkinson Disease Association, Inc.
1250 Hylan Boulevard
Suite 4B
Staten Island, NY 10305

(800) 223-2732 (toll-free) or (718) 981-8001
http://www.apdaparkinson.com

National Parkinson's Foundation
Bob Hope Parkinson Research Center
1501 NW 9th Avenue, Bob Hope Road
Miami, FL 33316
(800) 327-4545 (toll-free) or (305) 547-6666
http://www.parkinson.org

Parkinson's Disease Foundation
710 West 168th Street
New York, NY 10032
(800) 457-6676 (toll-free)
http://www.pdf.org

United Parkinson's Foundation and International Tremor Foundation
833 West Washington Boulevard
Chicago, IL 60607
(312) 733-1893

Caap-Ahlgren, Marianne, and Ove Dehlink. "Insomnia and Depressive Symptoms in Patients with Parkinson's Disease: Relationship to Health-Related Quality of Life. An Interview Study of Patients Living at Home," *Archives of Gerontology and Geriatrics* 32 (2001): 23–33.

Freed, Curt R., M.D. et al. "Transplantation of Embryonic Dopamine Neurons for Severe Parkinson's Disease," *New England Journal of Medicine* 344, no. 19 (2001): 710–719.

Marjama-Lyons, Jill M., M.D., and William C. Koller, M.D., Ph.D. "Parkinson's Disease: Update in Diagnosis and Symptom Management," *Geriatrics* 56, no. 8 (2001): 24–35.

Sveinbjornsdottir, Sigurlaug M.D. et al. "Familial Aggregation of Parkinson's Disease," *New England Journal of Medicine* 343, no. 24 (2000): 1,765–1,770.

Young, Rosabel, M.D., M.S. "Update on Parkinson's Disease," *American Family Physician* (April 15, 1999).

pension Regular amount (usually weekly, biweekly, or monthly) paid to retired workers. In past years, corporations provided for payments to retired workers; however, for the majority of current workers today, this practice has largely been abandoned. Despite this, people who are currently seniors may be receiving RETIREMENT pensions from large and medium-size corporations.

personal emergency device   Special equipment that a person can manipulate or activate in some way to notify others remotely that the individual is either in danger or is hurt and requires assistance. This can be very helpful for older or disabled people who are at risk for physical harm from FALLS.

The personal emergency device is usually small and portable and should be kept in a place that is nearby and accessible to the older or disabled person. ASSISTED-LIVING FACILITIES often insist that their residents wear their devices at all times. When activated, the personal emergency device will inform a previously determined service that the individual is in trouble, and they will contact emergency services.

Anyone considering a personal emergency device should be sure to find out the following information:

- What is the cost for the device?
- Is there a monthly fee or other fees for the service?
- How is the device used?
- Who will be contacted if the device is activated?
- If the device is accidentally set off, will there be an additional charge?

personal hygiene   Basic body care such as bathing, brushing or combing hair, and cleaning teeth. Very poor personal hygiene is one possible sign of DEMENTIA or ALZHEIMER'S DISEASE, particularly if the individual was neat and clean in past years. Poor personal hygiene may also be a sign of DEPRESSION or of another medical problem that makes it difficult or impossible for an individual to manage such basic tasks. Although serious medical conditions must be excluded with a deterioration of personal hygiene, it is also true that often addressing psychological issues can make a large impact on the individual's outward appearance.

See also ACTIVITIES OF DAILY LIVING.

pets   Animals that live with a family and that are often regarded with great affection, as compared to animals that are raised for food by farmers or that are used for other specific noncompanionship purposes. Some studies have shown that pet owners are healthier than non-pet-owners and may have lower blood pressure. In addition, when individuals focus on caring for their pets, they often spend less time paying attention to their "aches and pains," and ultimately have an improved sense of well-being.

In one study, reported in a 1996 issue of the *Journal of Nutrition for the Elderly,* on seniors ages 60 and older, researchers found that the pet owners had lower triglyceride levels and that dog owners walked significantly more than nonowners.

People of all ages receive love from and give love to their pets. For the older person who may feel isolated and alone, pets can particularly provide companionship and meaning. The pet may also be a link to a beloved spouse or partner who has died because they both enjoyed interacting with the pet together years ago. Some (but very few) nursing homes bring in animals, such as cats and dogs, for residents to befriend, and in a few nursing homes, pets live there permanently. If the older person cannot bring a pet to the nursing home, experts say that it can help the older person to be allowed to talk about their grief over the loss of a pet.

It can be very difficult for older persons when their pets die or when they must give up their pets to move into a nursing home or other place where pets are not allowed. Pets provide unquestioning love and affection, and older people benefit from the tactile experience of petting their animals. Studies have shown that blood pressure actually drops when pet owners pet their animals.

Some older people will delay or refuse to have surgery because they cannot find someone to care for their pets. When older people who are not cognitively impaired say that they will not have needed surgery, or when they refuse to move to a nursing home despite their serious medical needs, family members and others should inquire if they are worried about what would happen to the pets and if that is the reason for refusing needed medical treatment.

Of older people who are concerned about their pet, Christine Adamec states in *When Your Pet Dies,* "It's also a good idea to have the person carry a card with the name of their pets and instructions on who should be called in the event the elderly person becomes ill or some emergency occurs. The possession of this card alone could give peace of mind to an elderly person and make him or her more willing to seek out needed medical attention."

For further information about the importance of pets, contact:

Delta Society, the Human-Animal Connection
289 Perimeter Road East
Renton, WA 98055
(425) 226-7357

Christine Adamec. *When Your Pet Dies: Dealing with Your Grief and Helping Your Children Cope.* Lincoln, Neb.: iUniverse.com, 2000.

Dembicki, Diane, Ph.D. and Jennifer Anderson, Ph.D., R.D. "Pet Ownership May Be a Factor in Improved Health of the Elderly," *Journal of Nutrition for the Elderly* 15, no. 3 (1996): 15–31.

pharmacies   Retail facilities that fill prescriptions for medications and that also offer over-the-counter medications and remedies. Many also offer other devices such as blood-pressure monitors and other medical devices. It is a good policy for people of any age to obtain all or most of their prescriptions from one pharmacy. This is particularly true for older people, who may be taking many different drugs prescribed by different doctors, some of which could cause a MEDICATION INTERACTION. Often, when a patient uses only one pharmacy and the pharmacist and technicians are familiar with the patient and his or her medications, errors in medication combination usage can be reduced or eliminated entirely.

Patients will frequently receive a list of possible side effects of their medications at their pharmacies, as well as prescription-bottle labels that provide warnings, such as to avoid alcohol, desist from driving, take the drug with food.

See also ADVERSE DRUG EVENT.

physical restraints   Items that are used to hold individuals down, sometimes against their will. In the past, individuals in nursing homes were routinely restrained, but federal and state laws and regulations in the United States have forced the decreased use of restraints. The key problem with restraints is that they may increase the probability of bed sores and may exacerbate other medical problems such as ARTHRITIS and aspiration pneumonia. Also, if individuals are capable of handing toileting and personal hygiene, it is best to allow them to do so. It is a form of AGEISM to assume that all older people who are ill invariably need to be restrained.

Physical restraints may be used if a person requires medical treatment but is thrashing about and is difficult or impossible for medical staff to treat. The federal government provides guidelines for when physical restraints may and may not be used with MEDICARE patients. Unfortunately, these guidelines are sometimes misused, and even patients who need to be restrained for their own safety (to avoid falling out of bed or out of a chair) may sometimes not be restrained. This is a very difficult issue in many care facilities.

In the past, many older people in nursing homes were physically restrained in wheelchairs. However, this widespread restraint was often unnecessary and contributed to health problems such as INCONTINENCE.

physicians   Medical doctors or osteopathic doctors. Older people may need to see a wide variety of physicians, such as CARDIOLOGISTS, ENDOCRINOLOGISTS, NEPHROLOGISTS, NEUROLOGISTS, ONCOLOGISTS, physiatrists (physical-medicine doctors), and RHEUMATOLOGISTS, to help them with both acute and chronic ailments.

In 1999, there were 756.7 million visits to U.S. physicians in their offices for an overall rate of 278.5 visits per 100 persons. Patients age 75 and older had the highest rate of physician office visits: 678.7 visits per 100 persons. Chronic medical problems were the cause for about half of all physician visits for people older than age 65.

Cherry, Donald K., M.S., Catharine W. Burt, Ed.D., and David A. Woodwell, Division of Health Care Statistics. "National Ambulatory Medical Care Survey: 1999 Summary," *Advance Data from Vital and Health Statistics,* no. 322 (July 17, 2001).

population   Numbers of people. Based on the 2000 U.S. Census, there were 35 million people older than age 65 in the United States in 2000, a 12 percent increase over 1990 when there were 31.2 million seniors in the United States. There were 14.4 million men older than age 65 and 20.6 older women in 2000. The largest population increase was seen among people age 85 and older, which increased 38 percent, from 3.1 million to 4.2 million.

The senior population of every state increased from 1990 to 2000, with the exception of the District of Columbia, which showed a decline. States with the largest population increases of older individuals were, in this order: Nevada (72 percent increase), Alaska (60 percent increase), Arizona (39 percent up), and New Mexico (30 percent more seniors). The state which has had the least increase was Rhode Island (1 percent).

Some parts of the country have a very high concentration of seniors; for example, Clearwater, Florida, with 21.5 percent of its population age 65 and older, has the highest concentration of older people in the United States. The city of Clearwater's high concentration of older citizens is followed by the cities of Cape Coral, Florida (19.6 percent), Honolulu, Hawaii (17.8 percent), and St. Petersburg, Florida (17.4 percent).

Hertzel, Lisa, and Annetta Smith. "The 65 Years and Over Population: 2000," *United States Census 2000,* U.S. Census Bureau, C2KRD/-1-10 (October 2001).

poverty   Extremely low income, considered to be at the subsistence (survival) level. The income levels that constitute poverty in the United States are determined by the Department of Health and Human Services. In 2002, the poverty rate for a one-person household was $8,860, and it was $11,940 for a two-person household.

In some states, such as Alaska and Hawaii, the income levels are higher because of the higher cost of living in those states. For example, the 2002 poverty rate in Alaska was $11,080 for one person and $14,930 for two people. The 2002 poverty rate in Hawaii was $10,200 for one person and $13,740 for two people.

The numbers of older people who live below the poverty level vary considerably by race, with AFRICAN AMERICANS having higher rates of poverty than CAUCASIANS. (See Table 1.) For example, among black Americans, nearly 23 percent (22.7 percent) of

people who are age 65 and older are living at or below the poverty level. However, among older white Americans, only about 8 percent (7.6 percent) in this group are at this level of poverty. Poverty rates for people in races other than black or white are about 18 percent (17.8 percent).

PERCENTAGE OF POPULATION AGE 65 AND OLDER IN 1999 BELOW POVERTY LEVEL, BY RACE

Total	Black	White	Other
9.7	22.7	7.6	17.8

Source: Department of Health and Human Services

prescription assistance programs   Programs that provide prescribed medications to low-income individuals who cannot afford needed drugs. Many of these individuals are at or slightly above the POVERTY level and have no access to any programs that pay for all or part of the cost of their prescription medicines. In a 1999 survey of pharmaceutical companies, the corporations reported that they had provided $500 million worth of free prescription drugs to 1.5 million people in 1998.

Prescription assistance programs are important because many older individuals cannot afford the drugs that they need. As of this writing, MEDICARE does not pay for medications, and Medicare recipients must either join a program that covers payments (if they can) or must pay for the medications themselves. MEDICAID does pay for medications that are on an approved list of drugs in the state program.

Many pharmaceutical companies and some nonprofit organizations have special programs to assist people who cannot afford needed but expensive medications. According to a 2000 report by the General Accounting Office, half the programs that were contacted in their study required the physician to apply for free medications on behalf of the patient; the other programs required applications forms to be completed by the patient or the patient's advocate. Some programs required the applicant to provide verification of their low-income status; others relied on the physician to have performed that evaluation.

Once approved, most of the programs send the drug to the physician; others send the drug to the patient or send the patient a voucher to obtain the drug from a pharmacy. Copayments are rarely required of patients who are approved in these programs.

The GAO concludes, "Drug companies characterize their programs as a last-resort source of prescription drugs, and most programs are not designed to provide long-term prescription drug coverage."

Innovative Programs

Some companies have created their own programs; for example, in January 2002, Pfizer announced that it would provide key drugs that they produce to elderly consumers who will pay a $15 monthly copayment. The older individuals must be Medicare recipients with an annual income of $18,000 if living alone and $24,000 if a couple. As of this writing, Wal-Mart and CVS drugstores have agreed to participate in this program.

Glaxo, another huge pharmaceutical company, has a similar program, and it is likely that other pharmaceutical companies will also develop their own programs.

General Accounting Office. "Prescription Drugs: Drug Company Programs Help Some People Who Lack Coverage," GAO-01-137, November 2000.

prescription medication A drug that is ordered by a medical doctor for a medical condition. The majority of people older than age 65 take prescribed medications, and some people take four or more drugs.

One large-scale study in Sweden provided some fascinating insights about prescribed drug use among older people. This 1994 study of 4,642 nonhospitalized people age 65 and older in Tierp, Sweden, was reported in a 2001 issue of *The Annals of Pharmacotherapy.* Researchers found that the majority (78 percent) were taking prescribed medications.

The average age of the research subjects was 75.7 years. The average person who used prescribed drugs took 4.3 medications. (Men used 3.8 drugs, and women used 4.8 drugs per year.) More than a third of the subjects (39 percent) used five or more prescription medications per year. The types of drugs used most frequently were those for the cardiovascular system, the nervous system, or the gastrointestinal system.

Cardiovascular drugs were used by the largest group (47 percent), including diuretics and beta blockers. The use of such drugs was greatest among people ages 75–84 years old.

More than a third (37 percent) used forms of nervous system drugs, most frequently opium-based painkilling drugs (14.8 percent) and hypnotics/sedatives (14.2 percent). Drugs in the anxiolytic (anti-anxiety) class were also used, although women used them about three times as frequently as men.

About 34 percent of those who used prescribed drugs took medications for the gastrointestinal system. The largest type of medication for this system was antiulcer drugs, followed by antidiabetic medications.

The top three medical diagnoses for the subjects were HYPERTENSION (14.6 percent), DIABETES (8.9 percent), and heart failure (6.7 percent).

Jorgensen, Tove, et al. "Prescription Drug use, Diagnoses, and Healthcare Utilization Among the Elderly," *The Annals of Pharmacotherapy* 35 (2001): 1,004–1,009.

preventive care Actions that are taken to avoid illnesses or to minimize the effects of existing chronic or acute illnesses. For example, if a person has a problem with OBESITY, in most cases, a steady weight loss will improve health conditions such as DIABETES and ARTHRITIS. In fact, some individuals who are at risk for developing diabetes may eliminate their risk altogether by achieving a weight loss prior to the onset of the illness.

Regular visits to OPHTHALMOLOGISTS, dentists, and other health-care providers will enable individuals to take preventive action when early signs of illness are identified by medical professionals.

Individuals can also take preventive action against disease by giving up SMOKING and taking care to get regular EXERCISE suitable to their physical abilities and preapproved by their physicians. Using certain over-the-counter drugs such as aspirin may reduce the risk of STROKE or HEART ATTACK.

prostate cancer A disease in which malignant cells are found in the prostate gland, a male sex gland about the size of a walnut that is located below and adjacent to the bladder and in front of the rectum. (The gland may swell to the size of a lemon if it is enlarged.) The primary function of the prostate gland is to contribute to the seminal fluid. This milky white fluid is ejaculated at the time of a male orgasm during sex.

If diagnosed with prostate cancer in the early stages, most men can be treated and will recover completely. However, prostate cancer is the second leading cause of cancer deaths among men in the United States. (LUNG CANCER is the number-one cause of cancer deaths among males.)

An estimated 198,100 new cases of prostate cancer were diagnosed in the United States in 2001, and about 31,500 men died. However, the five-year survival rate for prostate cancer is much higher than in other cancers: about 93 percent for whites and 84 percent for blacks, the best survival rate for any form of cancer. Blacks have a poorer survival rate in nearly all forms of cancer.

Depending on how advanced the cancer and also depending on the health of the individual man, prostate cancer is usually treated with surgery, radiation treatment, or hormone treatment. Chemotherapy is rarely used with patients who have prostate cancer, although some experimental drugs are being used in advanced cases. Very experienced physicians sometimes use cryotherapy (freezing) or microwave (heating) therapy.

In some cases, no treatment is given for prostate cancer because of an individual's advanced age or ill health. (This is called "watchful waiting.") Low-grade prostate cancer is usually a slow-growing cancer, and if a man has a life expectancy of less than 10 more years, then doctors may decide that the treatment would make the patient feel worse than the disease does.

High-grade prostate cancer, however, will require some form of therapy, depending on the age of the patient and the grade and stage of the cancer. It is important to note that older men can have very aggressive forms of prostate cancer. It should never be assumed that prostate cancer is inevitably a slow-growing cancer; only an experienced physician can make the determination. Men who have any possible symptoms of prostate cancer should not delay informing their doctors about these symptoms.

Most at Risk

About 80 percent of the men who are diagnosed with prostate cancer are older than 65 years. According to the CENTERS FOR DISEASE CONTROL AND PREVENTION (CDC), most men with prostate cancer die from other diseases, such as heart attack and STROKE.

As mentioned, AFRICAN-AMERICAN men have the greatest risk of death from prostate cancer, with more than double the risk of white men and six times the risk for Asians/Pacific Islander men, although the reasons for this are unknown. According to the National Cancer Institute, African-American males have the highest rates of prostate cancer in the world.

There are also genetic risks associated with prostate cancer; for example, according to the National Cancer Institute, the risk for developing prostate cancer is increased if a man's father or brother has had prostate cancer. If a man has three or more relatives who have prostate cancer, his risk is increased by 10 times. The risk is also increased if the man has female relatives who have had BREAST CANCER.

TABLE 1   RISK OF DEATH FROM PROSTATE CANCER BY RACE IN THE UNITED STATES, PER 100,000 MEN OF THE SAME RACE

African American	48.7
Caucasian	19.6
Hispanic	14.5
American Indian	11.3
Asian/Pacific Islander	8.0

Source: "At A Glance: Prostate Cancer: The Public Health Perspective 2001," Centers for Disease Control and Prevention, 2001.

Symptoms

A man who has prostate cancer often has no symptoms, and a physician may notice a problem for the first time upon performing a rectal examination. Some men have mild to moderate symptoms. Some symptoms of prostate cancer that may occur (and which may also be symptoms of other problems, such as a bladder infection or another noncancerous disease) are:

- Frequent urination
- Difficulty with urination
- Painful urination
- Weak urinary flow
- Blood in the urine or semen
- Frequent pain in the lower back, upper thighs, or hips

Diagnosis

A "digital rectal examination" by the doctor may detect abnormalities that should be further screened for prostate cancer. Most men detest these examinations, but they can be life savers for affected men. During the examination, the doctor inserts the lubricated finger of a gloved hand into the rectum to feel the prostate gland for any lumpy or hard areas.

The exam is performed more easily if the man relaxes. This examination can be performed during an annual physical examination and may be performed by an internist, a urologist, or any physician experienced in performing rectal examinations. (All doctors are trained how to perform rectal examinations in medical school, but some doctors do not perform them on a regular basis. It is best to be examined by someone who is experienced and confident.)

Doctors should order a special blood test called a prostate-specific antigen (PSA) test. PSA is an enzyme produced by the prostate gland, and it increases if the gland enlarges or if cancer is present. Thus, if the PSA test is above normal, it may indicate cancer, although it may also indicate prostatitis (inflammation of the prostate) or a benign growth. The PSA test may also fail to detect some early prostate cancers.

Interestingly, the PSA blood test is also performed on a periodic basis in men who have had complete removals of their prostate glands because of prostate cancer. The reason for this is that there should be *no* prostate cells when there is no prostate gland. A rising PSA level is an indicator that cancer may be spreading because the cancer cells are elsewhere in the body.

Doctors do not agree on whether all men older than a certain age should be screened for prostate cancer using the PSA, nor is there any federal standard recommendation for the PSA similar to federal guidelines for mammograms to detect breast cancer in women. However, because of the prevalence of the disease and the fact that risk increases with age, it seems logical that men older than age 65 should have an annual rectal examination and a PSA test.

If a rectal examination and/or a PSA indicates that cancer may be present, the doctor orders a biopsy of the prostate gland; a transrectal ultrasound test may also be ordered. According to leading prostate cancer expert and author Patrick Walsh, M.D., the ultrasound test alone cannot determine whether a man has prostate cancer; it can merely assist the doctor in performing the biopsy more effectively.

If cancer is present, the biopsy will also determine how advanced the cancer is and how fast it is growing. Doctors will "stage" the cancer with regard to how advanced the current cancer is and how aggressively it is growing in the system. This information will help doctors determine what treatment to recommend.

One system that doctors use to categorize how fast the prostate cancer is growing is called the Gleason scale, named after the physician who devised it. This system uses a grading score of 2 to 10, with higher scores meaning more aggressive cancers.

According to the National Cancer Institute, there are four basic stages of prostate cancer. They are known as either Stages I-IV or A-D. Stage 1 (A) is a cancer that is not detected in a rectal examination and that is usually found by accident. The patient has no symptoms.

Stage II (B) is a more advanced case and can be detected during a rectal examination performed by the doctor. The patient may show an elevated PSA test. At this stage, the cancer is believed to be confined to the prostate gland.

At Stage III (C), the cancer has spread beyond the prostate gland to surrounding body tissues. The glands that make semen may also be cancerous. At Stage IV (D), the cancer has advanced (metastasized) still further to the lymph nodes or to other areas of the body. Most physicians use the TNM system to stage prostate cancer, which evaluates the aggressiveness of the tumor and whether cancer has advanced (metastasized) to the nodes or beyond the prostate to the bones and other organs.

Treating Prostate Cancer

Prostate cancer may initially be diagnosed by a urologist, an internist, a family doctor, or any other type of medical doctor; however, treatment is usually provided by a urologist. If radiation is needed, radiation oncologists provide this treatment. If chemotherapy is needed, it is provided by medical oncologists.

The choices of treatment for prostate cancer are usually surgery, radiation, or hormonal therapy. Some doctors consider "watchful waiting" to be a form of treatment. Watchful waiting is also referred to as delayed treatment. This means that no treatment is provided at present, but the patient is monitored.

Most urologists agree that watchful waiting is only appropriate for men whose life expectancy is less than 10 years or who have other severe medical problems, although some doctors use watchful waiting in some men whose tumors are considered to be at an early stage or growing slowly. However, experts say this is a dangerous policy to take because a tumor may suddenly begin growing very aggressively, without the knowledge of the patient or doctor.

Surgical Treatment   Many doctors believe that surgical treatment is the best option for most men who have been diagnosed with localized (confined to the gland) prostate cancer. In some cases, the doctor may remove part of the prostate gland in men who cannot have the entire prostate removed because of their age or ill health. However, in most cases, the doctor performs a "radical prostatectomy" and removes the entire gland.

The radical prostatectomy brings a risk of ERECTILE DYSFUNCTION and/or INCONTINENCE to the patient. Dr. Walsh of Johns Hopkins University innovated a nerve-sparing procedure in which the nerve bundles that control erection are saved and male potency can be preserved in many cases. Incontinence is also less likely to be a problem with this procedure. Other physicians, such as Dr. Scardino at Sloan-Kettering in New York, have pioneered surgery to preserve sexual potency by transplanting nerves from the man's leg to the pelvic area.

After prostate surgery, men can no longer produce semen, and they can no longer father children. When they have an orgasm, no fluid will be ejaculated.

Treatment with Hormones   Surgery is not the best choice for some men, especially if the cancer has advanced beyond the prostate. Instead, they may be treated with a variety of hormones, including luteinizing hormone-releasing hormone agonists (leuporolide, goserelin, and buserelin), which prevent testosterone from being converted to the active form, and antiandrogens (flutamide and bicalutamide). Drugs that block the adrenal glands from making androgens may also be used to treat patients, such as ketoconazole and aminoglutethimide. These hormones are used to block testosterone, which makes cancer grow faster.

These drugs may cause side effects such as nausea and vomiting, diarrhea, breast growth, and soreness; anemia may also occur. The man may also experience menopauselike symptoms, such as mood swings and hot flashes, and osteoporosis may also develop. Some of the drugs that are administered, such as ketoconazole, can lead to liver problems.

Hormonal treatment is usually only effective for several years at best because prostate cancer can continue to grow even without male hormones, albeit more slowly than with male hormones.

Treatment with Radiation   Doctors may also treat localized prostate cancer with radiation therapy, using special high-energy X rays aimed at the body by a machine or by radiation that is actually implanted into the body in tiny radioactive seeds. Radiation is also used to treat bone pain experienced with advanced cancer.

If radiation therapy is provided by a machine, patients usually go to a clinic or hospital five days a week for a number of weeks that are determined by the doctor. The patient is placed in a special body cast so that he cannot move about while the X rays are aimed at specific mapped areas of the body.

If implant radiation (interstitial brachytherapy) is used (also called implanted seeds), the procedure is performed on an outpatient basis. Although the risk of ejaculating radioactive pellets after they are implanted is extremely low, doctors advise men who have undergone the procedure to avoid intercourse or to use condoms.

Radiation therapy may cause impotence, immediately or a year or two later (from scarring), although this is less likely to occur than with non-nerve sparing surgery. Internal radiation may also cause temporary incontinence. Permanent or temporary hair loss of the radiated area may occur. There may be some bowel problems, such as a feeling of urgency. The radiated area may also become reddened, sore, and dry.

It should also be noted that some doctors are combining therapies; for example, using hormone therapy that is followed several months later by radiation therapy. The hormone therapy may work to reduce the size of the prostate and improve the results with radiation therapy. However, each person should consult with his own physician for treatment recommendations.

Questions for Patients

According to the National Cancer Institute, patients who have been diagnosed with prostate cancer should be sure to ask their doctors questions, including (but not limited to) the following questions before any treatment for prostate cancer is started:

- What is the stage and grade of my disease?
- What are my treatment choices?
- Are there new treatments under study now?
- Should I enroll in a clinical trial?
- What are the risks and benefits of each form of treatment?
- Will the treatment affect my sex life?
- Is it likely that I will have urinary problems?
- What are the side effects of each treatment?
- Should I expect to change my normal activities, and if so, how and for how long?

Emotional Issues

Virtually all men who are diagnosed with prostate cancer are very upset and fearful. Obtaining current information and listening carefully to the doctor's recommendations will help men overcome feelings of hopelessness or powerlessness. Talking with others who have undergone the procedure may help. The prognosis is very good for most men, but decisions about their treatment do need to be made in a timely manner. Often, a referral to a psychologist or counselor experienced in treating men with cancer can be of great benefit to patients with prostate cancer.

Future Clinical Tests

Studies are under way to determine if and how prostate cancer can be prevented. As of this writing in 2002, the National Cancer Institute is preparing to launch the Selenium and Vitamin E Cancer Prevention Trial (SELECT), the largest-ever study on prostate cancer prevention. They are recruiting 32,400 healthy men, most age 55 and older, to test the effects of Vitamin E and Selenium in preventing the onset of prostate cancer.

Men at 400 sites in the United States, Canada, and Puerto Rico will participate in this study, which is expected to take 12 years to complete.

The researchers are particularly seeking African-American men to participate in their study because of the very high rate of prostate cancer among black men. As a result of this high rate, black men older than age 50 (rather than age 55 for all others) will be recruited.

Prior studies have suggested that Vitamin E and selenium have decreased the rate of prostate cancer. In a 1996 study on the effect of selenium in preventing skin cancer, researchers found that although selenium did not prevent skin cancer, it did decrease the incidence of prostate cancer by 60 percent. In a 1998 clinical trial in Finland, Finnish smokers who took Vitamin E had a 32 percent lower incidence of prostate cancer. The SELECT study will help determine if selenium and/or Vitamin E has a protective effect on a large number of men.

For more information on SELECT, contact the National Cancer Institute. In Canada:

Canadian Cancer Society's Information Service
(888) 939-3333
http://cancer.gov/select

For more information on prostate cancer, contact the following organizations:

American Foundation for Urologic Disease
1128 N. Charles Street
Baltimore, MD 21201
(800) 828-7866

National Cancer Institute
Building 31, Room 10A03
31 Center Drive, MSC 2580
Bethesda, MD 20892
(800) 4-CANCER (800) 422-6237

Lange, Paul H., M.D., and Christine Adamec. *Prostate Cancer for Dummies.* New York: John Wiley & Sons, 2003.

National Cancer Institute. "Prostate Cancer," NIH Publication No. 00-1576 (December 2000).

Walsh, Patrick C., M.D., and Janet Farrar Worthington. *Dr. Patrick Walsh's Guide to Surviving Prostate Cancer.* New York: Warner Books, 2001.

prostate diseases (noncancerous) Disorders of the prostate gland, not including PROSTATE CANCER. The two primary prostate noncancerous disorders are benign prostatic hyperplasia (BPH) and prostatitis. Both of these disorders are very common medical problems among men older than age 65. Neither is known to cause prostate cancer.

BPH

Benign prostatic hyperplasia is an abnormal growth of noncancerous prostate cells, and it causes the prostate to enlarge. The condition also impedes the flow of urine because of the close proximity of the prostate gland to the bladder. At least half of all men in the United States ages 60–70 years have BPH, and 90 percent of men older than age 70 have BPH.

If the case is not severe, it may not require any treatment. BPH may, however, cause an elevated prostate-specific antigen (PSA) level, which may raise concerns of prostate cancer. Further testing will rule out cancer.

Men who have symptomatic BPH may have a need for frequent urination and may also feel that they cannot completely empty their bladders. The man straining to urinate so that he can completely empty his bladder can intensify his BPH symptoms. In the worst case, the urethra (the tube inside the penis that leads to the bladder) becomes completely blocked, and the man will not be able to urinate at all. In this case, he will require an emergency catheterization, in which a tube is inserted to withdraw the urine. This procedure may be performed in the doctor's office or in an emergency-room setting. The catheterization will also help temporarily to improve the man's flow of urine. Some men who have BPH also experience a problem with bleeding.

BPH is usually treated by UROLOGISTS. The diagnosis is based on a man's symptoms. The doctor may order a urinalysis to check for infection; tests to measure urinary flow or the amount of urine that is left in the bladder after urinating; a cystosocopy, which involves the insertion of a special viewing tube up the urethra so the doctor can see the bladder; and ultrasound tests.

There are a variety of treatments for BPH. In some cases, especially if the BPH is not severe, doctors may take no action and may follow up patients later. They may also advise patients to avoid alcohol and caffeine and to limit their fluid intake before bedtime to reduce the risk of being wakened by an urgent need to urinate.

Doctors may also prescribe drugs to treat BPH, such as alpha blockers to relax the prostate muscles. Some alpha-blocker drugs that doctors may prescribe are Hytrin (terazosin), Cardura (doxazosin), and Flomax (tamsulosin hydrochloride). Physicians also use Proscar (finasteride), a drug that causes a shrinking of the prostate, thus easing the obstruction.

If the BPH is causing a serious problem, the doctor may recommend surgery. Physicians may perform a transurethral resection of the prostate (TURP), in which prostate tissue is removed. A small number of men (about 5 percent) become incontinent and/or impotent after this procedure.

In another surgical procedure, transurethral incision of the prostate (TUIP), the doctor inserts a stent to keep the bladder passage open.

In a very small number of cases (less than 5 percent), the doctor may perform a prostatectomy, removing the entire prostate gland.

prostatitis An inflammation of the prostate that can occur to men of any age, prostatitis is usually caused by a bacterial infection and is treated with antibiotics. Affected men may have difficulty with urination and may also experience a burning sensation when they urinate. In addition, they may have pain in the lower back. Prostatitis is sometimes accompanied by chills and fever, which usually clear up when the antibiotics act to kill the bacteria that caused these symptoms. Some men suffer from chronic prostatitis. They may need to be on a maintenance (small daily) dose of antibiotics.

National Cancer Institute. "Understanding Prostate Changes: A Health Guide for All Men," NIH Publication No. 99-4303 (September 1999).

psychiatrists Medical doctors who treat psychiatric problems such as ANXIETY, DEPRESSION, and PARANOIA. Psychiatrists may also treat patients with DEMENTIA or ALZHEIMER'S DISEASE, although NEUROLOGISTS usually treat these conditions.

Psychiatrists are extremely skilled in the use of medications that act on the brain, such as Prozac (fluoxetine), an antidepressant, and other medications. Some psychiatrists are also quite skilled in alternative therapies for mental disorders, including counseling and even electroconvulsive therapy (ECT).

quest for youth Attempts to look or act much younger than one's actual age. It is very difficult for some older individuals to accept their aging status. The high value placed on younger people in the United States may be partially or largely responsible for this disaffection with aging.

Some older people may resort to plastic surgery for face lifts or other body changes. Many older women continue to dye their hair, even when they are in their 80s or 90s. Many older people refuse to wear HEARING AIDS because they think they make them appear aged, frail, and disabled. As a result, they cannot hear much of what others say, and their DRIVING may be impaired.

R

rage   Extreme and irrational anger. Older people who frequently exhibit rages may be suffering from DEMENTIA or ALZHEIMER'S DISEASE. Sometimes, people with DEPRESSION turn their distress outward into a rage and may commit crimes such as SPOUSE ABUSE. The person who is prone to rages should be thoroughly examined by a physician to rule out any underlying and treatable medical problems. Often, patients suffering from chronic painful conditions may have outbursts due to their frustration over loss of body function and image.

It can be very difficult or impossible for FAMILY CAREGIVERS to cope with these rages; instead, they may feel compelled to move the older person into a NURSING-HOME environment.

Often, by removing the underlying medical problem or by simply treating a patient's PAIN or depression, the episodes of rage will resolve.

rehabilitation   Planned and often assisted recovery from an illness or accident. Many older people experience FALLS and may need assistance with rehabilitation after hospitalization, such as physical therapy, occupational therapy, and speech therapy. Other individuals suffer from STROKES and may need help to relearn basic activities of living, such as dressing, feeding themselves, and toileting. They may also need speech therapy and other forms of therapy.

Some NURSING HOMES provide temporary rehabilitative assistance for individuals who have received treatment in a hospital and are not ill enough to remain in the hospital but are too sick to return home.

Di Libero, F., et al. "Comorbidity and Rehabilitation," *Archives of Gerontology and Geriatrics* 32 (2001): 15–22.

relaxation therapy techniques   Methods to overcome stress, such as MEDITATION or TAI CHI. Other relaxation techniques include hypnotherapy and progressive muscle relaxation. Studies have shown that effective relaxation can not only alleviate stress but can also improve the overall physical health among people of all ages. Psychologists and other therapists can teach patients to perform relaxation techniques. Such simple activities as correct deep breathing can have a significant impact on a patient's overall well-being.

religion   Belief in a higher power and acceptance of an accompanying value system. Religion may provide great solace to older individuals, helping them to accept their losses and to transcend the pain and difficulties that may be associated with their aging. In addition, members of the clergy as well as members of the faith group may help older people when they are ill or have other needs, bringing them food or visiting them in the hospital when they are ill.

respite services   Temporary paid or volunteer care, allowing the usual caregiver some time off. Adult day services may provide respite for FAMILY CAREGIVERS. Temporary ASSISTED-LIVING care or care in a NURSING HOME may also be provided under the respite care program in the state.

Respite care may mean that HOME HEALTH CARE is provided to the ailing older person, allowing the family caregiver an opportunity to tend to his or her own needs or take a long-delayed vacation. Some family caregivers have neglected their own health care and even delayed needed surgery because they could not find anyone to care for their older family member.

In the United States, the Older Americans Act Amendments of 2000 (Public Law 106-501) established the National Family Caregiver Support Program. About $125 million was funded for fiscal year 2001, and about $113 million of that amount was provided to states to work with agencies in the community on respite-care programs.

Some support groups offer their own respite-care programs, with volunteer office staff.

For further information, contact the state aging agency, or call the national Eldercare Locator at (800) 677-1116, available Monday through Friday from 9 A.M. to 8 P.M. eastern time.

restraints   See PHYSICAL RESTRAINTS.

retirement   Leaving a full-time job. Many older workers are retired, although not all collect a PENSION, and some continue to work part-time or full-time in other jobs. The U.S. Census Bureau performed a comparison of the standard (statutory) age of retirement in 24 countries, including the United States, and found that the actual age of retirement may be higher or lower than the generally accepted standard age. For example, in the United States, the standard age of retirement is age 65. However, the actual age of retirement is 61.6 for women and 63.6 for men. (As of this writing, reduced retirement benefits may be received by eligible Americans ages 62–64.)

In Iceland, the standard retirement age is 67 for men and women, but the average age of retirement is 69.5 for men and 66.0 for women. At the other extreme, in Belgium, the standard age of retirement is 65 for men and 60 for women; however, the average male Belgian retires at age 57.6, and the average female Belgian at 54.1 years.

See also WORK.

Kinsella, Kevin, and Victoria A. Velkoff. *An Aging World: 2001.* Washington, D.C.: U.S. Census Bureau, 2001.

reverse mortgages   A financial arrangement in which the owner of a house that is completely paid up makes an arrangement with a bank or other entity to receive a monthly payment. Rather than paying a monthly mortgage payment (as with a "forward mortgage"), instead with a reverse mortgage, the homeowner receives a monthly payment or sometimes a lump sum from the bank, mortgage company, or other loaning entity. In most cases, the owner may live in the house until death. After the person dies, the ownership of the house will revert to the lender. The homeowner usually must be age 62 years or older to qualify for such a mortgage.

The homeowner must still pay the taxes and home insurance and make or pay for any repairs to the home.

According to a 2001 booklet released by the AARP, an organization for older Americans, there are three primary types of reverse mortgages, including a single-purpose mortgage, a federally insured mortgage, and a proprietary mortgage.

The single-purpose mortgage is used for only one reason, such as to repair the house or to cover the cost of long-term care. This type of mortgage is not common.

The federally insured mortgage, also called a Home Equity Conversion Mortgage (HECM), is the most common type of reverse mortgage; it is available in every state, and the homeowner can use the money he or she has received for any reason. These loans are backed by the Federal Housing Administration (FHA).

The proprietary reverse mortgage is the least common type of reverse mortgage. It provides the most amount of money but is usually limited to people whose homes are significantly more valuable than other homes in the area.

AARP. "Home Made Money: A Consumer's Guide to Reverse Mortgages," 2001.

rheumatoid arthritis (RA)   A very debilitating and crippling form of ARTHRITIS that is experienced by more than 2 million Americans, most of whom (an estimated 75 percent) are female. Rheumatoid arthritis is an autoimmune disorder, which means that the individual's own immune system attacks itself. It may have a genetic basis as well; research continues on the causes of RA. Most patients with RA are treated by a RHEUMATOLOGIST, a medical doctor who specializes in arthritis. The treatment is usually coordinated with the patient's primary-care physician; however, sometimes, a pain specialist or a NEUROLOGIST is brought in to assist in the management of this painful condition.

Risk Factors

RA may strike people of any age, but it is more likely to have its onset in individuals between the ages 20–45. The disease causes severe inflammation and pain, and it eventually results in tissue destruction of bone and cartilage, although some physicians believe that early and aggressive treatment may delay or even prevent the most extreme consequences of the disease.

A majority (about 80 percent) of those who have RA become disabled after about 20 years, which means that individuals whose RA began at age 45 will be completely disabled by age 65. If the RA begins sooner, it becomes a disability before people enter their senior years. With new medications, the prognosis should improve. Many people with RA also suffer from OSTEOPOROSIS.

Symptoms of RA

Most people who have RA have both severe morning stiffness and pain and swelling in the joints, as well as identifiable nodules present in the joints. Long-term RA produces characteristic distortions in the finger joints, visible to the physician as well as to the lay person.

A 2001 article on RA in the *New England Journal of Medicine* explained the inflammation problem in this way, "The inflammatory process is usually tightly regulated, involving both mediators that initiate and maintain inflammation and mediators that shut the process down. In states of chronic inflammation, an imbalance between the two mediators leaves inflammation unchecked, resulting in cellular damage. In the cause of rheumatoid arthritis, this damage is manifested by the destruction of cartilage and bone."

Diagnosis of RA

The disease is diagnosed based on the patient's symptoms as well as physical signs, such as apparent inflammation and the presence of nodules. Laboratory tests are also used for diagnosis. The majority (about 60 percent) of RA patients test positive for rheumatoid factor in the blood. X-ray tests are also helpful to outline the severity of joint damage.

Recommended Treatments

Medications are the mainstay treatment, and the goals are to alleviate pain as well as to delay progression of the disease. Also recommended are lifestyle changes, such as weight loss, EXERCISE, heat and cold therapy, massage therapy, and physical therapy.

In the early stages of RA, patients may be treated with over-the-counter nonsteroidal antiinflammatory medications (NSAIDs), such as ibuprofen. If such drugs provide little or no relief, then prescribed NSAIDs are usually tried. Such drugs can cause stomach upset or ulcers over the long term.

Another class of antiinflammatory drugs is the COX-2 inhibitors. These drugs are less likely to cause gastrointestinal upset, although it can still occur. Drugs such as Bextra, Celebrex, and Vioxx fall into this category. Corticosteroids are also often prescribed, such as prednisone or hydrocortisone. These drugs have side effects, among them weight gain, blood-sugar changes, CATARACTS, blood-pressure elevation, and calcium wasting from the bones.

When the illness advances further, other different and very strong drugs are usually required, such as drugs in the disease-modifying antirheumatic disease (DMARD) class, including hydroxychloroquine, methotrexate, sulfasalazine, or intramuscular gold injections. Other newer drugs that may be prescribed are Enbrel (etanercept) and Remicade (inflixamab), which both work to block inflammation.

People who have RA should not drink alcohol because it can interact with their medications and cause serious liver damage. (See also ALCOHOLISM.) They should also check with their doctors before taking SUPPLEMENTS or using any form of ALTERNATIVE MEDICINE because such drugs can cause dangerous interactions with the other medicines that RA patients may take.

For further information, contact the following organizations:

Arthritis Foundation
1330 West Peachtree Street
Atlanta, GA 30309
(800) 283-7800 or (404) 965-7537
http://www.arthritis.org

National Institute on Arthritis and Musculoskeletal and Skin Diseases Information Clearinghouse
1 AMS Circle
Bethesda, MD 20892
(301) 495-4484 or (877) 226-4267 (toll-free)
http://www.nih.gov/niams

Choy, Ernest H.S., M.D., and Gabriel S. Panayi, M.D., Sc.D. "Cytokine Pathways and Joint Inflammation in Rheumatoid Arthritis," *New England Journal of Medicine* 344, no. 12 (March 22, 2001): 907–916.

Farhey, Yolanda, M.D., and Evelyn Hess, M.D. "Controlling Pain in Rheumatoid Arthritis and Fibromyalgia," *Women's Health in Primary Care* 4, no. 7 (July 2001): 469–473.

Infante, Ricardo, M.D., and Robert G. Lahita, M.D., Ph.D. "Rheumatoid Arthritis: New Disease-Modifying and Anti-Inflammatory Drugs," *Geriatrics* 56, no. 3 (2000): 30–40.

rheumatologist Medical doctor who specializes in treating patients who have diseases of the joints or soft tissues such as ARTHRITIS, including OSTEO-ARTHRITIS and RHEUMATOID ARTHRITIS, and also autoimmune disorders.

role reversal Refers to the feeling that some ADULT CHILDREN have toward their aging parents, that they, the "children" have now become parents to their increasingly dependent elders. One risk that comes with this feeling is to infantilize the older person, believing that he or she can perform almost nothing when the older person may actually still be capable of achieving some tasks without assistance.

If FAMILY CAREGIVERS or others take over virtually all tasks, then the older person may lapse into a LEARNED-HELPLESSNESS role. This means that he or she will assume that they cannot do tasks, and they will do less and less for themselves. This can lead to feelings of ANXIETY and DEPRESSION.

See also AGEISM.

rosacea Skin condition that is mostly found among fair-skinned people and which causes a characteristic reddening of the face, which may appear like a blushing. In addition to facial redness, this skin condition also causes bumps and pimples and is called adult acne by some. In most cases, rosacea is observed on the face, although it may occur in the neck and upper chest as well. In about half of the cases, the eyes are also affected, and individuals may feel that their eyes are irritated, according to the National Institute of Arthritis and Musculoskeletal and Skin Diseases.

Some cases of rosacea are severe; others are much less noticeable. An estimated 13 million Americans have rosacea. Both women and men may develop rosacea, but when it occurs to men, it is usually far more severe than when seen among women.

Hypothesized Causes

The cause of rosacea is unknown, although there are many theories that are yet unproven. Some experts believe that a tiny mite, *Demodex folliculorum,* is the cause, and that these mites clog the skin and cause it to become inflamed. Others believe there may be link between the development of rosacea and *Helicobacter pylori,* a bacterium that lodges in the stomach and other parts of the body. Still other researchers believe that rosacea may be caused by a problem with the immune system.

Some patients with rosacea develop an enlarged nose, similar to the nose of W.C. Fields, an early 20th-century actor who had rosacea. However, studies indicate that only about 21 percent of males and 8 percent of females with rosacea will develop rhinophyma (enlarged nose).

Diagnosis and Treatment

The illness is usually diagnosed by the individual's characteristic facial appearance. Patients may be treated by their primary-care providers, although dermatologists are the best choice to treat this disease.

Treatment may include antibiotics such as tetracycline or doxycline, although most patients stop taking these drugs because they can cause severe gastrointestinal problems. Skin ointments that contain metronidazole are also prescribed by many doctors who treat rosacea.

Some physicians have found success with a low dose (250 mg) of oral azithromycin three times a week, although clinical studies have yet to be performed on its efficacy with rosacea. Patients with rosacea may also benefit from soap substitutes and mild soaps. Facial peels and specialized skin treatments may be an option for some patients.

Patients with rosacea are advised to make lifestyle changes; for example, alcohol usually exacerbates the condition and should be avoided altogether; some foods, such as tomatoes, chocolate, and caffeinated beverages, may cause a flareup of rosacea; excessive sun may also cause rosacea to flare, and patients are advised to either avoid the sun or to wear a strong sunscreen. Excessive stress may also cause a flareup of rosacea, and patients may benefit from RELAXATION THERAPY, TAI CHI, or other methods to manage daily stress.

Women with rosacea should avoid cosmetics or other facial products that contain alcohol or any other ingredients that irritate the skin.

For more information, contact the following organizations:

American Academy of Dermatology
P.O. Box 4014
Schaumburg, IL 60168
(847) 330-0230
http://www.aad.org

National Arthritis and Musculoskeletal and Skin Diseases Information Clearinghouse (NAMSIC)
1 AMS Circle
Bethesda, MD 20892
(301) 495-4484
http://www.niams.nih.gov

National Rosacea Society
800 South Northwest Highway
Suite 200
Barrington, IL 60010
(888) NO-BLUSH (toll-free)
http://www.rosacea.org

National Institutes of Health, National Institute of Arthritis and Musculoskeletal and Skin Diseases. "Questions and Answers About Rosacea," April 1999. www.niams.nih.gov/hi/topics/rosacea.htm

Walsh, Nancy. "Rosacea Responds Favorably to Oral Azithromycin," *OB/GYN News* (May 1, 2001).

safety issues Aspects that affect the personal safety of individuals. As people age, they become more prone to FALLS and other accidents around the home and outside the home. If safety issues are not addressed, the probability of injuries is increased. For older people, an unsafe environment may also be a fatal environment. People who have ALZHEIMER'S DISEASE and DEMENTIA are at risk for safety hazards, as are other older individuals with DISABILITIES.

sandwich generation A term used to denote people who are still young enough to have minor children in the home and yet also have the responsibility for providing assistance and, sometimes, care and support to their aging parents. The term is used to indicate the pressure that such individuals feel, torn between their obligations to their children and to their parents.

See also ADULT CHILDREN; BABY BOOMERS.

savings/depletion of savings Many seniors have money saved in the bank in the form of bank accounts, certificates of deposit, or other financial instruments. Unfortunately, because of these liquid assets, older people can be vulnerable to scams and other CRIMES. In addition, because of their loneliness and feelings of isolation, some older people turn to GAMBLING, and a small number spend all or most of their "nest egg" on gambling casinos, bingo parlors, and lottery tickets.

Another problem is an increased use of credit cards by younger seniors, who may charge medical expenses, living expenses, or other fees, and later may be unable to pay the bills. Increasing numbers of seniors are turning to credit-counseling agencies or must even file for bankruptcy. States determine the laws on bankruptcy; however, there are federal laws that protect the consumer with regard to consumer credit, such as the Fair Credit Reporting Act. The Federal Trade Commission enforces this law.

Many states have laws that protect older consumers or offer them special benefits, such as money to pay utility bills or tax relief on property-tax payments. However, many older consumers either do not know about such opportunities, or they are too embarrassed to take advantage of them. Such people do not want to be perceived as "charity cases," even when they are in dire need of such charity.

Consumers are also entitled to read their credit reports. Consumers who are unemployed or who fit other criteria may receive their individual credit report at no fee. The three major credit-reporting companies are as follows:

Equifax
P.O. Box 74021
Atlanta, GA 30374
(800) 685-1111 (toll-free)

Experian (formerly TRW)
P.O. Box 2104
Allen, TX 75013
(888) 397-3742 (toll-free)

Trans Union
P.O. Box 1000
Chester, PA 19022
(800) 916-8800 (toll-free)

According to *Guide to Surviving Debt*, a publication of the National Consumer Law Center (1999), in dealing with debt collectors, it is important to pay for food and essential medical expenses first, followed by bills related to housing, such as the mortgage, rent, taxes, and insurance. After those bills are paid, says the NCLC, consumers should pay whatever is required (which may not be the full bill) to keep utilities, such as water, electricity, and so forth, turned on. Car payments should be next if the car is essential. The authors warn that consumers should not move up a bill's priority solely or primarily because a creditor is threatening either a lawsuit or the individual's credit rating.

For further information, contact the National Consumer Law Center at:

77 Summer Street
10th Floor
Boston, MA 02110
(617) 542-8010
or
1629 K Street, NW
Suite 600
Washington, DC 20006
(202) 986-6060

Dugas, Christine. "American Seniors Rack Up Debt Like Never Before," *USA Today* (April 26, 2002).
Federal Trade Commission. "Fair Credit Reporting" (March 1999). www.ftc.gov/bcp/online/pubs/credit/fcra.htm
Loonin, Deanne, and Jonathan A. Sheldon. *Guide to Surviving Debt.* Boston, Mass.: National Consumer Law Center, 1999.

self-esteem   Positive feelings about oneself and one's competency. Older individuals may find themselves unable to achieve tasks that were simple for them in the past, and this can cause a deterioration in their self-esteem. They are also affected by how others in society treat them. If an attitude of AGEISM is pervasive in the society and most people see older people as burdensome or useless, older individuals may take on this attitude as well.

self-neglect   Failure to care for oneself. Self-neglect may be relatively minor, such as failing to bathe, or it can be extremely serious, such as failing to eat or to take needed medications.

Self-neglect may be a sign of DEPRESSION, or it may stem from a physical inability to perform these tasks. Loss of interest in ACTIVITIES OF DAILY LIVING

and general hygiene may also be the first signs of senile DEMENTIA.

senior centers   Community organizations in the United States that offer information and opportunities for social interactions for older individuals. They also provide information on health and wellness, transportation services, educational opportunities, and chances to act as volunteers to others.

Some senior centers are defined as *multipurpose senior centers* by the ADMINISTRATION ON AGING because they provide comprehensive information on health, education, and nutrition and opportunities for social and recreational interactions with others. About 73 percent of all senior centers nationwide are multipurpose senior centers, compared to 30 percent in the early 1980s.

There are about 10,000 senior centers in the United States, and of these about 6,100 receive federal funding under the OLDER AMERICANS ACT. Most activities that are offered at senior centers are available to seniors for free of charge, or they involve low fees to cover for example, some expenses for trips to places outside the immediate area.

septicemia   A bacterial infection in the blood that is serious and can be life threatening. If the person goes into "septic shock," in which he or she becomes cold and clammy and unresponsive, the risk of death is increased to 50 percent or higher. Septicemia usually stems from infections of the respiratory, gastrointestinal, or genitourinary tract. This infection is most frequently associated with meningitis, pneumonia, and other bacterial infections. Infections that end up involving the heart valves can produce a constant source of recurrent infections in the bloodstream.

Risk Factors
Hospitalization and a weakened immune system are the primary risk factors for the development of septicemia in older individuals.

Symptoms of Septicemia
The primary symptoms of septicemia are high fever and chills, very rapid breathing (hyperventilation), and an accelerated heart rate. The person may also

experience a very low body temperature (HYPOTHER-MIA) or low blood pressure (HYPOTENSION). In most cases of septicemia, it is obvious to most lay people that the individual is very sick, although they will usually not be able to identify the cause of the illness.

Diagnosis and Treatment

The physical examination will reveal indicators of septicemia. Laboratory tests such as a blood culture, urine culture, and a complete blood count (CBC) will aid in diagnosis. In addition, a spinal tap of the patient's cerebrospinal fluid will indicate the presence of infection in the nervous system.

Treatment for septicemia usually is the administration of broad spectrum antibiotics and the provision of fluid replacement. Intravenous therapy in the hospital is usually required because the individual is much too ill to receive outpatient treatment.

sex Intimate relations with others. Many older people continue to enjoy sexual relations with other people despite the popular stereotype that most senior citizens are either uninterested or unable to have a sexual relationship or that they have both problems. However, some older men do experience problems with ERECTILE DYSFUNCTION, which are often correctable. Older women may experience some vaginal discomfort from INFECTIONS or from dryness due to MENOPAUSE. Medications may help resolve these problems.

See also MARRIAGE/REMARRIAGE.

shingles (herpes zoster) An extremely painful and relatively rare disease that usually appears in late middle age to the older years and that results from a reactivation of the same virus (varicella zoster) that causes chicken pox in children or adolescents. The virus may have remained dormant in the cranial or spinal nerves for decades until it was reactivated.

Not everyone who has had chicken pox as a child experiences this reactivation, and it is more likely to appear among people who are ill and/or receiving chemotherapy. People older than age 80 have a greatly increased risk of developing shingles than younger individuals. The incidence of shingles is about 1 in 1,000 before age 20 and increases to 4.5 to 11 per 1,000 after age 80.

The onset of shingles usually comes in the form of a rash. "Acute herpetic neuralgia," a condition of severe pain that accompanies the rash, may last up to 30 days. Subacute neuralgia may occur up to four months after the onset of shingles, whereas postherpetic neuralgia may occur more than four months after the initial appearance of shingles.

Some experts believe that the pain of shingles may be caused by damage to the central nervous system as well as by inflammation of the nerves.

The pain of shingles may precede the rash or may follow it by a few days. The rash lasts from two to four weeks. The pain is considered to be burning or stabbing by most patients. Some simply describe it as a distortion of sensation.

Patients may also suffer from impaired sleep, poor appetite, DEPRESSION, and anxiety. However, the sensations often change during the course of an attack to include numbness, itching, burning, and stinging. Ultimately, the discomfort often becomes a deep and constant aching.

Treatment of Shingles

Patients older than age 65 need to be treated by a pain management expert and may require a combination of medications, including such medications as antiviral drugs, opiods, antidepressants, corticosteroids, and anticonvulsants.

Antiviral medications may include such drugs as Zovirax (acyclovir), Valtrex (valacyclovir Hcl), and Famvir (famciclovir). Opioid drugs may include MS-Contin (morphone sulfate), Dilaudid (hydromorphone), methadone, or OxyContin (oxycodone). Antidepressants may include such drugs as Elavil (amitriptyline), Norpramine (desipramine), or Aventyl or Pamelor (nortriptylines). Prednisone is the usual corticosteroid drug that is used, and Neurontin (gabapentin) is the usual anticonvulsant that is prescribed.

The patient may also be given topical agents to apply to the skin, such as Zostrix (capsaicin) or Lidoderm, which is a bandage that allows lidocaine, the numbing medication, to soak into the affected area.

Patients and their physicians should not delay treatment, thinking that they will feel better because, in most cases, patients continue to feel worse. It is easier to block pain at the beginning of the onset than when the disease is more firmly established. Antivirals should be started within 72 hours of the onset of the illness.

Bajwa, Zahid H., M.D., and Charles C. Ho, M.D. "Herpetic Neuralgia: Use of Combination Therapy for Pain Relief in Acute and Chronic Herpes Zoster," *Geriatrics* 56, no. 12 (December 2001): 18–24.

Raeder, Carla K., and Mary S. Hayney. "Immunology of Varicella Immunization in the Elderly," *The Annals of Pharmacotherapy* 34, no. 2 (2001): 228–234.

Stankus, Seth John, MAJ, MC, USA, Michael Dlugopolski, MJ, MC, USA, and Deborah Packer, MAJ, MC, USA. "Management of Herpes Zoster (Shingles) and Postherpetic Neuralgia," *American Family Physician* 61 (2000): 2,437–2,444, 2,447–2,448.

skilled-nursing facilities (nursing homes) Long-term-care facilities that provide continuing care for older and disabled individuals who require skilled-nursing care. According to data from the 2000 Census in the United States, the percentage of people living in nursing homes who were age 65 and older declined from 5.1 percent in 1990 to 4.5 percent in 2000. There were about 1.47 million nursing-home residents who are age 65 and older in the United States, and most (65 percent) live in privately owned facilities.

In 1997, Medicaid paid for the largest proportion (56 percent) of nursing-home care, followed by private insurance or family payments (26 percent). Medicare covered the cost in 15 percent of the cases, and other charitable and financial organizations paid for the fees in the remaining 3 percent of cases.

Residents of Nursing Homes

In the United States, more than half of all nursing-home residents are 85 years and older. Most residents are white women, although the percentage of AFRICAN AMERICANS who live in nursing homes has increased from about 6 percent in 1985 to 9 percent by 1997. Most residents are admitted to nursing homes because of circulatory diseases or for mental disorders such as DEMENTIA or ALZHEIMER'S DISEASE.

Many residents need ASSISTIVE DEVICES, such as a wheelchair (62 percent) or a walker (22 percent).

(See Table 3 on assistive devices that are needed by nursing-home residents.) About 42 percent of nursing-home residents are INCONTINENT, experiencing difficulty controlling their bowels and bladder. Nearly all (96.2 percent) need help with bathing and showering, and most need help with dressing and other ACTIVITIES OF DAILY LIVING.

Most residents receive medical care and nursing care, as well as a variety of other services. (See Table 5, which includes services commonly received by many nursing-home residents.)

Falls in Nursing Homes

FALLS are a common problem in nursing homes. According to the National Center for Injury Prevention and Control, a division of the CENTERS FOR DISEASE CONTROL AND PREVENTION (CDC), about half of all nursing-home residents experience falls each year, and an average 100-bed skilled-nursing facility has 100–200 falls of their residents that are reported; however, many falls occurring to residents are not reported for a variety of reasons; for example, the fall may be regarded as a minor one.

Of all the falls that occur to all people who are age 85 and older in the United States, about 20 percent of them occur to residents in nursing homes. About 10 to 20 percent of the falls that occur to residents in nursing homes result in serious injuries, and between 2 and 6 percent cause FRACTURES. The CDC says that about 1,800 falls in nursing homes each year are fatal.

The most common causes of falls in nursing homes are weakness and gait problems, which represent the cause in about 24 percent of the falls. An estimated 16–27 percent of nursing-home falls are caused by environmental hazards, such as wet floors, lack of bed rails, improper bed height, poor lighting, and other usually correctable conditions.

PHYSICAL RESTRAINTS were used in the past to prevent older residents from falling, but experts report that they may actually increase the risk for falls because they may cause deconditioning and muscle atrophy. Most nursing homes in the United States have reduced the use of physical restraints among their residents because of federal regulations enacted in 1990.

Physical condition and EXERCISE can help to reduce the risk of falls by nursing-home residents.

TABLE 1 NUMBER AND PERCENT DISTRIBUTION OF ELDERLY NURSING-HOME RESIDENTS 65 YEARS AND OLDER BY SELECTED DEMOGRAPHIC CHARACTERISTICS, ACCORDING TO SEX: UNITED STATES, 1997

Resident characteristic	Both sexes	Male	Female	Both sexes	Male	Female
	Number			Percent distribution		
Total	1,465,000	372,100	1,092,900	100.0	100.0	100.0
Age						
65–74 years	198,400	80,800	117,700	13.5	21.7	10.8
75–84 years	528,300	159,300	368,900	36.1	42.8	33.8
85 years and older	738,300	132,000	606,300	50.4	35.5	55.5
Race						
White	1,294,900	315,800	979,100	88.4	84.9	89.6
Black	137,400	44,800	92,500	9.4	12.0	8.5
Other	18,000	*7,400	*10,600	1.2	*2.0	*1.0
Unknown	14,700	*	*10,600	1.0	*	*1.0
Hispanic origin						
Hispanic	32,100	*11,100	20,900	2.2	*3.0	1.9
Non-Hispanic	1,339,900	338,900	1,001,000	91.5	91.1	91.6
Unknown	93,000	22,100	71,000	6.4	5.9	6.5
Marital status						
Married	248,800	140,200	108,600	17.0	37.7	9.9
Widowed	924,400	131,000	793,400	63.1	35.2	72.6
Divorced/separated	98,200	34,600	63,600	6.7	9.3	5.8
Never married/single	173,800	61,300	112,500	11.9	16.5	10.3
Unknown	19,800	*	14,800	1.4	*	1.4
Living arrangement prior to admission						
Private residence	472,100	114,600	357,500	32.2	30.8	32.7
Retirement home	33,900	*	28,600	2.3	*	2.6
Board and care/residential facility	67,300	15,300	51,900	4.6	4.1	4.8
Nursing home	179,000	47,600	131,400	12.2	12.8	12.0
Hospital	651,300	172,400	478,900	44.5	46.3	43.8
Mental health facility	19,000	*5,900	13,100	1.3	*1.6	1.2
Other or unknown	42,400	*11,000	31,500	2.9	*2.9	2.9

* Data do not meet standard reliability or precision (sample size less than 30) and are therefore not reported. If asterisk precedes a number, data should not be assumed reliable because the sample size is between 30–59 or the sample size is greater than 59 but has a relative standard error over 30 percent.
NOTES: Numbers may not add to totals because of rounding. Percents are based on the unrounded figures.

TABLE 2 NUMBER AND PERCENT DISTRIBUTION OF ELDERLY NURSING-HOME RESIDENTS 65 YEARS AND OLDER BY SELECTED FACILITY CHARACTERISTICS, ACCORDING TO SEX: UNITED STATES, 1997

Facility characteristic	Both sexes	Male	Female	Both sexes	Male	Female
	Number			Percent distribution		
Total.	1,465,000	372,100	1,092,900	100.0	100.0	100.0
Ownership						
Proprietary	948,400	242,400	706,100	64.7	65.1	64.6
Voluntary nonprofit.	399,700	87,600	312,000	27.3	23.6	28.6
Government and other	116,900	42,100	74,800	8.0	11.3	6.8
Certification						
Certified by Medicare and Medicaid	1,246,800	311,900	934,800	85.1	83.8	85.5
Certified by Medicare only	46,200	*11,400	34,800	3.2	*3.1	3.2
Certified by Medicaid only	135,700	37,000	98,700	9.3	9.9	9.0
Not certified	36,400	11,800	24,600	2.5	3.2	2.3
Bed size						
Fewer than 50 beds	57,000	15,100	41,900	3.9	4.1	3.8
50 - 99 beds	364,600	95,000	269,600	24.9	25.5	24.7
100 - 199 beds	766,700	185,400	581,300	52.3	49.8	53.2
200 beds or more	276,700	76,600	200,100	18.9	20.6	18.3
Census region						
Northeast	346,500	84,600	261,900	23.7	22.7	24.0
Midwest	452,100	114,000	338,100	30.9	30.6	30.9
South	477,400	122,200	355,200	32.6	32.8	32.5
West	189,000	51,400	137,600	12.9	13.8	12.6
Metropolitan Statistical Area (MSA)						
MSA	1,006,500	245,100	761,500	68.7	65.9	69.7
Not MSA	458,500	127,000	331,400	31.3	34.1	30.3
Affiliation[1]						
Chain	821,500	210,000	611,400	56.1	56.4	56.0
Independent	635,000	160,200	474,800	43.4	43.1	43.5

* Data should not be assumed reliable because the sample size is between 30–59 or the sample size is greater than 59 but has a relative standard error more than 30 percent.
1 Excludes unknown.
NOTES: Numbers may not add to totals because of rounding. Percents are based on unrounded figures.

TABLE 3 NUMBER AND PERCENT OF ELDERLY NURSING-HOME RESIDENTS 65 YEARS AND OLDER BY USE OF SELECTED AIDS, CONTINENCE, VISION AND HEARING STATUS, AND SEX: UNITED STATES, 1997

Functional status	Both sexes	Male	Female	Both sexes	Male	Female
	Number			Percent		
Total.	1,465,000	372,100	1,092,900	· · ·	· · ·	· · ·
Aids used						
Glasses	973,400	230,100	743,200	66.5	61.9	68.0
Hearing aid	155,600	39,400	116,200	10.6	10.6	10.6
Transfer equipment	185,000	52,000	133,000	12.6	14.0	12.2
Wheelchair.	913,300	227,500	685,800	62.3	61.2	62.7
Cane	95,400	34,000	61,300	6.5	9.2	5.6
Walker	369,100	82,600	286,500	25.2	22.2	26.2
Oxygen.	84,500	28,100	56,500	5.8	7.5	5.2
Brace (any type)	46,200	12,200	34,100	3.2	3.3	3.1
Commode	121,600	25,400	96,200	8.3	6.8	8.8
Other aids or devices	250,100	69,800	180,300	17.1	18.6	16.5
Continence status						
Difficulty controlling both bowels and bladder . .	647,200	156,400	490,900	44.2	42.0	44.9
Difficulty controlling bowels.	18,900	*6,600	12,200	1.3	*1.8	1.1
Difficulty controlling bladder	189,700	44,600	145,100	13.0	12.0	13.3
Vision						
Not impaired	959,200	254,200	705,000	65.5	68.3	64.5
Impaired	396,700	93,000	303,700	27.1	25.0	27.8
Unknown[1]	109,100	24,900	84,100	7.5	6.7	7.7
Hearing						
Not impaired	1,005,800	256,500	749,300	68.7	68.9	68.6
Impaired	347,600	90,800	256,800	23.7	24.4	23.5
Unknown[1]	111,600	24,800	86,800	7.6	6.7	7.9

· · · Category not applicable.
* Data should not be assumed reliable because the sample size is between 30–59 or the sample size is greater than 59 but has a relative standard error more than 30 percent.
1 Includes those for whom status could not be determined (e.g., comatose patients)
NOTES: Numbers may not add to totals because of rounding. Percents are based on the unrounded figures.

TABLE 4 NUMBER AND PERCENT OF ELDERLY NURSING HOME RESIDENTS 65 YEARS AND OLDER BY DEPENDENCY IN ACTIVITIES OF DAILY LIVING AND INSTRUMENTAL ACTIVITIES OF DAILY LIVING AND SEX: UNITED STATES, 1997

Functional status	Both sexes	Male	Female	Both sexes	Male	Female
	Number			Percent		
Total.	1,465,000	372,100	1,092,900	. . .	. . .	. . .
Received assistance with ADLs[1]						
Bathing or showering	1,409,300	351,400	1,057,900	96.2	94.4	96.8
Dressing	1,277,600	318,900	958,700	87.2	85.7	87.7
Eating.	658,800	159,300	499,500	45.0	42.8	45.7
Transferring in or out of bed or chair.	372,100	87,300	284,800	25.4	23.5	26.1
Using toilet room	822,600	196,300	626,300	56.2	52.8	57.3
Number of dependencies in ADLs[1]						
None	44,000	17,600	26,800	3.0	4.6	2.5
1.	115,000	28,900	86,100	7.9	7.8	7.9
2.	210,400	59,400	151,000	14.4	16.0	13.8
3.	513,500	129,200	384,300	35.1	34.7	35.2
4.	446,300	108,600	337,700	30.5	29.2	30.9
5.	135,800	28,700	107,100	9.3	7.7	9.8
Received assistance with IADLs[1]						
Care of personal possessions	1,130,100	287,200	842,900	77.1	77.2	77.1
Managing money.	1,057,900	266,500	791,400	72.2	71.6	72.4
Securing personal items	1,115,800	278,100	837,700	76.2	74.7	76.7
Using telephone	910,500	233,500	677,000	62.2	62.8	61.9
Number of dependencies in IADLs[1]						
None	161,700	42,500	119,200	11.3	11.7	11.2
1.	110,400	29,000	81,500	7.7	8.0	7.6
2.	138,300	32,700	105,600	9.7	9.0	9.9
3.	253,600	65,200	188,400	17.7	18.0	17.7
4.	766,700	193,800	572,800	53.6	53.4	53.7

· · · Category not applicable.
1 ADL is activities of daily living, and IADL is instrumental activities of daily living.
NOTES: Numbers may not add to totals because of rounding. Percents are based on the unrounded figures.

TABLE 5 NUMBER AND PERCENT OF ELDERLY NURSING HOME RESIDENTS 65 YEARS AND OLDER BY SERVICES RECEIVED AND SEX: UNITED STATES, 1997

Service received	Both sexes	Male	Female	Both sexes	Male	Female
	Number			Percent		
Total	1,465,000	372,100	1,092,900	...	...	...
Dental care	267,200	73,300	193,900	18.2	19.7	17.7
Equipment or devices	743,100	188,700	554,400	50.7	50.7	50.7
Medical services	1,334,400	340,700	993,800	91.1	91.6	90.6
Mental health services	242,200	69,200	173,000	16.5	18.6	15.8
Nursing services	1,425,600	362,700	1,062,900	97.3	97.5	97.3
Nutritional services	1,084,700	278,900	805,800	74.0	75.0	73.7
Occupational therapy	277,500	75,800	201,600	18.9	20.4	18.5
Personal care	1,333,600	339,000	994,500	91.0	91.1	91.0
Physical therapy	399,100	110,400	288,700	27.2	29.7	26.4
Prescribed or nonprescribed medicines	1,371,800	348,400	1,023,400	93.6	93.6	93.6
Social services	1,029,200	258,900	770,400	70.3	69.6	70.5
Speech or hearing therapy	118,700	37,000	81,700	8.1	9.9	7.5
Transportation	282,400	79,900	202,600	19.3	21.5	18.5
Other services	202,700	50,500	152,100	13.8	13.6	13.9

··· Category not applicable.

NOTE: Numbers may not add to totals because of rounding.

Gait and balance therapy may also help. Environmental modifications may also be made, such as lowering bed heights, installing grab bars in the shower and handrails in hallways, and other improvements.

Doctors may wish to review prescribed medications among nursing-home residents, considering their benefits and risks, and, if possible, limiting drugs that make it more likely for nursing-home residents to fall.

Some nursing homes use technological devices that cause an alarm to go off if a nursing-home resident gets out of bed unassisted.

Fear and Abuse

Many older Americans fear being compelled to live in a nursing home and actively seek to avoid it. Perhaps some of their fears are justified. In recent years, public officials have become increasingly concerned about problems of ABUSE and NEGLECT experienced by nursing-home residents.

In a study reported in a 2001 issue of the *Journal of the American Medical Association (JAMA)*, researchers reported on the levels of pain in nursing-home residents in 1999, based on nationwide data from skilled-nursing facilities. The researchers looked at pain data at an initial point and then 60 to 180 days later. They found that 41 percent of the residents who were in pain in the first assessment were in severe pain 60 to 180 days later.

The researchers believed that the provided pain estimates were low, and they stated, "We believe that these results underestimate the true pain burden experienced by nursing-home residents because the data were reported by nursing-home staff rather than by patients."

They also stated, "The high rate of persistent pain is consistent with previous research noting that pain is often not appropriately treated in nursing-home residents. Untreated pain results in impaired mobility, depression, and diminishes quality of life. These population results indicate that pain control represents an often neglected need of this vulnerable population."

Sometimes, nursing-home employees react to the perceived "bad behavior" of residents, particularly those residents who are hostile and combative. Some residents are aggressive because of their illnesses, and these residents are more likely to be attacked by others; for example, a GAO study released in 2002 revealed that if an older person with dementia slaps a nursing-home worker in some states and the worker strikes back, this is not considered abuse by staff members.

Nursing Homes for Military Veterans

The VETERANS ADMINISTRATION oversees skilled-nursing facilities for military veterans, and according to the VA, in fiscal year 2000, the Department of Veterans Affairs spent about $1.9 billion on nursing-home care. The demand for nursing-home care provided by the VA is projected to triple from 2000 to 2010 because of many aging veterans. Most of the VA nursing-home funds (73 percent) were spent on the VA's own 134 nursing homes throughout the country. The balance was spent on care in 94 state-owned and state-operated nursing homes or 3,400 nursing homes under contract to the VA. A GAO report on VA nursing homes indicates that more oversight is needed.

Experiments in Nursing Homes

Some skilled-nursing facilities have experimented with allowing animals in the facility, such as cats or dogs. Proponents say that the addition of pets for the residents allows them to feel as if they are in a more homelike atmosphere and that the presence of the pets can calm them and make them happier. Someone other than the residents must be responsible for the care and feeding of the animals, but some studies have shown that the staff also likes to have pets in the facility.

Gabrel, Celia S., M.S., Division of Health Care Statistics. "Characteristics of Elderly Nursing Home Current Residents and Discharges: Data from the 1997 National Nursing Home Survey," National Center for Health Statistics, no. 312 (April 25, 2000).

General Accounting Office. "Nursing Homes: More Can Be Done to Protect Residents from Abuse," GAO-02-312 (March 2002).

General Accounting Office, Report to Congressional Requesters. "VA Long-Term Care: Oversight of Community Nursing Homes Needs Strengthening," GAO-01-768 (July 2001).

Lurie, Stephen J., M.D., Ph.D., senior ed., and Jody W. Zylke, M.D., contributing ed. "Research Letter: Persistent Pain in Nursing Home Residents," *Journal of the American Medical Association (JAMA)* 285, no. 16 (April 25, 2001). http://jama.ama-assn.org/issues/v285n16/ffull/jlt0425-6.html.

National Center for Injury Prevention and Control. "Falls in Nursing Homes: Fact Sheet," Centers for Disease Control and Prevention (CDC) (December 19, 2000).

Sahyoun, Nadine R., Ph.D., R.D. et al. "The Changing Profile of Nursing Home Residents: 1985:1997," *Aging Trends,* no. 4 (no volume listed) National Center for Health Statistics (March 2001): 1–8.

skin cancer Malignant tumor of the skin, and the most commonly occurring form of cancer in the United States. More than a million cases of skin cancer are diagnosed each year in the United States, but only malignant melanoma is usually fatal. Instead, most patients with skin cancer survive, and only about 9,800 patients die every year.

Types of Skin Cancer

The three main types of skin cancer are basal cell, squamous, and malignant melanoma. Basal cell and squamous cancers are highly curable. Malignant melanoma is far more dangerous and is responsible for about 75 percent of all skin-cancer deaths. However, if caught in the early stages, malignant melanoma is generally curable.

Those at Risk

Although anyone can develop skin cancer, there are certain groups of people who are most at risk. They include people who:

• Are light complexioned
• Have a family history of skin cancer
• Have had chronic sun exposure
• Have a history of sunburns in early life
• Have atypical moles or many moles
• Have freckles

Prevention of Skin Cancer

Experts at the CENTERS FOR DISEASE CONTROL AND PREVENTION (CDC) say that skin cancer can often be prevented with simple precautionary measures, such as seeking shade from direct sunlight, wearing hats or shirts, and regularly using sunscreen. Older individuals should not be seeking to develop their tans.

Symptoms of Skin Cancer

Pain, itching, redness, and/or scaling skin are all common symptoms. Older individuals may also have noncancerous problems with their skin due to DEHYDRATION or to sun exposure.

Diagnosis

The doctor diagnoses skin cancer based on the appearance of the skin and a biopsy of the affected area. Patients may also need to have lymph nodes examined in the affected area, as well as special X rays, to determine if the skin cancer has spread to other parts of the body.

Treatment

Skin cancer is treated by excision of the affected area. Sometimes, the cancer is removed at the same time as the biopsy is taken. Radiation therapy and topical chemotherapy may also be used. For cases of melanoma, which is the more malignant form of skin cancer, it is essential at the time of the biopsy and of the cancer removal that all of the surrounding tissue is clear of the tumor. A special type of surgery, MOSE, using the aid of the microscope, can help to accomplish this task.

Jerant, Anthony F., M.D. et al. "Early Detection and Treatment of Skin Cancer," *American Family Physician* 62 (2000): 357–368, 381–382.

National Cancer Institute. "Skin Cancer," NIH Publication No. 95-1564 (September 28, 1998).

sleep disorders   Abnormal sleep patterns or difficulty in attaining sleep. Some common sleep problems are insomnia and sleep apnea. Insomnia is difficulty in falling asleep; sleep apnea is a serious illness in which the person actually stops breathing for short periods of time. Sleep apnea can be fatal but is treatable when detected. Some studies have indicated that as many as half or more of men and women age 65 and older have chronic sleep problems.

A lack of sleep can lead to serious problems such as FALLS, accidents with DRIVING, and an increased risk for developing illnesses. In addition, sleep disorders can lead to excessive daytime somnolence, which can cause other problems, such as accidents. In addition, individuals may appear sluggish or demented, when in reality they are just sleep deprived.

Possible Causes

Many older people have difficulty sleeping because of their pain from illnesses or because of medications that they take that may impair sleeping; for example, diuretic drugs that cause the person to need to urinate frequently can impede normal sleep patterns. Decongestants and some corticosteroid drugs can interfere with sleep.

Older individuals who are not sleeping well may have emotional problems. They may suffer from DEPRESSION, STRESS, or anxiety. Sometimes, their own habits can lead to sleep problems; for example, napping on some days but not others can interfere with the circadian cycle, an internal "clock" that tells the body when to sleep and when to wake up. An excessive intake of caffeine in the evening from consuming coffee, tea, or other caffeinated beverages can also impair getting to sleep.

People with certain diseases are more likely to suffer from sleep disorders than others. For example, studies indicate that people with PARKINSON'S DISEASE have a high rate of insomnia. Because of their difficulty with movements, they often have to wake up just to roll over.

People who have ALZHEIMER'S DISEASE also often have a sleep reversal problem where they are awake at night and then they want to sleep during the day. Also, they may experience "sundowning," in which the person becomes even more confused and disoriented at night when there are fewer available environmental cues to help to orient the patient.

Sleep apnea is another common cause of sleep disorders among older people, according to the authors of *The Promise of Sleep*. The authors state that apnea "should be one of the first thing doctors consider when elderly patients have problems with sleepiness, high blood pressure or cognitive problems—but doctors almost never do this." Sleep apnea is a temporary and periodic halt in breathing, which can be dangerous and even fatal.

Some individuals suffer from "restless-legs syndrome," in which they feel that they must constantly move their legs because the legs feel irritated or otherwise uncomfortable. This disorder can impair normal sleep. Permax (pergolide) is a medication that has been used successfully to treat people with restless-legs syndrome. Other drugs that may help are Parlodel (bromocriptine), Tegretol (carbamazepine), Klonopin (clonazepam), Catapres (clonidine), Mirapex (pramipexole), Requip (ropinirole), and Sinemet (carbidopa/levadopa).

Diagnosis

To be certain of the diagnosis of a sleep disorder, a physician may prescribe an evaluation with a nighttime sleep study. Such a study is performed by the patient going to a sleep laboratory and sleeping there overnight while various monitors take readings. An accurate diagnosis of a sleep disorder is the cornerstone of appropriate therapy.

Treatment

The treatment of sleep disorders is directed to the cause. If the cause is, for example, sleep apnea, then weight loss may help. Often a simple oxygen device can be curative. Some patients may also need surgery. If the cause is depression, sedating antidepressants may help.

There are also general sleep medications, such as Ambien or Sonata, which may be beneficial for those who have trouble with insomnia or frequent awakenings. Some individuals have also had success with taking melatonin, an over-the-counter remedy available in most pharmacies and health-food stores. Valerian is an herbal remedy that has been used with success by others. Some patients have used kava kava, another herbal remedy, in the past; however, the Food and Drug Administration (FDA) issued an alert against kava kava in 2002, noting that the drug had caused hepatitis and liver damage in some individuals; several deaths also occurred subsequent to taking this herb. It is *not* recommended for people of any age.

Note: patients should always inform their doctors *before* they start taking melatonin, valerian, or any other herbal remedy or over-the-counter drug, to ensure that the remedy is safe and will not cause any bad reaction with other drugs the person is taking.

Dement, William C., M.D., Ph.D. and Christopher Vaughan. *The Promise of Sleep.* New York: Dell, 2000.
Neubauer, David N., M.D. "Sleep Problems in the Elderly," *American Family Physician* (May 1, 1999).

smoking   Use of nicotine products such as cigarettes, cigars, or pipe tobacco. Smoking is the most preventable cause of death and disease among people age 65 and older in the United States and it is also a global problem as well.

Smoking health risks have been known for decades. In 1964, the Surgeon General's first report on smoking and health revealed that smoking caused lung cancer. Every package of cigarettes that smokers purchase in the United States today includes a warning from the Surgeon General about the dangers of smoking.

Most people who smoke use cigarettes, but some smoke pipes or cigars, and others use oral forms of tobacco. All of these substances are dangerous, with a high risk for oral cancers and other severe health problems. They should not be considered safer than smoking cigarettes.

Addiction to Smoking

Although it is not commonly thought of as an addiction, the reality is that the key substance in tobacco, nicotine, is more rapidly addicting than heroin. Within just 10 seconds of inhaling the smoke from a cigarette, the nicotine is delivered to the brain, causing a cascade of pleasurable reactions. Some of the key effects of nicotine are to cause the brain to release adrenaline, which in turn makes the smoker's blood pressure, breathing, and heart rate go up. Nicotine also induces dopamine to be released, which is a brain chemical that enhances pleasure.

Other substances in cigarettes are tar and carbon monoxide, both substances that are harmful to the heart and respiratory systems. According to the CENTERS FOR DISEASE CONTROL AND PREVENTION (CDC), researchers have identified at least 43 substances in tobacco smoke that are cancer causing (carcinogenic).

Because tobacco products are so addicting, it is very difficult for many people who have begun to smoke to end their habit, even in the face of disease and death as well as harm to nonsmoking family members who must ingest secondhand smoke and face similar, albeit reduced, health risks.

Smoking and Death

Smoking has a profound effect on the lives of the smokers, their families and society at large. Smoking causes an estimated 430,000 deaths in the United States each year, and of these deaths, 70 percent of the individuals are age 65 and older. About 90 percent of all LUNG CANCER deaths can be directly attributed to smoking. In Canada, about 47,000 people die each year from smoking-related illnesses, and the majority are older people.

In looking at all deaths of smokers, the federal government in the United States estimates that at least half of all male deaths and about 43 percent of all female deaths are caused by smoking. In addition to the deaths caused by health problems attributed to smoking, each year more than 400 people age 65 and older die from fires started by smoking. Smoking is the primary cause of the deaths of older people in fires.

People who smoke are also more likely to consume alcohol, and the combined health effects of smoking and drinking can be very devastating. Excessive drinking, added to smoking, increases the risk for HYPERTENSION, KIDNEY DISEASE, STROKE, and many other health problems.

Statistics on Older People Who Smoke

According to the National Center for Health Statistics, about 3.7 million older people in the United States smoke. This is 9.7 percent of all people age 65 and older, including 10.2 percent of older men and 9.3 percent of older women. This is a lower percentage of smokers than found among younger individuals, (24 percent of Americans ages 45–64 years old smoke), but it is still high considering the severe health risks that are directly and indirectly attributable to smoking. Also, it is not known how many smokers died before they attained the age of 65 years. In addition, the harmful effects of smoking for many years are cumulative; therefore, these problems become more severe in older patients who have smoked for longer periods of time.

People of all races smoke, and white males are the heaviest smokers. However, African-American men who smoke have about a 50 percent greater risk than Caucasian men of developing lung cancer and an increased risk of death from lung cancer. African-American men also have a greater risk of suffering from stroke, another health condition associated with smoking, than faced by white men.

Most people who smoke started their habit as teenagers and quickly became addicted. Many older people who continue to smoke today began to smoke before the health risks were known, although repeated health warnings have occurred for decades. For example, in the mid-1960s, more than half of all males (54 percent) were smokers, and 34 percent of all females were smokers. Today, many of these individuals are experiencing the severe health consequences of smoking and many have already died because of their habit.

Health Problems Associated with Smoking

As mentioned, smoking is the single largest cause of lung cancer, the form of cancer that kills the most men and women in the United States as well as other countries. Other forms of cancer, such as ORAL CANCER and throat cancer, are directly attributable to smoking. In addition, smoking has been associated with BREAST CANCER and other forms of cancer.

Smoking also causes EMPHYSEMA and aggravates problems such as ASTHMA, CARDIOVASCULAR DISEASE, DIABETES, CHRONIC OBSTRUCTIVE PULMONARY DISEASE (COPD), and hypertension. Smoking is also associated with stroke and RHEUMATOID ARTHRITIS. Some studies show a link between smoking and the subsequent development of DEMENTIA among older people.

Smoking is also associated with the development of CATARACTS, GLAUCOMA, and other serious eye diseases that can lead to BLINDNESS. Smokers are more likely to suffer from hearing-loss problems. Smokers are also more likely to experience ERECTILE DYSFUNCTION.

If Older Smokers Quit

Many older smokers believe that it is "too late" to quit smoking or that there would be no health advantage to smoking cessation. However, in most cases (with the exception of terminally ill patients), they are wrong. If the older smoker stops smoking even when he or she is elderly, improvements will occur, such as a decrease in a risk of HEART DISEASE. After only 24 hours of not smoking, the risk for a HEART ATTACK drops. In about three months, lung function improves by as much as one-third. Within one to nine months of stopping smoking, chronic coughing and congestion improves, as do problems with shortness of breath.

Smoking-Cessation Products

Some people can stop smoking "cold turkey," but most people need help with quitting smoking. There are numerous products available to help the smoker stop smoking. There are both over-the-counter and prescribed medications that are effective.

Nicotine replacement drugs are one popular choice, and about 25 to 30 percent of those who use these products are not smoking a year later, which is about twice the success rate over people who try to quit smoking without medications or some other form of therapy. These over-the-counter drugs offer a dose of nicotine to the patient as a substitute for the nicotine found in the cigarette, cigar, or other form of tobacco and are available in the form of gum or skin patches.

The theory behind these drugs is that the patient is theoretically "weaned off" tobacco by the steady decrease of nicotine delivered to the brain. Note: it is very dangerous for the patient to use a nicotine replacement drug *and* to continue to smoke; this could result in an overdose of nicotine.

Nicotine replacement drugs in the forms of nasal sprays or inhalers are also available by prescription.

Zyban Sustained Release (bupropion), another antismoking drug, is a prescribed drug that is also used as an antidepressant. It affects the brain centers and theoretically enables smoking cessation. The key side effects are insomnia and dry mouth. Some studies have indicated that taking Zyban *and* a nicotine replacement drug can boost the success rate of ending smoking to as high as 50 percent; however, such a plan must be made only with the active involvement of an individual's physician.

Before using any over-the-counter or prescribed smoking-cessation drug, patients should discuss with their physicians the pros and cons of the drug and any actions they should take or problems they should report.

Other Smoking-Cessation Options

Some smokers are able to end their habit with the help of psychological therapy or hypnotherapy. Many therapists say that it is best for smokers to change their cues to smoking; for example, if smokers normally woke up and had a cup of coffee and a cigarette, they should perform another activity to replace this one, such as going for a walk, and if smokers normally smoked at restaurants, they should ask to be seated in the nonsmoking section, where they must refrain from smoking. Also, finding a substitute habit to replace the hand-to-mouth habit of smoking can be very effective.

It can be difficult to stop smoking when all or most of the smoker's friends continue to smoke. It may be hard to ask them to refrain from smoking around the individual or to smoke outdoors. Nevertheless, when the severe health consequences are considered, these are not unreasonable requests.

Smoking Cessation Programs Being Studied

The federal government is conducting research to see if acupuncture may help people give up smoking, and pharmaceutical companies are testing antismoking medications that would radically decrease the effect of nicotine on the brain. If effective, these drugs would theoretically make it easier for the smoker to give up smoking because the strongly pleasurable rush would no longer occur.

Medicare Testing of Stop-Smoking Program

In 2002 the CENTERS FOR MEDICARE AND MEDICAID SERVICES (CMS, formerly the Health Care Financing Administration) began to recruit smokers age 65 and older in seven demonstration sites in Alabama, Florida, Missouri, Ohio, Oklahoma, Nebraska, and Wyoming. According to CMS, these states were selected because of their high number of Medicare beneficiaries and a high number of smokers, among other reasons. An estimated 43,500 Medicare beneficiaries will be studied. The study is expected to be completed in 2004.

The program will test different options for smoking cessation, including reimbursement for provider (physician) counseling only; reimbursement for provider counseling, and an FDA-approved prescription or over-the-counter drug; and a telephone counseling "quitline," reimbursement for nicotine replacement therapy, and the usual care provided to people who smoke. According to the CMS, smokers older than age 65 are less likely than younger smokers to perceive the health consequences of their smoking; however, once they decide to quit smoking, they are *more* likely to succeed with cessation than younger smokers are.

Based on the results of the trial, Medicare may begin to provide coverage on smoking cessation subsequent to analysis of the findings.

Smoking Expected to Cause Many Deaths in China

Smoking is not only the cause of many health problems in the United States and Canada but it is also a severe problem in countries throughout the world. For example, in China, an estimated two-thirds of all males older than age 25 smoke, according to a 1998 article in the *British Medical Journal.* (Few Chinese women smoke.) At the current rate of smoking, it is estimated that 100 million males will die from smoking-related illnesses. Half will die in middle age, and the other half will die when they are in their senior years.

According to Bo Qi Lu and colleagues who wrote the *British Medical Journal* article, about 70 percent of all deaths from cancer have been from lung cancer, esophageal cancer, and stomach and liver cancer, and each disease was prominently found among smokers.

In China, of the deaths attributed to smoking among men older than age 70, 46.6 percent of deaths were from lung cancer, followed by deaths from chronic obstructive pulmonary disease [COPD] (27.4 percent). Among women older than age 70 in China, of deaths attributed to smoking, 20.1 percent were from lung cancer, and 8.6 percent were from COPD.

Qi Liu, Bo, et al. "Emerging Tobacco Hazards in China:1. Retrospective Proportional Mortality Study of One Million Deaths," *British Medical Journal* 317, (November 21, 1998): 1,411–1,422.
U.S. Department of Health and Human Services. "Cigarette Smoking Among Adults—United States, 1999," *Morbidity and Mortality Weekly Report* 50, no. 40 (October 12, 2001): 869–874.
———. *Reducing Tobacco Use: A Report of the Surgeon General,* U.S. Department of Health and Human Services, Centers for Disease Control and Prevention, National Center for Chronic Disease Prevention and Health Promotion, Office on Smoking and Health (2000).
———. "With Understanding and Improving Health and Objectives for Improving Health," *Healthy People 2010.* 2nd ed., 2 vols. Washington, D.C.: U.S. Government Printing Office, November 2000.

Social Security Administration (SSA) A very large federal organization in the United States that administers the OLD-AGE, SURVIVORS, AND DISABILITY INSURANCE PROGRAM (OASDI). This program provides financial and medical benefits to older individuals and to disabled people of all ages who qualify. In addition, family members of the beneficiary, such as their spouses and minor children, may also receive benefits.

Most Americans age 65 and older are recipients of OASDI benefits. According to the Office of the Chief Actuary of the Social Security Administration, about 91 percent of the population age 65 and older in the United States received retirement benefits as of January 2002.

The SSA also administers Supplemental Security Insurance (SSI), a program for individuals of all ages who are disabled and low income and that may provide a small monthly payment and MEDICAID coverage.

Originally called the Social Security Board when old age assistance programs were first legislated in 1935, the organization subsequently was named the Social Security Administration in 1946. The SSA was under the control of the Department of Health, Education and Welfare, later renamed the Department of Health and Human Services, for many years.

The Social Security Administration became an independent cabinet-level organization in 1995.

In 2001, there were 38,071,751 people receiving OASDI benefits, including 31,027,701 retired workers and their dependents and 7,044,050 survivors of deceased workers.

Social Security Administration. "A Brief History of Social Security" (August 2000).

special clothing Clothing that is easier to use than standard clothes, such as shirts with velcro fasteners or zippers rather than buttons, or skirts or pants that have elasticized waistbands and are washable. Nonskid shoes can help to prevent FALLS. Many older people require special clothing because of physical disabilities that make it difficult for them to dress and undress themselves.

Disorders such as ARTHRITIS, PARKINSON'S DISEASE, STROKE, or even tremor can make it virtually impossible for some individuals to handle even the simplest tasks, including dressing themselves.

See also ACTIVITIES OF DAILY LIVING.

spouse abuse   Physical assault of a husband or a wife, although most references to spouse abuse refer to a husband assaulting a wife. The abuser may have a psychiatric problem such as DEPRESSION or may be acting out in a rage that stems from ALZHEIMER'S DISEASE or DEMENTIA.

stomach cancer   Malignancy found in the stomach, a major organ of the digestive system. Also known as gastric cancer. About 24,000 people in the United States are newly diagnosed with stomach cancer, and about 13,500 people die of the disease each year. New studies indicate that the common stomach bacteria *Helicobacter pylori* may be implicated in gastric cancer.

Risk Factors

Most stomach cancer patients are older than 50 and are male. African Americans have a higher risk of stomach cancer than whites. There may also be a genetic risk to stomach cancer.

Symptoms

There may be few or no symptoms of stomach cancer. If symptoms do occur, they may be vague or easily ignored. Some symptoms which may occur are:

- Abdominal pain or discomfort
- Indigestion or heartburn
- Nausea and vomiting
- Constipation or diarrhea
- Bloated feeling after eating
- Appetite loss
- Weakness and fatigue
- Vomiting blood or having blood in the stool

Note: these above symptoms may also indicate a temporary problem or another health problem other than stomach cancer, and they are not clear-cut symptoms of stomach cancer. People with such symptoms should consult with their physicians for a medical evaluation and a diagnosis.

Diagnosing Stomach Cancer

A variety of laboratory tests may screen for stomach cancer. The fecal occult blood test checks for unseen or "hidden" blood in the stool. Blood in the stool does not necessarily indicate cancer, and further screening would be indicated.

An upper gastrointestinal (GI) X ray of the esophagus (the food tube that leads to the stomach) and the stomach can outline the stomach for the doctor and help detect tumors. An endoscopy is another screening procedure in which a special tube is passed through the mouth and into the esophagus and then the stomach. The doctor can see inside the stomach and can also remove tissue for a biopsy. If cancer is present, a biopsy will also help the doctor determine how advanced the cancer is and how fast it is growing.

Treatment for Stomach Cancer

The most common form of treatment is surgery in which the surgeon removes all or part of the stomach (gastrectomy or partial gastrectomy) and also tissue surrounding the stomach. After a total gastrectomy, the doctor connects the esophagus to the small intestine. A gastrectomy is a major operation and may require considerable recovery time. Patients may also have to change their diets, either temporarily or permanently. Patients who have had total gastrectomies will need injections of Vitamin B_{12} because they can no longer naturally absorb the vitamin through food.

Some patients who have had gastric surgery may experience "dumping syndrome," which causes cramps, nausea, and vomiting shortly after eating because the food enters the small intestine too quickly. Also, frequent diarrhea is another complication. Smaller and more frequent meals may help resolve this problem, as well as avoiding foods high in sugar content.

Chemotherapy is another option for patients who have been diagnosed with stomach cancer.

Cancer-killing drugs (chemotherapy) are administered to the patient to fight the disease. Chemotherapy for stomach cancer patients may be by injection or by mouth. Patients may experience nausea, vomiting, and hair loss, which usually end when the chemotherapy is completed.

Radiation therapy is also a form of treatment for stomach cancer. High-energy rays are directed at the cancerous part of the body. Radiation therapy may be given for five days a week for about five to six weeks, although the appropriate time frame is best determined by the doctor. Radiation therapy patients may experience nausea and vomiting, and the radiated area may be reddened and sore. They may also be very fatigued.

National Cancer Institute. "Stomach Cancer," NIH Publication No. 94-1554 (December 12, 2000).

stress   Sustained state of high emotion, based on real or imagined problems. Stress usually exacerbates existing medical problems, particularly CHRONIC DISEASES; for example, painful conditions such as ARTHRITIS often become more painful when an individual is under high stress.

Although many medical problems that older people face may be difficult or impossible to resolve, it is often possible to reduce their stressful effects through such methods as RELAXATION THERAPY, TAI CHI, and participation in a RELIGION. Psychological counseling is often quite helpful at alleviating stress.

stroke   A sudden and life-threatening loss of blood flow to a part of the brain and that results in damage or death of brain cells. Also known as a brain attack. An ischemic stroke occurs when the blood supply to the brain is interrupted, and there is a loss of oxygen to brain tissue. A hemorrhagic stroke occurs when a blood vessel leading to the brain or inside the brain bursts. Some strokes are considered minor; others are regarded as major events.

Stroke is a leading cause of DEATH among people older than age 65 in the United States and is the third-leading cause of death among people of all ages in the United States. Older people (age 65 and older) have a greater risk of having a stroke than younger individuals, and they represent about 72 percent of all individuals who have strokes in the United States. Yet, many individuals are unaware of the high stroke risk for older people, nor do they realize the urgency of taking immediate action.

Stroke is the third-most-common cause of death among CAUCASIAN, AFRICAN-AMERICAN, ASIAN-AMERICAN and HISPANIC-AMERICAN people older than age 65. It is the fourth-leading cause of death among NATIVE AMERICANS.

According to the AMERICAN HEART ASSOCIATION (AHA), about 89 percent of all deaths from strokes occur to people who are age 65 and older. According to the AHA, 961,000 Americans were discharged from hospitals with a first diagnosis of stroke in 1999. Of these patients, 73 percent were age 65 and older.

In 2001, Congress appropriated money for the CENTERS FOR DISEASE CONTROL AND PREVENTION (CDC) to establish the Paul Coverdell National Acute Stroke Registry. Some states, such as Georgia, Ohio, Massachusetts, and Michigan are developing their own statewide stroke registries. The information gained from these registries should help physicians improve their treatments and reduce rates of death and disability among stroke victims.

Life or Death
Immediate Action

Very prompt medical attention often means the difference between continued life and death for the person who has had a stroke. If patients who have had strokes receive medical attention within one to three hours, their chances of survival are greatly increased because stroke victims who are treated right away may receive a medication that dissolves the blood clots that obstruct arteries, a common cause of a stroke. Immediate medical attention may also improve the prognosis for later health as well as decrease the severity of the problems that most stroke patients suffer from.

Risk Factors

The key risk factors for suffering from a stroke are found among people who have:

- DIABETES
- HYPERTENSION (high blood pressure)
- History of heart disease, particularly atrial fibrillation or irregular heartbeat in the left upper chamber of the heart
- History of transient ischemic attacks (TIAs), or ministrokes
- Cigarette SMOKING: heavy smokers are at greatest risk
- OBESITY
- Age older than 65 years
- High consumption of alcohol
- Race (whites have a higher risk of new and recurrent strokes until much older ages. See Table 1.)

As can be seen from Table 1, there are both age and gender differences in the risk for suffering from a stroke. Nonblack females younger than age 74 have a much lower risk of suffering from new or recurrent strokes than nonblack males, or 6.2 per 1,000 people for women versus 14.4 for nonblack males. At age 74 and thereafter, however the stroke risk for these women rises to nearly the rate for men, or 22.7 for every 1,000 women versus 24.6 for every 1,000 men.

African-American women, however, face a significantly *higher* risk for stroke than black men at all points of old age. From ages 65 to 74, black men have a stroke risk rate of 11.9 per 1,000, but the rate for black women is 16.1. (The rate for black women in this age group is also higher than that for nonblack males.)

Among black women ages 75–84, the stroke rate still exceeds that for black men and is 22.4 per 1,000 versus 17.5 for black males. Within this age group, the stroke rate for black women is about the same as for nonblack women and lower than that for nonblack men.

The key point to keep in mind from this statistical data is that among people ages 65–74, black women are at the highest risk of suffering from stroke, and they continue to be at high risk at age 75 and beyond. The risk for nonblack women, however, is low from ages 65 to 74, but after that age, the rate radically increases.

TABLE 1   ANNUAL RATES PER 1,000 POPULATION OF NEW AND RECURRENT STROKES, BY AGE, GENDER AND RACE, 1999

	Nonblack Men	Nonblack Women	Black Men	Black Women
Ages 65–74	14.4	6.2	11.9	16.1
Ages 75–84	24.6	22.7	17.5	22.4
Ages 85 and older	27.9	30.6	40.8	Unknown

Source: American Heart Association. *2002 Heart and Stroke Statistical Update,* 2001.

Danger Symptoms of Stroke

According to the National Institute of Neurological Disorders and Stroke in Bethesda, Maryland, if anyone has one or more of any of the following danger symptoms, immediate emergency attention should be sought. In the United States, the individual or others should call 911 for emergency assistance. The patient should not drive, nor should others take the person to the hospital. Instead, in most cases, an ambulance would be best.

The danger symptoms of stroke are:

- Sudden confusion in understanding speech or in speaking
- Sudden numbness in the face, leg, or arm, especially if it is on one side of the body only
- Sudden blindness or difficulty seeing in one or both eyes
- Sudden inability or a severe difficulty in walking
- Sudden blindness or difficulty seeing in one or both eyes

Consequences of Stroke

A stroke may cause the following medical consequences:

- Temporary or permanent paralysis
- Cognitive (thinking) problems
- Language deficits
- Pain
- Emotional problems
- Death: About 15 percent of stroke victims die soon after the stroke, and stroke is the third-leading cause of death in the United States.

Diagnosis of Stroke

When an individual has possible stroke symptoms, doctors generally use radiologic methods to verify if the person has actually had a stroke and, if a stroke has occurred, to determine its level of severity. Physicians may use computed tomography (CT) scans of the brain to determine if an acute stroke has occurred. Another diagnostic device is the magnetic resonance imaging (MRI) scan, which can detect tiny aftereffects of a stroke, such as an increase in the water content of the brain tissue.

Physicians may also use ultrasound to image the carotid arteries in the neck. These images will assist the doctor in identifying any blockages or clots. Another diagnostic technique that is increasingly used is magnetic resonance angiography (MRA), which can detect blockages of both the carotid arteries (anterior) and the vertebral arteries (posterior). The MRA is a way of using an MRI to view a blood vessel without needing intravenous "dye" contrast that could damage the kidneys.

Treatment of Stroke

Stroke victims need immediate hospitalization and stabilization of their vital signs, especially of their blood pressure.

Medications for Stroke   Medications such as antiplatelet agents and anticoagulants are often prescribed for stroke patients. Two common anticoagulants, as of this writing, are warfarin and heparin. Calcium channel blocker medications and other medications may be prescribed for stroke victims to prevent further strokes. Many physicians place stroke patients on long-term ASPIRIN THERAPY to reduce the risk of any further strokes. The dose may be as small as a baby aspirin, depending on the patient and the previous medical history. Patients who were taking aspirin prior to the stroke may be changed to another medication plus aspirin.

In a study published in a 2001 issue of the *New England Journal of Medicine,* researchers studied 196 patients taking warfarin and 176 taking aspirin, both groups taking the drugs for stroke prevention. The researchers concluded that both therapies were equally effective in preventing stroke or death.

Surgery Sometimes Required   In rare cases, the stroke patient may require emergency surgery to treat an acute stroke or to repair damage that has already occurred. Surgery is generally required only when the patient is suffering from life-threatening bleeding in the brain and surgery is needed to relieve the pressure on the brain.

After the Stroke

Although the stroke itself is dangerous and frightening, the aftereffects of the stroke may be difficult as well. Many patients will require at least some degree of rehabilitation, including physical therapy, occupational therapy, and speech therapy. Counseling may be necessary to assist the patient to cope with ANXIETY and DEPRESSION that may occur. FAMILY CAREGIVERS will also need to adjust their schedules to accommodate the temporarily (or permanently) lost abilities of their loved one.

Physical therapists may assist patients in regaining their lost abilities in performing such basic skills as walking, sitting, ambulating from one position to another, and similar ACTIVITIES OF DAILY LIVING.

Occupational therapists may help the stroke victim master a broad range of tasks that they were previously capable of performing, such as reading and writing, bathing, dressing, and other daily life activities that must be relearned because of damage sustained from the stroke. Often, patients can no longer feed themselves subsequent to a stroke, and they need to relearn this skill as well.

Speech therapists can often help the patient who can continue to think rationally but who currently has major difficulty in thinking or saying the words they mean to express, as well as improve the motor function of the mouth and tongue to help with the mechanics of speech.

Lifestyle Changes   If the stroke victim was a smoker, physicians will urge him or her to stop smoking immediately and permanently to reduce the risk of further strokes. A broad array of other lifestyle recommendations may be made, depending on the individual needs of the patient.

For further information, contact the following organizations:

American Stroke Association
7272 Greenville Avenue
Dallas, TX 75231-4596
(800) AHA-USA1 (242-8721) (toll-free)
(888) 4STROKE (toll-free)
http://www.americanheart.org/

Brain Aneurysm Foundation
295 Cambridge Street
Old Forge Realty Building
Boston, MA 02114
(617) 723-3870

National Rehabilitation Information Center
1010 Wayne Avenue
Suite 800
Silver Spring, MD 20910-5633
(800) 346-2742
http://www.naric.com

National Stroke Association
9707 East Easter Lane
Englewood, CO 80112-3747
(303) 649-9299 or (800) STROKES (toll-free)
http://www.stroke.org

Stroke Clubs International
805 12th Street
Galveston, TX 77550
(409) 762-1022
See also CHOLESTEROL.

American Heart Association. *2002 Heart and Stroke Statistical Update,* 2001.
Brott, Thomas, M.D., and Julien Bogousslavsky, M.D. "Treatment of Acute Ischemic Stroke," *New England Journal of Medicine* 343, no. 10 (September 7, 2000): 710–722.
Centers for Disease Control and Prevention (CDC). "Preventing Heart Disease and Stroke: Addressing the Nation's Leading Killers 2002" (2002).
Mohr, J.P., M.D., et al. "A Comparison of Warfarin and Aspirin for the Prevention of Recurrent Ischemic Stroke," *New England Journal of Medicine* 345, no. 20 (November 15, 2001): 1,444–1,451.
Weinberger, Jesse, M.D. "Prevention and Management of Cerebrovascular Events in Primary Care," *Geriatrics* 57, no. 1 (January 2002): 38–43.

substance abuse Generally refers to the excessive use of alcohol or drugs. When older people are substance abusers, they are generally abusers of legal substances, such as alcohol or prescribed medications. Some people become addicted to PAINKILLING MEDICATIONS, particularly those that are controlled drugs, such as Vicodin (oxycodone). Some antianxiety drugs, such as Xanax (alprazolam), can also lead to addiction.

It may be difficult to locate rehabilitative sources for older individuals who are substance abusers. Families may also tacitly ignore substance abuse out of fear or embarrassment or not knowing what to do about it.

See also ALCOHOLISM; DRUG ABUSE.

suicide Ending one's own life. Suicide is different from ASSISTED SUICIDE, in which another person performs an act that ends life with the permission of the person whose life is ended. Some older people, particularly men, commit suicide-homicides, in which they take their own lives after murdering their spouses, without the consent or knowledge of the spouse.

The weapon of choice for men who end their lives is usually some form of firearm: guns are used in 78 percent of the suicides of males older than age 65. Guns are used in 36 percent of the suicides of older women.

In the United States, people older than age 65 have the highest suicide rate of all age groups, and the suicide rate increases with age. According to the National Institute of Mental Health (NIMH), the highest suicide rate of 64.9 deaths per 100,000 people is found among white men age 85 and older. The national rate for all ages is 10.6 per 100,000 people. According to the CENTERS FOR DISEASE CONTROL AND PREVENTION (CDC), among adults older than age 65, men represent 83 percent of all suicides.

Country-by-Country Age Comparison of Suicide Rates

In comparing the United States to other countries in terms of suicide, some countries have a much higher suicide rate. According to *An Aging World,* a report released by the U.S. Census Bureau in 2002, in comparing suicide rates for selected age groups in 23 countries in 1997, the suicide rate per 100,000 population of males who were age 75 and older was 45 per 100,000 in the United States and 27 per 100,000 in Canada. But the suicide rate was radically higher in Hungary, at 131 per 100,000. This high rate was followed by the rate in Bulgaria of 116.

The lowest suicide rate for older males was found in Ireland, of 22 per 100,000 men age 75 and older.

As for older women, suicide rates are much lower worldwide for women than for men, although they are higher in some countries than in others. For women age 75 and older, the suicide rate was 5 per 100,000 in the United States and 4 per 100,000 in Canada, Bulgaria, and Hungary tied for the highest suicide rates of older women, at 50 per 100,000 each, followed by rates of 33 per 100,000 each for older women in Japan and Singapore. The lowest suicide rates for older women were in Israel, at 1 per 100,000 population of older women, and Ireland, at 2 per 100,000 population.

Demographic Aspects in the United States

Suicide rates in the United States are highest among elderly men who are widowed or divorced. Men in this group have almost three times (2.7) the risk of committing suicide over the risk found among married men of the same age. The risk for suicide is also increased for older women who are divorced or widowed, although it is not quite as dramatic. Women who are 65 or older and who are divorced or widowed have about twice the risk (1.8) of suicide than that found among married women of the same age.

Causes of Suicide

Many older people who commit suicide have problems with DEPRESSION; others have severe medical problems, such as CARDIOVASCULAR DISEASE, STROKE, DIABETES, and CANCER. They may also have problems with ALCOHOLISM or the abuse of prescription drugs. Some people may have a combination of medical issues, such as cancer and depression.

Advance Warning Signs

Studies indicate that there may be warning signs ahead of time, although busy physicians may not see them. In studies of older adults who committed suicide, 20 percent had seen their primary-care physician that day, and 40 percent had seen their doctor within the last week.

Physicians sometimes mistakenly believe that depression is a normal part of aging and/or illness, and they either fail to treat depression altogether or they do not refer patients to other doctors, such as psychiatrists and neurologists, who treat depression. In the defense of doctors, depression is not always an easy diagnosis, and many people may mask their feelings and not report them to their physician.

Homicide-Suicides

Another form of suicide is the homicide-suicide, in which someone ends the life of another person and then commits suicide. Nearly all homicide-suicides involve a husband who murders his wife and then kills himself.

According to a paper written by Donna Cohen of the Department of Aging and Mental Health at the Florida Mental Health Institute in the University of South Florida, about 500 homicide-suicides (1,000 deaths) occur each year nationwide among people who are age 55 and older. Cohen says these are not pacts of love, nor are they acts of altruism. In fact, the victim rarely knows what is planned. Often, the victim is murdered in her sleep. In most cases, says Cohen, the homicide-suicide occurs because the male perpetrator actively fears a threat to the relationship, such as an imminent move of one or both parties to a nursing home. Other motives are a real or imagined change in health or increased marital conflict.

Cohen says that there are clues to a possible homicide-suicide that others can identify and act upon. Some key clues are:

- A marriage of long standing, the husband playing a dominant role
- A male caregiver whose wife has ALZHEIMER'S DISEASE or DEMENTIA
- A husband and wife who have many medical problems, one or both of whom are becoming more ill
- Consideration of a move to a NURSING HOME or ASSISTED-LIVING FACILITY
- A couple who is increasingly socially isolated from family and friends

Cohen says that adult children and others should take note if the husband exhibits the following behavioral patterns:

- He says that he is feeling hopeless or helpless.
- He loses interest in former activities.
- He talks about harming his wife.

Giving away important items and crying for no reason are other indicators of a possible suicide-homicide plan. Family members should ask the individual if he has thought about suicide or homicide-suicide, and they should also offer their help so that the individual does not feel compelled to go through with the crimes.

If the person says he has a plan to carry out the act of suicide and/or homicide, then this is a red flag for family members. Any guns in the house should be removed. The relative should call a crisis hotline or suicide crisis center or contact the elderly person's physician.

Cohen, Donna, Ph.D. "Homicide-Suicide in Older Persons: How You Can Help Prevent a Tragedy," Tampa, Fla.: Department of Aging and Mental Health, Florida Mental Health Institute, University of South Florida, 2001.

Kinsella, Kevin, and Victoria A. Velkoff. *An Aging World: 2001.* Washington, D.C.: U.S. Census Bureau, 2001.

supplements Refers to vitamins, minerals, and herbal medications and remedies, all of which can be found in health food stores, pharmacies, and even supermarkets in most areas of the United States. Clinical studies are finding that some supplements, such as Vitamin E and Selenium, may be beneficial to the body and may even prevent serious diseases such as CANCER, especially PROSTATE CANCER. Research on their use is ongoing.

It is extremely important for patients to inform their doctors of any supplements they are taking because these drugs may interact with or impede other medications that they are taking for various illnesses. However, many individuals are unaware of the importance of sharing this information and instead are under the mistaken impression that all "natural" drugs are also safe.

See also ALTERNATIVE MEDICINE.

de Jong, Nynke, Ph.D., et al. "Dietary Supplements and Physical Exercise Affecting Bone and Body Composition in Frail Elderly Persons," *American Journal of Public Health* 90, no. 6 (2000): 947–954.

surgery Procedure involving an incision in the skin and some other action, which may be a minor procedure or may be as complex as a kidney transplant or brain surgery. Surgery may be very dangerous for older people because they may react badly to anesthesia; they may also be frail in some cases, and doctors may fear that they may not survive the surgery. In some cases, ADULT CHILDREN may oppose surgery for their patients; however, as long as the patient is not mentally incompetent, whether or not the surgery is performed should be a decision left to the patient and his or her doctor.

syncope Temporary unconsciousness, popularly referred to as fainting. It is not the same as dizziness or vertigo, where there is usually no loss of consciousness. Syncope is also different from a seizure, although it may be difficult sometimes even for a physician to tell the difference. It may also be hard to determine the cause among people older than age 65 because they may have more than one chronic ailment and may be taking more than one medication.

Some signs that may precede syncope are:

- Sweating
- Nausea
- Extreme stress
- Palpitations

Causes of Syncope

Heart disease (vasovagal attack or neurocardiogenic attack) may result in a temporary loss of consciousness. Cardiac causes of syncope are associated with an increased death rate, and thus the patient with syncope should be evaluated and treated as soon as possible. Low blood pressure (HYPOTENSION) may have caused the syncope. Another cause of syncope is bradycardia, or slow heart rate. If the heart does not pump enough blood, or if it pumps the blood too slowly, this problem may occur. However, in at least half the cases, the cause of the syncope is not determined. In some cases, particularly when individuals are taking medications, the drug itself may cause a "fainting spell."

Diagnosis

The physician will evaluate the person based on symptoms and medical history. Laboratory tests and an electrocardiogram will usually be ordered to rule out HEART DISEASE. In some cases, a stress test will also be ordered, as well as a Holtes monitor, which is a device that can measure heart rhythm for a 24-hour period. The doctor may order an electroencephalogram of the brain if there is a chance of a seizure disorder or other neurological problem. Often, the physician may want to check a magnetic resonance imaging (MRI) scan of the brain to rule out other causes of loss of consciousness.

Treatment

The treatment for syncope depends on what the doctor believes is the cause of the fainting. If the cause is believed to be medications, then the doctor will reevaluate the necessity of the drug and if it is deemed needed, the dosage. A lower dosage may be indicated.

If the problem is cardiac in nature, a CARDIOLOGIST will be consulted; if neurologic in nature, a NEUROLOGIST will be sought. In some few cases, the patient may need a PSYCHIATRIST, for treatment of panic disorder or ANXIETY. Also, because syncope may be very frightening, the physician may want to have the patient obtain counseling to help deal with this problem. Maintaining adequate hydration is also very important in treating this condition.

Kapoor, Wishwa N., M.D, M.P.H. "Syncope," *New England Journal of Medicine* 343 (December 21, 2000): 1,856–1,862.

tai chi Also known as "t'ai chi" or "t'ai chi chuan." A form of Chinese martial arts credited to Chinese martial artist Chang San Feng in the 1400s. It primarily comprises simple and flowing movements that can be performed by most people and that resemble animal movements, such as a crane, a tiger, or a snake; for example, one movement involves standing on one leg. These movements are low impact and involve little risk for the person practicing them.

According to Dr. Cheng in his article for *The Physician and Sportsmedicine,* the movements should be performed for 20 to 30 minutes a minimum of three times a week to obtain maximum benefit.

Tai chi has been found to be particularly beneficial to some elderly patients. Studies have shown that the numbers of injuries and FALLS can be significantly reduced when older individuals receive training in and practice the basic principles of tai chi. These exercises may also help to improve the mobility and flexibility of adults who have ARTHRITIS.

An analysis of a variety of exercise programs among older individuals found that tai chi was very effective in improving balance and reducing the number of falls among older individuals. The analysis of 2,328 nursing home and community-dwelling senior residents, ages 60–75 years, was reported by Dr. Michael A. Province et al. in the *Journal of the American Medical Association (JAMA).* The authors concluded that of various exercise programs, tai chi training was most effective in reducing the number of injuries from falls. Those who participated in tai chi reduced their risk by about 25 percent.

Cheng, John, M.D. "Tai Chi Chuan: A Slow Dance for Health," *The Physician and Sportsmedicine* 27, no. 6 (1999).
Iknoian, Therese, and Manny Fuentes. *T'ai Chi For Dummies.* New York: Hungry Minds, 2001.
Province, Michael A., M.D. et al. "The Effects of Exercise on Falls in Elderly Patients: A Preplanned Meta-analysis of the FICSIT Trials," *Journal of the American Medical Association (JAMA)* 273, no. 3 (1995): 1,341–1,347.

taxes Fees paid to state, federal, county, and other government entities on homes, cars, wages, goods, and services that are purchased or on income that is received. Older individuals are usually subject to state and federal income tax; however, they may receive extra benefits. Some states allow exemptions of part of the tax on private homes or offer other tax breaks to senior citizens. Sometimes, senior citizens are unaware of these benefits, or they may be too embarrassed to take advantage of them.

telephone reassurance services A service that provides individuals, usually volunteers, who telephone homebound disabled or older individuals to verify that the seniors who are living alone are well and do not need anything. Sometimes, the volunteers arrange to call at a specific time, and if the individual doesn't answer, then they call a family member, the police, or someone else. Sometimes, religious organizations provide such services, and other times, nonsectarian organizations offer them. Sometimes, neighbors on a street set up their own informal telephone reassurance service, arranging what actions to take if the older person does not respond.

To find a telephone reassurance service in a particular area, contact the national ELDER-CARE LOCATOR.

temporary help Assistance that is provided on a nonpermanent basis, such as short-term nursing assistance, HOME HEALTH CARE, housekeeping help, or other forms of aid. Temporary help may be needed by people who have been discharged from the hospital but who are not yet fully able to manage on their own.

terminal illness Illness that doctors predict will generally lead to certain death, such as various forms of advanced CANCER or KIDNEY FAILURE.

thyroid disease An abnormality of the thyroid, which is a butterfly-shaped gland that is located in the front of the neck. The key thyroid disorders are hyperthyroidism, which is an excess of thyroid hormone, and hypothyroidism, which is an insufficient amount of thyroid hormone. When they have thyroid disease, older people are more likely to have abnormally low levels of thyroid, although it is possible for them to have overly high levels.

Risk Factors

It is important to screen for hypothyroidism among symptomatic individuals because the symptoms of severe hypothyroidism (lethargy, weakness, and confusion) may be confused with those of DEMENTIA. Hypothyroidism is relatively easy to treat by administering thyroid medication.

Causes of Thyroid Disease

Many thyroid diseases are autoimmune disorders, which means that the body has mistakenly attacked the thyroid gland as it would a foreign invader, either overproducing or underproducing thyroid hormone, depending on the form of the disease.

In fewer cases, thyroid disease results from reactions to some medications, such as lithium (which is usually prescribed for manic depression) or amiodarone (which may be given for some heart conditions), both of which may trigger hypothyroidism. Much more rarely, a disorder of the hypothalamus or the pituitary gland may cause hypothyroidism.

Symptoms of Hyperthyroidism

Hyperthyroidism, or excessively high levels of thyroid hormone, may be detected by a physician when a patient has some or all of the symptoms listed below. Hyperthyroidism is dangerous because it can stress the heart and the body unnecessarily.

Note: these symptoms may also indicate many other diseases, and, thus, only an experienced physician can perform the diagnosis. In most cases, an endocrinologist should treat thyroid disease.

- Elevated heart rate (pulse) of more than 100 beats per minute
- Enlarged thyroid
- Increased requirement for insulin and worsening of blood glucose levels, if the person has diabetes
- Insomnia/nightmares
- Weight loss despite a greater appetite
- Heavy sweating
- Extreme nervousness and irritability/anxiety
- Heat intolerance
- Shaking hands
- Decreased menstruation or no menstruation prior to menopause or surgical removal of the uterus

Symptoms of Hypothyroidism

There are basic symptoms common to many people whose thyroid levels are low. However, these symptoms may also indicate other diseases. Common symptoms of hypothyroidism are:

- Chronic constipation
- Puffy face, especially under the eyes
- Dry and itchy skin, doughy skin
- Depression/lack of energy/apathy
- Sensitivity to cold temperatures
- Decreased need for insulin in those who have DIABETES
- Muscle cramps and aches
- More frequent bowel movements (although not diarrhea)

The most common form of hypothyroidism is Hashimoto's thyroiditis. This is an autoimmune condition in which the body mistakenly makes antibodies (proteins) against the enzyme in the thyroid. Initially, it can cause *hyper*thyroidism, but more frequently this disease will result in *hypo*thyroidism because of the ongoing damage to the thyroid gland.

Diagnosing Thyroid Disease

If doctors believe that patients may have thyroid disease based on the symptoms displayed, then they will usually order a blood test known as a TSH (thyroid-stimulating hormone) assay. This will determine whether the thyroid levels are high, low, or within the normal range. Although one might think that high TSH levels mean hyperthyroidism, the reverse is true. The lower the TSH outside the normal range, the more hyperthyroid a person is. The higher the TSH outside the normal range, the more hypothyroid the person is.

Treating Thyroid Disease

The treatment of thyroid disease depends on the type of disease. Treatment may be very simple, such as prescribing supplemental thyroid hormone to the hypothyroid patient and following up with periodic blood tests to ensure that the blood levels of thyroid are in the normal range. Conversely, if the person has excessive levels of thyroid, the physician may attempt to suppress the thyroid function through various means, such as with prescribing antithyroid pills or radioactive iodine. In some cases, surgery will become necessary. Generally, a subtotal thyroidectomy is performed, leaving part of the thyroid gland intact. Sometimes, a total thyroidectomy is performed.

toileting   Ability to manage defecation and urination on one's own. INCONTINENCE of feces or urine is a problem of some older individuals, who may need to wear adult diapers. This can be a degrading prospect for adults who retain their full mental abilities. Complications of incontinence can also occur, including skin breakdown and sores, infections, and a wide variety of psychological issues such as DEPRESSION over the loss of bladder control.

Often incontinence can be treated with medication or surgery.

A surprisingly high number of women suffer from a form of bladder incontinence called stress incontinence. This often occurs after childbirth but progresses with advancing age. Often, such simple activities as coughing or sneezing or even laughing out loud can produce incontinence among women with this condition. It is easily remedied with gynecological or urological care (often without surgery). Many women fail to discuss this particular medical problem with their doctors because of embarrassment.

transplanted organs   Organs taken from another person, usually one who is recently deceased, and that are placed into an ill person whose own organ has failed or will fail imminently. Doctors have successfully transplanted hearts, lungs, kidneys, pancreases, and other organs. In very rare cases, a dual transplant is performed, such as a pancreas and kidney transplant.

In some cases, live donors can be used, such as when a kidney transplant is performed. Because healthy people have two kidneys, they are able to donate one kidney and continue to live. When transplants occur, direct donations of kidneys are usually offered by close family members to their very sick relatives, although sometimes nonrelated individuals donate their kidneys. Other organs, such as the heart or the pancreas, cannot be donated from a live donor because individuals need these organs to sustain their own lives.

Individuals who have received transplanted organs must take antirejection drugs for the rest of their lives. It is hoped that in the future, researchers will be able to use an individual's own body tissue to regenerate healthy organ tissue.

See also KIDNEY FAILURE.

transportation   Means of moving from one place to another. The primary forms of local transportation are private automobiles, buses, and taxis. Some people who live in large cities have access to subways. Public transportation may be difficult to manage for older people who are disabled. They may find it difficult to move as fast as others can move on and off of public transportation. They may continue DRIVING beyond the time when they should stop driving because of physical disabilities such as poor eyesight or hearing loss or poor reaction time.

Transportation is very important to noninstitutionalized older individuals because they need a means to shop, see their physicians, attend religious services, visit friends, and so forth. Most older people drive cars, but some limit their nighttime driving because they cannot see well enough. Others must give up driving altogether for health reasons. When people can no longer drive themselves to various places and must depend on others, they generally restrict the number of places they go to. This can cause a feeling of severe isolation and loss. This can also lead to a perceived or real loss of independence.

In general, people who have the most transportation problems fit the following criteria:

- Female
- Older than age 70, with the problem increasing as the person ages
- Without a car or other means of transportation
- Sickly
- Lower income
- Socially isolated

tuberculosis An infectious disease that primarily affects the lungs as well as other body parts and which is a concern to public health departments in the United States, Canada, and the world.

Once considered by developed nations to be a disease of the past, tuberculosis resurfaced in the late 20th century as a problem yet again. However, after a peak of 26,673 total cases nationwide in the United States in 1992, the numbers of affected people began to drop dramatically to 16,377 total cases in 2000. Of these cases, 3,534 cases (21.5 percent) were found among individuals age 65 and older. The largest racial grouping of older people who had tuberculosis were whites (40 percent), followed by blacks and Asian/Pacific Islanders, (22 percent each), Hispanics (14 percent), and other groups with the disease.

Tuberculosis is most heavily concentrated among seven states, where 59 percent of all cases were found in the period 1992–2000: California, Florida, Georgia, Illinois, New Jersey, New York, and Texas.

Some experts worry that the drop in the number of tubercular patients may mean interest in combating tuberculosis will decline. Dr. Small and Dr. Fujiwara wrote, in their 2001 article on tuberculosis in the *New England Journal of Medicine,* "Despite the resurgence of tuberculosis in the late 1980s and early 1990s, we have been given a second, perhaps final, chance to eliminate the disease in the United States. The levels of public awareness and political support for this goal are high, but with recent declines in rates of tuberculosis, there is a renewed risk of complacency."

TUBERCULOSIS CASES AND PERCENTAGE OF POPULATION AMONG PEOPLE AGE 65 AND OLDER, 1995–2000

	Number of Cases	Percentage of Total Cases in the United States
1995	5,351	23%
1996	5,103	24%
1997	4,691	24%
1998	4,393	24%
1999	4,028	23%
2000	3,534	22%

Source: *Reported Tuberculosis in the United States, 2000,* Centers for Disease Control and Prevention (CDC)

Risk Factors

People who are most vulnerable to developing tuberculosis generally fit at least some of these categories:

- People older than age 65
- Immigrants from countries with a high rate of TB
- Health workers in contact with tuberculosis patients in a hospital or nursing home
- Homeless people
- Those living with someone who has tuberculosis
- Those with a serious chronic illness (DIABETES, CANCER, or a KIDNEY DISEASE)
- Drug abusers
- Those infected with HIV

Symptoms of Tuberculosis

People with TB may have a chronic cough and they may cough up blood. They may also be fatigued and lose weight. They may also have no symptoms at all unless the disease becomes active in the body.

Diagnosis of TB

Physicians who suspect that their patients may have tuberculosis can test for the disease with the Mantoux method, a TB skin test. The skin is checked 48 hours later; a raised reddened area indicates that TB may be present. There are false positives, so people with a positive TB skin test will then need to have a chest X ray to determine if TB is present in the lungs. A chest X ray may also be taken to confirm the diagnosis, and when treatment is completed, another chest X ray should be taken for comparison purposes.

Treatment of TB

Patients with active TB may need to be hospitalized. Patients with chronic TB can usually take medication, and often the drugs are administered or overseen by workers from the public health department of the state. There are five different antimicrobial drugs that are most commonly prescribed: isoniazid, rifampin, pyrazinamide, ethambutol, and streptomycin. Second-line (less commonly chosen drugs) that are also prescribed to treat tuberculosis are capreomycin, ciprofloxacin, clofazimine, cycloserine, ethionamide, kanamycin, levofloxacin, ofloxacin, aminosalicyclic acid, rifabutin, and rifapentine.

Most patients take a combination of isoniazid, rifampin, and pyrazinamide daily for about eight weeks, according to Drs. Small and Fujiwara in their 2001 article in the *New England Journal of Medicine.* Then they take isoniazid and rifampin for 16 weeks.

If the tuberculosis is drug resistant, the physician may treat with rifampin, pyrazinamide, and ethambutol for about six months. Treatment is more extensive if HIV is also present.

Patients on isoniazid are advised that they should not consume alcohol during treatment, nor should they take Tylenol (acetaminophen) because the TB drug interacts with both alcohol and Tylenol and can cause liver damage.

Division of Tuberculosis Elimination, Centers for Disease Control and Prevention. "Reported Tuberculosis in the United States, 2000" (2001).

Jerant, Anthony F., M.D., Michelle Bannon, P.S.-C, M.P.H., and Stephen Rittenhouse, CPT, MC, USA. "Identification and Management of Tuberculosis," *American Family Physician* 61 (2000): 2,667–2,678, 2,681–2,682.

Small, Peter M., M.D. and Paula I. Fujiwara, M.D., M.P.H. "Management of Tuberculosis in the United States," *The New England Journal of Medicine* 345, no. 3 (July 19, 2001): 189–200.

ulcers, peptic

ulcers, peptic Painful erosions of the lining of the stomach or the small intestine. Being age 65 and older is a risk factor for the development of an ulcer. Other risk factors include as follows:

- Living in an institution or crowded environment
- Being AFRICAN AMERICAN or HISPANIC AMERICAN in the United States
- Living in an area with poor water sanitation
- Living in a developing/poor (also known as a less-developed) country

Cause of Ulcers

Contrary to continued popular belief, most stomach ulcers are caused by bacteria called *Helicobacter pylori* (HP), not STRESS. Two Australian physicians, Dr. Marshall and Dr. Warren, made this discovery in 1982. Dr. Marshall actually consumed some HP himself, subsequently developed gastritis, and then successfully treated himself with antibiotics. However, Marshall and Warren's theory was ridiculed by physicians around the globe for years because "everyone" knew that stress or a bad diet caused ulcers.

It was not until 1994 that the National Institutes of Health Consensus Development Conference determined that the connection between HP and the development of ulcers was a valid one, and they subsequently recommended that patients with ulcers caused by HP should be treated with antibiotics.

Ulcers may also result from a side effect of medications, particularly nonsteroidal antiinflammatory drugs (NSAIDs) taken for such chronic illnesses as OSTEOARTHRITIS. Ulcers caused by regular doses of NSAIDs may have no symptoms, but this does not mean there is no real problem.

Other Causes of Ulcers

Some ulcers are caused by chemotherapy or radiation treatment for CANCER. Zollinger-Ellison syndrome is a rare disease that causes some ulcers.

According to Anil Minocha, M.D., and Christine Adamec in their book *How to Stop Heartburn,* ulcer treatment has two primary aspects. (Some patients have both an ulcer and GASTROESOPHAGEAL REFLUX DISEASE, commonly known as heartburn). The first aspect is: "Heal the ulcer and improve symptoms using an HS [histamine blocker] agent or Carafate (sucralfate). A superior alternative to these drugs is a PPI [proton pump inhibitor medication] (Prilosec, Prevacid, Aciphex, Nexium, or Protonix). This treatment continues for six to 12 weeks, depending upon the location and the cause of the ulcer." The second treatment aspect is to prevent the ulcer from recurring.

Surgery

In rare cases, surgery is performed on an ulcer, especially if it is a complicated ulcer and there is excessive bleeding. It is also possible (rarely) for the ulcer to penetrate through the wall of the stomach or the small intestine, leading to pancreatitis or bleeding.

Minocha, Anil, M.D., and Christine Adamec. *How to Stop Heartburn: Simple Ways to Heal Heartburn and Acid Reflux.* New York: John Wiley & Sons, 2001.

United Kingdom (UK) Refers to England, Scotland, Northern Ireland, and Wales. There are large numbers of seniors in the United Kingdom. According to the U.S. Census Bureau, about 16 percent of the total population of the UK are age 65 and older. (The percent of older people is about 13 percent (12.6 percent) in the United States and also in

Canada (12.7 percent). (See Appendix II for population data of older individuals in countries throughout the world.)

The National Health Service (NHS) provides universal health-care coverage for older citizens in the United Kingdom, including home health care; however, there is a "means test," and people with assets that exceed a set fee are not eligible for free residential care. (A means test is also used for the low-income recipients of MEDICAID, in the United States.)

A disadvantage of universal health care may be that some individuals have to wait for nonemergency medical care longer than they would like. According to a survey of five countries performed by the Commonwealth Fund and reported in 2000, more than half (51 percent) of older people in England said that they had to wait five weeks or more for nonemergency care, in contrast to 40 percent of older individuals in Canada, 19 percent in Australia, and 7 percent in the United States.

Anderson, Gerard F., Ph.D. and Peter S. Hussey. "Health and Population Aging: A Multinational Comparison," Johns Hopkins University (October 1999).

Schoen, Cathy, et al. "The Elderly's Experiences with Health Care in Five Nations: Findings from the Commonwealth Fund," 1999 International Health Policy Survey (May 2000).

urinary problems/difficulties Medical problems with the bladder, the urethra, or other parts of the urinary tract system. Older individuals commonly have a variety of urinary problems, including urinary tract infections or URINARY INCONTINENCE as well as BLADDER CANCER.

If the urinary difficulty is infectious, it can usually be cleared up with a course of antibiotics. Men may suffer from prostatitis, an inflammation of the prostate gland that is usually treatable with antibiotics. Sometimes, a UROLOGIST will need to be consulted, and in some cases, SURGERY may be necessary.

Some common symptoms of a urinary tract infection, the most common form of urinary medical disorder, are:

- Pain and strain with urination
- Blood in the urine (although it may not be visible to the patient)

- BACK PAIN
- Fever

Urinary tract infections are usually relatively easy to cure, although some people suffer from recurrent infections. This is especially true of people with DIABETES or women after MENOPAUSE. Some patients may need to take a maintenance dose (low dose) of antibiotics if they are prone to urinary tract infections.

urinary incontinence Difficulty or inability to control urination. Although older men may experience this problem, it is more commonly seen among older women. The risk for urinary incontinence increases with age.

Types of Urinary Incontinence

There are four basic types of urinary incontinence, including stress incontinence, urge incontinence, functional incontinence, and overflow incontinence.

Stress incontinence is almost solely seen among women, although men who have undergone a prostatectomy (usually because of PROSTATE CANCER treatment) may develop this problem. It is typically characterized by the loss of urine when the person laughs, sneezes, or takes other actions that cause pressure on the bladder. MENOPAUSE and lower estrogen levels can also increase the risk for stress incontinence. Weak pelvic ligaments usually cause this form of incontinence.

Urge incontinence, which is the most common form of incontinence seen among older people, is a sudden loss of urine with no pressure on the bladder, and this problem may occur during sleep or when a person hears water running. Physicians also call urge incontinence by other terms, such as *reflex incontinence, spastic bladder,* or *overactive bladder.*

This condition may result from damage to the nerves that support the bladder. Some diseases, such as PARKINSON'S DISEASE or ALZHEIMER'S DISEASE, can weaken bladder nerves.

Functional incontinence refers to problems that a person has that prevent them from proper toileting, such as a person with Alzheimer's disease who does not think ahead that they need to use the toilet. A person in a wheelchair with normal cognitive abilities may have difficulties in getting to a toilet in time, despite laws on ACCESSIBILITY to facilities.

Overflow incontinence is a condition in which the bladder leaks or "overflows" urine. This problem may be caused by a blocked urethra, the tube that carries urine from the bladder. Damage to the nerves from diseases such as DIABETES can also cause overflow incontinence. Most people with overflow incontinence are men.

There are also combinations of factors, and a person can have two or more forms of incontinence. This is generally known as mixed incontinence.

Symptoms

The key symptom of urinary incontinence is a lack of control over urination. The urine loss may be a dribble or a flood, depending on the individual and the causes of the incontinence.

Diagnosis

UROLOGISTS are the primary type of doctors who diagnose and treat urinary incontinence. The doctor will take a complete medical history and perform a physical examination to check for obvious blockages, poor reflexes, and fecal impaction, all of which may be causing the problem.

The doctor will usually ask the patient to cough and will check to see if there is an involuntary loss of urine.

A urinalysis is ordered to check for possible infection and blood tests will also check for infection. Creatinine levels (which may indicate a KIDNEY DISEASE), electrolyte levels, and other tests may be ordered.

The doctor may also order procedures or tests to determine the degree of the problem. A cystoscopy is a physical examination of the inside of the bladder. An ultrasound test can also provide information about the bladder. The doctor can also check urine flow and determine if, after voiding, the patient is retaining urine in the bladder with urodynamics, which measure bladder pressure and urine flow.

Transient Incontinence

Sometimes, incontinence is a temporary problem. It may be caused by a variety of factors, including medications, infection, extreme urinary output as a result of diabetes, and other causes.

Treatment

Once the cause has been determined, treatment can begin. If the cause is an infection, antibiotics will be prescribed. If menopause appears to be the primary cause, then oral or topical hormone replacement therapy may be indicated. If the cause appears to be weak bladder muscles, the doctor will often recommend that female patients use Kegel exercises, which are tightening exercises of the bladder muscles. Alternatively, biofeedback, using a probe inserted into the vagina, can also be quite helpful in helping the female patient with retraining the pelvic muscles. In some cases, such as after a prostatectomy men are advised to use Kegel exercises to strengthen their bladder muscles.

Medications may also be prescribed to control incontinence or the constant urge to urinate without the presence of infection. One commonly prescribed medication is Detrol A (a long-acting form of tolterodine tartrate).

Bladder training may also be recommended if the individual is not intellectually impaired by dementia. Patients can be trained to increase the amount of time from when they feel they need to urinate to when they use the toilet. According to Jonathan M. Vapnek, in his 2001 article in *Geriatrics* on urinary incontinence,

"For example, if the urge [to urinate] rises approximately every hour, ask patients to try to hold off for 10 minutes per urge episode and do this for one week. Then raise the duration to 20 minutes and do that for a week. The goal is to increase the voiding interval from 2 to 4 hours over a 2-month period. Another approach involves increasing the intervals during the day with the objective of decreasing or eliminating them at night." Note: this approach should not be followed unless the patient's physician specifically recommends it.

"Scheduled TOILETING" is another approach, which may work better with individuals who have cognitive problems. The individual is taken to the toilet every two to four hours and encouraged to urinate.

In severe cases of incontinence, surgery may be performed.

Most doctors also recommend lifestyle changes. Avoidance of alcohol and caffeine is usually recommended to help control the bladder.

*Avoiding Diapers Is Best,
If Possible*

Some nursing home staff and some caregivers may believe that it is easier for older people to wear adult diapers if they have any problem with incontinence. The problem with this belief is that many cases of incontinence can be treated and that not treating them will often cause individuals' conditions to worse. It will also often cause feelings of hopelessness and helplessness, also known as LEARNED HELPLESSNESS. The individual may develop problems with DEPRESSION and low SELF-ESTEEM.

For more information, contact the following organizations:

American Foundation for Urologic Disease
The Bladder Health Council
1128 North Charles Street
Baltimore, MD 21201
(800) 242-2383 (toll-free) or (410) 468-1800

American Uro-Gynecologic Society
2025 M Street NW
Suite 800
Washington, DC 20036
(202) 367-1167

Vapnek, Jonathan M., M.D. "Urinary Incontinence: Screening and Treatment of Urinary Dysfunction," *Geriatrics* 56, no. 10 (2001): 25–29.

urologist   Physician who specializes in diseases of the bladder and the genitourinary tract, such as BLADDER CANCER and URINARY INCONTINENCE. Urologists also treat men who have difficulties with the prostate gland, such as infections of the prostate or PROSTATE CANCER. They also treat women who may suffer from frequent bladder infections or other bladder illnesses.

uterine cancer   Malignancy of the uterus. Also known as endometrial cancer. According to the National Cancer Institute, uterine cancer constitutes 6 percent of all cancers contracted by women in the United States.

Risk Factors

It is unknown what causes uterine cancer; however, there are patterns among women who develop the disease. Risks are highest for women who:

- Are older than age 50
- Are menopausal
- Are using hormone replacement therapy, particularly estrogen with progesterone
- Have never been pregnant
- Have HYPERTENSION
- Have DIABETES
- Are obese
- Are taking the drug tamoxifen to prevent or treat BREAST CANCER
- Have had COLORECTAL CANCER

Symptoms of Uterine Cancer

Symptoms may be vague. The most common symptom is vaginal bleeding after menopause has occurred. The vaginal discharge may be mostly watery at first and later more clearly includes blood. Other symptoms may include:

- Pain during intercourse
- Pelvic pain
- Painful or difficult urination

Diagnosis

The doctor usually a gynecologist, must perform a pelvic examination as part of the diagnosis of uterine cancer. The physician may also perform an annual Pap smear; however, the Pap smear is generally considered a more reliable test for cervical cancer than for uterine cancer.

If uterine cancer is suspected, the doctor may perform a transvaginal ultrasound test and also a biopsy. Additional tests may also be ordered, such as a CT scan, a magnetic resonance imaging (MRI) scan, or a colonoscopy or sigmoidoscopy.

If cancer is diagnosed, the doctor will "stage" it, which means that the cancer will be evaluated in terms of how far advanced it is. For example, if the cancer remains inside the uterus but is not in the cervix (the least advanced stage), it is considered Stage I. However, if the cancer has expanded to the cervix, it is Stage II.

If the cancer has gone beyond the uterus but still remains in the pelvis, and it has not yet attacked either the bladder or rectum, then it is Stage III cancer. In Stage IV cancer, the cancer has gone farther and is into the bladder, the rectum, or other parts of the body.

Treatment

Uterine cancer usually requires a hysterectomy, or the removal of the uterus. In most cases of older women, the ovaries are removed as well because they are also at risk for developing cancer. Some women with uterine cancer are treated with radiation therapy.

National Cancer Institute. "What You Need to Know About Cancer of the Uterus," NIH Publication No. 01-1562 (July 30, 2001).

vaginal cancer   Malignancy of the vaginal lining. This is a rare form of cancer that represents less than 2 percent of all reproductive system cancers and is primarily seen in women older than age 50. Only about 600 people die of vaginal cancer in the United States each year. About 2,300 new cases are diagnosed every year. Other than the fact that most cases occur in older women, risk patterns are unknown.

Symptoms

The older woman with vaginal cancer may experience some or all of the following symptoms or signs:

- Vaginal bleeding or discharge
- Painful or difficult urination
- Pelvic pain or pain with intercourse
- White raised patches on the vaginal surface

These above symptoms may occur with many problems that a woman may experience and should be diagnosed by a medical doctor, preferably a gynecologist.

Diagnosing and Treating Vaginal Cancer

This form of cancer is diagnosed with a pelvic examination, a Pap smear, and, if cancer is suspected, a biopsy. When vaginal cancer is diagnosed, surgery is the most frequently chosen option of treatment. Laser surgery of the cancerous tissue or more massive surgery may be indicated, depending on the staging of the cancer (how advanced it is).

Altman, Roberta, and Michael J. Sarg, M.D. *The Cancer Dictionary.* New York: Facts On File, 2000.

varicose veins   Enlarged veins caused by pooling of blood in the veins. The condition is usually found in the legs, although it can also occur elsewhere. Women are more susceptible to varicose veins than are men. The condition is aggravated by prolonged standing.

Symptoms

The most common symptoms are feelings of pain and heaviness in the legs. Other symptoms of varicose veins are:

- Visibly enlarged veins
- Swelling of the ankles
- Ankle skin that is discolored
- Ulcerated skin near the ankle

Diagnosis and Treatment

In addition to direct observation of the legs, the doctor may also order an ultrasound examination. Patients with varicose veins are treated conservatively at first: they are told to sit and sleep with their legs raised and to wear elastic support hose.

If the patient experiences a great deal of pain, physicians may order vein stripping and removal of the varicose veins. Sclerotherapy of the veins, which is an injection of a solution that closes the vein, may also be ordered.

Veterans Administration (VA)   Federal organization in the United States that manages benefits and programs for eligible people who have served in the U.S. military. The VA operates hospitals, clinics, and nursing homes. It also approves monthly payments to some individuals who became disabled during military service.

Nursing-Home Care

According to the General Accounting Office (GAO), in fiscal year 2000, the Department of Veterans

Affairs (VA) spent an estimated 10 percent of its health-care budget, or $1.9 billion, on providing nursing-home care for military veterans. This expenditure is expected to rise further as the number of older veterans age 85 and older will increase from 422,000 in 2000 to about 1.3 million military veterans by 2010.

The VA owns and operates 134 nursing homes nationwide, and they also pay for veterans' care in 94 state-owned nursing homes. About 3,400 nursing homes are under contract to the VA.

For further information, contact:

Department of Veterans Affairs (VA)
Office of Public Affairs
810 Vermont Avenue, NW
Washington, DC 20420
(800) 827-1000 (toll-free) or (800) 829-4833 (toll-free, TTY)
http://www.va.gov

veterans, military People who previously served in the military and who were honorably discharged. Veterans in the United States who have varying levels of service-connected disabilities may be eligible to receive medical care and payments from the VETERANS ADMINISTRATION. Their spouses or children may also receive some benefits.

Veterans with Diabetes and Other Serious Diseases

Veterans who developed or were diagnosed with DIABETES during their military service or within one year after leaving the military may be eligible for additional compensation. Also, special rules apply to Vietnam veterans who have developed Type 2 diabetes since their discharge from military service. (See section below.)

Some evidence from the Institute of Medicine (IOM) has indicated a possible link between a possible exposure to Agent Orange and other herbicides that were used during the Vietnam War and the subsequent development of diabetes or PROSTATE CANCER in veterans who served in the country of Vietnam.

As a result of the report from the IOM, in November 2000, the U.S. Department of Veterans Affairs (VA) ruled that military veterans who had served in

Vietnam and were subsequently diagnosed with diabetes could be eligible for disability compensation. According to VA estimates, an estimated 178,000 veterans with diabetes (including some veterans age 65 and older, although an age breakout was not provided) may be eligible for this compensation.

In addition to diabetes, the VA considers other conditions as service connected for veterans who served in Vietnam, including PROSTATE CANCER and respiratory cancers.

For further information, contact the local office of the Veterans Administration, or contact the national office at their toll-free number of (800) 827-1000 (http://www.va.gov). A pamphlet that can be downloaded is available at: http://www.va.gov/agentorange.

VA Death Benefits

When military veterans die, their survivors may be eligible for death benefits to cover a very small portion of funeral costs. Spouses are also entitled to receive a flag to honor the deceased veterans. The flags are available at no charge from the postal service. (Funeral directors usually obtain the flags for the spouse of the deceased veteran.) Veterans may also be buried in a national cemetery at no cost to the survivors, other than the fees charged by the funeral doctor to prepare the remains. A small monument is also provided at no charge.

visiting nurse Nurse who works for a home health-care agency that provides nursing services to individuals who are too ill to go to a clinic or a physician's office. This service enables people to recover at home from surgery or an injury and also helps people who have chronic health problems that need periodic attention. The service is often covered by MEDICARE, MEDICAID, or state agencies, although donations may be accepted as well.

For further information, contact the Visiting Nurse Associations of American (VNAA) at:

11 Beacon Street
Suite 910
Boston, MA 02108
(617) 523-4042 or (888) 866-8773 (toll-free)
http://www.vnaa.org/

vitamin deficiency Insufficient intake or decreased absorption of a vitamin, such as Vitamin B_{12} or C. Chronic vitamin deficiency can cause disease and even misdiagnosis. For example, a deficiency of Vitamin B_{12} may cause a person to exhibit symptoms commonly associated with ALZHEIMER'S DISEASE. If a person is older than age 70, the physician may conclude that some form of DEMENTIA is the most likely diagnosis; however, blood tests to rule out a vitamin deficiency are clearly indicated before such a diagnosis should be made.

Vitamin deficiencies may be caused by an inadequate intake of certain types of foods that contain the needed vitamins, or the problem may stem from the body's inability to use the vitamins in the food. In such cases, the individual may need to take supplemental vitamins. However, older individuals should not take supplemental vitamins without first discussing this option with their physicians to ensure that the vitamins will not affect the action of other medications that they may be taking. Patients should also discuss the appropriate dosages of vitamins needed. For example, high doses of Vitamin C could be harmful because they may cause clotting problems in some individuals, particularly those who are taking blood thinning drugs such as Coumadin (warfarin).

If physicians suspect that a patient has a vitamin deficiency, blood tests can be ordered to determine if there is such a deficiency. In the event that a vitamin deficiency is found, patients can then receive supplemental vitamins, either orally or by injection, depending on the type of vitamin that is needed and the extent of the deficiency; for example, Vitamin B_{12} is usually administered by injection, while Vitamin C can be taken orally.

wandering Leaving an area and traveling in a random and unplanned path. People who have ALZHEIMER'S DISEASE or DEMENTIA are noted for having problems with wandering away from where they live and with getting lost. Some individuals wander very far off or may even drive to another state. Often, if lost individuals with Alzheimer's disease or dementia are not found within several days, they may die from DEHYDRATION or exposure.

The first 48 hours that the person is gone are the most critical when the individual has dementia. It is a situation that is completely different from other "missing persons" cases in which the individuals involved may have voluntarily and with sound mind decided to leave their families.

weakness Difficulty or inability in moving a body part. Weakness in an arm, for example, may mean that the individual is having difficulty manipulating the arm. Weakness may be due to muscle wasting or disease. There may be damage to the brain, spinal cord, nerve roots, or twigs (the smallest nerve fibers), or there may be direct involvement of the muscles. Individuals who have chronic weakness may need to be evaluated by a NEUROLOGIST.

weather, impact on elders Effect of weather changes on an older person. Seniors may react more strongly to extremes of temperature. Others react to changes in air pressure or to inclement weather. Many people say that they can feel "in their bones" when the weather is starting to become worse. These patients usually are referring to a drop in the barometric pressure that causes joint capsules to swell. If the joints have ARTHRITIS pain and inflammation, the swelling can lead to further pain;

thus, such patients will often correctly predict weather changes.

Extremes of weather can be very difficult on older people who are disabled or have chronic illnesses. Cold weather affects breathing and can harm the skin. If older people do not stay warm, they can develop HYPOTHERMIA, or unusually low body temperature. This condition can be dangerous and even fatal. Very warm weather can lead to DEHYDRATION or heat exhaustion, heat stroke, and HYPERTHERMIA.

wheelchairs Special devices that transport disabled individuals of all ages. Often, they are motorized and relatively easy to manipulate. Most public facilities in the United States are wheelchair accessible, which means that there are ramps or other means (such as elevators) so that an individual in a wheelchair may enter the facility. Public bathrooms in the United States should also be wheelchair accessible.

It is very important for the individual to obtain a wheelchair that is physically comfortable and that the user can learn to operate easily. Wheelchairs are not a case of "one size fits all."

widows/widowers Married people whose spouse has died. A widow is a woman whose husband has died, and a widower is a man whose wife has died. The widow/widower may be eligible for pension payments, insurance payments, veteran's death benefits, and other money payable in the event of the death of a spouse. In some cases, the surviving spouse is unaware of insurance policies or financial plans that the deceased person had made, although this is more likely to be true in the case of an older woman who survives her spouse.

The surviving spouse should check all papers and documents of the deceased person to review the financial situation. Of course, it is far preferable that ESTATE PLANNING occurred before the death of the loved one so that he or she can explain their plans before then.

See also MARRIAGE/REMARRIAGE.

wills Legal documents that list a plan for how individuals wish their property to be disposed of after their deaths. Many older people fail to prepare a will, assuming that such legal matters are only for the very wealthy; however, anyone who owns a home or has any other ASSETS and who wishes to assure that their children or others will receive those assets after their deaths should prepare a will. ATTORNEYS can assist with this preparation, although in some states, particularly if the estate is small, individuals can fill out a form provided by the state government.

See also "DEATH TAX"; ESTATE PLANNING.

work Paid employment. Most older individuals in the United States are either retired or work only part-time, and this pattern is also true in countries worldwide. According to the U.S. Census Bureau, older women are more likely to work part-time than older men, although older men are more likely to continue to be in the workforce than are older women. The Census Bureau reports that older people represent only from 1 percent to 7 percent of the total workforce in any country.

The Census Bureau reports that in 1999, 16.9 percent of males age 65 and older and 8.9 percent of U.S. females were in the workforce. This is a higher rate than in some other countries and a lower rate than in other countries; for example, in Austria, only 2.0 percent of females age 65 and older and 4.6 percent of men in the same age group are part of the labor force. (See Appendix II to view statistics on the United States, Canada, and other countries and the labor force participation of their older citizens.)

Some older individuals are capable of working and wish to work, but they may face attitudes of AGEISM on the part of others. There may also be cultural constraints against working; for example, if the

unemployment rate is high, then there may be subtle or overt pressures for the jobs to go to younger men and women who are still supporting their families rather than to older and retired individuals. Another factor may be that companies need workers who are familiar with using computers and other devices that are commonly accepted by younger workers but which may be seen as threatening or difficult to learn by some older workers.

Age discrimination is another possible factor. Although age discrimination is illegal in the United States, companies sometimes give other reasons (or no reasons) for failing to hire an older person.

World Health Organization (WHO) A global health organization. WHO was formed in 1948 and is based in Geneva, Switzerland. The organization tracks major diseases as well as mortality (death) rates throughout the globe. The main headquarters is located in Geneva at the following address:

Avenue Appia 20
1211 Geneva 27
Switzerland
(+00 41 22) 791 21 11
http://www.who.int/m/topics/contact_who/en/index.html

WHO Regional Office addresses and member countries are as follows:

Regional Office for Africa (AFRO)
Parirenyatwa Hospital
PO Box BE 773
Harare
Zimbabwe
(00 263 4) 703580, 703684, 707493, 706591
http://www.whoafr.org

Member countries: Algeria, Angola, Benin, Botswana, Burkina Faso, Burundi, Cameroon, Cape Verde, Central African Republic, Chad, Comoros, Congo, Côte d'Ivoire, Equatorial Guinea, Eritrea, Ethiopia, Gabon, Gambia, Ghana, Guinea, Guinea-Bissau, Kenya, Lesotho, Liberia, Madagascar, Malawi, Mali, Mauritania, Mauritius, Mozambique, Namibia, Niger, Nigeria, Rwanda, Sao Tomé and Príncipe, Senegal, Seychelles, Sierra Leone, South Africa,

Swaziland, Togo, Uganda, United Republic of Tanzania, Zaire, Zambia, and Zimbabwe

Regional Office for Americas (AMRO/PAHO):
525 23rd Street, NW
Washington, DC 20037
(202) 974-3000
http://www.paho.org

Member countries: Antigua and Barbuda, Argentina, Bahamas, Barbados, Belize, Bolivia, Brazil, Canada, Chile, Colombia, Costa Rica, Cuba, Dominica, Dominican Republic, Ecuador, El Salvador, Grenada, Guatemala, Guyana, Haiti, Honduras, Jamaica, Mexico, Nicaragua, Panama, Paraguay, Peru, Puerto Rico (associate member), Saint Kitts and Nevis, Saint Lucia, Saint Vincent and the Grenadines, Suriname, Trinidad and Tobago, United States of America, Uruguay, and Venezuela

Regional Office for Southeast Asia (SEARO):
World Health House
Indraprastha Estate
Mahatma Gandhi Road
New Delhi 110002
India
(0091) 11.331.7804 or 11.331.7823
http://www.whosea.org

Member countries: Bangladesh, Bhutan, Democratic People's Republic of Korea, India, Indonesia, Maldives, Myanmar (Burma), Nepal, Sri Lanka, and Thailand

Regional Office for Europe (EURO):
8, Scherfigsvej
DK-2100 Copenhagen 0
Denmark
(0045) 39.17.17.17
http://www.who.dk

Member countries: Albania, Andorra, Armenia, Austria, Azerbaijan, Belarus, Belgium, Bosnia and Herzegovina, Bulgaria, Croatia, Czech Republic, Denmark, Estonia, Finland, France, Georgia, Germany, Greece, Hungary, Iceland, Ireland, Israel, Italy, Kazakhstan, Kyrgyzstan, Latvia, Lithuania, Luxembourg, Malta, Monaco, Netherlands, Norway, Poland, Portugal, Republic of Moldova, Romania, Russian Federation, San Marino, Slovakia, Slovenia, Spain, Sweden, Switzerland, Tajikistan, the Former Yugoslav Republic of Macedonia, Turkey, Turkmenistan, Ukraine, United Kingdom, Uzbekistan, and Yugoslavia.

Regional Office for the Eastern Mediterranean (EMRO):
WHO Post Office
Abdul Razak Al Sanhouri Street
Nasr City
Cairo 11371
Egypt
202 670 25 35
http://www.who.sci.eg

Member countries: Afghanistan, Bahrain, Cyprus, Djibouti, Egypt, Islamic Republic of Iran, Iraq, Jordan, Kuwait, Lebanon, Libyan Arab Jamahiriya, Morocco, Oman, Pakistan, Qatar, Saudi Arabia, Somalia, Sudan, Syrian Arab Republic, Tunisia, United Arab Emirates, and Yemen

Regional Office for the Western Pacific (WPRO):
P.O. Box 2932
1000 Manila
Philippines
(00632) 528.80.01
http://www.wpro.who.int

Member countries: Australia, Brunei Darusslam, Cambodia, China, Cook Islands, Fiji, Japan, Kiribati, Lao People's Democratic Republic, Malaysia, Marshall Islands, Federated States of Micronesia, Mongolia, Nauru, New Zealand, Niue, Palau, Papua New Guinea, Philippines, Republic of Korea, Singapore, Solomon Islands, Tokelau (associate member), Tonga, Tuvalu, Vanuatu, and Vietnam.

X Y Z

X rays Radiological films that are taken to detect FRACTURES and other medical problems. Physicians order X rays when they believe that there may be a break or damage to the bones and/or to the supporting structures of the body.

yard work Managing the area around one's house, such as mowing the lawn and trimming shrubs. Yard work becomes increasingly arduous for individuals as they age, although they may find it difficult to acknowledge this difficulty. Sometimes, yard work is the only exercise that some older individuals get. Many older people find great joy in caring for their plants and flowers and maintaining a pleasant appearance of their yard.

See also GARDENING.

zinc A common mineral. Some older individuals may develop a deficiency in zinc. Some experts believe that zinc deficiencies can lead to EATING DISORDERS. Zinc deficiencies are readily treatable with replacement zinc; however, older people and their CAREGIVERS should not self-diagnose or self-treat by purchasing zinc SUPPLEMENTS. Instead, they should consult with their physicians to determine if supplemental zinc is indicated and, if so, in what amount.

APPENDIXES

APPENDIX I
20 QUESTIONS ABOUT GLOBAL AGING

1. *True or false?* In the year 2000, children under the age of 15 still outnumbered elderly people (age 65 and older) in almost all nations of the world.

2. The world's elderly population is increasing by approximately how many people each month?

   a. 50,000   b. 300,000
   c. 500,000   d. 800,000

3. Which of the world's developing regions has the highest aggregate percentage of elderly?

   a. Africa   b. Latin America
   c. The Caribbean   d. Asia (excluding Japan)

4. China has the world's largest total population (more than 1.2 billion people). Which country has the world's largest elderly (65+) population?

   a. Japan   b. Germany
   c. China   d. Nigeria

5. *True or false?* More than half of the world's elderly today live in the industrialized nations of Europe, North America, and Japan.

6. Of the world's major countries, which had the highest percentage of elderly people in the year 2000?

   a. Sweden   b. Turkey
   c. Italy   d. France

7. *True or false?* Current demographic projections suggest that 35 percent of all people in the United States will be at least 65 years of age by the year 2050.

8. *True or false?* The number of the world's " oldest old" (people aged 80 and over) is growing more rapidly than that of the elderly as a whole.

9. More than one-third of the world's oldest old live in which three countries?

   a. Germany, the United States, and the United Kingdom
   b. India, China, and the United States
   c. Japan, China, and Brazil
   d. Russia, India, and Indonesia

10. Japan has the highest life expectancy at birth among the major countries of the world. How many years can the average Japanese baby born in 2000 expect to live?

    a. 70 years   b. 75 years
    c. 81 years   d. 85 years

11. *True or false?* Today in some countries life expectancy at birth is less than 40 years.

12. What are the leading killers of elderly women in Europe and North America?

    a. Cancers
    b. Circulatory diseases
    c. Respiratory diseases
    d. Accidents

13. *True or false?* Elderly women outnumber elderly men in all developing countries.

14. There are more older widows than widowers in virtually all countries because:

    a. Women live longer than men
    b. Women typically marry men older than themselves
    c. Men are more likely than women to remarry after divorce or the death of a spouse
    d. All of the above

15. In developed countries, recent declines in labor-force participation rates of older (55 and older) workers are due almost entirely to changing work patterns of

    a. Men   b. Women   c. Men and women

16. What proportion of the world's countries have a public old-age security program?

    a. All
    b. Three-fourths
    c. One-half
    d. One-fourth

17. Approximately what percent of the private sector labor force in the United States is covered by a private pension plan (as opposed to or in addition to Social Security)?

    a. 10 percent
    b. 25 percent
    c. 33 percent
    d. 60 percent

18. In which country are elderly people least likely to live alone?

    a. The Philippines
    b. Hungary
    c. Canada
    d. Denmark

19. *True or false?* In developing countries, older men are more likely than older women to be illiterate.

20. *True or false?* In most nations, large cities have younger populations (i.e., a lower percentage of elderly) than the country as a whole.

ANSWERS

1. **True**. Although the world's population is aging, children still outnumber the elderly in all major nations except six: Bulgaria, Germany, Greece, Italy, Japan, and Spain.

2. **d**. The estimated change in the total size of the world's elderly population between July 1999 and July 2000 was more than 9.5 million people, an average of 795,000 each month.

3. **c**. The Caribbean, with 7.2 percent of all people aged 65 or older. Corresponding figures for other regions are: Asia (excluding Japan), 5.5 percent; Latin America, 5.3 percent; and Africa, 3.1 percent.

4. **c**. China also has the largest elderly population, numbering nearly 88 million in 2000.

5. **False**. Although industrialized nations have higher percentages of elderly people than do most developing countries, 59 percent of the world's elderly now live in the developing countries of Africa, Asia, Latin America, the Caribbean, and Oceania.

6. **c**. Italy, with 18.1 percent of all people age 65 or over. In Monaco, a small principality of about 32,000 people located on the Mediterranean, more than 22 percent of residents are age 65 and over.

7. **False**. Although the United States will age rapidly when the baby boomers (people born between 1946 and 1964) begin to reach age 65 after the year 2010, the percent of population age 65 and over in the year 2050 is projected to be slightly above 20 percent (compared with about 13 percent today).

8. **True**. The oldest old are the fastest growing component of many national populations. The world's growth rate for the 80+ population from 1999 to 2000 was 3.5 percent, while that of the world's elderly (65+)population as a whole was 2.3 percent (compared with .3 percent for the total [all ages] population).

9. **b**. India has roughly 6.2 million people age 80 and over, China has 11.5 million, and the United States 9.2 million. Taken together, these people constitute nearly 38 percent of the world's oldest old.

10. **c**. 81 years, up from about 52 in 1947.

11. **True**. In some African countries (e.g., Malawi, Swaziland, Zambia, and Zimbabwe) where the HIV/AIDS epidemic is particularly devastating, average life expectancy at birth may be as much as 25 years lower than it otherwise would be in the absence of HIV/AIDS.

12. **b**. Circulatory diseases (especially heart disease and stroke) typically are the leading cause of death as reported by the World Health Organization. In Canada in 1995, for example, 44 percent of all deaths occurring to women at age 65 or older were attributed to circulatory disease. The percentage was virtually the same for elderly men.

13. **False**. Although there are more elderly women than elderly men in the vast majority of the world's countries, there are exceptions such as India, Iran, and Bangladesh.

14. **d**. All of the above.

15. **a**. From the late 1960s until very recently, labor force participation rates of older men in developed countries were declining virtually everywhere, whereas those for women were often holding steady or increasing. But because older men work in much greater numbers than do older women, increases in female participation were more than offset by falling male participation.

16. **b**. Of the 227 countries/areas of the world with populations of at least 5,000, 167 (74 percent) reported having some form of an old age/disability/survivors program circa 1999

17. **d**. The share of the private sector U.S. labor force covered by private pension plans was about 60 percent in the mid-1990s. However, not all employees who are covered by such plans actually participate in them.

18. **a**. The Philippines. The percentage of elderly people living alone in developing countries is usually much lower than that in developed countries; levels in the latter may exceed 40 percent.

19. **False**. Older women are less likely to be literate. In China in 1990, for example, only 11 percent of women age 60 and older could read and write, compared with half of men age 60 and older.

20. **We do not know**. Some literature from developed countries suggests that the statement is false; evidence from certain developing countries suggests that it is true. Both the Census Bureau's International Programs Center and the National Institute on Aging's Behavioral and Social Research Program would be most interested in empirical input from interested parties. Understanding global aging is a dialectical process.

APPENDIX II
POPULATION TABLES

TABLE I TOTAL POPULATION, PERCENT ELDERLY, AND PERCENT OLDEST OLD: 1975, 2000, 2015, 2030
(in thousands)

Country	1975				2000			
	Total population	Percent of population 65+	Percent of population 80+	80+ as a percent of 65+	Total population	Percent of population 65+	Percent of population 80+	80+ as a percent of 65+
United States	220,165	10.5	2.1	20.4	275,563	12.6	3.3	26.5
Western Europe								
Austria	7,579	14.9	2.3	15.5	8,131	15.4	3.4	22.2
Belgium	9,796	13.9	2.3	16.4	10,242	16.8	3.5	20.8
Denmark	5,060	13.4	2.4	18.0	5,336	14.9	4.0	26.7
France	52,699	13.5	2.5	18.3	59,330	16.0	3.7	23.3
Germany	78,679	14.8	2.2	14.6	82,797	16.2	3.5	21.6
Greece	9,047	12.2	2.1	17.1	10,602	17.3	3.5	20.2
Italy	55,441	12.0	1.9	16.0	57,634	18.1	4.0	22.2
Luxembourg	362	13.0	2.2	17.0	437	14.0	3.0	21.2
Norway	4,007	13.7	2.5	18.2	4,481	15.2	4.4	28.6
Sweden	8,193	15.1	2.7	17.8	8,873	17.3	5.0	29.2
United Kingdom	56,226	14.0	2.4	17.0	59,508	15.7	4.0	25.5
Eastern Europe								
Bulgaria	8,722	10.9	1.4	12.8	7,797	16.5	2.2	13.2
Czech Republic	9,997	12.9	1.7	13.5	10,272	13.9	2.4	17.1
Hungary	10,532	12.6	1.7	13.3	10,139	14.6	2.5	17.4
Poland	34,022	9.5	1.2	12.4	38,646	12.3	2.1	16.8
Russia	134,233	8.9	1.2	14.0	146,001	12.6	2.0	15.9
Ukraine	49,016	10.5	1.6	15.0	49,153	13.9	2.2	16.0
North America/Oceania								
Australia	13,900	8.7	1.5	17.4	19,165	12.4	3.0	24.0
Canada	23,209	8.4	1.6	19.3	31,278	12.7	3.1	24.8
New Zealand	3,083	8.7	1.4	16.4	3,820	11.5	2.9	25.0
Asia								
Bangladesh	76,582	3.6	0.3	8.4	129,194	3.3	0.5	15.0
China	927,808	4.4	0.6	12.5	1,261,832	7.0	0.9	13.1
India	620,701	3.8	0.3	8.1	1,014,004	4.6	0.6	13.1
Indonesia	135,666	3.2	0.3	8.6	224,784	4.5	0.4	10.0
Israel	3,455	7.8	1.0	12.3	5,842	9.9	2.4	23.9
Japan	111,524	7.9	1.1	13.5	126,550	17.0	3.7	21.7
Malaysia	12,258	3.7	0.5	13.3	21,793	4.1	0.5	13.5
Pakistan	74,734	3.0	0.3	10.9	141,554	4.1	0.5	13.3
Philippines	43,010	2.7	0.4	13.4	81,160	3.6	0.5	13.6
Singapore	2,263	4.1	0.4	9.7	4,152	6.8	1.5	21.3
South Korea	35,281	3.6	0.4	10.1	47,471	7.0	1.0	13.9
Sri Lanka	13,603	4.1	0.5	13.2	19,239	6.5	1.0	15.6
Thailand	41,359	3.0	0.3	10.9	61,231	6.4	0.9	13.9
Turkey	40,025	4.5	0.4	7.9	65,667	6.0	0.9	15.2
Latin America/Caribbean								
Argentina	26,049	7.6	0.9	12.1	36,955	10.4	2.2	21.7
Brazil	108,167	3.9	0.5	12.5	172,860	5.3	0.8	15.3
Chile	10,337	5.3	0.8	14.5	15,154	7.2	1.2	16.8
Colombia	25,381	3.6	0.4	11.8	39,686	4.7	0.6	12.2
Costa Rica	1,968	3.4	0.5	13.6	3,711	5.2	0.9	17.9
Guatemala	6,018	2.8	0.4	13.1	12,640	3.6	0.5	13.5
Jamaica	2,013	5.8	0.8	14.5	2,653	6.8	1.5	21.6
Mexico	59,099	4.0	0.7	17.9	100,350	4.3	0.6	14.9
Peru	15,161	3.5	0.3	9.1	27,013	4.7	0.7	15.0
Uruguay	2,829	9.6	1.6	16.9	3,334	12.9	2.7	21.2
Africa								
Egypt	38,841	4.2	0.4	9.7	68,360	3.8	0.4	10.2
Kenya	13,741	3.7	0.5	12.8	30,340	2.7	0.4	13.0
Liberia	1,609	3.7	0.9	23.3	3,164	3.4	0.6	16.8
Malawi	5,244	2.2	0.2	8.0	10,386	2.8	0.3	9.9
Morocco	17,305	3.7	0.5	14.2	30,122	4.6	0.7	14.2
Tunisia	5,668	3.5	0.5	13.1	9,593	6.0	0.8	13.3
Zimbabwe	6,143	2.6	0.3	9.9	11,343	3.5	0.5	14.7

TABLE I TOTAL POPULATION, PERCENT ELDERLY, AND PERCENT OLDEST OLD: 1975, 2000, 2015, 2030
(in thousands) *(continued)*

Country	2015				2030			
	Total population	Percent of population 65+	Percent of population 80+	80+ as a percent of 65+	Total population	Percent of population 65+	Percent of population 80+	80+ as a percent of 65+
United States	312,524	14.7	3.8	25.8	351,326	20.0	5.3	26.4
Western Europe								
Austria	8,316	18.8	4.9	26.2	8,278	25.2	7.0	27.9
Belgium	10,336	19.4	5.7	29.3	10,175	25.4	7.3	28.8
Denmark	5,521	18.9	4.4	23.6	5,649	23.0	7.1	30.8
France	61,545	18.8	5.8	30.9	61,926	24.0	7.5	31.2
Germany	85,192	20.2	5.4	26.6	84,939	25.8	7.2	28.1
Greece	10,735	20.6	6.3	30.5	10,316	25.4	7.8	30.8
Italy	56,631	22.2	6.8	30.5	52,868	28.1	9.0	32.1
Luxembourg	519	15.3	4.1	27.1	580	19.8	5.2	26.2
Norway	4,767	17.4	4.6	26.3	5,018	22.0	6.6	30.0
Sweden	8,900	21.4	5.7	26.8	8,868	25.1	8.6	34.3
United Kingdom	61,047	18.4	4.9	26.8	61,481	23.5	7.0	29.7
Eastern Europe								
Bulgaria	6,663	20.2	4.6	23.0	5,668	25.9	7.2	27.8
Czech Republic	10,048	18.8	4.2	22.3	9,409	24.7	7.4	30.0
Hungary	9,666	17.6	4.3	24.2	9,034	22.5	6.3	27.9
Poland	38,668	15.0	3.8	25.1	37,377	22.2	5.5	24.8
Russia	141,073	13.8	3.1	22.7	132,859	20.5	4.1	20.0
Ukraine	45,294	15.0	3.2	21.1	42,273	19.7	4.2	21.5
North America/Oceania								
Australia	21,697	15.8	4.1	25.9	23,497	21.1	6.0	28.5
Canada	35,653	16.1	4.3	26.8	39,128	22.9	6.2	26.9
New Zealand	4,396	13.7	3.5	25.7	4,768	17.8	5.0	28.2
Asia								
Bangladesh	160,486	4.4	0.6	12.5	184,478	7.2	1.0	13.5
China	1,397,414	9.5	1.7	18.0	1,483,121	16.0	2.9	18.3
India	1,241,572	5.9	0.9	14.5	1,437,103	9.0	1.4	15.7
Indonesia	275,152	6.2	1.1	16.9	312,592	10.9	1.7	15.6
Israel	6,992	11.1	3.0	26.6	7,873	14.9	3.9	26.5
Japan	125,843	24.9	7.0	28.2	116,740	28.3	11.1	39.3
Malaysia	28,414	5.9	0.8	14.3	35,306	9.4	1.6	16.9
Pakistan	185,715	4.5	0.7	15.0	226,251	6.5	0.9	14.4
Philippines	106,098	4.9	0.7	14.6	129,448	7.7	1.2	15.9
Singapore	6,646	8.7	2.1	24.1	9,047	14.8	3.0	20.4
South Korea	52,239	11.3	2.2	19.3	53,763	19.5	4.2	21.3
Sri Lanka	21,527	9.5	1.7	17.7	22,937	15.2	3.1	20.2
Thailand	68,139	9.8	1.8	18.0	71,311	16.4	3.1	19.3
Turkey	76,685	7.9	1.6	19.9	84,195	12.9	2.4	18.7
Latin America/Caribbean								
Argentina	42,916	11.8	3.1	26.0	47,229	14.7	4.0	27.3
Brazil	192,313	8.1	1.5	18.7	203,489	13.2	2.7	20.6
Chile	17,405	10.7	2.1	19.3	18,915	16.4	3.7	22.3
Colombia	49,189	6.5	1.0	15.6	57,666	11.5	1.8	15.9
Costa Rica	4,583	7.3	1.4	19.2	5,272	12.8	2.4	18.9
Guatemala	18,105	4.1	0.7	17.8	24,038	5.6	1.0	17.6
Jamaica	2,992	7.4	1.8	24.1	3,353	12.5	2.3	18.7
Mexico	121,712	6.3	1.0	16.6	139,125	10.2	1.9	18.7
Peru	33,551	6.4	1.2	18.3	39,253	9.9	1.9	19.0
Uruguay	3,730	13.5	3.8	28.2	4,109	15.5	4.4	28.1
Africa								
Egypt	85,219	5.1	0.6	11.9	99,583	8.0	1.1	14.2
Kenya	33,612	3.8	0.6	16.6	34,836	5.2	1.1	20.7
Liberia	4,655	4.0	0.8	21.1	6,745	4.2	1.0	24.9
Malawi	12,017	3.1	0.4	12.7	12,817	3.2	0.6	17.5
Morocco	37,832	5.5	1.0	17.4	44,664	9.1	1.4	15.2
Tunisia	11,174	7.6	1.5	19.8	12,322	12.7	2.3	17.7
Zimbabwe	10,548	5.0	1.0	20.2	9,086	6.4	1.8	27.7

Source: United Nations, 1999 and U.S. Census Bureau, 2000a.

TABLE II POPULATION BY AGE: 2000 AND 2030 (in thousands)

Country	All ages	0 to 24 years	25 to 54 years	55 to 64 years	65 to 69 years	70 to 74 years	75 to 79 years	80 years and over
		2000						
United States	275,563	97,064	119,662	24,001	9,436	8,753	7,422	9,225
Western Europe								
Austria	8,131	2,325	3,629	926	347	332	294	278
Belgium	10,242	3,033	4,432	1,052	521	462	383	358
Denmark	5,336	1,594	2,340	610	219	194	167	212
France	59,330	18,852	25,513	5,471	2,711	2,466	2,100	2,216
Germany	82,797	22,309	36,224	10,813	4,104	3,592	2,846	2,911
Greece	10,602	3,088	4,480	1,195	605	521	341	371
Italy	57,634	14,873	25,640	6,696	3,093	2,766	2,253	2,313
Luxembourg	437	133	199	44	19	17	12	13
Norway	4,481	1,435	1,937	426	167	164	156	196
Sweden	8,873	2,655	3,674	1,010	380	363	343	447
United Kingdom	59,508	18,549	25,496	6,138	2,585	2,347	2,018	2,373
Eastern Europe								
Bulgaria	7,797	2,354	3,255	902	453	382	282	169
Czech Republic	10,272	3,250	4,505	1,093	448	409	323	244
Hungary	10,139	3,207	4,336	1,113	479	420	326	257
Poland	38,646	13,915	16,676	3,319	1,616	1,372	953	794
Russia	146,001	49,232	64,197	14,160	5,996	6,182	3,299	2,936
Ukraine	49,153	16,052	20,607	5,647	2,080	2,294	1,377	1,096
North America/Oceania								
Australia	19,165	6,629	8,427	1,727	668	633	509	573
Canada	31,278	10,154	14,322	2,838	1,147	1,012	822	984
New Zealand	3,820	1,417	1,637	324	124	116	91	110
Asia								
Bangladesh	129,194	76,298	42,947	5,645	1,744	1,206	710	643
China	1,261,832	515,155	572,082	86,822	34,926	25,426	15,908	11,513
India	1,014,004	536,947	373,956	56,037	18,477	13,785	8,627	6,175
Indonesia	224,784	113,419	88,231	13,080	4,616	2,872	1,559	1,006
Israel	5,842	2,617	2,257	391	168	152	120	138
Japan	126,550	34,782	53,858	16,385	7,031	5,812	4,012	4,670
Malaysia	21,793	11,583	8,175	1,152	353	260	151	119
Pakistan	141,554	86,109	43,165	6,485	2,317	1,637	1,071	770
Philippines	81,160	46,410	28,087	3,717	1,220	820	504	401
Singapore	4,152	1,333	2,281	253	98	76	49	61
South Korea	47,471	18,091	22,191	3,875	1,365	895	594	460
Sri Lanka	19,239	8,759	7,933	1,295	455	358	244	195
Thailand	61,231	25,879	27,045	4,386	1,591	1,086	699	545
Turkey	65,667	32,182	25,619	3,935	1,514	1,099	721	597
Latin America/Caribbean								
Argentina	36,955	16,326	13,856	2,946	1,209	1,026	761	831
Brazil	172,860	84,691	68,842	10,136	3,501	2,594	1,693	1,403
Chile	15,154	6,733	6,194	1,133	391	310	210	184
Colombia	39,686	19,897	15,867	2,071	742	546	338	225
Costa Rica	3,711	1,888	1,438	193	70	53	35	34
Guatemala	12,640	7,922	3,765	496	184	132	79	62
Jamaica	2,653	1,312	1,027	135	56	48	36	39
Mexico	100,350	54,699	36,241	5,092	1,722	1,197	757	642
Peru	27,013	14,735	9,606	1,409	500	351	223	189
Uruguay	3,334	1,348	1,257	298	138	118	84	91
Africa								
Egypt	68,360	37,706	24,572	3,509	1,162	748	401	261
Kenya	30,340	20,064	8,423	1,021	340	237	146	108
Liberia	3,164	1,985	929	141	43	29	19	18
Malawi	10,386	6,955	2,757	385	126	85	49	28
Morocco	30,122	16,826	10,472	1,434	538	393	262	197
Tunisia	9,593	4,834	3,638	542	223	173	106	77
Zimbabwe	11,343	7,281	3,238	422	156	112	74	59

TABLE II POPULATION BY AGE: 2000 AND 2030 (in thousands) *(continued)*

Country	All ages	2030 0 to 24 years	25 to 54 years	55 to 64 years	65 to 69 years	70 to 74 years	75 to 79 years	80 years and over
United States	351,326	115,218	128,484	37,305	19,844	17,878	14,029	18,569
Western Europe								
Austria	8,278	1,916	3,034	1,244	636	500	367	582
Belgium	10,175	2,553	3,683	1,357	709	628	501	744
Denmark	5,649	1,515	2,076	760	357	295	246	400
France	61,926	16,405	22,599	8,073	3,775	3,435	3,005	4,635
Germany	84,939	20,074	31,104	11,886	6,502	5,192	4,036	6,145
Greece	10,316	2,287	3,814	1,594	692	620	503	807
Italy	52,868	10,165	18,788	9,033	4,115	3,307	2,685	4,775
Luxembourg	580	164	229	72	35	29	22	30
Norway	5,018	1,405	1,856	653	295	261	217	331
Sweden	8,868	2,210	3,267	1,167	555	482	424	763
United Kingdom	61,481	16,077	22,663	8,296	4,215	3,336	2,598	4,296
Eastern Europe								
Bulgaria	5,668	1,096	2,240	866	381	362	315	408
Czech Republic	9,409	1,933	3,718	1,436	583	532	512	696
Hungary	9,034	2,012	3,662	1,330	485	506	472	566
Poland	37,377	9,260	15,184	4,642	2,087	2,267	1,882	2,056
Russia	132,859	35,650	53,589	16,428	8,288	7,776	5,681	5,446
Ukraine	42,273	11,383	17,099	5,479	2,553	2,292	1,683	1,783
North America/Oceania								
Australia	23,497	6,643	8,941	2,960	1,356	1,212	975	1,410
Canada	39,128	10,368	14,987	4,800	2,581	2,249	1,728	2,414
New Zealand	4,768	1,400	1,914	607	233	209	166	238
Asia								
Bangladesh	184,478	71,167	84,043	16,060	5,248	3,821	2,356	1,783
China	1,483,121	437,787	588,812	219,501	84,958	59,230	49,367	43,466
India	1,437,103	558,161	614,683	135,423	49,013	35,886	23,744	20,194
Indonesia	312,592	112,472	132,916	33,067	12,612	9,740	6,450	5,335
Israel	7,873	2,724	3,154	825	327	288	246	310
Japan	116,740	25,589	40,441	17,661	7,094	6,391	6,562	13,002
Malaysia	35,306	15,017	13,891	3,063	1,236	919	617	563
Pakistan	226,251	95,929	98,625	17,008	5,826	4,186	2,568	2,109
Philippines	129,448	55,474	53,369	10,581	3,738	2,814	1,877	1,596
Singapore	9,047	2,345	4,158	1,204	468	360	239	274
South Korea	53,763	14,515	20,967	7,819	3,470	2,959	1,803	2,231
Sri Lanka	22,937	7,102	9,580	2,771	1,142	945	694	703
Thailand	71,311	21,219	28,987	9,441	3,927	3,189	2,303	2,245
Turkey	84,195	26,295	36,793	10,231	3,940	2,899	2,002	2,036
Latin America/Caribbean								
Argentina	47,229	16,082	19,374	4,834	1,963	1,705	1,376	1,895
Brazil	203,489	66,334	87,458	22,898	9,091	7,080	5,099	5,530
Chile	18,915	5,863	7,817	2,133	1,006	823	582	691
Colombia	57,666	21,940	23,069	6,034	2,481	1,872	1,217	1,053
Costa Rica	5,272	1,796	2,248	554	235	188	124	127
Guatemala	24,038	12,128	9,105	1,455	493	368	252	238
Jamaica	3,353	1,062	1,447	425	158	110	73	78
Mexico	139,125	52,128	58,225	14,646	5,165	3,700	2,621	2,639
Peru	39,253	14,952	16,694	3,735	1,394	1,031	711	736
Uruguay	4,109	1,444	1,593	434	183	156	119	179
Africa								
Egypt	99,583	38,878	43,516	9,212	3,144	2,261	1,437	1,136
Kenya	34,836	15,729	15,402	1,902	610	472	349	373
Liberia	6,745	3,958	2,213	292	92	69	50	70
Malawi	12,817	6,856	5,087	466	144	111	81	71
Morocco	44,664	17,220	19,141	4,225	1,546	1,180	735	618
Tunisia	12,322	3,806	5,428	1,517	581	442	270	278
Zimbabwe	9,086	4,622	3,566	317	146	147	127	161

Source: U.S. Census Bureau, 2000a.

TABLE III LABOR FORCE PARTICIPATION OF OLDER INDIVIDUALS WORLDWIDE, BY SEX

Country	Year	Males 60 to 64 years	Males 65 years and over	Females 60 to 64 years	Females 65 years and over
United States	1970	73.0	24.8	36.1	10.0
	1980	60.4	19.3	34.0	8.2
	1982	57.9	17.7	34.2	7.9
	1991	54.8	15.8	35.1	8.6
	1996	54.3	16.9	38.2	8.6
	1999	54.8	16.9	38.8	8.9
Western Europe					
Austria	1971	44.9	8.0	13.2	3.2
	1981	23.3	3.1	9.5	1.8
	1988	14.2	1.8	5.7	0.9
	1996	16.7	4.6	8.7	2.0
Belgium	1970	79.3	6.8	7.6	2.2
	1977	42.1	4.2	5.8	1.2
	1981	32.3	3.3	5.7	1.0
	1997	18.4	1.9	4.6	0.7
	1999	18.6	2.8	6.7	0.8
Denmark	1970	81.3	23.5	24.9	4.6
	1976	79.3	24.0	30.1	4.8
	1979	62.0	16.3	32.5	4.3
	1986	49.6	12.8	26.6	3.3
	1996	42.0	18.5	20.5	8.7
France	1975	54.6	10.7	27.9	5.0
	1982	39.1	5.0	22.3	2.2
	1984	29.9	4.3	18.0	2.1
	1990	18.1	2.8	16.7	1.5
	1996	16.4	2.3	15.2	2.0
Germany	1970	68.8	16.0	17.7	5.7
	1980	44.2	7.4	13.0	3.0
	1988	34.5	4.9	11.1	1.8
	1996	28.7	4.4	11.3	1.6
	1999	30.3	4.5	12.7	1.6
Greece	1971	(NA)	33.4	(NA)	8.4
	1981	61.7	26.2	13.4	5.0
	1987	53.5	14.0	22.0	5.1
	1997	47.8	10.7	20.3	3.4
	1998	45.4	9.7	21.2	3.6
Italy	1971	40.6	13.4	9.9	3.2
	1981	29.1	6.9	8.0	1.5
	1989	35.2	7.9	9.8	2.2
	1996	30.6	6.0	8.2	1.8
	1998	31.7	6.3	8.1	1.7
Luxembourg	1970	45.5	10.1	12.0	4.0
	1981	28.0	6.5	12.4	2.8
	1987	21.2	3.8	10.3	1.0
	1996	16.7	2.5	5.1	0.9
	1999	15.5	1.9	11.7	0.6
Norway	1970	73.6	15.7	628.0	73.7
	1980	62.7	12.6	632.2	72.9
	1985	72.7	27.1	35.9	14.0
	1989	64.9	23.6	44.1	11.8
	1996	62.5	16.5	48.9	9.3
	1999	61.1	13.4	49.5	8.8
Sweden	1970	75.7	15.2	25.7	3.2
	1975	68.5	11.0	35.1	3.5
	1980	65.9	8.1	41.4	2.6
	1985	63.2	11.3	45.6	3.1
	1996	59.7	(NA)	49.8	(NA)
	1999	55.5	(NA)	46.5	(NA)
United Kingdom	1971	86.4	19.4	27.8	6.4
	1981	74.6	10.7	22.5	3.7
	1986	53.4	7.5	18.8	2.7
	1993	52.2	7.4	24.7	3.5
	1999	(NA)	(NA)	(NA)	(NA)

Country	Year	Males 60 to 64 years	Males 65 years and over	Females 60 to 64 years	Females 65 years and over
Eastern Europe					
Bulgaria	1975	33.6	10.3	8.2	1.7
	1985	39.2	15.2	16.5	4.3
	1992	11.1	4.5	4.7	2.1
Czech Republic	1970	33.3	14.6	18.2	5.2
	1980	46.3	19.5	21.5	6.5
	1991	28.4	11.6	16.2	4.9
	1997	30.3	8.9	13.3	2.7
	1999	27.5	7.2	12.9	2.7
Hungary	1970	43.7	16.7	17.1	5.8
	1980	13.2	4.0	8.7	2.9
	1996	9.2	4.3	6.0	2.1
	1999	10.6	3.8	5.5	81.6
Poland	1970	83.0	56.4	51.1	33.0
	1978	62.4	34.9	37.4	19.4
	1996	33.4	15.3	19.2	8.5
Russia	1989	35.4	14.2	20.4	6.4
	1992	38.1	20.7	21.0	11.0
	1996	19.0	(NA)	7.2	(NA)
	1999	29.2	6.4	16.0	2.5
Ukraine	1989	32.0	10.9	15.3	4.5
	1995	34.3	(NA)	22.1	(NA)
	1999	28.3	9.8	16.7	6.0
North America/Oceania					
Australia	1971	75.6	22.2	16.0	4.2
	1976	68.4	16.8	18.2	5.1
	1981	53.1	12.3	15.5	4.9
	1986	44.8	9.0	13.6	3.0
	1997	45.7	10.1	18.9	2.9
	1999	46.7	9.6	18.3	3.1
Canada	1971	74.1	23.6	29.1	8.3
	1976	69.1	19.2	27.6	6.9
	1981	68.8	17.3	28.3	6.0
	1986	59.9	14.6	27.5	4.7
	1996	44.7	10.3	23.8	3.5
	1999	46.6	9.9	26.0	3.4
New Zealand	1971	69.2	21.3	15.5	3.5
	1976	57.9	16.2	13.9	2.8
	1981	45.7	10.9	11.7	1.9
	1989	33.8	10.6	14.4	3.5
. . . .	1992	33.5	8.8	15.7	2.9
	1997	50.5	8.9	29.3	3.0
	1999	57.4	10.4	32.5	3.9
Africa					
Egypt	1976	77.9	40.9	2.2	1.0
	1986	68.3	25.5	2.0	0.7
	1995	76.4	36.5	6.6	2.1
	1998	61.8	33.5	6.5	2.1
Liberia	1974	80.3	66.0	23.7	16.2
	1984	85.8	69.7	49.5	32.5
Malawi	1977	(NA)	83.6	(NA)	55.3
	1987	94.2	85.3	84.3	71.9
Morocco	1971	63.3	33.5	7.7	3.8
	1982	68.9	42.1	11.2	5.3
	1990	38.1	(NA)	8.9	(NA)
	1995	33.5	(NA)	7.7	(NA)
	1999	43.7	(NA)	13.0	(NA)
Tunisia	1975	66.5	38.0	8.6	4.8
	1984	59.2	38.5	4.4	3.5
	1994	54.6	31.5	7.3	3.3
	1997	54.1	34.0	7.7	3.5

TABLE III LABOR FORCE PARTICIPATION OF OLDER INDIVIDUALS WORLDWIDE, BY SEX (continued)

Country	Year	Males 60 to 64 years	Males 65 years and over	Females 60 to 64 years	Females 65 years and over	Country	Year	Males 60 to 64 years	Males 65 years and over	Females 60 to 64 years	Females 65 years and over
Zimbabwe	1969	43.1	24.9	9.0	2.7	Thailand	1970	74.6	44.6	47.5	21.2
	1982	69.1	(NA)	31.5	(NA)		1976	54.9	(NA)	23.2	(NA)
	1992	77.5	52.0	40.0	21.7		1980	67.8	39.3	43.1	19.0
Asia							1994	47.2	(NA)	23.5	(NA)
Bangladesh	1974	(NA)	84.2	(NA)	3.3		1997	46.4	(NA)	26.0	(NA)
	1981	84.7	68.7	4.5	3.6		1999	43.9	(NA)	21.1	(NA)
	1986	93.4	70.4	9.0	10.9	Turkey	1970	83.0	67.8	47.6	35.1
	1995	88.9	71.2	41.1	27.1		1975	76.8	64.9	40.7	27.9
China	1982	63.7	30.1	16.9	4.7		1980	67.4	43.9	36.3	20.8
	1990	63.7	33.6	27.4	8.4		1988	59.2	33.8	20.9	10.9
India	1971	73.8	(NA)	10.5	(NA)		1996	54.0	33.6	23.4	13.3
	1981	65.0	(NA)	14.0	(NA)	**Latin America/**					
	1991	71.4	42.3	20.8	8.2	**Caribbean**					
Indonesia	1971	79.3	62.9	35.2	24.5	Argentina	1970	57.2	29.1	10.3	4.7
	1976	87.5	69.7	48.4	31.2		1980	51.9	17.9	9.8	3.2
	1980	76.7	53.4	32.9	19.0		1989	56.1	23.5	11.2	3.7
	1988	79.2	56.3	46.1	25.4		1995	63.2	27.6	22.6	8.9
	1992	79.7	56.8	42.7	25.1	Brazil	1970	73.5	49.8	11.4	6.3
	1996	87.9	56.1	42.7	26.3		1980	57.5	21.8	10.3	2.8
	1999	66.5	(NA)	34.0	(NA)		1986	44.6	(NA)	99.5	(NA)
Israel	1972	(NA)	34.5	(NA)	7.2		1996	46.9	(NA)	18.5	(NA)
	1983	78.2	32.2	22.0	9.2		1998	47.5	(NA)	19.1	(NA)
	1989	66.3	21.4	19.0	6.3	Chile	1970	72.1	42.4	11.1	6.5
	1996	59.0	16.9	19.9	5.1		1982	61.5	25.5	10.1	4.5
	1999	56.4	14.6	23.6	4.6		1992	66.6	31.5	19.2	6.3
Japan	1970	85.8	54.5	43.3	19.7		1997	69.0	27.9	17.1	6.9
	1975	85.4	49.7	39.2	15.8		1999	69.2	27.4	21.0	6.5
	1980	81.5	46.0	38.8	16.1	Colombia	1973	72.9	49.6	12.4	8.1
	1985	78.3	41.6	37.9	15.2		1985	58.4	(NA)	16.7	(NA)
	1989	71.4	35.8	39.2	15.7		1996	51.7	24.4	15.7	6.1
	1996	74.5	36.7	39.0	15.4		1999	55.4	25.2	19.3	5.4
	1999	74.1	35.5	39.8	14.9	Costa Rica	1973	86.0	57.1	7.8	3.9
Malaysia	1970	66.1	46.6	25.1	13.7		1984	69.6	38.9	6.9	3.1
	1980	69.5	49.7	26.7	19.0		1989	45.3	(NA)	6.4	(NA)
	1991	53.3	31.8	14.6	6.7		1996	51.4	21.1	9.1	2.8
	1999	59.2	(NA)	20.8	(NA)		1999	58.2	26.7	11.8	3.8
Pakistan	1972	85.6	65.7	8.6	8.9	Guatemala	1973	87.7	69.8	10.2	7.1
	1981	75.7	(NA)	2.3	(NA)		1981	85.8	66.9	9.0	6.5
	1989	81.0	55.7	9.4	2.4		1987	88.5	63.3	20.6	13.7
	1994	78.8	52.7	11.8	7.4		1994	81.6	61.9	11.0	7.9
Philippines	1970	79.3	56.5	28.6	17.7	1998–9		87.2	71.4	41.0	28.8
	1975	84.3	62.6	19.6	13.7	Jamaica	1975	(NA)	64.7	(NA)	27.0
	1978	(NA)	60.6	(NA)	23.1		1978	(NA)	65.6	(NA)	30.7
	1983	(NA)	60.1	(NA)	28.0		1982	64.7	37.9	23.7	9.8
	1989	(NA)	59.0	(NA)	29.4		1988	(NA)	52.4	(NA)	24.9
	1996	(NA)	57.3	(NA)	29.0		1990	(NA)	53.6	(NA)	23.6
	1999	(NA)	54.5	(NA)	29.8	Mexico	1970	81.5	67.1	14.4	11.8
Singapore	1970	55.6	31.9	13.4	6.5		1980	85.6	68.6	24.1	18.6
	1980	52.5	28.6	11.3	6.4		1988	77.5	58.4	23.2	16.9
	1989	48.2	20.7	11.0	5.0		1996	74.1	52.0	23.8	14.1
	1996	48.6	21.7	14.9	5.2		1999	77.3	52.4	25.9	14.6
South Korea	1970	67.9	35.1	26.9	10.6	Peru	1972	83.9	61.5	13.4	8.5
	1975	68.3	34.4	33.6	12.0		1981	88.5	63.2	23.4	12.5
	1980	68.9	40.6	31.3	13.0		1989	75.0	34.6	23.9	12.0
	1989	65.6	39.0	41.6	18.1		1999	72.5	41.1	38.2	19.2
	1992	71.0	42.3	44.9	19.6	Uruguay	1975	58.9	20.9	12.2	3.6
	1996	54.5	(NA)	29.2	(NA)		1985	51.8	16.2	13.3	3.6
	1999	65.5	40.2	46.3	21.4		1995	59.3	19.4	23.9	6.7
Sri Lanka	1971	63.4	40.3	8.4	3.6						
	1981	56.6	35.7	6.9	3.8						
	1996	38.6	(NA)	7.8	(NA)						
	1999	43.3	(NA)	9.8	(NA)						

NA–Not available

TABLE IV   POPULATION 65 YEARS AND OLDER, FOR 2000

Area	Total population	Population 65 years and older	
		Number	Percent
United States	**281,421,906**	**34,991,753**	**12.4**
Alabama	4,447,100	579,798	13.0
Alaska	626,932	35,699	5.7
Arizona	5,130,632	667,839	13.0
Arkansas	2,673,400	374,019	14.0
California	33,871,648	3,595,658	10.6
Colorado	4,301,261	416,073	9.7
Connecticut	3,405,565	470,183	13.8
Delaware	783,600	101,726	13.0
District of Columbia	572,059	69,898	12.2
Florida	15,982,378	2,807,597	17.6
Georgia	8,186,453	785,275	9.6
Hawaii	1,211,537	160,601	13.3
Idaho	1,293,953	145,916	11.3
Illinois	12,419,293	1,500,025	12.1
Indiana	6,080,485	752,831	12.4
Iowa	2,926,324	436,213	14.9
Kansas	2,688,418	356,229	13.3
Kentucky	4,041,769	504,793	12.5
Louisiana	4,468,976	516,929	11.6
Maine	1,274,923	183,402	14.4
Maryland	5,296,486	599,307	11.3
Massachusetts	6,349,097	860,162	13.5
Michigan	9,938,444	1,219,018	12.3
Minnesota	4,919,479	594,266	12.1
Mississippi	2,844,658	343,523	12.1
Missouri	5,595,211	755,379	13.5
Montana	902,195	120,949	13.4
Nebraska	1,711,263	232,195	13.6
Nevada	1,998,257	218,929	11.0
New Hampshire	1,235,786	147,970	12.0
New Jersey	8,414,350	1,113,136	13.2
New Mexico	1,819,046	212,225	11.7
New York	18,976,457	2,448,352	12.9
North Carolina	8,049,313	969,048	12.0
North Dakota	642,200	94,478	14.7
Ohio	11,353,140	1,507,757	13.3
Oklahoma	3,450,654	455,950	13.2
Oregon	3,421,399	438,177	12.8
Pennsylvania	12,281,054	1,919,165	15.6
Rhode Island	1,048,319	152,402	14.5
South Carolina	4,012,012	485,333	12.1
South Dakota	754,844	108,131	14.3
Tennessee	5,689,283	703,311	12.4
Texas	20,851,820	2,072,532	9.9
Utah	2,233,169	190,222	8.5
Vermont	608,827	77,510	12.7
Virginia	7,078,515	792,333	11.2
Washington	5,894,121	662,148	11.2
West Virginia	1,808,344	276,895	15.3
Wisconsin	5,363,675	702,553	13.1
Wyoming	493,782	57,693	11.7

Source: U.S. Census Bureau

APPENDIX III
IMPORTANT ORGANIZATIONS

AARP
601 E Street, NW
Washington, DC 20049
(800) 424-3410 or (202) 434-2277
http://www.aarp.org

Administration on Aging (AoA)
Department of Health and Human Services (DHHS)
330 Independence Avenue, SW
Washington, DC 20201
(202) 619-0724
http://www.aoa.gov

Agency for Healthcare Research & Quality (AHRQ)
Publications Clearinghouse
P.O. Box 8547
Silver Spring, MD 20907
(800) 358-9295
http://www.ahrq.gov

Alliance for Aging Research
2021 K Street, NW
Suite 305
Washington, DC 20006
(202) 293-2856
http://www.agingresearch.org

Alzheimer's Disease and Related Disorders Association, Inc.
919 North Michigan Avenue
Suite 1100
Chicago, IL 60611
(800) 272-3900 or (312) 335-8700
(312) 335-8882 (TTY)
http://www.alz.org

Alzheimer's Disease Education and Referral (ADEAR) Center
P.O. Box 8250
Silver Spring, MD 20907
(800) 438-4380 or (301) 495-3311
http://www.alzheimer's org

American Academy of Family Physicians (AAFP)
11400 Tomahawk Creek Parkway
Leawood, KS 66211
(800) 274-2237 (toll-free)
http://familydoctor.org

American Academy of Neurology
1080 Montreal Avenue
St. Paul, MN 55116
(651) 695-1940
http://www.aan.com

American Academy of Ophthalmology
P.O. Box 7424
San Francisco, CA 94120
(800) 222-3937 or (415) 561-8500
http://www.eyenet.org

American Academy of Orthopaedic Surgeons
P.O. Box 2058
Des Plaines, IL 60017
(800) 824-BONE (toll-free)
http://www.aaos.org

American Academy of Physical Medicine and Rehabilitation
One IBM Plaza
Suite 2500
Chicago, IL 60611
(312) 464-9700
http://www.aapmr.org

American Association for Geriatric Psychiatry
7910 Woodmont Avenue
Suite 1050
Bethesda, MD 20814
(301) 654-7850
http://www.aagponline.org

American Association of Cardiovascular and Pulmonary Rehabilitation
7600 Terrace Avenue
Suite 203
Middleton, WI 53562
(608) 831-6989
http://www.aacvpr.org

American Association of Homes and Services for the Aging (AAHSA)
2519 Connecticut Avenue, NW
Washington, DC 20008
(202) 783-2242
http://www.aahsa.org

American Association of Critical Care Nurses (AACN)
100 Columbia
Aliso Viejo, CA 92656
(800) 899-2226 (toll-free)
http://www.aacn.org

American Association of Homes and Services for the Aging (AAHSA)
2519 Connecticut Avenue, NW
Washington, DC 20008
(202) 783-2242
http://www.aahsa.org

American Association of Neurological Surgeons
5550 Meadowbrook Drive
Rolling Meadows, IL 60088
(847) 378-0500 or (888) 566-2267 (toll-free)
http://www.aans.org

American Back Society
St. Joseph's Professional Center
2647 International Boulevard
Suite 401
Oakland, CA 94601
(510) 536-9929
http://www.americanbacksoc.org

American Bar Association Commission on the Legal Problems of the Elderly
740 15th Street, NW
Washington, DC 20005
(202) 662-8690
http://www.abanet.org/elderly

American Brain Tumor Association
2720 River Road
Suite 146
Des Plaines, IL 60018

(800) 886-2282 (toll-free) or (847) 827-9910
http://www.abta.org

American Cancer Society
1599 Clifton Road, NE
Atlanta, GA 30329
(800) 227-2345 or (404) 320-3333
http://www.cancer.org

American Chiropractic Association
1701 Clarendon Boulevard
Arlington, VA 22209
(800) 986-4636 or (703) 276-8800
http://www.amerchiro.org

American Chronic Pain Association
P.O. Box 850
Rocklin, CA 95677
(916) 632-0922
http://www.theacpa.org

American College of Obstetricians and Gynecologists (ACOG)
409 12th Street, SW
P.O. Box 96920
Washington, DC 20090
(202) 863-2518
http://www.acog.org

American College of Physicians, American Society of Internal Medicine (ACP-ASIM)
190 North Independence Mall West
Philadelphia, PA 19106
(800) 523-1546 or (215) 351-2400
http://www.acponline.org

American College of Surgeons (ACS)
633 North St. Clair Street
Chicago, IL 60611
(312) 202-5000
http://www.facs.org

American Council of the Blind
1155 15th Street, NW
Suite 1004
Washington, DC 20005
(800) 424-8666 or (202) 467-5081
http://www.acb.org

American College of Rheumatology
1800 Century Place
Suite 250
Atlanta, GA 30345

(404) 633-3777
http://www.rheumatology.org

American Dental Association
211 East Chicago Avenue
Chicago, IL 60611
(312) 440-2593
http://www.ada.org

American Diabetes Association
1701 North Beauregard Street
Arlington, VA 22311
(800) DIABETES or (703) 549-1500

American Dietetic Association
216 West Jackson Boulevard
Chicago, IL 60606
(800) 366-1655 or (312) 899-0040
http://www.eatright.org

American Federation for Aging Research (AFAR)
1414 Sixth Avenue
18th Floor
New York, NY 10019
(212) 752-2327
http://www.afar.org

American Foundation for the Blind
11 Penn Plaza
Suite 300
New York, NY 10001
(800) AFB-LINE
(212) 502-7662 (TTY)
http://www.afb.org

American Foundation for Suicide Prevention
120 Wall Street
22nd Floor
New York, NY 10005
(212) 363-3500 or (888) 333-2377
http://www.afsp.org

American Foundation for Urologic Diseases
1128 North Charles Street
Baltimore, MD 21201
(410) 468-1800
http://www.afud.org

American Geriatrics Society
350 Fifth Avenue
New York, NY 10118
(800) 247-4779
http://www.americangeriatrics.org
   or www.healthinaging.org

American Health Assistance Foundation
15825 Shady Grove Road
Suite 140
Rockville, MD 20850
(800) 437-2423 or (301) 948-3244
http://www.ahaf.org

American Health Care Association (AHCA)
1201 L Street, NW
Washington, DC 20005
(202) 842-4444
http://www.ahca.org

American Health Foundation
1 Dana Road
Valhalla, NY 10595
(914) 592-2600
http://www.ahf.org

American Heart Association (AHA)
7272 Greenville Avenue
Dallas, TX 75231
(800) 242-8721 or (888) 4-STROKE
http://www.americanheart.org

American Hospital Association (AHA)
One North Franklin
Chicago, IL 60606
(312) 422-3000
http://www.aha.org

American Institute for Cancer Research
1759 R Street, NW
Washington, DC 20009
(202) 328-7744 or (800) 843-8114
http://www.aicr.org

American Lung Association
1740 Broadway
New York, NY 10019
(800) LUNG-USA or (212) 315-8700
http://www.lungusa.org

American Medical Association (AMA)
515 North State Street
Chicago, IL 60610
(800) 621-8335 or (312) 464-5000
http://www.ama-assn.org

American Menopause Foundation
350 Fifth Avenue, Suite 2822
New York, NY 10118
(212) 714-2398
http://www.americanmenopause.org

American Mental Health Counselor's Association
801 N. Fairfax Street, Suite 304
Alexandria, VA 22314
(703) 548-6002
http://www.amhca.org

American Nurses Association
600 Maryland Avenue, SW
Suite 100 West
Washington, DC 20024
(202) 554-4444
http://www.nursingworld.org

American Occupational Therapy Association, Inc.
4720 Montgomery Lane
P.O. Box 31220
Bethesda, MD 20824
(800) 729-2682 or (301) 652-2682
(800) 377-8555 (TTY)
http://www.aota.org

American Optometric Association
243 North Lindbergh Boulevard
St. Louis, MO 63141
(800) 365-2219 or (314) 991-4100
http://www.aaoanet.org

American Pain Society
4700 West Lake Avenue
Glenview, IL 60025
(847) 375-4715
http://www.ampainsoc.org

American Parkinson Disease Association (APDA)
1250 Hylan Boulevard
Suite 4B
Staten Island, NY 10305
(800) 223-2732
http://www.apdaparkinson.org

American Pharmaceutical Association
2215 Constitution Avenue, NW
Washington, DC 20037
(800) 237-2742 (toll-free) or (202) 628-4410
http://www.pharmacyandyou.org

American Physical Therapy Association (APTA)
111 North Fairfax Street
Alexandria, VA 22314
(800) 999-2782, ext. 3395 or (703) 684-2782
http://www.apta.org

American Podiatric Medical Association
9312 Old Georgetown Road
Bethesda, MD 20814
(800) 366-8227 (toll-free) or (301) 571-9200
http://www.apma.org

American Psychiatric Association
1400 K Street, NW
Washington, DC 20005
(202) 682-6000
http://www.psych.org

American Psychological Association
750 First Street, NE
Washington, DC 20002
(800) 374-2721 or (202) 336-5500
http://www.apa.org

American Red Cross
430 17th Street, NW
Washington, DC 20006
(800) 435-7669 (toll-free)
http://www.redcross.org

American Society on Aging
833 Market Street
Suite 511
San Francisco, CA 94103
(800) 537-9728 or (415) 974-9600
http://www.asaging.org

American Speech-Language-Hearing Association
10801 Rockville Pike
Rockville, MD 20852
(800) 498-2071
(800) 638-8255 (TTY)
http://www.asha.org

American Tinnitus Association
P.O. Box 5
Portland, OR 97207
(800) 634-8978 (toll-free)
http://www.ata.org

Anxiety Disorders Association of America
11900 Parklawn Drive
Suite 100
Rockville, MD 20852
(301) 231-9350
http://www.adaa.org

Arthritis Foundation
National Office
1330 West Peachtree Street
Atlanta, GA 30309

(800) 283-7800 or (404) 965-7537
http://www.arthritis.org

Assisted Living Federation of American (ALFA)

11200 Waples Mill Road
Suite 150
Fairfax, VA 22030
(703) 691-8100
http://www.alfa.org

Association for Gerontology in Higher Education (AGHE)

1030 15th Street, NW
Suite 240
Washington, DC 20005
(202) 289-9806
http://www.aghe.org

Better Hearing Institute

50210B Backlick Road
Annandale, VA 22003
(800) EAR-WELL or (703) 684-3391
http://www.betterhearing.org

Better Vision Institute

1655 North Fort Myer Drive
Arlington, VA 222098
(800) 424-8422 (toll-free) or (703) 243-1508
http://www.visionsite.org

B'Nai B'rith

1640 Rhode Island Avenue, NW
Washington, DC 20036
(800) 500-6533 or (202) 857-6600
http://www.bnaibrith.org

Brookdale Center on Aging (BCOA) of Hunter College

1114 Avenue of the Americas
40th Floor
New York, NY 10036
(646) 366-1000
http://www.brookdale.org

Cancer Research Foundation of America

1600 Duke Street
Suite 110
Alexandria, VA 22314
(703) 836-4412 or (800) 227-2732
http://www.preventcancer.org

Catholic Charities USA (CCUSA)

1731 King Street
Suite 200
Alexandria, VA 22314
(703) 549-1390
http://www.catholiccharitiesusa.org

Catholic Golden Age (CGA)

National Headquarters
P.O. Box 249
Olyphant, PA 18447
(800) 836-5699
http://www.catholicgoldenage.org

Center for Social Gerontology

2307 Shelby Avenue
Ann Arbor, MI 48103
(734) 665-1126
http://www.tcsg.org

Center for the Study of Aging

706 Madison Avenue
Albany, NY 12208
(518) 465-6927

Center for Substance Abuse Treatment

5600 Fishers Lane
6th Floor Rockwall II
Rockville, MD 20857
(301) 443-5700
http://www.samhsa.gov/csat

Centers for Disease Control and Prevention (CDC)

1600 Clifton Road
Atlanta, GA 30333
(800) 311-3435 or (404) 639-3311
http://www.cdc.gov

Children of Aging Parents (CAPS)

1609 Woodborne Road
Suite 302A
Levittown, PA 19057
(800) 227-7294 or (215) 945-6900
http://www.caps4caregivers.org

Clearinghouse on Abuse and Neglect of the Elderly (CANE)

University of Delaware
College of Human Services, Education and Public Policy
Department of Consumer Studies
Newark, DE 19716
(302) 831-3525
http://www.elderabusecenter.org/clearing/index.html

Colorectal Cancer Network
P.O. Box 182
Kensington, MD 20895
(301) 879-1500
http://www.colorectal-cancer.net

Community Transportation Association
of America (CTAA)
1341 G Street, NW
10th Floor
Washington, DC 20005
(202) 628-1480
http://www.ctaa.org

Continuing Care Accreditation Commission
2519 Connecticut Avenue, NW
Washington, DC 20008
(202) 508-9459
http://www.ccaconline.org

Cremation Association of North America
401 North Michigan Avenue
Chicago, IL 60611
(312) 644-6610
http://www.cremationassociation.org

Delta Society
289 Perimeter Road East
Renton, WA 98055
(425) 226-7357
http://www.deltasociety.org

Department of Veterans Affairs (VA)
Office of Public Affairs
810 Vermont Avenue, NW
Washington, DC 20420
(800) 827-1000 or (800) 829-4833 (TTY)
http://www.va.gov

Disabled American Veterans
807 Maine Avenue, SW
Washington, DC 20024
(202) 554-3501
http://www.dav.org

Elderhostel
11 Avenue de Lafayette
Boston, MA 02111
(877) 426-8056 (toll-free) or (617) 426-7788
http://www.elderhostel.org

Equal Employment Opportunity
Commission (EEOC)
1801 L Street, NW
Washington, DC 20507

(800) 669-3362 (toll-free)
http://www.eeoc.gov

Family Caregiver Alliance
690 Market Street
Suite 600
San Francisco, CA 94104
(415) 434-3388
http://www.caregiver.org

Food and Drug Administration
(FDA)
HFE88
5600 Fishers Lane
Rockville, MD 20857
(888) 463-6332 (toll-free)
http://www.fda.org

Gerontological Society
of America
1030 15th Street, NW
Suite 250
Washington, DC 20005
(202) 842-1275
http://www.geron.org

Glaucoma Research Foundation
200 Pine Street
Suite 200
San Francisco, CA 94104
(800) 826-6693 or (415) 986-3162
http://www.glaucoma.org

Gray Panthers
733 15th Street, NW
Suite 437
Washington, DC 20005
(800) 280-5362 or (202) 737-6637
http://www.graypanthers.org

Huntington's Disease Society
of America (HDSA)
158 West 29th Street
7th Floor
New York, NY 10001
(800) 345-HDSA or (212) 242-1968, ext. 10
http://www.hdsa.org

Indian Health Service
Parklawn Building
Room 6-35
5600 Fishers Lane
Rockville, MD 20857
http://www.his.gov

International Hearing Society
16880 Middlebelt Road
Suite 4
Livonia, MI 48154
(800) 521-5247 or (734) 522-7200
http://www.hearingihs.org

International Tremor Foundation
7046 West 105th Street
Overland Park, KS 66212
(913) 341-3880
http://www.essentialtremor.org

**Japanese American Citizens League
(JACL)**
National Headquarters
1765 Sutter Street
San Francisco, CA 94115
(415) 921-5225
http://www.jacl.org

**Kansas Geriatric Education Center
on Aging**
University of Kansas Medical Center
3901 Rainbow Boulevard
Kansas City, KS 66160
(913) 588-1636
http://coa.kumc.edu/gec

Legal Services for the Elderly (LSE)
130 West 42nd Street
17th Floor
New York, NY 10036
(212) 391-0120

**Lighthouse National Center for Vision
and Aging**
111 East 59th Street
New York, NY 10022
(800) 829-0500 (toll-free) or (212) 821-9495
http://www.lighthouse.org

Meals on Wheels Association of America
1414 Prince Street
Suite 302
Alexandria, VA 22314
(703) 548-5558
http://www.mowaa.org

MedicAlert Foundation
2323 Colorado Avenue
Turlock, CA 95832
(800) 432-5378 or (209) 668-3333
http://www.medicalert.org

Medicare Rights Center
1460 Broadway
11th Floor
New York, NY 10036
(212) 869-3850
http://www.medicarerights.org

**National Academy of Elder Law
Attorneys, Inc.**
1604 North Country Club Road
Tucson, AZ 85716
(520) 881-4005
http://www.naela.org

**National Adult Day Services
Association**
National Council on Aging, Inc.
409 3rd Street, SW
Suite 200
Washington, DC 20024
(202) 479-6682
http://www.ncoa.org/nadsa

National Alliance for Caregiving
4720 Montgomery Lane
Suite 642
Bethesda, MD 20814
(301) 718-8444
http://www.caregiving.org

National Alliance for Hispanic Health
1501 16th Street, NW
Washington, DC 20036
(202) 387-5000
http://www.hispanichealth.org

**National Alliance for the Mentally Ill
(NAMI)**
Colonial Place Three
2107 Wilson Boulevard
Suite 300
Arlington, VA 22201
(800) 950-NAMI or (703) 524-7600
http://www.nami.org

**National Alliance for Breast Cancer
Organizations (NABCO)**
9 East 37th Street
10th Floor
New York, NY 10016
(212) 889-0606 or (888) 806-2226
http://www.nabco.org

**National Arthritis and Musculoskeletal
and Skin Diseases Information Clearinghouse**
National Institute of Arthritis and Musculoskeletal
and Skin Diseases (NIAMS)
National Institutes of Health (NIH)
1 AMS Circle
Bethesda, MD 20892
(877) 22-NIAMS or (301) 495-4484
http://www.nih.gov/niams

**National Asian Pacific Center on Aging
(NAPCA)**
1511 3rd Avenue
Suite 914
Seattle, WA 98101
(206) 624-1221
http://www.napca.org

**National Association for Continence
(NAFC)**
P.O. Box 8310
Spartanburg, SC 29305
(800) 252-3337 (toll-free)
http://www.nafc.org

**National Association of Area Agencies
on Aging**
927 15th Street, NW
Sixth Floor
Washington, DC 20005
(202) 296-8130
http://www.n4a.org

**National Association of Community
Health Centers**
1330 New Hampshire Avenue, NW
Suite 122
Washington, DC 20036
(202) 659-8008
http://www.nachc.com

**National Association for Hispanic Elderly
(Asociacion Nacional Por Personas Mayores)**
234 East Colorado Boulevard
Suite 300
Pasadena, CA 91101
(626) 564-1988

**National Association for Home Care
(NAHC)**
228 7th Street, SE
Washington, DC 20003
(202) 547-7424
http://www.nahc.org

**National Association of Area Agencies
on Aging (N4A)**
927 15th Street, NW
6th Floor
Washington, DC 20005
(800) 677-1116 or (202) 296-8130
http://www.n4a.org

**National Association of Nutrition and
Aging Service Programs**
1101 Vermont Avenue, NW
Suite 1001
Washington, DC 20005
(202) 682-6899
http://www.nanasp.org

**National Association of Professional Geriatric
Care Managers**
1604 North Country Club Road
Tucson, AZ 85716
(520) 881-8008
http://www.caremanager.org

**National Association of Social Workers
(NASW)**
750 First Street, NE
Suite 700
Washington, DC 20002
(800) 638-8799 or (202) 408-8600
http://www.naswdc.org

**National Association of State Units on
Aging (NASUA)**
1225 I Street, NW
Suite 725
Washington, DC 20005
(202) 898-2578
http://www.nasua.org

**National Association of the Deaf
(NAD)**
814 Thayer Avenue
Silver Spring, MD 20910
(301) 587-1788 or (301) 587-1789 (TTY)
http://www.nad.org

National Brain Tumor Foundation
414 Thirteenth Street
Suite 700
Oakland, CA 94612
(510) 839-9777
http://www.braintumor.org

National Cancer Institute (NCI)
National Institutes of Health (NIH)
Public Inquiries Office
Building 31, Room 10A03
31 Center Drive, MSC 2580
Bethesda, MD 20892
(800) 4CANCER or (800) 332-8615 (TTY)
http://www.nci.nih.gov

National Caucus and Center on Black Aged, Inc. (NCBA)
1424 K Street, NW
Suite 500
Washington, DC 20005
(202) 637-8400
http://wwwncba-blackaged.org

National Center for Complementary and Alternative Medicine (NCCAM) Clearinghouse
National Institutes of Health (NIH)
P.O. Box 8218
Silver Spring, MD 20907
(888) 644-6226
http://www.nccam.nih.gov

National Center on Elder Abuse (NCEA)
1225 I Street, NW
Suite 725
Washington, DC 20005
(202) 898-2586
http://www.elderabusecenter.org

National Citizen's Coalition for Nursing Home Reform
1424 16th Street, NW
Suite 202
Washington, DC 20036
(202) 332-2275
http://www.nccnhr.org

National Clearinghouse for Alcohol and Drug Information
11426 Rockville Pike, Suite 200
Rockville, MD 20852
(800) 729-6686
http://www.health.org

National Coalition for Adult Immunization
4733 Bethesda Avenue
Suite 750
Bethesda, MD 20814
(301) 656-0003
http://www.nfid.org/ncai

National Coalition for Cancer Survivorship (NCCS)
1010 Wayne Avenue
Suite 770
Silver Spring, MD 20910
(877) 622-7937
http://www.cansearch.org

National Council on Aging, Inc. (NCOA)
409 3rd Street, SW
Suite 200
Washington, DC 20025
(202) 479-1200
http://www.ncoa.org

National Council on Alcoholism and Drug Dependence (NCADD)
20 Exchange Place
Suite 2902
New York, NY 10005
(800) NCA-CALL or (212) 269-7797
http://www.ncadd.org

National Diabetes Information Clearinghouse (NDIC)
National Institute of Diabetes and Digestive and Kidney Diseases (NIDDK)
National Institutes of Health (NIH)
1 Information Way
Bethesda, MD 20892
(800) 860-8747 or (301) 654-3327
http://www.niddk.nih.gov

National Digestive Diseases Information Clearinghouse (NDIC)
National Institute of Diabetes and Digestive and Kidney Diseases (NIDDK)
National Institutes of Health (NIH)
2 Information Way
Bethesda, MD 20892
(800) 891-5389
http://www.niddk.nih.gov

National Elder Health Care Resource Center
University of Colorado Health Sciences Center
Campus Box A011-13
4455 East 12th Avenue
Denver, CO 80220
(303) 315-9228
http://www.uchsc.edu/ai/nehcrc

National Family Caregivers Association (NFCA)
10400 Connecticut Avenue, #500
Kensington, MD 20895
(800) 896-3650 or (301) 942-2302
http://www.nfaacares.org

National Federation of Interfaith Volunteer Caregivers
One West Armour Boulevard
Suite 202
Kansas City, MO 64111
(816) 931-5442
http://www.NFIVC.org

National Foundation for Depressive Illness, Inc.
P.O. Box 2257
New York, NY 10116
(212) 268-4260 or (800) 239-1265
http://www.depression.org

National Gerontological Nursing Association (NGNA)
7794 Grow Drive
Pensacola, FL 32514
(800) 723-0560 (toll-free)
http://www.ngna.org

National Health Information Center (NHIC)
Office of Disease Prevention and
   Health Promotion (ODPHP)
Department of Health and Human Services
P.O. Box 1133
Washington, DC 20013
(800) 336-4797 (toll-free)
http://www.health.gov/NHIC

National Heart, Lung, and Blood Institute (NHLBI) Information Center
P.O. Box 30105
Bethesda, MD 20824
(800) 575-WELL or (301) 592-8573
http://www.nhlbi.nih.gov

National Hispanic Council on Aging
2713 Ontario Road, NW
Washington, DC 20009
(202) 265-1288
http://www.nhcoa.org

National Hospice and Palliative Care Foundation
1700 Diagonal Road
Suite 300
Alexandria, VA 22314
(800) 338-8619 or 703-516-4928
http://www.hospiceinfo.org

National Indian Council on Aging (NICOA)
10501 Montgomery Boulevard NE
Suite 210
Albuquerque, NM 87111
(505) 292-2001
http://www.nicoa.org

National Information and Referral Support Center (NIRSC)
1225 I Street, NW
Suite 725
Washington, DC 20005
(202) 898-2578
http://www.nasua.org

National Institute of Mental Health
NIMH Public Inquiries
6001 Executive Boulevard
Room 8184, MSC 9663
Bethesda, MD 20892
(301) 443-4513
http://www.nimh.nih.gov

National Institute on Aging (NIA)
31 Center Drive, MSC 2292
Building 31, Room 5C27
Bethesda, MD 20892
(301) 496-1752
http://www.nia.nih.gov/

National Institute on Deafness and Other Communications Disorders
National Institutes of Health (NIH)
Office of Communication and Public Liaison
Bethesda, MD 20892-2320
(800) 241-1044 (toll-free) or (301) 496-7243

National Institute of Nursing Research (NINR)
Office of Science Policy and Public Liaison
National Institutes of Health (NIH)
31 Center Drive
Building 31, Room 5B10
Bethesda, MD 20892
(301) 496-0207
http://www.nih.gov/ninr

National Interfaith Coalition on Aging (NICA)
National Council on Aging (NCOA)
409 3rd Street, SW
Suite 200
Washington, DC 20024
(800) 424-9046 or (202) 479-1200
http://www.ncoa.org

National Kidney Foundation
30 East 33rd Street
New York, NY 10016
(800) 622-9010 or (212) 889-2210
http://www.kidney.org

National Legal Support for Elderly People with Mental Disabilities Project
Judge David L. Bazelon Center for Mental
   Health Law
1101 15th Street, NW
Suite 1212
Washington, DC 20005
(202) 467-5730 or (202) 467-4232 (TTY)

National Long-Term Care Ombudsman Resource Center
National Citizens' Coalition for Nursing
   Home Reform
1424 16th Street, NW
Suite 202
Washington, DC 20036
(202) 332-2275

National Mental Health Association
1021 Prince Street
Alexandria, VA 22314
(703) 684-7722
http://www.nmha.org

National Multiple Sclerosis Society
733 Third Avenue
6th Floor
New York, NY 10017
(800) 344-4867 (toll-free)
http://www.nmss.org

National Organization for Rare Disorders (NORD)
P.O. Box 8923
New Fairfield, CT 06812
(800) 999-6673 or (203) 746-6518
http://www.rarediseases.org

National Osteoporosis Foundation
1232 22nd Street, NW
Washington, DC 20037
(202) 223-2226
http://www.nof.org

National Ovarian Cancer Coalition (NOCC)
500 Northeast Spanish River Boulevard
Suite 14
Boca Raton, FL 33431
(561) 393-0005 or (888) 682-7426
http://www.ovarian.org

National Policy and Resource Center on Women and Aging
Heller Graduate School
Brandeis University
   Mail Stop 035
P.O. Box 9110
Waltham, MA 02254
(781) 736-3866
http://www.brandeis.edu/heller/National/ind.html

National Rehabilitation Information Center (NARIC)
1010 Wayne Avenue
Suite 800
Silver Spring, MD 20910
(800) 346-2742 (toll-free)
http://www.naric.com

National Resource Center on Native American Aging
P.O. Box 9037
Grand Forks, ND 58202
(800) 896-7628 (toll-free)
http://www.und.edu/dept/ncrnaa

National Resource Center on Supportive Housing & Home Modifications
USC Andrus Gerontology Center
3715 McClintock Avenue
Los Angeles, CA 90089
(213) 740-1364
http://www.homemods.org

National Self-Help Clearinghouse
365 Fifth Avenue
Suite 3300
New York, NY 10016
(212) 817-1822
http://www.selfhelpweb.org

National Senior Citizens Law Center
1101 14th Street, NW
Suite 400
Washington, DC 20005
(202) 289-6976
http://www.nsclc.org

National Senior Games Association (NSGA)
3032 Old Forge Drive
Baton Rouge, LA 70808
(225) 766-6800
http://www.nationalseniorgames.org

National Sleep Foundation
1522 K Street, NW
Suite 500
Washington, DC 20005
(202) 347-3471
http://www.sleepfoundation.org

National Stroke Association
9707 East Easter Lane
Englewood, CO 80112
(800) STROKES or (303) 754-0930
http://www.stroke.org

National Women's Health Network
514 10th Street, NW
Suite 400
Washington, DC 20004
(202) 347-1140
http://www.womenshealthnetwork.org

Native Elder Health Care Resource Center
University of Colorado Health Sciences Center
Campus Box A011-13
4455 East 12th Avenue
Denver, CO 80220
(303) 315-9228
http://www.uchs.edu/ai/nehcrc

North American Menopause Society (NAMS)
P.O. Box 94527
Cleveland, OH 44101
(440) 442-7550
http://www.menopause.org

Office of the U.S. Surgeon General
5600 Fishers Lane, Room 18-66
Rockville, MD 20857
(301) 443-4000
http://www.surgeongeneral.gov

Older Women's League
666 11th Street, NW
Suite 700
Washington, DC 20001
(800) TAKE-OWL or (202) 783-6686
http://www.owl-national.org

Organization of Chinese Americans
1001 Connecticut Avenue, NW
Suite 601
Washington, DC 20036
(202) 223-5500
http://www.ocanatl.org

Ovarian Cancer National Alliance (OCNA)
910 17th Street, NW
Suite 413
Washington, DC 20006
(202) 331-1332
http://www.ovariancancer.org

Pancreatic Cancer Action Network
P.O. Box 1010
Torrance, CA 90505
(877) 272-6226
http://www.pancan.org

Parkinson's Disease Foundation
833 West Washington Boulevard
Chicago, IL 60607
(800) 457-6676 or (312) 733-1893

Prevent Blindness America
500 East Remington Road
Schaumburg, IL 60173
(800) 331-2020 (toll-free) or (847) 843-2020
http://www.preventblindness.org

Self Help for Hard of Hearing People, Inc.
7910 Woodmont Avenue
Suite 1200
Bethesda, MD 20814
(301) 657-2248
http://www.shhh.org

Senior Job Bank
P.O. Box 30064
Savannah, GA 31410
http://www.seniorjobbank.org

Skin Cancer Foundation
254 Fifth Avenue
Suite 1403
New York, NY 10016

(212) 725-5176 or (800) 754-6490
http://www.skincancer.org

Social Security Administration (SSA)
Office of Public Inquiries
6401 Security Boulevard
Baltimore, MD 21235
(800) 772-1213 (toll-free)
http://www.ssa.gov

Society for Neuroscience
11 Dupont Circle, NW
Suite 500
Washington, DC 20036
(202) 462-6688
http://www.sfn.org

SPRY Foundation
10 G Street, NE
Suite 600
Washington, DC 20002
(202) 216-0401
http://www.spry.org

Substance Abuse and Mental Health Services Administration (SAMSHA)
Department of Health and Human Services
5600 Fishers Lane
Rockville, MD 20857
(800) 729-6686 or (800) 487-4889 (TTY)
http://www.samhsa.gov

United Seniors Health Council
409 Third Street, NW
Suite 200
Washington, DC 20024
(800) 637-2604
http://www.unitedseniorshealth.org

Visiting Nurse Association of America (VNAA)
11 Beacon Street
Suite 910
Boston, MA 02108
(888) 866-8773 or (617) 523-4042
http://www.vnaa.org

Well Spouse Foundation
30 East 40th Street
New York, NY 10016
(800) 838-0879 or (212) 685-8815
http://www.wellspouse.org

APPENDIX IV
STATE AND TERRITORY AGENCIES ON AGING

ALABAMA

Alabama Department of Senior Services
RSA Plaza
Suite 470
770 Washington Avenue
Montgomery, AL 36130-1851
(334) 242-5743
http://www.adss.state.al.us/

ALASKA

Alaska Commission on Aging
Division of Senior Services
Department of Administration
P.O. Box 110209
Juneau, AK 99811-0209
(907) 465-3250

AMERICAN SAMOA

Territorial Administration on Aging
Government of American Samoa
Pago Pago, American Samoa 96799
(011) 684-633-2207

ARIZONA

Aging and Adult Administration
Department of Economic Security
1789 West Jefferson Street,
#950A
Phoenix, AZ 85007
(602) 542-4446

ARKANSAS

Division Aging and Adult Services
Arkansas Department of Human Services
P.O. Box 1437, Slot 53
1417 Donaghey Plaza South
Little Rock, AR 72203-1437
(501) 682-2441
http://www.state.ar.us/dhs/aging

CALIFORNIA

California Department of Aging
1600 K Street
Sacramento, CA 95814
(916) 322-5290
http://www.aging.state.ca.us

COLORADO

Aging and Adult Services
Colorado Department of Social Services
1575 Sherman Street, Ground Floor
Denver, CO 80203
(303) 866-2800
http://www.cdhs.state.co.us/oss/aas/index1.html

CONNECTICUT

Division of Elderly Services
25 Sigourney Street
10th Floor
Hartford, CT 06106-5033
(860) 424-5298
http://www.dss.state.ct.us

DELAWARE

Delaware Division of Services for Aging and Adults with Physical Disabilities
Department of Health and Social Services
1910 North DuPont Highway
New Castle, DE 19720
(302) 577-4791
http://www.dsaapd.com/index.htm

DISTRICT OF COLUMBIA

District of Columbia Office on Aging
One Judiciary Square
9th Floor
441 Fourth Street, NW
Washington, DC 20001
(202) 724-5622
http://www.ci.washington.dc.us/aging/aghome.htm

FLORIDA

Department of Elder Affairs
Building B
Suite 152
4040 Esplanade Way
Tallahassee, FL 32399-7000
(850) 414-2000
http://www.elderaffairs.state.fl.us/

GEORGIA

Division of Aging Services
Department of Human Resources
Two Peachtree Street, NE
36th Floor
Atlanta, GA 30303-3176
(404) 657-5258
http://www.state.ga.us/Departments/DHR/
    aging.html

GUAM

**Division of Public Health
    & Social Services**
P.O. Box 2816
Agana, Guam 96910
(011) 671-475-0263

HAWAII

Hawaii Executive Office on Aging
250 South Hotel Street
Suite 109
Honolulu, HI 96813-2831
(808) 586-0100
http://www.hawaii.gov/health/coa/

IDAHO

Idaho Commission on Aging
P.O. Box 83720
Boise, ID 83720-0007
(208) 334-3833
http://www.idahoaging.com/

ILLINOIS

Illinois Department on Aging
421 East Capitol Avenue
Suite 100
Springfield, IL 62701-1789
(217) 785-3356
http://www.state.il.us/aging/

INDIANA

Bureau of Aging and In-Home Services
Division of Disability, Aging and Rehabilitative Services
Family and Social Services Administration
402 W. Washington Street,
#W454
P.O. Box 7083
Indianapolis, IN 46207-7083
(317) 232-7020
http://www.state.in.us/fssa/elderly/index.html

IOWA

Iowa Department of Elder Affairs
Clemens Building
3rd Floor
200 Tenth Street
Des Moines, IA 50309-3609
(515) 242-3333
http://www.state.ia.us/elderaffairs/

KANSAS

Department on Aging
New England Building
503 S. Kansas Avenue
Topeka, KS 66603-3404
(785) 296-4986
http://www.k4s.org/kdoa

KENTUCKY

Office of Aging Services
Cabinet for Families and Children
Commonwealth of Kentucky
275 East Main Street
Frankfort, KY 40621
(502) 564-6930
http://chs.state.ky.us/aging/

LOUISIANA

Governor's Office of Elderly Affairs
P.O. Box 80374
Baton Rouge, LA 70898-0374
(504) 342-7100
http://www.gov.state.la.us/departments/elderly.htm

MAINE

Bureau of Elder and Adult Services
Department of Human Services
35 Anthony Avenue
State House—Station #11

Augusta, ME 04333
(207) 624-5335
http://www.state.me.us/dhs/beas

MARYLAND

Maryland Department on Aging
State Office Building
Room 1007
301 West Preston Street
Baltimore, MD 21201-2374
(410) 767-1100
http://www.mdoa.state.md.us/

MASSACHUSETTS

Massachusetts Executive Office of Elder Affairs
One Ashburton Place
5th Floor
Boston, MA 02108
(617) 727-7750
http://www.stae.ma.us/elder/

MICHIGAN

Michigan Office of Services to the Aging
611 W. Ottawa, North Ottawa Tower
3rd Floor
P.O. Box 30676
Lansing, MI 48909
(517) 373-8230

MINNESOTA

Minnesota Board on Aging
444 Lafayette Road
St. Paul, MN 55155-3843
(651) 296-1531 or (800) 882-6262 (toll-free)
http://www.mnaging.org

MISSISSIPPI

Division of Aging and Adult Services
750 North State Street
Jackson, MS 39202
(601) 359-4925

MISSOURI

Division on Senior Services
Department of Health and Social Services
P.O. Box 1337
615 Howerton Court
Jefferson City, MO 65102-1337
(573) 751-3082
http://www.dss.state.mo.us/da/da.htm

MONTANA

Senior and Long Term Care Division
Department of Public Health and Human Services
P.O. Box 4210
111 Sanders
Room 211
Helena, MT 59620
(406) 444-4077
http://www.dphhs.state.mt.us/sltc

NEBRASKA

Department of Health and Human Services
Division on Aging
P.O. Box 95044
1343 M Street
Lincoln, NE 68509-5044
(402) 471-2307
http://www.hhs.state.ne.us/ags/agsindex.htm

NEVADA

Nevada Division for Aging Services
Department of Human Resources
State Mail Room Complex
3416 Goni Road
Building D-132
Carson City, NV 89706
(775) 687-4210
http://www.state.nv.us/hr/aging/

NEW HAMPSHIRE

Division of Elderly and Adult Services
State Office Park South
129 Pleasant Street
Brown Building #1
Concord, NH 03301
(603) 271-4680
http://www.dhhs.state.nh.us/

NEW JERSEY

Department of Health and Senior Services
New Jersey Division of Senior Affairs
P.O. Box 807
Trenton, NJ 08625-0807
(609) 943-3436

NEW MEXICO

State Agency on Aging
La Villa Rivera Building
228 East Palace Avenue

Ground Floor
Santa Fe, NM 87501
(505) 827-7640
http://www.nmaging.state.nm.us/

NEW YORK

New York State Office for the Aging
2 Empire State Plaza
Albany, NY 12223-1251
(800) 342-9871 (toll-free) or (518) 474-5731
http://aging.state.ny.us/nysofa

NORTH CAROLINA

Department of Health and Human Services
Division of Aging
2101 Mail Service Center
Raleigh, NC 27699-2101
(919) 733-3983
http://www.state.nc.us/DHR/DOA.home.htm

NORTH DAKOTA

Department of Human Services
Aging Services Division
600 South 2nd Street
Suite 1C
Bismarck, ND 58504
(701) 328-8910

NORTH MARIANA ISLANDS

CNMI Office on Aging
P.O. Box 2178
Commonwealth of the Northern Mariana Islands
Saipan, MP 96950
(670) 233-1320/1321

OHIO

Ohio Department on Aging
50 West Broad Street
9th Floor
Columbus, OH 43215-5928
(614) 466-5500
http://www.state.oh.us/age

OKLAHOMA

Aging Services Division
Department of Human Services
P.O. Box 25352
312 NE 28th Street
Oklahoma City, OK 73125

(405) 521-2281
http://www.okdhs.org/aging

OREGON

Senior and Disabled Services Division
500 Summer Street, NE
3rd Floor
Salem, OR 97301-1073
(503) 945-5811
http://www.sdsd.hr.state.or.us

PENNSYLVANIA

Pennsylvania Department of Aging
Commonwealth of Pennsylvania
Forum Place
555 Walnut Street
5th Floor
Harrisburg, PA 17101-1919
(717) 783-1550
http://www.aging.state.pa.us

PUERTO RICO

Commonwealth of Puerto Rico
Governor's Office of Elderly Affairs
Call Box 50063
Old San Juan Station, PR 00902
(787) 721-5710

RHODE ISLAND

Department of Elderly Affairs
160 Pine Street
Providence, RI 02903-3708
(401) 222-2858

SOUTH CAROLINA

Office of Senior and Long-Term Care Services
Department of Health and Human Services
P.O. Box 8206
Columbia, SC 29202-8206
(803) 898-2501
http://www.dhhs.state.sc.us

SOUTH DAKOTA

Office of Adult Services and Aging
Richard F. Kneip Building
700 Governors Drive
Pierre, SD 57501-2291
(605) 773-3656
http://www.state.sd.us/social/ASA/index.htm

TENNESSEE

Commission on Aging and Disability
Andrew Jackson Building
9th Floor
500 Deaderick Street
Nashville, TN 37243-0860
(615) 741-2056
http://www.state.tn.us/comaging

TEXAS

Texas Department on Aging
4900 North Lamar
4th Floor
Austin, TX 78751-2316
(512) 424-6840
http://www.texas.gov/agency/340.html

UTAH

Division of Aging and Adult Services
Box 45500
120 North 200 West
Salt Lake City, UT 84145-0500
(801) 538-3910
http://www.hsdaas.state.ut.us/SrvAge.htm

VERMONT

Vermont Department of Aging and Disabilities
Waterbury Complex
103 South Main Street
Waterbury, VT 05671-2301
(802) 241-2400
http://www.dad.state.vt.us

VIRGINIA

Virginia Department for the Aging
1600 Forest Avenue
Suite 102
Richmond, VA 23229
(804) 662-9333
http://www.aging.state.va.us

VIRGIN ISLANDS

Virgin Islands Department of Human Services
Knud Hansen Complex
Building A
1303 Hospital Ground
Charlotte Amalie, VI 00802
(340) 774-0930

WASHINGTON

Aging and Adult Services Administration
Department of Social and Health Services
P.O. Box 45050
Olympia, WA 98504-5050
(360) 725-2310
http://www.aasa.dshs.wa.gov

WEST VIRGINIA

West Virginia Bureau of Senior Services
Holly Grove
Building 10
1900 Kanawha Boulevard East
Charleston, WV 25305
(304) 558-3317
http://www.state.wv.us/seniorservices

WISCONSIN

Bureau of Aging and Long Term Care Resources
Department of Health and Family Services
1 West Wilson Street
Room 450
Madison, WI 53707
(608) 266-2536
http://www.dhfs.state.wi.us/Aging

WYOMING

Office on Aging
Wyoming Department of Health
6101 Yellowstone Road
Suite 259B
Cheyenne, WY 82002-0710
(307) 777-7986

APPENDIX V
STATE LONG-TERM CARE OMBUDSMAN PROGRAMS

ALABAMA

State Long-Term Care Ombudsman
Alabama Department of Senior Services
RSA Plaza
Suite 470
770 Washington Avenue
Montgomery, AL 36130
(334) 242-5743
(334) 242-5594 (fax)

ALASKA

State Long-Term Care Ombudsman
Alaska Mental Health Trust Authority
550 West 7th Avenue
Suite 1830
Anchorage, AK 99501
(907) 334-4480
(907) 334-4486 (fax)

ARIZONA

State Long-Term Care Ombudsman
Aging and Adult Administration
Department of Economic Security
1789 West Jefferson
2SW, 950A
Phoenix, AZ 85007
(602) 542-6454
(602) 542-6575 (fax)

ARKANSAS

State Long-Term Care Ombudsman
Arkansas Division of Aging & Adult Services
P.O. Box 1437, Slot 1412
Little Rock, AR 72201
(501) 682-8952
(501) 682-8155 (fax)

CALIFORNIA

State Long-Term Care Ombudsman
Department of Aging
1600 K Street
Sacramento, CA 95814
(916) 323-6679
(916) 323-7299 (fax)

COLORADO

State Long-Term Care Ombudsman
The Legal Center
455 Sherman Street,
Suite 130
Denver, CO 80203
(800) 288-1376 (toll-free) or (303) 722-0300, ext. 217
(303) 722-0720 (fax)

CONNECTICUT

State Long-Term Care Ombudsman
Department on Aging
Connecticut Department of Social Services
25 Sigourney Street
10th Floor
Hartford, CT 06106
(860) 424-5200, ext. 5221
(860) 424-4808 (fax)

DELAWARE

State Long-Term Care Ombudsman
Delaware Services for Aging and Adults
1901 North Dupont Highway
Main Administration Building Annex
New Castle, DE 19720
(302) 577-4791
(302) 577-4793 (fax)

DISTRICT OF COLUMBIA

State Long-Term Care Ombudsman
Legal Counsel for the Elderly
601 E Street, NW
4th Floor, Building A4-315
Washington, DC 20049
(202) 434-2140
(202) 434-6595 (fax)

FLORIDA

State Long-Term Care Ombudsman
Florida State Long-Term Care
    Ombudsman Council
600 South Calhoun Street
Holland Building,
Room 270
Tallahassee, FL 32301
(888) 831-0404
(813) 558-5598 (fax)

GEORGIA

State Long-Term Care Ombudsman
State Long Term Care Office
2 Peachtree Street, NW
9th Floor
Atlanta, GA 30303
(888) 454-5826
(404) 463-8384 (fax)

HAWAII

State Long-Term Care Ombudsman
Executive Office on Aging
250 South Hotel Street
Suite 406
Honolulu, HI 96813
(808) 586-0100
(808) 586-0185 (fax)

IDAHO

State Long-Term Care Ombudsman
Idaho Commission on Aging
P.O. Box 83720
3380 American Terrace
Suite 1
Boise, ID 83720
(208) 334-2220
(208) 334-3033 (fax)

ILLINOIS

State Long-Term Care Ombudsman
Illinois Department on Aging
421 East Capitol Avenue
Suite 100
Springfield, IL 62701
(217) 785-3143
(217) 524-9644 (fax)

INDIANA

State Long-Term Care Ombudsman
Division of Aging & Rehabilitation
    Services
402 West Washington Street
Room W454
P.O. Box 7083-W454
Indianapolis, IN 46207
(800) 545-7763 (toll-free)
(317) 232-7867 (fax)

IOWA

State Long-Term Care Ombudsman
Iowa Department of Elder Affairs
Clemens Building
200 10th Street
Des Moines, IA 50309
(515) 242-3327
(515) 242-3300 (fax)

KANSAS

State Long-Term Care Ombudsman
Office of the State Long-Term Care
    Ombudsman
610 SW 10th Street
2nd Floor
Topeka, KS 66612
(785) 296-3017
(785) 296-3916 (fax)

KENTUCKY

State Long-Term Care Ombudsman
Office of Aging Services, 5C-D
275 E. Main Street
Frankfort, KY 40621
(502) 564-6930
(502) 564-4595 (fax)

LOUISIANA

State Long-Term Care Ombudsman
Office of Elderly Affairs
412 N. 4th Street
3rd Floor
P.O. Box 80374
Baton Rouge, LA 70802
(225) 342-7100
(225) 342-7144 (fax)

MAINE

State Long-Term Care Ombudsman
Maine State Long-Term Care
  Ombudsman Program
1 Weston Court
P.O. Box 128
Augusta, ME 04332
(207) 621-1079
(207) 621-0509 (fax)

MARYLAND

State Long-Term Care Ombudsman
Maryland Department of Aging
State Office Building
301 West Preston Street
Room 1007
Baltimore, MD 21201
(410) 767-1100
(410) 333-7943 (fax)

MASSACHUSETTS

State Long-Term Care Ombudsman
Massachusetts Executive Office
  of Elder Affairs
1 Ashburton Place
5th Floor
Boston, MA 02108
(617) 727-7750
(617) 727-9368 (fax)

MICHIGAN

State Long-Term Care Ombudsman
Elderlaw of Michigan
221 North Pine
Lansing, MI 48933
(866) 485-9393
(517) 372-6401 (fax)

MINNESOTA

State Long-Term Care Ombudsman
Office of Ombudsman
  for Older Minnesotans
121 East Seventh Place
Suite 410
St. Paul, MN 55101
(800) 657-3591
(651) 297-564 (fax)

MISSISSIPPI

State Long-Term Care Ombudsman
Division of Aging & Adult Services
750 North State Street
Jackson, MS 39202
(601) 359-4928
(601) 359-9664 (fax)

MISSOURI

State Long-Term Care Ombudsman
Division on Aging
Department of Health & Senior Services
P.O. Box 570
615 Howerton Court
Jefferson City, MO 65102
(800) 309-3282
573-751-8687 (fax)

MONTANA

State Long-Term Care Ombudsman
Senior and Long Term Care Division
Department of Health & Human Services
P.O. Box 4210
111 Sanders, Room 211
Helena, MT 59620
(406) 444-4676
(406) 444-7743 (fax)

NEBRASKA

State Long-Term Care Ombudsman
Division of Aging Services
Montana Department of Health and
  Human Services
P.O. Box 95044
301 Centennial Mall South
Lincoln, NE 68509
(402) 471-2307
(402) 471-4619 (fax)

NEVADA

State Long-Term Care Ombudsman
Nevada Division for Aging Services
445 Apple Street
#104
Reno, NV 89502
(775) 688-2964
(775) 688-2969 (fax)

NEW HAMPSHIRE

State Long-Term Care Ombudsman
Division of Elderly & Adult Services
129 Pleasant Street
Concord, NH 03301
(603) 271-4375
(603) 271-5574 (fax)

NEW JERSEY

State Long-Term Care Ombudsman for Institutionalized Elderly
P.O. Box 807
Trenton, NJ 08625
(609) 943-4026
(609) 943-3479 (fax)

NEW MEXICO

State Long-Term Care Ombudsman
State Agency on Aging
1410 San Pedro, NE
Albuquerque, NM 87110
(505) 255-0971
(505) 255-5602 (fax)

NEW YORK

State Long-Term Care Ombudsman
New York State Office for the Aging
2 Empire State Plaza
Agency Building #2
Albany, NY 12223
(518) 474-7329
(518) 474-7761 (fax)

NORTH CAROLINA

State Long-Term Care Ombudsman
Division on Aging
2101 Mail Service Center
Raleigh, NC 27699
(919) 733-8395
(919) 715-0868 (fax)

NORTH DAKOTA

State Long-Term Care Ombudsman
Aging Services Division
Department of Health and Human Services
600 South 2nd Street
Suite 1C
Bismarck, ND 58504

(800) 451-8693
(701) 328-8989 (fax)

OHIO

State Long-Term Care Ombudsman
Department of Aging
50 West Broad Street
9th Floor
Columbus, OH 43215
(614) 466-1221
(614) 644-5201 (fax)

OKLAHOMA

State Long-Term Care Ombudsman
Aging Services Division, Department of Health Services
312 NE 28th Street
Suite 109
Oklahoma City, OK 73105
(405) 521-6734
(405) 521-2086 (fax)

OREGON

Office of the Long-Term Care Ombudsman
3855 Wolverine, NE
Suite 6
Salem, OR 97305
(503) 378-6533
(503) 373-0852 (fax)

PENNSYLVANIA

State Long-Term Care Ombudsman
Department of Aging
555 Walnut Street
5th Floor
P.O. Box 1089
Harrisburg, PA 17101
(717) 783-7247
(717) 772-3382 (fax)

RHODE ISLAND

State Long-Term Care Ombudsman
Alliance for Better Long-Term Care
422 Post Road
Suite 204
Warwick, RI 02888
(401) 785-3340
(401) 785-3391 (fax)

SOUTH CAROLINA

State Long-Term Care Ombudsman
Division on Aging
1801 Main Street
P.O. Box 8206
Columbia, SC 29202
(803) 898-2850
(803) 898-4513 (fax)

SOUTH DAKOTA

State Long-Term Care Ombudsman
Office of Adult Services & Aging
700 Governors Drive
Pierre, SD 57501
(605) 773-3656
(605) 773-6834 (fax)

TENNESSEE

State Long-Term Care Ombudsman
Commission on Aging
Andrew Jackson Building
9th Floor
500 Deaderick Street
Nashville, TN 37243
(615) 741-2056
(615) 741-3309 (fax)

TEXAS

State Long-Term Care Ombudsman
Department on Aging
4900 North Lamar Boulevard
4th Floor
P.O. Box 12786
Austin, TX 789751
(512) 424-6875
(512) 424-6890 (fax)

UTAH

State Long-Term Care Ombudsman
Division of Aging and Adult Services
Department of Social Services
120 North 200 West
Room 401
Salt Lake City, UT 84103
(801) 538-3924
(801) 538-4395 (fax)

VERMONT

State Long-Term Care Ombudsman
Vermont Legal Aid, Inc.
P.O. Box 1367
Burlington, VT 05402
(802) 863-5620
(802) 863-7152 (fax)

VIRGINIA

State Long-Term Care Ombudsman
Virginia Association of Area Agencies on Aging
530 East Main Street, Suite 428
Richmond, VA 23219
(804) 644-2804
(804) 644-5640 (fax)

WASHINGTON

State Long-Term Care Ombudsman
South King County Multi-Services Center
1200 South 336th Street
P.O. Box 23699
Federal Way, WA 98093
(253) 838-6810
(253) 815-8173 (fax)

WEST VIRGINIA

State Long-Term Care Ombudsman
Commission on Aging
1900 Kanawha Boulevard East
Charleston, WV 25308
(304) 558-3317
(304) 558-0004 (fax)

WISCONSIN

State Long-Term Care Ombudsman
Board on Aging and Long-Term Care
214 North Hamilton Street
Madison, WI 53703
(608) 266-8945
(608) 261-6570 (fax)

WYOMING

State Long-Term Care Ombudsman
Wyoming Senior Citizens, Inc.
756 Gilchrist
P.O. Box 94
Wheatland, WY 82201
(307) 322-5553
(307) 322-3283 (fax)

APPENDIX VI
NURSING HOME CHECKLIST

Name of Nursing Home: _____   **Date of Visit:** _____

	Yes	No	Comments
Basic Information			
The nursing home is Medicare-certified.			
The nursing home is Medicaid-certified.			
The nursing home has the level of care needed (e.g. skilled, custodial), and a bed is available.			
The nursing home has special services if needed in a separate unit (e.g. dementia, ventilator, or rehabilitation), and a bed is available.			
The nursing home is located close enough for friends and family to visit.			
Resident Appearance			
Residents are clean, appropriately dressed for the season or time of day, and well groomed.			
Nursing Home Living Spaces			
The nursing home is free from overwhelming unpleasant odors.			
The nursing home appears clean and well-kept.			
The temperature in the nursing home is comfortable for residents.			
The nursing home has good lighting.			
Noise levels in the dining room and other common areas are comfortable.			
Smoking is not allowed or may be restricted to certain areas of the nursing home.			
Furnishings are sturdy, yet comfortable and attractive.			

	Yes	No	Comments
Staff			
The relationship between the staff and the residents appears to be warm, polite, and respectful.			
All staff wear name tags.			
Staff knock on the door before entering a resident's room and refer to residents by name.			
The nursing home offers a training and continuing education program for all staff.			
The nursing home does background checks on all staff.			
The guide on your tour knows the residents by name and is recognized by them.			
There is a full-time Registered Nurse (RN) in the nursing home at all times, other than the Administrator or Director of Nursing.			
The same team of nurses and Certified Nursing Assistants (CNAs) work with the same resident 4 to 5 days per week.			
CNAs work with a reasonable number of residents.			
CNAs are involved in care planning meetings.			
There is a full-time social worker on staff.			
There is a licensed doctor on staff. Is he or she there daily? Can he or she be reached at all times?			
The nursing home's management team has worked together for at least one year.			
Residents' Rooms			
Residents may have personal belongings and/or furniture in their rooms.			
Each resident has storage space (closet and drawers) in his or her room.			
Each resident has a window in his or her bedroom.			
Residents have access to a personal telephone and television.			
Residents have a choice of roommates.			
Water pitchers can be reached by residents.			
There are policies and procedures to protect resident's possessions.			

	Yes	No	Comments
Hallways, Stairs, Lounges, and Bathrooms			
Exits are clearly marked.			
There are quiet areas where residents can visit with friends and family.			
The nursing home has smoke detectors and sprinklers.			
All common areas, resident rooms, and doorways are designed for wheelchair use.			
There are handrails in the hallways and grab bars in the bathrooms.			
Menus and Food			
Residents have a choice of food items at each meal. (Ask if your favorite foods are served.)			
Nutritious snacks are available upon request.			
Staff help residents eat and drink at mealtimes if help is needed.			
Activities			
Residents, including those who are unable to leave their rooms, may choose to take part in a variety of activities.			
The nursing home has outdoor areas for resident use and staff help residents go outside.			
The nursing home has an active volunteer program.			
Safety and Care			
The nursing home has an emergency evacuation plan and holds regular fire drills.			
Residents get preventive care, like a yearly flu shot, to help keep them healthy.			
Residents may still see their personal doctors.			
The nursing home has an arrangement with a nearby hospital for emergencies.			
Care plan meetings are held at times that are convenient for residents and family members to attend whenever possible.			
The nursing home has corrected all deficiencies (failure to meet one or more Federal or State requirements) on its last state inspection report.			

APPENDIX VII
GOVERNMENT HEALTH AGENCIES IN CANADA

Each province or territory in Canada manages its own health agency. The following is a list of government health agencies throughout Canada.

ALBERTA

Alberta Health Insurance Plan
P.O. Box 1360
Edmonton, Alberta
T5J 2N3
(780) 427-1432
http://www.health.gov.ab.ca/talk/index.htm

BRITISH COLUMBIA

Ministry Office
P.O. Box 9050 Stn. Provincial Government
Victoria, British Columbia
V8W 9E2
(250) 952-3456

MANITOBA

Manitoba Health
300 Carlton Street
Winnipeg, Manitoba
R3B 3M9
(800) 392-1207 (toll-free) or (204) 786-7101

NEW BRUNSWICK

Department of Health and Wellness
P.O. Box 5100
Fredericton, New Brunswick
E3B 5G8
(506) 453-2536
http://www.gnb.ca/0051/contacts-e.asp

NEWFOUNDLAND

Newfoundland Medical Care Plan
P.O. Box 5000
20 High Street
Grand Falls-Windsor, Newfoundland
A2A 2Y4
(709) 292-4000

NORTHWEST TERRITORIES

Department of Health and Social Services
Government of the Northwest Territories
Box 1320
Yellowknife, Northwest Territories
Z1A 2L9
(867) 920-6173
http://www.hlthss.tov.nt.ca/Content/contact.htm

NOVA SCOTIA

Department of Health
P.O. Box 488
Halifax, Nova Scotia
B3J 2R8
(902) 424-3377
http://www.gov.ns.ca/heal/about.htm

NUNAVUT

Nunavik Regional Board of Health and Social Services
P.O. Box 900
Kuujjuaq
(819) 964-2222

ONTARIO

Ontario Ministry of Health and Long-Term Care
80 Grosvenor Street
11th Floor
Toronto, Ontario
M7A 1S2
(800) 268-1154 (toll-free) or (416) 314-5518
http://www.gov.on.ca/health/english/tools/feedback.html

PRINCE EDWARD ISLAND

Health and Social Services
11 Kent Street

Second Floor, Jones Building
P.O. Box 2000
Charlottetown, Prince Edward Island
C1A 7N8
(902) 368-4900

SASKATCHEWAN

Saskatchewan Health
3475 Albert Street
Regina, Saskatchewan
S4S 6X6
(306) 787-3251

YUKON

Health and Social Services
Government of Yukon
Box 2703
Whitehorse, Yukon
Y1A 2C6
(867) 667-3673
http://www.hss.gov.yk.ca

APPENDIX VIII
HEALTH ORGANIZATIONS IN CANADA

Arthritis Society (National Office)
393 University Avenue
Suite 1700
Toronto, Ontario
M5G 1E6
(416) 979-7228
http://www.arthritis.ca

Canadian Cancer Society
National Office
10 Alcorn Avenue
Suite 200
Toronto, Ontario
M4V 3B1
(416) 961-7223
http://www.cancer.ca/english/ContactUs.asp

Canadian Diabetes Association
National Office
15 Toronto Street
Suite 800
Toronto, Ontario
M5C 2E3
(800) BANTING (toll-free) or (416) 363-3373
http://www.diabetes.ca

**Canadian Hospice Palliative
  Care Association**
43 Bruyere Street
Suite 131C
Ottawa, Ontario
K1N 5C8
(613) 241-3663
http://www.cpca.net

Canadian Lung Association
3 Raymond Street
Suite 300
Ottawa, Ontario
KR 1A3
(613) 569-6411
http://www.lung.ca/ca

Canadian MedicAlert Foundation
2005 Sheppard Avenue East
Suite 800
Toronto, Ontario
M2J 5B4
(800) 668-1507 (toll-free, English)
(800) 668-6381 (toll-free, French)

Canadian Mental Health Association
National Office
2160 Yonge Street
3rd Floor
Toronto, Ontario
M4S 2Z3
(416) 484-7750
http://www.cmha.ca

Division of Aging and Seniors
Health Canada
Address Locator: 1908A1
Ottawa, Ontario
K1A 1B4
(613) 952-7606

Health Canada
Brooke Claxton Building,
Tunney's Pasture
P.L. 0906C
Ottawa, Ontario
K1A 0K9
(613) 957-2991
http://www.hc-sc.gc.ca/english

**Heart and Stroke Foundation
  of Canada**
222 Queen Street
Suite 1402
Ottawa, Ontario
K1P 5V9
(613) 569-4361
http://ww2.heartandstroke.ca

Osteoporosis Society of Canada
33 Laird Drive
Toronto, Ontario
M4G 3S9
(800) 463-6842 (toll-free)
http://www.osteoporosis.ca

Parkinson Society Canada
4211 Yonge Street
Suite 316
Toronto, Ontario
M2P 2A9
(416) 227-9700
http://www.parkinson.ca/home.html

BIBLIOGRAPHY

AARP. "Home Made Money: A Consumer's Guide to Reverse Mortgages," 2001.

Adamec, Christine. *The Unofficial Guide to Eldercare*. New York: Macmillan, 1999.

———. "When Parents of Parents Remarry," *Single Parent* 27, no. 8 (October 1984): 20–21.

———. *When Your Pet Dies: Dealing with Your Grief and Helping Your Children Cope*. Lincoln, Nebr.: iUniverse.com, 2000.

Agrawal, Sangeeta, et al. "Gallstones, from Gall Bladder to Gut," *Postgraduate Medicine* 108, no. 3 (September 1, 2000): 143–153.

Altman, Roberta, and Michael J. Sarg, M.D. *The Cancer Dictionary*. New York: Facts On File, 1999.

Alward, Wallace L.M., M.D. "Medical Management of Glaucoma," *New England Journal of Medicine* 339, no. 18 (October 29, 1998): 1,298–1,307.

American Heart Association. *2002 Heart and Stroke Statistical Update,* 2001.

Anders, Kelly. "Elder Fraud: Financial Crimes Against the Elderly," National Conference of State Legislatures, July 1999.

Andersen-Ranberg, Karen, Lone Vasegaard, and Bernard Jeune. "Dementia Is Not Inevitable: A Population-Based Study of Danish Centenarians," *Journal of Gerontology: Psychological Sciences* 56B, no. 3 (2001): P152–P159.

Apte, Minoti V., M.D., M. Med. Sci., et al. "Alcohol-Related Pancreatic Damage: Mechanisms and Treatment," *Alcohol Health & Researcher World* 21, no. 1 (1997): 13–20.

Aparasu, Rajender R., and Jane R. Mort. "Inappropriate Prescribing for the Elderly: Beers Criteria-Based Review," *The Annals of Pharmacotherapy* 34 (2000): 338–346.

Aronow, Wilbert S., M.D. "Cholesterol 2001: Rationale for Lipid-Lowering in Older Patients with or without CAD," *Geriatrics* 56, no. 9 (2001): 22–30.

Baine, William B., M.D., William Yu, M.A., and James P. Summe, M.S. "Epidemiologic Trends in the Hospitalization of Elderly Medicare Patients for Pneumonia, 1991–1998," *American Journal of Public Health* 91, no. 7 (2001): 1,121–1,123.

Bajwa, Zahid H., M.D., and Charles C. Ho, M.D. "Herpetic Neuralgia: Use of Combination Therapy for Pain Relief in Acute and Chronic Herpes Zoster," *Geriatrics* 56, no. 12 (December 2001): 18–24.

Ballard, Harold S., M.D. "The Hematological Complications of Alcoholism," *Alcohol Health & Research World* 21, no. 1 (1997): 42–52.

Baran, Daniel, M.D. "Osteoporosis: Efficacy and Safety of a Bisphosphonate Dosed Once Weekly," *Geriatrics* 56, no. 3 (2001): 28–32.

Barnes, Peter J., D. Sc, "Chronic Obstructive Pulmonary Disease," *New England Journal of Medicine* 343 no. 4 (July 27, 2000): 269–280.

Beckles, G.L.A., and P.E. Thompson-Reid, eds. *Diabetes and Women's Health Across the Life Stages: A Public Health Perspective*. Atlanta, Ga.: U.S. Department of Health and Human Services, Centers for Disease Control and Prevention, National Center for Chronic Disease Prevention and Health Promotion, Division of Diabetes Translation (2001).

Beers, Mark H., M.D., and Robert Berkow, M.D., eds. *The Merck Manual of Geriatrics*. Whitehouse Station, N.J.: Merck Research Laboratories, 2000.

Biondi, David M., D.O., and Joel R. Saper, M.D. "Geriatric Headache: How to Make the Diagnosis and Manage the Pain," *Geriatrics* 55, no. 12 (2000): 40–50.

Blackman, Donald K., Ph.D., et al. "Overview: Surveillance for Selected Public Health Indicators Affecting Older Adults—United States," *MMWR* 48, no. SS-8 (December 17, 1999): 1–158.

Blinder, J., Barry F. Chaitin, and Renee S. Goldstein, eds. *The Eating Disorders: Medical and Psychological Bases of Diagnosis and Treatment*. New York: Aperture, 1988.

Bode, Christiane, Ph.D., and J. Christian Bode, M.D. "Alcohol's Role in Gastrointestinal Tract Disorders," *Alcohol Health & Research World* 21, no. 1 (1997): 76–93.

Bond, John H. M.D. "Polyp Guideline: Diagnosis, Treatment, and Surveillance for Patients with Colorectal Polyps," *American Journal of Gastroenterology* 95, no. 11 (November 2000): 3,053–3,063.

Brennan, Penny L., and Rudolf H. Moos. "Late-Life Drinking behavior: The Influence of Personal Characteristics, Life Context, and Treatment," *Alcohol Health & Research World* 20, no. 3 (1996): 197–105.

Brogden, Mike, and Preeti Nijhar. *Crime, Abuse and the Elderly*. Portland, Oreg.: Willan Publishing, 2000.

Brott, Thomas, M.D., and Julien Bogousslavsky, M.D. "Treatment of Acute Ischemic Stroke," *New England Journal of Medicine* 343, no. 10 (September 7, 2000): 710–722.

Bryer, Thomas. "Characteristics of Motor Vehicle Crashes Related to Aging," in *Mobility and Transportation in the Elderly.* New York: Springer Publishing, 2000.

Burkhardt, Jon E., et al. "Mobility and Independence: Changes and Challenges for Older Drivers: Executive Summary," Administration on Aging (July 1998).

Butler, Robert N., et al. "Anti-Aging Medicine: Efficacy and Safety of Hormones and Antioxidants," *Geriatrics* 55, no. 7 (2000): 48.

Butler, Robert, M.D. "Global Ageing: Challenges and Opportunities of the Next Century," *Ageing International* 23, no. 1 (1996): 12–32.

Caap-Ahlgren, Marianne, and Ove Dehlink. "Insomnia and Depressive Symptoms in Patients with Parkinson's Disease: Relationship to Health-Related Quality of Life. An Interview Study of Patients Living at Home," *Archives of Gerontology and Geriatrics* 32 (2001): 23–33.

Campbell, A. John, et. al. "Randomised Controlled Trial of a General Practice Programme of Home Based Exercise to Prevent Falls in Elderly Women," *British Medical Journal* 315 (1997): 1,065–1,070.

Caregivers Advisory Panel. "National Family Caregivers (NFCA) Survey of Self-Identified Family Caregivers," P.O. Box 1206, Charlestown, R.I. 02813 (September 2001).

Carr, David B. M.D. "The Older Adult Driver," *American Family Physician* 61 (2001): 141, 146, 148.

Casper, Lynn M., and Kenneth R. Bryson. "Co-resident Grandparents and Their Grandchildren: Grandparent Maintained Families," Population Division, U.S. Bureau of the Census, Washington, D.C., Population Division Working Paper No. 26 (March 1998).

Cassel, Christine K., M.D. "Successful Aging: How Increased Life Expectancy and Medical Advances Are Changing Geriatric Care," *Geriatrics* 56, no. 1 (2001): 35–39.

Cassell, Dana K., and David H. Gleaves, Ph.D. *The Encyclopedia of Obesity and Eating Disorders.* New York, Facts On File, 2000.

Centers for Disease Control and Prevention. "At a Glance: Colorectal Cancer: The Importance of Prevention and Early Detection, 2001" (2001).

Centers for Disease Control and Prevention, Health Resources and Services Administration, Indian Health Service, National Institutes of Health. "Oral Health," in *Healthy People 2010.* Washington, D.C.: National Institutes of Health, 2000.

Cherry, Donald K., M.S., Catharine W. Burt, Ed.D., and David A. Woodwell, Division of Health Care Statistics. "National Ambulatory Medical Care Survey: 1999 Summary," *Advance Data from Vital and Health Statistics,* no. 322 (July 17, 2001).

Choy, Ernest H.S., M.D., and Gabriel S. Panayi, M.D., Sc.D. "Cytokine Pathways and Joint Inflammation in Rheumatoid Arthritis," *New England Journal of Medicine* 344, no. 12 (March 22, 2001): 907–916.

Chu, Neelima V., M.D., and Steven V. Edelman, M.D. "Diabetes and Erectile Function," *Clinical Diabetes* 19, no. 1 (Winter 2001): 45–47.

Cohen, Robert I., M.D., Pradeep Chopra, M.D., and Carole Upshur, Ed.D. "Low Back Pain, Part 2: Guide to Conservative, Medical, and Procedural Therapies," *Geriatrics* 56, no. 11 (November 2001): 38–47.

Collins, Kim A., M.D., et al. "Elder Abuse and Neglect," *Archives of Internal Medicine* 160, no. 11 (June 12, 2000).

———. "Elder Abuse and Neglect," *Archives of Internal Medicine* 160, no. 11 (June 12, 2000).

Committee on Nutrition Services for Medicare Beneficiaries, Food and Nutrition Board. *The Role of Nutrition in Mainting Health in the Nation's Elderly: Evaluating Coverage of Nutrition Services of the Medicare Population.* Washington, D.C.: National Academy Press, 2000.

Cooper, James W., ed. *Diabetes Mellitus in the Elderly.* New York: The Haworth Press, 1999.

Couch, Robert B., M.D. "Prevention and Treatment of Influenza," *New England Journal of Medicine* 343 (December 14, 2000): 1,778–1,787.

Cumming, Robert G., et al. "Prospective Study of the Impact of Fear of Falling on Activities of Daily Living, SF-36 Scores, and Nursing Home Admission," *Journal of Gerontology: Medical Sciences* 55A, no. 5 (2000): M299–M305.

Davis, Katherine M., MSN, CS, NP-C, and Elizabeth Mathew, MSN, NP-C, CS. "Pharmacologic Management of Depression in the Elderly," *Nurse Practitioner* 23, no. 6 (1998): 16018, 16026, 16028.

DeAngelis, Lisa M., M.D. "Brain Tumors," *New England Journal of Medicine* 344, no. 2 (January 11, 2001): 114–123.

Decalmer, Peter, and Frank Glendenning, Eds. *The Mistreatment of Elderly People.* London: Sage Publications, 1997.

Dembicki, Diane, Ph.D., and Jennifer Anderson, Ph.D., RD. "Pet Ownership May Be a Factor in Improved Health of the Elderly," *Journal of Nutrition for the Elderly* 15, no. 3, (1996): 15–31.

Dement, William C., M.D., Ph.D., and Christopher Vaughan. *The Promise of Sleep.* New York: Dell, 2000.

Desbiens, Norman A., et al. "Stress in Caregivers of Hospitalized Oldest-Old Patients," *Journal of Gerontology: Medical Sciences* 56A, no. 4 (2001): M231–M235.

Deyo, Richard A., M.D., M.P.H., and James N. Weinstein, D.O. "Low Back Pain," *New England Journal of Medicine* 344, no. 5 (February 1, 2001): 363–370.

Di Libero, F., et al. "Comorbidity and Rehabilitation," *Archives of Gerontology and Geriatrics* 32 (2001): 15–22.

Division of Aging and Seniors, Health Canada. "Canada's Aging Population" (2002).

Division of Tuberculosis Elimination, Centers for Disease Control and Prevention. "Reported Tuberculosis in the United States, 2000" (2001).

Drexler, Andrew J., M.D., and Carolyn Robertson, APRN, MSN. "Type 2 Diabetes: How New Insights, New Drugs Are Changing Clinical Practice," *Geriatrics* 56, no. 6 (2001): 20–33.

Drive and Motor Vehicle Services Branch, Oregon Department of Transportation. "HB 2446: Older Driver Study. Preliminary Literature Review" (January 2000).

Duxbury, Andrew S. "Gait Disorders in the Elderly: Commonly Overlooked Diagnostic Clues," *Consultant* 37 (September 1997): 2,337–2,351.

Edelstein, Stephanie, and Karen Gaddy, American Bar Association, Commission on Legal Problems of the Elderly. *Assisted Living: Summary of State Statutes. Volume I: Guide and Table to State Summaries.* Washington, D.C.: AARP, 2000.

Engstrom, John W., M.D., and Michael J. Aminoff, M.D. "Evaluation and Treatment of Orthostatic Hypotension," *American Family Physician* 56, no. 5 (October 1, 1997).

Epstein, Murray, M.D. "Alcohol's Effect on Kidney Function," *Alcohol Health & Research World* 20, no. 3 (1996): 84–92.

Farhey, Yoland, M.D., and Evelyn Hess, M.D. "Controlling Pain in Rheumatoid Arthritis and Fibromyalgia," *Women's Health in Primary Care* 4, no. 7 (July 2001): 469–473.

Feinberg, Steven D., M.D., "Prescribing Analgesics: How to Improve Function and Avoid Toxicity When Treating Chronic Pain," *Geriatrics* 55, no. 12 (2000): 44–62.

Fine, Stuart L., M.D., et al. "Age-Related Macular Degeneration," *The New England Journal of Medicine* 342, no. 7 (2000): 483–492.

Fong, Donald S., M.D., M.P.H. "Age-Related Macular Degeneration: Update for Primary Care," *American Family Physician* 61 (2000): 3,035–3,042.

Fox, Sarah A., Ed.D., M.S.P.H., et al. "Targeted Mailed Materials and the Medicare Beneficiary: Increasing Mammogram Screening Among the Elderly," *American Journal of Public Health* 91, no. 1 (2001): 55–61.

Fox-Grage, Wendy, Judith Riggs, and Suzanne Linnane. "Alzheimer's Disease and Related Dementias: A Legislative Guide," National Conference of State Legislatures (March 2000).

Frisoni, Giovanni B., et al "Mild Cognitive Impairment in the Population and Physical Health: Data on 1,435 Individuals Aged 75 to 95," *Journal of Gerontology: Medical Sciences* 55A, no. 6 (2000): M322–M328.

Furman, Joseph M., M.D., Ph.D., and Stephen P. Cass, M.D., M.P.H. "Benign Paroxysmal Positional Vertigo," *New England Journal of Medicine* 341, no. 21 (November 18, 1999): 1,599–1,596.

Gabrel, Celia S., M.S., Division of Health Care Statistics. "Characteristics of Elderly Nursing Home Current Residents and Discharges: Data from the 1997 National Nursing Home Survey," National Center for Health Statistics, no. 312 (April 25, 2000).

———. "An Overview of Nursing Home Facilities: Data from the 197 National Nursing Home Survey," no. 311 (March 1, 2000).

Gan, Sandra C., M.D., et al. "Treatment of Acute Myocardial Infarction and 30-Day Mortality Among Women and Men," *New England Journal of Medicine* 343 (2000): 8–15.

General Accounting Office. "Nursing Homes: More Can Be Done to Protect Residents from Abuse," GAO-02-312 (March 2002).

———. "Prescription Drugs: Drug Company Programs Help Some People Who Lack Coverage," GAO-01-137 (November 2000).

General Accounting Office, Report to Congressional Requesters. "VA Long-Term Care: Oversight of Community Nursing Homes Needs Strengthening," GAO-01-768 (July 2001).

Gitter, Andrew, M.D., and Robert McAnnely, M.D. "The Value of Information Resulting from Instrumented Gait Analysis: The Physiatrist," www.vard.org/mono/gait/gitter.htm.

Glasgow, Nina. "Older Americans' Patterns of Driving and Using Other Transportation," *Rural America* 15, no. 3 (2000): 26–31.

Gratton, Brian. Urban Elders: *Family, Work, and Welfare Among Boston's Aged, 1890–1950.* Philadelphia: Temple University Press, 1986.

Gray, Shelly L., Jane E. Mahoney, and Dave K. Blough. "Medication Adherence in Elderly Patients Receiving Home Health Services Following Hospital Discharge," *The Annals of Pharmacotherapy* 35 (2001): 539–545.

Haber, Carole. *Beyond Sixty-Five: The Dilemma of Old Age in America's Past.* Cambridge, England: Cambridge University Press, 1983.

Hanlon, Joseph T., Leslie A. Shimp, and Todd P. Semla. "Recent Advances in Geriatrics: Drug-Related Problems in the Elderly," *The Annals of Pharmacotherapy* 34 (2000): 360–365.

The Hartford. "At the Crossroads: A Guide to Alzheimer's Disease, Dementia & Driving," Hartford, Conn., 2000.

Heart and Stroke Foundation of Canada. *The Changing Face of Heart Disease and Stroke in Canada.* Ottawa, Canada: Heart and Stroke Foundation, 1999.

Hennessy, C. H., Dr., Ph, MA, et al. "The Older Year," in *Diabetes and Women's Health Across the Life Stages: A Public Health Perspective,* GLA Beckles, and P.E. Thompson-Reid, eds. Atlanta, Ga.: U.S. Department of Health and Human Services, Centers for Disease Control and Prevention, National Center for Chronic Disease Prevention and Health Promotion, Division of Diabetes Translation, 2001.

Hertzel, Lisa, and Annetta Smith. "The 65 Years and Over Population: 2000," *United States Census 2000.* U.S. Census Bureua, C2KRD/-1-10, October 2001.

Hunter, Melissa H., M.D., and Dana E. King, M.D. "COPD: Management of Acute Exacerbations and Chronic Stable Disease," *American Family Physician* 64 (2001)L 603–612, 621–622.

Hyman, David J., M.D., M.P.H., and Valory N. Pavlik, Ph.D. "Characteristics of Patients with Uncontrolled Hypertension in the United States," *New England Journal of Medicine* 345, no. 7 (August 16, 2001): 479–486.

Iknoian, Therese, and Manny Fuentes. *T'ai Chi For Dummies.* New York: Wiley Publishing. 2001.

Inglehart, John K. "The Centers for Medicare and Medicaid Services," *New England Journal of Medicine* 345, no. 26 (December 27, 2001): 1,920–1,921.

Infante, Ricardo, M.D., and Robert G. Lahita, M.D., Ph.D. "Rheumatoid Arthritis: New Disease-Modifying and Anti-Inflammatory Drugs," *Geriatrics* 56, no. 3 (2000): 30–40.

In't Veld, Bas A., M.D., Ph.D., et al. "Nonsteroidal Antiinflammatory Drugs and the Risk of Alzheimer Disease," *New England Journal of Medicine* 345, no. 21 (November 22, 2001): 1,515–1,521.

"Interactions Between Alcohol and Various Classes of Medications," *Alcohol Research & Health* vol. 23, no. 1 (1999) 46–47.

Istre, Gregory R., M.D., et al. "Deaths and Injuries from House Fires," *New England Journal of Medicine* 344, no. 25 (June 25, 2001): 1,911–1,916.

Ivey, David C., Elizabeth Wieling, and Steven M. Harris. "Save the Young-the Elderly Have Lived Their Lives: Ageism in Marriage and Family Therapy," *Family Process* (July 22, 2000.)

Jerant, Anthony F., M.D., et al. "Early Detection and Treatment of Skin Cancer," *American Family Physician* 62 (2000): 357–368, 381–382.

Jerant, Anthony F., M.D., Michelle Bannon, P.S.-C, M.P.H., and Stephen Rittenhouse, CPT, MC, USA. "Identification and Management of Tuberculosis," *American Family Physician* 61 (2000): 2,667–2,678, 2,681–2,682.

Johansson, K., et al. "Alzheimer's disease and apolipo-protein E e 4 Allele in Older Drivers Who Died in Automobile Accidents," *Lancet* 349 (1997): 1,143–1,144.

Jong, Nynke de, Ph.D., MSc, et al. "Dietary Supplements and Physical Exercise Affecting Bone and Body Composition in Frail Elderly Persons," *American Journal of Public Health* 90, no. 6 (2000): 947–954.

Jorgensen, Tove, et al. "Prescription Drug Use, Diagnoses, and Healthcare Utilization Among the Elderly," *The Annals of Pharmacotherapy* 35 (2001): 1,004–1,009.

Kanaan, Nbil, M.D., and Raja Sawaya, M.D. "Nocturnal Leg Cramps: Clinically Mysterious and Painful—But Manageable," *Geriatrics* 56, no. 6 (June 2001): 34–42.

Kandel, Joseph, M.D., and David B. Sudderth, M.D. *The Arthritis Solution.* Rocklin, Calif.: Prima Publishing, 1997.
———. *Back Pain What Works! A Comprehensive Guide to Preventing and Overcoming Back Problems.* Rocklin, Calif.: Prima Publishing, 1996.

Kane, Robert L., Joseph G. Ouslander, and Itamar B. Abrass. *Essentials of Clinical Geriatrics.* New York: McGraw Hill, 1999.

Kapoor, Wishwa N. M.D., M.P.H. "Syncope," *New England Journal of Medicine* 343 (December 21, 2000): 1,856–1,862.

Kelley, George A., and Kristi Sharpe Kelley. "Aerobic Exercise and Resting Blood Pressure in Older Adults: A Meta-analytic Review of Randomized Controlled Trials," *Journal of Gerontology: Medical Sciences* 56A, no. 5 (2001): M298–M303.

Kennedy, Gary. *Geriatric Mental Health Care: A Treatment Guide for Health Professionals.* New York: Guilford Press, 2000.

Kiilavuori, K., et al. "The Effect of Physical Training on Skeletal Muscle in Patients with Chronic Heart Failure," *The European Journal of Heart Failure* 2 (2000): 53–63.

Kinsella, Kevin, and Victoria A. Velkoff. *An Aging World: 2001.* Washington, D.C.: U.S. Census Bureau, 2001.

Koenig, Harold G., M.D., and Maragatha Kuchibhatla, Ph.D. "Use of Health Services by Medically Ill Depressed Elderly Patients After Hospital Discharge," *American Journal of Geriatric Psychiatry* 7, no. 1 (1999): 48–56.

Kranzler, Jay D., M.D., Ph.D., Judith F. Gendreau, M.D., and Srinivas G. Rao, M.D., Ph.D. "The Psychopharmacology of Fibromyalgia: A Drug Development Perspective," *Psychopharmacology Bulletin* 36, no. 1 (2002): 165–213.

Kremer, Berry, et al. "A Worldwide Study of the Huntington's Disease Mutation: Tee Sensitivity and Specificity of Measuring CAG Repeats," *New England Journal of Medicine* 330, no. 20 (May 19, 1994): 1,401–1,406.

Krouse, Laurel H., M.D., Ph.D. "Elder Abuse," eMedicine. Available online. URL: www.emedicine.com/emerg/topic160.htm. Dowloaded June 5, 2001.

La, Shih-Wei, Chee-Keong Tan, and Kim-Choy Ng. "Epidemiology of Hyperglycemia in Elderly Persons," *Journal of Gerontology: Medical Sciences* 55A, no. 5 (2001): M257–M259.

Lang, Ariel J., Ph.D., and Murray B. Stein, M.D. "Anxiety Disorders: How to Recognize and Treat the Medical Symptoms of Emotional Illness," *Geriatrics* 56, no. 5 (2001): 24–34.

Lange, Paul H., M.D., and Christine Adamec. *Prostate Cancer for Dummies.* New York: John Wiley & Sons, 2003.

Leipzig, Rosanne M., M.D., Ph.D. "Prescribing: Keys to Maximizing Benefit While Avoiding Adverse Drug Effects," *Geriatrics* 56, no. 2 (2001): 30–34.

Lieberman, David A., M.D., et al. "Use of Colonoscopy to Screen Asymptomatic Adults for Colorectal Cancer," *New England Journal of Medicine,* 343, no. 3 (July 20, 2000): 162–168.

Little, D'Arcy, M.D., CCFP, and Munir A. Jamal, M.D., FRCSC. "Damaged DNA and Cellular Apotosis: The Story on Bladder Cancer in the Elderly," *Geriatrics and Aging* 4, no. 2 (2001): 14–15, 19.

Lohmander, L. Stefan, "What Can We Do About Osteoarthritis?" *Arthritis Research* 2 (2000): 95–100.

Loonin, Deanne, and Jonathan A. Sheldon. *Guide to Surviving Debt.* Boston, Mass.: National Consumer Law Center, 1999.

Lurie, Stephen J., M.D., Ph.D., senior ed., and Jody W. Zylke, M.D., contributing ed. "Research Letter: Persistent Pain in Nursing Home Residents," *Journal of the American Medical Association (JAMA)* 285, no. 16 (April 25, 2001). http://jama.ama-assno.org/issues/v285n16/ffull/jlt0425-6.html.

Maheshwari, Alok, M.D., et al. "Acute MI: Age-Related Presentations and Treatment Options," *Geriatrics* 55, no. 2 (2000): 32–40.

Makalinao, Jose Mari R., M.D., and Suzanne D. Fields, M.D. "Chronic Heart Failure: Examining Consensus Recommendations for Patient Management," *Geriatrics* 55, no. 12 (2000): 53–58.

Manek, Nisha J., M.D., M.R.C.P., and Nancy E. Lane, M.D. "Osteoarthritis: Current Concepts in Diagnosis and Management," *American Family Physician* 61 (2000): 1,795–1,804.

Marjama-Lyons, Jill M., M.D., and William C. Koller, M.D., Ph.D. "Parkinson's Disease: Update in Diagnosis and Symptom Management," *Geriatrics* 56, no. 8 (2001): 24–35.

Marottoli, Richard A., et al. "Driving Cessation and Changes in Mileage Driven Among Elderly Individuals," *Journal of Gerontology* 48, no. 5 (1993): S255–S260.

Marshall, Charles E., M.D., Donna Benton, Ph.D., and Joselyn M. Brazier, M.D. "Elder Abuse: Using Clinical Tools to Identify Clues of Mistreatment," *Geriatrics* 55, no. 2 (2000): 42–53.

Mattson, Mark P. "Huntington's Disease: Accomplices to Neuronal Death." *Nature* 415, (January 24, 2002): 377–379.

McAlindon, Timothy E., DM, et al. "Glucosamine and Chondroitin for Treatment of Osteoarthritis: A Systematic Quality Assessment and Meta-analysis," *Journal of the American Medical Association (JAMA)* 283, no. 11 (March 15, 2000): 1,469–1,475.

McCaig, Linda F., M.P.H., and Catherine W. Burt, Ed.D., Division of Health Care Statistics. "National Hospital Ambulatory Medical Care Survey: 1999 Emergency Department Summary," National Center for Health Statistics, no. 320 (June 25, 2001).

McCarberg, Bill H., M.D., and Keela A. Herr, Ph.D., RN. "Osteoarthritis: How to Manage Pain and Improve Patient Function," *Geriatrics* 56, no. 10 (2001): 14–24.

McLaughlin, Mary Ann, M.D., M.P.H. "The Aging Heart: State-of-the-Art Prevention and Management of Cardiac Disease," *Geriatrics* 56, no. 6 (2001): 45–49.

Meneilly, Graydon S., and Daniel Tessier. "Diabetes in Elderly Adults," *Journal of Gerontology* 56A no. 1 (2001): M5–M13.

Mense, Siegfried, David G. Simons, and I. Jon Russell. *Muscle Pain: Understanding Its Nature, Diagnosis, and Treatment.* Baltimore, Md.: Lippincott Williams & Wilkins, 2001.

Middlemiss, Carol. "Gastroesophageal Reflux Disease: A Common Condition in the Elderly," *Nurse Practitioner* 22, no. 11 (November 1998): 51–60.

Minino, Arialdi M., M.P.H., and Betty L. Smith, B.S. Ed, Division of Vital Statistics. "Deaths: Preliminary Data for 2000," *National Vital Statistics Reports* 49, no. 12 (October 9, 2001): 1–39.

Minocha, Anil, M.D., FACP. *The Gastroenterology Resident Pocket Survival Guide.* McLean, Va.: International Medical Publishing, 1999.

Minocha, Anil, M.D., and Christine Adamec. *How to Stop Heartburn: Simple Ways to Heal Heartburn and Acid Reflux.* New York: John Wiley & Sons, 2001.

Parks, Susan Mockus, M.D., and Karen D. Novielli, M.D. "A Practical Guide to Caring for Caregivers," *American Family Physician* 62 (2000): 2,613–2,620, 2,621–2,622.

Mohr, J.P., M.D., et al. "A Comparison of Warfarin and Aspirin for the Prevention of Recurrent Ischemic Stroke," *New England Journal of Medicine* 345, no. 20 (November 15, 2001): 1,444–1,451.

Morley, John W. "Editorial: Diabetes Mellitus: A Major Disease of Older Persons," *Journal of Gerontology: Medical Sciences* 55A, no. 5 (2000): M255–256.

Mouton, Charles P., M.D., M.S., et al. "Common Infections in Older Adults," *American Family Physician* 63 (2001): 257–268.

Mullick, Tarun, M.D., and Joel E. Richter, M.D. "Chronic GERD: Strategies to Relieve Symptoms and Manage Complications," *Geriatrics* 55, no. 11 (2000): 28–43.

Munson, Martha Little, M.S., Division of Health Care Statistics. "Characteristics of Elderly Home Health Care Users: Data from the 1996 National Home and Hospice Care Survey," National Center for Health Care Statistics, no. 309 (December 22, 1999).

Myers, Jonathan, Ph.D., et al. "Exercise Capacity and Mortality Among Men Referred for Exercise Testing," *New England Journal of Medicine* 346, no. 11 (March 14, 2002): 793–801.

National Cancer Institute. "Annual Report to the Nation on the Status of Cancer, 1973–1998, Featuring Cancers with Recent Increasing Trends," *Journal of the National Cancer Institute* 93, no. 11 (2001): 824–842.

———. "Bladder Cancer," NIH Publication No. 01–1559 (September 7, 2001).

———. "Cancer of the Colon and Rectum," NIH Publication No. 99–1552 (1999).

———. "Stomach Cancer," NIH Publication No. 94–1554 (December 12, 2000).

———. "Understanding Prostate Changes: A Health Guide for All Men," NIH Publication No. 99–4303 (September 1999).

———. "What You Need to Know About Cancer of the Uterus," NIH Publication No. 01–1562 (July 30, 2001).

National Cancer Institute of Canada. *Canadian Cancer Statistics 2001.* Toronto, Canada, 2001.

National Center for Injury Prevention and Control. "Falls in Nursing Homes: Fact Sheet," Centers for Disease Control and Prevention (CDC) (December 19, 2000).

National Cholesterol Education Program, National Heart, Lung, and Blood Institute. "Detection, Evaluation, and Treatment of High Blood Cholesterol in Adults (Adult Treatment Panel III): Executive Summary," NIH Publication No. 01–3670 (May 2001).

National Institute of Arthritis and Musculoskeletal and Skin Diseases (NIAMS). "Questions & Answers about Arthritis Pain," National Institutes of Health, NIH Publication No. 01–4856 (February 2001).

National Institutes of Health, National Institute of Arthritis and Musculoskeletal and Skin Diseases. "Questions and Answers About Rosacea" (April 1999). www.niams.nih.gov/hi/topics/rosacea/rosacea.htm.

National Institutes of Health News Release. "Folic Acid Possibly a Key Factor in Alzheimer's Disease Prevention" (March 1, 2002).

Neoptolemos, J.P., et al. "Adjuvant Chemoradiotherapy and Chemotherapy in Resectable Pancreatic Cancer: A Randomised Controlled Trial," *Lancet* 358, no. 92993 (November 10, 2001): 1,576–1,585.

Office of Safety and Traffic Operations R & D, Federal Highway Administration. "Older Driver Highway Design Handbook" (January 1998).

Olsen, Richard V., Ph.D., et al. "Alzheimer's and Related Dementias Homes That Help: Advice from Caregivers for Creating a Supportive Home." Newark, N.J.: Architecture and Building Science Research Group, School of Architecture, New Jersey Institute of Technology, 1993.

Orwoll, Eric, M.D., et al. "Alendronate for the Treatment of Osteoporosis in Men," *New England Journal of Medicine* 343 (2000): 604–610.

Oscar-Berman, Marlene, Ph.D., et al. "Impairments of Brain and Behavior: The Neurological Effects of Alcohol," *Alcohol Health & Research World* 21, no. 1 (1997): 65–75.

Ostir, Glen V. "Disability in Older Adults 1: Prevalence, Causes, and Consequences," *Behavioral Medicine* (Winter 1999): 147–156.

"Pain Drug Use Among American Elders," *Executive Health's Good Health Report* 34, no. 2 (November 1997): 1.

Palmore, Erdman, Ph.D. "The Ageism Survey: First Findings," *The Gerontologist* 41, no. 5 (2001): 572–575.

Panda, Mukta, and Norman A. Desbiens. "Pain in Elderly Patients: How to Achieve Control," *Consultant* 41, no. 12 (October 1, 2001): 1,597–1,608.

Patz, Edward F., M.D., Philip C. Goodman, M.D., and Gerold Bepler, M.D., Ph.D. "Screening for Lung Cancer," New England Journal of Medicine 343, no. 22 (November 30, 2000): 1,627–1,633.

Perrino, Carrol S., Ph.D., and Anthony Saka, Ph.D., P.E. "The Risky Driver: An Annotated Bibliography of Recent Research," Morgan State University National Transportation Center (April 1998).

Petit, William Jr., and Christine Adamec. *The Encyclopedia of Diabetes.* New York: Facts On File, 2002.

Petrella, Robert J., M.D., Ph.D. "Exercise for Older Patients with Chronic Disease," *Physicians & Sportsmedicine* 27, no. 11 (October 15, 1999): 79–101.

Physicians' Desk Reference. *The PDR Guide to Nutritional Supplements: An Authoritative A-to-Z Guide to the 100 Most Popular Therapies and Nutraceuticals.* New York: Ballantine Books, 2001.

Pipher, Mary, Ph.D. *Another Country: Navigating the Emotional Terrain of Our Elders.* New York: Berkley Publishing Group, 1999.

Pittman, Joel R., Pharm. D., and Michael H. Bross, M.D. "Diagnosis and Management of Gout," *American Family Physician* (April 1, 1999).

Portis, Andrew J., M.D., and Chandru P. Sundaram, M.D. "Diagnosis and Management of Kidney Stones," *American Family Physician* 63 (2001): 1,329–1,338.

Porter, Ray, Ed. *Cambridge Illustrated History of Medicine.* Cambridge, United Kingdom: Cambridge University Press, 1996.

Prevent Blindness America. "Vision Problems in the U.S.: Prevalence of Adult Vision Impairment and Age-Related Eye Disease in America," (2002).

Prusiner, Stanley B., M.D., "Shattuck Lecture: Neurodegenerative Diseases and Prions," *New England Journal of Medicine* 344, no. 20 (May 17, 2001): 1,516–1,526.

Puisieux, François, et al. "Ambulatory Blood Pressure Monitoring and Postprandial Hypotension in Elderly Persons with Falls or Syncopes," *Journal of Gerontology: Medical Sciences* 55A, no. 9 (2000): M535–M540.

Qi Liu, Bo, et al. "Emerging Tobacco Hazards in China: 1. Retrospective Proportional Mortality Study of One Million Deaths," *British Medical Journal* 317, (November 21, 1998): 1,411–1,422.

Raeder, Carla K., and Mary S. Hayney. "Immunology of Varicella Immunization in the Elderly." *The Annals of Pharmacotherapy* 34, no. 2 (2001): 228–234.

Rigaud, Anne-Sophie, and Bernard Forette. "Hypertension in Older Adults," *Journal of Gerontology: Medical Sciences* 56A, no. 4 (2001): M217–M225.

Rigler, Sally K., M.D. "Alcoholism in the Elderly," *American Family Physician* 61 (2000): 1,710–1,716.

Rosenthal, Bruce P., O.D. "Screening and Treatment of Age-Related and Pathologic Vision Changes," *Geriatrics* 56, no. 12 (December 2001): 27–31.

Rubenstein, Laurence Z., et al. "Effects of a Group Exercise Program on Strength, Mobility, and Falls Among Fall-Prone Elderly Men," *Journal of Gerontology: Medical Sciences* 55A, no. 6 (2000): M317–M321.

Rubenstein, Laurence Z., M.D., M.P.H., Christopher M. Powers, Ph.D., P.T., and Catherine H. MacLean, M.D., Ph.D. "Quality Indicators for the Management and Prevention of Falls and Mobility Problems in Vulnerable Elders," *Annals of Internal Medicine* 135 (2001): 686–693.

Russell, J. Neil, Ph.D., et al. "Trends and Differential Use of Assistive Technology Devices: United States, 1994," Centers for Disease Control and Prevention, National Center for Health Statistics, Advance Data Number 292 (November 13, 1997).

Ruth, Roger A., and Robino Hamill-Ruth. "A Multidisciplinary Approach to Management of Tinnitus and Hyperacusis," *The Hearing Journal* (November 2001).

Sahyoun, Nadine R. Ph.D., R.D., et al. "The Changing Profile of Nursing Home Residents: 1985: 1997," *Aging Trends* (no volume listed), no. 4 National Center for Health Statistics (March 2001): 1–8.

Sandhu, Satinderpal K., M.D., and Sherif B. Mossad, M.D. "Influenza in the Older Adult: Indications for the Use of Vaccine and Antiviral Therapy," *Geriatrics* 56, no. 1 (2001): 43–51.

Sargent, Daniel J., Ph.D., et al. "A Pooled Analysis of Adjuvant Chemotherapy for Resected Colon Cancer in Elderly Patients," *New England Journal of Medicine* 345, no. 15 (October 11, 2001): 1,091–1,097.

Schaie, K. Warner, Ph.D., and Martin Pietrucha, Ph.D., eds. *Mobility and Transportation in the Elderly.* New York: Springer Publishing, 2000.

Scogin, Forrest, Mark Floyd, and Jennifer Forde. "Anxiety in Older Adults," in *Psychopathology in Later Adulthood,* Susan Krauss Whitbourne, ed. New York: John Wiley & Sons, 2000.

Shaefer, David C., M.D., Ph.D., and Lawrence J. Cheskin, M.D. "Constipation in the Elderly," *American Family Physician* (September 15, 1998).

Shirey, Lee, et al. "Alzheimer's Disease and Dementia: A Growing Challenge," *Challenges for the 21st Century: Chronic and Disabling Conditions* 1, no. 11 (September 2000): 1–6.

Shumway-Cook, Anne, et al. "Predicting the Probability for Falls in Community-Dwelling Older Adults," *Physical Therapy* 77, no. 8 (1997): 812–820.

Simon, Harvey B., "Hyperthermia," *New England Journal of Medicine* 329, no. 7 (August 12, 1993): 483–487.

Small, Peter M., M.D., and Paula I. Fujiwara, M.D., M.P.H. "Management of Tuberculosis in the United States," *The New England Journal of Medicine* 345, no. 3 (July 19, 2001): 189–200.

Smith, Douglas L., M.D. "Anemia in the Elderly," *American Family Physician* (October 1, 2000).

Smith S. D., et al. "Urine Detection of Survivin and Diagnosis of Bladder Cancer," *Journal of the American Medical Association (JAMA)* 285 (2001): 324–328.

South-Paul, Jeannette E., Col., MC, USA. "Osteoporosis: Part I: Evaluation and Assessment," *American Family Physician* 63 (2001): 897–904, 908.

———. "Osteoporosis: Part II: Nonpharmacologic and Pharmacologic Treatments," *American Family Physician* 63 (2001): 1,121–1,128.

Standridge, John, M.D., FAAFP, Assistant Professor, Department of Family Medicine, University of Tennessee, College of Medicine, Chattanooga, Tenn. "Alcohol Abuse in the Elderly," Continuing Medical Education activity, published by the Southern Medical Association (November 1998).

Stankus, Seth John, MAJ, MC, USA, Michael Dlugopolski, MJ, MC, USA, and Deborah Packer, MAJ, MC, USA. "Management of Herpes Zoster (Shingles) and Postherpetic Neuralgia," *American Family Physician* 61 (2000): 2,437–2,444, 2,447–2,448.

Starr, Cynthia. "Emerging Cardiac Risk Factors" *Patient Care* 35, no. 10 (May 30, 2001): 38–50.

Staud, Roland, M.D., and Christine Adamec. *Fibromyalgia for Dummies.* New York: Hungry Minds, 2002.

Stevens, Judy A., Ph.D., and Sarah Olson, M.S. "Reducing Falls and Resulting Hip Fractures Among Older Women," *MMWR* 49 (2000): 1–12.

Stevens, Judy A., M.S., M.PH., Ph.D., et al. "Surveillance for Injuries and Violence Among Older Adults," *Morbidity & Mortality Weekly Report* 48, no. SS-8 (December 17, 1999): 27–50.

Strauss, Peter J., and Nancy M. Lederman. *The Elder Law Handbook: A Legal and Financial Survival Guide for Caregivers and Seniors.* New York: Facts On File, 1996.

Sveinbjornsdottir, Sigulraug, M.D., et al. "Familial Aggregation of Parkinson's Disease," *New England Journal of Medicine* 343, no. 24 (2000): 1,765–1,770.

Swagerty, Daniel L., Jr., M.D., M.P.H., and Deborah Hellinger, D.O. "Radiographic Assessment of Osteoarthritis," *American Family Physician* 64 (2001): 279–286.

Tatara, Toshio, Ph.D., principal investigator, et al. *The National Elder Abuse Incidence Study: Final Report*, The National Center on Elder Abuse, 1998.

Tideiksaar, Rein, "Preventing Falls: How to Identify Risk Factors, Reduce Complications," *Geriatrics* 51, no. 2 (1996): 43–51.

U.S. Department of Agriculture. "Food Insufficiency and the Nutritional Status of the Elderly Population," *Nutrition Insights* 18 (May 2000).

U.S. Department of Health & Human Services. "Cigarette Smoking Among Adults—United States, 1999," *Morbidity and Mortality Weekly Report* 50, no. 40 (October 12, 2001): 869–874.

———. *Healthy People 2010.* 2nd ed. "With Understanding and Improving Health and Objectives for Improving Health." 2 vols. Washington, D.C.: U.S. Government Printing Office, November 2000.

———. *Reducing Tobacco Use: A Report of the Surgeon General.* U.S. Department of Health and Human Services, Centers for Disease Control and Prevention, National Center for Chronic Disease Prevention and Health Promotion, Office on Smoking and Health, 2000.

U.S. Department of Justice, Civil Rights Division, Disability Rights Section. "A Guide to Disability Rights Laws" (August 2001).

U.S. General Accounting Office Report to Congressional Requesters. "VA Long-Term Care: Oversight of Community Nursing Homes Needs Strengthening," GAO-01-768 (July 2001).

Vaillant, George E., M.D. *Aging Well: Surprising Guideposts to a Happier Life from the Landmark Harvard Study of Adult Development.* Boston: Little, Brown & Company, 2002.

Van Den Berge, Greet, M.D., Ph.D., et al. "Intensive Insulin Therapy in Critically Ill Patients," *New England Journal of Medicine* 345, no. 19 (November 8, 2001): 1,359–1,367.

Vapnek, Jonathan M., M.D. "Urinary Incontinence: Screening and Treatment of Urinary Dysfunction," *Geriatrics* 56, no. 10 (2001): 25–29.

Vernon, Jack A., Ed. *Tinnitus Treatment and Relief.* Needham Heights, Mass.: Allyn & Bacon, 1998.

Vita, Anthony J., et al. "Aging, Health Risks, and Cumulative Disability," *New England Journal of Medicine* 338, no. 15 (April 9, 1998): 1,035–1,041.

Wagner, Gorm, et al. "Sildenafil Citrate (VIAGRA®) Improves Erectile Function in Elderly Patients with Erectile Dysfunction: A Subgroup Analysis," *Journal of Gerontology: Medical Sciences* 56A, no. 2 (2001): M113–M119.

Wallach, Frances R., M.D. "Infectious Disease: Update on Treatment of Pneumonia, Influenza, and Urinary Tract Infections," *Geriatrics* 56, no. 9 (2001): 43–47.

Walling, Anne D. "Diagnosing Biliary Colic and Acute Cholecystitis," *American Family Physician* 62, no. 6 (September 15, 2000): 1,386.

Walsh, Nancy. "Rosacea Responds Favorably to Oral Azithromycin," *OB/GYN News* (May 1, 2001).

Walsh, Patrick C., M.D., and Janet Farrar Worthington. *Dr. Patrick Walsh's Guide to Surviving Prostate Cancer.* New York: Warner Books, 2001.

Weathermon, Ron, Pharm.D., and David W. Crabb, M.D. "Alcohol and Medication Interactions," *Alcohol Health & Research World* 20, no. 3 (1996): 40–54.

Weinberger, Jesse, M.D. "Prevention and Management of Cerebrovascular Events in Primary Care," *Geriatrics* 57, no. 1 (January 2002): 38–43.

Whitbourne, Susan Krauss, Ph.D. *The Aging Individual.* New York: Springer Publishing Company, 1996.

Whitbourne, Susan Krauss, ed. *Psychopathology in Later Adulthood.* New York: John Wiley & Sons, 2000.

Yates Shayna M., and Tim A. Dunnagan. "Evaluating the Effectiveness of a Home-Based Fall Risk Reduction Program for Rural Community-Dwelling Older Adults," *Journal of Gerontology: Medical Sciences* 56A (2001): M226–M230.

Young, Melinda G. "Chronic Pain Management in the Elderly," *Patient Care* 18 (September 30, 2000): 31–49.

Young, Rosabel, M.D., M.S. "Update on Parkinson's Disease," *American Family Physician* (April 15, 1999).

Zakhari, Sam, Ph.D. "Alcohol and the Cardiovascular System," *Alcohol Health & Research World* 21, no. 1 (1997): 21–29.

INDEX